JOINING TOGETHER

Eleventh Edition

JOINING TOGETHER

Group Theory and Group Skills

DAVID W. JOHNSON
University of Minnesota

FRANK P. JOHNSON

Boston   Columbus   Indianapolis   New York   San Francisco   Upper Saddle River
Amsterdam   Cape Town   Dubai   London   Madrid   Milan   Munich   Paris   Montreal   Toronto
Delhi   Mexico City   São Paulo   Sydney   Hong Kong   Seoul   Singapore   Taipei   Tokyo

Vice President and Editorial Director: Jeffery W. Johnston
Senior Acquisitions Editor: Meredith D. Fossel
Associate Editor: Anne Whittaker
Editorial Assistant: Andrea Hall
Vice President, Director of Marketing: Margaret Waples
Senior Marketing Manager: Christopher Barry
Senior Managing Editor: Pamela D. Bennett
Project Manager: Kerry Rubadue
Senior Operations Supervisor: Matthew Ottenweller
Senior Art Director: Diane Lorenzo

Text Designer: S4Carlisle Publishing Services
Cover Designer: Diane Lorenzo
Photo Coordinator: Carol Sykes
Permissions Administrator: Rebecca Savage
Cover Art: Superstock
Full-Service Project Management: S4Carlisle Publishing Services
Composition: S4Carlisle Publishing Services
Printer/Binder: STPCourier
Cover Printer: STP Courier
Text Font: 9.5/12 pts, Trump Mediaeval LT Std

Credits and acknowledgments for materials borrowed from other sources and reproduced, with permission, in this textbook appear on appropriate page within text.

Every effort has been made to provide accurate and current Internet information in this book. However, the Internet and information posted on it are constantly changing, so it is inevitable that some of the Internet addresses listed in this textbook will change.

Library of Congress Cataloging-in-Publication Data
Johnson, David W.
  Joining together : group theory and group skills / David W. Johnson, Frank P. Johnson.—11th ed.
    p. cm.
  ISBN 978-0-13-267813-1—ISBN 0-13-267813-6 1. Social groups. 2. Leadership. 3. Group relations training. I. Johnson, Frank P. (Frank Pierce) II. Title.
  HM716.J64 2013
  302'.14—dc23
                                                                      2012005131

10 9 8 7 6 5 4 3 2 1

ISBN 13: 978-0-13-267813-1
ISBN 10:   0-13-267813-6

This book is dedicated to our parents,
Roger W. Johnson and Frances E. Johnson,
who created the basic group to
which we first belonged.

ABOUT THE AUTHORS

Frank P. Johnson graduated from Ball State University with a Bachelor of Science in Education and received a Masters of Divinity from Andover Newton Theological School in Boston and his Doctor in Ministry degree from Louisville Presbyterian Theological School. He has 35 years experience in the field of Applied Behavioral Science, with professional recognition from National Training Laboratories Institute (NTL) Institute of Applied Behavioral Science, Association for Creative Change, Consultant/Trainers Southwest, and the Mid-Atlantic Association for Training and Consulting. Frank was employed for 13 years at the University of Maryland Counseling Center, teaching group counseling, and, during that time was a Clinical Assistant Professor in the Maryland School of Psychiatry and Human Behavior. He has written many journal articles, contributed chapters to books, and is the co-author of *Joining Together: Group Theory and Group Skills*. Frank also has been a consultant with a variety of organizations, including educational, governmental, religious, and industrial. From 1984–1996 he was employed at Ethyl Corporation as a Human Resources Development Associate. Since his retirement from Ethyl, Frank has served as an Interim Minister in several churches and is now employed as a Chaplain for Canon Hospice in Baton Rouge, Louisiana.

David W. Johnson is a Professor of Educational Psychology at the University of Minnesota. He is Co-Director of the Cooperative Learning Center. David received his doctoral degree from Columbia University. He has authored over 500 research articles and book chapters and is the author of over 50 books. David is a past-editor of the *American Educational Research Journal*. He held the *Emma M. Birkmaier Professorship in Educational Leadership* at the University of Minnesota from 1994 to 1997 and the *Libra Endowed Chair* for Visiting Professor at the University of Maine in 1996–1997. He received the American Psychological Association's 2003 Award for Distinguished Contributions of Applications of Psychology to Education and Practice. In 2007 David received (with his brother Roger) *Brock International Prize in Education* administered by the College of Liberal Studies at the University of Oklahoma. In 2008 David received the *Distinguished Contributions to Research in Education Award* from the American Education Research Association. In 2010 he received the *Jeffrey Rubin Theory To Practice Award*, awarded by the International Association for Conflict Management and the Program on Negotiation at the Harvard Law School. In 2011 David received the A. M. Wellner Lifetime Achievement Award from the National Register of Health Service Providers in Psychology. For the past 40 years, David has served as an organizational consultant to schools and businesses throughout the world. He is a practicing psychotherapist.

PREFACE

We, the authors, know a great deal about groups. We grew up in one. There are seven children in our family. Frank is the oldest. David is in the middle. We are five years apart in age. Although Frank was very bossy as a child and refused to believe that David was not supposed to clean up his room, our relationship survived. As part of a group of seven children, we raised each other and learned about group dynamics in the trenches of trying to decide as a group who gets the extra piece of pie, who sits by the windows in the car, who decides which game we are going to play, who sweeps and who mops, and whether we go to sleep with the light on or off.

Families are not the only group setting. Within all organizations and social systems, and throughout all walks of life, groups are the key setting in which things get done. The need for knowledge of group dynamics and skills in being part of small groups is more important than ever. Our original reasons for writing *Joining Together* included introducing readers to both (a) the theory and research findings needed to understand how to make groups effective and (b) the skills required to apply that knowledge in practical situations. Expertise in working in groups is based on an integration of such knowledge and skills. *Joining Together* is more than a book reviewing current knowledge in the area of small groups, and it is more than a book of skill-building exercises. The theory and exercises are integrated into an inquiry or experiential approach to learning about the dynamics of small groups. Throughout one's life, choices, opportunities, and successes are created by knowledge of group dynamics and mastery of the skills required to apply that knowledge in practical situations.

What we know about group functioning is dynamic, not static. It is constantly being revised and updated as new insights are translated into revised theoretical explanations for group behavior and new lines of research. Significant advances in the field continue to be achieved. Much has changed since we published the first edition of this book in 1975. Some theories have been disconfirmed in the intervening years. Other theories have been refined or subsumed into new conceptual systems. This book reflects the new developments in theory and research by taking an updated look at what we know about group dynamics. Although the readers of this book are diverse, *Joining Together* remains focused on the characteristic dynamics found in virtually all groups. Examples are used from all walks of life. Because this book is intended to serve as an introduction to group dynamics, we have maintained a balanced, integrative stance when presenting theories and research findings.

NEW TO THIS EDITION

- New sections on controversy and creativity, including updated research on the theory of constructive controversy, the creative process, and a brand new diagnostic tool for evaluating the ways in which readers make decisions.
- New set of exercises on the dynamics of intergroup conflict and negotiation.

- All new section on Restorative Justice, covering additional and related topics of Distributive Justice, Procedural Justice, and Scope of Justice.
- Focus on new technologies: the phenomenon of online groups and digital decision-making skills.
- New sections on intergroup dependence, positive social relationships, psychological health, and self-esteem.
- Expanded discussion of potential problems in decision making.
- Greater focus on minority influence, group goals, and diversity.

ACKNOWLEDGMENTS

The authors wish to thank many people for their help in writing this book and in preparing the manuscript. We owe much to the social psychologists who have influenced our theorizing and to the colleagues with whom we have conducted various types of laboratory-training experiences. We have tried to acknowledge sources of the exercises included in this book whenever possible. Some of the exercises presented are so commonly used that the originators are not traceable. If we have inadvertently missed giving recognition to anyone, we apologize. Special thanks are extended to our wives, Linda Mulholland Johnson and Jane Miley Johnson, who contributed their support to the development and writing of this book.

We also would like to thank the reviewers of *Joining Together: Group Theory and Group Skills*, Eleventh Edition. They include:

Fred Bemak, George Mason University;
Cecilia Garza, Texas A&M International University;
Susan Carol Losh, Florida State University;
Jennifer M. Smith, Western Kentucky University;
Carolyn Vos Strache, Pepperdine University.

BRIEF CONTENTS

CONTENTS

CHAPTER 12

Leading Growth and Counseling Groups   473

CHAPTER 13

Team Development, Team Training   498

CHAPTER 14

Epilogue   527

LIST OF EXERCISES

CHAPTER ONE

Group Dynamics

BASIC CONCEPTS TO BE COVERED IN THIS CHAPTER

In this chapter a number of concepts are defined and discussed. The major ones are in the following list. Students should divide into pairs. Each pair is to (1) define each concept, noting the page on which it is defined and discussed, and (2) ensure that both members understand its meaning. Then combine into groups of four. Compare the answers of the two pairs. If there is disagreement, look up the concept in the chapter and clarify it until all members agree on and understand the definition.

CONCEPTS

1. Group
2. Group dynamics
3. Group effectiveness
4. Interdependence
5. Role
6. Norm
7. Status
8. Sequential-stage theory of group development
9. Recurring-phase theory of group development
10. Primary group
11. Reference group
12. Group processing

 ## GROUP DYNAMICS AND ME

Although the scientific investigations of group work are but a few years old, I don't hesitate to predict that group work—that is, the handling of human beings not as isolated individuals, but in the social setting of groups—will soon be one of the most important theoretical and practical fields. . . . There is no hope for creating a better world without a deeper scientific insight into the . . . essentials of group life.

Kurt Lewin (1943)

Membership in groups is inevitable and universal. All day long we interact first in one group and then in another. Our family life, our leisure time, our friendships, and our careers are all filled with groups. We are born into a group called the family, and we would not survive the first few years of our lives, the first few weeks, or even the first few minutes without membership in this group. Within our family and peer groups, we are socialized into ways of behaving and thinking, educated, and taught to have certain perspectives on ourselves and our world. Our **personal identity** is derived from the way

Importance of Groups	Nature of Groups	Types of Groups
• We are small-group beings • We live in groups • Groups and quality of life	• Group orientation • Individual orientation	• Pseudo • Traditional • Effective • High performance
Group Structure	**Stages of Group Development**	**Basic Elements of Effectiveness**
• Roles • Norms	*Sequential Stages* • Forming • Norming • Storming • Performing • Adjourning	• Positive interdependence • Individual accountability • Promotive interaction • Social skills • Group processing
	Recurring Stages • Task and emotional expressions • Depend, pair, fight or flight • Affection, inclusion, control	**Field of Group Dynamics** • Nature of group dynamics • History of group dynamics • Kurt Lewin • Nature of book

Dynamics of Promotive Interaction

- Creating clear, operational, mutual goals members are committed to
- Communicating ideas and feelings accurately and clearly
- Distributed participation and leadership
- Equal access to power based on expertise, access to information
- Decision procedures flexibly matched with situational needs
- Controversy used to promote creative problem solving, critical thinking
- Conflicts are faced, encouraged, and resolved constructively.

Figure 1.1 Nature of group dynamics.

in which we are perceived and treated by other members of our groups. As humans we have an inherent social nature: Our life is filled with groups from the moment of our birth to the moment of our death.

Group dynamics is the area of social science that focuses on advancing knowledge about the nature of group life. It is the scientific study of the nature of groups, behavior in groups, group development, and the interrelations between groups and individuals, other groups, and larger entities. Knowledge of group dynamics has the potential to change the way we think about groups and, consequently, the way we function in groups. The purposes of this book, therefore, are to help you understand the theory and research on group dynamics and improve your own small-group skills.

As a starting point, Figure 1.1 provides a helpful summary of the nature of group dynamics. The different concepts and terms listed in Figure 1.1 are discussed throughout this chapter and the rest of the book. After reviewing the information

SELF-DIAGNOSIS

Each of the following seven statements describes an action related to group effectiveness. For each statement mark

5 if you always behave that way   **2** if you seldom behave that way
4 if you frequently behave that way   **1** if you never behave that way
3 if you occasionally behave that way

WHEN I AM A MEMBER OF A GROUP

_____ **1.** I clarify the group's goals and ensure that the goals are formulated so that members "sink or swim" together and are committed to achieving them.

_____ **2.** I facilitate communication by modeling good sending and receiving skills and ensuring that communication among all group members is distributed and two-way.

_____ **3.** I provide leadership by taking whatever action is needed to help the group achieve its goals and maintain good working relationships among members, and I encourage all other members to do the same.

_____ **4.** I use my expertise and knowledge to influence the other group members to increase their efforts to achieve our mutual goals, and I let myself be i by other members who are knowledgeable and have relevant expertise

_____ **5.** I suggest different ways of making decisions (such as majority vote or d depending on (a) the availability of time and resources, (b) the size and s of the decision, and (c) the amount of member commitment needed ment the decision.

_____ **6.** I advocate my views and challenge the views of others in order to cr quality, creative decisions.

_____ **7.** I face my conflicts with other group members and present the conflict lems to be jointly solved. If we are unable to do so, I request the hel group members to help us resolve the conflicts constructively.

_____ **Total Score**

provided in Figure 1.1, think carefully about each of the statements listed in the Self-Diagnosis on page 3. These statements are designed to make you think concretely about your current understanding of groups and how you participate in them.

EXERCISE 1.1

YOUR SOLITARY ACTIVITIES

1. List everything you do in a typical day from the moment you wake up until the moment you fall asleep.
2. Delete from your list all the activities you perform with groups of people and see what is left.
3. Form a group of three and discuss the results.

EXERCISE 1.2

WHO AM I?

We are all members of groups. If we are asked to describe who we are, most of us include information about the groups to which we belong. "I'm a student at the University of Minnesota," "I'm a member of the hockey team," "I'm a Johnson," "I'm a male," "I'm an American," and so forth. Membership in groups may be formal ("I'm an employee of IBM"), aspiring ("I want to be rich"), marginal ("Sometimes I'm invited to Ralph's parties, sometimes I'm not"), voluntary ("I'm a Baptist"), and nonvoluntary ("I'm a female"). To a large extent, our memberships define who we are as individuals.

1. We can all describe ourselves in many ways. Write ten different answers to the question "Who am I?" on a sheet of paper. Answer in terms of groups you belong to, beliefs you hold, and your roles and responsibilities.
2. Rank your answers from most important to your sense of self to least important to your sense of self.
3. Form a group of three and share your self-descriptions. Count how many memberships are represented in the triad. Discuss the role of groups in your view of who you are as a person.
4. Count how many group memberships are represented in the class.

EXERCISE 1.3

WHAT IS A GROUP?

The definition of a group is controversial. The purpose of this exercise is to structure a critical examination of the different definitions. The procedure is as follows:

1. The class forms groups of seven members.
2. Each member receives a sheet containing one of the seven definitions that appear on the following pages. Without interacting with the other group members, each member is to proceed as follows:
   a. Study his or her definition until it is thoroughly understood.
   b. Plan how to teach the definition to the other members of the group.
   c. Give three examples of groups that meet the criterion contained in the definition.
   d. Give three examples of two or more people in close proximity who do not meet the criterion contained in the definition.
   e. Explain in what way(s) his or her group (doing this exercise) meets the criterion contained in the definition.

   Allow ten minutes for this phase of the exercise.
3. Each group meets to derive a single definition of the concept group. Up to twenty minutes is allowed for this phase.
4. Each group reads its definition to the entire class.
5. If there is substantial disagreement, the class forms new groups (composed of one member from each of the previous groups). The task of the new group is to arrive at one definition of the concept group, each member representing the definition of his or her former group.
6. Each group reads its definition to the entire class.

WHAT IS A GROUP?

It takes two flints to make a fire.

Louisa May Alcott

In a bus trapped in a traffic jam, six passengers begin to talk to each other, comparing reactions and sharing previous similar experiences. They start to develop a plan of action to get the bus out of the heavy traffic. Is this a group? In Yellowstone National Park it is deep winter. Several cross-country skiers glide through an isolated, snow-covered valley. They are studying winter ecology and photography. Periodically they cluster around a professional photographer as he explains the ways the winter scenes can be photographed. The vacationers admire and discuss the beautiful winter scenery as they photograph it. Is this a group? Do groups exist at all? How do you tell when you are a member of a group?

In reading a book on group dynamics, you first need to understand what a group is. We all know that groups exist, but confusion and disagreements abound when we try to define the word *group*. Many social scientists think they know exactly what a group is. The trouble is, they do not agree with one another. The reasoning behind seven of the most common definitions of the word *group* is discussed in the following sections. Notice where and how the definitions are the same and where and how they are different.

Goals

A **group** may be defined as a number of individuals who join together to achieve a goal. Groups exist for a reason. People join groups in order to achieve goals they are unable to achieve by themselves. It is questionable whether a group can exist unless there is a mutual goal that its members are trying to achieve. Freeman, as early as 1936, pointed out that people join groups in order to achieve common goals. Other social scientists who have defined group this way are Mills and Deutsch:

> To put it simply, they [small groups] are units composed of two or more persons who come into contact for a purpose and who consider the contact meaningful (Mills, 1967, p. 2).

> A psychological group exists (has unity) to the extent that the individuals composing it perceive themselves as pursuing promotively interdependent goals (Deutsch, 1949a, p. 136).

Interdependence

A **group** may be defined as a collection of individuals who are interdependent in some way. According to this definition, the individuals are not a group unless an event that affects one of them affects them all. Social scientists who have defined group in this way believe as follows:

> A group is a collection of individuals who have relations to one another that make them interdependent to some significant degree. As so defined, the term group refers to a class of social entities having in common the property of interdependence among their constituent members (Cartwright & Zander, 1968, p. 46).

> By this term [group] we generally mean a set of individuals who share a common fate, that is, who are **interdependent** in the sense that an event which affects one member is likely to affect all (Fiedler, 1967, p. 6).

Interpersonal Interaction

A **group** may be defined as a number of individuals who are interacting with one another. According to this definition, a group does not exist unless interaction occurs. Social scientists who have defined group in this way state the following:

> For a collection of individuals to be considered a group there must be some interaction (Hare, 1976, p. 4).

> A group is a number of people in interaction with one another, and it is this interaction process that distinguishes the group from an aggregate (Bonner, 1959, p. 4).

> We mean by a group a number of persons who communicate with one another often over a span of time, and who are few enough so that each person is able to communicate with all the others, not at secondhand, through other people, but face-to-face (Homans, 1950, p. 1).

Perception of Membership

A **group** may be defined as a social unit consisting of two or more persons who perceive themselves as belonging to a group. According to this definition, the persons are not a group unless they perceive themselves to be part of a group. Social scientists who have defined group in this way posit the following:

> A small group is defined as any number of persons engaged in interaction with one another in a single face-to-face meeting or series of such meetings, in which each member receives

some impression or perception of each other member distinct enough so that he can, either at the time or in later questioning, give some reaction to each of the others as an individual person, even though it be only to recall that the other was present (Bales, 1950, p. 33).

We may define a social group as a unit consisting of a plural number of separate organisms (agents) who have a collective perception of their unity and who have the ability to act and/ or are acting in a unitary manner toward their environment (M. Smith, 1945, p. 227).

Structured Relationships

A **group** may be defined as a collection of individuals whose interactions are structured by a set of roles and norms. According to this definition, the individuals are not a group unless role definitions and norms structure their interactions. Social scientists who have defined group in this way are McDavid and Harari, and Sherif and Sherif:

A social-psychological group is an organized system of two or more individuals who are interrelated so that the system performs some function, has a standard set of role relationships among its members, and has a set of norms that regulate the function of the group and each of its members (McDavid & Harari, 1968, p. 237).

Mutual Influence

A **group** may be defined as a collection of individuals who influence each other. Individuals are not a group unless they are affecting and being affected by each other and, therefore, the primary defining characteristic of a group is interpersonal influence.

Motivation

A **group** may be defined as a collection of individuals who are trying to satisfy some personal need through their joint association. According to this definition, the individuals are not a group unless they are motivated by some personal reason to be part of a group. Individuals belong to the group in order to obtain rewards or to satisfy personal needs. It is questionable that a group could exist unless its members' needs are satisfied by their membership. Social scientists who have defined group in this way write as follows:

We define "group" as a collection of individuals whose existence as a collection is rewarding to the individuals (Bass, 1960, p. 39).

The definition which seems most essential is that a group is a collection of organisms in which the existence of all (in their given relationships) is necessary to the satisfaction of certain individual needs in each (Cattell, 1951, p. 167).

Some of these definitions may be overly specific or may overlap. What each implies, however, is that not every collection of people is a group. The *Oxford English Dictionary* (1989) defines a *group* as a number of persons or things regarded as forming a unit on account of any kind of mutual or common relation or classified together on account of a common degree of similarity. On the basis of the preceding definitions, a **small group** may be defined as two or more individuals in face-to-face interaction who are aware of their positive interdependence as they strive to achieve mutual goals,

WHAT IS THE BEST WAY TO DEFINE A GROUP?

Following are the seven definitions of the concept *group*. Rank them from most accurate (1) to least accurate (7). Write down your rationale for your ranking. Find a partner and share your ranking and rationale, listen to his or her ranking and rationale, and cooperatively create a new, improved ranking and rationale. Then find another pair and repeat the procedure in a group of four.

Rank	Definition
_____	A **group** is a number of individuals who join together to achieve a goal.
_____	A **group** is several individuals who are interdependent in some way.
_____	A **group** is a number of individuals who are interacting with one another.
_____	A **group** is a social unit consisting of two or more persons who perceive themselves as belonging to a group.
_____	A **group** is a collection of individuals whose interactions are structured by a set of roles and norms.
_____	A **group** is a collection of individuals who influence each other.
_____	A **group** is a collection of individuals who are trying to satisfy some personal need through their joint association.

aware of their membership in the group, and aware of the others who belong to the group. Though there may be some groups that do not fully fit this definition, the most commonly recognized examples of groups do.

A distinction can be made between small and large groups. Whereas the definition of a small group usually includes member interaction, a group may also involve large numbers of members who have some common characteristic without actually meeting one other (such as a reference group, discussed later in this chapter). A community can be a large group, as can individuals with the same ethnic heritage.

Groups may be contrasted with aggregates. An **aggregate** is a collection of individuals who are present at the same time and place but who do *not* form a unit or have a common degree of similarity. Individuals standing on a street corner, the members of an audience at a play, and students listening to a lecture are aggregates, not groups.

Do Groups Even Exist?

Not everyone believes that groups exist. One of the more interesting social science debates centers on the nature of groups. There are two contrasting positions: the group orientation and the individual orientation. Those who support group orientation focus on the group as a whole, as something separate from the individual group members. In explaining the actions of group members, social scientists focus on the influences of the group and the larger social system of which the group is a part. They believe that when people come together as a group, they form a new social entity with its own rules, attitudes, beliefs, and practices.

Supporters of the individualist orientation, however, focus on the individual in the group; without individuals, groups do not exist. In order to explain the functioning of the group, social scientists study the attributes, cognitions, and personalities of the group members. One of the first supporters of an individualist orientation, Floyd Allport (1924), argued that groups do not think, feel, or act—only people do, and therefore groups are not real entities and are not deserving of study. See the Group Orientation versus Individualistic Orientation comparison table for more information about these two positions.

Group Orientation	Individualistic Orientation
The *group orientation* focuses on the group as a whole. In explaining the actions of group members, social scientists focus on the influences of the group and the larger social systems of which it is part. Emile Durkheim (1898, p. 104), arguing that groups were entities different from individuals, stated, "If, then, we begin with the individual, we shall be able to understand nothing of what takes place in the group." He posited that small *primary groups* (small groups characterized by face-to-face interaction, interdependence, and strong group identification such as families and very close friends) are the building blocks of society, and he worked upward from this level to an analysis of social systems in general. He was convinced that a group mind or collective consciousness-dominated individual will in many situations. Le Bon (1895) believed that a group mind exists separate from the minds of individual members. Cartwright and Zander (1968) maintained that a group can be emotionally healthy or pathological. Cattell (1951) described groups as possessing different personalities. Lewin (1935), as a Gestalt psychologist, noted that a group cannot be understood by considering only the qualities and characteristics of each member. When individuals merge into a group, something new is created that must be seen as an entity in itself. Changes in one aspect of a group will necessarily lead to changes in the other group features.	The *individualistic orientation* focuses on the individual in the group. In order to explain the functioning of the group, psychologists focus on the attitudes, cognitions, and personalities of the members. Floyd Allport (1924) argued that groups do not think, feel, or act (only people do), and therefore groups are not real and are not deserving of study. He said, "Groups have no nervous systems, only individuals have nervous systems." To Allport, groups are no more than (a) shared sets of values, ideas, thoughts, and habits that exist simultaneously in the minds of several persons or (b) the sum of the actions of each member taken separately. His *coup de grâce* was his observation, "You can't stumble over a group." Many social scientists have agreed with Allport and have taken a rather cavalier approach to the attributes that determine whether a collection of people is a group. Groups have also been defined on the basis of individual perceptions of other members (Bales, 1950), individual reward (Bass, 1960), and individual purpose and meaning (Mills, 1967). Much of the research on groups, furthermore, has used individual members as the unit of analysis.

Solomon Asch (1952) adopted a middle ground by comparing groups to water. He argued that in order to understand the properties of water, it is important to know the characteristics of its elements, hydrogen and oxygen. This knowledge alone, however, is not sufficient to understand water—the combination of hydrogen and oxygen must be examined as a unique entity. Similarly, groups must be studied as unique entities, even though it is important to know the characteristics of the individual members.

Although supporters of the individualistic orientation may argue that groups are not important, evidence suggests that groups evoke stronger reactions than an individual engaging in the same behavior. Actions by groups and individuals elicit differing preferences for redress (Abelson, Dasgupta, Park, & Banaji, 1998). When individuals are perceived to be part of a cohesive group (as opposed to an aggregate of unrelated individuals), observers express stereotypic judgments about the individuals and infer that their behavior was shaped by the presence of others (Oakes & Turner, 1986; Oakes, Turner, & Haslam, 1991; Wilder, 1977, 1978a). A misogynist statement made by an individual, for example, provokes a different reaction than a misogynist statement made by a group. Social scientists of both the individualistic and group persuasions have been productive in generating theories of group functioning and conducting research to validate or disconfirm the theories.

BARRIERS TO CAPITALIZING ON THE POWER OF GROUPS

Directions: Consider the following five sources of resistance to using small groups. Rate yourself from 1 to 5 on each source.

1————————2————————3————————4————————5

Low	Middle	High
Not a Concern of Mine	Somewhat a Concern	Consistently and Strongly a Concern

Causes of Missed Opportunities to Capitalize on the Power of Groups

_____   **Belief that isolated work is the natural order of the world.** Such a myopic focus blinds individuals to the realization that no one person could have built a cathedral, achieved America's independence from England, or created a supercomputer.

_____   **Resistance to taking responsibility for others.** Many individuals do not easily (a) take responsibility for the performance of colleagues or (b) let colleagues assume responsibility for their work.

_____   **Confusion about what makes groups work.** Many individuals may not know the difference between effective and ineffective groups.

_____   **Fear that they cannot use groups effectively.** Not all groups work. Most adults have had experiences with ineffective and inefficient committees, task forces, and clubs, and know how bad groups can be. When many educators weigh the potential power of learning groups against the possibility of failure, they choose to play it safe and rely on isolated work.

_____   **Concern about the time and effort required to change.** Using groups requires individuals to apply what is known about effective groups in a disciplined way. Learning how to do so and engaging in such disciplined action may seem daunting.

THE IMPORTANCE OF GROUPS

No man is an island, entire of itself.

John Donne

Humans are small-group beings. We always have been and we always will be. Human evolution has depended on individuals coming together in various types of groups to live, work, and govern. For 200,000 years humans lived in small hunting-and-gathering groups. For 10,000 years humans lived in small farming communities. In the last 1,000 or so years, large cities have developed. Each of these living conditions depends on cooperative efforts of group work for its success. In fact, our ability to function effectively in groups may be the reason humans exist today. This ability certainly played a large role in the manner humans developed.

Two recent branches of the human species are Neanderthals and Cro-Magnons (modern humans). Our origins are somehow linked with the fate of the Neanderthals. We have never been proud of our extinct predecessors, partly because of their looks. Nevertheless, the Neanderthals represent a high point in the human story. Their lineage goes back to the earliest members of the genus *Homo.* They were the original pioneers. Over thousands of years, Neanderthals moved out of Africa by way of the Near East into India, China, Malaysia, and southern Europe. In recent times, around 150,000 years ago, they pioneered glacial landscapes and became the first humans to cope with climates hospitable only to woolly mammoths and reindeer.

There is no anatomical evidence that the Neanderthals were cerebrally inferior to us (the Cro-Magnons). In fact, they had a larger brain than we do. There is no doubt whatsoever that they were our physical superiors. Their strongest individuals could probably lift weights of half a ton or so. Physically, we are quite puny in comparison. But we gradually replaced the Neanderthals during an overlapping period of a few thousand years. It may have mainly been a matter of attrition and population pressure. As the glaciers from Scandinavia advanced, northern populations of Neanderthals moved south while our ancestors were moving north out of Africa. About 40,000 years ago we met in Europe. We flourished and they vanished about 30,000 years ago.

There are numerous explanations for the disappearance of the Neanderthals. Perhaps they evolved into us. Perhaps we merged through intermarriage. Perhaps there was an intergroup competition for food, with the Neanderthals unable to meet our challenge and dying off in marginal areas. Perhaps the Neanderthals were too set in their ways and were unable to evolve and refine better ways to cooperate while we were continually organizing better cooperative efforts to cope with changing climatic conditions.

During the time our ancestors coexisted with the Neanderthals, Cro-Magnons developed highly sophisticated cooperative efforts characterized by social organization, group-hunting procedures, creative experimentation with a variety of materials, sharing of knowledge, division of labor, trade with other communities, and transportation systems. We sent out scouts to monitor the movements of herds of animals we preyed upon. The Neanderthals probably did not. We cached supplies and first aid materials to aid hunting parties far away from our home bases. The

Neanderthals apparently did not. Neanderthals probably engaged their prey chiefly in direct combat. We developed more efficient ways of hunting, such as driving animals over cliffs. We developed more sophisticated tools and weapons to kill from a distance, such as the spear and the bow and arrow. The Neanderthals probably did not. The Neanderthals used local materials to develop tools. We were more selective, often obtaining special fine-grained and colorful flints from quarries as far as 250 miles away through trade networks. We improved the toolmaking process through experimentation and sharing knowledge with other communities. The Neanderthals probably did not. The Neanderthals used stone almost exclusively for tools. We used bone and ivory to make needles and other tools. We "tailored" our clothes and made ropes and nets. Our ability to obtain more food than we needed spawned the formation of far-ranging trade and social networks. These more complex forms of cooperation directly led to the accumulation of wealth and the creation of artistic efforts, laws, and storytelling to preserve traditions. Whether we replaced or evolved from the Neanderthals, our ingenuity was evident in organizing cooperative efforts to increase our standard of living and the quality of our lives. We excelled at organizing effective group efforts.

Groups and the Quality of Life

Our ancestors' lives were improved greatly and dramatically by living in groups, but what about us today? It is fair to say that the quality of contemporary life is related directly to **group effectiveness.** With so many of our activities and social interactions taking place within groups—be it our risk-management group at work, our weekend softball team, or the people we live with—almost every aspect of modern life is affected by group dynamics. Knowledge of group dynamics, therefore, is a tool that can make our lives better and more meaningful, because it can help us build effective groups in every part of our lives.

Understanding Group Dynamics Is Central to Maintaining a Viable Family. For thousands of years, family life has been one of the sustaining values of civilization. Anthropologist Margaret Mead observed that the family is the toughest institution humans have, and it is one of our core small groups. The structure of the family, however, has changed significantly in the last hundred years. First came the demise of the extended family. More recently, the nuclear family has been on the decline as more single-parent households form. Today, one child in four is raised by a single parent. Obviously, creating sustainable families is a hard task in our modern climate. In order to build and maintain a constructive family life within the diverse demands of modern life, individuals need to have a thorough knowledge of group dynamics and small-group skills.

A Knowledge of Group Dynamics Is Central to Effective Businesses and Industries. During the first half of the twentieth century, mass production made the United States the world leader in manufacturing. By the end of the twentieth century, however, many businesses had turned to the high productivity generated by small groups. Today, many companies rely on employees working in teams to design and launch new products, conduct research and training, handle employee issues, facilitate interdepartmental communication, and much more. Furthermore, the dramatic new technologies made available in the past two decades now enable groups to work between offices, across towns, and around the world. What makes organizations viable today is their ability to create teams dominated by a culture of learning, continuous improvement, and adaptation. In turn, what makes people viable employees is their ability to work in small groups and produce results (see Chapter 13).

Understanding Group Dynamics Is Central to Education. Over the past few generations, the teaching paradigm has changed from lecture and individual work to cooperative learning (Johnson, Johnson, & Holubec, 2008). Instead of listening to a teacher's lecture and taking notes, students now work in small groups to help one another learn a specific lesson or task. Instead of comparing students to one another and encouraging **competition,** cooperative group-based work allows students to work together in a manner that benefits all of them. Cooperative learning has been shown to produce higher achievement, more positive relationships, and greater psychological health than competitive or individualistic learning (Johnson & Johnson, 1989; see Chapter 11).

A Knowledge of Group Dynamics Is Central to the Long-Term Maintenance of Psychological Health. Simply by watching television commercials or flipping through the pages of almost any magazine, we can infer that the country is experiencing an epidemic of depression, anxiety, and mental illness. Prescription drugs, various forms of therapy, and a host of other products and services advertised in the media are aimed at treating these problems. This proliferation is more than a marketing trend, however; surveys indicate the rate of depression over the last two generations has increased roughly tenfold. People, especially young people, are experiencing much more depression, feeling hopeless, giving up, being passive, having low self-esteem, and committing suicide. Being involved in supportive groups, however, can help prevent the occurrence of psychological problems. Networks of friends and family, group activities, and other types of productive group interaction can help people feel more connected to the world around them, making them less depressed and anxious. Furthermore, group therapy and counseling groups are a preferred method of treatment for psychological problems (see Chapter 12).

In short, knowing group dynamics theory and having small-group skills can change your life. They can make you more employable and lead to greater career success. They can improve your friendships. They can lead to more caring and loving family relationships and greater competence as parents. They can promote greater psychological health and increased ability to cope with stress and adversity.

As you continue reading about groups—how they operate and are constructed, and why a group is effective and productive—what you are learning is the nature of groups. To that end, you should focus on the following ideas:

1. The nature of group structure
2. The relationship between group structure and group productivity
3. How the dynamics of the group determine its effectiveness
4. The ways groups develop over time

GROUP STRUCTURE

Imagine you are an ecologist whose career has been dedicated to studying ecosystems around the world. You have encountered many diverse habitats in your studies, from thick rain forests to parched deserts. They all had a set of common features: topography, weather patterns, plants, animals, and their interconnections. You have observed, for example, that plants and animals sharing certain territories develop elaborate divisions of labor and broad symbioses. You also have learned that plants and animals adapt over time to be uniquely suited for survival in their particular habitats. Thus, you expect to find a basic ecological structure when you travel to a new habitat.

Now imagine you are studying small groups. Although many diverse types of groups may be found, when you approach a new group you look for the basic features that characterize all groups. These features include a purpose that defines the territory of the group and binds the members together, a definable pattern of communication among members, different members performing different functions that fit into an overall division of labor, procedures for managing conflicts, expectations concerning acceptable and unacceptable behavior by group members, and the adaptation of the group to the organization, society, and culture within which it is based. Once the basic structure has been identified, the nature of interpersonal relations in the group can be understood as clearly as can the functioning of an ecosystem.

Just like ecosystems, groups have a structure. Groups function as their members interact, and whenever two or more individuals join together to achieve a goal, a group structure develops. Observers of groups who want to know how a group truly functions look beyond the group's unique features to its basic structure, a stable pattern of interaction among members. Two aspects of group interaction are especially important to understanding how a group is structured: differentiated roles and integrating norms. Within any group, no matter which organization, society, or culture it belongs to, the

GROUP STRUCTURE

Definition		Example
Roles	Expectations defining the appropriate behavior of an occupant of a position toward other related positions	President, vice president, secretary; summarizer, recorder
Norms	Common beliefs regarding group members' appropriate behavior, attitudes, and perceptions; rules, implicit or explicit, that regulate the behavior of group members	Promptness, courtesy, reciprocity, responsibility

group's roles and norms structure the interaction among group members. Roles differentiate the responsibilities of group members, whereas norms integrate members' efforts into a unified whole.

Roles: Differentiation Within Groups

Think of a group you have belonged to, and answer this question: Did everyone in the group act the same way or perform the same functions? In all likelihood, your answer is "no." A considerable degree of differentiation usually exists within groups, meaning different members work on different tasks and are expected to accomplish different things. In other words, different group members play different roles.

Roles define the formal structure of the group and differentiate one position from another. Formally, a **role** may be defined as a set of expectations governing the appropriate behavior of an occupant of a position toward occupants of other related positions. Often such roles are assigned in a relatively formal manner, such as appointing a president, secretary, treasurer, and so on. At other times, individuals drift into various roles on the basis of their interests and skills. Once a role is assumed, however, the member is expected (by other group members) to behave in certain ways. Members who conform to their role requirements are rewarded, whereas those who deviate are punished.

Roles ensure that the task behaviors of group members are interrelated appropriately so that the group's goals are achieved. The roles usually are complementary in that one cannot be performed without the other (e.g., the roles of "teacher" and "student"). The expectations that define a role include rights and obligations; the obligations of one role are the rights of other roles. One of the obligations of being a teacher, for example, includes structuring a learning situation, whereas one of the rights of being a student is to have learning situations structured by the teacher. Within a group, expectations of the obligations that accompany a particular role can conflict; this is called **role conflict.** What a principal expects from a teacher and what students expect from a teacher, for example, can be contradictory. Contradictory expectations, therefore, can create one type of role conflict.

A second type of role conflict occurs when the demands of one role are incompatible with the demands of another role. Every person is required to play multiple roles, and almost everyone belongs to more than one group. Sometimes such role conflict can provide great drama. Back in the Old West, for example, Sheriff Pat Garrett was called on to arrest the famous outlaw Billy the Kid. Billy the Kid also happened to be one of Garrett's best friends, but Garrett shot him anyway. This situation, although extreme, illustrates how roles can influence our actions in ways that make us act contrary to our private feelings or vested interests.

Stanley Milgram provided an important example of role incompatibility with his famous studies on obedience to authority (1974). In these studies, he placed paid adult subjects in the role of teacher and gave them the responsibility of giving "learners" an electric shock when they committed a memory error. Milgram began his study with the intention of showing that teachers would refuse to comply with the requirements of their role if those requirements went against their own personal beliefs. Once the study was under way, however, the findings showed a different situation. Although almost all teachers began to express reluctance and show signs of stress as the intensity of the shock increased and the learner cried out in pain, the majority of the teachers continued to administer the shocks. Over 60% of subjects administered the maximum shock (450 volts) to the learner. Even when the teachers were compelled to hold the learners' hands to the shock plate, 30% continued to administer the shocks. Milgram's results point out that many people can commit a variety of costly, harmful, and even immoral actions if role pressure is severe enough.

Different social roles usually are associated with different degrees of status. **Status** can be thought of as the degree to which an individual's contribution is crucial to the success and prestige of the group, how much power and control over outcomes that individual has, and the extent to which the person embodies some idealized or admired characteristic (such as being physically attractive). In many subhuman and some human groups, status is determined by physical dominance. In other groups, status may be determined by wealth, education, or any other determinant the group deems valuable.

Although status and power ordinarily go hand in hand, they need not. In a series of experiments, Johnson and Allen (1972) separated status and power from each other. They found that having high status and high power in an organization results in an enhanced self-perception that leads to altruistic behavior but disdain for the worker. On the other hand, when an individual has high status but low power in an organization that rewards high power, he or she engages in selfish behavior (usually by deviating from the prescribed norms in order to increase his or her own rewards) but has respect for the workers.

Whatever determines status within a certain group, status differences have a number of important effects on group processes. High-status individuals are likely to be valued by the group and treated more tolerantly. These group members, therefore, often are less affected by group norms and peer pressure than are lower-status members, in part because high-status individuals are less likely to expect punishment for their improper actions (Johnson & Allen, 1972). High-status members also have disproportionately strong influence over group decisions and judgments, whereas those low in status tend to be ignored, even when they offer intelligent and creative advice. In fact, a situation in which a low-status person has a critical insight or piece of information but is ignored by the rest of the decision-making group is not uncommon.

Norms: Integration of Members' Actions

Whereas roles differentiate members' rights and obligations from one another, norms integrate the actions of all group members. **Norms** are rules, implicit or explicit, established by groups to regulate the behavior of all members. Norms tell group members how to behave, or how not to behave, in various situations. In short, the norms of a group are the group's common belief regarding appropriate behavior, attitudes, and perceptions for its members. These prescribed modes of conduct and one common belief not only guide the behavior of group members but also help group interaction by specifying the kinds of responses that are expected and acceptable in particular situations. Norms thus provide a basis for predicting the behavior of other members and serve as a guide for a members' own behavior.

All groups have norms, and they may be set formally or informally. A group of students who party together, for example, often has common ideas about what is acceptable and unacceptable behavior at a party. More formally organized groups, such as classes, have norms about absence, tardiness, accomplishment of assigned work, and appropriate times to speak. In any group, some norms specify the behavior expected of all group members and others apply only to individuals in specific roles. In the classroom, for instance, some norms govern both the teacher's and the students' behavior, but others may apply only to the teacher or only to the students. Because norms refer to the expected behavior sanctioned by a group, they have an "ought to" or "must" quality: Group members must not disrupt the group's work, group members ought to participate in discussions, and so on.

The norms of any group vary in importance. Norms that have a low effect on the objectives and values of the group usually allow for a greater range of behavior and bring less severe pressures for members to conform than do norms more relevant to group functioning. Because most groups insist on adherence to their norms as a basic requirement for membership, individuals wishing to join or remain in specific groups generally follow these "rules of the game." If they do not, they soon may find themselves on the outside looking in.

For a group norm to influence a person's behavior, the person must recognize that it exists, be aware that other group members accept and follow the norm, and accept and follow it himself or herself. A regulation that all members should be on time for group meetings, for example, becomes a norm only to the extent that the individual group member accepts it, sees other group members accepting it, and sees them enforcing the regulation among themselves. At first a person may conform to a group norm because the group typically rewards conforming behavior and punishes nonconforming behavior. Later the person may internalize the norm and conform to it automatically, even when no other group members are present.

Norms cannot be imposed on a group. Instead, they develop out of the interaction among group members. This concept of norms being social products was demonstrated ingeniously by Muzafer Sherif in 1936. When a fixed point of light is viewed in total darkness, it appears to move spontaneously, a perceptual phenomenon known as the *autokinetic effect*. Sherif utilized this phenomenon to study how group norms develop and how group members come to form coherent, shared beliefs about new events. Leading individuals into a totally dark room, Sherif turned on a tiny light and asked participants, first individually and then in groups, to note how much the light moved. When tested in groups, the participants reached consensus in their judgments on the amount of movement. Sherif, however, was able to increase or decrease subjects' estimates of movement dramatically if he paid accomplices to offer particularly large or small estimates. Once a group decision was made about how much the light was moving, the norm persisted even when the group was not present. That is, individual participants continued to use the group judgment as a frame of reference to evaluate the perceived movement of the light. The important lesson Sherif's study demonstrates is many of the judgments and values that seem to belong to individual group members actually are shaped by the judgments of other group members.

Another classic study about the effect of group norms on the beliefs and values of group members was conducted by Theodore Newcomb in 1943. Born in 1903, Newcomb was a pioneer of social psychology and a cofounder of the social psychology program at the University of Michigan. He conducted a number of studies on how the college experience affected students, the most famous of which was his study of group norms at Bennington College. The students, all females from mostly well-to-do and politically conservative families, lived in a community where most of the faculty and older students were somewhat materialistic and politically liberal. A majority of the Bennington students became progressively more liberal over their careers, but some did not. Newcomb was able to relate the student's ultimate political orientation to the group she identified with—liberal if she thought of herself as primarily a member of the campus community and conservative if her primary identification was with her family. Newcomb's study marks the point where the study of reference groups began. A **reference group** is a group people identify with, compare their attitudes to, and use as a means of evaluating those attitudes.

CREATING PRODUCTIVE GROUPS

Although this discussion of structure, rules, and norms may suggest the opposite, there is nothing magical about working in a group. Some groups are highly effective and achieve amazing goals, while others are highly ineffective and waste everyone's time. The authors have studied various types of groups for more than thirty years. We have interviewed thousands of members in a wide variety of organizations in a number of different countries to discover how groups are being used and where and how groups work best. Using our research and the findings of other researchers, such as Katzenbach and Smith (2003), we have developed a group performance curve to clarify the difference between ineffective and effective groups (Figure 1.2). Four types of groups appear on the curve: pseudogroups, traditional work groups, effective groups, and high-performance groups. The performance curve begins with the individual members of the group and portrays their performance relative to each group type. The purpose of the curve is to illustrate that the productiveness of any small group depends on how the group is structured (Katzenbach & Smith, 2003).

As the following explanations of the four groups featured on the performance curve point out, groups can be created in a variety of ways and for a multitude of reasons. In those very roots of group development, though, may also lie many of the reasons why one group is productive and another group is not. Attention must be paid to the reasons for the group's existence, its structure, and its motivations.

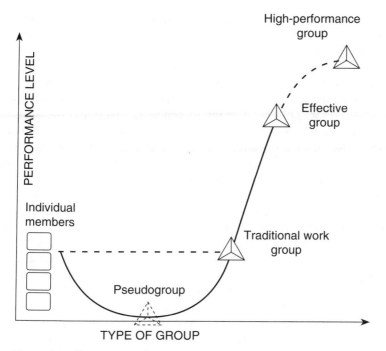

Figure 1.2 The group performance curve.

A **pseudogroup** is a group whose members have been assigned to work together but who have no interest in doing so. They believe they will be evaluated by being ranked from the highest performer to the lowest performer. Although members talk to one another, they actually are competing. They see one another as rivals who must be defeated, block or interfere with one another's performance, hide information, attempt to mislead and confuse, and distrust one another. As a result, the sum of the whole is less than the sum of the potential of the individual members. In other words, members would be more productive if they were working alone. Furthermore, the group does not mature because members have no interest in or commitment to one another or to the group's future. An example of a pseudogroup might be a regional sales team that is told to work together to increase profits, only to find out that the top salesperson will receive three times the bonus any other team member will receive.

A **traditional work group** is a group whose members are assigned to work together and accept that they have to do so. Members believe that they will be evaluated and rewarded as individuals, not as members of the group. The work is structured so that very little joint work is required. Members interact primarily to clarify how the work is to be done. They seek one another's information but have no motivation to inform their groupmates. Members are accountable as separate individuals, not as members of a team. Some members loaf, seeking a free ride on the efforts of their more conscientious groupmates. The conscientious members then feel exploited and do less. The result is the sum of the whole is more than the sum of the potential of some of the members, but the more hard-working and conscientious members would perform better if they worked alone. An example of this might be a study group designated by the teacher, in which some students do research for an upcoming test while others do nothing.

An **effective group** is more than the sum of its parts. It is a group whose members commit themselves to maximizing their own and one another's success. Members are assigned to work together, and they are happy to do so. They believe their success depends on the efforts of all group members. An effective group has a number of defining characteristics, including positive interdependence that unites members to achieve clear operational goals, two-way communication, distributed leadership, and power based on expertise. In addition, effective groups feature a decision-making process that allows group members to challenge one another's information and reasoning and to resolve conflicts constructively. Members of effective groups hold one another accountable to do their fair share of the work, promote one another's success, appropriately engage in small-group skills, and determine how effectively they are working together.

A **high-performance group** meets all the criteria for an effective group and out performs all reasonable expectations, given its membership. What differentiates a high-performance group from an effective group is the level of commitment members have to one another and to the group's success. Jennifer Futernick, who is part of a high-performance, rapid-response team at McKinsey & Company, calls the emotion that binds her teammates together a form of love (Katzenbach & Smith, 2003). Ken Hoepner of the Burlington Northern Intermodal Team (also described by Katzenbach & Smith, 2003) stated, "Not only did we trust each other, not only did we respect each other, but we gave a damn about the rest of the people on this team. If we saw somebody

TYPES OF GROUPS

Demonstrate your understanding of the different types of groups by matching the definitions with the appropriate group. Find a partner and check your answers; explain why you believe your answers to be correct.

	Type of Group	Definition
_____	Pseudogroup	a. A group in which members work together to accomplish shared goals. Members perceive that they can reach their goals if and only if the other group members also reach their goals.
_____	Traditional group	b. A group whose members have been assigned to work together but who have no interest in doing so. The structure promotes competition at close quarters.
_____	Effective group	c. A group that meets all the criteria for being an effective group and outperforms all reasonable expectations, given its membership.
_____	High-performance group	d. A group whose members agree to work together but see little benefit from doing so. The structure promotes individualistic work with talking.

vulnerable, we were there to help." As these examples demonstrate, members' mutual concern for one another's personal growth enables high-performance groups to perform far above expectations and also to have a lot of fun. Unfortunately, high-performance groups are rare; most groups never achieve this level of development.

EXERCISE 1.4

SAVING THE WORLD FROM DRACULA

A problem-solving situation is used to provide an introduction to group dynamics.

1. Form heterogeneous groups of four.
2. Read the situation sheet, "The Danger of Dracula."
3. Create a plan of attack to stop Count Dracula from initiating a new reign of terror by vampires. Rank the items listed on the "Saving the World from Dracula Ranking Sheet." Your goal is to rank items from most important (1) to least important (12) and write out a rationale as to why you ranked the items as you did.
   a. Working by yourself, individually, rank the items from most important (1) to least important (12). Write out a rationale explaining your ranking.
   b. Working *cooperatively* in your group, rank the items again, coming to consensus. Write out a rationale explaining the group's ranking. There should be one ranking and rationale from the group.
4. Score your own and your group's ranking (see p. 533 in Appendix for answer key):
   a. Compute the absolute difference (ignore plus and minus signs) between your individual ranking and the experts' ranking.
   b. Compute the absolute difference (ignore plus and minus signs) between your group's ranking and the experts' ranking.
   c. A perfect ranking will have a score of zero. The lower your score, the more accurate your ranking. The criteria for success are:

0–20	Excellent
21–30	Good
31–40	Poor
41+	Terrible

5. When the group has solved the problem, answer the following questions:
   a. What is the group's goal?
   b. What were the patterns of communication among group members?
   c. How did leadership emerge in the group? Who provided what types of leadership in your group?
   d. What determined how influential each member was in the group?
   e. What method of decision making was used, and how effective was it?
   f. Why or why not did members challenge each other's conclusions?
   g. What conflicts arose among group members and how were they managed?
   h. How do you simultaneously participate in a group and observe the processes the group uses to complete its tasks?
   i. What actions by group members helped and what actions hindered the team in completing its task?

continued on next page

continued from previous page

THE DANGER OF DRACULA

You are a group of scientists who specialize in public health. Your mandate is to prevent epidemics and threats to the general health of the public. Your current concern is the possibility of a proliferation of vampires resulting from the release of Count Dracula from his grave, where he has been trapped for over a hundred years.

Voivode Dracula (1431–1476) was Vlad III, Prince of Wallachia (a province of Romania bordered to the north by Transylvania and Moldavia, to the east by the Black Sea, and to the south by Bulgaria). Dracula was known as a brilliant, courageous, cunning, and clever general who defeated the Turkish army. He was also known as Vlad the Impaler, for impaling tens of thousands of victims on sharpened stakes. In 1459, on St. Bartholomew's Day, for example, Dracula had 30,000 of the citizens of the city of Brasov impaled, arranging the stakes in various geometric formations in front of the city. He was also a noted statesman and scholar. His mighty brain, iron resolution, and immense cruelty made him a formidable adversary. Although he supposedly was killed in battle in 1476 by the Turks, it soon became apparent that he had instead become a vampire. Dracula adopted the title of Count and terrorized that region of Europe until he was imprisoned in his grave in the late 1800s by a team of English scientists and adventurers. The exact whereabouts of his grave were hidden to prevent any misguided soul from freeing him.

Archaeologists excavating an ancient castle in Transylvania have uncovered Count Dracula's crypt and coffin. They plan to open the casket, and when they do they will release Count Dracula once more into the world. Not believing in the danger, the archaeologists are inviting television crews to film the opening, hoping the publicity will help them raise money. You, however, know the truth. Vampires do exist, and once released, Count Dracula will create at least five more vampires a day, each of whom will in turn create five more vampires a day. In a very short time, vampires could be terrorizing the whole world. Your group has the responsibility of preventing this world disaster by destroying Count Dracula before he can begin. Your plan must include:

a. The procedures you will use to destroy Dracula
b. The procedures you will use to protect yourself from Dracula
c. A description of Dracula's strengths and weaknesses that must be overcome and exploited
d. The time of day Dracula will be destroyed

Pooling the resources of your group, you have 12 relevant items. **Your task is to rank these items according to their importance to your quest to prevent a reign of terror by Count Dracula,** starting with 1 for the most important item and ending with 12 for the least important item. Separating items into four categories may help (see table below).

How to Destroy Dracula	Protection Procedures	Dracula's Strengths and Weaknesses	When (Time) We Will Destroy Dracula

SAVING THE WORLD FROM DRACULA RANKING SHEET

Rank the following items according to their importance for saving the world from Dracula, starting with 1 for the most important to 12 for the least important.

	1	2	3	4	2–4	3–4
Item		**Your Ranking**	**Group Ranking**	**Experts' Ranking**	**Individual Difference Scores**	**Group Difference Scores**
1. Oak stake						
2. Diagram/map of Dracula's castle and key to Dracula's crypt						
3. Human ability to cooperate						
4. Table detailing sunrise and sunset in Transylvania						
5. 44-Magnum revolver and shells						
6. Branch of wild rose						
7. Sharp ax and several cloves of garlic						
8. Tickets: plane to Budapest, train to Transylvania, car to castle						
9. Collapsible steel cage						
10. Cross, holy water, communion wafers						
11. Two high-intensity flashlights						
12. Herbs mixed by a witch at midnight under a full moon						
Total						

HOW TO CREATE AN EFFECTIVE GROUP

I will pay more for the ability to deal with people than for any other ability under the sun.

John D. Rockefeller

To be effective overall, a group must do three things: achieve its goals; maintain good working relationships among members; and adapt to changing conditions in the surrounding organization, society, and world. To create such a group you should use the following set of guidelines. These guidelines provide direction for building an effective group, a framework for diagnosing how well a group is functioning, and a means for motivating group members to improve. For further clarification, Table 1.1 lists the guidelines and Table 1.2 offers a comparison of effective and ineffective groups.

Guideline 1: Establish Clear, Operational, and Relevant Group Goals that Create Positive Interdependence and Evoke a High Level of Commitment from Every Member. Groups exist for a reason: People want to achieve goals they are unable to achieve by themselves. In effective groups, goals must be stated clearly so that all members understand the nature of the goals. Additionally, goals must be operational so that members understand how to achieve them. Goals also must be relevant to members' needs, so that they commit themselves to achieving the goals. Finally, the group's goals must create positive interdependence among members. Group goals and social interdependence are discussed in Chapter 3.

Guideline 2: Establish Effective Two-Way Communication by Which Group Members Communicate their Ideas and Feelings Accurately and Clearly. Communication is the basis for all human interaction and group functioning, and it is especially important when groups of people are working toward a common goal. Group members must send and receive messages effectively in order to exchange information and transmit meaning. Effective communication also can decrease misunderstandings and discord among group members. Effective communication depends on minimalizing competition among members and establishing two-way communication. Communication among group members is discussed in Chapter 4.

TABLE 1.1 **Guidelines for Creating Effective Groups**

1. Establish clear, operational, relevant group goals that create positive interdependence and evoke a high level of commitment from every member.

2. Establish effective two-way communication within which group members communicate their ideas and feelings accurately and clearly.

3. Ensure that leadership and participation are distributed among all group members.

4. Ensure that the use of power is distributed among group members and that patterns of influence vary according to the needs of the group as members strive to achieve their mutual goals.

5. Match the method of decision making with (a) the availability of time and resources, (b) the size and seriousness of the decision, and (c) the amount of member commitment needed to implement decision. The most effective way of making a decision is usually by consensus.

6. Encourage structured controversies in which group members advocate their views, disagree, and challenge each other's conclusions and reasoning in order to create high-quality, creative decisions.

7. Ensure that members face their conflicts of interests and use integrative negotiations and mediation to resolve them constructively.

TABLE 1.2   **Comparison of Effective and Ineffective Groups**

EFFECTIVE GROUPS	INEFFECTIVE GROUPS
Goals are clarified and modified so that the best possible match between an individual's goals and the group's goals is achieved; goals are structured cooperatively so all members are committed to achieving them.	Members accept imposed goals; goals are competitively structured so that each member strives to outperform the others.
Communication is two-way, and the open and accurate expression of both ideas and feelings is emphasized.	Communication is one-way, and only ideas are expressed; feelings are suppressed or ignored.
Participation and leadership are distributed among all group members; goal accomplishment, internal maintenance, and developmental change are underscored.	Leadership is delegated and based on authority; participation is unequal, with high-power members dominating; only goal accomplishment is emphasized.
Ability and information determine influence and power; contracts are built to make sure that individuals' goals and needs are fulfilled; power is equalized and shared.	Position determines power; power is concentrated in the authority system; obedience to authority is the rule.
Decision-making procedures are matched with the situation; different methods are used at different times; consensus is sought for important decisions; involvement and group discussions are encouraged.	Decisions are always made by the highest authority; there is little group discussion; members' involvement is minimal.
Structured controversy in which members advocate their views and challenge each other's information and reasoning is seen as the key to high quality and creative decision making and problem solving.	Disagreement among members is suppressed and avoided; quick compromises are sought to eliminate arguing; groupthink is prevalent.
Conflicts of interest are resolved through integrative negotiations and mediation so agreements are reached that maximize joint outcomes and leave all members satisfied.	Conflicts of interest are resolved through distributive negotiations or avoidance; some members win and some members lose or else conflict is ignored and everyone is unhappy.
Interpersonal, group, and intergroup skills are stressed; cohesion is advanced through high levels of inclusion, affection, acceptance, support, and trust; individuality is endorsed.	The functions of group members are stressed; individuality is deemphasized; cohesion is ignored; rigid conformity is promoted.

Guideline 3: Ensure that Leadership and Participation Are Distributed Among All Group Members. All members of a group are responsible for providing leadership. Equal participation and leadership ensures that all members are invested in the group's work, committed to implementing the group's decisions, and satisfied with their membership. Shared leadership and participation also enables the group as a whole to use the resources of every individual, thereby increasing the cohesiveness of the group. Leadership is discussed in Chapter 5.

Guideline 4: Ensure that Power Is Distributed Among Group Members and that Patterns of Influence Vary According to the Needs of the Group. In effective groups, members' power is based on expertise, ability, and access to information, not on authority or personality characteristics. Power struggles among group members can distract the group from its purpose and goals, ultimately making the group useless. To prevent power struggles, every member of the group must have some power of influence in some part of group work. As a group evolves and new goals are set, the distribution of power also needs to evolve. To this end, group members should form coalitions that help fulfill personal goals on the basis of mutual influence and interdependence. Power is discussed in Chapter 6.

Guideline 5: Match Decision-Making Procedures with the Needs of the Situation.
Groups can make decisions in a variety of ways, but there must be a balance between the time and resources a group has available and the method of decision making it uses. A jury deciding a death penalty case, for example, would require a unanimous decision, whereas a church group deciding when to hold its next meeting may not. Balance also is needed among the size and seriousness of the decision, the commitment needed to put it into practice, and the method used for making the decision. The most effective way of making a decision usually is by consensus (unanimous agreement). Consensus promotes distributed participation, the equalization of power, constructive controversy, cohesion, involvement, and commitment. Decision making is discussed in Chapter 7.

Guideline 6: Engage in Constructive Controversy by Disagreeing and Challenging One Another's Conclusions and Reasoning, thus Promoting Creative Decision Making and Problem Solving.
In order to make effective decisions, members must present the best case possible for each major course of action and subject all other alternatives to critical analysis. Controversies over opposing ideas and conclusions are beneficial for groups, because they promote involvement in the group's work, quality and creativity in decision making, and commitment to implementing the group's decisions. Controversies also help ensure that minority and dissenting opinions receive serious discussion and consideration. Controversy and creativity are discussed in Chapter 8.

Guideline 7: Face Your Conflicts and Resolve them in Constructive Ways.
Conflicts of interest may result from incompatible needs or goals, scarce resources, and competitiveness. Five basic strategies can be used to manage conflicts of interest: **withdrawal,** forcing (win–lose negotiations), **smoothing, compromise,** and problem solving (integrative negotiations). Members of effective groups face their conflicts and engage in integrative problem-solving negotiations to resolve them. When problem-solving negotiations fail, mediation may occur. When they are resolved constructively, conflicts are an important and indispensable aspect of increasing group effectiveness. Conflicts of interest are discussed in Chapter 9.

THE DEVELOPMENT OF GROUPS OVER TIME

All groups change over time. The kinds of developmental changes seen in most groups have been described by well over one hundred theories. Most of these theories have taken one of two approaches: **recurring-phase theories** and **sequential-stage theories.**

(Hill & Gruner, 1973; Shambaugh, 1978). Recurring-phase theories focus on the issues that dominate group interaction again and again. Robert Freed Bales (1965), for example, stated that equilibrium has to exist between task-oriented work and emotional expressions to build better relationships among group members. The group tends to oscillate between these two concerns, sometimes striving for more solidarity and sometimes striving for a more work-oriented focus. Wilfred Bion's (1961) recurring-phase theory stated that groups focus on three basic themes: dependency on the leader, pairing among members for emotional support, and fight-flight reactions to a **threat** to the group. William Schultz (1966) proposed that group development occurs as members concern themselves with three issues: affection, inclusion, and control.

Sequential-stage theories discuss the typical order of the phases of group development. Richard Moreland and John Levine (1982, 1988) suggested that group members go through predictable, sequential stages of membership: prospective member, new member, full member, marginal member, and ex-member. At each stage, the member is concerned with a different aspect of group life. For example, the new member attempts to change the group to meet his or her needs while the group attempts to mold the new member to fit the group's needs. Later on, the full member engages in role negotiation in order to find a niche that is most comfortable.

Another famous sequential-stage theory, offered by Worchel, Coutant-Sassic, and Grossman (1992), proposed six stages to group development. The initial stage is discontent, when individuals feel that their present group(s) are not meeting their needs. The second stage is a precipitating event that brings members together. In the third stage, members begin to identify with the group. In the fourth stage, attention turns to group productivity. In the fifth stage, attention shifts to the individual group member, who negotiates with the group to expand task efforts to meet personal goals. In the sixth and final stage, the group begins to disintegrate.

Probably the most famous sequential-stage theory was formulated by Bruce W. Tuckman (1965; Tuckman & Jensen, 1977). Tuckman reviewed over fifty studies on group development conducted in a variety of settings (mostly therapy and training groups of limited duration). Although the description of the stages the groups went through varied widely on the surface, Tuckman found a surprising amount of agreement beneath the diversity and hypothesized five stages: forming, storming, norming, performing, and adjourning.

Tuckman theorized that groups focus on specific issues at each of the five stages, and this focus influences members' behaviors. The *forming stage* is a period of uncertainty in which members try to determine their place in the group and the procedures and rules of the group. Conflicts begin to arise during the *storming stage* as members resist the influence of the group and rebel against accomplishing the task. Members often confront their various differences, and conflict management becomes the focus of attention. During the *norming stage,* the group establishes some consensus regarding a role structure and group norms for appropriate behavior. Cohesion and commitment increase. In the *performing stage,* the group members become proficient in working together to achieve the group's goals and more flexible in patterns of working together. The group disbands in the *adjourning stage.* Of all the sequential-stage theories, Tuckman's seems the most useful and has created the most interest.

Virtually all the studies that Tuckman reviewed involved group leaders who were passive and nondirective and who made no attempt to intervene in the group process.

Most groups, however, have a coordinator, team leader, or instructor who tries to ensure that the group functions productively. In applying Tuckman's conclusions to such groups, the authors (with the help of Roger Johnson and other colleagues) identified seven stages of development: (1) defining and structuring procedures, (2) conforming to procedures and getting acquainted, (3) recognizing mutuality and building trust, (4) rebelling and differentiating, (5) committing to and taking ownership for the goals, procedures, and other members, (6) functioning maturely and productively, and (7) terminating. Each of these stages is discussed in turn.

Defining and Structuring Procedures

When a group begins, the members are usually concerned about what is expected of them and the nature of the group's goals. Group members want to know what is going to happen; what is expected of them; whether or not they will be accepted, influential, and liked; how the group is going to function; and who the other group members are. Group members expect the coordinator to explain how the group is to function in a way that reassures them that their personal needs will be met. When a group first meets, therefore, the coordinator should define the procedures to be used, define the group's goals, establish the interdependence among members, and generally organize the group and announce the beginning of the group's work.

Conforming to Procedures and Getting Acquainted

As group members follow the prescribed procedures and interact around the task, they become acquainted with one another and familiarize themselves with the procedures until they can follow them easily. They also learn the strengths and

SUMMARY OF THE COORDINATOR'S ROLE

1. Introduce, define, and structure the group.
2. Clarify procedures, reinforce members for conforming to the procedures, and help members become acquainted.
3. Emphasize and highlight the positive interdependence among group members, and encourage them to engage in both trusting and trustworthy behaviors.
4. Accept the rebellion by and differentiation among group members as a normal process. Use integrative negotiations to help members establish their independence from another and the prescribed procedures.
5. Help members commit themselves to and take ownership of the group's goals and procedures.
6. Be a consultant to the group, providing resources for the group to function effectively.
7. Signal termination and help the members move on to future groups.

weaknesses of the other group members. During this stage the group members are dependent on the coordinator for direction and clarification of the group's goals and procedures. The coordinator should also stress the following group norms: (1) take responsibility for one's own performance and the performance of the other members of the group, (2) provide help and assistance to other members, (3) respond to other members in an accepting, supportive, and trustworthy way, (4) make decisions through consensus, and (5) confront and solve problems in group functioning. During this stage the goals and procedures of the group are the coordinator's. The group members conform to the prescribed procedures and interact with one another, but they are not committed personally to the group's goals and each other.

Recognizing Mutuality and Building Trust

The third stage of group development is marked by group members recognizing their interdependence and building trust. A sense of mutuality is built as group members recognize they "sink or swim together." Members begin to take responsibility for one another's performance and appropriate behavior. Trust is built through disclosing one's thoughts, ideas, conclusions, and feelings, and having the other group members respond with acceptance, support, and reciprocation of the disclosures. Trust is discussed at length in Chapter 3 and in Johnson (2003).

Rebelling and Differentiating

Relationships among group members are often built through a cycle of establishing independence and becoming friendly, then differentiating themselves from each other through conflict, and finally committing themselves to a relationship. The fourth stage of group development is marked by group members rebelling against the coordinator and procedures and differentiating themselves from one another through disagreements and conflicts. On the road to maturity a group will go through a period (sometimes short, sometimes long) of challenging the authority of the coordinator. This is an ordinary occurrence in group development and should be expected. This swing toward independence contrasts sharply with the dependence demonstrated by members during stage 2. Group members may wish to test and challenge the coordinator's sincerity and commitment or attempt to establish their independence by doing the opposite of the group procedures.

Rebelling and differentiating are important methods by which group members establish boundaries and autonomy (Johnson, 1979, 1980a). As they are natural parts of the development process, the coordinator needs to deal with both in an open and accepting way. Some advice for doing so includes the following:

1. Do not tighten control and try to force conformity to prescribed procedures; reason and negotiate.
2. Confront and problem solve when members become counterdependent and rebellious.

3. Mediate conflicts among members, helping the group establish members' autonomy and individuality.
4. Work toward members taking ownership of the procedures and committing themselves to one another's success.

Coordinating a group at this stage is like teaching a child to ride a bicycle: One runs alongside to prevent the child from falling, but one must let loose so the child can learn to balance on his or her own.

Committing to the Group's Goals, Procedures, and Members

During this stage, dependence on the coordinator is replaced by dependence on the other members of the group, and conformity to the prescribed procedures is replaced by personal commitment to the collaborative nature of the experience. The group shifts from being the coordinator's group to being the members' group. Group norms become internalized and motivation becomes intrinsic rather than extrinsic. Group members promote each other's efforts to achieve the group's goals and provide each other with support and assistance.

Functioning Maturely and Productively

As the group achieves maturity, autonomy, and productivity, a group identity emerges. Group members collaborate to achieve goals while ensuring that their relationships with each other are maintained at a high-quality level. The coordinator becomes a consultant to the group rather than a directive leader. The relationships among group members continue to improve, as does the relationship between the coordinator and the members. In the maturely functioning group, all the guidelines for effective groups are met. Many groups never reach this stage.

Terminating

The life of every group is finite. Goals are met, projects are finished, and the group members go their separate ways. For groups that have matured into cohesive, effective groups, where strong emotional bonds exist among group members, the termination of the group may be quite upsetting. Nevertheless, group members deal with the problems of separating so that they can leave the group experience behind them and move on to new experiences.

Length of Each Stage

Not all stages last the same amount of time. Many groups move very quickly through the first five stages, spend considerable time functioning maturely, and then terminate quickly. Other groups never seem to progress past the rebelling and differentiating stage. Figure 1.3 shows the average amount of time groups tend to spend in each stage.

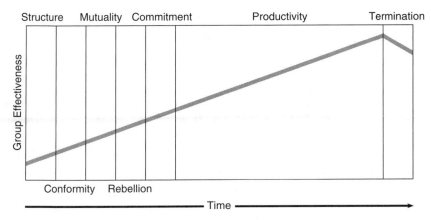

Figure 1.3   Stages of group development.

Conclusion

Both the sequential-stage and the recurring-phase perspectives are useful for understanding group development, and they are not contradictory. A group may move through various stages while dealing with basic themes that surface as they become relevant to the group's work. Because the issues underlying the themes are never completely resolved, they can recur later.

EXERCISE 1.5

ARE GROUPS BENEFICIAL OR HARMFUL?

Some controversy exists over whether group membership is constructive or destructive. The purpose of this exercise is to structure a critical discussion of the issue.

1. **Assignment to Groups:** Assign participants to groups of four. Each group is to write a short statement summarizing and explaining its position on whether individual or group decision making is more effective.
2. **Assignment to Pairs and Positions:** Divide each group into two pairs:
   a. Pair One takes the position that individuals are superior to groups in making decisions and uses Briefing Sheet One.
   b. Pair Two takes the position that groups are superior to individuals in making decisions and uses Briefing Sheet Two.
3. Participants review the procedure and guidelines for constructive controversy.
4. Conduct the exercise and monitor participants to ensure that the procedures are skillfully followed.
5. Participants process their experience.

TASKS

1. Make the best case possible for your assigned position. Ensure it gets a fair and complete hearing.
2. Critically analyze and challenge the opposing positions. Ensure the information and logic stands up under critical scrutiny.
3. Reach a consensus on the group's best reasoned judgment about the issue.

continued on next page

continued from previous page

PROCEDURE

1. **Prepare Positions:** Working with your partner, prepare a persuasive presentation that makes the best case possible for your assigned position. The presentation should have three parts: a thesis statement (your position), a rationale (your information organized in a logically compelling way), and a conclusion (your position). In preparing your presentation, use the overview of social-psychological research, applicable text material, and what you know from other sources. You have ten minutes to prepare a forceful and persuasive three-minute presentation and your arguments for the open discussion. Both members of the pair have to be ready to give the presentation.

2. **Present Positions:** Meet with a person representing the opposing position. Give a three-minute presentation of the best case possible for your position. Be persuasive. Listen to the other person's three-minute presentation; take notes and ask for clarification of anything that is not fully understood.

3. **Advocate, Attack, and Defend Discussion:** Continue to advocate the best case possible for your position. Critically analyze and challenge the opposing position. Point out the shortcomings in its information and logic. Defend your position from the attacks of the opponent. The discussion should focus on theory, research, and facts, not on opinions and impressions. You have ten minutes to discuss the issue.

4. **Reverse Perspectives:** Give a two-minute presentation of the best case possible for the opposing position. Summarize the opposing position (information and logic). The summary should be complete and accurate. Add any additional information you may have that supports the opposing position. Listen to the opponent's presentation of your position and correct anything that is incorrectly understood.

5. **Write a Joint Report:** Drop all advocacy. Reach a consensus on the nature of your best reasoned judgment about the issue. Write one statement summarizing and explaining your joint conclusions on whether individual or group decision making is more effective. The best reasoning from both sides should be synthesized or integrated into your best reasoned judgment. Base your conclusions on theory, research, and facts.

RULES FOR CONSTRUCTIVE CONTROVERSY

1. I am critical of ideas, not individuals. I challenge and refute the ideas of the opposing pair, but I do not indicate that I personally reject the members of the pair.
2. I focus on reaching the best decision possible, not on "winning." I remember that we are all in this together.
3. I encourage everyone to participate and to master all the relevant information.
4. I listen to everyone's ideas, even if I don't agree.
5. I paraphrase or restate what someone has said if it is not clear to me.
6. I first bring out all the ideas and facts supporting both sides, and then I try to put them together in a way that makes sense.
7. I try to understand both sides of the issue.
8. I change my mind when the evidence indicates that I should do so.

BRIEFING SHEET ONE: GROUPS ARE GOOD FOR HUMANS

1. Under most conditions, the productivity of groups is higher than the productivity of individuals working alone.
2. Groups make more effective decisions and solve problems more effectively than individuals working alone.
3. It is through group memberships that the values of altruism, kindness, consideration for others, responsibility, and so forth are socialized in us.
4. The quality of emotional life in terms of friendship, love, camaraderie, excitement, joy, fulfillment, and achievement is greater for members of groups than for individuals acting alone.
5. The quality of everyday life is higher in groups because of the advantages of specialization and division of labor. Our material standard of living—for example, our housing, food, clothing, transportation, entertainment, and so forth—would not be possible for a person living outside of a society.
6. Conflicts are managed more productively in groups. Social influence is better managed in groups. Without group standards, social values, and laws, civilization would be impossible.
7. A person's identity, self-esteem, and social competencies are shaped by the groups of significance to him or her.
8. Without cooperation, social organization, and groups of various kinds, humans would not survive. Humans have a basic social nature, and our survival and evolution are the results of the effectiveness of our groups.
9. Friendship, love, companionship, meaning, purpose, cooperation, and all that is good in life occur in groups.

BRIEFING SHEET TWO: GROUPS ARE NOT GOOD FOR HUMANS

1. People in groups are more likely to take greater risks than they would alone. Groups tend to take more extreme positions and indulge in more extreme behavior than their members would alone.
2. In groups there is sometimes a diffusion of responsibility such that members take less responsibility for providing assistance to someone in need or for rewarding good service.
3. In large groups individuals can become anonymous and therefore feel freer to engage in rowdy, shocking, and illegal behavior. When one member engages in impulsive and antisocial behavior, others may do likewise. Riots are often initiated and worsened by such modeling effects.
4. Being identified as part of a group may increase the tendency of nonmembers to treat one in impersonal and inhumane ways. It is easier, for example, to drop a bomb on the "enemy" than on a person.
5. Group contagion often gives rise to collective panic.
6. Millions of people have been swept into mass political movements only to become unhappy victims of the distorted visions of their leaders.
7. Groups often influence their members to conform. One type of conformity, obedience to authority, can cause a person to act in cruel and inhumane ways to others. The identity of the individual can be threatened when conformity is too extreme.
8. It is within groups that injustice, abuse, bullying, stereotypes, scapegoating, and all antisocial actions occur.

THE FIELD OF GROUP DYNAMICS

Close cooperation between theorists and practitioners can be accomplished . . . if the theorist does not look toward applied problems with highbrow aversion or with a fear of social problems, and if the applied psychologist realizes that there is nothing so practical as a good theory.

Kurt Lewin (1951, p. 169)

Understanding of the field of group dynamics is not complete until one understands (1) its roots in theory, research, and practice and (2) the nature of the field's primary founder, **Kurt Lewin.**

Like all scientific fields, the field of group dynamics is a combination of theory, research, and practice. **Theory** identifies the characteristics of effective groups, research validates or disconfirms the theories, and practical procedures based on the validated theory are implemented in the "real world" to see if they work. The theory, research, and practical applications of group dynamics are not separate and succinct processes; they all interact and enhance each other (Figure 1.4). Theory both guides and summarizes research. Research validates or disconfirms theory, thereby leading to its refinement and modification. Practice is guided by validated theory, and practical applications of the theory reveal inadequacies that lead to refining of the theory, conducting new research studies, and modifying the application to emphasize the interactions among theory, research, and practice.

What happens among group members is dynamic, not static. Social scientists interested in groups analyze the dynamics within groups by constructing theories and conducting research to test the theories. They then apply the validated theory to real-world situations to see if they work.

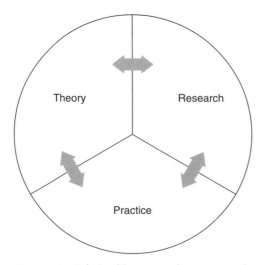

Figure 1.4   Relationship among theory, research, and practice.
Source: D. W. Johnson & R. T. Johnson, *Cooperation and competition: Theory and research* (Edina, MN: Interaction Book Company, 1989). Reprinted with permission of the authors.

Theory	Guides and summarizes research
Research	Validates or disconfirms theory, thereby leading to its refinement and modification
Practice	Guided by validated theory; applications of the theory reveal inadequacies that lead to refining of the theory, conducting new research studies, and modifying the application

History of the Field of Group Dynamics

The study of group dynamics is a relatively young field, one that is rooted in a wide range of traditionally separate fields. Although the earliest existing philosophical literature contains a great deal of wisdom about the nature of groups, and although the basic assumptions of group dynamics were discussed from the sixteenth through the nineteenth centuries, the field of group dynamics is a twentieth-century, North American development. Interested scientists came from many different disciplines and branches of the social sciences. The field of group dynamics, therefore, is the common property of all the social sciences.

While its roots go back to the late 1800s, group dynamics gained prominence as a field of study in the early 1940s. After a worldwide depression, the rise of dictatorships in Europe, and World War II, most Americans were worried about the fate of their country and the future of democracy. A general agreement existed that the country needed a better understanding of how democratic organizations could be made to function more effectively. Scientists had helped win the war, many people said, and now research should improve democracy. The field of group dynamics was thought to have significant potential for doing so. The health of a democratic society was seen as depending on the effectiveness of its component groups. Strengthening the family, the community, and the multitude of groups within our society was viewed as the primary means of ensuring the vitality of our democracy. For Americans, the scientific study of how groups functioned was needed to maintain a democratic form of government and solve current social problems.

The drive to strengthen democracy by using the scientific method to strengthen groups resulted in two interrelated movements within psychology. The first movement was the scientific study of group dynamics. Searching for ways to strengthen democracy, a new group of specialists called *social psychologists* developed experimental methods of studying group dynamics and began to conduct studies of group discussion, group productivity, attitude change, and leadership. The second movement was the application of group dynamics theory and research to develop methods for training leaders and group members in the social skills needed to promote effective functioning of democratic groups.

In the late nineteenth century, researchers on group dynamics focused on the question, "What change in an individual's normal solitary performance occurs when other people are present?" Norman Triplett, an Indiana University psychologist, studied the records of the Racing Board of the League of American Wheelmen. Triplett observed that cyclists' times were faster when they were racing against each other than when the cyclists simply raced against the clock. He hypothesized that the presence of other people (i.e., competitors) acted as a stimulant to the performer. If the hypothesis was valid, Triplett reasoned, it would hold for activities other than bicycle racing. Creating an analogy to bicycle racing, Triplett (1898) asked children to wind fishing reels and compared their performance when alone with their performance when another child was present. The children performed faster when the audience was present. This experiment was the first attempt to investigate the impact of social interdependence (i.e., competitive versus individualistic efforts) on achievement on a motor performance task.

Triplett's work later resulted in research on social facilitation-impairment (Zajonc, 1965), social interdependence (Johnson & Johnson, 1989), and social loafing (Harkins & Szymanski, 1987). **Social facilitation** researchers, for example, were interested in the question, "Does the impact of an audience differ on simple versus complex tasks?" If you were running a mile, would an audience make you run faster or slower? If you were asked to assemble a complex new machine you had never seen before, would an audience increase or decrease the speed with which you assembled the machine? Allport (1924), Moede (1920), and others found that on simple tasks, an audience increased an individual's speed of performance, whereas on complex tasks, an audience decreased an individual's speed of performance.

Another line of research, which became prominent in the late 1920s and 1930s, focused on the question, "Are individuals or groups more productive on problem-solving and decision-making tasks?" (Gordon, 1924; Shaw, 1932; Watson, 1928). Overall, the results indicated that groups are more productive than are individuals. The descendants of this tradition are the research on social interdependence (Deutsch, 1962; Johnson & Johnson, 1989), jury decision making (e.g., Kerr et al., 1976), minority influence in groups (e.g., Moscovici, 1985a), conformity (e.g., Asch, 1951), and group polarization (e.g., D. Myers, 1978).

By the end of the 1930s, the field of group dynamics had advanced rapidly, due largely to the efforts of Kurt Lewin and three sociologists. Muzafer Sherif (1936) studied the impact of group norms on perception of an ambiguous stimulus. In an ingenious experiment he demonstrated that the judgments made by individuals were influenced by the judgments of their fellow group members. Sherif (1906–1988) was born in Turkey and first came to the United States in 1929 to do graduate work at Harvard. He studied briefly in Germany, where he became opposed to Nazism. When he returned to the United States in 1934, he completed a doctorate at Columbia University under Gardner Murphy. Returning to Turkey, he increasingly got into trouble for his criticisms of Nazism in the German and Turkish governments. He was imprisoned in 1944, but his American colleagues secured his release and facilitated his immigration to the United States in 1945. He taught at Princeton University until 1949, when he moved to the University of Oklahoma, where he became director of the Institute for Group Relations.

Theodore Newcomb (1903–1984) was born in Ohio and, after graduating from Oberlin College, received his doctorate at Columbia University, where he worked with Goodwin Watson and Gardner Murphy. He spent most of his career at the University of Michigan, making many contributions to the field of group dynamics. He is considered one of the originators in the field because of his famous Bennington field study. As previously discussed, during the years 1935–1939, Theodore Newcomb (1943) investigated the impact of social norms on political issues on the students at Bennington College. His research laid the foundation for the study of reference groups.

In 1937, W. F. Whyte moved into one of the slums of Boston and began a three-and-a-half-year study of social clubs, political organizations, and racketeering. Whyte (1943) reported in vivid detail the structure, culture, and functioning of the Norton Street gang and the Italian Community Club. His study dramatized the great significance of groups in the lives of individuals and in the functioning of larger social systems. One of his most interesting findings was that expectations for performance in a given activity within the group (i.e., bowling) were stabilized in line with relative status of group members, in spite of the fact that some low-status members exhibited high skill in the task when they played against individuals outside their own group. Whyte also demonstrated the power of research conducted by a participant-observer (i.e., someone involved in the situation who makes systematic observations of the behavior of the other participants).

Although the early contributions of Sherif, Newcomb, and Whyte were important influences on the formation of the field of group dynamics, in the 1930s and 1940s the field was defined and popularized by Lewin's pioneering work, which demonstrated that the behavior of individuals should be understood in terms of the nature of the groups to which they belong (Lewin, 1943, 1948). The most influential study of group dynamics in the late 1930s was that of Lewin, Lippitt, and White (1939), which focused on the influences of different leadership patterns on groups and group members. Groups of 10- and 11-year-old children met regularly for several weeks under the leadership of an adult, who behaved in one of three ways: democratically, autocratically, or in a laissez-faire manner. The effects of these leadership patterns on the behavior of group members were large and dramatic. Severe forms of scapegoating, for example, occurred in the autocratic groups, and at the end of the experiment, the children in some of those groups destroyed the things they had constructed. This study made it clear that important social issues could be produced in the laboratory and studied experimentally.

Following this study, Lewin and his associates conducted a series of research studies aimed at developing a theory of group dynamics. Their studies focused on the effects of fear and frustration on organized versus unorganized groups (French, 1941), the impact of training on the behavior of leaders of youth groups (Bavelas, 1942), group decision-making procedures as a means of improving industrial production (Marrow, 1957), and group decision-making procedures as a means of changing eating habits related to wartime food shortages (Lewin, 1943; Radke & Klisurich, 1947). Group dynamics research was gaining popularity at this time and was being applied to an ever-increasing list of problems.

In the 1950s, Bales and his colleagues conducted research on the patterning of group members' responses and the nature of roles within a group in small discussion groups (Bales, 1950, 1953; Bales & Slater, 1955). Bavelas (1948) and Leavitt (1951) examined information exchange by imposing network structures on decision-making groups and observing their effects on subsequent productivity. Schachter (1951) researched group reactions to the opinions of deviates. Deutsch (1949a, 1949b, 1962) investigated cooperation and competition and the nature of trust.

In the 1950s, the seeds that ended the group dynamics movement were planted. Festinger's theories of informal social communication (1950) and social comparison (1954) focused social psychology on the individual (not the group) as the primary unit analysis. Social psychology began to examine how attitudes, values, personality, and thoughts internal to an individual guided and influenced social behavior. This individualistic trend was accelerated by the emergence of several other theoretical perspectives during the late 1950s, such as attribution theory (Heider, 1958), cognitive dissonance (Festinger, 1957), and persuasion (Hovland, Janis, & Kelley, 1953).

In the 1960s and 1970s, most social psychologists saw the individual as a simpler unit than the group on which to base the study of social interaction. Statistical and methodological difficulties in group research pushed researchers toward the study of individual variables. Psychologists were disposed to deconstruct social variables into smaller segments (the individual) rather than integrating them into larger social structures. They preferred to use single-factor explanations for behavior rather than multifactor explanations. Studies that involved the systematic observation of groups in naturalistic settings were seen as too difficult and expensive to conduct, analyze, and interpret.

In the 1980s and 1990s, however, the investigation of group dynamics experienced a revival. Many of the pragmatic, methodological, and statistical difficulties that thwarted group research in the 1950s and 1960s were either ameliorated or largely overcome. A number of group issues, such as cooperation, conflict resolution, distributive justice, intergroup relations, and cross-cultural interaction, became major research foci of social psychology (Deutsch, 1985; Tjosvold, 1991a; Tjosvold & Johnson, 1982). In industrial psychology, the determinants of work-group productivity and modes of effective leadership was the focus of considerable research (Hackman & Oldham, 1980; Tjosvold, 1991b). Clinical psychologists emphasized the client–therapist relationship and the treatment of families as dysfunctional systems (e.g., Johnson & Matross, 1977; Wolman & Stricker, 1983). In sociology, research focused on the possession and use of power, dominance hierarchies, and group structure (e.g., Berger, Rosenholtz, & Zelditch, 1980). In Europe, interest focused on group issues such as minority influence (Moscovici, 1985a) and intergroup relations (Tajfel, 1981).

The growth of the field of group dynamics can be seen in the number of studies published in the field. From 1890 to 1940, there had been a gradual growth in the number of published studies on group behavior from one per year to approximately thirty per year. By the late 1940s, fifty-five studies were being published annually, and by the end of the 1950s, the rate had skyrocketed to about 150. During the 1960s and 1970s, the number of research studies on group dynamics persisted at about 125 per year. Group dynamics became one of the dominant fields in the social sciences. In the twenty-first century, interest in group dynamics is on the rise.

Kurt Lewin and the Field of Group Dynamics

As previously stated, Kurt Lewin was at the heart of the group dynamic movements and consequently was one of the most important psychologists of the twentieth century. Lewin was born on September 9, 1890, in the tiny village of Mogilno in the

Prussian province of Posen, now part of Poland. In 1914, he completed his doctoral studies in philosophy and psychology at the University of Berlin. He then joined the Kaiser's army as a private in the infantry and fought for four years in World War I, during which time he was promoted to lieutenant and given an Iron Cross for bravery. At the end of the war, he returned to the University of Berlin to teach and to become part of the Psychological Institute, where Max Wertheimer, Kurt Koffka, and Wolfgang Kohler were formulating Gestalt theory. Lewin became one of the Gestaltists, but his interests were in the area of motivation and his work tended to be directed toward practical application. In 1933, as Hitler was rising to power, Lewin migrated to the United States. He subsequently worked at Cornell University, the University of Iowa, and the Massachusetts Institute of Technology, where he founded and headed the famous Research Center for Group Dynamics (which later moved to the Institute for Social Research at the University of Michigan). On February 11, 1947, Lewin died suddenly of a heart attack.

In his advocacy of the study of group dynamics, Lewin was noted for three things: his development of theory, his early championing of the use of experimental methodology, and his insistence that theory and research be relevant to social practice.

Kurt Lewin was, above all, a theorist. Lewin's contributions to theory in group dynamics included (1) an emphasis on building conceptual systems that explained the dynamics observed in groups and (2) creating a field theory analysis of the field (Lewin, 1943, 1948). Borrowing concepts and language from force-field physics, Lewin theorized that individuals locomote through different regions of their life-space, being either impelled by forces or drawn by valences that exist along power vectors. Some of the strongest forces and valences an individual experiences stem from groups. From this theoretical orientation, he and his associates and students formulated a wide variety of theories and research programs that defined the field of group dynamics.

Lewin was an innovative researcher who had a genius for thinking of ways to study his ideas experimentally. He was convinced that the use of experimental methods in researching the dynamics of groups would revolutionize the field, and he was right.

Lewin saw the interests of the theorist and those of the practitioner as being inextricably interrelated. He believed that social science theory should do more than advance knowledge; it should also provide guidelines for action. To this end, Lewin coined the term **action research** to indicate using the scientific method to answer research questions that have significant social value. He urged social scientists to develop theories that can be applied to important social problems. Lewin saw group dynamics theory as one way to bridge the gaps between theoretical science, public policies, and democratic practices. He had a profound faith in democracy, which to him was much more than just a political system. It was also a way of life, based on mutual participation and continual interaction in decision making for purposeful change. He wanted to conduct and inspire research that made a difference in the real world of human affairs.

Although Lewin did not create the field of group dynamics, he was the major source of much of the theorizing, the development of innovative experimental research methods, and the practical application in the field. Both the content of this book and the entire field of group dynamics are heavily influenced by Lewin and his work.

ONLINE GROUPS

The future of most groups (and relationships) may be online. Online groups can be developed and maintained through such avenues as e-mail, designated sites such as Facebook and MySpace, blogging, texting, tweeting, and playing massive multiplayer and other games. Online interaction can supplement face-to-face groups or be the setting in which new groups are created. Online interaction can maintain previous face-to-face groups as people move to different geographic locations. New groups can be created that are entirely online. Increasingly online interaction will include the options of real-time voice chat and video (i.e., as bandwidth expands, video will become free and easy to use).

A number of points can be made about online groups and their connection to face-to-face groups:

- Online groups are real groups. There are actual people who read the e-mails, respond to comments on a blog, receive and send tweets, and so forth. Online groups involve interacting with real people, just in a different medium.
- Groups are based on the amount of time members spend interacting with each other; more and more group time is going to be online. There is only so much time a person can spend each day on his or her groups. It is a zero-sum situation. Every minute a person spends interacting online is one minute less he or she can spend on face-to-face groups, and vice versa. Trends indicate that people will be spending more of their group time online rather than face-to-face. This means that much of a person's cooperative efforts will either be online or will include online elements.
- Electronic media offer the opportunity to expand the number of a person's groups very quickly and very easily. The barriers to entry into groups are low and the opportunity to do so is high. A person can easily find other people with needed expertise and resources on the Internet. Entering one website may provide access to dozens of people to interact with about an area of mutual interest. It is difficult, if not impossible, to suddenly have access to large numbers of potential collaborators in face-to-face situations. The ease of creating groups enhances the ability of individuals to find collaborators and identify people who have resources essential for completing a cooperative project. In many ways, cooperation is enhanced by the Internet and online groups.
- Personal geography is less relevant in Internet groups. No matter where one lives, it is possible to find collaborators all over the world. Thus, diversity of workforce or school may be less important to many people because they can find diverse colleagues on the Internet. Cooperation and constructive conflict are enhanced by diverse perspectives and resources, so the quality of cooperation and constructive conflict can be considerably enhanced by Internet groups.
- It is easy to interact with lots of people simultaneously on the Internet. The same e-mail can be sent to dozens, even hundreds, of people. What a person posts on a Facebook page can be read and responded to by dozens, even hundreds, of friends. In contrast, most face-to-face groups have limited membership.

The speed at which communication can take place will enhance cooperation. If competitive messages are sent, however, more people can be alienated more quickly. In competitive and individualistic situations, communication tends to be avoided and trust tends to be low.

- In online groups, people primarily know a person through what the person discloses about him- or herself. New avenues of assessing the nature of other group members will be developed, such as speed of keyboarding and responding, cleverness in phrasing responses, patterns of wording in messages, sense of humor, creativity in writing, and so forth.

- Online groups can be highly positive and fulfilling. The arrival of an e-mail can bring joy, the honest disclosure of thoughts and feelings can be liberating, and support from online colleagues can be quite powerful. Not all online groups are positive, however. There can be cyber bullying and other negative interactions online. But the vast majority of online groups seem to be quite positive, resulting in laughter, good humor, cheerfulness, joy, and fun. Such behaviors reflect positive groups.

- Material posted on the Internet spreads rapidly and widely. That means people have to be more concerned about (a) what they post on the Internet and (b) their privacy in public and face-to-face groups. Interaction with another group member can be recorded once and sent to dozens, hundreds, and thousands of people. Pictures taken at a party can show up on a company's website twenty years later. The nature of the Internet will make group members more cautious about their behavior and what they post on group sites.

- Online groups focus attention on ethics, manners, and values. As part of developing online groups, new systems of ethics and manners are being developed. In addition, online interactions (like face-to-face interactions) affect values. For example, in a recent study in the United States, Japan, Singapore, and Malaysia, the more participants played a prosocial online game, the more they tended to behave in prosocial ways after they stopped playing the game. Conversely, when participants played a violent online game, they were more likely to behave in competitive, obstructive ways afterwards. In other words, the nature of present group interaction will influence future group interaction.

THE NATURE OF THIS BOOK AND HOW TO USE IT

This is not a book that you can read with detachment. It is written to involve you with its content. By reading this book, you will learn the theoretical and empirical knowledge now available on group dynamics, and you will learn how to apply this knowledge in practical ways within the groups to which you belong. In this book we directly apply existing theory and research to the learning of effective group skills. The book defines the skills needed for effective group functioning; it also provides opportunities for readers to practice these skills for themselves and to receive feedback on their performance. As you participate in the exercises, use diagnostic procedures to assess your current skill levels, and discuss the relevant theory and research provided, you bridge the gap between theory and practice.

The purpose of this book is to bring together the theory on group dynamics, the research testing that theory, and structured exercises aimed at building practical group skills and illuminating the meaning of the theory and research presented. The central aim of each chapter is to review the most important theory and research on a given topic, analyze basic issues in group dynamics, and provide structured skill-building exercises and other instructional aids. Most chapters begin with a discussion task involving the concepts presented in the chapter. A short diagnostic instrument is presented at the beginning of each chapter to help you become more aware of your current behavior in the area under discussion. In addition, most chapters contain a controversy exercise in which you and your classmates argue different sides of one of the central issues of the chapter. At the end of many of the chapters there is a procedure for examining the changes in your knowledge and skills.

In using this book you should diagnose your present knowledge and skills in the areas that are covered, actively participate in the exercises, reflect on your experiences, read the chapters carefully, and integrate the information and experiences into action theories related to group dynamics. You then should plan how to continue your skill- and knowledge-building activities after you have finished the book.

KEEPING A PERSONAL JOURNAL

A *journal* is a personal collection of writing and thoughts that have value for the writer. Keeping a journal is an important part of using this book. You may wish to record what you are learning about group dynamics and about how you behave in group situations. A journal has to be kept up on a regular basis. Entries should be valuable to the author, have some possibilities for sharing with others, and reflect significant thinking. Such a journal will be of great interest to you after you have finished this book. The purposes of the journal are:

1. To record what you are learning about group dynamics that has personal meaning. You may also wish to include specific information you have learned about the social psychology of groups, effective behavior in groups, and the extent to which you have developed the group skills you want.

2. To record how you behave in group situations.

3. To collect thoughts related to the book's content (the best thinking often occurs when you are driving to or from school, about to go to sleep at night, and so forth).

4. To collect newspaper and magazine articles and references relevant to the topics covered in each chapter.

5. To keep summaries of conversations and anecdotal material that are unique, interesting, or illustrate things related to group dynamics.

The journal is an important part of this book. It is not an easy part. The entries should be important to you in your effort to make this course useful to you and your fellow participants. You may be surprised how writing sharpens and organizes your thoughts.

(*Note:* If you publish your journal, as did John Holt, Hugh Prather, and others, all we ask is a modest 10% of the royalties.)

LEARNING CONTRACT

Before beginning the next chapter, we would like to propose a learning contract. The contract is as follows:

> I understand that I will be taking an experiential approach to learning about group dynamics and to developing the skills needed to function effectively in groups. I willingly commit myself to the statements hereunder.

1. I will use the structured experiences in this book to learn from. This means I am willing to engage in specified behaviors, seek out feedback about the impact of my behavior on others, and analyze my interpersonal interactions with other class members in order to make the most of my learning.

2. I will make the most of my learning by (a) setting personal learning goals that I will work actively to accomplish, (b) being willing to experiment with new behavior and to practice new skills, (c) being open about my feelings and reactions to what is taking place, (d) seeking out and being receptive to feedback, and (e) building conclusions about the experiences highlighted in the exercises.

3. I will help others make the most of their learning by (a) providing feedback in constructive ways, (b) helping to build the conditions (such as openness, trust, acceptance, and support) under which others can experiment and take risks with their behavior, and (c) contributing to the formulation of conclusions about the experiences highlighted in the exercises.

4. I will use professional judgment in keeping what happens among group members in the exercises appropriately confidential.

Signed: _____

YOUR SKILL LEVEL

Before continuing on to Chapter 2, it is a good idea for you to assess your current group skill level. Doing so provides you with a baseline of what your current skills are, indicates areas you may need to work on, and serves as a point of comparison for later in the book when you learn more about group dynamics. Answer the following questions, describing yourself as accurately as you can:

1. How do you see yourself as a group member? What is your pattern of behavior in functioning within groups?

2. What are your strengths in functioning in groups?

3. What situations within groups do you have trouble with and why? How do you feel when faced with them? How do you handle them? How would you like to handle them?

4. What group skills do you wish to improve? What changes would you like to make in your present group behavior? What new strengths in group behavior would you care to develop? What new group skills would you like to acquire?

SUMMARY

Group dynamics is the scientific study of behavior in groups. Group dynamics is central to human existence, as humans are small-group beings. Groups are ubiquitous in our lives, and it is inevitable that you now belong to many, many groups. Because you spend so much time in various groups, the effectiveness of your groups relates directly to the quality of your life. Therefore, you need a working knowledge of group dynamics and the small-group skills required to put that knowledge to use in school, at work, during leisure activities, at home, in your neighborhood, and in every other arena of your life. To begin with, you must know what is and is not a group. That is harder than it seems, as social scientists have yet to agree on a single definition. Generally, however, a small group is two or more individuals in face-to-face interaction, all aware of their positive interdependence as they strive to achieve mutual goals, all aware of their membership in the group, and aware of the others who belong to the group.

All groups have a basic structure that includes roles and norms. Group productivity depends on five basic elements (positive interdependence, individual accountability, promotive interaction, appropriate use of social skills, group processing). Not all groups are effective. To be effective, groups members have to (1) ensure each other's commitment to clear mutual goals that highlight members' interdependence, (2) ensure accurate and complete communication among members, (3) provide leadership and appropriate influence, (4) flexibly use decision-making procedures that ensure all alternative courses of action receive a fair and complete hearing and that each person's reasoning and conclusions are challenged and critically analyzed, and (5) resolve their conflicts constructively. Groups develop over time and pass through stages, although there is little agreement as to what those stages are.

The field of group dynamics is about 110 years old in North America. One of the most important figures in the field of group dynamics is Kurt Lewin. His work, more than anyone else's, shows the interrelationships between knowledge of group dynamics and actual small-group skills. The purpose of this book is to bring together the theory on group dynamics, the research testing them, and structured exercises aimed at helping readers master practical group skills. The experiential learning procedures used in creating this integration of theory, research, and practical skills are discussed in the next chapter.

CHAPTER TWO

Experiential Learning

BASIC CONCEPTS TO BE COVERED IN THIS CHAPTER

In this chapter a number of concepts are defined and discussed. The major ones are in the following list. Students should divide into pairs. Each pair is to (1) define each concept, noting the page on which it is defined and discussed, and (2) ensure that both members understand its meaning. Then combine into groups of four. Compare the answers of the two pairs. If there is disagreement, look up the concept in the chapter and clarify it until all members agree on and understand the definition.

CONCEPTS

1. Experiential learning
2. Procedural learning
3. Action theory
4. Psychological success
5. Role playing
6. Participant–observer
7. Content
8. Process
9. Observing
10. Feedback

PROCEDURAL LEARNING

Knowing is not enough; we must apply. Willing is not enough;
we must do.

Goethe

One learns by doing the thing; for though you think you know it,
you have no certainty until you try.

Sophocles

The hand is the cutting edge of the mind.

Jacob Bronowski, *Ascent of Man*

This chapter is a bit different from the other chapters in this book, but it is key to your overall experience with the material presented. This book is designed to be an interactive experience, because developing group skills is a hands-on process. As Kurt Lewin so strongly believed, it is the combination of theory and practice that makes for truly effective learning. Given the importance of the exercises in this book to its overall mission, it is helpful to discuss the theory of learning on which these exercises are built. In this chapter, therefore, experiential learning is explained and the use of experiential learning to learn new skills is discussed.

Experiential learning involves reflecting on one's experience to generate and continually update an action theory that guides the effectiveness of one's actions. A form of experiential learning is **procedural learning,** which involves conceptually learning what a skill is and when it should be used, and then practicing the skill to eliminate errors in its execution until an automated level of mastery is attained. Increasing your expertise in group dynamics requires procedural learning. Learning how to implement group dynamics theory and research is very similar to learning how to play tennis or golf, how to perform brain surgery, or how to fly an airplane. Procedural learning involves a progressive refinement of knowledge and skill as the procedures are practiced, practiced, and practiced. It involves more than simply reading material for a recognition level or even a total-recall level of mastery. *Procedural learning* exists when you study group dynamics to:

1. Understand the conceptual nature of the skill
2. Use the skill
3. Obtain feedback about your performance
4. Use the skill again in a modified way until you eliminate errors in using the skill and attain an automated level of mastery

It is the procedural nature of mastering group dynamics that makes this book different from most other textbooks. This may seem strange at first. Traditionally, there has been a separation between "head" learning and "hand" learning. In learning group dynamics, however, you should remember Jacob Bronowski's (1973) observation that it is the "hand" that drives the subsequent evolution of conceptual understanding, revealing the conceptual nature of the procedure being used. To *understand*, you have to *do*.

Thus, from using group skills you gain an understanding of what group dynamics are and how useful they can be.

Procedural learning is based on experiential learning. The Russian cognitive theorist L. S. Vygotsky (1962) stated that learning from experience is the process whereby human development occurs. Your development and continual improvement of group skills depends on your participation in the skill-building exercises included in this book. Those exercises, and the links they provide to the theory and research discussed, are based on experiential learning. In experiential learning, the responsibility for your learning lies with you, not with the teacher or instructor. Experiential exercises are structured so that you can experiment with your behavior, try things out, see what works, build skills, and develop action theories out of your own experiences. Appropriate theory is then presented so that you can summarize your learning and build conceptual frameworks within which you can organize what you know. Although experiential learning is a stimulating and involving activity, it is important to remember always that experience alone is not beneficial. You learn from the combination of experience and the conceptualization of your experiences.

This chapter discusses the nature of action theories and experiential learning and presents the procedures through which group skills are learned. In addition, directions for how to conduct a skill training experience and the ethics of doing so are discussed. First of all, to understand experiential learning you must first know what an action theory is.

 ## ACTION THEORIES

Change and growth take place when a person has risked himself and dares to become involved with experimenting with his own life.

Herbert Otto

All humans need to become competent in taking action and simultaneously reflecting on their action in order to learn from it. Integrating thought with action requires that we plan our behavior, engage in it, and then reflect on how effective we were. When we learn a pattern of behavior that effectively deals with a recurrent situation, we tend to repeat it over and over until it functions automatically. Such habitual behavioral patterns are based on theories of action. An **action theory** is a theory as to what actions are needed to achieve a desired consequence in a given situation. All theories have an "if–then" form. An action theory states that in a given situation, if we do x, then y will result. Our theories of action are normative. They state what we ought to do if we wish to achieve certain results. Examples of action theories can be found in almost everything we do. If we smile and say hello, then others will return our smile and greeting. If we apologize, then the other person will excuse us. If we steal, then we will be punished. If a person shoves us, then we should shove back. All of our behavior is based on theories that connect our actions with certain consequences.

In essence, we build an action theory. As our behavior becomes habitual and automatic, our action theories become tacit (we are not able to put them into words).

KURT LEWIN AND EXPERIENTIAL LEARNING

The use of experiential procedures to learn about behavior in groups was greatly influenced by Lewin. When Lee Bradford and Ken Benne were looking for help in training community leaders in leadership and group decision-making skills, they approached Kurt Lewin. What resulted was the experiential learning method. One of Lewin's characteristics was to discover valuable concepts and principles by observing his own and other people's experiences. The most trivial event, the most casual comment, might spark a thought in Lewin's mind that would result in a new theoretical breakthrough in the social psychology of groups. Those associating with Lewin never knew when he might make an important discovery, and this produced an excitement rare in a relationship with a colleague or teacher. Students and colleagues learned from Lewin how important it is to examine one's own experiences for potential principles about the way in which groups develop and work. Thus, Lewin's personal style focused on experiential learning.

Much of Lewin's research highlighted the importance of active participation in groups in order to learn new skills, develop new attitudes, and obtain new knowledge about groups. His research demonstrated that learning is achieved most productively in groups whose members interact and then reflect on their mutual experiences. In this way members are able to spark one another's insights and creativity in deriving conclusions about group dynamics. From Lewin, therefore, came an emphasis on studying one's own experiences in order to learn about group dynamics, on discussing mutual experiences to increase mutual learning and creativity, and on behaving democratically in structuring learning situations.

When our behavior becomes ineffective, we become aware of our action theories and modify them.

As children we are taught action theories by parents and other socializing agents. As we grow older we learn how to modify our action theories and develop new ones. We learn to try to anticipate what actions will lead to what consequences, to try out and experiment with new behaviors, to experience the consequences, and then to reflect on our experiences to determine whether our action theory is valid or needs modification. Experiential learning is a procedure based on the systematic development and modification of action theories.

We all have many action theories, one for every type of situation we regularly find ourselves in. This does not mean that we are aware of our action theories. An action is usually based on tacit knowledge—knowledge that we are not always able to put into words. Because most of our action theories function automatically, we are rarely conscious of our assumed connections between actions and their consequences. One of the purposes of this book is to help you become more conscious of the action theories that guide how you behave in small-group situations, to test these theories against reality, and to modify them to make them more effective.

GAINING EXPERTISE THROUGH EXPERIENTIAL LEARNING

Aesop tells the story of the lion, the bear, and the fox. The bear was about to seize a stray goat when the lion leaped from another direction on the same prey. The bear and the lion then fought furiously for the goat until they had received so many wounds that both sank down, unable to continue the battle. Just then the fox dashed up, seized the goat, and made off with it as fast as he could go, while the lion and the bear looked on in helpless rage. "How much better it would have been," they said, "to have shared in a friendly spirit." The bear and the lion had learned from their direct experience an important lesson in the advantages of cooperation over competition.

We all learn from our experiences. From touching a hot stove we learn to avoid heated objects. We learn about interpersonal relationships by socializing and dating. In fact, our knowledge about dealing with others primarily comes from actual experience interacting with people. Along these lines, many aspects of group dynamics also can be learned only by experience. Hearing a lecture on resisting group pressure, for example, is not the same as actually experiencing group pressure. Seeing a movie on how to manage conflict is not the same as facing an angry neighbor who is yelling in your face. It takes more than listening to explanations to learn group skills; experience is key to formulating group skills that serve you well.

Experiential learning involves generating an action theory from your own experiences and then continually modifying it to improve your effectiveness. The purpose of experiential learning is to alter the learner's **cognitive structures,** modify the learner's attitudes, and expand the learner's repertoire of behavioral skills. These three outcomes are interconnected and change as a whole, not as separate parts. Working on any one part in the absence of the other two is ineffective:

1. Information and knowledge can generate interest in changing, but that does not bring about change. Knowing a rationale for change is not sufficient to motivate a person to change.
2. Firsthand experience alone does not generate valid knowledge. For hundreds of years, for example, scientists believed the world consisted of four elements: earth, air, fire, and water (in China there were five elements: earth, air, fire, water, and metals). Experience with different types of gases and different types of matter did not generate a correct theory of physics. In addition to experience, there must be a theoretical system that the experience tests out, and reflection on the meaning of the experience.
3. More than engaging in a new behavior is needed to result in permanent change. New skills may be practiced and mastered, but they fade away unless action theories and attitudes also change.

The process of experiential learning can be represented as a four-stage cycle (Figure 2.1). Begin by engaging in behavior on the basis of your current action theory. You then assess the consequences of your actions through reflection and feedback. Next, you reflect on the effectiveness of your actions and reformulate or refine your action theory. Finally, you implement your revised action theory by engaging in a modified set of

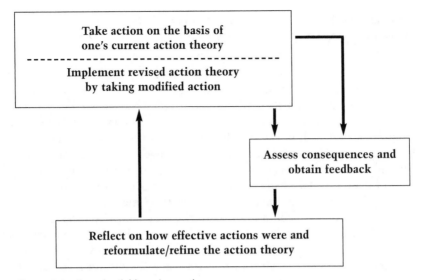

Figure 2.1   Experiential learning cycle.

behaviors. You repeat this process of continuous improvement until you develop expertise in using the skill. Furthermore, to engage in these four steps, you must believe that you are capable of implementing the behaviors specified by the theory, you perceive these behaviors as appropriate, and you have positive attitudes toward implementing the theory.

The four-stage experiential learning process discussed here is based on a number of principles that need to be understood and followed. These principles are based on the theories of Kurt Lewin (Lewin, 1935; Lewin & Grabbe, 1945).

Principle 1: Effective Experiential Learning Affects the Learner's Cognitive Structures (Action Theories), Attitudes and Values, Perceptions, and Behavioral Patterns. To learn to be a more effective decision maker, for example, the learner must develop (1) a concept of what decision making is (knowledge), (2) an action theory concerning what decision-making behaviors lead to effective group decision making, (3) positive attitudes toward new decision-making procedures, (4) a belief that the new decision-making actions are appropriate for the situation and that one is capable of performing them, and (5) the behavioral skills needed to perform the new decision-making actions.

Principle 2: People Believe More in Knowledge They Have Discovered Themselves Than in Knowledge Presented by Others. As mentioned in Chapter 1, Lewin was a great believer in experimental procedures whereby a person behaviorally validates or disproves a theory. He believed that such procedures needed to be introduced into the educational process so that students could test for themselves alternative behavioral patterns under controlled conditions. An approach to learning based on inquiry and discovery increases students' motivation to learn and their commitment to implement their conclusions in the future.

Principle 3: Learning Is More Effective When It Is an Active Rather Than a Passive Process. When a learner can take a theory, concept, or practice and "try it on for size," he or she understands it more completely, integrates it more effectively with past learning, and retains it longer. Many concepts, such as mathematical procedures, are never really learned until one uses them.

Principle 4: New Action Theories, Attitudes, and Behavioral Patterns Cannot Be Accepted Using a Piecemeal Approach; One's Entire Cognitive-Affective Behavioral System Has to Change. Theories, attitudes, and behavioral patterns are interconnected, and they change as a whole rather than as separate parts. Like any system, a cognitive-affective behavioral system demands coherence, consistency, orderliness, and simplicity. Trying to change only a part of the system is not effective. Only when the whole system changes can the new learning fully be accepted and integrated.

Principle 5: It Takes More Than Information to Change Action Theories, Attitudes, and Behavioral Patterns. Telling people about the need or desire for change does not mean they will change. Providing a rationale for change is not sufficient to motivate people to change. Likewise, reading a book or listening to a lecture does not result in mastery and retention of the material, does not promote attitude change, and does not increase social skills. What information can do is generate someone's interest in learning more about the desired changes.

Principle 6: It Takes More Than Firsthand Experience to Generate Valid Knowledge. As Lewin Stated, for Thousands of Years People Experienced the Effects of Gravity Without Coming to the Correct Theory of Gravity. Simply experiencing something, even something as profound as gravity, is not enough to understand it. In addition to experience, there must be a theoretical system tested by experience and reflection on the meaning of the experience.

Principle 7: Behavioral Changes Are Temporary Unless the Action Theories and Attitudes Underlying Them Are Changed. New behavioral skills may be practiced and mastered, but without changes in the person's action theories and attitudes, the new behavior patterns will fade away. Consider the classic case of embarking on a plan to lose weight. A person starts off by cutting calories and exercising four or five times a week, but soon the caloric intake is rising and the exercise is down to once or twice a week. Research suggests, however, that if the person looks at the dietary changes and exercise as a new way of living rather than as a short-term fix, he or she is more likely to lose weight permanently.

Principle 8: Perceptions of Oneself and One's Social Environment Must Change Before Changes in Action Theories, Attitudes, and Behavior Can Take Place. Lewin believed that behavior, action theories, and attitudes all are steered by perception. Your perceptions of yourself and your immediate situation affect how you behave, what you believe, and how you feel. Before learners engage in specific behaviors, they must believe they are capable of doing them. They also must see the behaviors as being appropriate to the situation.

Principle 9: The More Supportive, Accepting, and Caring the Social Environment, The Freer a Person Is to Experiment with New Behaviors, Attitudes, and Action Theories. As the need to justify oneself and protect oneself against rejection decreases, it becomes easier to experiment with new ways of behaving, thinking, and valuing. Learning situations should be designed to provide learners with a safe environment for trying out new behaviors and attitudes.

Principle 10: In Order for Changes in Behavior Patterns, Attitudes, and Action Theories to Be Permanent, both the Person and the Social Environment Have to Change. The person's role definitions, the expectations of the person held by colleagues and friends, and the general values of the career and social settings all must change if the person is to maintain these changed behaviors, attitudes, and action theories. To this end, **team training** is more effective than individual training because it changes both individuals and their social environment at the same time.

Principle 11: It Is Easier to Change a Person's Action Theories, Attitudes, and Behavioral Patterns in a Group Context Than in an Individual Context. Another benefit of learning new skills and behaviors in a group is that group members provide a level of encouragement and validation that is not present when only one person is being changed. Group members can rely on one another for support and discuss their experiences as they go through the process together.

Principle 12: A Person Accepts a New System of Action Theories, Attitudes, and Behavioral Patterns When He or She Accepts Membership in a New Group. New groups with new role definitions and expectations for appropriate behavior are helpful tools for educational efforts. A person becomes socialized by internalizing the normative culture of the groups to which he or she belongs. As the person gains membership in a new group, a new normative culture is accepted and internalized.

Experiential learning procedures are especially useful when you want to learn new skills. In the following sections, we review motivations for learning new skills and how we go about the learning.

EXPERIENTIAL LEARNING AND MOTIVATION

All men by nature desire to learn.

> Aristotle

Before we dive into the discussion of how people learn new skills and concepts, let's think about what motivates people to learn. We spend most of our lives learning new skills and ideas, whether they come on the job, in school, or in social settings. But what do we hope to gain from learning new things? Do we learn simply so we can gain recognition, promotion, or material success? Or do we learn to fulfill an internal need to know more or a desire for personal betterment? If someone offered you the opportunity either to earn $500,000 or to experience a sense of accomplishment and satisfaction from climbing Mt. Everest, which would you choose?

What leads to psychological success in a learning situation? In short, you will feel successful when you are encouraged to take as much responsibility for your own behavior as you can handle. You must believe that you are in control of or at least have some influence over your learning in order to feel psychological success. To this end, Kurt Lewin, Dembo, Festinger, and Sears (1944) found evidence that you can experience psychological success (as opposed to psychological failure) if:

1. You have the opportunity to define your goals.
2. These goals are based on your central needs and values.
3. You have the opportunity to define the paths to goal accomplishment.
4. In setting the goals you have a realistic level of aspiration, that is, the goals are challenging but not impossible to achieve.

Experiential learning offers the opportunity for experiencing success by allowing you to decide what aspects of your experience you wish to focus on, what skills you wish to develop, and how you conceptualize the conclusions drawn from your experience. This is quite different from the traditional lecture approach to learning, in which you are a passive listener and the instructor **controls** the material being presented. When an instructor decides what material is presented and how it is presented without letting learners have any influence over the decision, learners experience psychological failure no matter how entertaining the presentation is.

Although the primary motivation for learning in experiential situations is psychological success, extrinsic factors encourage further learning. The approval and support of other learners are examples of extrinsic factors that motivate learning, and the two types of factors—psychological success and extrinsic factors—can operate simultaneously. As you participate in the exercises in this book, your learning will accelerate if other participants give you approval and recognition for successful learning. Likewise, you should make a conscious effort to give approval to other readers who are seriously trying to increase their own group skills. Few influences on our behavior are more powerful than the support and approval of a group of friends or acquaintances. Using such group influences to help individuals learn is one of the most constructive ways available to assure the development of group skills and knowledge.

LEARNING GROUP SKILLS

For things we have to learn before we can do them, we learn by doing them.

Aristotle

People are not born with a full set of skills, nor do those skills magically appear when we need them. We have to learn them. Learning how to participate in and lead a group is no different from learning how to play the piano or throw a football. All skills are learned the same way, according to the following steps:

1. *Understand why the skill is important and how it can be of value to you.* Before you want to learn a skill, you must see a need for it. You need to know that you will be better off with the skill than without it.

2. *Understand what the skill is, what component behaviors you have to engage in to perform the skill, and when the skill should be used.* To learn a skill, you must have a clear idea of what the skill is and how to perform it. Novices often find it helpful to observe someone who has mastered the skill perform it several times while describing it step by step.

3. *Find situations in which you can practice the skill over and over again while a "coach" watches and tells you how well you are performing it.* Guided practice in how to develop a skill is key to learning it, and there are four levels of guided practice. The *first* level consists of practicing successive approximations of the group skill while others provide scaffolding on how to do so. *Scaffolding* is support, in the form of reminders, prompts, and suggestions, that helps you approximate the expert use of the group skills. As you practice the skills again and again, the scaffolding gradually fades until you use the skill by yourself, which is called *soloing*. The *second* level consists of using the group skills while articulating and explaining how to do so to your coach. Doing so ensures that the scaffolding is internalized and that self-monitoring and self-correction take place. The *third* level is independent practice, in which you perform the skill while self-monitoring and self-correcting your efforts. In effect, you give yourself feedback. This solidifies your sense of self-sufficiency and your commitment to use the skills. *Finally*, you decontextualize the skills by using them in a variety of groups and in a variety of situations other than the one in which you learned them. Try practicing the skill for a short time each day for several days until you are sure you have mastered it completely.

4. *Assess how well the skill is being implemented.* The key to assessing how well you engage in the skill is to understand that you can never fail. Rather, your behavior approximates what you ideally wish and, through practice and experiential learning, the approximations get closer and closer to the ideal. To put it simply, you have to sweat in practice before you can perform in concert. You cannot expect to learn a skill the first time you try it, and those initial attempts are part of the process of gaining expertise. Long-term success is inevitable when those initial attempts are followed by practice,

feedback, and reflection on how to implement the group skills more competently. Practice, feedback, and reflection enable you to compare how well you
are doing with how well you want to do.

5. *Keep practicing until the skill feels real and it becomes an automatic habit
   pattern.* Most skill development goes through the following steps:
   a. Self-conscious, awkward engagement in the skill. Practicing any new skill
      feels awkward, and group skills are no exception. The first few times some-
      one throws a football, plays a violin, or leads a discussion, it feels strange.
   b. A feeling of phoniness while engaging in the new skill. After a while the awk-
      wardness passes, and enacting the skill becomes easier. Many individuals,
      however, still feel that the skill is unauthentic at this point. Encouragement
      is needed to move them through this stage.
   c. Skilled but mechanical use of the skill.
   d. Automatic, routine use in which the skill is integrated fully into your behav-
      ioral patterns. At the point, the skill should feel like second nature to you.
   You have to practice a new skill long enough to go through these stages of development. The more you use a skill, the more natural it feels. With time and
   patience, you will be able to apply the skill to real situations and gain the fire
   and life that sometimes may be lacking when you practice.

6. *Load your practice toward success.* Set up small goals along the way to mastering your skill so you can feel a sense of accomplishment as you practice. Meeting
   these smaller goals can help keep you motivated to accomplish the larger goal. If
   you were training for a marathon, for example, you'd mark a certain completion
   time or distance covered as points of success, even if they weren't the final goal.

7. *Get friends to encourage you to use the skill.* Your friends can help you learn
   by giving you encouragement to do so. The more encouragement you receive,
   the easier it is be for you to continue developing the skill.

8. *Help others learn the skill.* One of the best ways to gage how completely you
   have learned a skill is to try teaching the skill to someone else. Breaking down
   what you have learned in order to teach it to someone else illustrates how thoroughly you understand the concepts and theory behind the skill. Furthermore,
   teaching a skill to someone else can help you see aspects of the skill in new
   ways that can improve your own performance.

The skill-learning steps outlined here do not follow a prescribed timeline. Rather,
they depend on the person, the skill, and the situation. Most skill learning begins with
a period of slow learning, followed by a period of rapid improvement, then a period in
which performance remains about the same (a plateau), then another period of rapid
improvement, and so forth. Plateaus are quite common in skill learning, and you have
to continue practicing the skill until the next period of rapid improvement begins. The
goal for skill learning is to engage the small-group skills automatically and naturally.

It is up to you, after engaging in learning exercises, to practice the skills until you
feel comfortable performing them. The extent of your learning and skill development
rests entirely on your commitment to use this book in fruitful ways. To help you in your
group skills development, the next three sections discuss various methods of experiential learning that can help you successfully complete the exercises found in this book.

ROLE PLAYING

Role playing is a vital training tool for mastering new skills. It can simulate real-life situations, making it possible to try new ways of handling situations without suffering any serious consequences if the methods fail. The purpose of role playing is to bring patterns of behavior and their consequences into focus by allowing participants to experience the situation concretely, identify effective and ineffective behavior, gain insight into their behavior, and practice the skills required to manage the situation constructively.

Role playing involves setting up an imaginary setting in which individuals are asked to adopt certain roles and act out a situation. Participants act and react in terms of the assumptions they are asked to adopt, the beliefs they are asked to hold, and the characters they are asked to play. The outcome of a role-playing situation is not determined in advance and the situation is not rehearsed. Initial instructions are given and the actors determine what happens.

You do not have to be a good actor to participate in a role-playing exercise. You only need to accept the initial assumptions, beliefs, background, or assigned behaviors and then let your feelings, attitudes, and behavior change as circumstances seem to require. The role-play instructions simply lay out what the situation is and who the characters are; they do not provide a script. Once the setup is understood, you and the situation take over.

Your experiences in participating in role playing may lead you to change your attitudes and future behaviors. You may have emotional experiences that were not expected when the role playing began. The more real the role playing and the more effective the exercise, the more emotional involvement you will feel and the more you will learn. If you are used to being a leader, for example, and are cast as an outsider in a certain role-playing situation, you may gain insight into the frustrations and anxiety that can accompany an outsider status.

When you engage in the role-playing exercises presented in subsequent chapters, questions may be raised that are not answered in your briefing sheets. When this happens, you are free to make up facts or experiences that apply to the circumstances. Do not, however, make up experiences or facts that do not fit the role. In addition, you should not consult or look at your role instructions after the initial read-through.

Once the action has started, you should be yourself.

When you are leading a role-playing exercise, you should keep three important points in mind. *First*, help the participants get into the situation and their roles by introducing them in such a way that the players are emotionally involved. Introduce the scene to the role players. *Second*, always discuss the role playing when it is finished. How could the conflict have been prevented? How did the characters feel in the situation?

Was the solution satisfactory? What other solutions might have worked? *Third*, be sure to "de-role" after the role playing has ended. Some participants will have trouble getting into their role and other participants will have trouble getting out of their role. Announce clearly that the role play is over and that participants should reflect on and analyze the role play, not continue it.

 LEARNING HOW TO BE A PARTICIPANT–OBSERVER

What Is a Participant–Observer?

A **participant–observer** is a person who is skilled enough to both participate in group work and observe group process at the same time (Figure 2.2). When a group is working, a distinction is commonly made between:

1. **Content:** What is being discussed in order to achieve the group's goals
2. **Process:** The sequence of group members' actions that take place over time and are aimed at achieving the group's goal

Ideally, a competent group member actively participates in the group's work while also observing the process being used to achieve the group's goals. To do so, a group member must function on two levels—as participant and as observer. Periodically, the group should stop its task work and discuss the process being used. Members continuously improve the group by (1) discussing the quality of the process being used, (2) reflecting on its effectiveness in achieving the group's goals and maintaining effective working relationships among members, and (3) setting goals for improving the process. Such reflection and discussion are aimed at (1) streamlining the group's process to make it simpler (reducing complexity) and (2) eliminating unskilled and inappropriate

GROUP PROCESSING

Receive feedback
Analyze and reflect
Set improvement goals
Celebrate

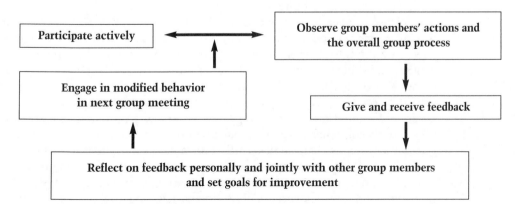

Figure 2.2 Participant–observer.

actions (error-proofing the process). The process a group uses to achieve its goals includes setting clear goals that create positive interdependence, communicating effectively, providing leadership, using appropriately decision-making procedures, resolving conflicts constructively, and so forth. A person highly skilled in process observation can participate in group work and observe group process at the same time, thus becoming a participant–observer. The steps in developing competence in being a participant observer are:

1. Observing
2. Giving and receiving feedback
3. Reflecting and setting goals for improvement
4. Modifing behavior in the next group meeting
5. Repeating the cycle over and over again automatically in every group you are a member

Learning How to Observe

Learning how to be a participant–observer begins with learning how to observe the process the group is using to achieve its goals. The process includes goal setting, communication, leadership, use of power, decision making, and conflict resolution. You gain competence in observing by consciously engaging in formal observation methods (discussed following) that focus on each part of the process. You do this hundreds of times on a wide variety of observation schedules until the observation procedures become internalized, that is, until they become an automatic habit.

Observing is aimed at describing and recording behavior as it occurs. From the behavior of group members an observer can make inferences about the group process—the way in which the group is functioning. The problem with observation is the potential for lack of objectivity by the observers (Hastorf & Cantril, 1954). Each group member is biased in ways that may affect his or her perception and assessment of what is taking place in the group. A solution to the problem of bias is the use of structured coding systems, which require observers to categorize each group behavior into an objectively definable category. Doing so at least ensures that observers are looking at the same behaviors on the same scale.

Four steps usually are involved in observation. The first step is to prepare for observing, and it requires a bit of planning and forethought so the actual observation produces useful results. Step one starts with the group deciding which member behaviors, actions, and skills are to be observed. Refer back to the guidelines for creating effective groups shown in Table 1.1 for a refresher; it details aspects of the group process that should be observed. At this point, the group also should choose a member to be an observer. If more than one group is being observed, a sampling plan should be made that describes in what order the groups will be observed and for how long. Next, the group finds or constructs an observation form or checklist that lists the behaviors, actions, and skills the group wants observed for a particular aspect of group process. For example, a group may choose to use an observation form that measures discussion, participation, and feedback specifically in the decision-making part of the group process.

Numerous observation sheets are included in this book. The observer should be shown the form so the best results are generated.

In step two, the observer watches and records how often each member performs the specified behaviors. When there is more than one observer, each may be able to focus on only some of the group members. *In step three,* the observer looks at how often group members engage in the specified behaviors and then infers how well the group is functioning in that aspect of group process under observation. Step four is to summarize the observations in a clear and useful manner and then present the summary to the group as feedback. The group then can use the feedback as a jumping-off point for discussion and revision of group process.

When you observe a group process in action, the results are reported back to the group members in the form of feedback. **Feedback** is information on actual performance that individuals compare with criteria for ideal performance. When feedback is given skillfully, it generates energy, directs the energy toward constructive action, and transforms the energy into action toward improving the performance of the teamwork skills. Member performance improves, and the discrepancy between ideal and real performance decreases. Members tend to feel empowered and become even more effective the next time. The feedback checklist included here may help in assessing the effectiveness of feedback.

By the time you finish this book, you will have developed skills in observing the group process. At first, the observation tasks specified in the exercises might seem difficult, but gradually you should find them to be easier and more helpful as your skills develop. Because effective future behavior depends on awareness of the nature and consequences of current behavior, there is no substitute for direct observation in developing skills and group effectiveness. Simply put, by observing what is happening today, you can avoid repeating the same mistakes tomorrow. Any effective group member must be aware of the group process while participating in the group, and it is through observation practice that such skills are developed.

FEEDBACK CHECKLIST

Feedback	Yes	No
Is feedback given?		Was not given or received; start over.
Is feedback generating energy in students?		Students are indifferent; start over.
Is energy directed toward identifying and solving problems so that performance is improved?		Energy used to resist, deny, avoid feedback; start over.
Do students have opportunities to take action to improve performance?		No, students are frustrated and feel like failures; start over.

CONSTRUCTING AN OBSERVATION PROCEDURE

Observation forms are used to answer the question, "How often are certain actions or events happening?" Observation forms are used to tally and count the number of times a behavior, action, or event is observed in a specified time period. The form has to be designed so that all potential observers can use it (e.g., it must be age appropriate). A structured (formal) observation form is created in the following way:

1. Define exactly what behaviors, actions, skills, or events are being observed (such as individual contributes ideas, encourages participation, checks for understanding, gives group direction). All observers have to be looking for the same thing.

2. Determine the time period during which data will be collected. One group may be observed for fifty minutes or each group may be observed for two minutes. Observations may be summarized after one class session or after several class sessions.

3. Enter the actions to be observed in the first column (each action or skill is placed in a separate row; the final row is reserved for the total of the columns).

4. Make an additional column for each member of the group and make a final column to record the total for each row on the form.

5. Make sure all columns are clearly labeled and wide enough to enter data.

CONDUCTING SKILL-TRAINING EXERCISES

A Typical Skill-Training Session

Before discussing how to conduct a skill-training session, it may be helpful to review the overall structure of a group exercise. A typical session would involve the following procedures:

1. Participants are presented with an introduction by a coordinator, who then conducts a warm-up discussion. The introduction should include the objectives of the session, an outline of what will happen, and a description of the specific skills the participants will be learning. The warm-up discussion sets the stage for the exercise, involves participants, and promotes some sort of emotional connection among participants. The warm-up could take the form of a brief exchange of current feelings among participants or an interesting anecdote about group skills told by the coordinator. The expectations of the participants should be set at this point.

2. The exercise is conducted.

3. After the exercise is completed, the participants are asked to conceptualize, analyze, and summarize their experience. This step may be structured through discussion questions or data feedback about how each person and the group behaved. All participants should share what they learned and explain how it applies to their life. Participants also should explore the theoretical principles into which they gained insight as a result of their experience.

4. In a general session, participants should talk over the experience and summarize their ideas about their experience. The coordinator should integrate appropriate theory and cognitive frameworks into the participants' statements. The emphasis at this point is on integrating the important learnings, theory, and research with their experiences.

5. The coordinator should then discuss the issues of applying the learnings and skills to the participants' specific life situations.

6. The overall success of the session in accomplishing its objectives should be evaluated.

7. At the end of the session, the coordinator needs to provide a sense of closure. This can be achieved through a short, fun, involving experience, or the coordinator may simply say that the training exercise is over.

Designing a Skill-Training Session

A skill-training program could involve any number and combination of the exercises presented in this book. It could consist of a single exercise or of several exercises drawn from different chapters. It could last a few minutes or several days. Whatever the length of the session and the number of exercises used, the basic design of the training process is the same. The following elements need to be considered when you, as a coordinator, design a skill-training session:

1. Examine the coordinator-participant relationship. Useful questions to be cleared up include, "What is the purpose of the session?" "Why is the coordinator conducting it?" "What is the contract between the coordinator and the participants?" "What is the relationship between the coordinator and the participants?" Review your motivations as a coordinator, hidden agendas (if any), explicit and implicit assumptions about the session and the participants, and your limitations and competencies. It also is helpful to know the following information about the participants:

   a. *Expectations:* What do the participants hope, believe, or fear might happen or not happen?

   b. *Experience:* What kind of previous training have the participants had?

   c. *Relevance:* How might the learnings be used after the session?

   d. *Relationships:* What are the participants' past and future relationships with one another?

   e. *Needs:* What specific learnings, and what general kinds of learnings, do the participants want or need?

   f. *Vital data:* Sex, age, marital status, general attitudes, physical or emotional problems and pressures, back-home support possibilities, and so on.

   g. *Motivation:* What is the level of the participants' motivation?

   h. *Recruitment:* How were the participants recruited? Did they all voluntarily agree to attend the session?

2. Specify the desired outcomes of the session; they usually are discussed as objectives or goals. They should specify who is to be trained and what is to be the direction and magnitude of the desired learning. Clearly specified goals are

useful when you are deciding on the components of the session and its evaluation. All the criteria for clear goals provided in Chapter 4 are important when you are stating the session's objectives. Participants should be able to spell out the knowledge they will try to achieve.

3. Detail the constraints on the session, including the available time periods, location, and facilities, as well as everyone's range of competencies.

4. Generate a list of alternative exercises and activities that can be used in the skill-training session. Sometimes plans need to be changed on the fly to accommodate unforeseen changes in the group or unplanned directions; you always should have a few backups in place. These alternatives may include a variety of exercises and theory sessions. This list can be put together from two sources: the desired outcomes of the session and the resources and preferences of the coordinators. All the exercises in this book and in *Reaching Out* (Johnson 2006) are possibilities.

5. Make a tentative design for the session. Evaluate it in terms of these questions:
   a. Is it appropriate for accomplishing the desired outcomes?
   b. Are the activities within the group's range of competencies?
   c. Is there an opportunity for participants to express their needs and/or expectations?
   d. Does it enable the participants to make the transition from the "outside" world to the session and then back to the "outside" world?
   e. Does it encourage the transfer of learning?
   f. Does it have high personal relevance for the participants, and can it enable them to function better in their day-to-day life?
   g. If there is more than one coordinator, does it allow time for each of you to conduct a portion of the exercises and confer with one another?
   h. Are high- and low-tension activities placed appropriately within the design?
   i. Do the assumptions about the participants' skills and backgrounds match reality?
   j. Does the overall design provide a sense of continuity and appropriate transitions among activities?
   k. Are participants able to see the relationship between the exercises and the desired outcomes of the session?
   l. Does it allow for a logical flow of experiences?
   m. Does it offer flexibility in case of unexpected and emerging needs?
   n. Is it consistent with the principles of experiential learning?
   o. Is there opportunity for ongoing participant feedback and evaluation?
   p. Are you prepared to recognize and deal with unanticipated learning outcomes?
   q. Are all the necessary materials and facilities available?

6. Make sure you are highly committed to the final design. If more than one coordinator is conducting the session, assign responsibilities. Arrange for the materials and facilities.

7. If there is more than one coordinator, assess how you function as a staff. See if any team development needs to take place among the staff before the skill-training sessions begin.

Evaluation

Evaluation is the process of determining how successful or unsuccessful a group was in achieving its goal or objective. In the case of a skill-training session, it is the process of gathering evidence about whether the desired outcomes of the session were achieved, what unanticipated lessons were learned, and how the activities involved in the session contributed to its success or failure. An evaluation must include a clear operational statement of the desired outcomes, ways to measure how closely the desired outcomes were achieved, and what activities and coordinator behaviors, contributed to the session's success or failure. Evaluations also should highlight what the coordinators could do to improve their own competencies. Time must be allotted for the participants to give feedback on the effectiveness of the session. Finally, time must be set aside following the session during which the data are analyzed and conclusions are drawn.

When you are conducting an evaluation, it is helpful to know such things as the emotional reactions of the participants (How do they feel about their experiences?), the specific or significant lessons they have learned, and the amount of increased participant competence each has in performing the skills. Furthermore, evaluations can uncover important information from the participants' perspectives, such as what future experiences the participants now see the need for, the degree to which their desired outcomes were achieved, their reactions to various parts of the session, and what the coordinators did that was helpful or unhelpful.

A variety of data-collection procedures can and should be used to evaluate a session. Coordinators can use interviews, general statements made by the participants, questionnaire responses, observation of how skills were applied, and so on to draw conclusions. Although not all sessions have to be evaluated at a high level of proficiency, more than the general impressions of the coordinators should be used. To this end, participant input can be invaluable. At the very least, the coordinators should be able to direct the same session in the future in a more effective and efficient way.

Helpful Guidelines

When conducting the exercises in this book, the coordinator has a set of general responsibilities that include the following:

1. Organizing the materials, procedures, and facilities he or she will need in order to manage the exercise.
2. Introducing, ending, and tying together the experiences involved in the exercise.
3. Preventing the group from becoming sidetracked by keeping time in a task-oriented way.
4. Restating and calling attention to the main learnings of the exercise, which include relating the experiences to the theory.
5. Setting a climate of experimentation, acceptance, openness, and warmth so that participants feel safe trying out new skills and improving their competencies.
6. Serving as an anchor point by being reliable, knowledgeable, trustworthy, and responsible.
7. Modeling the skills she or he wishes to teach.

8. Following the general outlines of experiential learning.
9. Being enthusiastic about the value of the exercise.
10. Knowing and understanding the material well.
11. Making sure everyone understands his or her instructions and responsibilities.
12. Being sensitive to the differences in participation, needs, and styles of the participants.
13. Remaining flexible so that the preplanned procedures do not interfere with the participants' learning.
14. Enjoying herself or himself and making sure that she or he also learns and benefits from the exercises.

As you proceed through the book and encounter various types and forms of group skill exercises, refer back to this discussion of how to role play, how to be a participant–observer, and how to conduct and design a skill-training session. With the procedures and guidelines at hand, you can use the provided exercises and then move on to create new ones. As you put the procedures to work and move through the exercises to build your group skills, you learn firsthand how valuable experiential learning can be.

ETHICS OF EXPERIENTIAL LEARNING

To maintain the integrity of any knowledge being transmitted as well as the integrity of everyone involved in a learning experience, it is necessary to enact and follow a code of ethics. All learning activities require either an implicit or explicit code of ethics. Researchers in the field of group development have paid a great deal of attention to the ethics of group leaders, but thus far they have given little consideration to the ethics of conducting experiential learning activities.

The most serious ethical issue involved in teaching group skills is determining the value and necessity of such cognitive and behavioral changes for the participants. Attempting to teach another person carries with it a responsibility to work in the person's best interests and meet his or her needs. It should also be noted that the only way to promote ethical standards in teaching–learning relationships is for the teachers to enforce their code of ethics on themselves and to use good judgment in what they themselves do. As long as a teacher's behavior is based on care, respect, and regard for participants, ethical violations can be minimized. Persons leading experiential learning activities therefore must develop a personal code of ethics to which they hold themselves accountable. The following points should provoke some thought as to what that personal code of ethics might include.

The Contract: Informed Consent and Mutual Agreement

1. The coordinator's intentions and objectives should be communicated clearly to the participants. The participants should understand that they are going to participate in an experiential exercise in which they are expected to examine their own behaviors and the behaviors of others and then analyze the behaviors for learning purposes.

2. The nature of the contract should be easily understood by the coordinator and the participants. The number of exercises, the length of each session, and the appropriateness and the objectives of each exercise should be agreed upon.

3. The point at which the contract is terminated should be clear to both the coordinator and the participants.

The Activities

When conducting activities, you, as the coordinator, should:

...ticipants' *freedom of choice.* Participation should be voluntary. ...and sit on the sidelines as the exer-

...the exercise. Have an explicit reason ...d to explain the reason clearly. ...ose exercises that you are competent

...hen appropriate to the participants'

...tyles and personal needs and deal with ...f your role. Be aware of the impact of

...participants' feelings and reactions to ...learn from the experience. Allow ad-...n of the session.

...participants. Doing so could damage ...continue to encourage participants to ...es, and face conflicts to improve their ...uld originate with the participants, not

...revealed in the activity will not be used ...rticipants.

...hological stress. Make responsible deci-...know where psychological services are sions when such problems ...... available.

10. *Solicit feedback that you can use to improve your performance.* Open your sessions to competent professionals who are interested in the effectiveness of experiential learning.

11. *Conduct follow-up interviews* with participants to determine the impact of the sessions and to assess reactions to the sessions.

The Coordinator's Knowledge, Skills, and Needs

1. *Knowledge:* The coordinator's actions need to be based on empirically validated theory. Folklore, superstition, common sense, fads, popular gimmicks, and personal experiences are not adequate bases for teaching others. The coordinator

should understand thoroughly the principles of experiential learning, the steps in skill development, and the knowledge the exercise is designed to teach.

2. *Experience:* The coordinator should have some experience and skill in conducting exercises and helping participants reflect on their own and other's behavior. Knowing the steps of experiential learning is not enough: The coordinator should also have some skills and competencies in applying the principles of experiential learning.

3. *Clear explanations:* At any time during the exercises the coordinator should be able to explain the relevant theory and the way in which current activities relate to the theory. This does not mean that the coordinator will not use intuition when conducting an exercise, but the coordinator should be able to reconstruct the theory behind his or her intuitive actions.

4. *Self-awareness:* The coordinator should be aware of his or her personal needs and deal with them productively. The coordinator should also be aware of the impact of his or her personal needs and styles on the participants and the instructional activities.

Final Notes

Your ability to conduct and coordinate experiential learning exercises will improve as you apply the material in this book with intelligence and caution. If you are interested in other skill-building exercises, see Johnson (1991, 2006) and Johnson and Johnson (1997). You do not have to be a skilled teacher to conduct the exercises contained in this book, but constant concern for increasing your knowledge and skills in experiential learning is helpful.

The preceding statements are meant to be guidelines, not rigid rules. The only effective way to enforce ethical standards in educational activities is for the persons conducting the educational problems to enforce their code of ethics on themselves and use good judgment in what they do. Again, as long as a coordinator's behavior is based on care, respect, and regard for the participants, ethical violations probably can be avoided. We hope that the preceding guidelines help the users of this book build a personal code of ethical conduct.

SUMMARY

To master the field of group dynamics you must conceptually learn the relevant theory and research and master the skills that put that knowledge into action. Such procedural learning results from skill-building experiences as well as academic study. Procedural learning involves a progressive refinement of knowledge and skill as the procedures are practiced, practiced, and practiced. In other words, this book focuses on both "head" and "hand" learning.

Experiential learning begins with the formulation of an action theory. Action theories specify what actions are needed to achieve a desired consequence in a given situation. The next step is to take action and engage in the relevant group skills. The success or failure of the actions is assessed. On reflection, the action theory is refined and reformulated. The group skills are then used again in a modified and improved way. This cycle is repeated over and over again as the skills are refined and continuously improved on. This continuous improvement process eventually results in expertise in the use of group skills as changes in cognitive understanding, attitudes, and behavioral patterns result. While learning experientially, you experience psychological success.

When mastering group skills, you need to observe how other group members are using them as you participate fully in the group. Such participant observation enables you to know when to use various group skills and how to help others to do so in order to improve the overall functioning of the group. In order to learn the group skills discussed in this book, you need to conduct the skill-building exercises competently and ethically.

CHAPTER THREE

Group Goals, Social Interdependence, and Trust

BASIC CONCEPTS TO BE COVERED IN THIS CHAPTER

In this chapter a number of concepts are defined and discussed. The major ones are in the following list. Divide into heterogeneous pairs. Each pair is to (1) define each concept, noting the page on which it is defined and discussed, and (2) ensure that both members of the pair understand the meaning of each concept. Then combine into groups of four. Compare the answers of the two pairs. If there is disagreement, look up the concept in the chapter and clarify it until all members agree on and understand the definition.

CONCEPTS

1. Goal
2. Goal structure
3. Group goal
4. Operational goal
5. Level of aspiration
6. Hidden agenda
7. Social interdependence
8. Cooperative efforts
9. Competitive efforts
10. Individualistic efforts
11. Social judgment theory
12. Group cohesion
13. Psychological health
14. Distributive justice
15. Merit distribution of benefits
16. Equality distribution of benefits
17. Need distribution of benefits
18. Trust
19. Trusting
20. Trustworthy

 # INTRODUCTION

The honor of one is the honor of all. The hurt of one is the hurt of all.

Creek Indian Creed

Aesop tells a story of a man who had four sons. The father loved them very much, but they troubled him greatly, for they were always fighting with one another. Nothing the father said stopped their quarreling. "What can I do to show my sons how wrong it is to act this way?" the father thought. One day he called his sons to him and showed them a bundle of sticks. "Which of you, my sons, can break this bundle of sticks?" he asked them. All the boys tried in turn, but not one of them could do it. Then the father untied the bundle and gave each son a single stick. "See if you can break that," he said. Of course, they could easily do it. "My sons," the father said, "each of you alone is weak. He is as easy to injure as one of these sticks. But if you will be friends and stick together, you will be as strong as the bundle of sticks."

Since our beginnings, humans have joined together to achieve goals that each could not achieve alone. While elephants have size and cheetahs have speed, it is our ability to engage in cooperative enterprises to achieve mutual goals that distinguishes us as a species. Social interdependence defines the ways in which the goals of individuals are related. Social interdependence is the heart of all human interaction, and cooperation is the heart of all small-group efforts.

To be effective, groups must set group goals that all members commit themselves to cooperate in achieving. There are two steps to do so. First, operational goals and the paths to achieving the goals must be clearly specified and measurable. Second, positive interdependence (i.e., cooperation) must be structured among group members. Underlying both of these steps is the concept of trust, which is essential to creating groups that successfully meet their goals. The complex relationship among these three elements—group goals, social interdependence, and **trust**—is the topic of this chapter.

EXERCISE 3.1

ORIENTATIONS TOWARD SOCIAL INTERDEPENDENCE

This exercise has two purposes: (1) to make you more aware of your orientation toward goal interdependence with others and (2) to make your group more aware of members' orientations toward social interdependence. The procedure is as follows:

1. Working by yourself, complete the following questionnaire.
2. Using the scoring table that follows the questionnaire, determine your score and then determine the group average for each scale.
3. Have a group discussion concerning the orientations toward social interdependence of group members.

SOCIAL INTERDEPENDENCE QUESTIONNAIRE

For each item, indicate your *general* perceptions about each statement. In the appropriate space, write down the number that most accurately describes your actions.

continued on next page

continued from previous page

1 = never	4 = mostly
2 = seldom	5 = always
3 = sometimes	

1. I like to compare myself with others to see who is best.
2. In my situation, people spend a lot of time working by themselves.
3. In my situation, people share their ideas and resources with one another.
4. In my situation, people are motivated to see who can do the best job.
5. In my situation, individuals like to work by themselves.
6. In my situation, individuals learn lots of important things from one another.
7. In my situation, individuals want to do better than others.
8. In my situation, it bothers individuals when they have to work with one another.
9. In my situation, individuals help one another do a good job.
10. In my situation, individuals are encouraged to outperform one another.
11. In my situation, individuals would rather work alone than work together.
12. In my situation, individuals believe that they are more productive when they work with one another.

Competitive	*Individualistic*	*Cooperative*
1. _____	2. _____	3. _____
4. _____	5. _____	6. _____
7. _____	8. _____	9. _____
10. _____	11. _____	12. _____
Total _____	Total _____	Total _____

EXERCISE 3.2

ARE GROUP GOALS NECESSARY?

There has been some controversy over whether group goals are necessary. The purpose of this exercise is to structure a critical discussion of the issue. The procedure is as follows:

1. **Assignment of Positions:** The class forms groups of four. Each group is ultimately to write a report summarizing its position on whether
   a. Groups cannot function without goals.
   b. Group goals are of no use.
   The report is to contain the group's overall conclusions and the facts and rationale supporting its position. The supporting facts and rationale may be obtained from this chapter, the entire book, and outside reading.
2. **Preparation Pairs:** Each group divides into pairs. One pair is assigned the position that groups cannot function without goals and the other pair is assigned the position that group goals are of no use. Each pair reviews the supporting sections of this chapter, the procedure for the exercise, and the guidelines for constructive controversy (p. 32). They prepare a persuasive "best-case" rationale for their assigned position that includes as many facts and research findings as possible. Ten minutes are allowed for this phase.
3. **Presentations:** One member of each pair changes chairs. A "group goals are necessary" person should be seated with a "group goals are unnecessary" person. The "group goals are necessary" person has up to three minutes to present the best case possible for the

position, being as forceful and persuasive as possible. The "group goals are unnecessary" person takes notes and asks for clarification of anything that is not fully understood. The "group goals are unnecessary" person then presents.

4. **Open Discussion** (Refute and Rebut): There is an open discussion of whether or not group goals are necessary. Each side presents as many facts and research findings as it can to support its point of view. Members listen critically to the opposing position and ask for supporting facts for any conclusions made by the opponent. Participants should ensure that all the facts supporting both sides are brought out and discussed. The guidelines for constructive controversy should be followed. A period of about ten minutes is allowed for this phase.

5. **Perspective Reversal:** Members of each pair change chairs. The "group goals are necessary" person presents in three minutes the best case possible for the "group goals are unnecessary" position. He or she should be as forceful and persuasive as he or she can and add new arguments or facts if possible. The "group goals are unnecessary" person then similarly presents the best case possible for the "group goals are necessary" position.

6. **Synthesis and Integration:** Participants drop all advocacy and come to their best reasoned judgment as to whether group goals are necessary. The pair members summarize the information and arguments for each position and come to an agreement. Each pair prepares a short presentation on its conclusion to the rest of the class. Since other groups will have other conclusions, each group may need to explain the validity of its position to the class. About ten minutes are allowed for this phase.

7. **Whole Class Discussion:** The coordinator samples the decisions made by the groups of four by having several of them present their position to the class. The class then discusses similarities and differences among the positions and the coordinator summarizes what the participants have learned about group goals.

BRIEFING SHEET: GROUPS CANNOT FUNCTION WITHOUT GOALS

Your position is that a group cannot function without having at least one goal that is understood and accepted by several of its members. To support your position, use the rationale given below, any material from this chapter that is applicable, and your outside reading.

Group goals guide the actions of members and allow them to plan and coordinate their efforts. Group goals direct, channel, guide, energize, motivate, and coordinate the behavior of group members. Groups cannot exist unless the activities of their members are directed toward achieving something (a goal). It is the power of goals to **influence** members to engage in needed behaviors that makes goals essential to an effective group. All in all, groups cannot function effectively or even exist without goals.

BRIEFING SHEET: GROUP GOALS ARE OF NO USE

Your position is that a goal is not useful to a group and is a concept that has no basis in reality. To support your position, use the rationale given below, any material from this chapter that is applicable, and your outside reading.

Group goals are often stated in such vague terms that they could not possibly be effective guides for the actions of members. When asked, many group members cannot accurately describe the group's goals, and thus the goals can have no impact on these persons. Often, goals do not determine members' efforts because the goals seem unrelated to what group members actually do. Appraisals of group process, moreover, usually reveal that groups have not achieved their goals, which suggests that the goals are not the true motivators of members' actions. It may even be that groups do not try to accomplish anything; they just exist. All in all, goals are of no use to a group.

 ## WHAT IS A GOAL?

No wind favors him who has no destined port.

Montaigne

On September 17, 1868, Major George A. Forsyth and fifty handpicked scouts were camped on Beecher's Island (a small island in the dry bed of the Arikaree River) in eastern Colorado Territory. Full-scale war had just erupted with the Indian tribes of the Great Plains. Forsyth and his scouts had left Fort Hays in Kansas to find the enemy, but the Native Americans found Forsyth first. On that morning, the Cheyenne war chief known as Roman Nose led over 700 Cheyenne and Oglala warriors in a dawn attack on Forsyth's camp. Many of Forsyth's men and all his horses were killed or wounded. Forsyth was shot in both legs and a bullet creased his skull. They were trapped on the island. By September 25, as a result of stealthy sniping and repeated charges, half of Forsyth's men were casualties. Wondering whether he would live to see another morning, Forsyth lay stretched out beside the rotting carcass of his dead horse. A horrific stench rose from the dead men and animals all around him. The overall goal of Forsyth and his scouts was to survive. They did have, however, a number of short-term goals. They had to construct a barrier to protect them from enemy fire. They used the dead horses. They had to maintain group unity and support in order to instill morale and hope as well as mount an effective defense. They had to ensure there was adequate water, shelter, food, and caring for the wounded. Luckily, the weather was mild enough that shelter was not a necessity. They had enough water on the island to survive. After several days, however, the scouts began to eat their horses' decaying flesh.

As it became more and more difficult to accomplish their subgoals, the overall goal of survival seemed less and less likely. The situation seemed hopeless. Suddenly, the Indians withdrew. Puzzled, the survivors soon saw why. A company of cavalry was galloping toward the island. Unknown to Forsyth, two of his scouts had slipped through the besieging Indians and traveled to Fort Wallace in Kansas. Captain Louis H. Carpenter, a Civil War comrade of Forsyth, immediately mounted a company of cavalry for a rescue expedition. Carpenter's troopers were officially known as Company H of the 10th Calvary, but to their Indian foes they were the "Buffalo Soldiers." Rather than fight these soldiers, Roman Nose decided to withdraw. Over the course of three

WHY GOALS ARE IMPORTANT

1. **Goals are guides for action.** They direct, channel, and determine what members and teachers do.

2. **Goals motivate behavior.** Goals are motivators and energizers. No goals, no motivation.

3. **Goals provide the basis for resolving conflicts.** Conflicts among group members are resolved on the basis of what members want to accomplish.

4. **Goals are a prerequisite for assessment and evaluation.** Without knowing what the purpose of the activity is, no assessment can be conducted.

decades, the Buffalo Soldiers gained a reputation of being the most professional, experienced, and effective troops on the frontier.

Groups exist to achieve goals. The goal may be to build a better mousetrap, climb a mountain, or win a baseball game. A **goal** is an ideal, a desired place toward which people are working, a state of affairs that people value. The goals of individuals are related through social interdependence. Individuals' goal attainments can be positively related (i.e., cooperation), negatively related (i.e., competition), or independent from one another (i.e., **individualistic** efforts). When a positive correlation exists among individuals' goal attainments, a group goal results. A **group goal** is a future state of affairs desired by enough members of a group to motivate them to work toward its achievement.

Goals are not intellectual, cold, or analytical. They focus group members' passions and ignite the flame of inspired work. Group goals create a compelling vision of the future that will be uniquely possible if all work together for a common purpose. A **vision** is an ideal and unique image of the future. The vision enlists the emotions of group members and points them toward coordinated efforts. The vision binds members through a shared emotional commitment. Group goals breathe life into group members' hopes and dreams and enable them to see the exciting possibilities of their joint efforts.

Do Group Goals Exist?

Do groups have goals, or are there only the various individual goals of the group's members? Social psychologists have hotly debated this issue for decades. Many social scientists believe that a group goal is a combination of the individual goals of all group members. People become group members because they have certain goals and motives that they wish to express or fulfill through group membership. These personal goals are not always clear to the member—he or she may be completely aware, partially aware, or totally unaware of his or her goals and motives during a group meeting.

On the other hand, Lewin (1944) noted that there are situations in which group members do seem to act to maximize joint outcomes or accomplish group goals rather than to maximize their individual outcomes or achieve their individual goals. Both Horwitz (1954) and Pepitone (1952) conducted studies that indicated that group members become motivated to achieve a group goal and are personally satisfied when the group does so. The success of the group, rather than their personal gain, seems to be the major source of their satisfaction. Emmy Pepitone (1980) concluded from these and other studies that group goals can be identified, they function as an important source of member interdependence in groups, and they denote a central focus that is present most of the time and readily identifiable as an objective reality. Group goals provide a unity, a common fate, that cannot readily be identified simply by noting the individual goals of group members. More recent studies (Matsui, Kakuyama, & Onglateo, 1987; Mitchell & Silver, 1990) indicate that group goals, compared with individual goals, result in higher group performance, goal acceptance, and cooperation among group members. Numerous other studies have demonstrated that individuals do focus on joint outcomes rather than individual outcomes when they are placed in situations requiring cooperation with others.

No definitive answer exists as to whether group goals are entities in and of themselves or simply a combination of the individual goals of members. Perhaps the safest conclusion is both group and individual goals exist and the group goals are relevant to the individual needs of the members. Group members may typically

EXERCISE 3.3

YOUR GOAL-RELATED BEHAVIOR

This exercise examines goal-related behavior in problem-solving groups. Working by yourself, answer the following three questions. Be honest. Check as many responses to each question as are characteristic of your usual behavior. Then form a triad with two of your classmates and discuss your answers and why you answered them as you did. Develop as much awareness of your behavior in goal-related situations as possible.

1. When I am a member of a group that does not seem to have a clear awareness of what its goals are or how they are to be achieved, I usually:
   _____ Feel uninterested and refuse to attend meetings.
   _____ Ask the designated leader to stop messing around and tell the group what it is supposed to be doing.
   _____ Ignore the situation and be extra nice to the other members.
   _____ Take over the conversation and tell the other group members what the group's goals are; propose that members review the group's goals and in return they will be told what to do to achieve the goals.
   _____ Initiate a group discussion to clarify each member's understanding of the group goals until all group members clearly understand what they are and what actions the group needs to take to accomplish them.

2. When a member of a group that has a clear understanding of its goals but seems to have little commitment to accomplishing them, I usually:
   _____ Refuse to have anything to do with the other member and avoid him or her.
   _____ Make fun of the other group member until he or she becomes more committed.
   _____ Pretend that there is nothing wrong and be nice to the other person.
   _____ Propose a compromise in which the person works harder and the group expects less.
   _____ Initiate a group discussion in which the group goals are considered and reformulated to make them more relevant to each member's goals.

3. When I am a member of a group that has conflicting opinions on what its goals should be, or that has members with conflicting needs and motives, I usually:
   _____ Simply withdraw and wait for them to work out their differences.
   _____ Tell the leader to decide who is right and who is wrong and tell the losers to shutup.
   _____ Try to smooth over the differences and ask everyone to be nice and keep their differences to themselves.
   _____ Propose a 50/50 compromise where everyone gets half of what they want.
   _____ Figure out how much cooperative and competitive behavior exists in the group and give the group feedback based on my observations in an attempt to increase cooperativeness among its members.
   _____ Start a group discussion on the different positions, goals, and motives of group members and seek a solution that is acceptable to everyone.

try to achieve both individual and group goals. The degree to which members' actions simultaneously promote individual and group goal accomplishment determines the effectiveness of the group. The situation is complicated by the fact that most groups and individuals have multiple goals and different members value different goals at different times and even the same member places different values on the same goal at different times.

START GOALS

If a man does not know to which port he is sailing,
no wind is favorable.

Seneca

For a goal to be accomplished, all group members must be committed to achieving it. There are two ways to induce member commitment to the group's goals. The first is to ensure that the goals meet the START criteria (Table 3.1). To be effective, goals need to be specific (so it is clear what needs to be done next), measurable (so progress can be tracked), challenging, relevant, and aimed at competencies that will be transferred to other situations. The second way is to involve group members in the process of forming the goals. The more involved members are in creating the goals, the greater their ownership of and commitment to the goals. Other factors influencing commitment are how desirable the goal seems (the benefits group members receive if the goal is accomplished) and the ways in which members relate to one another in working toward the accomplishment of the goal (some ways of relating are more fun and involving than others).

TABLE 3.1   **START Goals**

GOAL CHARACTERISTIC	DEFINITION OF CHARACTERISTIC
S **Specific**	Goals have to be specific enough that they are clearly understood and a plan to achieve them can be developed. Specific goals indicate what needs to be done next.
T **Trackable and measurable**	Members must be able to determine the extent to which they have achieved the goals. Goals must be operationalized so that the steps to achieving them are clear and understandable.
A **Achievable but challenging**	Goals must be challenging enough that the group has a 50/50 chance of achieving them. Group must be able to achieve the goals if they work hard enough and have sufficient teamwork.
R **Relevant**	Goals must be relevant to the members' interests and the interests of other stakeholders in the group. Members must see the goals as meaningful and be personally committed to achieving them.
T **Transfer**	Goals must be aimed at having members take what is learned and transfer it to other situations. Whatever skills members master today should be usable in other situations tomorrow.

CLEAR AND UNCLEAR GOALS

This exercise contrasts the behavioral consequences of having clear and unclear goals. Approximately one hour is needed to complete it. The procedure is as follows:

1. Seat the participants in groups of six to eight, formed into circles.
2. Introduce the exercise as focusing on clear and unclear group goals.
3. Have each group select an observer, who reports to a designated place for instructions. While the observers are being briefed, urge the group members to get acquainted with one another.
4. Give each observer a copy of the observation guide and tell observers that the groups will work on two tasks. The first task will be unclear, the second one clear. Their job is to make careful observations of group behavior on the two tasks. The observers then return to their groups but sit outside the circle.
5. Brief all groups as follows: "We are going to study group behavior by working on two brief tasks. Your observer will not participate but will report to you at the end of the second task. Your first task will take about eight minutes. I will give you a warning a minute before the time is up. The task is to list the most appropriate goals to govern the best developmental group experiences in order to maximize social development in a democratic society."
6. While the groups work on the task, the observers should take notes. After seven minutes give the warning, and after eight minutes end the discussion.
7. Give the second task: "List as many of the formally organized clubs or organizations that exist in a typical community as you can." State that the groups will have six minutes to work on the task. At the end of five minutes give a one-minute warning, and after six minutes end the discussion.
8. Give a copy of the observation guide to all participants. Then have each group discuss its experience, using the information obtained by the observers as its major resource. This discussion should last ten to fifteen minutes.
9. Form clusters by asking one group to pull its chairs in a circle around another group. The inner group becomes group A and the outer group becomes group B. Instruct group A to produce a list of characteristics of clear and unclear goals, with one person recording them in two columns. Allow six minutes for this task. Group B is to listen to group A, take notes, and be ready to add to the list. After six minutes, instruct group B to comment on the list and have both groups jointly select the four or five most important characteristics of clear and unclear goals from the list. Give them nine minutes to do so.
10. Groups A and B then change places, with group B now in the center. Group B is told to list behavioral symptoms of each of the characteristics of the listed clear and unclear goals, beginning with the most important characteristics. After nine minutes, group A joins the discussion, which should take another six minutes.
11. Each cluster presents its work to the other group. Hold a general discussion on the nature of group goals and their consequences in feeling and behavior, using the material in the following section.

OBSERVATION GUIDE

During this exercise the groups will work on two tasks. The first task will be unclear, and the second will be clear. Your job as an observer is to make careful notations of group behavior on the two tasks. When you understand the form, return to your group but sit outside the circle.

	First Task	Second Task
1. Number of times a member clarified the goal or asked that it be clarified.		

2. Assessment of the "working climate" of the group:
Was it cooperative, hostile, pleasant, critical, accepting, and so forth?
    At the beginning?
    At the middle?
    At the end?		

3. Frequency of verbal behavior not directly related to getting the job done (side conversation, jokes, comments).		
4. Frequency of nonverbal behavior not related to getting the task done (looking around the room, horseplay, bored withdrawal, hostility).		
5. How much progress did the group make in getting the task done? (Make an estimate.)		

CLARITY OF GOALS

Goal accomplishment depends on members' coordinating and synchronizing their actions. To do so, the goal and the actions required to achieve the goal must be clear. Goals become clarified as they are made more specific, operational, workable, measurable, and observable. Exercise 3.4, Clear and Unclear Goals, provides you with a list of the characteristics of each kind of goal as well as the behavioral symptoms of groups with clear and unclear goals. Some symptoms of unclear goals are a high level of group tension, joking or horseplay, distraction by side issues, and the failure to use good ideas. When goals are unclear, meetings may be pointless and trivial issues may be discussed at length (Wright, 1979). When truck drivers who hauled logs to the mill were told to "do their best" when loading the logs, they carried about 60% of what they legally could haul. They later were encouraged to carry 94% of the legal limit, and they met this specific goal. In financial terms, this clarification of goals earned the company more than a quarter of a million dollars (Latham & Baldes, 1975).

OPERATIONAL GOALS

The secret of success is constancy of purpose.

Benjamin Disraeli

Goals are made more clear when they are stated in operational terms. **Operational goals** are goals for which specific steps to achievement are identifiable (i.e., observable, countable, and specific). **Nonoperational goals** are goals for which the specific steps required to achieve them are not discernable (i.e., nonobservable, noncountable, and ambiguous). An example of an operational goal is "Name three qualities of a good group member." An example of a nonoperational goal is "Make conclusions about the theoretical and empirical findings of qualities of effective actions by a group member." An operational goal has indicators that will make it evident when it has been achieved. The goal "Name three qualities of a good group member" is operational in that when you have listed three items, and if they refer to group membership, you will know the goal has been reached. The goal "Make conclusions about the theoretical and empirical findings of qualities of effective actions by a group member" is nonoperational in that it may be difficult to tell when such a goal has been achieved. Whatever indicators are used to tell when a group has accomplished its goals, several of them are better than one. Usually, the goal of a problem-solving group will have indicators that reflect both the accomplishment of the goal (profit, new members gained, problems solved) and maintaining working relationships among group members (group cohesion, effective communication, effective decision making, high level of trust among members).

Operational goals have several advantages. The first advantage is in facilitating communication among its members and between the group and other groups. A goal must be stated in such a way that it succeeds in telling what the group intends to accomplish, and this communication is successful when any knowledgeable person can look at the group's behavior or products and decide whether or not the goal has been reached. Second, operational goals help guide the group in planning and carrying out its tasks. Operational goals help a group select and organize the appropriate resources and methods it will need in working on its tasks. Third, operational goals help the group evaluate both the group process and the group product. By specifying the criteria for goal accomplishment, the group can evaluate its progress. Fourth, when goals are operational, conflicts about what actions the group members should take are more likely to be decided by rational, analytic processes.

For most groups, clear goals cannot always be determined in advance. Groups often discuss their stated goals until a consensus exists concerning how they can be operationalized. Through such discussions, commitment to goals is built and the goals become acceptable to the group members. Usually, the more time a group spends clarifying and operationalizing its goals, the less time is needed to achieve them.

GROUP GOALS AND LEVEL OF ASPIRATION

Group goals reflect the members' aspirations. **Level of aspiration** is the compromise between ideal goals and more realistic expectations. Kurt Lewin and his associates developed a theory of level of aspiration to explain how people set goals for themselves and their groups (Lewin, Dembo, Festinger, & Sears, 1944). The theory generally predicts that individuals enter situations with an ideal outcome in mind (for example, earning a B in a course of study) but revise their goals upward after success and downward after failure (if they get A's on the first two tests, they change their goal to aspire for an A, but if they get C's on the first two tests, they change their goal to aspire for a C). As they gain experience, individuals revise their ideal expectations to match the reality of the situation.

Groups, like individuals, develop levels of aspirations. Alvin Zander conducted a series of studies with populations as diverse as teams of high school boys batting a ball (Zander & Medow, 1963) and United Fund chapters setting their fund-raising goals (Zander, 1971). He demonstrated that groups set goals that are slightly optimistic and revise their goals as feedback about performance levels becomes available. Groups tend to lower their level of aspiration somewhat less after failure than they raise it after success. In the United Fund study, only 40% of the chapters that failed to reach their goal lowered their goal for the next year. Of the chapters that succeeded in reaching their goal, 80% raised their goal. While this optimistic bias is constructive in most circumstances, there are times when it leads to a cycle of failure. When unsuccessful United Fund chapters set over-optimistic goals year after year, the continued failure decreased morale, work enjoyment, and group efficiency.

DEALING WITH HIDDEN AGENDAS

Consensus about what the group's goals should be usually helps group functioning, whereas disagreement about what the group's goals should be usually interferes with group functioning. Individual group members with similar goals are usually happier with the group and its tasks than members of groups with heterogeneous individual goals. Individual goals that are markedly different from the group's goals may become **hidden agendas**—personal goals that are unknown to other group members and are at cross-purposes with the dominant group goals. Hidden agendas are present in almost every group and often can hinder group effectiveness. Groups, therefore, usually strive to increase consensus among group members as to the nature of the group's goals. Some procedures for doing this are as follows:

1. When you first form a group, thoroughly discuss its goals, even when they are prescribed by superiors or by the constitution of the group. Such a discussion will clarify the members' understanding of the goals and help clear away any misunderstandings concerning the tasks necessary to reach them. During the discussion the group should reword, reorganize, and review the goals until the majority of members feel a sense of "ownership" of the goals.

2. As the group progresses in its activities, remember that it is continuously working on two levels at once: toward the achievement of the group's goals and toward the achievement of individual members' goals. Look for hidden agendas. The recognition of a group problem is the first step in diagnosing and solving it.

3. Bear in mind that there are conditions under which hidden agendas should be brought to the surface and rectified, and conditions under which they should be left undisturbed. A judgment must be made about the consequences of bringing hidden agendas to the attention of the entire group. Hidden agendas should

be given different amounts of attention at different times, depending on their influence on the group's effectiveness and on the nature of the group and its members.

4. Do not scold or pressure group members when hidden agendas are recognized. They are present and legitimate and are simply problems to be solved.

5. Evaluate the ability of the group to deal productively with hidden agendas. As groups mature, their ability to resolve hidden agendas is typically increased.

HELPING GROUPS SET EFFECTIVE GOALS

Still the question recurs, "Can we do better?" The dogmas of the quiet past are inadequate to the stormy present. The occasion is piled high with difficulty, and we must rise with the occasion. As our case is new, so we must think anew, and act anew.

   Abraham Lincoln, Annual Message to Congress, December 1, 1862

Two methods of helping groups set effective goals are the survey-feedback method and program evaluation and review method. The **survey-feedback method** begins with interviewing group members about group goals and the priorities of the group. These

CHARACTERISTICS OF EFFECTIVE GROUP GOALS

1. The extent to which the goals are operationally defined so that they are measurable and observable. Members need to know what they are supposed to do.

2. The extent to which group members see the goals as being meaningful, relevant, realistic, acceptable, and attainable.

3. The extent to which the goals create positive interdependence among group members.

4. The degree to which both group goals and individual members' goals can be achieved by the same tasks and activities.

5. The extent to which the goals are challenging and offer a moderate risk of failure.

6. How easily the goals can be modified and clarified.

7. How long a group has to attain the goals.

interviews are conducted before a periodic meeting of the group (e.g., annually or semi-annually). On the basis of the information collected, a group meeting is held to set goals and priorities for the next six months or year. During this meeting the group plans its short-term goals, ranks the goals in terms of priority, defines specific responsibilities for working on the tasks, and sets goals for increasing group effectiveness. Special attention is paid to identifying and solving relationship problems among members that might hinder goal achievement.

In program evaluation and review, or the **critical path method,** groups specify the end state they want to achieve. Working backward from this final goal, the group details what must happen immediately before the goal is achieved and what tasks and subgoals are needed to accomplish the goal. The group decides which of the activities and subgoals are most critical for final goal accomplishment and allocate resources accordingly. A timetable for accomplishing each subgoal is set. The whole process is then reviewed and responsibilities assigned.

EXERCISE 3.5

COOPERATIVE, COMPETITIVE, AND INDIVIDUALISTIC GOAL STRUCTURES

The purposes of this exercise are (1) to provide an experiential definition of the three goal structures and (2) to direct participants' attention to the contrasting patterns of interaction created by these three structures. (The correct answers are in the Appendix on p. 534.) The procedure for the coordinator is as follows:

1. Assign participants to heterogeneous groups of three.
2. Conduct a competitive task experience as follows:
   a. State that the members of each triad are to compete to see who is best in identifying how many squares are in a certain geometric figure. The criterion for winning is simply to identify more correct squares than the other two triad members identify. Ask the participants to turn their square figure right side up, and tell them to begin.
   b. At the end of four or five minutes, instruct the participants to stop. Ask them to determine who is the winner of each triad, ask the winners to stand, and then have everyone applaud.
   c. Tell the participants to turn away from their triad and, working by themselves, write down (1) how they felt during the competition and (2) what they noticed during the competition. Give them another three or four minutes to do this.
3. Conduct an individualistic task experience as follows:
   a. State that participants are to work individualistically to find as many two-sided figures in a geometric figure as they can. All participants who find 95% of the biangles will receive an evaluation of "excellent," all those who find 90% will receive an evaluation of "good," and so forth. Tell the participants to turn their biangles right side up and begin.
   b. At the end of four or five minutes, ask the participants to stop. Then announce the number of biangles in the figure. Ask the participants to leave their triad and, working by themselves, describe (1) how they felt and (2) what they noticed during this task. Give them another three or four minutes to do this.

continued on next page

continued from previous page

4. Conduct a cooperative task experience as follows:

    a. State that the participants are to re-form their triads and work as a group to identify as many triangles in a geometric figure as they can, making sure that all members of the triad can correctly identify all the triangles. When they are finished, the members of each triad should sign the group's paper to indicate their agreement with the group's answer. All members of the groups finding 95% of the triangles will receive an evaluation of "excellent," all members of the groups finding 90% of the triangles will receive an evaluation of "good," and so forth. Tell the participants to turn their triangle figures right side up and begin.

    b. At the end of nine or ten minutes, tell the participants to stop. Inform them of the number of triangles in the figure. Then ask them to turn away from their triad and, working by themselves, write down (1) how they felt and (2) what they noticed during the cooperative task. Give the participants four minutes to do this.

Goal Structure and Interaction Among Group Members

	Goal Structures		
	Cooperative	**Competitive**	**Individualistic**
Interaction			
Communication			
Facilitation of others' efforts			
Peer influence			
Utilization of others' resources			
Divergent thinking			
Emotional involvement in task			
Acceptance and support among members			
Trust among members			
Conflict management			
Division of labor			
Fear of failure			

5. Instruct the participants to share their reactions to the three types of task situations with the other members of their triad. Give them ten or twelve minutes to do so. Then sample the reactions of the triads in a class discussion. Ask the participants to draw conclusions about the reactions of the triads to the three task experiences.

6. Instruct the triads to fill out the table on the basis of their experiences in the three goal structures and the comments made by the other triads. In the spaces provided, they should summarize their observations of the interaction that occurred in three task situations.

7. Review with the entire class the conceptual definitions of the three goal structures and discuss their views of the impact of each of these structures on group functioning and productivity.

Goal Structures Exercise: Biangles

Goal Structures Exercise: Squares

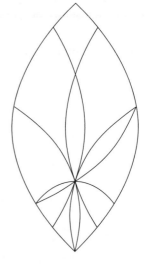

How did I feel?
What did I notice?

How did I feel?
What did I notice?

Goal Structures Exercise: Triangles

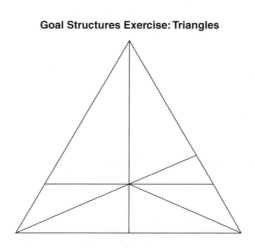

How did I feel?
What did I notice?

EXERCISE 3.6

SUBSISTENCE

The purpose of this exercise is to observe how unequal resources affect the development of cooperation or competition within a group. The exercise simulates the effects of poverty and affluence in a life-and-death situation. The procedure is as follows:

1. Form groups of seven. One member should volunteer to be the recorder, and another member should volunteer to be the observer. Each group should have five participants, one recorder, and one observer.
2. To play the game contained in this exercise, the group needs a pack of blank 3 × 5-inch index cards to serve as food cards. The group also needs a pack of hunting-and-gathering cards. The statements that should be written on these cards, one statement per card, can be found in the Appendix on pages 534–535.
3. The role of the observer is to record the frequency of the behaviors listed on the observation sheet. The frequencies are reported to the group during the concluding group discussion.
4. The role of the recorder is to:
   a. Read the Subsistence Instruction Sheet to the group.
   b. Review the rules with participants.
   c. Give each participant three food cards.
   d. Shuffle the hunting-and-gathering cards and place them in the center of the group.
   e. Distribute and collect food cards on the basis of the cards drawn.
   f. At the end of each round, collect one food card from each participant.
   g. Ensure that each participant announces how many food cards he or she has at the end of each round.
   h. Announce how many participants starved to death and who has the most food cards at the end of each week (seven rounds).
5. When the game is over, discuss the following questions:
   a. Who survived and who died?
   b. How was a cooperative or a competitive strategy decided on?
   c. How did participants feel about the impending death by starvation?
   d. How did the dead feel when they knew others could have saved them?
   e. How did the survivors feel when others died when they had extra food cards?
   f. Who organized the group to create a just distribution of food?
   g. What real-life situations parallel this exercise?

SUBSISTENCE INSTRUCTION SHEET

A severe drought has devastated your world. Because food is so scarce, you have banded to-gether into a hunting-and-gathering group. It is more efficient for several people to coordinate their hunting and gathering so that more territory can be covered in any one day. There are five members of your hunting-and-gathering group. The food cards in your hands represent all you have left of your dwindling food supply. Because you are already weakened by hunger, you must eat at the end of each day (round) or die. At that time, you must give up one food card. When you are out of cards, you will die of starvation. A member who does not have one food card at the end of a day (round) is considered to be dead and can no longer participate in the group. Members with only one food card may not talk. Only members with two or more food cards may discuss their situation and converse with one another. You may give food cards to one another whenever you wish to do so.

SUBSISTENCE EXERCISE RULES

1. The game begins when the recorder gives all participants three food cards, shuffles the hunting-and-gathering cards, and places them in the center of the group.
2. The purpose of the game is to gain points. You receive eight points if at the end of the week of hunting and gathering (seven rounds) you have more food cards than does any other participant in your group. If no one in your group has starved at the end of the week of hunting and gathering, all participants receive five points.
3. The game is played for a minimum of two weeks. At the beginning of each week, all participants begin with three food cards and with all five participants alive.
4. You draw one card during each round. You read it aloud to the group and receive from or give to the recorder the number of food cards indicated.
5. During a round you may give food cards to other participants if you wish to.
6. All participants read the hunting-and-gathering cards aloud. Only those with two or more food cards, however, may discuss the game with each other. Participants with one or no food cards must be silent.
7. At the end of each round, participants hold up their food cards and announce to the group how many food cards they have.
8. At the end of each round, participants give one food card each to the recorder. This symbolizes the food eaten during the day to stay alive.
9. If a participant cannot give a food card to the recorder at the end of a round, the participant dies of starvation and is excluded from further rounds during that week.
10. At the end of each week of hunting and gathering (seven rounds), the recorder announces who has the most food cards and how many participants starved to death. Points are then awarded.

Subsistence Record Sheet

Name	Round 1	Round 2	Round 3	Round 4	Round 5	Round 6	Round 7

Subsistence Observation Sheet

	Round 1	Round 2	Round 3	Round 4	Round 5	Round 6	Round 7
Number of cards given away							
Number of cards taken away							
Number of people starved							

continued on next page

continued from previous page

Subsistence Observation Sheet (Continued)

	Round 1	Round 2	Round 3	Round 4	Round 5	Round 6	Round 7
Cooperative strategy suggested							
Competitive comment							
Other							
Other							

GROUP GOALS AND SOCIAL INTERDEPENDENCE AMONG MEMBERS

Sandy Koufax was one of the greatest pitchers in the history of baseball. He was perhaps the only major-league pitcher whose fastball could be heard to hum. Opposing batters, instead of talking and joking in the dugout, would sit quietly and listen to hear Koufax's fastball hum. When it was their turn to bat, they were already intimidated. There was, however, a simple way for Koufax's genius to have been negated: by making the first author of this book, his catcher. To be great, a pitcher needs an outstanding catcher (his great partner was Johnny Roseboro). David is such an unskilled catcher that Koufax would have had to throw the ball much slower in order for David to catch it. This would have deprived Koufax of his greatest weapon. Placing Frank at a key defensive position in the infield or outfield, furthermore, would have seriously affected Koufax's success. Sandy Koufax was not a great pitcher on his own. Only as part of a team could Koufax achieve greatness. In baseball and in every other group, it takes a cooperative effort. Extraordinary achievement comes from a cooperative group, not from the individualistic or competitive efforts of isolated individuals.

Social interdependence to humans is like water to fish. Just as fish are immersed in water their entire lives, we, too, are immersed in social interdependence. And because we are immersed in it, social interdependence can escape our notice. Because we cannot imagine its absence, we often do not consider its presence and, therefore, regularly underestimate the role that social interdependence plays in human life. The following section, however, is designed to make you think about what social interdependence is, how we partake in it, and how it affects our daily lives. Some background on social interdependence theory, which has a long history in the field of social science, also is provided.

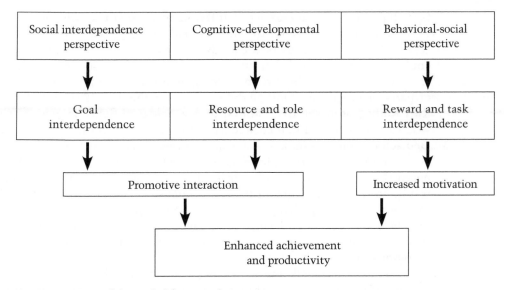

Figure 3.1   General theoretical framework.
Source: D. W. Johnson and R. Johnson, ***Cooperation and competition: Theory and research***
(Edina, MN: Interaction Book Company, 1989). Reprinted with permission of the authors.

Theoretical Orientations

Two are better than one, because they have a good reward for their
toil. For if they fall, one will lift up his fellow; but woe to him who is
alone when he falls and has not another to lift him up.... And though
a man might prevail against one who is alone, two will withstand him.
A threefold cord is not quickly broken.

Ecclesiastes 4:9–12

There are at least three general theoretical perspectives that have guided research on cooperation: cognitive-developmental, behavioral, and social interdependence (Figure 3.1). The cognitive-developmental perspective is largely based on the theories of Piaget and Vygotsky. Piaget proposed that when individuals cooperate on the environment, sociocognitive conflict occurs that creates cognitive disequilibrium, which in turn stimulates perspective-taking ability and cognitive development. Vygotsky proposed that knowledge is social, constructed from cooperative efforts to learn, understand, and solve problems. Behavioral theory states that productivity depends on group reinforcers and rewards. Skinner focused on group contingencies, Bandura focused on imitation, and Homans, Thibaut, and Kelley focused on the balance of rewards and costs in **social exchange** among interdependent individuals. While the cognitive-developmental and behavioral theoretical orientations have their followings, by far the most important theory dealing with cooperation and competition is social interdependence theory.

The historical roots of social interdependence theory can be traced to the emerging school of gestalt psychology at the University of Berlin in the early 1900s.

Gestalt psychology was part of the shift from mechanistic to field theories (Deutsch, 1968). As the *field* became the unit of analysis in physics, so did the *whole, or gestalt*, become the focus of the study of perception and behavior for gestalt psychologists. They posited that humans develop organized and meaningful views of their world by perceiving events as integrated wholes rather than as a summation of parts or properties. One of the founders of the gestalt school of psychology, Kurt Koffka, proposed that, similar to psychological fields, groups were dynamic wholes in which the interdependence among members could vary (Deutsch, 1968; Deutsch & Krauss, 1965).

Building on the principles of gestalt psychology, Kurt Lewin (1935, 1948) proposed that the essence of a group is the interdependence among members that results in the group being a *dynamic whole* so that a change in the state of any member or subgroup changes the state of any other member or subgroup. Group members are made interdependent through common goals. As members perceive their common goals, a state of tension arises that motivates movement toward the accomplishment of the goals.

Lewin's individuals and colleagues conducted research indicating that it is the drive for goal accomplishment that motivates cooperative and competitive behavior. Interrupted tasks are almost always resumed when people are free to do as they wish (Ovisankian, 1928); under certain conditions one activity can substitute for another in completing a task and, hence, release the tension connected with another, interrupted activity (Lissner, 1933; Mahler, 1933). Cooperative work that is interrupted and not completed can lead to a persisting force to recall that is not much different from the pressure to recall induced by interrupted individual work (Lewis, 1944; Lewis & Franklin, 1944). In the late 1940s, Morton Deutsch extended this work and formulated a theory of cooperation and competition (Deutsch, 1949a, 1962).

Morton Deutsch was born in 1920, graduated from City College of New York in 1939, and obtained a master's degree from the University of Pennsylvania in 1940. After serving in the United States Air Force from 1942 to 1945, he entered the doctoral program in social psychology at M.I.T. to study with Kurt Lewin. Following in Lewin's footsteps, Deutsch has become noted as an outstanding social psychologist because of his commitment to the development of theory about complex social issues, his ability to find ways to study these issues in a laboratory setting, and his dedication to the solution of social problems. Deutsch's (1949a) original theory has served as a major conceptual structure for the study of cooperation and competition from the start of his career to the present day. Since his initial theorizing, Deutsch has extended his theory of social interdependence to include trust, conflict resolution, and systems of distributive justice. Deutsch's theory has been extended and applied to education (Johnson, 1970, Johnson & Johnson, 1974, 1989, 2005a, 2009b) and business and industry (Tjosvold, 1986), and many other areas.

Social interdependence exists when the outcomes of individuals are affected by their own and others' actions (D. W. Johnson & R. Johnson, 1989, 2005a, 2009b). There are two types of social interdependence: positive (when the actions of individuals promote the achievement of joint goals) and negative (when the actions of individuals obstruct the achievement of each other's goals). Social interdependence may be differentiated from social dependence, independence, and helplessness. **Social dependence** exists when the goal achievement of person A is affected by person B's actions, but the reverse is not true. **Social independence** exists when the goal achievement of person A is unaffected by person B's actions and vice versa. *Social helplessness* exists when neither the person nor others can influence goal achievement. There are three ways interdependence can be structured in a situation (Deutsch, 1949a, 1962; Johnson, 2003; Johnson & Johnson, 1989, 2005a, 2009b):

1. Positive interdependence (i.e., cooperation): When a situation is structured so individuals' goal achievements are positively correlated, individuals perceive that they can reach their goals if and only if the others in the group also reach their goals. Thus, individuals seek outcomes that are beneficial to all those with whom they are cooperatively linked.
2. Negative interdependence (i.e., competition): When a situation is structured so individuals' goal achievements are negatively correlated, each individual perceives that when one person achieves his or her goal, all others with whom he or she is competitively linked fail to achieve their goals. Thus, individuals seek an outcome that is personally beneficial but detrimental to all others in the situation.
3. No interdependence (i.e., individualistic): When a situation is structured so there is no correlation among participants' goal attainments, each individual perceives that he or she can reach his or her goal regardless of whether other individuals attain or do not attain their goals. Thus, individuals seek an outcome that is personally beneficial without concern for the outcomes of others.

Deutsch (1949a, 1962) posited that positive interdependence creates the psychological processes of **substitutability** (i.e., the degree to which actions of one person substitute for the actions of another person), positive **cathexis** (i.e., the investment of positive psychological energy in objects outside of oneself, such as friends, family, and work), and inducibility (i.e., the openness to being influenced by and to influencing others). Negative interdependence tends to create nonsubstitutability, negative cathexis, and resistance to influence. No interdependence can be characterized by the absence of these three psychological processes.

Interaction Patterns

The basic premise of social interdependence theory is that the type of interdependence structured in a situation determines how individuals interact with one another which, in turn, determines outcomes. Positive interdependence tends to result in promotive interaction. **Promotive interaction** occurs as individuals encourage and facilitate each other's efforts to accomplish the group's goals. Promotive interaction is characterized by individuals (Johnson & Johnson, 1999a, 2005a) providing each other with help and assistance, exchanging needed resources such as information and materials, challenging each other's conclusions and reasoning, advocating the exertion of effort to achieve mutual goals, influencing each other's efforts to achieve the group's goals, and acting in trusting and trustworthy ways. Negative interdependence typically results in oppositional interaction. **Oppositional interaction** occurs as individuals discourage and obstruct one another's efforts to achieve. Individuals focus both on increasing their own success and on preventing anyone else from being more successful than they are. *No interaction* exists when individuals work independently without any interaction or interchange with one another. Individuals focus only on increasing their own success and ignore as irrelevant the efforts of others. Each of these interaction patterns creates different outcomes, as described in Table 3.2.

OUTCOMES OF SOCIAL INTERDEPENDENCE

Within Yosemite National Park lies the famous Half Dome Mountain. The Half Dome is famous for its 2,000 feet of soaring, sheer cliff wall. Unusually beautiful to the observer, and considered unclimbable for years, the Half Dome's northwest face was first

TYPES OF POSITIVE INTERDEPENDENCE

Positive Goal Interdependence: Individuals perceive that they can achieve their goals if and only if all the members of their group also attain their goals. Members of a group have a mutual set of goals that they are all striving to accomplish.

Positive Celebration/Reward Interdependence: The group celebrates success. A joint reward is given for successful group work and members' efforts to achieve.

Positive Resource Interdependence: Each member has only a portion of the information, resources, or materials necessary for the task to be completed and the members' resources have to be combined in order for the group to achieve its goal.

Positive Role Interdependence: Each member is assigned complementary and interconnected roles that specify responsibilities that the group needs in order to complete a joint task.

Positive Identity Interdependence: The group establishes a mutual identity through a name, flag, motto, or song.

Environmental Interdependence: Group members are bound together by the physical environment in some way. An example is putting people in a specific area in which to work.

Positive Fantasy Interdependence: A task is given that requires members to imagine that they are in a life-or-death situation and must collaborate in order to survive.

Positive Task Interdependence: A division of labor is created so that the actions of one group member have to be completed if the next team member is to complete his or her responsibility.

Positive Outside Enemy Interdependence: Groups are placed in competition with one another. Group members then feel interdependent as they strive to beat the other groups and win the competition.

TABLE 3.2 **Social Interdependence Theory**

PROCESS	COOPERATIVE	COMPETITIVE	INDIVIDUALISTIC
Interdependence	Positive	Negative	None
Interaction pattern	Promotive	Oppositional	None
Outcome 1	High effort to achieve	Low effort to achieve	Low effort to achieve
Outcome 2	Positive relationships	Negative relationships	No relationships
Outcome 3	Psychological health	Psychological illness	Psychological pathology

scaled in 1957 by Royal Robbins and two companions. This incredibly dangerous climb took five days, with Robbins and his companions spending four nights on the cliff, sleeping in ropes with nothing below their bodies but air. Even today, the northwest face is a death trap to all but the finest and most skilled rock climbers. And far above the ground, moving slowly up the rock face, are two climbers.

The two climbers are motivated by a shared goal of successfully climbing the northwest face. As they move up the cliff they are attached to one another by a rope (the life line). As one member (the lead climber) climbs, the other (the belayer) ensures that the two have a safe anchor and he or she can catch the lead climber if that climber falls. The lead climber does not begin climbing until the belayer says "go." Then the lead climber advances, puts in a piton, slips in the rope, and continues to advance. The pitons help the belayer catch the lead climber if the climber falls and they mark the path up the cliff. The lifeline goes from the belayer through the pitons up to the climber. When the lead climber has completed the first leg of the climb, he or she becomes the belayer and the other member of the team begins to climb. The pitons placed by the lead climber serve to guide and support the second member of the team up the rock face. The second member advances up the route marked out by the first member until the first leg is completed, and then leap-frogs and becomes the lead climber for the second leg of the climb. The roles of lead climber and belayer are alternated until the summit is reached.

All human life is like mountain climbing. The human species has a cooperation imperative—we desire and seek out opportunities to operate jointly with others to achieve mutual goals. We are attached to others through a variety of "lifelines" and we alternate supporting and leading others to ensure a better life for ourselves, our children, our neighbors, and all generations to follow. From cradle to grave we cooperate with others. Each day, from our first waking moment until sleep overtakes us again, we cooperate within family, work, leisure, and community by working jointly to achieve mutual goals.

Since the late nineteenth century, there have been hundreds of research studies conducted on social interdependence (Johnson, 2003; Johnson & Johnson, 1989, 2005a, 2009b). The numerous variables that are affected by cooperation can be subsumed within three broad and interrelated outcomes (see Figure 3.2) (Johnson, 2003; Johnson & Johnson, 1989): (a) effort exerted to achieve, (b) quality of relationships among participants, and (c) participants' psychological adjustment.

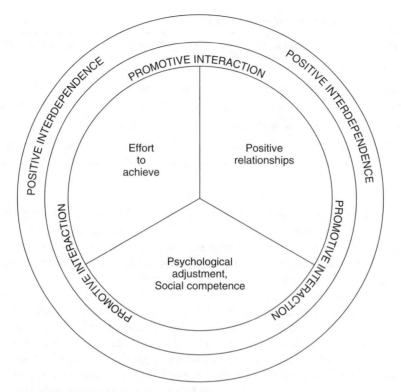

Figure 3.2 Outcomes of cooperation.
Source: D. W. Johnson and R. T. Johnson, *Cooperation and competition: Theory and research* (Edina, MN: Interaction Book Company, 1989). Reprinted with permission of the authors.

If research is to have impact on theory and practice, it must be summarized and communicated in a complete, objective, impartial, and unbiased way. In an age of information explosion, considerable danger exists that theories may be formulated on small and nonrepresentative samples of available knowledge, which can lead to fallacious conclusions that in turn lead to mistaken practices. A quantitative reviewing procedure, such as meta-analysis, allows for more definitive and robust conclusions. A **meta-analysis** is a method of statistically combining the results of a set of independent studies that test the same hypothesis and using inferential statistics to draw conclusions about the overall result of the studies. The essential purpose of a meta-analysis is to summarize a set of related research studies, so that the size of the effect of the **independent variable** on the dependent variable is known.

Amount and Characteristics of Research

The study of cooperative, competitive, and individualistic efforts is commonly recognized as the oldest field of research in U.S. social psychology. In the late 1800s, Triplett (1898) conducted a study on the factors associated with competitive performance. Since then, more than 1,200 studies have been conducted on the relative merits of cooperative, competitive, and individualistic efforts and the conditions under which each is appropriate. Many of the research studies have yielded findings with high internal validity, being carefully conducted by skilled investigators under highly controlled laboratory (31%) and field (65%) settings. When rated on the variables of random assignment to conditions, clarity of control conditions, control of the experimenter effect, control of the curriculum effect (same materials used in all conditions), and verification of the successful implementation of the independent variable, 51% of the studies met these criteria. This is one of the largest bodies of research within psychology, and it provides sufficient empirical research to test social interdependence theory's propositions.

Findings from the research on social interdependence have an external validity and generalizability rarely found in the social sciences. The more variations in places, people, and procedures the research can withstand and still yield the same findings, the more externally valid the conclusions. The research has been conducted over eleven decades by many different researchers with markedly different theoretical and practical orientations working in different settings. Participants in the studies varied from age three to older adults and have come from different economic classes and cultural backgrounds. Widely different research tasks, ways of structuring social interdependence, and measures of the dependent variables have been used. The duration of studies ranged from one session to more than 100 sessions. The research has been conducted in numerous cultures in North America (Caucasian, Black American, Native American, and Hispanic populations) and countries from all parts of the world. The research on social interdependence includes both theoretical and demonstration studies conducted in educational, business, and social service organizations. The diversity of the research gives social interdependence theory wide generalizability and considerable external validity.

The many diverse dependent variables examined in studies on social interdependence over the past 110 years can be subsumed within three broad categories (Johnson & Johnson, 1989, 2005a, 2009b): effort to achieve, positive interpersonal relationships, and psychological health.

EFFORT TO ACHIEVE

Two heads are better than one.

John Heywood

A meta-analysis of all studies found that the average person cooperating achieved at about two-thirds of a standard deviation above the average person performing within a competitive (effect size = 0.67) or individualistic (effect size = 0.64; Table 3.3) situation (Johnson & Johnson, 1989, 2005a, 2009b). All effect sizes were computed using Cohen's d and adjusted for sample size utilizing the procedure recommended by Hedges and Olkin (1985). When only studies yielding findings with high internal validity were included in the analysis, the effect

TABLE 3.3   **Mean Effect Sizes for Impact of Social Interdependence on Dependent Variables**

CONDITIONS	ACHIEVEMENT	INTERPERSONAL ATTRACTION	SOCIAL SUPPORT	SELF-ESTEEM
Total Studies				
Coop vs. Comp	0.67	0.67	0.62	0.58
Coop vs. Ind	0.64	0.60	0.70	0.44
Comp vs. Ind	0.30	0.08	−0.13	−0.23
High-Quality Studies				
Coop vs. Comp	0.88	0.82	0.83	0.67
Coop vs. Ind	0.61	0.62	0.72	0.45
Comp vs. Ind	0.07	0.27	−0.13	−0.25
Mixed Operationalizations				
Coop vs. Comp	0.40	0.46	0.45	0.33
Coop vs. Ind	0.42	0.36	0.02	0.22
Pure Operationalizations				
Coop vs. Comp	0.71	0.79	0.73	0.74
Coop vs. Ind	0.65	0.66	0.77	0.51

Note: Comp, Competition; Coop, Cooperation; Ind, Individualistic.

Source: D. W. Johnson and R. Johnson, *Cooperation and competition: Theory and research* (Edina, MN: Interaction Book Company, 1989). Reproduced by permission.

sizes were 0.88 and 0.61, respectively. Cooperative experiences promote more frequent insight into and use of higher-level cognitive and moral reasoning strategies than do competitive (effect size = 0.93) or individualistic (effect size = 0.97) efforts. Cooperators tend to spend more time on task than do competitors (effect size = 0.76) or participants working individualistically (effect size = 1.17). Competitors tended to spend more time on task than did participants working individualistically (effect size = 0.64). Cooperation, when compared with competitive and individualistic efforts, tends to promote greater long-term retention, higher intrinsic motivation and expectations for success, more creative thinking (i.e., process gain), greater transfer of learning, and more positive attitudes toward the task and school.

Besides higher achievement and greater retention, cooperation, compared with competitive or individualistic efforts, tends to result in more (Johnson, 2003; Johnson & Johnson, 1989):

1. Willingness to take on difficult tasks and persist, despite difficulties, in working toward goal accomplishment. In addition, there is intrinsic motivation, high expectations for success, high incentive to achieve based on mutual benefit, high epistemic curiosity and continuing interest in learning, and high commitment to achieve.

2. High achievement and long-term retention of what is learned.

3. Higher-level reasoning, critical thinking, and meta-cognitive thought. Cooperators are better able to *"sort sense from nonsense,"* and utilize the critical thinking abilities of grasping information, examining it, evaluating it for soundness,
and applying it appropriately. Cooperative situations promote more frequent
insight into and a greater use of higher level cognitive and moral reasoning
strategies than do competitive or individualistic experiences (effect sizes = 0.93
and 0.97 respectively).

4. Creative thinking and process gain. **Process gain** occurs when new ideas, solutions, or efforts are generated through group interactions; these ideas, solutions,
or efforts are not generated when persons work individually. In cooperative
groups, members more frequently generate new ideas, strategies, and solutions
that they would think of on their own.

5. Transfer of learning from one situation to another. **Group-to-individual transfer**
occurs when the competencies or information individuals learned within a
cooperative group is subsequently performed or utilized individually. What
individuals learn in a group today, they are able to do alone tomorrow.

6. Positive attitudes toward the tasks being completed. Cooperative efforts result
in more positive attitudes toward the tasks being completed and greater continuing motivation to complete the tasks. The positive attitudes extend to the
work experience and the organization as a whole.

7. Time on task. Over thirty studies measured time on task and found that
cooperators spent more time on task than did competitors (effect size = 0.76)
or individuals working individualistically (effect size = 1.17). Competitors
spent more time on task than did individuals working individualistically (effect
size = 0.64).

Not all research supporting the use of cooperation has been experimental. Balderston (1930) conducted a study of group-incentive plans in the workplace that relied on
written descriptions collected from a number of companies. In each instance, the pay
of all members depended on the productivity of the group as a whole. Balderston found
that this method of work doubled the efficiency of the workers, increased their pay
about 25%, and reduced their costs substantially compared to the flat rate previously
paid to each individual. The users of group-incentive methods stated that their plans
were valuable because they increased cooperation and team spirit among members,
reduced monotony on the job, and caused workers to focus on a common goal.

Kurt Lewin often stated, *"I always found myself unable to think as a single person."* Most efforts to achieve are a personal but social process that requires individuals
to cooperate and to construct shared understandings. Both competitive and individualistic structures, by isolating individuals from one another, tend to depress achievement
and productivity.

Process Gain or Loss

There has been some debate as to whether process loss or process gain occurs in cooperative groups (Hill, 1982). **Process loss** occurs when fewer ideas, fewer solutions,
and less effort on a learning or problem-solving task are generated within groups than

by persons working individualistically, whereas process gain occurs when interaction within groups generates greater efforts and a higher quantity and more novel ideas and problem solutions than working individualistically. The meta-analysis results indicate that not only do groups outperform individuals on most tasks and under most conditions (thus indicating process gain rather than process loss), individuals perform higher on individual measures of achievement after learning in cooperative groups than after learning alone (thus indicating greater group-to-individual transfer than individual-to-individual transfer) (Johnson & Johnson, 1989, 2005a, 2009b). Correspondingly, there is evidence that cooperative groups engage in collective induction, inducing general principles that none of the group members could induce alone (Ames & Murray, 1982).

POSITIVE RELATIONSHIPS AND SOCIAL SUPPORT

A faithful friend is a strong defense, and he that hath found him, hath found a treasure.

Ecclesiastics 6:14

We are created, not for isolation, but for relationships. Caring and committed relationships are not a luxury, they are a necessity. Recent national surveys indicate that it is feeling valued, loved, wanted, and respected by others that give life meaning and purpose and it is intimate relationships that create happiness.

More than 180 studies have compared the impact of cooperative, competitive, and individualistic efforts on interpersonal attraction. Cooperative efforts, when compared with competitive (effect size = 0.67) and individualistic (effect size = 0.60) experiences, promoted considerably greater interpersonal attraction among individuals (Johnson & Johnson, 1989, 2005a, 2009b). This remains true when only the methodologically high-quality studies are examined (effect sizes = 0.82 and 0.62, respectively) and when the studies focusing on relationships between white and minority participants (effect sizes = 0.52 and 0.44, respectively) and relationships between participants who were disabled and nondisabled (effect sizes = 0.70 and 0.64, respectively) are examined. Since the 1940s, furthermore, more than 106 studies comparing the relative impact of cooperative, competitive, and individualistic efforts on social support have been conducted. Cooperative experiences promoted greater task-oriented and personal social support than did competitive (effect size = 0.62) or individualistic (effect size = 0.70) experiences. This was still true when only the methodologically high-quality studies are examined (effect sizes = 0.83 and 0.72, respectively).

Much of the research on interpersonal relationships has been conducted on relationships between white and minority individuals and between nonhandicapped and handicapped individuals (Johnson, 2003b; Johnson & Johnson, 1989). There have been over forty experimental studies comparing some combination of cooperative, competitive, and individualistic experiences on cross-ethnic relationships and over forty similar studies on mainstreaming of handicapped individuals (Johnson, 2003b; Johnson & Johnson, 1989, 2005a, 2009b). Their results are consistent: Working cooperatively creates far more positive relationships among diverse and heterogeneous individuals than does working competitively or individualistically.

An extension of social interdependence theory, **social judgment theory,** focuses on relationships among diverse individuals (Johnson, 2003b; Johnson & Johnson, 1989). The social judgments that individuals make about one another increase or decrease the liking they feel toward one another. Such social judgments are the result of either a process of acceptance or a process of rejection (Johnson, 2003b; Johnson & Johnson, 1989). The **process of acceptance** is based on the individuals promoting mutual goal accomplishment as a result of their perceived positive interdependence. The promotive interaction tends to result in frequent, accurate, and open communication; accurate understanding of one another's perspective; inducibility; differentiated, dynamic, and realistic views of one another; high self-esteem; success and productivity; and expectations for positive and productive future interaction. The **process of rejection** results from oppositional or no interaction based on perceptions of negative or no interdependence. Both lead to an absence of or inaccurate communication; egocentrism; resistance to influence; monopolistic, stereotyped, and static views of others; low self-esteem; failure; and expectations of distasteful and unpleasant interaction with others. The processes of acceptance and rejection are self-perpetuating. Any part of the process tends to elicit all the other parts of the process.

The positive relationships among members promoted by cooperative efforts result in a high level of group cohesion. **Group cohesion** is the mutual attraction among members of a group and the resulting desire to remain in the group. Highly cohesive groups are characterized by greater ease in setting goals (Festinger, Schachter, & Back, 1950), greater likelihood in achieving those goals (Seashore, 1954; Wolfe & Box, 1988), and greater susceptibility to being influenced by group mates (Schachter, Ellertson, McBride, & Gregory, 1951). The more cohesive a group is, the more its members are likely to stay in the group, to take part in group activities, and to try to recruit new, like-minded members (Levine & Moreland, 1998; Mobley, Griffith, Hand, & Miglino, 1979; Sprink & Carron, 1994). The impact of group cohesiveness on group performance is stronger for small groups and real groups. Group performance seems to be driven predominantly by members' commitment to successful task performance, and doing well on a task tends to increase group cohesiveness (Mullen & Cooper, 1994; Figure 3.3). When a task requires close cooperation among group members (such as a football team executing a difficult play or a military unit carrying out a complicated maneuver), cohesiveness increases performance (Gully, Devine, & Whitney, 1995). As cohesiveness increases, absenteeism and turnover of membership decrease, member commitment to group goals increases, feelings of personal responsibility to the group increase, willingness to take on difficult tasks increases, motivation and persistence in working toward goal achievement increase,

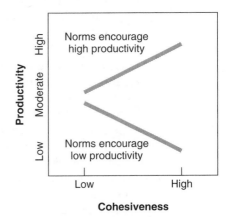

Figure 3.3 The hypothesized link between productivity and cohesiveness.

satisfaction and morale increase, willingness to endure pain and frustration on behalf of the group increases, willingness to defend the group against external criticism or attack increases, willingness to listen to and be influenced by colleagues increases, commitment to one another's professional growth and success increases, and productivity increases (Johnson, 2003b; Johnson & Johnson, 1989, 2005a, 2009b; Watson & Johnson, 1972).

An important question is whether the relationships formed within cooperative groups will continue voluntarily in subsequent nontask situations. A number of studies have demonstrated that when individuals were placed in postinstructional, free-choice situations, there was more cross-ethnic interaction (Johnson & Johnson, 1989) and more cross-handicap interaction (Johnson & Johnson, 1989, R. Johnson & D. W. Johnson, 1981, 1989; R. Johnson, D. W. Johnson, DeWeerdt, Lyons, & Zaidman, 1983; R. Johnson, D. W. Johnson, Scott, & Ramolae, 1985; Johnson & Johnson, 1989) when individuals had been in a cooperative rather than a competitive or individualistic situation. In other words, the relationships formed within cooperative groups among heterogeneous peers do seem to generalize to post-task situations.

Another question is whether the quality of interpersonal relationships among students is related to academic achievement. Roseth, D. W. Johnson, and R. Johnson (2008) conducted a meta-analysis on 148 studies involving more than 17,000 early adolescents. The studies were conducted in eleven different countries. They found that positive peer relationships explained 33% of the variation in academic achievement, and when only the moderate- and high-quality studies were included, positive peer relationships explained 40% of the variation in achievement. It seems that if teachers want to increase early adolescents' achievement, they should facilitate the development of friendships. Another question is whether there is a relationship among cooperative experiences, social interdependence dispositions, and harm-intended aggression, victimization, and prosocial behavior (Choi, D., W. Johnson, & R. Johnson, 2011). Two hundred and seventeen students from third to fifth grades completed a series of questionnaires. A path analysis was conducted among the variables. The results indicate that cooperative experiences predicted cooperative predispositions, the absence of individualistic predispositions, and engagement in prosocial behavior. Cooperative predispositions predicted the engagement in prosocial behavior and the absence of engaging in harm-intended aggression. If schools wish to prevent bullying and increase prosocial behaviors, the use of cooperative learning and efforts to help students become more predisposed to engage in cooperation seem to be important strategies.

Besides liking one another, cooperators give and receive considerable social support (Johnson, 2003b; Johnson & Johnson, 1989, 2005a, 2009b). Since the 1940s, over 106 studies comparing the relative impact of cooperative, competitive, and individualistic efforts on social support have been conducted. Cooperative experiences promoted greater task-oriented and personal social support than did competitive (effect size = 0.62) or individualistic (effect size = 0.70) experiences. Social support tends to promote achievement and productivity, physical health, psychological health, and successful coping with stress and adversity.

PSYCHOLOGICAL HEALTH AND SELF-ESTEEM

All for one, one for all.

Alexandre Dumas

The third set of variables researched includes psychological health, self-esteem, and social competencies. **Psychological health** is the ability to develop, maintain, and appropriately modify interdependent relationships with others to succeed in achieving goals (Johnson, 2003; Johnson & Johnson, 1989). To manage social interdependence, individuals must correctly perceive whether interdependence exists and whether it is positive or negative, be motivated accordingly, and act in ways consistent with normative expectations for appropriate behavior within the situation. Eight studies have been conducted that directly measure the relationship between social interdependence and psychological health (see Johnson & Johnson, 1989, 2005a, 2009b). The samples included university individuals, older adults, suburban high school seniors, juvenile and adult prisoners, stepcouples, Olympic hockey players, and Chinese business managers. The results indicate that working cooperatively with peers and valuing cooperation result in greater psychological health than do competing with peers or working independently. More specifically, cooperativeness is positively related to emotional maturity, well-adjusted social relations, strong personal identity, ability to cope with adversity, social competencies, basic trust and optimism about people, self-confidence, independence and autonomy, higher self-esteem, and increased **perspective-taking skills** (the ability to understand how

a situation appears to other people). Competitiveness was in some cases positively and in some cases negatively related to psychological health, including conditional self-esteem and egocentrism. Individualistic attitudes were negatively related to a wide variety of indices of psychological health, especially a wide variety of pathology, basic self-rejection, and egocentrism.

Social interdependence theory has been extended to self-esteem (Johnson, 2003; Johnson & Johnson, 1989). A process of self-acceptance is posited to be based on (a) internalizing perceptions that one is known, accepted, and liked as one is, (b) internalizing mutual success, and

(c) evaluating oneself favorably in comparison with peers. A process of self-rejection may occur from (a) not wanting to be known, (b) low performance, (c) overgeneralization of self-evaluations, and (d) the disapproval of others. There have been more than eighty studies comparing the relative impact of cooperative, competitive, and individualistic experiences on self-esteem. Cooperative experiences promote higher self-esteem than do competitive (effect size = 0.58) or individualistic (effect size = 0.44) experiences, even when only the methodologically high-quality studies are examined (effect sizes = 0.67 and 0.45, respectively). D. W. Johnson and Norem Hebeisen (1981) studied 821 white, middle-class, high school seniors in a midwestern suburban community. They found that cooperative experiences tend to be related to beliefs that a person is intrinsically worthwhile, others see the person in positive ways, the person's attributes compare favorably with those of his or her peers, and he or she is a capable, competent, and successful person. Competitive experiences tend to be related to conditional self-esteem based on whether one wins or loses. Individualistic experiences tend to be related to basic self-rejection.

Psychological health includes internalizing constructive values. There are values inherent in social interdependence. Cooperative, competitive, and individualistic efforts have inherent value systems that are taught by the flow of day-to-day life within schools (Johnson & Johnson, 2000, 2008, 2010). The values inherently taught by cooperative efforts include commitment to one's own and others' success and well-being, commitment to the common good, and the view that facilitating and promoting the success of others is a natural way of life. Engaging in competitive efforts inherently teaches the values of getting more than others, beating and defeating others, seeing winning as important, and believing that opposing and obstructing the success of others is a natural way of life. The values inherently taught by individualistic experiences are commitment to one's own self-interest and the view that others' well-being is irrelevant. Schools inculcate numerous values in students and the instructional methods used influence the values that students develop.

A number of studies have related cooperative, competitive, and individualistic experiences to perspective-taking ability (Johnson, 2003; Johnson & Johnson, 1989, 2005a, 2009b). Cooperative experiences tend to increase perspective-taking ability whereas competitive and individualistic experiences tend to promote **egocentrism** (being unaware of perspectives other than your own) (effect sizes of 0.61 and 0.44, respectively).

Social competence is an important aspect of psychological health. Social skills and competencies (e.g., individuals' abilities to provide leadership, build and maintain trust, communicate effectively, make effective decisions, and manage conflicts constructively) tend to increase more within cooperative than in competitive or individualistic situations (Johnson, 2003b; Johnson & Johnson, 1989). Employability and career success depend largely on such social skills. These skills also provide the basis for building and maintaining life-long friendships, loving and caring families, and cohesive neighborhoods. One of the most important sets of social competencies involves managing conflicts. Social interdependence theorists note that both positive and negative interdependence create conflicts among individuals (Deutsch, 1973; Johnson & Johnson, 2005b, 2007; Tjosvold, 1991b). In cooperative situations, conflicts occur over how best to achieve mutual goals. In competitive situations, conflicts occur over who will win and who will lose. Two of the conflict resolution programs implemented in schools to teach students how to manage conflicts constructively are (1) the Teaching Students to Be Peacemakers program, in which students are taught how to resolve conflicts of interests constructively by engaging in integrative negotiations and peer mediation (Johnson & Johnson, 2005b) and (2) the Academic Controversy program, in which students are taught how to challenge intellectually each other's ideas, reasoning, and conclusions (Johnson & Johnson, 2007). The research on both programs indicates that conflicts that occur within the context of positive (as opposed to negative) interdependence might result in a wide variety of positive outcomes (such as higher achievement, more frequent use of higher-level reasoning, more accurate perspective taking, more integrative agreements, greater liking for each other, and more positive attitudes toward conflict).

The higher the level of an individual's psychological pathology (e.g., depression, anger, anxiety), the less able he or she is to develop and maintain caring and committed relationships. The association between antisocial behavior and rejection by the normal peer group, for example, is well documented (Bierman, 2004; Williams, Forgas, & von Hippel, 2005). Inappropriately aggressive behavior leads to rejection by peers (Coie & Kupersmidt, 1983; Dodge, 1983). Rejected children are also deficient in a number of social-cognitive skills, including peer group entry, perception of peer group norms, response to provocation, and interpretation of prosocial interactions (Bierman, 2004; Williams, Forgas, & von Hippel, 2005). Among children referred to child guidance clinics, 30 to 75% (depending on age) are reported by their parents to experience peer difficulties (Achenback & Edelbrock, 1981). These difficulties are roughly twice as common among clinic children as among nonreferred youngsters. Moreover, referred children have fewer friends and less contact with them than nonreferred children, their friendships are significantly less stable over time, and their understanding of the reciprocities and intimacies involved in friendships is less mature (Selman, 1981).

Finally, it is through cooperative efforts that many of the attitudes and values essential to psychological health (such as self-efficacy) are learned and adopted.

RECIPROCAL RELATIONSHIPS AMONG THE THREE OUTCOMES

The reason we were so good, and continued to be so good, was because he (Joe Paterno) forces you to develop an inner love among the players. It is much harder to give up on your buddy, than it is to give up on your coach. I really believe that over the years the teams I played on were almost unbeatable in tight situations. When we needed to get that six inches we got it because of our love for one another. Our camaraderie existed because of the kind of coach and kind of person Joe was.

David Joyner

Each of the outcomes of cooperative efforts (effort to achieve, quality of relationships, and psychological health) influences the others and, therefore, they are likely to be found together (Johnson, 2003; Johnson & Johnson, 1989, 2005a, 2009b): (1) Caring and committed friendships come from a sense of mutual accomplishment, mutual pride in joint work, and the bonding that results from joint efforts. The more individuals care about one another, the harder they will work to achieve mutual goals. (2) Joint efforts to achieve mutual goals promote higher self-esteem, self-efficacy, personal control, and confidence in one's competencies. The healthier psychologically individuals are, the better able they are to work with others to achieve mutual goals. (3) Psychological health is built on the internalization of the caring and respect received from loved ones. Friendships are developmental advantages that promote self-esteem, self-efficacy, and general psychological adjustment. The healthier people are psychologically (i.e., free of psychological pathology such as depression, paranoia, anxiety, fear of failure, repressed anger, hopelessness, and meaninglessness), the more caring and committed their relationships. Because each outcome can induce the others, you are likely to find them together. They are a package—each outcome is a door into all three.

MEDIATING VARIABLES: THE BASIC ELEMENTS OF COOPERATION

The truly committed cooperative group is probably the most productive tool that humans have. Creating and maintaining cooperative groups, however, is far from easy. Individuals fool themselves if they think well-meaning directives to "work together," "cooperate," and "be a team" will be enough to create cooperative efforts among members. There is a discipline to creating cooperation. Making teams work is like being on a diet. It does no good to diet one or two days a week. If you wish to lose weight, you have to control what you eat every day. Similarly, it does no good to structure a team carefully every fourth or fifth meeting. The basic elements that make cooperation work are a regimen that should be followed rigorously. The basic components of effective cooperative efforts are positive interdependence, individual and group accountability, face-to-face promotive interaction, appropriate use of social skills, and group processing.

Positive Interdependence: We Instead of Me

During a football game, the quarterback who throws the pass and the receiver who catches the pass are positively interdependent. The success of one depends on the success of the other. Both have to perform competently to assure their mutual success. If one fails, they both fail. They are positively interdependent. **Positive interdependence** exists when individuals perceive that they are linked with other people in such a way that they cannot succeed unless the others succeed (and vice versa) and/or that they must coordinate their efforts with the efforts of others to complete a task (Johnson, 2003; Johnson & Johnson, 1989, 2005a, 2009b). The discipline of using cooperative groups begins with structuring positive interdependence. Group members have to know that they *"sink or swim together"*—that is, they have two responsibilities: to maximize their own productivity and to maximize the productivity of all other group members. There are two major categories of interdependence: outcome interdependence and **means interdependence** (Johnson, 2003; Johnson & Johnson, 1989, 2005a, 2009b). When persons are in a cooperative or competitive situation, they are oriented toward a desired outcome, end state, goal, or reward. If there is no outcome inter-dependence (goal and reward interdependence), there is no reason for cooperation or competition. In addition, the means through which the mutual goals or rewards are to be accomplished specify the actions required on the part of group members. The way in which a goal is to be accomplished determines what courses of action members take and what roles they play. Means interdependence includes resource, role, and task interdependence (which are overlapping and not independent from one another).

Positive interdependence has numerous effects on individuals' motivation and productivity, not the least of which is to highlight the fact that the efforts of all group members are needed for group success. Group members who think their efforts are unnecessary for the group's success may reduce their efforts (Kerr, 1983; Kerr & Bruun, 1983; Sweeney, 1973), whereas group members who perceive their contribu-tions as being unique increase their efforts (Harkins & Petty, 1982). When goal, task, resource, and role interdependence are clearly understood, individuals realize that their unique contributions are required in order for the group to succeed. In addition, reward interdependence needs to be structured to ensure that one member's efforts do not make the efforts of other members unnecessary. If the highest score in the group determines group rewards, for example, low-performing members might see their ef-forts as unnecessary and contribute minimally while high-performing members may feel exploited, become demoralized, and decrease their efforts so as not to provide undeserved rewards for irresponsible and ungrateful "free-riders" (Kerr, 1983).

While positive interdependence is a necessity for group productivity (as well as many other outcomes of group efforts), the relative contribution of the various types of interdependence received very little attention until recently (Johnson, 2003; Johnson & Johnson, 1989, 1998, 2003, 2005a, 2009b). What is now known is:

1. Group membership in and of itself does not seem sufficient to produce higher achievement and productivity—positive interdependence is required (Hwong, Caswell, Johnson, & Johnson, 1993). Knowing that one's performance affects the success of groupmates seems to create "responsibility forces" that increase one's efforts to achieve.
2. Interpersonal interaction is insufficient to increase productivity—positive inter-dependence is required (Lew, Mesch, Johnson, & Johnson, 1986a, 1986b; Mesch, Johnson, & Johnson, 1988; Mesch, Lew, Johnson, & Johnson, 1986). Individuals achieved more under positive goal interdependence than when they worked individualistically but had the opportunity to interact with classmates.
3. Goal and reward interdependence seem to be additive (Lew, Mesch, Johnson, & Johnson, 1986a, 1986b; Mesch, Johnson, & Johnson, 1988; Mesch, Lew, Johnson, & Johnson, 1986). While positive goal interdepen-dence is sufficient to produce higher achievement and productivity than achieved by individualistic efforts, the combination of goal and reward in-terdependence is even more effective.
4. Both working to achieve a reward and working to avoid the loss of a reward pro-duced higher achievement than did individualistic efforts (Frank, 1984). There is no significant difference between the working to achieve a reward and working to avoid a loss.

5. Goal interdependence promotes higher achievement and greater productivity than does resource interdependence (Johnson, Johnson, Ortiz, & Stanne, 1991).

6. Resource interdependence by itself may decrease achievement and productivity compared with individualistic efforts (Johnson, Johnson, Stanne, & Garibaldi, 1990; Ortiz, Johnson, & Johnson, 1996).

7. The combination of goal and resource interdependence increased achievement more than that achieved by goal interdependence alone or by individualistic efforts (Johnson, Johnson, Stanne, & Garibaldi, 1990; Ortiz, Johnson, & Johnson, 1996).

8. Positive interdependence does more than simply motivate individuals to try harder, it facilitates the development of new insights and discoveries through promotive interaction (Gabbert, Johnson, & Johnson, 1986; D. Johnson & Johnson, 1981; D. Johnson, Skon, & Johnson, 1980; Skon, Johnson, & Johnson, 1981). Members of cooperative groups use higher-level reasoning strategies more frequently than do individuals working individualistically or competitively.

9. The more complex the procedures involved in interdependence, the longer it will take group members to reach their full levels of productivity (Ortiz, Johnson, & Johnson, 1996). The more complex the teamwork procedures, the more members have to attend to teamwork and the less time they have to attend to taskwork. Once the teamwork procedures are mastered, however, members concentrate on taskwork and outperform individuals working alone.

10. Studies on identity interdependence involving social dilemmas have found that when individuals define themselves in terms of their group membership, they are more willing to take less from common resources and to contribute more toward the public good (Brewer & Kramer, 1986; De Cremer & Van Dijk, in press; De Cremer & Van Vugt, 1999; Kramer & Brewer, 1984).

Entitativity

The degree of positive interdependence influences the perceived entitativity of the group. Entitativity is the perception that a group is a unified and coherent whole in which the members are bonded together (Campbell, 1958). The stronger the interdependence (e.g., common goals, common outcomes, interpersonal bonds, promotive interaction, behavioral influence, communication), the greater the perceived entitativity of a group (Gaertner & Schopler, 1998; Lickel et. al., 2000; Welbourne, 1999). Perceived entitativity, in turn, influences both group members and nonmembers, with group members perceiving the group as a unified and coherent whole and nonmembers perceiving the group to be a single entity (Johnson & Johnson, 1995a). The stronger the positive interdependence and the resulting entitativity, the stronger the identification with the group, the social identity derived from group membership, the self-esteem and self-worth derived from group membership, the qualities of the group that become incorporated into members' self-definitions, the group's influence on the member's perspective, the differentiation and clarity of boundaries between ingroup and outgroups, the ingroup bias, the vulnerability of self-esteem to attacks on the ingroup (i.e., prejudice against the ingroup may be seen as a threat to one's self-esteem), the empathy members feel for one another, and the helping and promotive actions of group members.

The entitativity created by positive interdependence not only affects group members' perception of their group, it also affects the perceptions of the group by nonmembers (Johnson & Johnson, 1995a). The higher a group's perceived entitativity, the more group membership influences the traits ascribed to members by nonmembers. Stereotypes and discriminatory behavior are built on such impressions. In addition, entitativity tends to result in perceived collective responsibility of ingroup members, either through commission (i.e., encouraging the member to engage in the behavior) or omission (i.e., failing to prevent the member from engaging in the behavior). *Collective responsibility* exists when members of a group are held responsible and sanctioned for the actions of a single member of a group. Highly interdependent groups are seen as highly responsible for the actions of any individual member. Finally, the greater the perceived entitativity of a group, the more likely conflicts based on incompatible goals (i.e., realistic conflicts) will arise. Realistic conflict, in turn, increases a group's entitativity as members band together against an outside threat.

Individual Accountability/Personal Responsibility

Within groups there may be a tension between the collective interest of the group and the interests of individual members. The benefits resulting from group action may accrue to all group members regardless of their individual contributions to the group's efforts (Rapoport & Bornstein, 1987). Because contributions entail personal costs involving time, physical and mental effort, and other resources, group members may have an incentive to "free ride" on the contributions of others. The problem is, of course, that if every group member decides to free ride, the group will be unsuccessful and everyone will suffer. One of the factors preventing free riding is a sense of responsibility to the group and the other group members.

Positive interdependence is posited to create "responsibility forces" that increase group members' feelings of responsibility and accountability for (a) completing one's share of the work and (b) facilitating the work of other group members (Deutsch, 1949a, 1962). When a person's performance affects the outcomes of collaborators, the person feels responsible for their welfare as well as his or her own (Matsui, Kakuyama, & Onglateo, 1987). Failing oneself is bad, but failing others as well as oneself is worse. The shared responsibility created by positive interdependence adds the concept of "ought" to group members' motivation—one ought to do one's part, contribute, and satisfy peer norms (Johnson & Johnson, 1989). Such feelings of responsibility increase a person's motivation to perform well. The more a person is liked and respected by groupmates, furthermore, the more responsibility he or she will feel toward groupmates (Wentzel, 1994).

Responsibility forces increase when there is group and individual accountability. **Group accountability** exists when the overall performance of the group is assessed and the results are given back to all group members to compare against a standard of performance. **Individual accountability** exists when the performance of each individual member is assessed, the results are given back to the individual and the group to compare against a standard of performance, and the member is held responsible by groupmates for contributing his or her fair share to the group's success. Hooper, Ward, Hannafin, and Clark (1989) found that cooperation resulted in higher achievement when individual accountability was structured than when it was not. Archer-Kath, Johnson, and Johnson (1994) found that by increasing individual accountability, perceived interdependence among group members may also be increased.

The lack of individual accountability may reduce feelings of personal responsibility. Members may reduce their contributions to goal achievement when the group works on tasks for which it is difficult to identify members' contributions, when there is an increased likelihood of redundant efforts, when there is a lack of group cohesiveness, and when there is lessened responsibility for the final outcome (Harkins & Petty, 1982; Ingham, Levinger, Graves, & Peckham, 1974; Kerr & Bruun, 1981; Latane, Williams, & Harkins, 1979; Moede, 1927; Petty, Harkins, Williams, & Lantane, 1977; Williams, 1981; Williams, Harkins, & Latane, 1981). If, however, there is high individual accountability and it is clear how much effort each member is contributing, if redundant efforts are avoided, if every member is responsible for the final outcome, and if the group is cohesive, then the social loafing effect vanishes.

Generally, as the group gets larger and larger, members are less likely to see their own personal contribution to the group as being important to the group's chances of success (Kerr, 2001; Olson, 1965). As group size increases, individual members tend to communicate less frequently, which may reduce the amount of information utilized in arriving at a decision (Gerard, Wilhelmy, & Conolley, 1968; Indik, 1965) and the communication may be less truthful, as members may alter their statements to conform to the perceived beliefs of the overall group (Gerard, Wilhelmy, & Conolley, 1968; Rosenberg, 1961). Social loafing, therefore, increases as the size of the group increases. The smaller the size of the group, on the other hand, the greater the individual accountability (Messick & Brewer, 1983). Morgan, Coates, and Rebbin (1970) found that group performance actually improved when one member was missing from five-person groups, perhaps because members believed that their contributions were more necessary.

Promotive (Face-to-Face) Interaction

As discussed previously in this chapter, promotive interaction occurs when group members encourage and facilitate each other's efforts to achieve the group's goals. Promotive interaction is characterized by members providing help and assistance, exchanging needed resources, challenging one another's conclusions and reasoning, acting in trusting and trustworthy ways, and feeling less anxiety and stress (Johnson, 2003; Johnson & Johnson, 1989).

Social Skills

Placing socially unskilled individuals in a group and telling them to cooperate will obviously not be successful. Individuals must be taught the interpersonal and small-group skills needed for high-quality cooperation, and be motivated to use them. To coordinate efforts to achieve mutual goals, individuals must get to know and trust one another, communicate accurately and unambiguously, accept and support one another, and resolve conflicts constructively (Johnson, 2006). Interpersonal and small-group skills form the basic nexus among individuals, and if individuals are to work together productively, and cope with the stresses and strains of doing so, they must have a modicum of these skills. Especially when groups function on a long-term basis and engage in complex, free exploratory activities over a prolonged period, the interpersonal and small-group skills of the members may determine the level of members' productivity.

In their studies on the long-term implementation of cooperation, Marvin Lew and Debra Mesch (Lew, Mesch, Johnson, & Johnson, 1986a, 1986b; Mesch, Johnson, & Johnson, 1993; Mesch, Lew, Johnson, & Johnson, 1986) investigated the impact on performance within cooperative groups of a reward contingency for using social skills, positive goal interdependence, and a reward contingency for academic achievement. In the cooperative skills conditions, individuals were trained weekly in four social skills. Each member of a cooperative group was given two bonus points toward the quiz grade if the teacher observed that all group members demonstrated three out of four cooperative skills. The results indicated that the combination of positive goal interdependence, an academic contingency for high-performance by all group members, and a social skills contingency, promoted the highest achievement. Archer-Kath, Johnson, and Johnson (1994) trained individuals in the social skills of praising, supporting, asking for information, giving information, asking for help, and giving help. Individuals received either individual or group feedback in written graph form on how frequently members engaged in the targeted behaviors. The researchers found that giving people individual feedback on how frequently they engaged in targeted social skills was more effective in increasing individuals' achievement than was group feedback. The more socially skillful individuals are, the more attention teachers pay to teaching and rewarding the use of social skills, and the more individual feedback people receive on their use of the skills, the higher the achievement tends to be in cooperative groups.

Not only do social skills promote higher achievement, they contribute to building more positive relationships among group members. Putnam, Rynders, Johnson, and Johnson (1989) demonstrated that when individuals were taught social skills, were observed by the teacher, and given individual feedback as to how frequently they engaged in the skills, their relationships became more positive, even between handicapped and nonhandicapped individuals.

Group Processing

Effective group work is influenced by whether or not groups periodically reflect on how well they are functioning and how they plan to improve their work processes. A **process** is an identifiable sequence of events taking place over time, and **process goals** refer to the sequence of events instrumental in achieving outcome goals. **Group processing** is reflecting on a group session to (a) describe what member actions were helpful and unhelpful and (b) make decisions about what actions to continue or change. The purpose of group processing is to clarify and improve the members' effectiveness in contributing to joint efforts to achieve the group's goals.

Yager, Johnson, Johnson, & Snider (1986) found that high-, medium-, and low-achieving participants achieved at a higher level on daily achievement, postinstructional achievement, and retention measures in the cooperation with group processing condition than did participants who engaged in cooperation without any group processing or individualistic efforts. Participants in the cooperation without group processing condition, furthermore, achieved higher on all three measures than did the participants in the individualistic condition. Putnam, Rynders, Johnson, and Johnson (1989) found that more positive relationships developed between handicapped and nonhandicapped participants when participants were taught social skills and engaged in group processing than when participants worked cooperatively without social skills training or group processing. These positive relationships carried over to post-instructional free-time situations. Johnson, Johnson, Stanne, and Garibaldi (1990) found that participants performed at a higher level on problem-solving tasks when they worked cooperatively than when they worked individually. These investigators conducted a study comparing cooperation with no processing, cooperation with both instructor processing (instructor-specified cooperative skills to use, observed, and gave whole class feedback as to how well participants were using the skills) and participant processing (the instructor specified cooperative skills to use, observed, gave whole class feedback as to how well participants were using the skills, and had groups discuss how well they interacted as a group) compared with cooperation with instructor processing only, cooperative with group processing only, and individualistic efforts. Participants performed at a higher level in all three cooperative conditions than did those in the individualistic condition. Finally, Archer-Kath, Johnson, and Johnson (1994) found that group processing with individual feedback was more effective than was group processing with whole group feedback in increasing participants' (a) achievement motivation, actual achievement, uniformity of achievement among group members, and influence toward higher achievement within cooperative groups, (b) positive relationships among group members and between participants and the teacher, and (c) participants' self-esteem and positive attitudes toward the subject area. Schippers, Hartog, and Koopman (2007) found that group processing makes teams more effective.

Group processing promotes individual self-monitoring, which can promote a sense of **self-efficacy** (i.e., the expectation of successfully obtaining valued outcomes through personal effort) rather than helplessness. Sarason and Potter (1983) examined the impact of individual self-monitoring of thoughts on self-efficacy and successful performance and found that having individuals focus their attention on self-efficacious thoughts is related to greater task persistence and less cognitive interference. They concluded that the more that people are aware of what they are experiencing, the more aware they will be of their own role in determining their success. The greater the sense of self- and joint-efficacy promoted by group processing, the more productive and effective group members and the group as a whole become.

Effective processing focuses group members on positive rather than negative behaviors. When people monitor their own and their collaborators' actions, they begin by deciding which behaviors to direct their attention toward. Individuals can focus either on positive and effective behaviors, or on negative and ineffective behaviors. Sarason and Potter (1983) found that when individuals monitored their stressful experiences, they were more likely to perceive a program as having been more stressful than did those who did not. But when individuals monitored their positive experiences, they were more likely to perceive the group experience as involving less psychological demands, were more attracted to the group and had greater motivation to remain members, and felt less strained during the experience and more prepared for future group experiences. When individuals are anxious about being successful, and are then told they have failed, their performance tends to decrease significantly. But when individuals anxious about being successful are told they have succeeded, their performance tends to increase significantly (Turk & Sarason, 1983).

In addition to the improvement in the efficiency and effectiveness of group efforts resulting from group processing, reflecting on the actions of group members who enhance or hinder the group's success may also result in other dynamics such as the compensation effect (i.e., an increase in performance that occurs when group members work harder to compensate for the real or imagined shortcomings of other group members), the reduction of social loafing through highlighting the unique and indispensable contributions of each group member, the clarification of the nature of the group's goals and their importance, the awareness that the group has the resources needed to succeed (thereby increasing collective efficacy), and involvement in the group's efforts (Johnson & Johnson, 2009b).

During group processing, members are expected to express respect for each other and each other's contributions to the group efforts (Johnson & Johnson, 2009b; Johnson, Johnson, & Holubec, 2008). The expression of respect toward a group member by group leaders tends to increase the group member's self-esteem, while the expression of respect among group members tends to increase members' efforts to achieve group goals when the group is devalued by an outgroup, beliefs that one is valued as a group member, commitment to the group and adherence to ingroup norms, and collective identification and group-serving behavior.

Finally, group processing may be seen as a form of team reflexivity, the extent to which group members overtly reflect upon and modify their functioning. Group functioning may include the strategies and processes used to achieve the group's goals. Reflexivity tends to be positively related to subjective and objective measures of group performance in the United Kingdom (Carter & West, 1998), Australia (Hirst, Mann, Bain, Pirola-Merlo, & Richter, 2004), Israel (Somech, 2006), China (Tjosvold, Tang, & West, 2004), and the Netherlands (Schippers et al., 2003). Carter and West (1998), for example, found that reflexivity predicted team effectiveness in a study involving nineteen BBC production teams. Gurtner, Tschan, Semmer, and Nägele (2007) found that three-person experimental groups in a reflexivity condition performed better than did groups in a control condition. A field study among fifty-nine work teams found that team reflexivity mediated the relationship between diversity and team performance, commitment, and satisfaction (Schippers et al., 2003). Tjosvold, Tang, and West (2004) found that group reflexivity increased subsequent innovation.

THE STABILITY OF COOPERATION

When positive interdependence, individual accountability, promotive interaction, appropriate use of social skills, and group processing are absent, group members may pursue their own self-interests. While group members benefit from mutual cooperation, under certain conditions each member may benefit more from exploiting the cooperative efforts of others (Axelrod, 1984). If all group members, however, attempt to exploit the cooperation of their groupmates, their benefits are considerably less than they would gain from cooperating. The temptation to exploit the cooperative efforts of other members is greatest when the life of the group is short, the time the group terminates is known, and the exploitation cannot be traced (and, therefore, the other group members cannot retaliate effectively).

There are four conditions that contribute to the stability of cooperation. First, group members must have a stake in their future interaction. Continuing interaction is what makes it possible for cooperation based on reciprocity to be stable. The shadow of the future is enlarged as the interactions become more frequent and more prolonged over time. Second, cooperators must be easily identifiable and the actions of each group member must be visible to all other group members (thereby ensuring retaliation if one member exploits the cooperative efforts of the others). Third, group members need to emotionally identify with their groupmates and with the group as a whole. Members must value one another's well-being and want to promote the long-term success of the group. Finally, group members must understand the value of reciprocity and are able and willing to reciprocate cooperation.

DISTRIBUTIVE JUSTICE: THE ALLOCATION OF BENEFITS AMONG GROUP MEMBERS

I am in Birmingham because injustice is here. . . Injustice anywhere is a threat to justice everywhere. We are caught in an inescapable network of mutuality, tied in a single garment of destiny.

Martin Luther King, Letter from the Birmingham Jail

The way in which benefits are distributed among group members can have a marked effect on how members behave toward one another in the future and how effective the group is. Depending on the circumstances, benefits may be distributed according to merit, equality, or need (Deutsch, 1975, 1979, 1985).

The **equity or merit view of distributing benefits** has been presented by Homans (1961) as a basic rule of distributive justice and equity theory. The rule is that in a just distribution, benefits will be distributed among individuals in proportion to their contributions; those members who contribute most to the group's success receive the greatest benefits. The underlying assumption is that productivity will increase when benefits (for example, bonuses, salaries, advancement, grades) are contingent on performance. Benefits are assumed to be a scarce resource (i.e., there are not enough benefits for every member to receive what he or she wants). The utilitarian value of a benefit increases with the number of persons who want the benefit; the benefit becomes a scarce commodity when its supply is far less than the demand for it. The symbolic meaning of the benefit may become far more important than the intrinsic value of the benefit. Children fight over being first in line not because of the intrinsic value of the position but rather because it symbolizes that they are a winner, superior to those who are positioned behind them.

The equity method is, in essence, an individual incentive plan aimed at motivating each group member to compete to be the most productive group member (who will then receive greater benefits than the other group members will receive). There are shortcomings to this way of distributing benefits. First, the competition it creates among group members typically has negative consequences for group productivity. Group members get involved in obstructing each other's efforts as well as striving to outperform each other. All the negative consequences of competition may surface within the group. Second, motivation to contribute to the group's efforts becomes extrinsic (to gain benefits) rather than intrinsic (to contribute to group's well-being). Third, it is based on a utilitarian, economic point of view, in which group members are of value only to the extent that they contribute to the group's success. A group member only has value if he or she contributes to the group's success, and the members that contribute a great deal are more valuable than members who contribute only a little. Members (including oneself) become depersonalized. Thus, if a member contributes little to group success and receives disproportionately small benefits, he or she is viewed (by self and others) as having little personal worth. Diesing (1962) describes such a situation as being alienated from oneself and others. Fourth, group members with a high number of qualities that give them an advantage often get higher benefits than members with few such qualities, and may attribute their success to their worthiness and effort (implying that those who have fewer resource attractors are less worthy and more lazy). Examples of such qualities are being born into a wealthy and famous family, being born with various cognitive and physical abilities that are genetically determined, and graduating from prestigious universities. Finally, a merit system often results in a situation in which the group members who are rewarded the most are given the power to distribute future benefits. Deutsch (1975, 1979, 1985) notes that this allows those who are in power to bias the system of allocation to perpetuate their disproportionate benefits and power even when they are no longer making relatively large contributions to the group's well-being.

An **equality system of distributive justice** distributes benefits to all group members equally. If a football team wins the Super Bowl, all members receive a Super Bowl ring. The equality system encourages cooperation among group members and, therefore, tends to result in mutual esteem, equal status, and mutual respect among members, as well as group loyalty and enjoyable, personal relationships among members (Deutsch, 1985). Sales clerks report a greater sense of teamwork and greater job satisfaction under a equality system, whereas the equity system tends to promote the avoidance of maintenance duties, competition for customers, and low morale (Babchuk & Good, 1951). Blau (1954) compared two groups of interviewers in an employment agency. In one, there was fierce competition to fill job openings. In the other, the interviewers worked cooperatively. Members of the competitive group, who were personally ambitious and extremely concerned about productivity, hoarded job notifications rather than posting them so everyone could see them, as they were supposed to do. Members of the cooperative group, by contrast, told one another about vacancies and encouraged one another to fill them. The cooperators ended up filling significantly more jobs.

The distribution of benefits according to need distributes benefits to the group members according to need. The member who has the largest family may receive the highest monetary bonus, the member who is grieving for the death of her parents may be asked to do the least work, or the member who has the least ability will be given the most support and assistance for completing his assigned tasks. Rawls (1971) pointed out that one of the natural duties of group members is to help another member who is in need or in jeopardy, providing the member can do so without excessive loss or risk to him- or herself. The assumption is that the gain to the member who needs help far outweighs the losses required by groupmates. Deutsch (1975, 1979, 1985) notes that a caring-oriented group will stress responsibility for one another, permissiveness toward members expressing their needs, heightened sensitivity to one another's needs, and support and nurturance.

Whatever the group's system of distributing benefits, it has to be perceived as "just" by group members. There is evidence that before a task is performed, members tend to believe that an equity system is fairest, but after a task is completed, an equality system tends to be viewed as the fairest (Deutsch, 1979, 1985; Johnson & Johnson, 1983; Johnson, Johnson, Buckman, & Richards, 1986; Wheeler & Ryan, 1973).

Conditions for Constructive Competition

There is considerable evidence that cooperation promotes higher achievement and greater productivity than do competitive efforts (Johnson & Johnson, 1989, 2005a, 2009b). There are many reasons why competitors achieve less than they would if they were working cooperatively. One reason is that when individuals are working toward competitive goals, they tend to engage in self-protective strategies such as self-worth protection, self-handicapping, and defensive pessimism. *Self-worth protection* involves withholding effort so that failure can be attributed to not trying rather than to incompetency (Mayerson & Rhodewalt, 1988; Rhodewalt, Morf, Hazlett, & Fairfield,, 1991; Thompson, Davidson, & Barber, 1995). *Self-handicapping* involves creating an impediment to one's performance (e.g., procrastination and unrealistically high expectations) so that an excuse is ready if one fails (Covington, 1992; McCown & Johnson, 1991). *Defensive pessimism* involves unrealistically low (a) expectations for succeeding and (b) valuing of the task, so that anxiety about succeeding is minimized (Cantor & Harlow, 1994; Cantor & Norem, 1989; Norem & Illingworth, 1993). Strategies such as these tend to lower achievement in competitive situations. Many of the discussions of competition, furthermore, portray it as so destructive that its elimination is recommended, especially from the school and the workplace (Kohn, 1992, 1993; Maehr & Midgley, 1991).

Other social scientists, however, have argued that competition can be constructive and should be encouraged when it is appropriately structured (Johnson & Johnson, 1974, 1978; Sherif, 1978). Social interdependence theory has been expanded to include the conditions under which competition can be constructive (Johnson & Johnson, 1974, 1978, 1989, 1999a, 2005a, 2009b; R. Johnson & Johnson, 1979; Stanne, Johnson, & Johnson, 1999). Indicators of constructive competition include effectiveness in completing the task, perceiving one's participation in the competition as being personally worthwhile above and beyond winning (i.e., increasing self-confidence, social support, and achievement), increasing willingness to take on more challenging tasks, strengthening the relationship with other competitors, improving morale, improving the ability of competitors to work together cooperatively in the future, insistence on participating in the competition, and enjoyment of the competition. The few attempts to identify the factors contributing to the potential constructiveness of competition have theorized that competition tends to be more constructive when (Johnson & Johnson, 1974, 1978, 1989, 1999a, 2005a, 2009b):

1. Winning is relatively unimportant. If winning is too important, high levels of anxiety result that interfere with performance, especially on motor tasks. Most individuals are likely to perceive their performance as a failure, and losing promotes the development of "competition learned helplessness," whereas winning can promote the development of "psychological burnout".
2. All participants have a reasonable chance to win. Motivation to achieve is based on the perceived likelihood of being able to achieve a challenging goal. Those who believe they cannot win will not try, and will cheat, avoid challenge, use superficial and effort-minimizing strategies, engage in impaired problem solving, use other self-handicapping strategies, and have less interest in and enjoyment of the experience.
3. There are clear and specific rules, procedures, and criteria for winning. Ambiguity in competition interferes with achievement as energy is directed toward worrying about what is fair and unfair.

In two field studies in business and industry, Tjosvold, Johnson, Johnson, and Sun (2003, 2006) found that variables related to constructive competition included the fairness of the rules, motivation to compete and win, perceiving that one's chances of winning were good, a strong positive relationship among competitors, acting fairly during the competition, and a history of confirming each other's competence. By controlling these factors, the constructiveness of competition may be enhanced.

Competition is the underlying basis for a number of other theories, such as realistic conflict theory and social dominance theory. Realistic conflict theory maintains that intergroup conflicts are rational in the sense that groups have incompatible goals and are in competition over scarce resources (Campbell, 1965; Sherif, 1966). Social dominance theory assumes that resources are limited and, therefore, individuals, groups, and species compete to acquire scarce resources (Charlesworth, 1966; Darwin, 1859). The competition for scarce resources results in a hierarchy of individuals within groups and among groups themselves.

Social dominance theory has been used to explain such dynamics as ingroup bias (Sidanius & Pratto, 1999) and bullying in schools. Social interdependence theory, therefore, may be linked to realistic conflict, social dominance, and other theories and phenomena assumed to be based on competition.

CONDITIONS FOR CONSTRUCTIVE INDIVIDUALISTIC EFFORTS

Perhaps the least-developed aspect of social interdependence is the conditions under which individualistic efforts are appropriate and effective. Social interdependence theory assumes that there are conditions under which individualistic efforts are more effective than cooperation and competition. Being able to work individualistically on one's own when it is appropriate is an important competence. Individualistic efforts may be most appropriate when (Johnson & Johnson, 1974, 1978, 1989, 1999, 2005a, 2009b):

1. Cooperation is too costly, difficult, or cumbersome due to the unavailability of skilled potential cooperators or the unavailable of the resources needed for cooperation to take place.
2. The goal must be perceived as important, relevant, and worthwhile.
3. Participants expect to be successful in achieving their goals.
4. Unitary, nondivisible, simple tasks need to be completed, such as the learning of specific facts or the acquisition or the performance of simple skills.
5. The directions for completing the task are clear and specific so participants do not need further clarification on how to proceed and how to evaluate their work.
6. What is accomplished will be used subsequently in a cooperative effort. Individualistic efforts can supplement cooperative efforts through a division of labor in which each person learns material or skills to be subsequently used in cooperative activities. Learning facts and simple skills to be used in subsequent cooperative efforts increases the perceived relevance and importance of individualistic tasks. It is the overall cooperative effort that provides the meaning to individualistic work. It is contributing to the cooperative effort that makes individualistic goals important.

MIXED-MOTIVE SITUATIONS

In most situations, group members usually have a mixture of cooperative, competitive, and individualistic motives. People need to be able to work cooperatively with peers, superiors, and subordinates, compete for fun and enjoyment, and work autonomously on their own. A player on a basketball team may be focused on the cooperative goal of ensuring the team wins, a competitive goal of being the best player on the team, and an individualistic goal of perfecting a jump shot. Mixtures of the three types of social interdependence are continually present in any situation. Which one dominates the situation, however, has important implications for individual, group, and organization productivity, morale, and well-being.

Cooperativeness needs to dominate group life. The effectiveness of a group can be easily damaged when an individual dominated by competitiveness joins the group (Kelley & Stahelski, 1970). First, the cooperative members begin behaving in com petitive ways, violating trust, hiding information, and cutting off communication. Second, all members begin competing. Third, the competitive person sees the formerly cooperative members as having always been competitive. Fourth, the cooperative members are aware that their behavior is being determined by the other's competitive behavior, but the competitive person is not aware of his or her impact on cooperative members.

EXERCISE 3.7

THE LEVEL OF ACCEPTANCE IN YOUR GROUP

The purpose of this exercise is to provide a way in which the level of acceptance in your group can be assessed and discussed. The procedure is as follows:

1. With the other members of your group, fill out the following questionnaire. Questionnaires should be unsigned so that no one's responses can be identified.
2. Tabulate the results in the summary table that follows the questionnaire.
3. Discuss the conclusions that can be drawn from the results. Consider these two questions:
   a. What is contributing to the present high or low level of acceptance in the group?
   b. How can the level of acceptance in the group be increased?

QUESTIONNAIRE: LEVEL OF ACCEPTANCE

Think about the ways in which the members of your group normally behave toward you. In the parentheses in front of the statements below, place the number corresponding to your perceptions of the group as a whole, using the following scale:

5 = They *always* behave this way.
4 = They *typically* behave this way.
3 = They *usually* behave this way.
2 = They *seldom* behave this way.
1 = They *rarely* behave this way.
0 = They *never* behave this way.

My fellow group members:

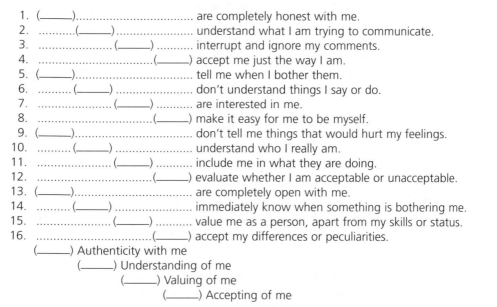

1. (_____)................................. are completely honest with me.
2. ....(_____)...................... understand what I am trying to communicate.
3. ....(_____)........... interrupt and ignore my comments.
4. ....(_____) accept me just the way I am.
5. (_____)................................. tell me when I bother them.
6. ....(_____)...................... don't understand things I say or do.
7. ....(_____)........... are interested in me.
8. ....(_____) make it easy for me to be myself.
9. (_____)................................. don't tell me things that would hurt my feelings.
10. ....(_____)...................... understand who I really am.
11. ....(_____)........... include me in what they are doing.
12. ....(_____) evaluate whether I am acceptable or unacceptable.
13. (_____)................................. are completely open with me.
14. ....(_____)...................... immediately know when something is bothering me.
15. ....(_____)........... value me as a person, apart from my skills or status.
16. ....(_____) accept my differences or peculiarities.
    (_____) Authenticity with me
        (_____) Understanding of me
            (_____) Valuing of me
                (_____) Accepting of me

continued on next page

continued from previous page

Total the number of points in each column. Statements 3, 6, 9, and 12 are reversed in the scoring; subtract from 5 the rating given to each before placing the remainder in each column.

Summary Table: Level of Acceptance

Score	Authenticity	Understanding	Valuing	Accepting
0–4	_____	_____	_____	_____
5–8	_____	_____	_____	_____
9–12	_____	_____	_____	_____
13–16	_____	_____	_____	_____
17–20	_____	_____	_____	_____

EXERCISE 3.8

HOW TRUSTING AND TRUSTWORTHY AM I?

When you are attempting to build a relationship with someone, there always is a risk that the person may react in a rejecting and competitive way. In order for two group members to trust each other, each has to expect the other to be trustworthy and each has to engage in trusting behavior. This exercise allows you to compare the way you see your trust-building behavior in the group with the way other members see it. The procedure is as follows:

1. Complete the following questionnaire. Score your responses.
2. Make a slip of paper for each member of your group. Fill out each slip as shown, rating the member from 1 (low) to 7 (high) on how open and accepting you perceive him or her to be. Base your rating on how you think the person has behaved during the entire time your group has met together.

MEMBER RECEIVING FEEDBACK: EDYTHE

1. Openness and sharing:	3
2. Acceptance, support, and cooperativeness:	6

3. Hand each member his or her slip. If there are six members in your group, you should receive five ratings of yourself, and each of the other members should likewise end up with five slips. Compute an average of how the other members see your behavior by adding all your ratings for openness and dividing up the number of slips. Then do the same with your ratings for acceptance.
4. Discuss with the other group members how similar your perception and their perceptions of your openness and acceptance are. If there is a difference between the two, ask the group to give you more specific feedback about your trust-building behavior in the group. Then discuss how to build trust with others in situations outside the group.

UNDERSTANDING YOUR TRUST ACTIONS QUESTIONNAIRE

The following is a series of questions about your behavior in your group. Answer each question as honestly as you can. There are no right or wrong answers. It is important for you to describe your behavior as accurately as possible. Answer between 1 (I never behave that way) and 7 (I always behave that way).

7 = I always behave that way.
6 = I almost always behave that way.
5 = I frequently behave that way.
4 = I behave that way as frequently as not.
3 = I occasionally behave that way.
2 = I seldom behave that way.
1 = I never behave that way.

When I Am a Member of a Group

_____ 1. I offer facts, give my opinions and ideas, and provide suggestions and relevant information to help the group discussion.

_____ 2. I express my willingness to cooperate with other group members and my expectations that they will also be cooperative.

_____ 3. I am open and candid in my dealings with the entire group.

_____ 4. I give support to group members who are on the spot and struggling to express themselves intellectually or emotionally.

_____ 5. I keep my thoughts, ideas, feelings, and reactions to myself during group discussions.

_____ 6. I evaluate the contributions of other group members in terms of whether their contributions are useful to me and whether they are right or wrong.

_____ 7. I take risks in expressing new ideas and current feelings during a group discussion.

_____ 8. I communicate to other group members that I am aware of and appreciate their abilities, talents, capabilities, skills, and resources.

_____ 9. I offer help and assistance to anyone in the group in order to bring up the performance of everyone.

_____ 10. I accept and support the openness of other group members, support them for taking risks, and encourage individuality in group members.

_____ 11. I share any materials, books, sources of information, or other resources I have with the other group members in order to promote the success of all members and the group as a whole.

_____ 12. I often paraphrase or summarize what other members have said before I respond or comment.

_____ 13. I level with other group members.

_____ 14. I warmly encourage all members to participate, giving them recognition for their contributions, demonstrating acceptance and openness to their ideas and generally being friendly and responsive.

SCORING THE TRUST QUESTIONNAIRE

In order to obtain a total score for trusting actions and trustworthy actions, write the score for each question in the appropriate blank and then total the scores for each column. Reverse the scoring for the starred questions (if you circled 2, write 6; if you circled 1, write 7; 4 remains the same).

continued on next page

continued from previous page

Trusting (Openness and Sharing) Actions	Trustworthy (Acceptance and Support) Actions
_____ 1.	_____ 2.
_____ 3.	_____ 4.
_____ 5.*	_____ 6.*
_____ 7.	_____ 8.
_____ 9.	_____ 10.
_____ 11.	_____ 12.
_____ 13.	_____ 14.
_____ **Total**	_____ **Total**

If you have a score of 35 or over, classify yourself as being trusting or trustworthy, whichever the case might be. If your score is less than 35, classify yourself as being distrustful or untrustworthy, whichever the case may be.

Always expresses acceptance, support, and cooperative intentions to other members

Expresses acceptance, support, and cooperative intentions more often than not

Expresses rejection, nonsupport, and competitive intentions more often than not

Always expresses rejection, nonsupport, and competitive intentions to other members

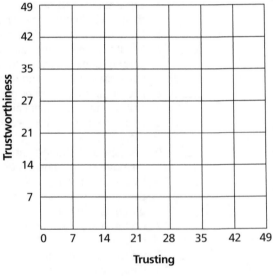

Trustworthiness (vertical axis): 7, 14, 21, 27, 35, 42, 49

Trusting (horizontal axis): 0, 7, 14, 21, 28, 35, 42, 49

Never is open with ideas and information and never shares materials and resources

More closed and nonsharing than not

More open and sharing than not

Always is open with ideas and always shares materials and resources

Johnson Trust Diagram

Plot the total scores in the Johnson Trust Diagram. Plot an × on the horizontal axis at the point representing your "trusting" total score. Plot an × on the vertical axis at the point representing your "trustworthy" total score. Then place an × at the point on the graph where the two scores intersect. This represents your level of trust. You may wish to plot the scores of all group members and compare how the "trusting" and "trustworthy" scores match.

EXERCISE 3.9

PRACTICING TRUST-BUILDING SKILLS

This exercise provides an opportunity to practice trust-building skills. Form a group with six members. Choose one member to be an observer. Complete the following task. Then listen carefully to the report of the observer on the interaction among group members, and analyze the dynamics of building trust.

GENETIC TRAITS TASK

Working as a group, estimate the number of people in your school who possess each of the following genetic traits. Establish the frequency of occurrence of each genetic trait, first in your group, then in the entire class. On the percentage of occurrence of each trait in your group and the class, estimate the number of people in your school who possess each trait.

Trait	Group	Class	School
1. Dimples in the cheeks versus no dimples			
2. Brown (or hazel) eyes versus blue, gray, or green eyes			
3. Attached vs. free earlobes (an earlobe is free if it dips below the point where it is attached)			
4. Little-finger bend versus no bend (place your little fingers together with your palms toward you; if your little fingers bend away from each other at the tips, you have a little-finger bend)			
5. Tongue roll versus no tongue roll (if you can curl up both sides of your tongue to make a trough, you have it, and it's not contagious)			
6. Hairy versus nonhairy middle fingers (examine the backs of the middle two fingers on your hands and look for hair between the first and second knuckles)			
7. Widow's peak versus straight or curved hairline (examine the hairline across your forehead and look for a definite dip or point of hair extending down toward your nose)			

continued on next page

continued from previous page

Observation Sheet

	1	2	3	4	5	Total
1. Contributes ideas						
2. Describes feelings						
3. Paraphrases						
4. Expresses acceptance and support						
5. Expresses warmth and liking						
Total						

"Trusting" behaviors = 1 and 2; "Trustworthy" behaviors = 3, 4, and 5.

DEVELOPING AND MAINTAINING TRUST

An essential aspect of group effectiveness is developing and maintaining a high level of trust among group members. The more members trust one another, the more effectively they can work together (Deutsch, 1962, 1973; Johnson, 1974). Group members openly express thoughts, feelings, reactions, opinions, information, and ideas when trust is high (Johnson, 2006). When the trust level is low, group members will be evasive, dishonest, and inconsiderate in their communications. Trust, however, is not a stable personality trait. Trust exists among individuals and is dynamic, increasing or decreasing with every action a group member makes.

Trust is a word everyone uses, yet it is a complex concept and difficult to define. Deutsch (1962) may have developed the best definition, which included the following elements:

1. You are in a situation in which a choice to trust another person can lead to either beneficial or harmful consequences. Thus, you realize there is a risk involved in trusting.
2. You realize that whether beneficial or harmful consequences result depends on the actions of another person.
3. You expect to suffer more if the harmful consequences result than you will gain if the beneficial consequences result. The loss will be greater than the gain.
4. You are relatively confident that the other person will behave in such a way that the beneficial consequences will result.

Sounds complicated, doesn't it? In fact, there is nothing simple about trust; it is a complex concept and difficult to explain. An example may help. Imagine you are a part of a cooperative group attempting to solve a problem. You begin to contribute to the discussion, knowing you will gain if you contribute good ideas that other members accept but lose if your ideas are laughed at and belittled. Whether you gain or lose depends on the behavior of other group members. You will feel more hurt if you are laughed at

	High Acceptance, Support, and Cooperativeness		Low Acceptance, Support, and Cooperativeness	
High Openness and Sharing	Person A	Trusting Confirmed	Person A	Trusting Disconfirmed
	Person B	Trustworthy Confirmed	Person B	Untrustworthy No risk
Low Openness and Sharing	Person A	Distrusting No risk	Person A	Distrusting No risk
	Person B	Trustworthy Disconfirmed	Person B	Untrustworthy No risk

Figure 3.4 The dynamics of interpersonal trust.

than you will feel satisfaction if your ideas are appreciated. Yet you expect the other group members to consider your ideas and accept them.

Building Interpersonal Trust

The trust that must exist in a group in order for it to work effectively is established through a sequence of trusting and trustworthy actions, as described in Figure 3.4. If person A takes the risk of being self-disclosing, he may be either confirmed or disconfirmed, depending on whether person B responds with acceptance or rejection. If person B takes the risk of being accepting, supportive, and cooperative, she may be confirmed or disconfirmed, depending on whether person A is disclosing or nondisclosing.

The crucial elements of trust are openness and sharing, on the one hand, and acceptance, support, and cooperative intentions on the other. Working cooperatively with others requires openness and sharing, which in turn are determined by the expression of acceptance, support, and cooperative intentions in the group. **Openness** is the sharing of information, ideas, thoughts, feelings, and reactions to the issue the group is pursuing. **Sharing** is the offering of your materials and resources to others in order to help them move the group toward goal accomplishment. **Acceptance** is the communication of high regard for another person and his contributions to the group's work. **Support** is the communication to another person that you recognize her strengths and believe she has the capabilities she needs to manage productively the situation she is in. **Cooperative intentions** are the expectations that you are going to behave cooperatively and that every group member will also cooperate in achieving the group's goals.

Interpersonal trust is *built* through risk and confirmation and is *destroyed* through risk and disconfirmation. Without risk there is no trust, and the relationships among group members cannot move forward. The steps in building trust are

1. Person A takes a risk by disclosing to person B his thoughts, information, conclusions, feelings, and reactions to the immediate situation.

2. Person B responds with acceptance, support, and cooperativeness and recipro-cates person A's openness by disclosing her own thoughts, information, con-clusions, feelings, and reactions to the immediate situation and to person A.

An alternative way in which trust is built is the following:

1. Person B communicates acceptance, support, and cooperativeness toward person A.
2. Person A responds by disclosing his thoughts, information, conclusions, feelings, and reactions to the immediate situation and to person B.

Being Trusting and Trustworthy

The level of trust within a group is constantly changing according to members' ability and willingness to be trusting and trustworthy. **Trusting behavior** is the willingness to risk beneficial or harmful consequences by making oneself vulnerable to other group members. More specifically, trusting behavior involves being self-disclosing and will-ing to be openly accepting and supportive of others. **Trustworthy behavior** is the willingness to respond to another person's risk taking in a way that ensures that the other person will experience beneficial consequences. This involves your acceptance of another person's trust in you. Expressing acceptance, support, and cooperative-ness and reciprocating disclosures appropriately are key aspects of being trustworthy in relationships with other group members. In considering members' trustworthy behavior, you should remember that accepting and supporting the contributions of other group members does not mean that you agree with everything they say. You can express acceptance and support for the openness and sharing of other members and at the same time express different ideas and opposing points of view.

Acceptance is probably the first and deepest concern to arise in a group. Accep-tance of others usually begins with acceptance of oneself. Group members need to ac-cept themselves before they can fully accept others. Acceptance is the key to reducing anxiety and fears about being vulnerable. Defensive feelings of fear and distrust are common blocks to the functioning of a person and to the development of constructive relationships. Certainly, if a person does not feel accepted, the frequency and depth of participation in the group will decrease. To build trust and to deepen relationships among group members, each member needs to be able to communicate acceptance, support, and cooperativeness.

The key to building and maintaining trust is being trustworthy. The more accept-ing and supportive you are of others, the more likely they are to disclose their thoughts, ideas, theories, conclusions, feelings, and reactions to you. The more trustworthy you are in response to such disclosures, the deeper and more personal the thoughts a person will share with you. When you want to increase trust, increase your trustworthiness.

Destroying Trust

Trust No One.

The X Files

For trust to develop, one person has to become vulnerable to see whether the other person abuses that vulnerability. Many such tests are necessary before the trust level between two people becomes very high. However, just one betrayal is often sufficient to establish distrust and, once established, distrust is resistive to change. Distrust is difficult to change because it leads to the perception that despite the other person's attempts to "make up," betrayal will recur in the future. Distrust typically reduces the commitment of group members to achieving the group's goals, increases social loafing, increases competition among group members, and leads to destructive conflict. Distrust is created when group members use rejection, ridicule, or disrespect as a response to one another's openness. Making a joke at the expense of the other person, laughing at his disclosures, moralizing about her behavior, being evaluative, or being silent and poker-faced all communicate rejection and will effectively silence the other group member and destroy some of the trust in the relationship. Distrust is also created when there is nonreciprocation of openness. If a group member is open and other members do not reciprocate, the member may feel overexposed and vulnerable. Finally, distrust is created when a group member refuses to disclose his or her thoughts, information, conclusions, feelings, and reactions. If a group member indicates acceptance and others are closed and guarded in response, the member will feel discounted and rejected.

EXERCISE 3.10

DEFINITIONS

Match the correct definition with the correct concept. Find a partner and (1) compare answers and (2) explain your reasoning for each answer.

_____	**1. Openness**	a. The willingness to risk beneficial or harmful consequences by making oneself vulnerable to other group members
_____	**2. Sharing**	b. The communication to another person that you recognize her strengths and believe she has the abilities she needs to manage the situation productively
_____	**3. Acceptance**	c. The expectations that you are going to behave cooperatively and that every group member will also cooperate in achieving the group's goals
_____	**4. Support**	d. The sharing of information, ideas, thoughts, feelings, and reactions to the issue the group is pursuing
_____	**5. Cooperative intentions**	e. The willingness to respond to another person's risk-taking in a way that ensures that the other person will experience beneficial consequences
_____	**6. Trustworthy behavior**	f. The communication of high regard for others and for their contributions to the group's work
_____	**7. Trusting behavior**	g. The offering of your materials and resources to others in order to help them move the group toward goal accomplishment

Re-establishing Trust After It Has Been Broken

How can trust, once lost, be regained? The following guidelines may help. To re-establish trust, group members should:

1. Increase positive outcome interdependence by establishing cooperative goals that are so compelling that all members will join in to achieve them. Such goals are often referred to as superordinate goals.
2. Increase resource interdependence so that it is clear that no one person has a chance for succeeding on their own.
3. Openly and consistently express cooperative intentions.
4. Reestablish **credibility** by making certain that actions match announced intentions. Group members must always keep their word.
5. Be absolutely and consistently trustworthy in dealing with other group members. Acceptance and support of other members are critical.
6. Periodically "test the waters" by engaging in trusting actions and making themselves vulnerable to the other members.
7. Apologize sincerely and immediately when they inadvertently engage in untrustworthy actions.
8. Strive to build a "tough but fair" reputation by:
    a. Initially and periodically responding cooperatively to other members who act competitively (even when they know in advance that the others plan to compete).
    b. Use a *tit-for-tat* strategy that matches the other person's behavior if the others continue to compete. When the competitors realize that their competitiveness is self-defeating and the best they can hope for is mutual failure, they may start cooperating.

Trusting Appropriately

Never trusting and *always* trusting are equally inappropriate. Trust is not always appropriate. There are times when it is inadvisable to disclose thoughts, feelings, or reactions to another person. There are people who will behave in untrustworthy ways if you make yourself vulnerable to them. When you have a mean, vicious, hostile boss who has taken advantage of your openness in the past, for example, it is inappropriate to engage in trusting behavior in the present. To master the skills in building and maintaining trust, therefore, you need to be able to tell when it is appropriate to be trusting and when it is not. You need the ability to size up situations and make an enlightened decision about when, whom, and how much to trust.

Trusting as a Self-Fulfilling Prophecy

Tom joins a new group expecting the members to dislike and reject him. He behaves, therefore, in a very guarded and suspicious way toward the other group members. His actions cause them to withdraw and look elsewhere for a friendly companion. "See," he then says, "I was right. I knew they would reject me." Sue, who joins the same group at the same time Tom does, expects the members to be congenial, friendly, and trustworthy. She is warm and friendly, openly discloses her thoughts and feelings, and generally is accepting and supportive of the other members. Consequently, she finds her fellow members to be all that she expected. Both Tom and Sue have made a self-fulfilling prophecy.

A **self-fulfilling prophecy** is, in the beginning, a false definition of a situation that evokes a new behavior, one that makes it possible for the originally false impression to come true. The assumptions you make about other people and the way in which you then behave often influence how other people respond to you, thus creating self-fulfilling prophecies in your relationships. People usually conform to the expectations others have for them. If other people feel that you do not trust them and expect them to violate your trust, they will often do so. If they believe that you trust them and expect them to be trustworthy, they will often behave that way. There is a lot to be said for assuming that other people are trustworthy.

Personal Proclivity to Trust

Although trust exists in relationships, not in people, there has been some attempt to measure individual differences in willingness to trust others. Rotter (1971) developed the *Interpersonal Trust Scale* to distinguish between people who have a tendency to

HELPFUL HINTS ABOUT TRUST

1. **Trust is a very complex concept to understand.** It may take a while before individuals fully understand it.

2. **Trust exists in relationships, not in someone's personality.** Although some people are more naturally trusting than others, and although it is easier for some people to be trust-worthy than others, trust is something that occurs *between* people, not *within* people.

3. **Trust is constantly changing as two people interact.** Everything you do affects the trust level between you and the other person to some extent.

4. **Trust is hard to build and easy to destroy.** It may takes years to build up a high level of trust in a relationship, then one destructive act can destroy it all.

5. **The key to building and maintaining trust is being trustworthy.** The more accept-ing and supportive you are of others, the more likely they will disclose their thoughts, ideas, theories, conclusions, feelings, and reactions to you. The more trustworthy you are in response to such disclosures, the deeper and more personal the thoughts a person will share with you. When you want to increase trust, increase your trustworthiness.

6. **Trust needs to be appropriate.** *Never* trusting and *always* trusting are inappropriate.

7. **Cooperation increases trust, competitive decreases trust.** Trust generally is higher among collaborators than among competitors.

8. **Initial trusting and trustworthy actions within a group can create a self-fulfilling prophecy.** The expectations you project about trust often influence the actions of other group members toward you.

trust others and those who tend to distrust. A high truster tends to say, "I will trust a person until I have clear evidence that he or she cannot be trusted." A low truster tends to say, "I will not trust a person until there is clear evidence that he can be trusted." High trusters, compared with low trusters, are (1) more trustworthy, (2) more likely to give others a second chance, respect the rights of others, and be liked and sought out as friends (by both low- and high-trust people), and (3) less likely to lie and be unhappy, conflicted, or maladjusted.

SUMMARY

Groups exist for a reason. People join groups to achieve goals they are unable to achieve by themselves. The personal goals of individual group members are linked together by positive interdependence. Group goals result. Group goals direct, channel, motivate, coordinate, energize, and guide the behavior of group members. To be useful, however, group goals have to be clear and operational. The group level of aspiration is continually being revised on the basis of success and failure.

The basis for group goals is the positive interdependence among group members. Social interdependence theory originated from Kurt Lewin's field theory and was formalized by Morton Deutsch. Hundreds of research studies have been conducted that have validated the theory. Within cooperative groups, as opposed to competitive and individualistic efforts, achievement is higher, relationships are more positive and committed, and psychological health, self-esteem, and social competences are higher. The key elements that power cooperation are positive interdependence, individual accountability, promotive interaction, social skills, and group processing.

An essential aspect of ongoing cooperation is the level of trust among members. Trust consists of two parts: being trusting and being trustworthy. Trust is built when a person takes a risk and acts in a trusting way and the other person responds supportively in a trustworthy way. The key to trust, therefore, is being trustworthy.

The cooperative effort to achieve group goals requires frequent, clear, and accurate communication. Group members must be able to communicate and listen clearly and effectively. You will learn how to do this in the next chapter.

CHAPTER FOUR

Communication Within Groups

BASIC CONCEPTS TO BE COVERED IN THIS CHAPTER

In this chapter a number of concepts are defined and discussed. The major ones are in the following list. Divide into heterogeneous pairs. Each pair is to (1) define each concept, noting the page on which it is defined and discussed, and (2) ensure that both members of the pair understand the meaning of each concept. Then combine into groups of four. Compare the answers of the two pairs. If there is disagreement, the members look up the concept in the chapter and clarify it until they all agree on the definition and understand it.

CONCEPTS

1. Group communication
2. Effective communication
3. Sender
4. Receiver
5. Message
6. Channel
7. Noise
8. Defensive behavior
9. Equilibrium theory
10. One-way communication
11. Two-way communication
12. Authority hierarchy
13. Informal communication network
14. Gatekeeper
15. Leveling
16. Sharpening
17. Assimilation
18. Communication network
19. Defensive communication
20. Group norms

INTRODUCTION AND DEFINITIONS

The brothers Grimm tell a tale about a valiant little tailor who, bothered by flies, swatted at them with a cloth. When he lifted up the cloth, seven flies lay dead under it. "Seven!" the tailor said, "Seven at one blow!" Proud of his success, he made himself a belt on which he embroidered, "Seven in one blow!" Later in the day he met the king, who read the words on the belt. "Seven men at one blow!" the king exclaimed, "This is a mighty warrior indeed! If you kill the two evil giants who are murdering and plundering the people of my kingdom, I will give you my only daughter in marriage and half my kingdom as well!" "What a fine offer," the little tailor said. "I am willing to slay your giants." The rest is history.

This breakdown in communication resulted in a little tailor marrying a princess and becoming a king. Not all misunderstandings are as benign. Failures to communicate effectively surround us every day, more often bringing problems and discomfort than riches, love, and position. In fact, breakdowns in communication bring such pain and difficulties that the study of group dynamics pays a great deal of attention to effective group communication.

In this chapter the nature of effective group communication is defined. To understand group communication, two factors must be discussed: the patterns of group communication and the variables that influence communication effectiveness (Figure 4.1). Group communication can be understood better as a pattern of interaction among members than as a specific set of skills. There have been three approaches to examining patterns of group communication: interaction analysis, one- versus two-way communication, and communication networks. The influences on communication effectiveness include cooperative versus competitive context, group norms, physical barriers, seating arrangements, and humor. Each of these topics is discussed in this chapter.

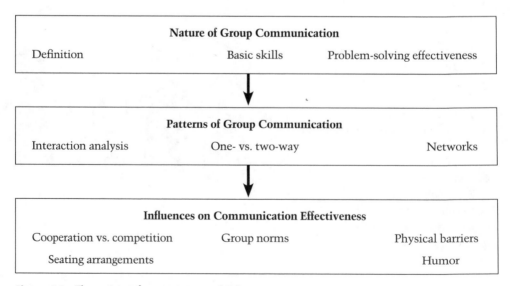

Figure 4.1   The nature of group communication.

EXERCISE 4.1

YOUR COMMUNICATION BEHAVIOR (I)

What is your communication behavior like in a group? How would you describe your communication actions? Begin a discussion of communication within groups by answering the following questions as honestly as possible:

1. If I, as group chairperson, were giving a set of instructions and the other group members sat quietly with blank faces, I would:
   _____ State the instructions clearly and precisely and then move on.
   _____ Encourage members to ask questions until I was sure that everyone understood what he or she was supposed to do.
2. If the group chairperson gave a set of instructions to the group that I did not understand, I would:
   _____ Keep silent and later ask another group member what he or she meant.
   _____ Immediately ask the chairperson to repeat the instructions and answer my questions until I was sure I understood what he or she wanted me to do.
3. How often do you let other group members know when you like or approve of something they say or do?
   Never   1 : 2 : 3 : 4 : 5 : 6 : 7 : 8 : 9   Always
4. How often do you let other group members know when you are irritated or impatient with, embarrassed by, or opposed to something they say or do?
   Never   1 : 2 : 3 : 4 : 5 : 6 : 7 : 8 : 9   Always
5. How often do you check out what other group members are feeling and how they are reacting rather than assuming that you know?
   Never   1 : 2 : 3 : 4 : 5 : 6 : 7 : 8 : 9   Always
6. How often do you encourage other group members to let you know how they are reacting to your behavior and actions in the group?
   Never   1 : 2 : 3 : 4 : 5 : 6 : 7 : 8 : 9   Always
7. How often do you check to make sure you understand what other group members mean before agreeing or disagreeing?
   Never   1 : 2 : 3 : 4 : 5 : 6 : 7 : 8 : 9   Always
8. How often do you paraphrase or restate what other members have said before responding?
   Never   1 : 2 : 3 : 4 : 5 : 6 : 7 : 8 : 9   Always
9. How often do you keep your thoughts, ideas, feelings, and reactions to yourself in group sessions?
   Never   1 : 2 : 3 : 4 : 5 : 6 : 7 : 8 : 9   Always
10. How often do you make sure that the rest of the group knows all the information you have about the current topic of discussion?
    Never   1 : 2 : 3 : 4 : 5 : 6 : 7 : 8 : 9   Always

These questions deal with several aspects of communication in groups that are discussed in this chapter. The first two questions refer to whether communication is one-way (from the chairperson to the rest of the group members) or two-way. Questions 3 and 4 focus on your willingness to give feedback to other group members on how you are receiving and reacting to their messages. Questions 5 and 6 refer to your willingness to ask for feedback about how other group members are receiving and reacting to your messages. Questions 7 and 8 focus on receiving skills, and questions 9 and 10 relate to your willingness to contribute (send) relevant messages about the group's work. Review your answers to these questions and summarize your present communication behavior in a group.

GROUP COMMUNICATION

Communication is the basis for all human interaction and for all group functioning. Our daily lives are filled with one communication experience after another. It is through communication that group members interact, and effective communication is a prerequisite for every aspect of group functioning. **Group communication** can be defined as a message sent by a group member to one or more receivers with the conscious intent of affecting the receivers' behavior (Johnson, 2006). A group member sends the message "It is time to vote" to evoke the response "Everyone in favor raise your right hand." Any signal aimed at influencing the receiver's behavior in any way is communication. **Effective communication** exists among group members when the receivers interpret the sender's message in the same way the sender intended it (Johnson, 2006). If John tries to communicate to the other group members that it is a wonderful day and he is feeling great by saying "Hi" with a warm smile, and if the other group members interpret John's "Hi" and smile as meaning John thinks it is a beautiful day and he is feeling good, then effective communication has taken place. If group members interpret John's "Hi" and smile as meaning he wants to initiate a group discussion, then ineffective communication has taken place.

The complexities of group communication are reflected in its pervasiveness and simultaneous nature. Communication is pervasive in all aspects of sensing other group members. Whenever group members see, hear, smell, or touch one another, communication takes place. In addition, communication is a simultaneous process in which members receive, send, interpret, and infer all at the same time. It is not a sequence of events in which a group member thinks up a message, sends it, and other group members receive it. The multiperson nature of group communication, furthermore, makes it difficult to create a theory of group communication.

Usually, communication models portray communication between two individuals because message exchange between two individuals is relatively orderly and meanings are fairly easy to understand. The analysis of communication in dyadic situations is helpful. Dyadic analyses, however, may be misleading, as they do not represent the complexity of group interactions, where multiple relationships must simultaneously be developed and managed, and do not exhaust the interesting possibilities of group communication (Keyton, 1999). In a dyad, communication is a two-way exchange (Figure 4.2). In a triad, however,

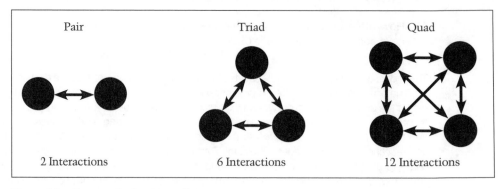

Figure 4.2 Communication in small groups.

there are six lines of communication. In a group of four, there are twelve interactions to keep track of. Creating a conceptual framework that illuminates the communication in groups of six, ten, twenty, or ninety individuals may be beyond current social science.

An attempt to illustrate the complexities of group communication is presented in Figure 4.3. In that figure, the process of communication within a small group is characterized by

1. The ideas, feelings, and intentions of the sender and the way he or she decides to behave lead him or her to send a message to the receivers. The communicator is referred to as the **sender** and the persons at whom the message is aimed are the **receivers.**
2. The sender encodes a message by translating ideas, feelings, and intentions into a message appropriate for sending. The **message** is any verbal or nonverbal symbol that one person transmits to others; it is subject matter being referred to in a symbolic way (all words are symbols).
3. The sender transmits the message to the receivers.
4. The message is sent through a channel. A **channel** can be defined as the means of sending a message to another person: the sound waves of the voice, the light waves that make possible the seeing of words on a printed page.
5. The sender perceives any discernible response of the receivers, thus receiving feedback.
6. The receivers decode the message by interpreting its meaning. The receivers' interpretation depends on how well they understand the content of the message and the intentions of the sender.

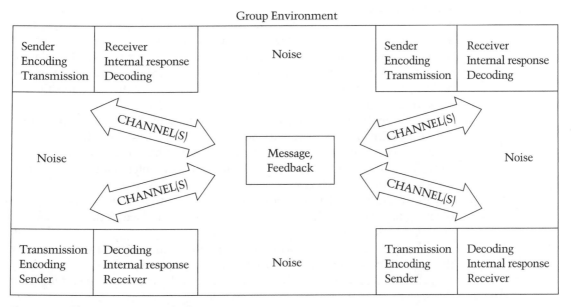

Figure 4.3 The group communication process.

7. The receivers respond internally to this interpretation of the message.
8. **Noise** is any element that interferes with the communication process. In the sender, noise refers to such things as his or her attitudes and frame of reference and the appropriateness of his or her language or other expression of the message. In the receiver, noise refers to such things as attitudes, background, and experiences that affect the decoding process. In the channel, noise refers to (a) environmental sounds, such as static or traffic, (b) speech problems, such as stammering, and (c) annoying or distracting mannerisms, such as a tendency to mumble. To a large extent, the success of communication is determined by the degree to which noise is overcome or controlled.

In the next sections, sending and receiving messages is reviewed.

SENDING AND RECEIVING MESSAGES

To send a message effectively, group members must phrase the message so that it reflects the following criteria (Johnson, 1974, 2006):

1. Clearly own your messages by using first-person singular pronouns (I, me, and my). Personal ownership involves taking responsibility for the ideas and feelings that one expresses. People disown their messages when they use phrases such as "most people," "some of our friends," and "our group."
2. Establish your credibility. **Sender credibility** refers to the receiver's perception of the trustworthiness of the sender's statements. A highly credible sender is one who is perceived to be (a) reliable as an information source, (b) motivated to tell the truth, (c) warm and friendly, (d) trustworthy, (e) in possession of expertise, and (f) dynamic.
3. Make your messages complete and specific. Include clear statements of all necessary information the receiver needs to understand the meaning of the message. Being complete and specific seems obvious, but people often do not communicate the frame of reference they are using, the assumptions they are making, the intentions they have in communicating, or the leaps in thinking they are making.
4. Make your verbal and nonverbal messages congruent. Every face-to-face communication involves both verbal and nonverbal messages. Usually these messages are congruent. The person who is saying that he appreciates your help is smiling and expressing warmth. Communication problems arise when a person's verbal and nonverbal messages are contradictory. If a person says, "Here is some information that may be of help to you" with a sneer on his face and a mocking tone of voice, the meaning you receive is confused by the two different messages being sent.
5. Be redundant. Sending the same message more than once and using more than one channel of communication (such as pictures and written messages as well as verbal and nonverbal cues) will help the receiver understand your messages.

6. Ask for feedback concerning the way your messages are being received. To communicate effectively, you must be aware of how the receiver is interpreting and processing your messages. The only way to be sure is to seek feedback continually as to what meanings the receiver is attaching to your messages.

7. Make the message appropriate to the receiver's frame of reference. Explain the same information differently to an expert in the field and a novice, to a child and an adult, to your boss and your coworker.

8. Describe your feelings by name, action, or figure of speech. When communicating your feelings it is especially important to be descriptive. You may describe your feelings by name ("I feel sad"), by actions ("I feel like crying"), or by figures of speech ("I feel down in the dumps"). Description will help communicate your feelings clearly and unambiguously.

9. Describe others' behavior without evaluating or interpreting. When reacting to the behavior of others be sure to describe their behavior ("You keep interrupting me") rather than evaluating it ("You're a rotten, self-centered egotist who won't listen to anyone else's ideas").

The skills involved in receiving messages include (1) communicating the intention of wanting to understand the ideas and feelings of the sender without evaluation and

(2) understanding and interpreting the sender's ideas and feelings. Communicating the intention to understand a message may be the more important, as the principal barrier to effective communication is the tendency to evaluate the message being received. Evaluative receiving makes the sender defensive and cautious and thereby decreases the openness of the communication. More specifically, the receiving skills are paraphrasing, checking one's perception of the sender's feelings, and negotiating for meaning (Johnson, 2006).

1. Paraphrase accurately and nonevaluatively the content of the message and the feelings of the sender. Restate the sender's expressed ideas and feelings in your own words, avoid any indication of approval or disapproval, neither add to nor subtract from the message, and indicate an understanding of the sender's frame of reference. Paraphrasing is the most basic and important skill in receiving messages.

2. Describe what you perceive to be the sender's feelings. Check your perception of the sender's feelings by tentatively identifying the perceived feelings without expressing approval or disapproval and without attempting to interpret them or

explain their causes. It is simply saying, "Here is what I understand your feelings to be; am I accurate?"

3. Negotiate the meaning of the sender's message. State your interpretation of the
   message and negotiate with the sender until there is agreement as to the message's meaning. Often the words contained in a message do not carry the actual
   meaning. A person may ask, "Do you always shout like this?" and really mean
   "Please quiet down." Sometimes, therefore, paraphrasing the content of a message will do little to communicate your understanding of it. You may wish to
   preface your negotiation for meaning with "What I think you mean is...."

A complete treatment of these basic receiving skills, so important to effective communication, can be found in Johnson (2006), which also contains exercises for developing
verbal and nonverbal competence in these receiving skills.

EXERCISE 4.2

WHO WILL BE PRESIDENT OF BEWISE COLLEGE?

The purposes of this exercise are to examine within a task-oriented group the communication
patterns, the pattern of information sharing, and the effects of collaboration and competition
on group problem solving. The exercise takes about one hour and twenty minutes to complete.
Participants are organized into groups of four role players and two observers.

Timetable		Materials	
Activity	*Minutes*	*Item*	*Number*
Introduction to exercise	10	Briefing sheet	1 per student
Briefing of observers	5	Set of data sheets	1 per group
Groups make decision	30	Candidate summary	1 per student
Whole class discussion	15	Observation sheet	1 per observer
Group processing	15		
Conclusions and closure	5		

An unlimited number of groups may be directed at the same time. The procedure for the
coordinator is as follows:

1. Introduce the exercise as focusing on communication within a problem-solving situation.
   Review the briefing sheet in a realistic manner to set the stage for the role playing.
2. Divide the class into groups of six. Ask two participants to volunteer to be observers. The
   other four members will choose the new president of Bewise College. Suggest that there
   is one correct decision. Tell them they must reach their decision independently of the other
   groups. Then distribute a briefing sheet, a candidate summary sheet, and one data sheet to
   each of the four participants. Be sure that the four different data sheets are distributed to
   different members in each group. **Emphasize that in the exercise, all communication
   in the group must be verbal.** A participant may read his or her data sheets out loud and
   may take notes on what other members say, but may not read other members' materials,

may not let other group members read his or her data sheet, and may not let other group members read his or her notes.

3. Instruct the observers in the use of the Patterns of Communication Observation Sheet. The four participants should read their materials while you are doing so. Distribute copies of the frequency chart, and brief observers on how they are used. All observers will need at least six copies of the observation form, so time should be allotted for them to make their extra copies.

4. Give the signal to begin the group meeting. You may introduce an element of competition by posting groups' solutions in order of completion and by posting the number of minutes used by each group to make their decision.

5. In a whole class discussion, have all the groups share their decision as to which candidate to hire and why. After all the groups have reported, review the correct answer, which appears on page 535 in the Appendix.

6. Have participants discuss the nature of communication within their groups. Review the observation sheets. Then ask the groups to discuss their experience, using the observations of the observers. Monitor the processing of each group and make notes about what students learned in order to provide examples of what participants learned from the experience. Here are some relevant questions for discussion:

   a. What were the patterns of communication within the group?
      1. Who spoke to whom and how frequently?
      2. Who talked, how often did they talk, and for how long?
      3. Who triggered whom in what ways?
      4. Who interrupted whom?
      5. Who encouraged whom to participate?
      6. What could have been done to gain more effective participation?
   b. Was the needed information easily obtained by all the group members? Did group members share their information appropriately, request one another's information, and create the conditions under which the information could be shared?
   c. Were the resources of all group members used? Was everyone listened to?
   d. How cooperative or competitive were the group members?
   e. How did the group make decisions?
   f. What problems did the group members have in working together?
   g. What conclusions about small-group communication may be made from the group's experience?

7. Summarize what the group members have learned, relate it to relevant material in the chapter, and provide closure by complementing the groups on the quality of their work (regardless of whether they made the right decision).

BEWISE COLLEGE BRIEFING SHEET

1. This is the first meeting of your group.
2. **There is verbal communication only.** The information you bring with you is all in your head. Do not read anyone else's materials and do not let anyone else read yours.
3. Assume there is a correct decision (there is one candidate you should hire).
4. Assume that all information in your data sheet and candidate summaries is correct.
5. The decision should be made by consensus. All members should agree on the candidate to hire and be able to explain the reasons why the candidate chosen will make the best president.
6. You must work on the problem as a group.

continued on next page

continued from previous page

PATTERNS OF COMMUNICATION OBSERVATION SHEET

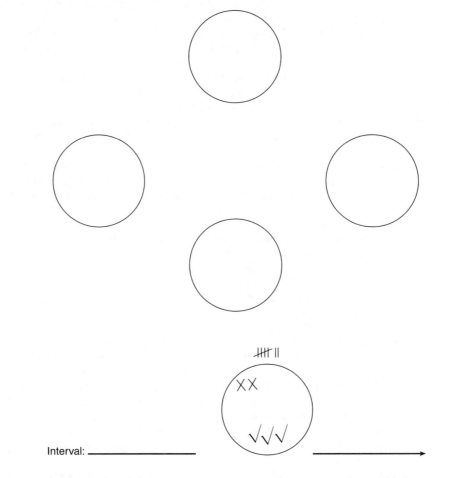

Interval: _____

Use one sheet for each five-minute interval. Label the circles with the names of the group members. Indicate a message from a sender to a receiver with an arrow. When someone sends a message to the entire group, indicate this with an arrow to the center. Indicate the frequency of message sending with tally marks (卌 II). Place an × in the member's circle every time he or she interrupts or overrides another group member, and place a check (✓) in the member's circle every time he or she encourages another member to participate.

BEWISE COLLEGE DATA SHEET 1

Your group is a committee consisting of board members, administrators, faculty, and students of Bewise College. Your group has been authorized by the Board of Regents to select a new president of the college from the list of candidates. Each of the represented groups (Board of Regents, administrators, faculty, students) has its own list of requirements for the new president. Insofar as is possible, your group is pledged to select a candidate who meets these requirements.

Bewise College was established in 1969. It is located in the heart of an industrial city with a population of about 100,000. In addition to a standard liberal arts curriculum, Bewise College offers a curriculum in which students can receive college credit for work and learning experiences outside the college. There is only one other college in the same city; it is the smallest college in the state, and until 1984 all students attending it were African Americans.

The new president faces a series of challenges. The Board of Regents sees the need for a president who can raise money to support the college. The college is now in a desperate financial position and has been losing money for the past two years. It may have to close if it cannot balance its budget. The college administrators want a president with administrative experience. The college is making budget cuts that will require a strong and experienced administrator to orchestrate.

BEWISE COLLEGE DATA SHEET 2

Your group is a committee consisting of board members, administrators, faculty, and students of Bewise College. Your group has been authorized by the Board of Regents to select a new president of the college from the list of candidates. Each of the represented groups (Board of Regents, administrators, faculty, students) has its own list of requirements for the new president. Insofar as is possible, your group is pledged to select a candidate who meets these requirements.

Bewise College was established in 1969. It is located in the heart of an industrial city with a population of about 100,000. In addition to a standard liberal arts curriculum, Bewise College offers a curriculum in which students can receive college credit for work and learning experiences outside the college. Within the state, only Brown College, Samuels College, and Holubec College are larger, making Bewise one of the largest colleges in the state. Samuels College is attended primarily by upper-class students from wealthy families. Andrews is the smallest college in the state.

The new president faces a series of challenges. The Board of Regents wants the new president to be an effective public relations person who can create a positive image of the college within the community, state, and world at large. Success in public relations primarily depends on the president's ability to make powerful public speeches to a wide variety of groups and organizations. The college administrators want an experienced administrator as president. They are very much afraid of a president who will not be a competent administrator. The college is launching a comprehensive assessment of faculty teaching performance. Administrative experience is needed to manage such a program.

BEWISE COLLEGE DATA SHEET 3

Your group is a committee consisting of board members, administrators, faculty, and students of Bewise College. Your group has been authorized by the Board of Regents to select a new president of the college from the list of candidates. Each of the represented groups (Board of Regents, administrators, faculty, students) has its own list of requirements for the new president. Insofar as is possible, your group is pledged to select a candidate who meets these requirements.

Bewise College was established in 1969. It is located in the heart of an industrial city with a population of about 100,000. In addition to a standard liberal arts curriculum, Bewise College offers a curriculum in which students can receive college credit for work and learning experiences outside the college. The students attending Bewise College are primarily minority group members, working-class and lower-income students, the elderly, and dropouts from other colleges and universities.

continued on next page

continued from previous page

The new president faces a series of challenges. The faculty wants a president who has teaching experience because they believe it will make the president sympathetic to the problems of the faculty. In addition, they see the necessity of having a president who comes from a background that would provide insights into the type of student attending Bewise College. Students are dissatisfied with and angry about the quality of teaching at Bewise College. The students, therefore, want a president with an education degree who can judge the teaching ability of faculty and insist on improvements.

BEWISE COLLEGE DATA SHEET 4

Your group is a committee consisting of board members, administrators, faculty, and students of Bewise College. Your group has been authorized by the Board of Regents to select a new president of the college from among the list of candidates. Each of the represented groups (Board of Regents, administrators, faculty, students) has its own list of requirements for the new president. Insofar as is possible, your group is pledged to select a candidate who meets these requirements.

Bewise College was established in 1969. It is located in the heart of an industrial city with a population of about 100,000. In addition to a standard liberal arts curriculum, Bewise College offers a curriculum in which students can receive college credit for work and learning experiences outside the college. The faculty at Bewise College consists primarily of young and dedicated, but inexperienced, instructors. Because universities are always larger than colleges, Bewise is smaller than the state university, but it is growing rapidly.

The new president faces a series of challenges. Faculty members are having a very difficult time in the classroom and want a president who has had experience in working with the type of students attending Bewise College. Faculty members are upset with the difficulty of teaching the types of students at Bewise College and are dissatisfied with student unresponsiveness to their teaching. The students have stated that the only qualification they will recognize as valid for judging faculty teaching ability is for the president to have an education degree. Students also see the necessity of having a president who comes from a background that would provide insights into the type of student attending Bewise College.

Bewise College Candidate Summary Sheet

Name	David Wolcott
Education	Graduated from Andrews College in liberal arts in 1982; received a master of education degree from Winfield University in English in 1984 and a doctorate in political science from Winfield University in 1993.
Employment	Instructor in English at Winfield University, 1984–1988; taught political science at James University, 1988–1997; representative in state legislature, 1990–1992; chairman of the department of political science at James University, 1995–1999; dean of students at James University, 1999–present.
Other	Is well known for his scholarship and intelligence.
Name	Roger Thornton
Education	Graduated from Samuels College in science in 1975; received a master of education degree in chemistry from Smith University in 1982 and a doctorate in administration from Smith University in 1986.

Name	**Roger Thornton**
Employment	High school chemistry teacher, 1982–1989; high school principal, 1989–1996; school superintendent, 1996–present.
Other	Very innovative and efficient administrator; very successful political speaker (the superintendent of schools is elected in his district); his father is vice president of a large bank.
Name	**Edythe Constable**
Education	Graduated from Brown College with a degree in liberal arts in 1985; received a master's degree in accounting from Smith University in 1990 and a doctorate in administration in 1998 from Smith University.
Employment	Insurance agent, 1985–1990; certified public accountant, 1990–1998; vice president of finance, Williams College, 1998–present.
Other	Taught accounting in night school for eight years; volunteer director of a community center in a lower-class neighborhood for four years; was highly successful in raising money for the community center; has a competing job offer from a public relations firm for which she has worked part-time for two years.
Name	**Frank Pierce**
Education	Graduated from Smith University with a degree in industrial arts in 1988; received a master of education degree in mathematics in 1991 from Smith University and a doctorate in administration from State University in 1997.
Employment	Neighborhood worker, 1988–1991; coordinator of parent-volunteer program for school system, 1991–1995; assistant superintendent for community relations, 1995–present.
Other	Has written a training program for industrial education.
Name	**Helen Johnson**
Education	Graduated from Brown College with a degree in social studies education in 1986; received a master of education degree in social studies in 1990 from Brown College.
Employment	Taught basic academic skills in a neighborhood center run by the school system, 1986–1990; chair of student teaching program, Smith University, 1990–1994; dean of students, Smith University, 1996–2000; vice president for community relations and scholarship fund development, Smith University, 2000–present; frequently asked to give speeches on Smith University throughout the state.
Other	Grew up in one of the worst slums in the state. Has written one book and several scholarly articles. Received award for fund-raising effectiveness.
Name	**Keith Clement**
Education	Graduated with a degree in biology education from Mulholland College in 1987; received a master's degree in administration from Mulholland College in 1989.
Employment	Biology teacher in a high school, 1986–1992; consultant in a fund-raising and public relations firm, 1992–present.
Other	Recognized as one of the leading fundraisers in the state. Entertaining speaker; has written a book on teaching working-class students; has done extensive volunteer work in adult education.

EXERCISE 4.3

SOLSTICE SHENANIGANS MYSTERY

The purpose of this exercise is to study the way in which information is communicated in problem-solving groups. A mystery situation is used. Each of the accompanying clues should be written on a separate card. (The answers appear on p. 536 in the Appendix.)

Timetable		Materials	
Activity	*Minutes*	*Item*	*Number*
Introduction to exercise	5	Deck of clue cards	1 per group
Briefing of observers	5	Observation sheet	1 per group
Groups make decision	20		
Whole class discussion	5		
Group processing	5		
Conclusions and closure	5		

1. Introduce the exercise as focusing on communication within a problem-solving situation. Set the stage for the exercise by announcing that each group has been formed to solve a crime.
2. Assign students to heterogeneous groups of five. One member should volunteer to be an observer. The observer's task is to record the communication patterns of the group, using the Patterns of Communication Observation Sheet.
3. The task of each group is to work cooperatively to solve a crime. Each group is to decide by consensus
   a. What was stolen?
   b. How was it stolen?
   c. Who was the thief?
   d. What was the thief's motive?
   e. When did the crime take place?
4. Each group receives a deck of cards. On each card is written a clue to the mystery. Keeping the cards face down so that the clues cannot be read, one member deals them all out so that each member has several clues.
5. Each group member is to read aloud the clues on his or her cards, but not show his or her cards to anyone else. Members may take notes, but may not look at the cards of other members. All communication in the group is to be verbal.
6. When a group has answered the preceding five questions concerning the crime, it may wish to answer the following two questions if the other groups are not yet done:
   a. What happened to the other items?
   b. Who was present at the party?
7. Each group is to discuss the communication patterns they used in solving the mystery. Members may use the following questions to structure the discussion:
   a. What were the patterns of communication within the group?
      1. Who spoke to whom, and how frequently?
      2. Who talked, how often did he/she talk, and for how long?
      3. Who triggered whom in what ways?
      4. Who interrupted whom?
      5. Who encouraged whom to participate?
      6. What could have been done to gain more effective participation?

b. Was the needed information easily obtained by all the group members? Did group members share their information appropriately, request one another's information, and create the conditions under which the information could be shared?

c. Were the resources of all group members used? Was everyone listened to?

d. How cooperative or competitive were the group members?

e. How did the group make decisions?

f. What problems did the group have in working together?

g. What conclusions about small group communication may be made from the group's experience?

8. Summarize what the group members have learned, relate it to relevant material in the chapter, and provide closure by complementing the groups on the quality of their work (regardless of whether they made the right decision).

SOLSTICE SHENANIGANS MYSTERY CLUES

Mr. Purloin showed great interest in Mrs. Klutz's expensive diamond ring.

Mr. Purloin danced all evening with Ms. Beautiful. Mrs. Klutz was always losing things.

Mrs. Klutz could not find her diamond ring after leaving the party.

The Hosts had a big party to celebrate the summer solstice.

The Hosts had a painting by Artisimisso.

Artisimisso was a sixteenth-century Italian artist.

Paintings by sixteenth-century Italian artists are quite valuable.

Mr. Avarice was heard to say that he would do anything for a valuable painting.

Mr. Klutz is a dealer in fine art.

Mr. Klutz needed money badly to keep his business from failing.

Mr. Klutz always carried his briefcase with him.

Mr. Avarice is known to be very rich.

All of Artisimisso's paintings are small.

Mrs. Klutz spent most of the evening in a dark corner of the patio with Mr. Handsome.

Ms. Perceptive saw something glitter in a corner of the patio as she was getting ready to leave the party.

Ms. Perceptive admired a painting by Artisimisso when she arrived at the party.

Ms. Perceptive noticed that the picture she admired was not there when she left the party.

Ms. Perceptive left the party at 10 p.m.

Ms. Wealthy brought her dog to the party.

Ms. Wealthy could not find what she had brought to the party.

The Neighbors owned three dogs.

The Neighbors found four dogs in their backyard after the party.

Mrs. Klutz admired the painting by Artisimisso when she left the party.

Mrs. Klutz left about 9:30 p.m.

Mr. Handsome was a kleptomaniac.

Mr. Handsome left the party twenty minutes after Mrs. Klutz.

Mr. and Mrs. Klutz left the party together.

Mr. Purloin was a jewel thief.

Ms. Beautiful noticed the painting when she left the party at 9:45 p.m.

Ms. Beautiful left the party with Mr. Purloin.

Ms. Wealthy and Mr. Avarice left the party together.

Ms. Wealthy left the party about the time Mr. Klutz did.

COMMUNICATION IN A PROBLEM-SOLVING GROUP

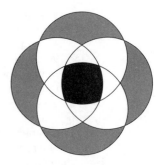

For any problem-solving group to be effective, the members have to obtain the information they need to solve the problem and then put the information together in such a way that results in an accurate or creative solution (Figure 4.4). In most problem-solving groups, some information is shared by everyone, some information is known only to a few members, and each member may have information that no one else in the group knows. Each member is responsible for communicating what he or she knows to the other members of the group. Each member is also responsible for seeking out the information known by the other members but not by that person. Thus, effective sending and receiving skills are both essential for all group members. What makes the exchange of information problematic is the noise that is usually present in problem-solving groups.

Figure 4.4 Communication of information. The black area represents information known to all group members; the gray areas represent information known to only one group member; the white areas represent information known to two or more members of the group.

The integration of members' information, ideas, experiences, and opinions is an essential part of problem solving in a group. How successfully group members integrate their resources depends to a large extent on three factors: (1) their sending and receiving skills, (2) the group norms about and procedures for communicating, and (3) the pattern of communication among group members. The views of communication patterns include interaction analysis, one- and two-way communication, and communication networks.

INTERACTION ANALYSIS

Many observation systems exist to examine the patterns of communication among group members. One of the most famous, which is discussed in depth in Chapter 5, is Bales' (1953) *equilibrium theory*. Bales posited that effective groups must maintain a balance between task and **socio-emotional activity** and developed an observation system known as interaction process analysis (IPA) to analyze the interaction among group members. The results of his research lead to various scholars compiling lists of task and socio-emotional roles in groups. If socio-emotional issues are not managed well, the resulting tension tends to inhibit the group's ability to achieve its goals. In a similar formulation, Homans (1950) analyzed a number of previous case studies and concluded that a group must balance activity in its external system (which deals with achieving its goals and adapting to its environment) with activity in its internal system (which deals with relations among group members and the development of the group).

Communication patterns in groups have been analyzed by Gouran and Hirokawa (1996), who posited that in effective decision making, communication serves two functions: promotive functions (promoting sound reasoning and critical thinking) and counteractive functions (preventing groups from making errors). Thus, communication among group members facilitates the pooling of information, identifying and remedying individual errors, and making persuasive arguments. The effectiveness of decisions tends to increase as group communication focuses on problem analysis, clear and realistic goal setting, and critical and realistic evaluation of information and alternatives.

The interaction among group members can be analyzed on three levels. The first level is the relative frequency and length of communication acts—who talked, how often, and for how long. The second level is who communicates to whom. The third level is who triggers whom in what ways. For example, whenever one member speaks, another may always speak next (even if the remarks are not initially directed to him) or may always interrupt the speaker. Knowing who interrupts whom gives the observer clues as to how members see their own status or power in the group relative to that of other members. Generally, high-authority members feel freer to interrupt low-authority members than vice versa.

EXERCISE 4.4

TRANSMISSION OF INFORMATION

The objective of this exercise is to compare the effectiveness of one-way and two-way communication. At least ten persons and two observers are required.

Timetable		*Materials*	
Activity	*Minutes*	*Item*	*Number*
Introduction to exercise	5	Observation sheet 1	1 per student
Briefing of class	10	Observation sheet 2	1 per student
One-way demonstration	10	Summary table 1	1 per student
Two-way demonstration	15	Summary table 2	1 per student
Whole class discussion	20	Summary graph	1 per student
Conclusions and closure	5		

1. Introduce the exercise as an example of information being passed from member to member within a group.
2. Ask ten persons to leave the room. They are to constitute two groups of five members each.
   a. *One-Way Communication:* The first group is to demonstrate one-way communication. Entering the room one by one, each is to listen to a brief story and repeat it to the next person in his or her own way without help from other participants or the group's observer. The receiver cannot ask questions or comment. He or she must simply listen to the story and then repeat it to the next person.
   b. *Two-Way Communication:* The second group is to demonstrate two-way communication. Entering the room one by one, each is to listen to the story and ask questions about it to clarify its meaning and to make sure that he or she knows what the story is about.

continued on next page

continued from previous page

The person then repeats the story to the next person in the group in his or her own way without help from other participants or the group's observer; the receiver can ask as many questions as he or she wants. You may wish to record the whole experience so that it can be played back for the participants' benefit.

3. After the ten participants have left the room, pass out copies of the accompanying observation sheets and a copy of "The Story" to the observers. Discuss the use of the observation sheet and read the story aloud. Explain the basic concepts of leveling, sharpening, and assimilation (these are discussed in the section on the effects of one-way communication on a message).

4. Begin the demonstration of one-way communication. Ask the first person to enter the room, read the story once, ask the second person to enter, have the first person repeat the story to the second person, and so on, until the fifth person repeats the story to the observers.

5. Begin the demonstration of two-way communication. Ask the first person to enter the room, read the story once, answer all questions he or she has about the story, ask the second person to enter, have the first person repeat the story to the second person and answer all of the second person's questions, and so on, until the fifth person repeats the story to the observers.

6. Reread the original story out loud.
   a. Using the results recorded by the observers and the following summary tables and summary graph, chart the percentages of original details retained correctly in the successive reproductions and compare the one-way and two-way communications.
   b. Discuss the results, incorporating the material in the sections on the characteristics of communication within an authority hierarchy and the effects of one-way communication on a message. Ask the group for further evidence that leveling, sharpening, and assimilation occurred.
   c. Ask what conclusions about one-way and two-way communication can be made on the basis of the results of the demonstration.
   d. Ask the group what conclusions can be made about communication in authority hierarchies.

Other stories can be used in this exercise. Often, the more the cultural background of the story differs from the listener's culture, the more the story is taken in. A story from the Eskimo culture that might be used in this exercise follows "The Story."

OBSERVATION SHEET: ONE-WAY COMMUNICATION

List in the first column the twenty specific details of the story (these appear in italics in the story). Verify the list when the coordinator reads the story to the first person. As person 1 repeats the story to person 2, note the mistakes in person 1's version by writing the wrong words or phrases in the proper row and column. To help in scoring, use a checkmark for details correctly reported and a zero for details left out. Repeat this procedure for the rest of the participants.

Detail	Original Story	Version 1	Version 2	Version 3	Version 4	Version 5
1						
2						
3						
4						
5						

Detail	Original Story	Version 1	Version 2	Version 3	Version 4	Version 5
6						
7						
8						
9						
10						
11						
12						
13						
14						
15						
16						
17						
18						
19						
20						

OBSERVATION SHEET: TWO-WAY COMMUNICATION

List in the first column the twenty specific details of the story (these appear in italics in the story). Verify the list when the coordinator reads the story to the first person. As person 1 repeats the story to person 2, note the mistakes in person 1's version by writing the wrong words or phrases in the proper row and column. To help in scoring, use a checkmark for details correctly reported and a zero for details left out. Repeat this procedure for the rest of the participants.

Detail	Original Story	Version 1	Version 2	Version 3	Version 4	Version 5
1						
2						
3						
4						
5						
6						
7						
8						
9						
10						
11						
12						
13						

continued on next page

continued from previous page

Detail	Original Story	Version 1	Version 2	Version 3	Version 4	Version 5
14						
15						
16						
17						
18						
19						
20						

THE WAR OF THE GHOSTS

One night two young men from Egulac went down to the river to hunt seals, and while they were there it became foggy and calm. Then they heard war cries, and they thought, "Maybe this is a war party." They escaped to the shore and hid behind a log. Now canoes came up, and they heard the noise of paddles, and they saw one canoe coming up to them. There were five men in the canoe and they said: "What do you think? We wish to take you along. We are going up the river to make war on the people."

One of the young men said, "I have no arrows."

"Arrows are in the canoe," they said.

"I will not go along. I might be killed. My relatives do not know where I have gone. But you," he said, turning to the other, "may go with them."

So one of the young men went, but the other returned home.

The warriors went on up the river to a town on the other side of Kalama. The people came down to the water and they began to fight, and many were killed. Presently the young man heard one of the warriors say, "Quick, let us go home. That Indian has been hit." Now he thought, "Oh, they are ghosts." He did not feel sick, but they said he had been shot.

So the canoes went back to Egulac, and the young man went ashore to his house and made a fire. And he told everybody: "Behold, I accompanied ghosts, and we went to fight. Many of our fellows were killed, and many of those who attacked us were killed. They said I was hit, but I did not feel sick."

He told it all, and then he became quiet. When the sun rose he fell down. Something black came out of his mouth. His face became contorted. The people jumped up and cried.

He was dead.

Summary Table: One-Way Communication

Person	Details Correct		Details Incorrect		Details Left Out		Total Details
	Number	Percentage	Number	Percentage	Number	Percentage	
1							
2							
3							
4							
5							

Summary Table: Two-Way Communication

Person	Details Correct		Details Incorrect		Details Left Out		Total Details
	Number	Percentage	Number	Percentage	Number	Percentage	
1							
2							
3							
4							
5							

SUMMARY GRAPH

On this graph, plot the percentages of original details retained correctly in one-way and two-way communication. Connect the one-way results with a solid line and the two-way results with a broken line.

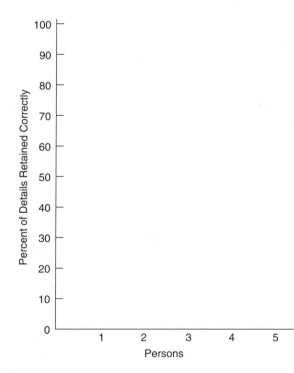

EXERCISE 4.5

ONE- AND TWO-WAY COMMUNICATION

This exercise contrasts the impact of one-way and two-way communication on communication effectiveness. For this exercise, each participant needs two sheets of paper and a pencil. The coordinator needs copies of the accompanying square arrangements, which are given on page 536 in the Appendix. The coordinator may wish to copy the three summary tables below onto a blackboard or a large sheet of paper.

Timetable		Materials	
Activity	**Minutes**	**Item**	**Number**
Introduction to exercise	5	2 sheets of paper	1 per student
Briefing of class	10	Pencil or pen	1 per student
One-way demonstration	10	2 diagrams	1 per class
Two-way demonstration	15	2 summary tables	1 per class
Whole class discussion	20		
Conclusions and closure	5		

1. Introduce the exercise as a comparison of the effectiveness of one-way and two-way communication.
2. Select a sender and two observers (if the group has less than seven members, select only one observer). The sender should be a person who communicates well and who speaks clearly and loudly enough to be heard.
3. *One-Way Communication:* Have the sender sit either with his or her back to the receivers or behind a screen:
   a. Give the sender the first square arrangement, being careful that the group members do not see it. Tell the sender to study the arrangement of squares carefully for two minutes in order to be prepared to instruct the group members on how to draw a similar set of squares on their paper.
   b. Ask the first observer to note the behavior and reactions of the sender during the exercise and to make notes for later comments.
   c. Ask the second observer to make notes on the behavior and reactions of the receivers. Facial reactions, gestures, posture, and other nonverbal behaviors may be observed.
   d. Give the group these instructions: "The sender is going to describe a drawing to you. You are to listen carefully to her instructions and draw what she describes as accurately as you can. You will be timed, but there is no time limit. You may ask no questions of the sender and give no audible response. You are asked to work independently."
   e. Display Table 1 at the front of the room. Then tell the sender to proceed to give the instructions for drawing the first arrangement of squares as quickly and accurately as she can. Make sure that there are no questions or audible reactions from the group members.

TABLE 1   **Accuracy of One- and Two-Way Communication**

ONE-WAY COMMUNICATION			TWO-WAY COMMUNICATION		
Correct	Guess	Actual	Correct	Guess	Actual
5					
4					
3					
2					
1					
0					

f. When the sender has completed giving the instructions for the first square arrangement, record the time it took her to do so in the proper space in Table 2. Ask all members of the group to write down the number of squares they think they have drawn correctly in relation to the preceding square.

TABLE 2   **Medians for One- and Two-Way Communication**

Medians	One-Way	Two-Way
Time elapsed		
Guess accuracy		
Actual accuracy		

4. *Two-Way Communication:* Instruct the sender to face the group members.
    a. Give the sender the second square arrangement and tell him or her to study the relationship of the squares in this new diagram for two minutes in preparation for instructing the receivers on how to draw it.
    b. Ask the first observer to note the behavior and reactions of the sender during the exercise and to make notes for later comments.
    c. Ask the second observer to make notes on the behavior and reactions of the receivers. Facial reactions, gestures, posture, and other nonverbal behaviors may be observed.
    d. Give the group these instructions: "The sender is going to describe another drawing to you. This time she will be in full view of you and you may ask as many questions as you wish. She is free to reply to your questions or amplify her statements as she sees fit. She is not, however, allowed to make any hand signals while describing the drawing. You will be timed, but there is no time limit. Work as accurately and rapidly as you can."
    e. Display Table 1 at the front of the room. Then tell the sender to proceed to give the instructions for drawing the first arrangement of squares as quickly and accurately as she can. Make sure that any receiver who wishes to ask questions does so. Audible reactions from the receivers are permitted.
    f. When the sender has completed giving instructions for the second figure, record the time in the appropriate space in Table 2. Ask the group members to guess the number of squares they have drawn correctly and to record the number on their papers.

continued on next page

continued from previous page

5. Score the accuracy of the drawings:
   a. Obtain a median for guessed accuracy on the first drawing by recording the number of group members who guessed zero, the number who guessed 1, and so on in Table1. Find the median guessed number by counting from zero the number of group members guessing each number until you reach half the members of the group. Then record the median in Table 2.
   b. Repeat this method to get the median of accurate guesses for the second drawing.
   c. Show the group members the master drawing for the first set of squares, and point out the relationship of each square to the preceding one. Each square must be in the exact relationship to the preceding one as it appears on the master drawing in order to be counted as correct. When this step has been completed, ask the members to count and record the actual number right. Have them make a similar count for the second square arrangement.
   d. Obtain the median for accuracy for the first and second arrangements and place them in Table 2.
6. Discuss the following questions with the class:
   a. What can be concluded from the results in terms of time, accuracy, and level of confidence?
   b. What did the observers record during the exercise? How did the behavior of the sender and the group members vary from one situation to the other? What were the group members and the sender feeling during the two situations?
   c. How does this exercise compare with situations you find yourself in at work, school, or home? How might you change your behavior in relating to your friends and acquaintances as a result of what you have experienced during this exercise?

COMMUNICATION NETWORKS

If a group is to function effectively, its members must be able to communicate easily and efficiently. Communication within the group needs to be arranged so that ideas, knowledge, and other information may flow freely among group members. To this end, a number of studies have been conducted on the physical arrangement of communication networks—that is, who can communicate with whom and whether the communication is direct or via another group member. More specifically, **communication networks** are representations of the acceptable paths of communication among members of a group or organization.

In the research studies, various communication networks are imposed on groups to determine their effects. Some of the networks that have been investigated are diagrammed in Figure 4.5. The dots represent individual group members and the lines represent links in the communication network. The most common procedure for imposing communication networks was first formulated by Alex Bavelas (1948). He suggested placing group members in cubicles connected by slots in their walls, through which written messages could be passed. When all slots are

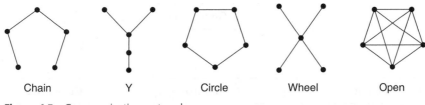

Figure 4.5 Communication networks.

open, every group member can communicate directly with every other member. Other patterns are formed merely by selection of the appropriate slots.

Communication networks have been found to influence the emergence of leadership, the development of organization, the morale of group members, and the efficiency of problem solving (Leavitt, 1951; Shaw, 1964). The group member who occupies a central physical position in a communication network usually has more information and emerges as the leader of the group and is better able to coordinate group activities. Members who occupy a central position in a communication network usually are more satisfied with the group's work than members who occupy fringe positions. Typically, the morale of a group is higher in decentralized (circle, open) communication networks than in centralized ones (chain, Y, wheel).

When a task is simple and requires only the collection of information, a centralized network is more efficient in terms of speed and lack of errors. But when the task is complex and requires the analysis of information, the decentralized networks are more efficient. The problem with centralized communication networks is the members in the central positions may receive more messages than they can handle. Furthermore, any extra demands that must be addressed by a member in a central position are likely to interfere with the efficiency of the network.

COMMUNICATION PATTERNS IN AN AUTHORITY HIERARCHY

An authority hierarchy may be found in every organization and in many groups. An *authority hierarchy* exists when role requirements are established in such a way that different members perform different roles, and members performing particular roles supervise the other members to make sure they fulfill their role requirements. If a group, for example, were divided into several committees, each responsible for a different aspect of the group's work, its role structure would look like Figure 4.6. In an authority hierarchy, a system of rewards and punishments is usually established so that a supervisor will have some power over the persons he or she is supervising. Although authority hierarchies are established to facilitate the effectiveness of the group, they often undermine communication, distributed participation and leadership, and equalization of power.

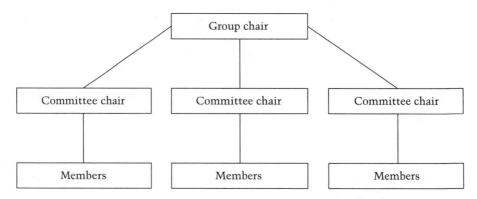

Figure 4.6   A group and its internal authority hierarchy.

To organize itself to accomplish its goals, maintain itself in good working order, and adapt to a changing world, a group structures the communication among members by scheduling meetings, requesting reports from group members, setting up conferences among members, and writing summaries of group progress. The communication network thus created determines the amount and type of information a group member can expect to receive from the other members. In any group, communication is selective, a communication network exists, incentives to use the network properly are present, and members are expected to use certain procedures for communicating with one another. The formal network is created to coordinate members' efforts to accomplish goals. Many groups, furthermore, establish an *informal communication network* based on patterns of friendship and social contact among group members.

In an authority hierarchy, communication procedures may be one-way, one-way-with-feedback, or two-way. **One-way communication** is characterized by a group chairperson giving instructions to the committee chairpersons, who pass the instructions on to the group members. The committee chairpersons are not allowed to communicate with the group chairperson and the group members are not allowed to communicate with the committee chairpersons. The receivers are passive, and communication effectiveness is determined by how the messages are created and presented. One-way communication tends to take less time than the other two procedures, but it tends to be less effective. Although it tends to be less frustrating for the sender, it tends to be unsatisfactory for the receivers.

In *one-way-with-feedback communication*, the chairperson presents the message and the group members give feedback on how well they understand it. The exchange is completed when the group members indicate to the chairperson that they have received the message correctly. No provision exists for mutual influence or exchange—that is, group members can provide feedback on their understanding of the message but not on whether they agree with it. This procedure tends to be faster than two-way communication and less frustrating for the chairperson, but it also is less effective and more frustrating for the group members.

Two-way communication is a reciprocal process in which each member may initiate messages and clarify other members' messages. In a two-way communication procedure, the chairperson and the other group members freely exchange ideas and information. Feelings of **resistance** or doubt can be discussed and resolved at the time they are experienced so they do not interfere with the group's work. Two-way communication encourages open and candid member interaction, distributed participation and leadership, consensual decision making, and other elements of group effectiveness. Although two-way communication tends to be more time consuming than the one-way procedures and more frustrating for the chairperson, it tends to be less frustrating for the group members and more effective for the whole group in the long run. Any goal-directed, problem-solving group that hopes to be effective should use two-way communication procedures.

Even when a two-way communication procedure is encouraged, the authority hierarchy will influence communication among group members. High-authority group members usually do most of the talking, and most of the messages are directed at them. Low-authority members often do not communicate with one another during a group meeting, preferring to address their remarks to high-authority members. Because they generally fear evaluation by those with power, members without power can be expected to take few risks, speak inconsequentially, and avoid frankness. High-authority members often hesitate to reveal vulnerabilities, a tendency that also decreases open and effective communication among group members. Thus, several influences push the group's use of communication procedures toward practices that thwart the kind of discussion needed to function effectively.

Informal Communication Networks and Gatekeepers

When one-way communication procedures are used in a group, comprehension of messages is often so poor that group members turn to the informal communication network to clarify what has been communicated. Some group members tend to be better at understanding messages from higher-ups, and other members seek them out and ask them what the higher-ups meant. Such members are known as *opinion leaders* or gatekeepers. A **gatekeeper** is a person who translates and interprets messages, information, and new developments to groupmates. There are two common types of gatekeepers. Information gatekeepers receive messages from superiors and outside sources and read, listen, and reflect on written reports and verbal messages to a greater extent than do other group members. Technological gatekeepers read more in their field and consult more with outside sources than do the other group members.

Gatekeepers frequently serve as translators by taking messages from superiors and rephrasing them into more understandable forms and into the specific meanings they have for different group members. When one-way communication procedures are being used, the original source often is not available for questioning and clarification of messages; therefore, group members must rely on gatekeepers to clarify the messages. Research on testimony in court cases indicates that people remember initial reports of events they witnessed better than the events themselves (Jones & Gerard, 1967). If the gatekeeper misconstrues the message, errors in understanding are amplified as interpretations are passed from member to member. Even within a two-way communication procedure, group members will at times be unable to clarify a message and will use gatekeepers to help them do so.

Effects on the Message of a One-Way Communication Procedure

What happens to information when it is passed through several persons with little or no clarification? The more the message is passed from person to person, the more distorted and changed it tends to become. Communicators attempt to simplify a message so that it fits into their frame of reference, interests, experience, and tasks. Three psychological processes characterize this simplification of a message (Allport & Postman, 1945; Bartlett, 1932):

1. **Leveling:** The receiver tends to reduce the amount of information he or she receives by remembering much less of the message than was presented by the sender. The message tends to grow shorter and more concise to be more easily understood. In successive versions, fewer words are used and fewer details are mentioned.

2. **Sharpening:** The receiver sharpens certain parts of the information so that a few high points are readily remembered even as most of the message is forgotten. Sharpening is the selective retaining, perceiving, and reporting of a limited number of details from a larger context. It is the reciprocal of leveling—one cannot exist without the other. Certain points become dominant, and all the others are grouped about them.

3. **Assimilation:** The receiver takes much of the message into his own frame of reference and personality. Thus, interpretations and memories of what was heard are affected by the receiver's own thoughts and feelings. This process involves not only changing the unfamiliar to some known context, but also leaving out material that seems irrelevant and substituting material that derives meaning from the receiver's own frame of reference.

Because these three processes are at work whenever one-way procedures are being used, inefficient and ineffective communication usually results. This is true even when gatekeepers supplement the procedure.

EXERCISE 4.6

COMMUNICATION NETWORKS

The purpose of this exercise is to compare the impact of five different communication patterns on productivity and morale. Each group member is to write down his or her reactions to each experience. Participants need to understand how to play poker.

Timetable		Materials	
Activity	Minutes	Item	Number
Introduction to exercise	5	Deck of cards	1 per group
5 communication networks	30	Paper and pen	1 per student
Group processing	15		
Whole class discussion	10		
Conclusions and closure	5		

1. Introduce the exercise as a structured experience in learning how communication networks affect communication among group members.
2. Assign students to heterogeneous groups of six. One member needs to volunteer to be an observer. The task of the observer is to time how long it takes the group to complete its task and to make notes about the behavior and apparent feelings of the participants.
3. **Chain:** The five participants in each group place themselves in a straight line with everyone facing the same way. Each member receives five cards from a regular deck of playing cards. **No verbal communication is allowed,** but members may write notes to the person in front of or behind them. Members may pass cards to the person in front of or behind them. The group task is to select one card from each member's hand in order to make the highest-ranking poker hand possible. After the group has decided on a poker hand, each member should write an answer to the following questions:
   a. How satisfied are you with the group and its work?
   b. How did you feel?
   c. What did you observe?
4. **Y:** The same task with the same rules is repeated, but this time the group members arrange themselves in a Y, with everyone facing toward the center person. Members may pass notes and cards only to the person on their left or right. **No verbal communication is allowed.** After the group has completed the task, each member writes answers to the same three questions.
5. **Circle:** The same task with the same rules is repeated, but this time the group members arrange themselves in a circle. Members may pass notes and cards only to the person on their left or right. **No verbal communication is allowed.** After the group has completed the task, each member writes answers to the same three questions.
6. **Wheel:** The same task with the same rules is repeated, but this time the group members arrange themselves in a wheel (see Figure 4.5). Members on the outside may pass notes and cards only to the person in the middle; the member in the middle may pass notes and

continued on next page

continued from previous page

cards to anyone. **No verbal communication is allowed.** After the group has decided on a poker hand, each member answers the same three questions.

7. **Open:** The same task is repeated, this time with the members sitting in a circle. Any member may communicate with anyone else in the group. Members may pass cards and notes to whomever they wish in the group. **No verbal communication is allowed.** After the group has decided on a poker hand, each member answers the same three questions.

8. **Group Processing:** Using the reactions group members wrote down after each experience and the observer's impressions, the group discusses and writes down the advantages and disadvantages of each communication pattern.
   a. What were the feelings of the members in the middle of a communication pattern? What were the feelings of those on the fringe?
   b. In what communication pattern was the shortest amount of time needed to arrive at a group poker hand?
   c. If you were in charge of a company, which communication pattern would you try to use?
   d. How many messages were sent in each type of communication pattern?
   e. Did each pattern have a leader? For those patterns that did, what position did the leader occupy?

9. **Whole Class Discussion:** Each group shares its conclusions with the rest of the class.

10. Summarize what the group members have learned, relate it to relevant material in the chapter, and provide closure by complementing the groups on the quality of their work.

INFLUENCES ON EFFECTIVENESS OF GROUP COMMUNICATION

There are a number of influences on the effectiveness of group communication. The most powerful is whether the group climate is primarily cooperative or competitive. Other influences on communication effectiveness include group norms, physical setting, seating arrangements, and humor. Each of these influences is discussed in the following sections.

EFFECTS OF COOPERATION AND COMPETITION ON COMMUNICATION

Within any group there tends to be a mixture of cooperative and competitive efforts. In some groups the interaction among members is almost purely cooperative, in some groups members' interactions are almost purely competitive, and in other groups members' interactions reflect a mixture of cooperation and competition.

When group members are working *cooperatively*, communication tends to be more frequent, open, complete, accurate, and honest (Deutsch, 1973; Johnson &

Johnson, 1974, 1989). The effectiveness of communication is enhanced by coopera-tors' long-term time orientation, focus on both achieving goals and good working relationships with others, interest in informing as well as being informed by others, and the frequent use of sending and receiving skills. Cooperators tend to perceive more accurately the intentions and actions of other group members. Mispercep-tions and misunderstandings occur less frequently and, when they do occur, are easier to correct and clarify. Effective communication is enhanced by the fact that in cooperative situations, individuals trust and like one another and therefore are willing to communicate effectively and respond helpfully to one another's wants, needs, and requests.

When group members are competing with one another, communication tends to be either lacking or deliberately misleading (Deutsch, 1973; Johnson & Johnson, 1989). Competition, therefore, gives rise to espionage for obtaining information other group members are unwilling to share and tactics to delude or mislead other group members. Competitors typically have a short-term time orientation, focus their energies on winning, tend to deny the legitimacy of others' needs and feel-ings, and consider only their own interests. Competitors tend to have a suspicious, hostile attitude toward one another that increases their readiness to exploit one another and refuse one another's requests. The more intense the competition, the more likely it is that communication will be ineffective.

An important aspect of competition is defensiveness. Gibb's (1961) eight-year study focused primarily on defensive communication within groups. Defensive communication is behavior that occurs when a person feels threatened or antici-pates a threat. Gibb demonstrated that evaluation, control, superiority, certainty, and neutrality create defensive communication. The use of defensive communica-tion by one group member tends to create similar defensive reactions in others. The more defensive the communication in a group, the more likely it is that mem-bers will misperceive the motives, values, and emotions of other members and the less efficient and effective communication tends to be.

PHYSICAL INFLUENCES ON COMMUNICATION

Physical factors can facilitate or block effective communication within a group. The group's environment can be a source of stress (Baum, Singer, & Baum, 1982; Halpern, 1995). The environment can be too hot, too cold, too impersonal, too big, too small, too noisy, or contain too many distractions. On the other hand, many people seek out environments to spend time in because doing so makes them feel better (Altman & Churchman, 1994; Carlopio, 1996) and even feel rejuvenated and energized (Hartig, Mang, & Evans, 1991; Herzog & Bosley, 1992).

Temperatures from the mid-60s to the mid-80s are viewed as comfortable, but temperatures outside this range can reduce productivity. If a room is too hot, physical effects such as exhaustion, aggressiveness, and even physical damage (such as heat stroke) can result. The same is true for noise. While sounds ranging from 0 to 50 deci-bels generally produce little irritation for the listener, sounds over 80 decibels may bother group members. While loud noise can be ignored for a short period of time, in general, the louder the noise, the more likely it is to produce distraction, irritation, and psychological stress (Cohen & Weinstein, 1981).

The effectiveness of group communication may be enhanced if members pay attention to where they meet, the acoustics of the meeting space, the time of day the meeting takes place, the duration of the meeting, and the ventilation, temperature, and lighting in the room. All these physical factors can enhance effective communication among members if skillfully managed.

 ## SEATING ARRANGEMENTS

Seating arrangements typically are taken for granted or unrecognized. They may, however, create a group ecology (Sommer, 1967). The way in which group members seat themselves in relation to one another exerts significant influences on their perceptions of status, patterns of participation, leadership activities, and affective reactions (Gardin, Kaplan, Firestone, & Cowan, 1973; Howells & Becker, 1962; R. Myers, 1969; Steinzor, 1950; Strodtbeck & Hook, 1961). Members who perceive themselves to have relatively high status in the group select positions (such as the head of the table) that are in accord with this perception. Members sitting at the end positions of a rectangular arrangement participate more in the group and are seen as having more influence on the group decision than members seated at the sides (Nemeth & Wachtler, 1974; Riess, 1982; Riess & Rosenfeld, 1980). The group's formal leader usually sits at the head of the table, and the member sitting at the head of the table is usually perceived to be the leader. There is a strong tendency for members to communicate with members facing them rather than with members adjacent to them. Easy eye contact among members enhances frequency of interaction, friendliness, cooperativeness, and liking for the group and its work. The more formal a seating arrangement, the more anxious members may feel.

HUMOR

Humor is an important influence on the effectiveness of group communication. Humor tends to promote cohesiveness and reduce tension in groups (Bloch, Browning, & McGrath, 1983). Smith and Powell (1988) found that group leaders who used self-disparaging humor were perceived to be more effective at relieving tension, better at encouraging member participation, and more willing to share opinions than leaders who used superior-targeted or subordinate-targeted disparaging humor. Dension and Sutton (1990), in a field study of operating room nurses, found that humor served two functions: It reduced tensions among surgical team members, and it provided variety when standard operating procedures were perceived as boring to surgical team members. Humor was more effective when higher-power members initiated it. Vinton (1989) reported that humor served three purposes in one work group: (1) Self-ridiculing jokes signaled to coworkers that one was willing to participate in a friendly, informal relationship, (2) teasing eased working relationships when members worked in cramped quarters, and (3) bantering helped lessen the status differentials that existed among the members. Taken together, these studies indicate that the effectiveness of group communication is enhanced by appropriate and usually self-directed humor.

EXERCISE 4.7

YOUR COMMUNICATION BEHAVIOR (II)

How would you now describe your communication behavior in a problem-solving group? What are your strengths in communicating, and in what areas do you still wish to build skills? Now that you have completed the exercises and read the material in this chapter, take twenty minutes or so to write a description of how you see your communication behavior in problem-solving groups. Include a description of the way you formulate and send messages, the receiving skills you use, the way in which you contribute your information and ideas to the group, the way in which you receive information about group meetings and group business, and so on.

After you have written your description, meet with two people who know you well and discuss it with them. Is it accurate? Can they add anything? Do they have other ideas that might help clarify your communication behavior?

SUMMARY

Group communication typically involves a multiperson exchange that is effective when the receivers interpret the sender's message in the same way the sender intended it. There are basic sending and receiving skills that all group members need to master. Sending skills include taking clear ownership for your messages, making your messages complete and specific, ensuring your verbal and nonverbal messages are congruent, building in redundancy, obtaining feedback as to how the message is received, adapting the message to the receiver's frame of reference, describing your feelings, and describing others' behavior with evaluation. Receiving skills include paraphrasing accurately and nonevaluatively the content of the message and the sender's feelings, describing your perception of the sender's feelings, and negotiating the meaning of the message until you and the sender agree.

Group communication is primarily analyzed according to the patterns of communication among group members and the factors that facilitate its effectiveness. There are three ways that communication patterns can be analyzed:

1. The interaction among members: The patterns of communication in groups are revealed by documenting (a) the length and frequency of each person's

    communication acts, (b) who speaks to whom, and (c) who triggers communication acts by whom in what ways.

2. The communication network in the group: Communication networks studied include circle, chain, Y, wheel, and open patterns. These patterns influence not only the flow of information in the group, but also who is perceived to be the leader, the way in which tasks are completed, the satisfaction and morale of group members, and the ease with which tasks are completed. The more complex the task, the more open communication patterns are needed.

3. The nature of one-way and two-way communication within authority hierarchies: Many groups have authority hierarchies. In an authority hierarchy, the pattern of communication may be one-way, one-way with feedback, or two-way. Two-way communication is the most desirable in terms of group effectiveness. One-way communication often results in the creation of informal communication networks characterized by gatekeepers or opinion leaders. One-way communication also results in receivers leveling, sharpening, and assimilating the message.

There are factors that influence the effectiveness of the patterns of communication in groups. Whether the communication takes place in a cooperative or a competitive context determines how effective and how defensive the patterns of communication are. The more cooperative the climate, the more effective communication tends to be. Group norms largely determine communication effectiveness. There are physical barriers to communicating effectiveness, such as the acoustics of the room, the seating patterns, ventilation, temperature, and lighting, and the duration of the meeting. Seating arrangements determine who is perceived to be the leader and who exerts influence.

You are now aware of the power and importance of group communication, the variety of patterns group communication may take, and the factors influencing communication effectiveness. The next chapter will discuss the nature of leadership within groups.

Leadership

BASIC CONCEPTS TO BE COVERED IN THIS CHAPTER

In this chapter a number of concepts are defined and discussed. The major ones are listed below. Divide the class into heterogeneous pairs. Each pair is to (a) define each concept, noting the page on which it is defined and discussed and (b) ensure that both members of the pair understand the meaning of each concept. Then combine into groups of four. Compare the answers of the two pairs. If there is disagreement, look up the concept in the chapter and clarify it until all members agree on and understand the definition.

CONCEPTS

1. Leadership
2. Trait approach to leadership
3. Charismatic leadership
4. Machiavellian leadership
5. Leadership styles
6. Initiating structure
7. Influence leadership
8. Role position approach to leadership
9. Distributed-actions approach to leadership
10. Task actions
11. Relationship actions
12. Member maturity
13. Telling
14. Selling
15. Participating
16. Delegating

WHAT IS LEADERSHIP?

Genghis Khan was probably the greatest conqueror in history. Between 1206 and 1258 A.D., he and his sons conquered nearly all of Asia and much of central Europe. If it were not for the death of his youngest son Ogadai in 1241, the rest of Europe would probably have been conquered. Genghis Khan's empire lasted for hundreds of years. So how did he lead nomadic tribes from the Mongolian desert to create the largest empire in history? The societies they conquered (including China and several Muslim empires) were far larger, were more culturally and technologically advanced, and had larger armies. Yet Genghis Khan prevailed. As a leader, he succeeded by choosing his Mongol officers on merit rather than class (in contrast to most armies of the Middle Ages), being open to new tools and ideas (he was more interested in acquiring trading routes and technology than subjects), and establishing a superior communication system with his subordinates (he developed a real-time signaling system of colored banners in battle that allowed him to give orders that were instantly understood by his soldiers). Historically, Genghis Khan was an exceptionally successful leader.

Leadership matters. Leaders shape people's lives, for good and for ill. The leaders of Enron, for example, impoverished thousands of employees and stockholders, stealing their livelihoods, destroying their retirement accounts, and ripping them apart with stress. On the other hand, Winston Churchill inspired his nation and the free world to resist tyranny and maintain their freedom. The English word *lead* is more than a thousand years old, and its meaning has changed little from its Anglo-Saxon root *laedare*, meaning "to lead people on a journey." To *lead* is to guide by influencing the destination and the direction for the group to go. The Oxford English Dictionary notes the appearance of the word "leader" in the English language as early as 1300, while the word "leadership" did not appear until about 1800. A **leader** is a person who can influence others to be more effective in working to achieve their mutual goals and maintain effective working relationships among members. **Leadership** is the process through which leaders exert such influence. Being a leader and exerting leadership takes skill. *Leadership skills* are your ability to help the group achieve its goals and maintain effective working relationships among members. Leadership is often contrasted with managing a group. The root origin of *manage* is a Latin word meaning "hand," and *managers* are individuals who "handle" the status quo.

The consequence of leadership is cooperation among individuals in pursuit of a common goal. The effects of leadership, however, are difficult to identify because successful goal achievement is the result of the coordinated efforts of many (not just the leader), and influenced by the actions of competitors, changes in weather patterns, discovery of new technologies, broad economic conditions, currency fluctuations, and many other factors beyond the control of the leader or the followers. Leadership may be illusionary. Many philosophers, such as Hegel and Spencer, believed that "great leaders" are merely puppets of social forces that shape events and history, regardless of who occupies positions of leadership. These two broad views of leaders and leadership (i.e., history is shaped by great leaders versus history is shaped by

EXAMPLE OF A LEADER: BENJAMIN FRANKLIN

Before Benjamin Franklin reached thirty years of age he had been chosen public printer for the colony of Pennsylvania, had founded the famous and influential Junto Club, created and published *Poor Richard's Almanac* (the most widely read publication in America), had founded the first circulating library, and had been elected grand master of the Freemasons Lodge of Pennsylvania. The next year he inaugurated the first fire-fighting company in Pennsylvania and was chosen clerk of the Pennsylvania Assembly. He was one of the most successful businessmen in the colonies, but had enough interest in scholarship and research to be the founder (at age thirty-seven) of the American Philosophical Society. He continued to serve in a variety of leadership posts in politics, the army, science, diplomacy, and education (founding the academy that became the University of Pennsylvania). At eighty he led the group enterprise of writing the Constitution of the United States. A biographer noted, "Nobody could approach him without being charmed by his conversation, humor, wisdom, and kindness" (Fay, 1929).

How would you explain Benjamin Franklin's success as a leader? Was it due to his (pick only one):

_____ **1.** Inborn, genetic traits?

_____ **2.** Style of leadership?

_____ **3.** Ability to influence others?

_____ **4.** Occupation of positions of authority?

_____ **5.** Ability to provide helpful behaviors in diverse situations?

In selecting one of these alternatives, you have decided on a theory of leadership. In this chapter we shall review each of these theories.

strong social forces regardless of who leaders are) have been the primary focus of the debate about leadership.

There is also a debate about whether leadership can be best understood as a quality of an individual or as a relationship between leaders and followers. Leadership may depend on a person's traits or style of doing things, or leadership might only exist between leaders and followers. Grint (2005) notes that it only requires followers to do nothing for leadership to fail. It may even be followers who teach leaders how to lead. Followers can play an active role in the relationship, empowering their leaders, influencing their leaders' behavior, and determining the consequences of the leaders' actions (Howell & Shamir, 2005).

In this chapter, the five major theories of effective leadership (genetic traits, style of leadership, ability to influence others, occupying a position of authority, and ability to provide situational leadership) are discussed (see Figure 5.1). Benjamin Franklin is used as an example of each leadership theory. The chapter ends with a discussion of organizational leadership.

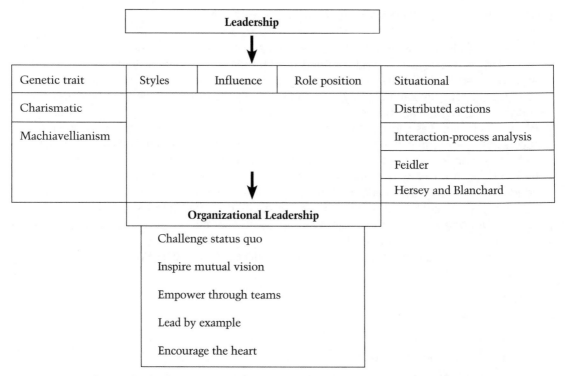

Figure 5.1 Small-group leadership.

WHO ARE YOUR HEROES?

Who is your ideal leader? Who does our society consider to be ideal leaders? Everyone has heroes whom they would like to imitate and be like. The strength and dedication of George Washington, the intellect and commitment of Thomas Jefferson, the courage of Harriet Tubman, the values and determination of Martin Luther King, Jr., may inspire us to wish to be like them. Who is your ideal leader? What qualities does our society believe the ideal leader must have?

Every society has a vision of what constitutes a leader. The ancient Egyptians, for example, attributed three qualities of divinity to their king (Frankfort, Frankfort, Wilson, & Jacobsen, 1949): "Authoritative utterance is in thy mouth, perception is in thy heart, and thy tongue is the shrine of justice." An analysis of leaders in Homer's *Iliad* resulted in four sets of ideal leadership qualities admired by ancient Greeks (Sarachek, 1968): (1) justice and judgment (Agamemnon), (2) wisdom and counsel (Nestor), (3) shrewdness and cunning (Odysseus), and (4) valor and action (Achilles).

1. Working by yourself, complete the following two tables.
2. Form a group of four. Compare answers and reach consensus about society's views of who are leaders and what characteristics they have.

Who Are Ideal Leaders?

Leaders Society Admires	Leaders I Admire	Leaders We Admire
1.	1.	1.
2.	2.	2.
3.	3.	3.
4.	4.	4.

What Are Qualities of Ideal Leaders?

Qualities Society Admires	Qualities I Admire	Qualities We Admire
1.	1.	1.
2.	2.	2.
3.	3.	3.
4.	4.	4.
5.	5.	5.
6.	6.	6.

EXAMPLE OF A HERO

King Alfred is the only king in English history who is given the title, "The Great." Alfred became King of Wessex in England in 849, a time when the Vikings had conquered the North and the Danes had conquered the East. It appeared that the Vikings and Danes might conquer all of England. Alfred, however, drove the Danes out of the South and West of England and united that part of England as never before. He became famous for courage and skill as a warrior who fought "like a wild boar." He built an efficient army and a navy that patrolled the English Channel, discouraging further invasions, and turned the attention of the Vikings and Danes toward the north of France. He then proceeded to repair the ravages of the Danish incursions. He rebuilt churches, imported foreign scholars, founded schools, began the compilation of the *English Chronicle,* and personally translated a number of books from the Latin including Bede's *History* (which celebrates the glory of the English church). He is known as a lawgiver and educator who was devoted to the welfare of his people. His code of law was the first to survive in its original form. He hoped for a day when all the youth in England would be devoted to learning. Alfred was the first great statesman to emerge clearly from the mists of early English history. He died in 900 and, due largely to his work, most of the tenth century in England was a golden age of peace and prosperity. Never again was England to have such a king.

EXERCISE 5.2

CONTROVERSY: WHAT IS THE NATURE OF LEADERSHIP?

The five views of leadership can be the basis for an academic controversy. The purpose of the controversy is to analyze critically the five views of leadership. The procedure is as follows:

Step 1   Forming Leadership Groups: Form leadership groups of five. The goals of the group are to:

a. Learn all five views of leadership.
b. Critically analyze each view of leadership.
c. Come to a consensus about the nature of leadership based on group members' best reasoned judgment.
d. Write a summary of the group's conclusions about the nature of leadership.

To achieve these goals, you need to participate in a structured controversy.

Step 2   Forming Preparation Pairs: In each group, members count off from 1 to 5. Each group pairs up with another group. Members of the two groups form preparation pairs. The "1s" become a pair, the "2s" become a pair, and so forth. Each preparation pair adopts one of the leadership theories:

1s	Genetic Traits View of Leadership
2s	Style View of Leadership
3s	Influence View of Leadership
4s	Position View of Leadership
5s	Distributed Actions View of Leadership

The pairs meet separately to (a) learn their position and (b) prepare a forceful, three-minute presentation of their position. Both members must contribute to building a persuasive case for their view of leadership. The purpose of the presentation is to persuade the other members of their leadership group to adopt the recommended view as the most valid and reasonable view of leadership. The presentation should include (1) a position statement: *"Our view is that a leader is someone who ..."* (2) a rationale supporting the position containing as many facts and research findings as possible, arranged in logical order to maximize their persuasiveness, and illustrated with a visual drawing: *"Because of a, b, and c, you must conclude that ..."* and (3) a conclusion that is a restatement of the position statement: *"Therefore, the most valid view of leadership is ..."*

Each person needs his or her own copy of the presentation. The pairs have about ten minutes for this phase of the exercise.

PREPARATION FORM

1. *"The most valid theory of leadership is"* (the theory assigned to me is):

_____

2. Because of (list the reasons why your theory is the most valid view of leadership, and then arrange the reasons in the most persuasive order):

	Reason	Most Persuasive Order
1.		
2.		
3.		
4.		
5.		
6.		

3. Therefore, you have to conclude that the most valid theory of leadership is:

_____

Step 3   Practice Pairs: Each person finds a new partner who has the same number and is prepared to present the same view. A number "1" finds another "1," a number "2" finds another "2," and so forth. The pair members share their presentation plan and their visual. Each person takes something from the other's preparation and adds it to his or her own in order to strengthen his or her presentation.

Step 4   Presenting the Best Case Possible for the Assigned Position: The leadership group of five meets. Each member presents the best case possible for his or her assigned position. The presentation is aimed at persuading the other members to adopt the position as the most valid view of leadership. The other group members should listen carefully, take notes, and ask for clarification of anything that is not fully understood. Each person has about three minutes to present his or her position (fifteen minutes total for a group of five).

MY PRESENTATION

_____ I will give a strong, enthusiastic, sincere appeal for the listeners to agree with me.
_____ I will make eye contact, speak clearly, and use appropriate gestures.
_____ I will keep my presentation within the time limits.
_____ I will create a visual to illustrate my points.

Step 5   Challenging the Validity of Each Position: The group of five has an open discussion (anyone can speak at any time) in which:

a. I continue to advocate the best case for their assigned position.
b. I continue to learn the other positions.
c. I challenge the validity of each of the other positions (give them a trial-by-fire) by critically analyzing (1) the theory, research, and assumptions of each position; and (2) the logic of the presentation. ("*Your position has the following flaws …*")
d. I defend my own position from the challenges of the other group members. ("*You are mistaken—my position is valid because …*").

continued on next page

continued from previous page

You should present as many facts and research findings as you can to support the position. Members should listen critically to the opposing position, asking for facts to support any conclusions made by the opposing pair. Participants should ensure that all the facts supporting both sides are brought out and discussed. The rules for constructive controversy should be followed. About ten minutes should be allowed for this phase.

My Analysis of the Theories

Persuasive Points	Criticisms
Theory One:	
Theory Two:	
Theory Three:	
Theory Four:	
Theory Five:	

Step 6   Reversing Perspectives: Each person presents the best case possible for the position of the next higher number (1 presents the 2 position, 2 presents the 3 position, 3 presents the 4 position, 4 presents the 5 position, 5 presents the 1 position). Be as forceful and persuasive as you can in arguing for the opposing position. Expand on the other position, adding new arguments or facts that the advocate did not present. You have about two minutes for the presentation (ten minutes total for the group of five).

Step 7   Synthesizing and Integrating the Five Positions: Group members drop all advocacy, synthesize and integrate the best information and reasoning from all five positions, and come to a consensus as to their view of leadership. Write down your best reasoned judgment as to the nature of leadership: (a) our group position, (b) our rationale arranged in a logical order, and (c) a conclusion that is the same as your position. About ten minutes should be allowed for your group for this phase.

OUR GROUP POSITION

1. Our group position is: _____

_____

_____

_____

2. Because of:
   a. _____
   b. _____
   c. _____
   d. _____

3. Therefore, you have to conclude that our conclusions are valid.

Step 8   Groups Present Their Positions to Entire Class: Each leadership group presents its final position to the entire class. Since other groups will have other conclusions, each group may explain the validity of its position to the class.

Step 9   Group Processing: Each leadership group discusses:

1. What leadership actions did each member take to help the group effectively advocate and challenge each of the leadership theories?
   a. _____
   b. _____
   c. _____
   d. _____
   e. _____

2. What can each member do to be even more effective next time?
   a. _____
   b. _____
   c. _____
   d. _____
   e. _____

3. What were the most fun parts of arguing about leadership?
   a. _____
   b. _____
   c. _____

4. What did I learn about myself as an arguer?
   a. _____
   b. _____
   c. _____

WHAT IS LEADERSHIP?

There are several different views of leadership. The following questionnaire measures your view. The procedure is:

1. Working by yourself, complete the following questionnaire.
2. Determine your score.
3. Form a group of four members. Compare your scores. Then read the following sections of this chapter.

continued on next page

continued from previous page

The statements listed below reflect various theories of leadership. Read each statement carefully. Using the following scale, indicate the degree to which you agree or disagree with each statement.

1 = Strongly Disagree
2 = Disagree
3 = Neither Disagree nor Agree
4 = Agree
5 = Strongly Agree

1. Leaders are born, not made.
   Strongly Disagree 1———2———3———4———5 Strongly Agree
2. Each leader has his or her own style.
   Strongly Disagree 1———2———3———4———5 Strongly Agree
3. The leader in a group is the person who is most able to influence the others.
   Strongly Disagree 1———2———3———4———5 Strongly Agree
4. Whoever has the most authority (power invested in a position) is the leader.
   Strongly Disagree 1———2———3———4———5 Strongly Agree
5. With training, anyone can learn to be a leader.
   Strongly Disagree 1———2———3———4———5 Strongly Agree
6. Great leaders with unique and inborn traits are discovered, not developed.
   Strongly Disagree 1———2———3———4———5 Strongly Agree
7. If you want to be a leader, know your style and go with it.
   Strongly Disagree 1———2———3———4———5 Strongly Agree
8. If you are appointed leader, then you are the leader, because subordinates are supposed to obey their superiors.
   Strongly Disagree 1———2———3———4———5 Strongly Agree
9. A leader persuades and inspires members to follow the leader's views of what needs to be done.
   Strongly Disagree 1———2———3———4———5 Strongly Agree
10. Leadership is acting in a way that helps the group achieve its goals and maintain good working relationships among members.
    Strongly Disagree 1———2———3———4———5 Strongly Agree
11. A good predictor of leadership ability is whether or not the person comes from a family of leaders.
    Strongly Disagree 1———2———3———4———5 Strongly Agree
12. To choose who should lead, decide which style of leadership is most effective.
    Strongly Disagree 1———2———3———4———5 Strongly Agree
13. The leader is the person who influences others to do what is best.
    Strongly Disagree 1———2———3———4———5 Strongly Agree
14. A leader makes sure that subordinates do their jobs.
    Strongly Disagree 1———2———3———4———5 Strongly Agree
15. Any member of a group may become a leader by taking actions that help the group complete its goal and maintain effective working relationships.
    Strongly Disagree 1———2———3———4———5 Strongly Agree
16. Leaders are "great persons" who become (or who are) members of elite social groups because of their outstanding inborn traits.
    Strongly Disagree 1———2———3———4———5 Strongly Agree

17. Some leaders are democratic. Some leaders are authoritarian. Every leader has his or her own style.
    Strongly Disagree 1———2———3———4———5 Strongly Agree
18. Leaders are leaders because they influence group members more than group members influence them.
    Strongly Disagree 1———2———3———4———5 Strongly Agree
19. Leaders are given the authority and power to punish and reward group members.
    Strongly Disagree 1———2———3———4———5 Strongly Agree
20. A leader varies his or her behavior from situation to situation to provide the appropriate leadership actions at the appropriate time.
    Strongly Disagree 1———2———3———4———5 Strongly Agree

WHAT IS LEADERSHIP?: SCORING

Genetic Traits	Style	Influence	Authority	Needed Functions
_____ 1	_____ 2	_____ 3	_____ 4	_____ 5
_____ 6	_____ 7	_____ 8	_____ 9	_____ 10
_____ 11	_____ 12	_____ 13	_____ 14	_____ 15
_____ 16	_____ 17	_____ 18	_____ 19	_____ 20
_____ Total	_____ Total	_____ Total	_____ Total	_____ Total

The higher the total score for each category, the more strongly you tend to believe in that explanation of leadership. The lower the total score in a category, the less strongly you tend to believe in that explanation of leadership.

TRAIT THEORIES OF LEADERSHIP

"I can call spirits from the vastly deep" (Glendower).
"Why, so can I, or so can any man; But will they come
when you do call them?" (Hotspur)

William Shakespeare, *Henry IV, Part I*

Perhaps Benjamin Franklin was one of the greatest leaders of the eighteenth century because he was genetically superior to his contemporaries. Throughout history many people have believed that leaders are born, not made, and great leaders are discovered, not developed. Especially in times of social upheaval, many people looked for a great leader who had unique, inborn traits. This is the **"great-person" theory of leadership.** Royalty, members of elite social classes, and older siblings are likely to believe in this theory of leadership. One of the strongest advocates was Aristotle, who stated, "From the moment of their birth, some are marked for subjugation and others for command." Leaders such as Napoleon and Mao Zedong were able to control the destinies of millions of people, perhaps because of their personal traits.

This point of view was advocated by Carlyle (1849), Galton (1869), and James (1880), who defined *leadership* as a unique aspect of extraordinary individuals whose actions and decisions are sometimes capable of radically changing the flow of history. This view is a persistent view of leadership in popular culture. Certain unique individuals are portrayed as transforming their societies. Galton, especially, argued that the unique attributes of these leaders are in their genetic makeup, being inherited from generation to generation. Since the qualities of leaders are immutable, leaders cannot be trained or developed. In the early twentieth century, there were many strong advocates of the trait theory of leadership. Wiggam (1931), for example, concluded that the survival of the fittest, and marriage among them, produce an aristocratic class that differs biologically from the lower classes and, therefore, a proportionately high birth rate among the abler classes was needed to ensure an adequate supply of superior leaders. Henry Ford remarked, "The question 'Who should be boss?' is like asking 'Who ought to be the tenor in the quartet?' Obviously, the man who can sing tenor." He was suggesting the boss is a person who has the natural ability to lead.

In response to these beliefs, hundreds of research studies were conducted to identify the personal attributes of leaders. In one of the more interesting studies, Frederick Adams Wood (1913), an American historian, examined 386 rulers in fourteen countries in Western Europe who lived between A.D. 1000 and the French Revolution. All of these rulers had absolute power over their kingdom. Each was classified as strong, weak, or mediocre on the basis of knowledge about his or her intellectual and personal characteristics (which presumably were independent of the strength or weakness of the leader's nation at that time). The condition of each country also was classified as prosperous, declining, or lacking a clear indication of either (this classification was based on the country's economic and political status, not on its artistic, educational, and scientific development). Wood found a relationship (correlations from +0.60 and +0.70) between the monarchs' personalities and the state of the countries: "Strong, mediocre, and weak monarchs are associated with strong, mediocre, and weak periods respectively" (p. 246). As with any correlation, however, a direct relationship between cause and effect cannot be inferred. Wood, however, clearly favored the interpretations that strong leaders cause their countries to flourish. This perspective guided most of the research on leadership until the early 1950s (Zaccaro, 2007), when researchers decided trait-based leadership approaches were insufficient to explain effective leadership (Mann, 1959; Stogdill, 1948). Stogdill (1948) was thought to have sounded the death knell of the trait view of leadership when he stated, "The evidence suggests that leadership is a relation that exists between persons in a social situation, and that persons who are leaders in one situation may not necessarily be leaders in other situations" (p. 65). Yet, in the 1980s, research emerged that brought the leader-trait view back into prominence (Zaccaro, 2007; Zaccaro, Kemp, & Bader, 2004). From this point of view, **effective and successful leaders** establish a direction for collective effort and then manage, shape, and develop the collective efforts in accordance with this direction.

This renewed interest in leader traits proposes first that leadership potential is based on multiple traits (not a select few) that operate in an integrated, coherent way. From this perspective, traits not only refer to personality attributes, but also motives, values, cognitive abilities, social and problem-solving skills, and expertise. The second is that the integrated expression of these traits must accommodate the current situation if they are to affect leader effectiveness. Because situations can radically change, the expression of the leader's traits must change. Thus, there may be some traits that are stable across different situations while other traits may be situationally bound. Because of the flexibility of a leader's behavior, persons who emerge as leaders in one situation may also emerge as leaders in much different situations.

There may be, however, some traits associated with effective leadership (see Table 5.1), such as persistence, tolerance for ambiguity, personal adjustment, social competence, self-confidence, initiative, sense of humor, drive, honesty, integrity, internal locus of control, achievement motivation, extroversion, and cognitive ability (Avolio, 2007; Bird, 1940; Den Hartog & Koopman, 2001; Kirkpatrick & Locke, 1991; Mann, 1959; Stogdill, 1974; Yukl, 2005). These findings are somewhat ambiguous, however, as many people with these traits never become leaders. While leaders tend to be more intelligent (i.e., cognitive ability) than followers, for example, many of the most intelligent people never obtain positions of leadership. A longitudinal study of 1,000 highly intelligent children from California showed that none attained high political office or the presidency of a corporation or college, only 5% were in Who's Who, and only 13% were in *American Men of Science* (Terman & Odor, 1947). And, despite the findings that leaders are better adjusted psychologically than nonleaders, many leaders (such as Adolf Hitler, Mussolini, and Stalin) showed signs of being emotionally disturbed.

TABLE 5.1 **Percentage of Significant Relationships Reported in a Positive or Negative Direction for 125 Studies, Representing 751 Findings on the Relationship of Various Personality Characteristics and Leadership**

PERSONALITY FACTORS AND NUMBER OF STUDIES OF EACH	NUMBER OF FINDINGS	PERCENT YIELDING SIG. POSITIVE RELATIONSHIP	PERCENT YIELDING SIG. NEGATIVE RELATIONSHIP	PERCENT YIELDING NEITHER
Intelligence, 28	(196)	46% (91)	1%* (1)	53% (104)
Adjustment, 22	(164)	30% (50)	2%* (2)	68% (112)
Extroversion, 22	(119)	31% (37)	5%* (6)	64% (76)
Dominance, 12	(39)	38% (15)	15%* (6)	46% (18)
Masculinity, 9	(70)	16% (11)	1%* (1)	83% (58)
Conservatism, 17	(62)	5% (3)	27%* (17)	68% (42)
Sensitivity, 15	(101)	15% (15)	1%* (1)	84% (85)

*Rounded upward.

Source: R. Mann, A review of the relationship between personality and performance in small groups, *Psychological Bulletin, 56,* 241–270, 1959. Reprinted with permission.

It seems that while several traits seem to differentiate between leaders and nonleaders, when the traits are considered singly they hold little diagnostic or predictive significance; rather, they have to be considered in combinations to be predictive (Stogdill, 1974). Clusters of traits may only matter, however, when they fit with the specific demands of the group, organization, or society. To rise to a leadership position may depend on being in the right place at the right time in the sense that one's clusters of traits match the demands of the current state of affairs (Stogdill, 1974; Weber, 1924/1947). A social crisis may be necessary for the emergence of a charismatic leader, whereas stability may be necessary for a bureaucratic leader to flourish. Certain types of events may trigger the emergence of certain types of leaders (Avolio, 2007). Regardless of a person's specific traits, however, the best predictor of leadership success is prior success in leadership roles. Perhaps the safest conclusion to draw from the trait studies of leadership is that individuals who have the energy, drive, self-confidence, and determination to succeed will become leaders because they work hard to get leadership positions.

Some leadership theorists hold the position that not all traits are fixed and may evolve over time, depending on the dynamic exchange between the leader and the followers, and the context (Avolio, 2007). Sternberg (2007) even defines the qualities of leadership (a synthesis of wisdom, intelligence, and creativity) as attributes that are modifiable, flexible, and dynamic rather than fixed, rigid, and static. Generally, trait theorists agree that traits are not an either/or issue, but rather a matter of degree in influencing a leader's effectiveness. The major problem with trait theories, however, is that an unlimited number of traits can be identified and an infinite number of interactions. Finally, the research has focused on "great men" as leaders and relatively neglected "great women."

In the extensive research trying to differentiate leaders from nonleaders on the basis of personal attributes, there has been considerable discussion and research on two major traits of some leaders: charisma and Machiavellianism.

Charismatic Leaders

The specific traits that define a leader have not been unambiguously identified, yet a handful of people have changed millions of lives and reshaped the world. Joan of Arc, for example, miraculously recruited French soldiers to follow her into battle. How this happened, the nature of heroic or charismatic leadership, is a mystery, an unsolved aspect of leadership. The dictionary defines **charisma** as "an extraordinary power, as of working miracles." Sometimes charismatic leaders seem to inspire their followers to love and be passionately devoted to them. Other times charismatic leaders offer their followers the **promise** and hope of deliverance from distress. Charismatic leaders are saviors who say in essence, "I will make you safe," "I will give you identity," or "I will give your life significance and meaning."

Charisma does not seem to be correlated with any one personality type. The personalities of Alexander the Great, Julius Caesar, George Washington, Robespierre, Simon Bolivar, Sun Yat-sen, and Mahatma Gandhi were widely different, yet all of these individuals were all able to inspire confidence in their followers and to demand from them the sacrifice even of life itself. Garibaldi won the loyalty of his Roman soldiers with an unusual appeal: "What I have to offer you is fatigue, danger, struggle, and death; the chill of the cold night in the fall air, and heat under the burning sun; no lodgings, no provisions, but forced marches, dangerous watch posts, and the continual struggle with the bayonet against batteries—those who love freedom and their country may follow me!" During World War II, Winston Churchill offered "blood, sweat, and tears," but sustained the faith and courage of millions.

Attempts to understand measure charisma have, by and large, failed. In general, a **charismatic leader** has (a) the ability to communicate an extraordinary power or vision to others or (b) unusual powers of practical leadership that enable the leader to achieve goals that alleviate followers' distress. The charismatic leader has a sense of mission, a belief in the social-change movement he or she leads, and confidence in him- or herself as the chosen instrument to lead the movement to its destination. The leader appears extremely self-confident in order to inspire others with the faith that the movement he or she leads will prevail and ultimately reduce their distress.

Machiavellianism

If charismatic leaders begin social movements and bring them to power, Machiavellian leaders consolidate and wield the power the charismatic leaders obtain. Niccolo Machiavelli (1469–1527) was a Florentine statesman whose treatise *The Prince* called on rulers to use craft, duplicity, and cunning as political principles for increasing their power and success. **Machiavellian leaders** believe (a) people are basically weak, fallible, and gullible, and not particularly trustworthy; (b) others are impersonal objects; and (c) one should manipulate others whenever it is necessary to achieve one's own ends. Machiavelli did not originate this approach. Throughout history there have been theorists who conceived of leadership essentially in terms of the possession and exercise of power for self-enhancement. After analyzing the historical literature on how political leaders should govern, Richard Christie (Christie & Geis, 1970) concluded that Machiavellian leaders who manipulate their followers for political and personal reasons have four characteristics: (1) They are not very emotionally involved in their interpersonal relationships, as it is easier to manipulate others if they are viewed as objects rather than as fellow humans. (2) Because they take a utilitarian rather than a moral view of their interactions with others, such leaders are not concerned with conventional morality. (3) Because successful manipulation of followers depends on an accurate perception of their needs and of reality in general, they are not psychologically pathological. Finally, (4) since the essence of successful manipulation is a focus on getting things done rather than achieving long-term ideological goals, Machiavellian leaders will have a low degree of ideological commitment.

Traits versus Relationships versus Context versus Chance

While there have been many attempts to downplay the importance of traits in the success and effectiveness of leaders, this perspective never disappears. There seems to be a bias, at least in Western societies, toward attributing events as being caused by individuals. Yet there are multiple objections to the **trait approach to leadership.** One defines leadership as a relationship existing between leaders and followers—no followers, no leader. A second objection views leadership as being determined by social forces, social movements, and changing social values. Leaders play out roles designed for them by these broad social forces. John W. Gardner (1990), for example, believed that leaders should be viewed as an integral part of a social system and cannot be separated from the historic context in which they arise, the setting in which they function (e.g., business, education, politics), and the system over which they preside (e.g., political, educational, economic).

Finally, there are theorists who believe that sheer chance may determine whether individuals become leaders. Leaders may emerge simply because they are in the right place at the right time. The invention of a new technology, a decision made by a business to sell part of the company, a plague that decimates a society, may all result in unique opportunities for leadership by whoever is present at the time.

Perhaps the question is not whether individual traits determine leader effectiveness. A more appropriate question is, "Under what conditions will individual traits influence leader effectiveness?"

Trait Theory of Leadership

Strengths	Weaknesses

LEADERSHIP STYLES

Perhaps Benjamin Franklin became a leader through his style of relating to others. Franklin was noted for his charm, conversational skills, humor, wisdom, and kindness. But was Franklin's leadership style the same as George Washington's or Thomas Jefferson's? Even casual observation of leaders in action reveals marked differences in their styles of leadership. *Style* refers to the way in which something is said or done. It is usually contrasted with the *substance* of the statements and actions. The style with which an action is executed can carry as many messages as does the substance of the action itself—style affects its legitimacy and credibility.

Three main styles of leadership have been identified: autocratic, democratic, and laissez-faire. **Autocratic leaders** dictate orders and determine all policy without involving group members in decision making. **Democratic leaders** set policies through group discussion and decision, encouraging and helping group members to interact, requesting the cooperation of others, and being considerate of members' feelings and needs. **Laissez-faire leaders** do not participate at all in their group's decision-making processes.

Aggressive acts were more frequent under autocratic and laissez-faire leaders than they were under a democratic leader. Hostility was thirty times as great in the autocratic groups than in either of the other two: Frequently one group member was made the target of hostility and aggression until he or she left the group, and then another member would be chosen to perform the same function. Nineteen of twenty members liked the democratic leader better than the autocrat, and seven of ten liked the laissez-faire leader better than the autocrat.

The pioneering study of whether leadership styles do in fact make a difference in group functioning was conducted by Lewin, Lippitt, and White (1939). Although the study has many shortcomings, it demonstrates strikingly that the same group behaves in markedly different ways under leaders with different leadership style. As discussed in Chapter 1, this study focused on groups of ten- and eleven-year-olds who were led by three adult leaders, each of whom adopted a different leadership style for a specified period. When the groups were under an autocratic leader, the children were more dependent on the leader and more egocentric in their peer relationships. When rotated to a democratic style of leadership, the same children took more initiative and responsibility, were friendlier, and continued to work when the leader was out of the room. Their interest in their work and in the quality of their product was higher. Aggressive acts were more frequent under autocratic and laissez-faire leaders than they were under a democratic leader. Hostility was thirty times as great in the autocratic groups as in either of the other two. Nineteen of twenty group members liked the democratic leader better than the autocrat, and seven of ten liked the laissez-faire leader better than the autocrat.

Since this classic study a number of researchers have investigated the relative impact of democratic and autocratic leaders on group functioning. In reviewing these studies, Stogdill (1974) noted that neither democratic nor autocratic leadership could guarantee increased productivity but member satisfaction is more strongly associated with a democratic style of leadership. Satisfaction with democratic leadership tends to be highest in small, interaction-oriented groups. Other studies have compared permissive, follower-oriented, participative, and considerate leadership styles with restrictive, task-oriented, directive, socially distant, and structured leadership styles. After reviewing the studies in each of these areas, Stogdill (1974) concluded:

1. Person-oriented styles of leadership are not consistently related to productivity.
2. Among the work-oriented leadership styles, socially distant, directive, and structured leader behaviors that tend to maintain role differentiation and let members know what to expect are consistently related to group productivity.

3. Among the person-oriented leadership styles, only those providing for member participation in decision making and showing concern for members' welfare and comfort are consistently related to group cohesiveness.
4. Among the work-oriented leadership styles, only the structuring of member expectations is related uniformly to group cohesiveness.
5. All of the person-oriented leadership styles tend to be related to member satisfaction.
6. Only the structuring of member expectations is related positively to member satisfaction among the work-oriented leadership styles.

Thus, the most effective style of leadership (i.e., it promotes group productivity, cohesiveness, and satisfaction) is showing concern for the well-being and contributions of group members while at the same time **initiating group structure** by clearly defining one's role as a leader and what one expects from the other members.

Two major shortcomings of the style approach to leadership are that different styles are effective under different conditions, and an unlimited number of styles may be identified. Certain conditions exist, for example, under which autocratic leadership seems more effective (such as when an urgent decision has to be made). In other conditions, a democratic style may be most effective (such as when considerable member commitment to the implementation of the decision needs to be built). Conditions even exist in which the laissez-faire style seems best (such as when the group

is committed to a decision, has the resources to implement it, and needs a minimum of interference to work effectively). Because different **leadership styles** are required in different situations, even with the same group, the attention of many social scientists has moved to **situational approaches to leadership**. But before considering such approaches, two other theories of leadership are briefly discussed.

In support of the style theories of leadership, however, is the notion of equifinality, which posits that there are many different ways that a person, group, or organization can behave and still achieve the same outcome. Equifinality implies that different leaders can behave in their own quite idiosyncratic and unique ways and still achieve the same outcome. Rather than trying to tailor their behavior to the situation, leaders may know how they prefer to operate and what they are able to do easily and well, and engage in those behaviors and still get key leadership tasks accomplished.

Style Theory of Leadership

Strengths	Weaknesses

INFLUENCE THEORY OF LEADERSHIP

A leader is a man who has the ability to get other people to do what they don't want to do, and like it.

Harry S. Truman

Leadership is the ability to decide what is to be done, and then to get others to want to do it.

Dwight D. Eisenhower

"Leadership appears to be the art of getting others to want to do something that you are convinced should be done."

Vance Packard, *The Pyramid Climbers*

Benjamin Franklin may have been an outstanding leader because he knew how to influence people. **Leadership** is influencing other group members. An influence approach to leadership implies that a reciprocal role relationship exists between leaders and followers in which an exchange, or transaction, takes place. Without followers there can

be no leader, and without a leader there can be no followers. As Homans stated, *"Influence over others is purchased at the price of allowing oneself to be influenced by others"* (1961, p. 286). The leader receives status, recognition, esteem, and other reinforcement for contributing his or her resources to the accomplishment of the group's goals. The followers obtain the leader's resources and ability to structure the group's activities toward the attainment of a goal. The leader provides structure, direction, and resources. The followers provide deference and reinforcement. Because both the leader and the followers control resources the other desires, each influences the other's behavior.

The interdependence of leader and followers has been demonstrated by a number of studies. Leaders tend both to talk more than other group members and receive more communications than do other group members (Zander, 1979). The person who talks the most in the group is the most likely to emerge as leader (the average correlation between participation and leadership is 0.65) (Burke, 1974; Stein & Heller, 1979). A member's proportion of talking time increases as his or her perceived leadership status increases and as members' support for his or her leadership increases (Bavelas, Hostoft, Gross, & Kite, 1965; Pepinsky, Hemphill, & Shevitz, 1958; Zdep & Oakes, 1967). Quantity of participation is seen as a sign of motivation, involvement, willingness to share resources with the group, and seriously trying to contribute to the group's goals (Sorrentino & Boutillier, 1975). The compliance of members is greater when a leader justifies his or her demands as being good for the group, has the power to punish members who do not do as he or she has asked, and has a legitimate right to make demands of subordinates (Michener & Burt, 1975). The success or failure of the group does not seem to affect a leader's ability to influence, nor does approval of him or her by subordinates.

Viewing leadership as a reciprocal influence between a leader and a set of followers does not mean that good leadership is based on domination. Hitler, for example, defined leadership as the ability to move the masses (through persuasion or violence). Ho Chi Minh believed a good leader must learn to mold, shape, and change the people just as a woodworker must learn to use wood. Both views are erroneous. Leaders do not influence through domination and coercion. The influence of leaders is directed toward persuading group members to cooperate in setting and achieving goals. Leadership, thus, is the art of ensuring that group members work together with the least friction and the most cooperation. This often means that leaders need to persuade and inspire members to follow the leader's views of what needs to be done in order to achieve the group's goals.

Influence Theory of Leadership

Strengths	Weaknesses

ROLE POSITION/GROUP STRUCTURE APPROACH TO LEADERSHIP

Perhaps Benjamin Franklin was known as a leader simply because he was appointed to various leadership positions. The **role position approach to leadership** posits that a person becomes a leader when he or she is put in a position of authority. Within groups, leadership begins with the formal role structure that defines the group's hierarchy of authority. **Authority** is legitimate power assigned to a particular position to ensure that individuals in subordinate positions meet the requirements of their organizational roles. Because organizations demand that subordinates obey their superiors when performing their roles, a person with authority influences his or her subordinates. In short, the person who is directly above you in the authority hierarchy is your leader.

There are, however, few leaders in an authority hierarchy who do not also have a boss. Thus, to the person's subordinates the person is a leader, but to the person's superiors the person is a follower. This reality means that individuals in formal leadership positions must continuously balance acting as if their own leader need not know what they are doing and mindlessly passing on to their subordinates whatever direction is given by their superiors. Very little research has been focused on balancing the roles of leader and follower simultaneously.

There are at least three problems with the role position approach to leadership. (1) Individuals are appointed to high-authority positions for a variety of reasons, not all of which have to do with leadership ability. If one wants to know who is likely to occupy a position of formal leadership, the place to look is the opportunity structure of the society. As is frequently noted, if you want to be king, your best bet is to be the son of a king or queen. (2) The theory does not explain how the leader can engage in nonleadership behaviors and how the subordinates can engage in leadership actions. Not all of the appointed leader's actions are leadership behavior. In addition, subordinates can provide leadership. (3) The role behavior of subordinates is influenced by outsiders who have no direct authority over them.

Authority-Position Theory of Leadership

Strengths	Weaknesses

EXERCISE 5.3

UNDERSTANDING YOUR LEADERSHIP ACTIONS: QUESTIONNAIRE

Each of the following items describes a leadership action. For each question, mark:

    5 if you always behave that way
    4 if you frequently behave that way
    3 if you occasionally behave that way
    2 if you seldom behave that way
    1 if you never behave that way

WHEN I AM A MEMBER OF A GROUP

_____ 1. I offer facts and give my opinions, ideas, feelings, and information in order to help the group discussion.

_____ 2. I make sure I understand what other group members say by restating it in my own words. I use good communication skills and help facilitate effective communication among group members.

_____ 3. I give direction to the group by calling attention to the tasks that need to be done and suggesting procedures for completing them. I organize role responsibilities for group members.

_____ 4. I promote the open discussion of conflicts among group members in order to resolve disagreements and mediate when the members seem unable to resolve the conflicts directly.

_____ 5. I tell jokes and make amusing comments in order to make members laugh and to increase the fun we have working together.

_____ 6. I summarize the contributions of group members into one condensed statement and integrate all the diverse actions of members into a unified whole.

_____ 7. I express support, acceptance, and liking for other members of the group, and give appropriate recognition and praise when another member has taken a constructive action in the group.

_____ 8. I ask for facts, information, opinions, ideas, and feelings from the other group members in order to use all the group's resources to complete the task.

_____ 9. I encourage all members of the group to participate. I try to give them the confidence to contribute actively to the group effort. I let them know I value their contributions.

_____ 10. I ask others to explain the group's answers and conclusions to ensure that they comprehend and understand the material being discussed by the group.

_____ 11. I give the group energy. I try to get group members excited about achieving our goals.

_____ 12. I observe the way the group is working and use my observations to help discuss how group members can work together better.

SCORING THE LEADERSHIP QUESTIONNAIRE

To obtain a total score for **task actions** and maintenance actions, write the score for each item in the appropriate column and then add the columns. You can plot your results in Figure 5.2.

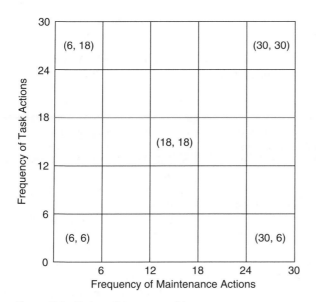

Figure 5.2 Task maintenance grid

Task Actions	**Maintenance Actions**
_____ 1. Information and opinion giver	_____ 2. Communication facilitator
_____ 3. Direction and role definer	_____ 4. Interpersonal problem solver
_____ 6. Summarizer	_____ 5. Tension reliever
_____ 8. Information and opinion seeker	_____ 7. Supporter and praiser
_____ 10. Checker for understanding	_____ 9. Encourager of participation
_____ 11. Energizer	_____ 12. Process observer
_____ **Total for Task Actions**	_____ **Total for Maintenance Actions**

TASK/MAINTENANCE PATTERNS

(6, 6) Only a minimum effort is given to getting the required work done. There is general noninvolvement with other group members. The person with this score may well be saying: "To hell with it all!" Or he or she may be so inactive in the group as to have no influence whatsoever on other group members.

(6, 30) High value is placed on keeping good relationships within the group. Thoughtful attention is given to the needs of other members. The person with the score helps create a comfortable, friendly atmosphere and work tempo. However, he or she may never help the group get any work accomplished.

(30, 6) Getting the job done is emphasized in a way that shows very little concern with group maintenance. Work is seen as important, and relationships among group members are ignored. The person with this score may take an army-drillmaster approach to leadership.

(18, 18) The task and maintenance needs of the group are balanced. The person with this score continually makes compromises between task needs and maintenance needs. Though a great compromiser, this person does not look for or find ways to creatively integrate task and maintenance activities for optimal productivity.

(30, 30) When everyone plans and makes decisions together, all the members become committed to getting the task done as they build relationships of trust and respect.

continued on next page

continued from previous page

MATCHING EXERCISE 1

To help you learn the task and maintenance actions, match the following terms with their definitions (answers appear on page 200).

Goal Actions

_____ 1. Information and opinion giver
_____ 2. Information and opinion seeker
_____ 3. Direction and role definer
_____ 4. Summarizer
_____ 5. Energizer
_____ 6. Checker for understanding

Relationship Actions

_____ 7. Encourager of participation
_____ 8. Communication facilitator
_____ 9. Tension reliever
_____ 10. Process observer
_____ 11. Interpersonal problem solver
_____ 12. Supporter and praiser

a. Makes sure all group members understand what other members say.
b. Pulls together related ideas or suggestions and restates them.
c. Offers facts, opinions, ideas, feelings, and information.
d. Expresses acceptance and liking for group members.
e. Uses observations of how the group is working to help discuss how the group can improve.
f. Lets members know their contributions are valued.
g. Asks for facts, opinions, ideas, feelings, and information.
h. Asks others to summarize the discussion to make sure they understand.
i. Encourages group members to work hard to achieve goals.
j. Calls attention to tasks that need to be done and assigns responsibilities.
k. Helps resolve and mediate conflicts.
l. Tells jokes and increases the group fun.

MATCHING EXERCISE 2: HOW WELL DO I UNDERSTAND FUNCTIONING (LEADERSHIP) SKILLS?

The goal and relationship leadership skills are listed in column 1 and statements expressing the skills are in column 2. For each skill, indicate which statement (*a* through *l*) expresses it.

Goal Actions

_____ 1. Information and opinion giver
_____ 2. Information and opinion seeker
_____ 3. Direction and role definer
_____ 4. Summarizer
_____ 5. Energizer
_____ 6. Checker for understanding

a. "Helen, my understanding of you is that you are suggesting that we define the problem before we try to solve it."
b. "How about giving our report on yoga while standing on our heads?"
c. "Three ideas have been suggested. Dale thinks we should play football, José thinks we should go to lunch, and Tai believes we should write a story about what we are doing."

Relationship Actions

____ 7. Encourager of participation
____ 8. Communication facilitator
____ 9. Tension reliever
____ 10. Process observer
____ 11. Interpersonal problem solver
____ 12. Supporter and praiser

d. "I think we should help resolve the conflict between David and Linda."

e. "George Washington was the first President of the United States and in my opinion, the best one."

f. "Francene has not said anything for the past five minutes. Is there a problem?"

g. "That is an important insight, Roger. It indicates you have really worked hard on the homework."

h. "Fire up! We can find a good solution. Let's put a little more effort into it."

i. "Frank, explain to us step-by-step how to solve question 12."

j. "We should first define the problem and second suggest solutions. We can then decide which solution to adopt."

k. "Roger, do you know who the fourth President of the United States was and what he is famous for?"

l. "Helen, I would like to hear what you think about this; you have good ideas."

SITUATIONAL THEORIES OF LEADERSHIP

Perhaps Benjamin Franklin became a renowned leader because he was able to vary his behavior from situation to situation to provide the appropriate leadership actions at the appropriate time. The situational theory of leadership posits that leadership is provided by group members varying their behavior to provide the actions a group needs at that specific time. Four situational theories are discussed here: the distributed- actions theory, Bales's interaction-process analysis, Fiedler's contingency theory, and Hersey and Blanchard's situational theory.

The Distributed-Actions Theory of Leadership

Not the cry, but the flight of the wild duck, leads the flock to fly and follow.

Chinese Proverb

The **distributed-actions theory of leadership** emphasizes that certain functions need to be provided if a group is to achieve its goals and maintain effective working relationships among members (Benne & Sheats, 1948). A *function* is an action that must take place in order for a group to be effective. At different times, different functions are needed. At one time, information may be needed, while at another time the information provided by members may need to be summarized and integrated. To help reach group goals, members must engage in the *goal-leadership actions* of contributing, asking for, summarizing, and coordinating information, structuring and directing the group's efforts, and providing the energy to motivate members. It does no good to achieve goals successfully if the manner of doing so alienates group members. In addition, group members must engage in the *relationship-leadership actions* of listening carefully and respectfully to one another, encouraging the participation of all members, facilitating communication, relieving tension, assessing the emotional climate of the group, and discussing how the group's work can be improved. Thus, any member provides leadership when he or she engages in an action that helps the group complete its goals and maintain effective working relationships, or arranges for someone else to engage in the needed functions (Benne & Sheats, 1948; Hackman, 2002; Hackman & Wageman, 2005; Johnson, 1970; Johnson & Johnson, 1997; McGrath, 1962).

Leadership, therefore, is specific to the situation. Each group member provides leadership by having the diagnostic skills to be aware that a given function is needed in the immediate situation in order for the group to function most effectively, have the flexibility to provide the diverse types of actions needed for different situations, and be able to utilize the abilities of other group members in providing the actions needed by the group. Responsibility for providing leadership needs to be distributed among all group members for at least three reasons. First, if members do not participate, then their ideas, skills, and information are not being utilized. This reduces the group's effectiveness. Second, members who participate become more committed to the group than do members who remain silent. Third, unequal patterns of participation can create relationship problems in the group as active members often become worried about or annoyed by the silent members and view them as unconcerned about goal achievement.

Many theorists note that without followers, there can be no leaders. Most, however, believe that leaders act and followers mainly react. The opposite is true as well. Leaders are also followers, and followers also exhibit leadership. The distributed functions theory of leadership is one of the few theories that make this explicit. A group member is not either a leader or a follower, he or she is both. The distinction between leaders and followers becomes moot, unnecessary, and unhelpful.

The distributed-actions theory of leadership is one of the most concrete and direct approaches available for improving your leadership skills and for improving the effectiveness of the groups to which you belong. Any group member can be taught the diagnostic skills and behaviors that help a group accomplish its goal and maintain

effective working relationships among members. There is, however, some criticism of the approach. There are so many different actions members can take to help in achieving goals and maintaining relationships that specific ones are hard to pin down. What constitutes leadership, then, depends on the view of the person who is listing the leadership behaviors. Finally, it is unclear whether this view of leadership is useful in understanding the leadership of larger and more complex entities, such as organizations and nations.

EXAMPLE OF A LEADER: HARRIET TUBMAN

Harriet Tubman was born a slave about 1820 in Bucktown, Maryland. Her grandparents had been brought from Africa to America sometime after 1725. Very early in life, Harriet developed a rebellious nature, perhaps from the hard work and many beatings she endured. She was determined to be free. At age fifteen she was beaten nearly to death with a 2-pound iron counterweight for helping another slave to escape. She never completely recovered, having a dent in her skull and seizures during which she would suddenly fall asleep. In 1849, Harriet escaped to Delaware and then to Pennsylvania. While working in Philadelphia, she became involved with the Underground Railroad—a network of routes, guides, and hiding places that helped runaway slaves reach freedom in the northern states. As early as 1850 she began working as a guide, or "conductor," for the railroad, risking her life over and over again to help others gain their freedom. She was given the name Moses for the frequency with which she conducted runaways to the North and was so successful that a reward of $40,000 was offered for her capture. In all, she helped at least 300 slaves escape. After the Fugitive Slave Law was passed in 1850, Harriet conducted escaped slaves all the way to Canada. During the Civil War she worked as a nurse, laundress, cook, and spy for the Union army in South Carolina. She spent the rest of her life working to feed and house needy blacks and to gain full freedom for them. She died at about the age of ninety-three on March 10, 1913. She embodies a leader whose actions spoke louder than words.

Bales's Interaction-Process Analysis

If you put five strangers together and assign them a task that requires them to cooperate, something quite remarkable but very predictable happens: The social interaction among them becomes patterned and a leadership structure emerges. One member tends to assume a *task-leadership role* that includes behaviors oriented primarily to task achievement (such as directing, summarizing, and providing ideas). Another member tends to assume a *social-emotional-leadership role* that includes behaviors oriented primarily to the expressive, interpersonal affairs of the group (such as alleviating frustrations, resolving tensions, and mediating conflicts).

Robert Bales (1950, 1952, 1955), in a series of studies in the late 1940s and early 1950s, was among the first to focus on task and social-emotional leadership. His work has been corroborated and extended by Burke (1972). The basic interaction-process theory consists of the following points:

1. When a group has a task to complete, its members engage in task-related behaviors on an unequal basis.
2. The members who are high on task behaviors tend to create some tension and hostility on the part of members who are less committed to the task.
3. There is a need for actions that help maintain effective working relationships among members.
4. Social-emotional actions are engaged in by members other than those high on task actions.
5. These differentiated roles (task and social-emotional) are stabilized and synchronized as the task and social-emotional leaders reinforce and support each other.

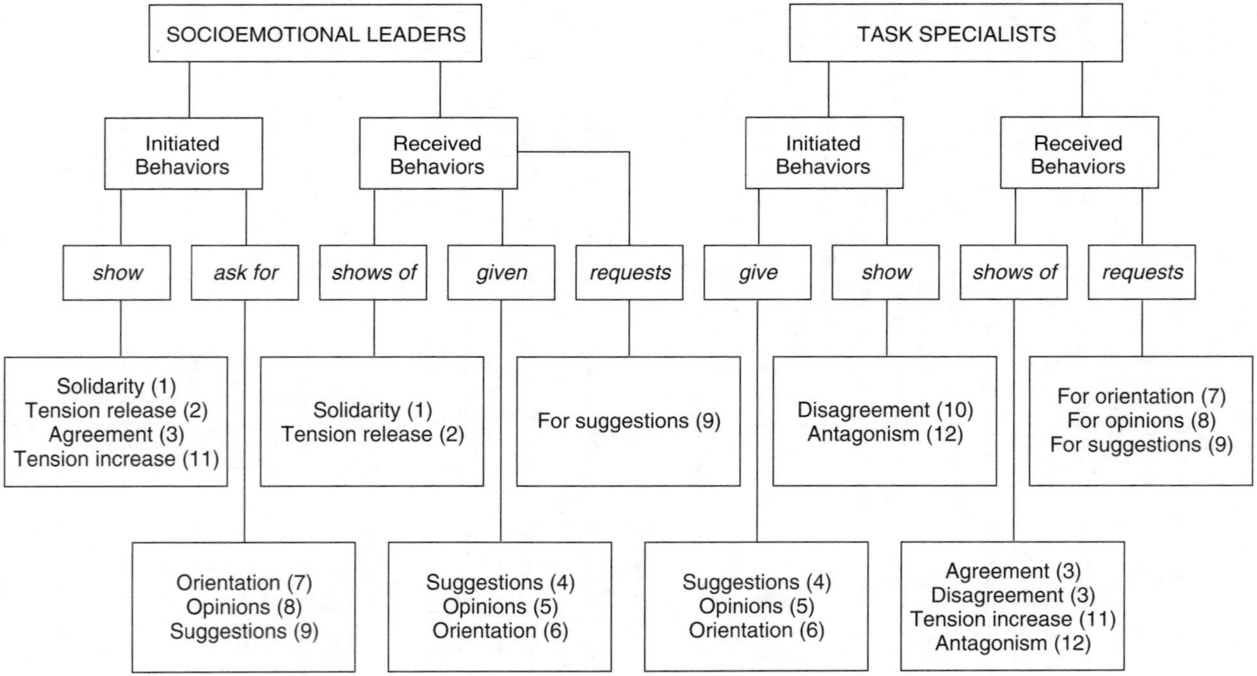

Figure 5.3 How behaviors differ for socioemotional leaders and task specialists. (Numbers in parentheses are category numbers from Bales's interaction process analysis.)

Bales developed an observational instrument for identifying task and social-emotional behaviors within a small group (Figure 5.3). The instrument consists of several categories that are designed to allow a systematic classification of all the acts of participation in a group.

Bales's (1950, 1952, 1955) research indicates that positive emotions (categories 1, 2, and 3) are usually expressed more than twice as often as negative emotions (10, 11, and 12). Opinions and information are much more often volunteered (46% of all participant behaviors observed) than asked for (7%). Problem-solving groups tend to progress through three stages: orientation (What is the problem?), evaluation (How do we feel about it?), and control (What should we do about it?). As the discussion moves from the intellectual examination of the problem (the orientation phase) to evaluation and decision (the control phase), emotions are expressed more often.

Fiedler's Contingency Theory of Leadership

Fred Fiedler (1964, 1967, 1969) was the first psychologist to present a model of leadership that dealt with both leader orientation and situational variables. Contingency models of leadership assume that there is an interaction between a leader's traits and the current situation. Fiedler defined a leader's effectiveness in terms of the group's performance in achieving its goals. He identified three key situational conditions in a group—leader-member relations, task clarity, and leader power—that determine which type of leadership is most beneficial for the group. Fiedler divided leaders into those who were task-oriented and those who were maintenance-oriented, arguing that orientations were rather enduring characteristics not subject to change or adaptation (i.e., traits). Task-oriented leaders emphasize the work the group needs to do; maintenance-oriented leaders focus on maintaining group participation. Fiedler found no consistent relationship between group effectiveness and leadership behaviors, as maintenance-oriented leaders were more effective in certain situations and task-oriented leaders more effective in other situations.

A *task-oriented leader* is effective under two sets of conditions. In the first, he or she is on good terms with the group members, the task is clearly structured, and the leader has a position of high authority and power. In this situation, the group is ready to be directed and is willing to be told what to do, and the leader can focus attention on completing the task. In the second set of conditions, the leader is on poor terms with group members, the task is ambiguous, and the leader has low authority and power. The leader's effectiveness then depends on taking responsibility for making decisions and directing group members. On the other hand, when moderately good or poor relations exist between the leader and the group members, when the leader has a position of moderate authority and power, and when the task is moderately clear, the *maintenance-oriented leader* who emphasizes member participation in decision making tends to be more effective.

There are some difficulties with Fiedler's theory. For example, how can a person tell if the situational conditions of leader-member relations, task clarity, and leader power are high, moderate, or low? Almost all group situations fall into the moderate range; in only the most extreme cases are the sets of conditions in the high or low categories. Moreover, are leader-member relations, task clarity, and leader power the only situational factors that group leaders should be aware of? What other elements of a given situation might influence leadership styles? A good leader always pays attention to the situational conditions that influence the group, modifying his or her behavior to make it effective. Finally, there are general weaknesses to contingency theories. Contingency models tend to become more and more complex as research identifies more and more potential moderators between personal and situations attributes. The more complete a contingency theory, therefore, the more complex it is and the less practically useful it will be.

EXERCISE 5.4

THE LEAST PREFERRED CO-WORKER SCALE

Fiedler (1978) developed an indirect measure of leadership style known as the *Least Preferred Co-Worker (LPC) Scale*. Think of a person with whom you have a difficult working relationship, someone you work with now, or someone you knew in the past. This person need not be the one you liked least but should be the person with whom you have had the most difficulty working.

On the LPC Scale following, circle the number that best describes where you would place yourself in the spectrum defined by each adjective pair. To calculate your total score, add up the numbers you have circled for each of the adjective pairs. Your score will fall somewhere between 16 and 128. If your score is 56 or less, you are a low-LPC leader. The lower your score, the more task oriented you are. If your score is 63 or above, you are a high-LPC leader. The higher your LPC score, the more relationship oriented you are. If your score falls between 56 and 63, you do not fit easily into either category and may call yourself socioindependent.

According to Fiedler (1978), people who describe their least preferred co-worker in very negative, rejecting terms are so oriented toward completing the task that it completely determines their perception of co-workers with whom they have trouble working. In effect, they say, "If I cannot work with you, if you frustrate my need to get the job done, then you cannot be good in other respects. You are unfriendly, unpleasant, cold, and nasty." People who describe their least preferred co-workers in positive terms are relationship oriented. In effect, they say, "Even though I cannot work with you, getting the job done is not everything, and I can still see you as friendly, relaxed, and interesting."

ORGANIZATIONAL LEADERSHIP

Whenever anyone asks me [how to be a leader] I tell them I have the secret to success in life. The secret to success is to stay in love. Staying in love gives you the fire to really ignite other people, to see inside other people, to have a greater desire to get things done than other people. A person who is not in love doesn't really feel the kind of excitement that helps them to get ahead and lead others and to achieve. I don't know any other fire, any other thing in life that is more exhilarating and is more positive a feeling than love is.

Army Major General John H. Stanford (Kouzes & Posner, 1987)

On July 15, 1982, Don Bennett, a Seattle businessman, was the first amputee ever to climb Mount Rainier (reported by Kouzes & Posner, 1987). He climbed 14,410 feet on one leg and two crutches. It took him five days. When asked to state the most important lesson he learned from doing so, without hesitation, he said, "You can't do it alone."

What did he mean? There were many ways in which others helped him achieve his goal, including his daughter. During one very difficult trek across an ice field, his daughter stayed by his side for four hours and with each new hop told him, "You can do it, Dad. You're the best dad in the world. You can do it, Dad." The encouragement by his daughter kept him going, strengthening his commitment to make it to the top. For groups and organizations the situation is similar. With colleagues cheering them on, members amaze themselves with what they can accomplish.

There is growth and decline. Staying the same is not an option. Growth takes leadership, not management. There is a difference. Some individuals manage, some individuals lead. Leaders take us on journeys to places we have never been before. Managers tend to handle the status quo. The metaphor of the journey may be the most appropriate metaphor for discussing the tasks of organizational leaders. Leading an organization involves five steps (Johnson & Johnson, 1994; Kouzes & Posner, 1987):

1. Challenging the status quo of the traditional competitive and individualistic models of management.
2. Inspiring a clear mutual vision of what the organization should and could be, a clear mission that all members are committed to achieving, and a set of goals that guide members' efforts.
3. Empowering members through teams. Being part of a team empowers each member to accomplish things beyond his or her individual expertise, both technically and interpersonally.
4. Leading by example by modeling the behaviors the leader recommends to the members of the organization, including teamwork and taking risks to increase expertise.
5. Encouraging the hearts of members to persist and keep striving when work gets difficult.

Challenging the Status Quo

Organizations and groups are sites for an inevitable and external conflict. On one side are the forces of maintenance and continuity (i.e., the status quo), which strive to create and sustain orderly and predictable procedures. Opposing them are the forces of innovation and discontinuity, which seek to alter established practices. Both forces seek the same goal of team and organizational productivity, and both forces are needed. The creative tension between the two is the force that produces considered and thoughtful development and change.

These same two forces operate within the individual member. Group members experience the conflict between the security of the past and the satisfaction of increased expertise and accomplishment. The status quo side wants to continue what was done in the past, while the enhanced expertise side strives for growth, change, and increased competence. Leaving the status quo and risking one's current success against the potential of being even better in the future requires courage.

In challenging the status quo, leaders highlight that if members are not working to increase their expertise, they are losing their expertise. **Expertise** is a process, not an end product. Any person or organization is constantly changing. If expertise is not growing, then it is declining. The minute a person believes he or she is an expert and stops trying to learn more, then he or she is losing expertise. Leaders must lead members toward enhanced expertise, not manage for bureaucratic control. And the clearest and most direct challenge to traditional competitive and individualistic actions is the adoption of cooperative teams within the organization. The organization needs to be transformed into an interlocking network of cooperative teams in order to increase productivity, promote more supportive and committed relationships, and increase members' psychological adjustment and self-esteem.

Creating a Mutual Vision

The second leadership responsibility is to create a joint vision of what the team or organization should and could be, a clear mission that all members are committed to achieving, and a set of goals that guide members' efforts. *To do so a leader must:*

1. Have a vision/dream of what the organization could be.
2. Communicate that vision with commitment and enthusiasm.
3. Make it a *shared* vision that staff members adopt as their own.
4. Make it a rational vision based on theory and research and sound implementation procedures.

Leaders enthusiastically and frequently communicate the dreams of the team and organization as being places where individuals share, help, encourage, and support each other's efforts to achieve and succeed—places where *we* dominates *me*. Working together to get the job done creates caring and committed relationships that propel members forward in their mutual search for excellence.

Leaders inspire a shared vision. It is the common vision that creates a basic sense of sink or swim together (i.e., positive interdependence) among members. Leaders breathe life into the hopes and dreams of others and enable them to see the exciting possibilities the future holds by striving for a common purpose. The vision and its advocacy, furthermore, have to be rational. The new practices have to be backed up with knowledge of the relevant research and theory. A person with no followers is not a leader, and people will not become followers until they accept a vision as their own. It is the long-term promise of achieving something worthwhile and meaningful that powers an individual's drive toward greater expertise. You cannot command commitment, you can only inspire it!

Empowering Members Through Teams

The most important of all the five leadership practices is empowering individuals by organizing them into cooperative teams. To be effective, a cooperative team must be carefully structured to include positive interdependence, face-to-face promotive interaction, individual accountability, social skills, and group processing (Johnson, Johnson, & Holubec, 2008).

The one-word test to detect whether someone is on the road to becoming a leader is *we*. Leaders do not achieve success by themselves. It is not *my* personal best that leaders inspire, it is *our* personal best. The most important thing a leader can do is to organize members so that they work together, for at least two reasons. The first is to promote committed and caring relationships among organization members. This is achieved through a team approach. Cooperative efforts result in trust, open communication, and interpersonal support, all of which are crucial ingredients for productivity. When trust is broken by competition, harsh feelings, criticism, negative comments, and disrespect, productivity suffers. The second is to empower staff members through teamwork. By organizing members into teams, leaders increase members' confidence that if they exert effort, they will be successful.

Leading by Example

One does not improve through argument but through examples....
Be what you wish to make others become. Make yourself, not your
words, a sermon.

Henri Frederic Amiel

Organizational leaders model teamwork and risk taking to increase productivity and technical and interpersonal expertise. Leaders practice what they preach. They walk their talk. They speak coherently about their vision and values and make their actions congruent with their words. They especially model taking on challenging tasks, failing, learning from mistakes, and trying again.

Encouraging the Heart

Love 'em and lead 'em.

Major General John H. Stanford,
Commander, U.S. Army

Leaders are vigilant about the little things that make a big difference. Each spring at Verstec, annual bonuses are given to about 2,000 nonmanagerial personnel (Kouzes & Posner, 1987). One year, the president arrived at the celebration dressed in a satin costume, riding atop an elephant, and

accompanied by the Stanford Marching Band. The president said, "If you are going to give someone a check, don't just mail it. Have a celebration."

This example may seem extreme, but it makes a difference when each member knows that his or her hard work and successes are perceived, recognized, and celebrated. Leaders search out "good news" opportunities and orchestrate celebrations. Members become exhausted, frustrated, and disenchanted. They often are tempted to give up. Leaders inspire staff members by giving them the courage and hope to continue the quest by:

1. Recognizing individual contributions to the common vision.
2. Celebrating individual and joint accomplishments frequently.

To give individual recognition and have a group celebration requires a cooperative organizational structure. In competitions, to declare one person a winner is to declare all others losers. Group celebrations do not take place in competitive/individualistic organizations. In such environments, praise may be perceived to be phony or satirical, and recognition may be the source of embarrassment and anxiety about future retaliation by colleagues. Within cooperative enterprises, however, genuine acts of caring draw people together and forward. Love of their work and each other is what inspires many members to commit more and more of their energy to their jobs. Establishing a cooperative structure and encouraging the development of caring and committed relationships among members may just be the best-kept secret of exemplary leadership.

Understanding Bad Leadership

There is an increasing interest in the dynamics of bad leadership. Much of this interest is based on research findings that poor leaders do not just have low scores on the same dimensions as good leaders, they exhibit entirely different patterns of behavior. Good and bad leadership may be qualitatively different phenomena (Kellerman, 2004; Sternberg, 2007).

WHAT IF YOU DO NOT WANT TO BE A LEADER?

If you follow the rules given below carefully, you can be guaranteed to never be a leader:

1. Be absent from group meetings as frequently as possible.
2. When you do attend, contribute nothing.
3. If you do participate, come on strong early in the discussion. Demonstrate your knowledge of everything, including your extensive vocabulary of big words and technical jargon.
4. Indicate that you will do only what you have to and nothing more.
5. Read the paper or knit during meetings.

TOWER-BUILDING

This exercise provides participants with an opportunity to observe leadership behavior in a situation of intergroup competition in which verbal communication is not allowed. Several groups are needed for this exercise, all of which should have at least seven members. The task of each group is to build a tower from supplied materials. A large room is needed so that the groups can work separately (but within sight of one another). The time needed to complete the exercise is approximately one hour. The procedure is as follows:

1. Two judges are selected to determine which tower is (a) the highest, (b) the strongest, (c) the most beautiful, and (d) the most clever.
2. The class forms groups of at least seven members.
3. Each group selects two of its members to observe leadership in the group. The observers are to note the following:
   a. How the group organizes for work.
   b. How decisions are made by the group.
   c. Whether participation and influence are distributed throughout the group or whether a few members dominate.
   d. What task and maintenance actions are needed to improve the functioning of the group.
   e. How the group reacts to winning or losing.
4. Each group receives a box of supplies containing construction paper, newsprint, tape, magazines, crayons, pipe cleaners, scissors, and glue.
5. The groups have twenty minutes to build their towers. This is a *nonverbal exercise: No talking among group members or between groups is allowed*.
6. During the twenty minutes, the judges meet to decide how they will evaluate the towers on the basis of the four criteria given. At the end of the twenty minutes, the judges decide which tower wins and award a box of candy (provided by the person conducting the exercise) to the winning group.
7. The groups meet with their observers and discuss the exercise. All impressions concerning how the group functioned and what leadership patterns were present and absent should be presented and reviewed.

HOLLOW SQUARE

The Hollow Square exercise is a problem-solving situation in which you can observe leadership functions. You can see the processes of group planning, the problems of communication between a planning group and an implementing group, and the problems with which an implementing group must cope when carrying out a plan it did not make itself. All of these processes require effective leadership behavior. The objectives of the exercise are to provide a

continued on next page

continued from previous page

problem-solving task in which you can observe leadership behavior, increase your awareness of the problems involved in using a formal hierarchy in group problem solving, and give you practice in observing groups and in giving the group feedback on your observations.

The exercise is carried out in clusters of ten to twelve people. Each cluster is divided into three subgroups: four persons are planners, four are implementers, and the rest are observers. The planners decide how they are going to instruct the implementers to do a task, the implementers carry out the task as best they can, and the observers watch the process of both groups in the two phases. Here is the specific procedure for the coordinator of the exercise:

1. Tell the participants the objectives of the exercise, and divide them into four-person planning teams, four-person implementing teams, and observers. Each team goes to a separate room or different parts of a large room (out of earshot) to await instructions.
2. Hand out the appropriate instruction sheets to each team. Give them adequate time to read them; then review them with each team. The observers should be fully briefed first, the planners next, and the implementers last.
3. The planners are given the general diagram sheet and the pieces of the puzzle and are instructed to begin phase I. Each planner is given four pieces of the puzzle. The exact distribution of the pieces is not crucial, but they should not have any labels marked on them. Phase I lasts forty-five minutes. All information the planners need to know is on their briefing sheet. The answer to how the puzzle fits together is on page 536.
4. At the end of phase I, the planning team gives the implementing team its instructions. The planners then are prohibited from giving any further help; they must remain silent and uninvolved as the implementing team works.
5. Implementers are to finish the task, phase II, according to their instructions, taking as much time as necessary.
6. When the task is completed, a discussion is held involving all the members of each cluster. This discussion is to include reports from the observers, planners, and implementers, and a comparison of similarities between the exercise and other organizational and group experiences of the members. Questions for the discussion should include:
   a. What leadership functions were present and absent in the planning and implementing teams? What were the consequences of their presence or absence?
   b. What leadership functions were needed for each type of activity?
   c. How could the functioning of each team have been improved?
   d. Were the leadership functions distributed among all the team members? Were participation and influence evenly distributed throughout the team?
   e. How was communication between the planning and implementing teams handled? How could it have been improved?
   f. How did it feel to wait for the planners' instructions, and how did it feel to watch the implementers carry them out?
7. The major points of the discussion should be summarized, with an emphasis on conclusions about the leadership functions being present, absent, and distributed within the teams. Other types of learning that typically take place during the exercise are:
   a. Planners often place limitations on team behavior that do not appear in the instructions, thereby making their task harder. They could, for example, ask the implementing team to observe their planning meeting.
   b. There is considerable frustration in planning something that others will carry out without your involvement. The commitment to implement a plan usually is built through the planning process, and when the planners cannot put the plan into effect, they often experience frustration.

c. Planning is so interesting and absorbing that planners can forget what their implementing team is experiencing. Implementers can become anxious because they do not know what the task will be, though this concern usually does not enter the minds of the planners.

d. Planners often fail to use all the resources at their disposal to solve the problem, such as getting the silent members of the planning team to participate.

e. Planners can spend so much time planning the task that they do not allow enough time to communicate their plans adequately to the implementers, which results in wasting much of the implementers' effort.

f. In communicating their plan to the implementing team, the planning team often does not take into account the implementers' anxieties, their need to be physically comfortable, and so on. Their preoccupation with giving information under pressure blinds them to the needs of the members of the implementing team, which reduces the effectiveness of the communication.

g. Implementers usually develop some antagonism or hostility toward their planners while they are waiting for their instructions. These feelings increase if they are given complex instructions in a short amount of time and are confused as they take responsibility for finishing the task.

INSTRUCTION SHEET FOR OBSERVERS

You will be observing a situation in which a planning team decides how to solve a problem and gives instructions to an implementing team. The problem consists of assembling sixteen flat pieces into a square that contains an empty square in its middle. The planning team is supplied with a general diagram of the assembled pieces. The planners are not allowed to put the puzzle together themselves; they are to instruct the implementing team on how to assemble the pieces in minimum time. You will be silent observers throughout the process. Half of you should observe the planners throughout the entire exercise, and half of you should observe the implementers. Observation sheets focusing upon task and maintenance leadership behaviors are provided to help you observe. Make sure you understand the behavioral roles before you begin. Some suggestions are:

1. Each observer should watch the general patterns of leadership behavior.
2. During phase I, consider the following questions:
   a. What kinds of behavior block or help the process?
   b. Are the team members participating equally?
   c. How does the planning team divide its time between planning and instructing?
   d. What group functions are not provided by the group members?
3. During the instructing process, note these behavioral questions:
   a. At the beginning of the instruction, how do the planners orient the implementers to their task?
   b. What assumptions made by the planning team are not communicated to the implementing team?
   c. How effective are the instructions?
   d. Does the implementing team appear to feel free to ask questions of the planners?
   e. What leadership functions are present and absent?
4. During the assembling period, seek answers to the following questions:
   a. How does the implementing team show that instructions were understood clearly or misunderstood?

continued on next page

continued from previous page

    b. What nonverbal reactions do planning team members show as they watch their plans being implemented or distorted?

    c. What leadership functions are present and absent?

5. You should each have two copies of the observation sheets, one for phase I and one for phase II.

INSTRUCTION SHEET FOR PLANNERS

Each of you will be given a packet containing four pieces of a puzzle. When all the pieces from all four packets are properly assembled, they will form a large square containing an empty place in the middle. A sheet bearing a diagram of the completed puzzle is provided for your team. Your task is to:

1. Plan how the sixteen pieces distributed among you can be assembled to solve the puzzle.
2. Decide on a plan for instructing your implementing team on how to carry out your plan for putting the puzzle together.
3. Call the implementing team, and begin instructing them at any time during the next forty minutes.
4. Give them at least five minutes of instructions; the implementing team must begin assembling the puzzle forty-five minutes from now.

Before you begin, read these rules:

1. During planning:
   a. Keep the pieces from your packet in front of you at all times.
   b. Do not touch the pieces or trade any of them with other persons, either now or during the instruction period.
   c. Do not assemble the square; that is the implementers' job.
   d. Do not mark any of the pieces.
2. During instruction:
   a. Give all instructions in words. Do not show the diagram to the implementers; hide it. Do not draw any diagrams yourselves, either on paper or in the air with gestures. You may give your instructions orally or on paper.
   b. The implementing team must not move the pieces until the signal is given to start phase II.
   c. Do not show any diagram to the implementers.
   d. After the signal is given for the assembly to begin, you may not give any further instructions; stand back and observe. You may not touch the pieces or in any way join in the implementers' work.

INSTRUCTION SHEET FOR IMPLEMENTERS

1. Your team will have the responsibility of carrying out a task in accordance with instructions given you by your planning team.
2. Your task will begin forty minutes from now.
3. Your planning team may call you in for instruction at any time during the next forty minutes.
4. If the planning team does not call you in during the next forty minutes, you must report to it on your own at the end of that time.

5. You may send notes to the planners, and they may send notes in reply.
6. Once you have begun the task of assembling the puzzle, your planning team is not allowed to give you any further instructions. Finish the assigned task as quickly as possible.
7. While you wait for a call from your planning team, do the following:
   a. Individually, write on a piece of paper the concerns you feel while waiting for instructions.
   b. As a group, think of anything that might help you follow instructions or keep you from doing so. Write actions that will help you on one sheet of paper and those that will hinder you on another.
   c. Make notes on how the four of you can organize as a team to receive and follow the instructions.
   d. Keep handy the sheets on which you have written these notes. You may find them useful during the discussion that takes place after you have completed the task.

EXERCISE 5.7

WHY I AM A LEADER!

Working individually, rank the five theories of leadership from:

a. Most difficult to least difficult to implement.
b. First choice to last choice for your personal plan to improve your leadership abilities.

Form a group of four members. Working cooperatively, rank the five theories, reaching consensus as to (a) their difficulty to implement and (b) the group's choice to improve members' leadership abilities.

Difficulty	Theory	My Personal Plan
_____	I plan to be genetically superior to most other people. They will realize I was born to lead, and they were born to follow me.	_____
_____	I plan to do things with such great style that I will be the leader of any group to which I belong.	_____
_____	I plan to know how to influence people so skillfully that they will gladly follow me.	_____
_____	I plan to be appointed or elected leader of every group to which I belong.	_____
_____	I plan to learn the goal and relationship skills required for groups to function effectively.	_____

SUMMARY

Small-group leadership may be defined in a variety of ways. It has been defined as a set of traits, a personal style, the ability to influence others, a role in an authority hierarchy, or the situational fulfillment of functions necessary for achieving the group's goals and maintaining effective working relationships among members. Organizational leadership involves a process of challenging the status quo, inspiring a mutual vision, empowering members through teams, leading by example, and encouraging the heart to persist.

The third guideline for creating an effective group is to ensure that leadership and participation are distributed among all group members. All members are responsible for providing leadership. The equalization of participation and leadership ensures that all members are involved in the group's work, committed to implementing the group's decisions, and satisfied with their membership. It also ensures that the resources of every member are utilized fully while increasing the cohesiveness of the group.

ANSWERS

Matching 1 (page 184): 1. c; 2. g; 3. j; 4. b; 5. i; 6. h; 7. f; 8. a; 9. l; 10. e; 11. k; 12. d.

Matching 2 (pages 184–185): 1. e; 2. k; 3. j; 4. c; 5. h; 6. i; 7. l; 8. a; 9. b; 10. f; 11. d; 12. g.

CHAPTER SIX

Using Power

BASIC CONCEPTS TO BE COVERED IN THIS CHAPTER

In this chapter a number of concepts are defined and discussed. The major ones are in the following list. Students should divide into pairs. Each pair is to (1) define each concept, noting the page on which it is defined and discussed, and (2) ensure that both members understand its meaning. Then combine into groups of four. Compare the answers of the two pairs. If there is disagreement, look up the concept in the chapter and clarify it until all members agree on and understand the definition.

CONCEPTS

1. Power
2. Constructive power
3. Destructive power
4. Dynamic interdependence view of power
5. Reactance
6. Trait factor view of power
7. Source effects (credibility, attractiveness)
8. Message effects
9. Receiver effects
10. Social dominance
11. Social exchange theory
12. Reward power
13. Coercive power
14. Legitimate power
15. Referent power
16. Expert power
17. Informational power
18. Oppression
19. Group norms
20. Group mind
21. Deindividuation

 **INTRODUCTION**

The price of greatness is responsibility.

Winston Churchill

In Orwell's fable, *Animal Farm*, the livestock of a farm overthrow their human masters and form an egalitarian system. At first, the ideology of the new order is summarized in seven simple maxims, including "All animals are equal." As the story unfolds, however, the pigs, who assume the managerial positions on the farm, soon take advantage of their new status and power to bestow all kinds of special treatment on themselves. For instance, they do none of the many arduous chores that are the essence of farm-work, and they claim as their own the farmhouse (which is the most comfortable spot on the farm). Eventually, the swine legitimize their behaviors by formally changing the farm's ideology. They delete six of the seven maxims, retaining only the equality principle, which they qualify with the addendum, "but some animals are more equal than others." In Orwell's world, the pigs, by assuming superior power and status, come to see themselves as privileged and meriting favorable treatment. What is true for pigs may also be true for humans.

Although we often may not want to admit it, power is a basic aspect of social life. It can be seized or given up, increased or lost. It can be used for good, evil, or trivial purposes. Power is a key element of every relationship we have, whether with family, friends, lovers, or coworkers. Yet many persons are unaware of the influence they exert on others, and many are unaware of how necessary and constructive mutual influence is in building effective groups and collaborative relationships. Being skillful in influencing other group members and taking responsibility for such influence are important parts of being a member of a group.

In this chapter we discuss the nature of power and its constructive and destructive uses. We also discuss direct ways of using power (Figure 6.1). These include the dynamic interdependence and the trait factor perspectives on power, the six bases of power, and the interaction between high- and low-power individuals. The discussion then moves on to indirect ways of using power, including group norms and the group mind.

THE IMAGE OF POWER

When you think of power, what images come to mind? Do you think of a football player, a great orator, a semi-truck, or a gun? Write down the images you have when you think of power. Find a partner. Share your images and listen carefully to your partner's images. Then choose the two images most illustrative of the concept *power*.

1. _____   4. _____

2. _____   5. _____

3. _____   6. _____

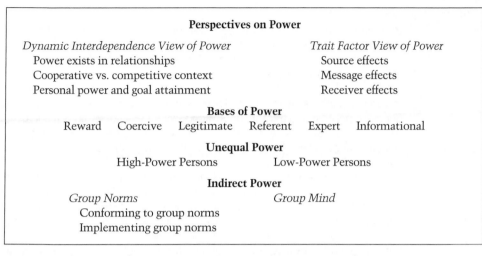

Perspectives on Power

Dynamic Interdependence View of Power   *Trait Factor View of Power*
  Power exists in relationships   Source effects
  Cooperative vs. competitive context   Message effects
  Personal power and goal attainment   Receiver effects

Bases of Power
Reward   Coercive   Legitimate   Referent   Expert   Informational

Unequal Power
High-Power Persons   Low-Power Persons

Indirect Power
Group Norms   *Group Mind*
  Conforming to group norms
  Implementing group norms

Figure 6.1   The nature of power: constructive versus destructive uses of power.

EXERCISE 6.1

IS POWER A PERSONAL OR A RELATIONSHIP ATTRIBUTE?

There has been some controversy over whether power is an attribute of a person or an aspect of a relationship between two or more persons. The purpose of this exercise is to structure a critical discussion of the issue. The procedure is as follows:

1. **Assignment of Positions:** The class forms groups of four. Each group is ultimately to write a report summarizing its position:

   Position A: Power is a personal attribute. Some people are born to wield power and some are not. Because of their innate personality and makeup, they are able to influence others and rise to positions of power.

   Position B: Power is an attribute of a relationship. For power to exist, there must be both an influencer and an influencee. In most situations, who is influencing whom to what degree changes constantly according to who has relevant information and expertise. As circumstances and situations change, the relationship changes and the relative power of group members changes.

   The report is to contain the group's overall conclusions and the facts and rationale supporting its position. The supporting facts and rationale may be obtained from this chapter, the entire book, and outside reading.

2. **Preparation Pairs:** Each group divides into pairs. One pair is assigned Position A (power is a personal attribute) and the other pair is assigned Position B (power is an attribute of a relationship). Each pair reviews the supporting sections of this chapter, the procedure for the exercise, and the guidelines for constructive controversy (p. 32). They prepare a persuasive "best-case" rationale for their assigned position that includes as many facts and research findings as possible. Ten minutes are allowed for this phase.

3. **Presentations:** One member of each pair changes chairs. A personal attribute person should be seated with a relationship attribute person. The personal attribute person has up

continued on next page

continued from previous page

    to three minutes to present the best case possible for the position, being as forceful and persuasive as possible. The relationship attribute person takes notes and asks for clarification of anything not fully understood. The relationship attribute person then presents.

4. **Open Discussion** (Refute and Rebut): There is an open discussion of whether power is a personal attribute or an aspect of a relationship. Each side presents as many facts and research findings as it can to support its point of view. Members listen critically to the opposing position and ask for supporting facts for any conclusions made by the opponent. Participants should ensure that all the facts supporting both sides are brought out and discussed. The guidelines for constructive controversy should be followed. About ten minutes are allowed for this phase.

5. **Perspective Reversal:** Members of each pair change chairs. The "personal attribute" person presents in three minutes the best case possible for the "relationship attribute" position. He or she should be as forceful and persuasive as he or she can and add new arguments or facts if possible. The relationship attribute person then similarly presents the best case possible for the personal attribute position.

6. **Synthesis and Integration:** Participants drop all advocacy and come to their best reasoned judgment as to whether power is an attribute of a person or a relationship. The pair members summarize the information and arguments for each position and come to an agreement. Each pair prepares a short presentation on its conclusion for the rest of the class. Because other groups will have other conclusions, each group may need to explain the validity of its position to the class. About ten minutes are allowed for this phase.

7. **Whole Class Discussion:** The coordinator samples the decisions made by the groups of four by having several of them present their position to the class. The class then discusses similarities and differences among the positions and the coordinator summarizes what the participants have learned about power and influence.

WHAT IS POWER?

The fundamental concept in social science is power, in the same sense in which energy is the fundamental concept in physics.

Bertrand Russell (1938, ch. 1)

In effective groups, the use of power tends to be distributed among group members, and patterns of influence tend to vary according to the needs of the group. Understanding the nature of power, however, is not easy. In the vast literature on power in philosophy, history, sociology, political science, anthropology, and psychology, there are many different definitions of power. Power has been conceived of as a quality of the person, the position, the place, the situation, or the relationship. Some individuals are viewed as having power because of their ability to dominate others through their physical prowess, verbal prowess, or charisma. Some positions are viewed as carrying power, such as the presidency of a corporation or the chair of a committee. Some places are viewed as sites of power, such as a church, mosque, or temple. Some view situations as determining the level of power of each person, such as when a nurse provides emergency medical aid to a general. Finally, some view power as a quality of the relationship in which both parties influence the other.

These diverse views of power make it difficult to define. In this book, **power** is defined as the capacity to affect the outcomes of oneself, others, and the environment (Coleman & Tjosvold, 2000). The use of power can be direct (within interpersonal interaction) or indirect (through group norms and values). The direct use of power can be examined from two points of view: the dynamic interdependence perspective and the trait factor perspective. In addition, the use of power can be purposeful or nonpurposeful. Sometimes power is deliberately wielded and sometimes it is an unintended side effect of one's actions. In this chapter, only the purposeful use of power is discussed.

When individuals work together to achieve mutual goals, the use of power is inevitable, essential, and distributed. When individuals interact, mutual influence inevitably goes on continuously, as individuals act and then react and adjust to one another's actions. They take turns talking, modify the expression of their attitudes and beliefs to take into account the reactions of other individuals, and speed up or slow down their activity to stay coordinated with one another. In addition, the use of power is essential to all aspects of group functioning. Goals cannot be established, communication cannot take place, leadership cannot exist, and decisions cannot be made without mutual influence. Power, furthermore, is distributed among all group members. Every group member has some influence over other members and what takes place in the group. Finally, the use of power may result in constructive or destructive outcomes. In the following section, the constructive use of power will be discussed.

WHAT IS POWER?

Following are five different views of power. Find a partner and (1) agree on the definition for each view of power and (2) choose the view of power that is most interesting to the two of you.

	Concept	Definitions
_____	Person	a. Power is a quality of a relationship in which each party influences the other.
_____	Position	b. Situational factors determine the level of power of each person.
_____	Place	c. Positions contain power, such as the presidency of a corporation or the chair of a committee.
_____	Situation	d. Power is a trait that some individuals have, usually because they were born with it.
_____	Relationship	e. Certain churches, mosques, or ancient sites such as Stonehenge have power.

Constructive versus Destructive Uses of Power

The use of power may be constructive or destructive. The constructiveness of the use of power may be determined by the following criteria (Deutsch, 1962, 1973):

1. Power is constructive when it is used to enhance, rather than reduce, the achievement of the group goals, the quality of relationships among members, and the group's adaptation to its environment.
2. Power is constructive when it is used for others' (not one's own) benefit and the common good.
3. Power is constructive when it is invited, not imposed, by others.

The use of power is most *constructive* when it increases group effectiveness, benefits all members of the group, and is encouraged by all group members. When power is used primarily for self-benefit or to force others to do something they do not wish to do, then the use of power tends to be *destructive*. There are circumstances in which the use of power for self-benefit can be encouraged by others, either because they are mislead or because they are willing to sacrifice for the person's well-being. There may also be times when the use of power will benefit others but is imposed on them against their will.

The dominant view of power tends to be that power is destructive. Lord Acton's observation, "Power tends to corrupt, and absolute power corrupts absolutely," is typical of this view. Some social scientists, however, believe that power is positive and essential for mutual enhancement and the achievement of mutual goals. Mary Parker Follett (1924, 1973), for example, believed that power could be grown and developed through co-action to achieve mutual goals and that doing so would enrich the soul and advance the humanity of every participant. Similarly, Deutsch (1949a, 1962) viewed power as an inherent aspect of cooperation and competition, with the success of cooperative efforts dependent on the constructive use of power among collaborators. Their views are best represented in the dynamic interdependence view of power.

THE DYNAMIC INTERDEPENDENCE VIEW OF POWER

Coercive power is the curse of the universe; co-active power,
the enrichment and advancement of every human soul.

Mary Parker Follett (1924, p. xii)

Dynamic means in a constant state of change; *interdependence* means that each member's actions affect the outcomes of other members. The **dynamic interdependence view of power** posits that who is influencing whom to what degree changes constantly as members strive to achieve the group's goals. Power is thus seen to exist in relationships, not in individuals (i.e., for power to exist, there must be both an influencer and an influencee) and to be almost always bidirectional (each group member can influence and be influenced by all other members). When any two people interact, they influence

and are influenced by one another. Insofar as the conditions the group faces are constantly changing and multiple issues are being dealt with at the same time, the power relations among group members are always changing and complex. At any moment, for example, one member may have more power on issue 1 than other members but less power on issues 2 and 3. As members coordinate their actions, the power of any member constantly shifts and changes.

The type and degree of interdependence among group members determine the power available to be used by group members. Interdependence may be positive or negative. The way in which power is used varies according to the type of interdependence existing among individuals.

Competitive Context

In a *competitive context*, power is used to gain advantage and to promote one's own success at the expense of others. Power often is thought of as being the successful influence of one person over another who originally is unwilling to perform the desired behaviors. Robert Dahl (1957), for example, states that power involves "an ability to get another person to do something that he or she would not otherwise have done" (p. 158). Such definitions implicitly view power as (Coleman & Tjosvold, 2000):

1. *A fixed-pie resource.* The amount of total power available is limited.
2. *A zero-sum resource.* The more power A has, the less is available for B.
3. *A commodity that should be hoarded.* Competitors tend to use their power in order to maximize the power differences between themselves and others. This is known as the *iron law of oligarchy* (individuals in power tend to remain in power) (Michels, 1915/1959). Concepts such as *powerholder* reflect this view that power is a commodity to be obtained and preserved. Powerholders often become preoccupied with seeking more and more power (McClelland, 1975, 1985).
4. *Acting in a unidirectional way.* A division exists between the powerful and the powerless, and the dominant person influences the subservient person, not vice versa.
5. *Being inherently coercive.* The dominant person overrides the subservient person's reluctance and resistance to engage in the targeted behavior.

DYNAMIC INTERDEPENDENCE APPROACH TO POWER

	Characteristics
Dynamic	Focuses on the changing nature and patterns of influence within a group as members strive to achieve mutual goals rather than on who possesses power.
Holistic	Assumes that power is a complex phenomenon that has to be studied as a whole and cannot be meaningfully broken into components.
Phenomenological	Stresses the immediate experience of group members and the ways they influence one another in the present rather than focusing on members' history and genetics.
Deductive	Applies and validates theoretical principles concerning the nature and use of power.
Distributed	Stresses that power is distributed among all group members and that every group member has some influence over every other group member and over what takes place in the group.
Inevitable	Assumes power exists in all relationships. In small groups, mutual influence goes on continuously as group members act and react and adjust to one another's actions.
Essential, Pervasive	Assumes the use of power is essential to all aspects of group functioning—goal setting, communication, leadership, decision making, conflict resolution.

The competitive view currently dominates most social scientists' and powerholders' understanding of power. Reliance on competitive, dominating strategies of power use, however, has negative consequences, such as the alienation and resistance of those subjected to the influence attempts, which increases the need for continuous scrutiny and control of the less powerful and limits the powerholder's ability and willingness to use other types of power that are based on trust and power sharing.

Resistance to the coercive use of power may be viewed as psychological reactance. **Reactance** is the need to reestablish a person's freedom whenever it is threatened. It is a motivational state aroused whenever persons feel their freedom has been abridged or threatened (Brehm, 1966). Threats to personal freedom motivate persons to take actions that help them regain their freedom and control, such as seeking to obstruct or negate the powerholder's influence and to sabotage the group's efforts and effectiveness.

The use of *coercive power* may escalate as it encounters resistance. The more the target of the influence resists, the greater the likelihood that the influencer will shift from a mild to a strong tactic (Gavin, Green, & Fairhurst, 1995; Kipnis, 1984;

Michener & Burt, 1975). This, in turn, will generate more resistance. The coercive use of power then escalates into more and more extreme forms, which usually decreases group effectiveness.

Cooperative Context

Four mountain climbers are ascending a rock face in the Italian Alps. Bound together by a rope, they give one another constant instructions on how to proceed. "Use the handhold on the right." "Put a piton in there." "Give me a little more rope." "Belay me." Each member of the team welcomes the suggestions of the other teammates and responds promptly and competently to the requests.

In a *cooperative context*, power is used to maximize joint benefits and enhance the group's effectiveness. Because they are working together to achieve mutual goals, group members are inducible. **Inducibility** is openness to influence (Deutsch, 1949a, 1962). In cooperative situations, when a member's influence will help other members achieve their goals, they tend to be open to the influence attempt. If, for example, your cat is in a tree and will not come down, and a friend brings over a ladder and asks you to help carry it over to the tree and set it up, you are quite willing to do so. Your friend's power to induce your help is quite high because it promotes the achievement of your goal. It is inducibility that allows group members to coordinate their actions. Inducibility also underlies the norm that group members should be receptive to one another's influence attempts and facilitate one another's actions that promote the achievement of the group's goals. What tends to result is an orientation toward enhancing mutual power. Mutual power is created and developed out of the interaction among group members and their commitment to achieving their mutual goals. Power is implicitly viewed as (Coleman & Tjosvold, 2000):

1. *Expandable.* Power is developed jointly and expands as individuals work together. As the positive interdependence and the ability of members to work together increase, so does the joint power to achieve the group's goals.
2. *Something to be shared.* Power and resources are shared with others in order to more effectively achieve the group's goals, out of genuine concern for other group members and because it is seen as morally right to do so.
3. *Acting in a bidirectional way.* Every group member influences all others. The more open an individual is to be influenced by others, the more open they are to the individual's attempts to influence them. Bidirectional influence tends to result in greater learning and integration of new information, as well as the discovery of creative ways to improve group effectiveness (Zajonc, 1960). Power differences tend to be minimized as members enhance one another's power in order to achieve their shared goals.
4. *Noncoercive.* In cooperative situations, group members want to be influenced by others in order to improve their effectiveness. They also wish to influence the other group members in order to promote their success in achieving the group's goals.
5. *Asymmetrical.* Positive interdependence among group members can be symmetrical (members are equally dependent on one another's resources) or

asymmetrical (one member is more dependent on the resources of another member than vice versa). In the complexities of group life, power is always asymmetrical on any one issue under one set of conditions.

6. *Based on expertise, competence, and access to information.* In cooperative situations, authority or personality characteristics are set aside in favor of who has the most expertise at this time on this particular issue.

In cooperative situations (compared with competitive and individualistic situations), individuals tended to be less coercive and more supportive and persuasive in their use of power (Tjosvold, 1981; Tjosvold, 1985a, 1985b; Tjosvold, Johnson, & Johnson, 1984), which results in more trusting and friendly relationships, greater exchange of resources, more time spent on tasks, greater productivity, and a stronger view of power as expandable (Richter & Tjosvold, 1981; Tjosvold, 1981, 1989, 1990a; Tjosvold, Coleman, & Sun, 2003). Cooperators (compared with competitors) tend to be more open to influence, more positive toward those who exercise power, and more appreciative of the way power is used (Tjosvold, 1995b). Cooperators also believed more strongly that power-holders used their power wisely and were more likable, fair, and trustworthy.

An alternative view of positive interdependence with small groups posits that the power of one group member over others depends on three factors: the benefits of working together to achieve mutual goals, the costs of doing so, and the availability of alternative groups in which the rewards may be higher and the costs lower (Cartwright, 1959; Thibaut & Kelly, 1959). In other words, the patterns of influence among group members change constantly as the group progresses toward its goals, the costs (in energy, emotion, time, and so forth) of working together vary, and alternative relationships and groups become available in which the goals of group members might be better achieved (Cartwright, 1959; Thibaut & Kelly, 1959). If the group members make progress toward achieving their goals and if the costs of working together go down so that no other group would be as rewarding, positive interdependence is high and the ability of members to influence one another increases. If, on the other hand, the group is not making progress toward goal accomplishment, if the costs to group members in terms of emotion and energy are high, and if other groups are available that are more effective and less demanding, positive interdependence is low and the ability of group members to influence one another decreases. In the latter case, members may even terminate their membership and join other groups, thereby reducing to zero the capacity of the original group members to influence and be influenced by them.

MOBILIZING POWER TO ACHIEVE GOALS

There is a story about a man, after a severe windstorm, attempting to move a tree from his driveway so that he could get his car out of the garage. His neighbor watched as he strained, but the tree did not move. "Are you using all your strength?" asked the neighbor. "Of course I am," replied the man. "Can't you see how I'm straining?" "Are you sure you are using all your strength?" asked the neighbor. "Yes! Yes! Yes!" replied the man. "No, you are not," said the neighbor. "You haven't asked me to help."

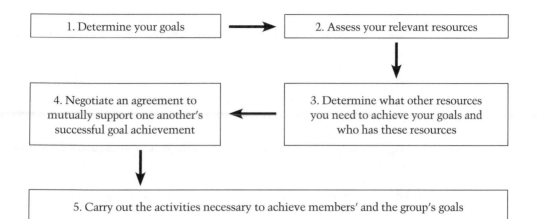

Figure 6.2 Mobilizing power to accomplish goals.

THE TRUTH ABOUT THE WORLD

When you:
  Have high aspirations
  Are engaged in a difficult task that is critically important
  But you have limited resources
You need partners (cooperative coalitions).

Most groups are formed because the group can accomplish goals that one individual working alone cannot. In working together, group members are dependent on the assistance of other members to achieve their own goals and have the power to promote or obstruct the goal achievement of other members. The achievement of goals typically requires the mobilization of the combined efforts of all group members. The process by which group members mobilize their power in order to accomplish their goals consists of five steps (Figure 6.2):

1. *Determining your goals:* The first step in using your power in a group is to clarify your personal goals. **Goals** are desired future states based on wants, needs, and interests. Typically, goals are sought consciously, but some are sought unconsciously. In order to plan how to attain your goals, you must be aware of them, accept them as valuable and worthwhile, and be willing to enlist the aid of other group members to accomplish them.
2. *Determining your relevant resources:* The second step in using your power is to contribute your resources to achieving the group's goals and your personal goals. You must be aware of your resources in order to understand (a) what other resources you need to achieve your goals, (b) how you can help other group members achieve their goals, and (c) how the resources of all members can be combined to achieve the group's goals.

3. *Determining your needed coalitions:* The third step in using your power is to assess what coalitions you need to secure the resources you must have to achieve your goals. Coalitions are formed by (a) identifying the group members who have the resources you need, (b) identifying how your resources could contribute to their goal accomplishment, and (c) negotiating a mutual support agreement in which each agrees to contribute to the other's success.

4. *Negotiating contracts:* The fourth step in using your power is to negotiate an agreement with the appropriate group members to mutually support one another's efforts to achieve goals. In planning how resources should be utilized to help achieve the goals, group members often develop formal or informal contracts with one another. The contract usually includes (a) the resources you want from the other group members, (b) the resources other group members want from you, and (c) how members should coordinate their effects to achieve the goals. In essence, the contracts are a plan for group members to apply their resources in certain ways toward the achievement of the group's goals.

5. *Implementing the contracts:* The fifth step in using your power is to carry out the activities necessary to achieve the goals.

EXERCISE 6.2

PERSONAL POWER AND GOAL ACCOMPLISHMENT

The purpose of this exercise is to give you an opportunity to experience the process just discussed (on p. 211) to increase your personal power step-by-step.

1. Form groups of four.
2. Reread step 1 (**Determining Your Goals**). Each person first should state all the goals that he or she might work toward in this group. After everyone has had a say, each member should state which three goals he or she would like the group to accomplish first. Write these goals down on a sheet of newsprint, and include your name. Then go on to the next step.
3. Reread step 2 (**Determining Your Resources**). You determine your resources by creating a list of your skills, talents, abilities, or personal traits that help you function more productively. The object is to increase your awareness of (a) your strengths, so that you may more consciously mobilize them to achieve your goals, and (b) other resources you need. The procedure for each group is as follows:
   a. Individually, think of all the things you do well, all the things you are proud of having done, and all the things about which you feel a sense of accomplishment. List all your positive accomplishments and your successes.
   b. Share your lists with one another. Then, with the help of the other group members, examine your past successes and identify the personal strengths you used to achieve them. Make a list of these strengths.
   c. After you have all made your list of strengths, give one another feedback about additional strengths. Add to each person's list the qualities, skills, and characteristics that person has overlooked or undervalued.

    d. Each member should then discuss the question, "What might be keeping me from using all my strengths?" The group helps members explore the ways in which they can free themselves from constraints on the use of their strengths.

    e. Review the material on self-acceptance and the acceptance of others in Johnson (2006).

4. Reread step 3 (**Determining Your Needed Coalitions**). As a group, look for similarities among your goals. Decide as a group on the three goals that are most in accord with the personal goals of each member. List them. Review the strengths listed in step 2. Try to determine what resources are needed for the accomplishment of each of the three goals, and who has them. In participating in this exercise you may experience either the frustration of finding little or no compatibility between your own goals and those of the other group members or the rejection of having your resources overlooked, undervalued, or underused. Do not at this point make any formal coalitions with other group members. Limit yourself to determining what coalitions are needed. Then go on to the next step.

5. Reread step 4 (**Negotiating Contracts**). Negotiate formal contracts with other group members and form open coalitions. In doing so, focus specifically on (a) what you want from the group members, (b) what the other group members want from you, and (c) what you exchange so that all members can accomplish their goals. Write your contracts down on a large piece of paper such as newsprint so that all members can see and read them. In essence, these contracts are a plan for group members to apply their resources cooperatively to achieve the group's goals.

6. Reread step 5 (**Implementing the Contracts**). Carry out the actions specified in the contract.

DISCUSSION

After completing the preceding steps, the groups should discuss their experiences. The following questions may be used to stimulate discussion:

1. What was the outcome of the five steps? To what extent were everyone's goals integrated in the group's goals, and to what extent were everyone's resources committed to the accomplishment of the group's goals?

2. What are the present reactions and feelings of each group member toward the five steps?

3. On the basis of the group's experiences, what conclusions can be made about the use of power in a group? Groups should write their answers down on newsprint-sized pieces of paper. When all groups have finished their discussion, the conclusions should be shared.

THE TRAIT FACTOR APPROACH TO POWER

One night, long, long ago, a princess lay down to sleep on a bed that had thirteen mattresses. At the bottom of the pile of mattresses a tiny pea had been placed. The princess tossed and turned all night, unable to sleep. This fairy-tale princess was unable to sleep because it is part of the nature of princesses to be disturbed by factors that those of us with mundane natures do not even notice. This story illustrates the *trait factor approach to power*, which views the capacity to exert power over other people as a

TRAIT FACTOR APPROACH TO POWER

	Characteristics
Static	Focuses more on continuity than on change.
Atomistic	Assumes that complex phenomena can be analyzed into component parts.
Historical	Assumes that causation of present behavior is a function of genetic and experiential factors acting cumulatively over relatively long periods of time.
Inductive	Stresses accounting for empirically observed phenomena more than seeking empirical validation for general theoretical statements.

genetically inherited trait or disposition. The princess is credited with having innate dispositions that differentiated her from all other women. Who can deny her divine spark?

The trait factor approach to power is based on the assumption that a person's genetic traits explain why the person is as he or she is, how the person became so, and why the person stays the same despite circumstances, fortune, and opportunities. Thus, just as some individuals are born with the ability to run fast, certain individuals are born with an inherent ability to influence others. Two of the trait factor approaches to power are the work on power and persuasion and the work on social dominance.

Power and Persuasion

Aristotle dealt at some length in his *Rhetoric* with the characteristics of an effective influencer and gave detailed advice on the techniques of persuasion. From the trait factor point of view, influence is a function of the characteristics of both the person exerting the influence and the person receiving the influence. The characteristics of the influence attempt itself may have some importance.

A major study of the trait factor approach to power was the Yale Attitude Change Program, which was headed by Carl Hovland (Hovland, Janis, & Kelley, 1953; Hovland, Lumsdaine, & Sheffield, 1949; McGuire, 1985). Most of the research in this program focused on the effects of a single attempt to influence people through mass media, such as a politician giving a speech to an audience, an announcer delivering a television commercial, or a health official warning the public about a health danger. In each of these situations, the contact between the communicator and the receiver of the communication is brief and not repeated, the communication is one-way (there is no interaction between the two parties), and the person delivering the message is presented as having some authority to do so.

Hovland's studies of wartime propaganda were organized around the question, "Who says what to whom with what effect?" Investigators usually break this question down into variables relating to the characteristics of the communicator, the characteristics of the communication, and the characteristics of the person receiving the message (i.e., *source, message,* and *receiver effects*). The exercise of power may be seen as a credible and attractive communicator's delivery of an effectively organized message to a vulnerable or influenceable audience. People are more likely to be influenced by individuals whom they perceive to be trustworthy, distribute resources fairly, and treat people with respect (Tyler, 1997; Tyler & Degoey, 1996). Messages are more effective if they are phrased to be two-sided, action-oriented, and discrepant with members' current beliefs. The powerholder is more effective if the less powerful individuals have low self-esteem, see their attitudes under modification as peripheral to them, have no **forewarning** of the influence attempt, role play positions that agree with the communicator's, have not been inoculated, are distracted while the message is presented, and are not very intelligent. Trait factor researchers assume that people process information rationally and are motivated to attend to a message, learn its contents, and incorporate it into their attitudes. The trait factor approach to influence, however, is weak both logically and empirically in situations where two or more individuals are constantly interacting. It is much less applicable in group situations, where individuals are working together to achieve a goal that requires everyone's input.

Social Dominance Theory

Social dominance theory is a trait factor theory of power directly based on competition. *Social dominance* is defined as the ability to control resources. Resources are anything essential for survival, growth, and development (Charlesworth, 1996). Resources are assumed to be limited, and therefore resource acquisition compels competition among group members, as well as among groups and species (Darwin, 1859/1959).

A social dominance hierarchy is created when members of a social group vary in their ability to acquire resources (Hawley, 1999). Each member's ability to compete successfully for limited resources—the trait ability—defines his or her position in the social hierarchy. A social dominance hierarchy is not an organizational method, then; it is a natural consequence of differences in individuals' abilities to compete. The competitive rule of thumb that helps determine social dominance hierarchies says, "Depending on who your opponent is, assert when you can prevail, yield when you cannot." This rule is seen as diminishing conflict among group members and minimizing the personal costs of interacting with other members.

Although young children may compete for resources through physical coercion and force, most people learn that aggression is unacceptable and adopt other, more socially accepted means of obtaining resources, such as persuasion or forming coalitions. The intent is to establish dominance (i.e., gain control of resources) while minimizing interpersonal conflict with other group members. Forming coalitions may be the most successful strategy for acquiring control of resources, as groups of individual who help one another do better than groups of individuals who do not (Campbell, 1965, 1978; Kropotkin, 1902). Social dominance theory assumes that groups are composed of self-interested individuals whose self-interests include balancing their own needs with the needs of others. Social relationships are viewed as resources in and of themselves, because individuals who have social contracts to collaborate will do better than those who do not. Thus, the most adaptive way to acquire resources may be to be a fair player, to consider others, to compromise, to be an overall good group member. Social dominance hierarchies are seen as developing naturally any time individuals have contact with one another.

Being dominant (reflecting relative competitive ability) is assumed to be correlated with health, vigor, productiveness, and reproductive success, presumably because dominant individuals are better able to fulfill their nutritional, social, and security needs than are other group members. Thus, the dominant individual within a social hierarchy becomes the focus of attention—admired, liked, viewed as an attractive social partner, and obeyed.

The motivation to dominate others and the ability to do so may be seen as traits that differentially appear in individuals. Social dominance theory, therefore, may be the clearest example of the trait factor approach to power.

THE BASES OF POWER

On November 1, 1095, Pope Urban II delivered a speech in an open field outside the town of Clermont, France, in which he urged the crowd to arm itself and drive the "wicked race" of pagans from the Holy Land. Moved by the pope's words, the crowd began to yell, "It is the will of God!" Urban's speech marked the beginning of the long series of wars known as the Crusades. Peter the Hermit organized the First Crusade in 1096. All over Europe huge groups of unarmed men, priests, monks, women, and children became captivated by the promise of salvation, the lure of riches, and the promise of adventure, and gathered to begin the trek to Jerusalem. Caught up in their religious fervor, few stopped to contemplate their chances for survival. Almost all of them died. Yet the Crusades lasted until 1291, when the Muslims regained full control of the Holy Land. What gave Pope Urban II the power to launch such a 200-year effort?

According to *social exchange theory*, power is based on the control of valuable resources. If a person has control over a resource you want, that person has power over you unless, of course, you have an alternative source for the resource. The type of resource under a person's control determines the basis for the person's power. The power bases typically are reward, coercive, legitimate, referent, expertise, and informational (French & Raven, 1959; Frost & Stahelski, 1988; Raven, 1992, 1993; Raven & Kruglanski, 1970).

Pope Urban II may have attained his power through the promise of heavenly rewards for participating in a Crusade. A person has **reward power** over other group members if he or she has the ability to deliver positive consequences or remove negative consequences in response to their behavior. Rewards can be higher salaries, food, gold stars, positive feedback, or salvation. A person's power is greater the more the group members value the reward, the more they believe that the person can dispense the reward, and the less chance they have of receiving the reward from someone else. The successful use of reward power results in group members complying with the powerholder's requests, seeking the powerholder out, liking the powerholder, and communicating effectively with the powerholder. Under certain conditions, however, the reward power can backfire. Too many rewards can create the suspicion that

RANKING BASES OF POWER

Find a partner. Working cooperatively, rank the following bases of power from most to least effective in influencing others. Compare your ranking with the ranking of another pair. Explain the reasoning underlying your ranking and listen to the other pair's rationale.

Rank	Base of Power
_____	Ability to deliver positive consequences or remove negative consequences in response to their behavior.
_____	Ability to mete out negative consequences or remove positive consequences in response to the behavior of group members.
_____	Possession of a position in the group or organization (such as president) or special role responsibilities (such as x-ray technician).
_____	Modeling behavioral patterns and personal qualities that others want to imitate out of respect, liking, and wanting to be liked.
_____	Possession of some special expertise that is useful in accomplishing the goal and that is not available anywhere else.
_____	Possession of resources or information that is useful in accomplishing the goal and that is not available anywhere else.

group members are being bribed or conned, which tends to result in dislike and/or resistance.

Pope Urban II may have attained his power from the threat of punishment (eternal damnation) if Christians did not participate in the Crusade. A person has **coercive power** over other group members if the person can mete out negative consequences or remove positive consequences in response to the behavior of group members. Punishments may include physical pain or isolation, withholding money or approval, or eternal damnation. Punishing a member who fails to go along with one's wishes often increases the pressure on group members to engage in the desired behavior. Coercive power, however, frequently causes group members to avoid and dislike the coercive person. Group members may do what the person wants, but they tend to avoid interacting with the person in the future. Only when the use of coercive power brings a conflict into the open to be resolved can coercion have positive effects.

Pope Urban II may have attained his power from his position as Pope. When a person has **legitimate power**, group members believe the person ought to have influence over them because of his or her position in the group or organization (such as an employer) or because of his or her special role responsibilities (such as those of a police officer). Group members who obey legitimate authorities accept the norms of the group and therefore comply through a sense of duty, loyalty, or even moral obligation. Group members invariably believe it their duty to follow the commands of a person with legitimate power. Individuals tend to have more legitimate power when they are perceived to be trustworthy, distributing resources fairly, and treating people with respect

DEFINING BASES OF POWER

Find a partner and, working cooperatively, match the following bases of power with their definitions. Compare answers with another pair.

_____	1. Reward	a. Group members believe the person has useful knowledge not available elsewhere.
_____	2. Coercive	b. Group members believe the person ought to have power because of his or her position or responsibilities.
_____	3. Legitimate	c. The person can deliver positive consequences or remove negative consequences.
_____	4. Reference	d. Group members believe the person has a special knowledge or skill and is trustworthy.
_____	5. Expert	e. Group members do what the person wants out of respect, liking, and wanting to be liked.
_____	6. Informational	f. The person can deliver negative consequences or remove positive consequences.

(Tyler, 1997; Tyler & Degoey, 1996). Legitimate power often is used to reduce conflict, such as when the person with legitimate power mediates or arbitrates or when those with less power simply conform to the person's wishes.

Pope Urban II may have attained his power because of the desire of Christians to emulate him and win his respect. When a person has **referent power**, group members identify with or want to be like the person and therefore do what he or she wants out of respect, liking, and wanting to be liked. Charismatic leaders have referent power, and they typically use it to demand new obligations that contradict established social norms and require self-sacrifice and united action (Hoffer, 1951; Weber, 1946). Generally, the more the person is liked, the more the group members identify with him or her.

Pope Urban II may have attained his power through his superior skills and abilities resulting from being God's representative on Earth. When a person has **expert power**, group members see the person as having skills and competencies useful for accomplishing the goal and not available anywhere else. The more a person is perceived to be an expert, the more influence he or she has within the group (Littlepage & Mueller, 1997). Group members may need to work together for some time before they can assess clearly one another's expertise. Over time, group members become more proficient at recognizing and utilizing the strengths of each group member (Littlepage, Robison, & Reddington, 1997; Littlepage & Silbiger, 1992), thereby improving their coordination of efforts and expertise (Goodman & Leyden, 1991). When a person successfully uses expert power, group members generally like the person, because they believe the person is correct in trying to influence them. If, on the other hand, the use of expertise fosters feelings of inadequacy in group members, it will tend to have negative effects.

Pope Urban II may have attained his power from his information about the will of God. When a person has **informational power**, group members believe the person has useful information not available anywhere else. Information resources include rational argument, factual data, and logic. The person's power is based on the logic of the person's arguments or the superiority of his or her demonstrated knowledge; it has effects similar to those that result from the use of expert power.

French and Raven argued that power may be drawn from these six key sources. Pope Urban II was powerful because he drew from all six bases of power. It should be noted that it is the *perception* of a group member's power base that affects the behavior of other members, not the actual resources. A member can have considerable resources that are unknown or ignored by other group members and therefore have little power over the others. On the other hand, a group member can have few resources but be seen as having many resources and thereby have a great deal of influence over the other group members.

CONFLICT MODEL OF SOCIAL INFLUENCE

The French social psychologist Serge Moscovici (1980, 1985a) proposed an intergroup conflict model of social influence in which power defines whether a group member is part of the majority or a minority. He assumes that both majority and minority members are sources and targets of influence attempts. Majority members tend to use their power to force minority members to yield and conform to the majority's expectations. Minority members tend to convert majority members to the minority's position. What defines the majority and the minority members is the amount of power they have. A *power majority* has the most control over how important resources are distributed (they may be the numerical minority). A *power minority* has little control over the distribution of important resources (they may be a numerical majority).

EXERCISE 6.3

UNEQUAL RESOURCES

This exercise gives participants a chance to observe how groups (1) use resources that have been distributed unequally and (2) negotiate to obtain the resources they need. It is conducted with four groups, each having two to four members. If there are enough participants to have more than one cluster of four groups, the coordinator may wish to add the element of competition between, as well as within, the clusters. The exercise should take less than one hour. The procedure for the coordinator is as follows:

1. Introduce the exercise as an experience with the use of resources needed to accomplish a task that have been distributed unequally among groups. Form the groups. For each cluster have at least two observers. Groups should be placed far enough away from one another so that their negotiation positions are not compromised by casual observation.

continued on next page

continued from previous page

2. Meet briefly with the observers and discuss what they might focus on. Any aspect of negotiation and problem solving can be observed.

3. Distribute an envelope of materials and a copy of the accompanying task sheet to each group. Explain that each group has different materials, but that each must complete the same tasks. Explain that the groups may negotiate for the use of materials and tools in any way that is agreeable to everyone. Emphasize that the first group to finish all the tasks is the winner. (If clusters are competing, there will be both a group winner and a cluster winner.) Give the signal to begin.

4. When the groups have finished, declare the winner. Then conduct a discussion on using resources, sharing, negotiating, competing, and using power. Ask the observers to participate in the discussion. Then ask each cluster to summarize its conclusions about the use of power that manifested itself during the exercise.

Group Materials

Group 1	Scissors, ruler, paper clips, pencils, two 4-inch squares of red paper, and two 4-inch squares of white paper.
Group 2	Scissors, glue, and two sheets each of gold paper, white paper, and blue paper, each 8 × 11 inches.
Group 3	Felt-tipped markers and two sheets each of green paper, white paper, and gold paper, each 8 × 11 inches.
Group 4	Five sheets of paper, 8 × 11 inches: one green, one gold, one blue, one red, and one purple.

UNEQUAL RESOURCES EXERCISE TASK SHEET

Each group is to complete the following tasks:

1. Make a 3 × 3-inch square of white paper.
2. Make a 4 × 2-inch rectangle of gold paper.
3. Make a 3 × 5-inch T-shaped piece of green-and-white paper.
4. Make a four-link paper chain, each link in a different color.
5. Make a 4 × 4-inch flag in any three colors.

The first group to complete all the tasks is the winner. Groups may negotiate with one another for the use of needed materials and tools on any mutually agreeable basis.

POWER AND PROBLEM SOLVING

In Exercise 6.3, the resources of the group were distributed unequally among members. This is the case in most groups; it is rare if not impossible to find a group in which every member has exactly the same resources. Yet, unequal distribution of resources does not mean that members are powerless. Every group member has some power; every member is able to influence other group members in some way. How a group manages power has an important bearing on group effectiveness.

The effectiveness of any group is improved when power is relatively mutual among its members and power is based on competence, expertise, and information. The ability of the group to solve problems increases as all group members come to believe they share equally in influencing the direction of the group effort, and as the group climate becomes relatively free of domination by a few of the most powerful members. When members have equal power, they are more cooperative in their interactions, more responsive to the cooperative initiatives of other members, and more committed to implementing the group decision. Studies have found that even within organizations, the satisfaction of subordinates increases when they believe they can influence particular aspects of the organization's decision making (Tjosvold, 1995b). Unequal power interferes with the trust and communication necessary for managing group conflicts constructively. Thus, the problem-solving ability of a group is improved when the group has dynamic power patterns that in the long run equalize influence among group members. A group's decisions are invariably of higher quality when power is based on competence, expertise, and relevant information, not on authority or popularity. The problem-solving capacity of many groups is seriously damaged when the member with the most authority is most influential at a time that calls for expertise and accurate information as the bases of power. When power is not distributed equally among group members, or when the use of authority dominates and expertise and informational bases of power are ignored, group effectiveness is undermined.

EXERCISE 6.4

POWER TO THE ANIMALS

The objective of this exercise is to examine the interaction among groups of different levels of power as they negotiate with one another. The exercise takes two hours. The coordinator should read the accompanying instructions regarding the distribution of marbles and then follow this procedure:

1. Introduce the exercise as one that highlights interaction among groups having unequal power. Divide the class into groups of twelve. Explain that within each group are three mammals, four birds, and five fishes; the status of the members in each group is determined by how well they negotiate—for marbles. (Even if there are more than twelve participants in a group, keep the number of mammals under five.) Hand out a copy of the general instructions to every participant.
2. Distribute twelve bags of marbles randomly within each group. Make sure that the members understand their instructions. Give them time to examine what marbles they have, warning them not to let other participants see the marbles. Then begin negotiation session 1, which is to last five minutes.
3. During the negotiation session write down on newsprint-sized sheets three headings: "Mammals," "Birds," and "Fishes." After five minutes, stop the negotiating and have the participants compute their scores. Take the three highest scores and place them, along with the persons' initials, under the heading "Mammals." (Even if there are more than twelve participants in a group, keep the number of mammals under five.) Place the

continued on next page

continued from previous page

    next four scores, together with the persons' initials, under the heading "Birds." Place the remaining five scores, with the persons' initials, under the heading "Fishes." Have each person make a name tag indicating what he or she is and put it on.

4. Begin negotiation session 2. After five minutes, end it and ask for scores. Read just the individual scores, placing the three highest in the Mammals column, the next four in the Birds column, and the next Five in the Fishes column. Members who change columns on the basis of their score will have to exchange their name tags.

5. Conduct negotiation session 3 in the same way.

6. Conduct negotiation session 4 in the same way.

7. Announce that the mammals now have the authority to make the rules for the exercise and that although anyone else can suggest rules, the mammals will decide which ones will be implemented. Inform the mammals that they may make any rules they wish, such as a rule that all marbles must be redistributed so that everyone has equal points, or a rule that all fishes and birds must give mammals the marbles they ask for whether they want to or not. Have the mammals record their rules on newsprint.

8. After the new rules are established, conduct negotiation session 5. Then allow five minutes for the mammals to discuss and make any rule changes.

9. Repeat this cycle twice. Then give the birds and the fishes copies of the list of strategies for influencing a high-power group. The birds and the fishes have ten minutes to discuss the strategies and decide which ones to adopt. Then continue with another negotiation session.

10. After the birds and the fishes have tried a variety of strategies, or when they refuse to continue, conduct a discussion of the experience. The following questions may be used as guides:

    a. What were your feelings and your reactions to the experience?

    b. Are there any parallels between the system set up by the game and the system in which we live?

    c. Would it have made much difference if the members who were fishes had been the mammals?

    d. Were the mammals acting with legitimate authority?

    e. Are there any parallels between the exercise and the relations among racial groups, rich and poor, and teachers and students?

    f. What negotiation strategies were used?

    g. What feelings arose from the unequal distribution of power? How did it feel to have high power? How did it feel to have low power? How did your experiences compare with the following discussions of high- and low-power group members?

    h. How did the strategies for changing the high-power group work? What contributed to their effectiveness or ineffectiveness?

    i. What conclusions about the use of power can be drawn from your experiences in the exercise?

DISTRIBUTION OF MARBLES

1. The total number of marbles needed is seventy-two (six times the number of group members).

2. The number of green marbles needed is five (the number of mammals plus two).

3. The number of yellow marbles needed is ten (the number of birds plus the number of fish plus one).

4. The number of red, white, and blue marbles needed is fifty-seven, nineteen of each.

Give each participant a bag of six marbles. Five bags are to contain one green marble, one yellow marble, and four marbles randomly selected from the colors red, white, and blue. Three bags are to contain one yellow marble and five marbles randomly selected from the colors red, white, and blue. The remaining four bags are to contain a random assortment of red, white, and blue marbles. These twelve bags are to be distributed at random within each group.

GENERAL INSTRUCTIONS

In this exercise there are three levels of power based on the number and kinds of marbles in each group. Group members have the chance to progress from one level of power to another by obtaining marbles through negotiation. The three members who get the most power will be declared the winners when the exercise ends. You will be given six marbles each. The scoring system for the marbles follows. Additional points are awarded if a member is able to get several marbles of the same color.

Color	Points	Number of a Kind	Points
Green	50	4	50
Yellow	25	3	30
Red	15	2	20
White	10	1	10
Blue	5		

For example, a person's total score if the person had six green marbles would be 300 (6 × 50) plus 50 (for six of a kind), or 350 points. The rules for negotiation are as follows:

1. You have five minutes to improve your score.
2. You improve your score by negotiating with other group members.
3. Members must be holding hands to have an agreement.
4. Only one-for-one trades are legal. Two-for-one or any other combination is illegal.
5. Once a member touches the hand of another member, a marble of unequal value (or color) must be traded. If two members cannot make an agreement, they will have to hold hands for the entire negotiating round.
6. There is no talking unless hands are touching. This rule must be strictly followed.
7. Members with folded arms do not have to negotiate with other members.
8. All marbles must be hidden. This rule must be strictly followed.

STRATEGIES FOR INFLUENCING A HIGH-POWER GROUP

1. Build your own organizations and resources in order to make the low-power group less vulnerable.
2. Form coalitions.
3. Change the attitudes of high-power group members through education or moral persuasion.
4. Use existing legal procedures to bring pressures for change.
5. Search for ways in which to make high-power group members dependent on the low-power group.
6. Use harassment techniques to increase the high-power group's costs of sticking with the status quo.

UNEQUAL POWER

One of the most common settings for analyzing power is in the relationship between high- and lower-power groups. Power includes the capacity to affect another person's outcomes (as well as one's own outcomes and the environment). *High power* is the capacity to have considerable effect on another person's outcomes, whereas *low power* is the capacity to have little effect on another person's outcomes. When the distribution of power is obviously unequal, the potential for its destructive use increases and the group tends to be less effective. High-power group members act and react differently than do low-power group members. The use of power, furthermore, has metamorphic effects on both the high- and low-power group members.

High-Power Members

In Greek mythology, the king of Phrygia, Midas, showed unusual kindness to Dionysus' teacher, Silenus. In appreciation, Dionysus offered to grant any wish King Midas wanted to ask. Midas requested that all he touched would turn to gold. When even his food became gold, he implored Dionysus for relief and was directed to bathe in the river Pactolus (which has since had golden sands). His touch returned to normal, King Midas had gained the wisdom to know that the exercise of power does not always turn out the way it is intended.

Life generally seems good for high-power persons. Everything goes well, every problem is solved easily, everyone seems to like and appreciate them and everything they do. High-power persons are typically happy and often do not see the degree to which power is involved in their relationships. They are convinced that low-power people really do like them, everyone communicates honestly with them, no one hides information from them, and they are really seen as "nice" people. When this enjoyable world is threatened by dissatisfaction expressed by low-power individuals, however, high-power people do not tend to react benevolently. They attempt to protect their superior power by rejecting demands for change and being uninterested in learning about the intentions and plans of low-power members, being inattentive to the communications of the low-power person, and being unresponsive to cooperative gestures by the low-power members (Tjosvold, 1978). They usually are hard to move toward cooperation, conciliation, and compromise, and they will largely ignore the efforts of their low-power individuals to increase cooperative problem solving. They attempt to protect their superior power by rejecting demands for change. High-power individuals tend to be more angered by a lower-power person's harm or insult than when the positions are reversed (Baumeister, Smart, & Boden, 1996). As Aristotle noted, people think it "right that they should be revered by those inferior to them" (Aristotle 1991, p. 143), and high-power members find it particularly vexing to be insulted or harmed by someone who should actually treat them with deference. To them, low-power persons do not "know their place" and insist on "rocking the boat" out of ignorance and spite.

In describing how high-power people react to low-power individuals, the acronym LEAD is useful. The L stands for the "*legitimize*" strategies high-power group members use to solidify their position and make it difficult for low-power members to reduce the differences in power between them. Once group members gain power, they tend to

HIGH-POWER STRATEGIES TO JUSTIFY THE STATUS QUO

L *Legitimize* own privileges and intimidate low-power individuals
E Self-*enhancement*
A *Attribute* low-power people's success to own control
D *Devalue* low-power individuals and their contributions

establish regulations and norms to legitimize their position and privileges and make illegitimate any attempt by others to change the status quo. High-power group members, for example, may establish norms as to where low-power individuals may live, what occupations they may have, and where they must go to school. This strategy may be described as the "power defines injustice" strategy, or the "might is right" strategy.

In addition, high-power group members tend to make the risk of attempting to change the power status quo so great that low-power members are deterred from trying to do so. They do so in two ways: by establishing severe penalties for those who attempt to change the status quo, and by offering low-power members a variety of benefits as long as they do not rebel. The latter seems to be more effective. The severe penalties strategy may be characterized as the "this-hurts-me-more-than-it-will-hurt-you" strategy, or the "if-only-you-would-behave-neither-of-us-would-go-through-this-suffering" strategy.

The E stands for self-*enhancement*. High-power group members tend to have high-self-esteem, based in part on a tendency to enhance their view of themselves and their capabilities. Having high power has been shown to result in an enhanced self-perception (Johnson & Allen, 1972). A meta-analysis indicates that as a person's power increases, self-evaluations become increasingly positive (effect size = 0.45) (Georgesen & Harris, 1998). High power seems to result in an egocentric or self-serving bias (Harris & Schaubroeck, 1988), resulting in inflating self-evaluations to maintain the benefits of high power, such as employment, promotions, and perks. Participants who were randomly assigned to central positions in a communication network (the more powerful positions) not only viewed themselves as powerful but also rated themselves as more capable than the participants who were randomly assigned peripheral positions (Stotle, 1978). High-power group members tend to feel more secure than low-power members (Tjosvold, 1978) and tend to receive inflated positive feedback from others, thereby producing an inflated sense of self-worth (Kipnis, Castell, Gergen, & Mauch, 1976).

The A stands for the *attribution* of low-power individuals' success to the guidance and intervention of the high-power individuals. The *power-devaluation theory* proposed by Kipnis and his colleagues (Kipnis, 1972; Kipnis, Castell, Gergen, & Mauch, 1976; Kipnis, Schmidt, Prince, & Stitt, 1981; Wilkinson & Kipnis, 1978) posits that as a person's power increases, he or she will make more attempts to influence others. As more influence attempts are made, the person comes to believe that he or she controls the low-power people's behavior and is the causal agent in producing the outcomes. The performances of low-power others are devalued and the high-power person takes responsibility for any successes associated with the work of the low-power group members.

The D stands for the tendency of high-power group members to *devalue* low-power members and their efforts to help the group achieve its goals, as well as a tendency to see the worst in others (Kipnis, Castell, Gergen, & Mauch, 1976; Tjosvold, 1978). High-power members have been shown to be altruistic toward but disdainful of low-power members (Johnson & Allen, 1972). A meta-analysis indicates that as a person's power increases, the performance ratings of others become increasingly negative (effect size = 0.29) (Georgesen & Harris, 1998). The devaluation of low-power group members by high-power members is reflected in the high-power members being uninterested in learning about the intentions and plans of low-power members (Tjosvold & Sagaria, 1978), less cooperative and more exploitative in response to low-power members' cooperation (Lindskold & Aronoff, 1980), and less likely to make concessions in negotiations (Lawler & Yoon, 1993). High-power members also see themselves as being entitled to a larger share of available resources due to their superior value (Murnighan & Pillutla, 1995). It is ironic that the greater a person's power, the more insufficient it is likely to seem, simply because the claims on it increase faster than the power to fulfill them (Halle, 1967). For example, the Ford Foundation, by far the richest of American foundations, is also the most inadequately endowed in terms of the expectations it is called on to meet.

The Metamorphic Effects of High Power. In Greek myths, the heroes typically become so arrogant (based on their past accomplishments) that they compare themselves to the gods. Having gained power from their heroic deeds, they seek even more, and in doing so they bring forth the jealousy of the gods, who engineer the hero's demise. Arachne, for example, believed she could weave better than Athena (goddess of wisdom and weaving). Athena was offended and came to Earth, where they had a contest over who could weave the best. Arachne won! In response, Athena turned her into a spider. The point of these myths is that obtaining power brings about a metamorphosis that eventually results in the person's downfall.

Using power tends to alter the high-power person (Kipnis, Castell, Gergen, & Mauch, 1976). First, the gaining of power becomes a goal in and of itself, apart from the larger goals that power is intended to fulfill, such as accomplishing the task. Second, the ease with which powerholders can exercise their power encourages them to use it for their own benefit, at the expense of those under their power. Third, powerholders received unwarranted positive feedback, even adulation, from others, which results in an inflated sense of self-worth. Fourth, power may lead to the devaluation of others, reflected in a tendency to see the worst in others. Fifth, having an inflated view of oneself may lead powerholders to overstep the bounds of the appropriate use of their power. The corporate scandals of 2002–2003 at Enron, Tyco, and WorldCom may be large-scale examples of high-power individuals devaluing others and serving only themselves.

One of the most dramatic examples of the tranformative effects of power is the Stanford Prison Study (Haney, Banks, & Zimbardo, 1973; Zimbardo, 1975). Zimbardo conducted a field study to explore the roles of guards and prisoners in a prison situation. From over 100 applications to participate in the two-week experiment, Zimbardo carefully selected twenty-four participants on the basis of extensive psychological testing to ensure they were "normal" and representative of intelligent, middle-class male youth. Stanford students were assigned randomly to be either guards or prisoners. The prisoners were "arrested" by uniformed police, booked, and transported to the mock prison constructed in the basement of the psychology building at Stanford University. The prisoners were dressed in a prison shirt, heavy ankle chain, and stocking cap. Guards wore khaki uniforms, clubs, whistles, and reflective sunglasses. The setting was made realistic with bars on the doors and strict visiting hours for anyone wanting to meet with the prisoners. The guards were simply instructed to keep order. The simulation had to be abandoned after only six days, however, because the treatment of the prisoners by the guards was far more aggressive and dehumanizing than had been expected. The guards seemed to enjoy thinking up new ways to degrade prisoners. The power these normal, bright, young, middle-class men had over their schoolmates transformed them in unexpected and negative ways.

Status and Power. High-status positions invoke a sense of privilege (Messe, Kerr, & Sattler, 1992). Occupants of high-status position come to believe they are entitled to special treatment simply because of the position they hold. Privilege behaviors seemed to be a central component of people's role schema for "supervisor," and due to this sense of privilege, supervisors expended less effort than subordinates on shared tasks and took more than an equal share of the rewards offered to the group.

High status does not always mean high power. Johnson and Allen (1972) demonstrated that having high status and high power results in an enhanced self-perception that leads to altruistic behavior but disdain for the low-power, low-status members. But when individuals had high status but low power, they felt underrewarded and attempted to obtain increased rewards from the group (they deviated from the prescribed norms in order to increase their own rewards) and emphasized the incompetence, uncooperativeness, lack of generosity, and unfairness of the high-power members (Johnson & Allen, 1972). They also tended to dislike their high-power groupmates and to respect low-power members.

Power Stereotyping Theory. An association exists between power and stereotyping (Fiske, 1993; Fiske & Morling, 1996). The general premise of *power stereotyping theory* is that people in positions of power are likely to stereotype subordinates because they pay less attention to them, perhaps due to lack of cognitive capacity (having high power requires attending to more people and more issues at the same time), viewing subordinates as unimportant because the high-power person's outcomes do not depend on the actions of subordinates, or having a dominant personality trait (which results in their attempting to control their interactions with others to such an extent that they ignore the actions and motivations of others). Regardless of its cause, decreases in attention make powerful individuals more likely to depend on stereotypes in interacting with low-power individuals.

Oppression. High-power group members often oppress low-power members. *Oppression* is the experience of repeated, widespread, systemic injustice, which may involve the legal system (as in slavery, apartheid, or the lack of right to vote), be embedded in unquestioned norms and rules, or even involve violence (Deutsch, 2006). Once established, oppression is often institutionalized into the structure of society (i.e., major economic, political, and cultural institutions as well as mass media and cultural stereotypes), where it exists and functions without the full, conscious awareness of high-power individuals. Perhaps the most dangerous form of oppression is moral exclusion—that is, defining low-power group members as outside of the moral community and therefore not entitled to fair outcomes or treatment. In the most extreme cases, oppression based on moral exclusion has led to genocide and enslavement; at a less extreme level, it has led to the marginalization of low-power individuals. What keeps oppression in place is the superior power of the oppressors, the systematic use of force (including official, semi-official, or unofficial violence and terror), control over the legal and legislative systems, control over socialization and indoctrination of new members, and control over the social production of meaning to legitimize oppression (i.e., control over history, religion, science, or ideology).

High-power group members tend to have the power to take the initiative in their interaction with low-power members (Harvey, 1999). High-power individuals can begin, modify, or end the relationship. They can decide when to begin or end a specific contact (such as a conversation), insist on being listened to, and insist on being given answers to reasonable and pertinent questions. Two of the major consequences of such interactions between high- and low-power individuals are the application of oppression when the use of power is challenged and erosion of the low-power person's self-esteem and identity. Treating a low-power individual as an inferior, day after day in interaction after interaction, creates a public image of that person being an inferior, which he or she may internalize into an image of self-inferiority. Correspondingly, the interactions produce a public image of superiority for the high-power person and a corresponding self-image of superiority. These public and self-images work to keep a system of oppression in place.

Low-Power Members

In describing how low-power people react to high-power individuals, the acronym CORE is useful.

The C stands for *cooperation, compliance,* and yielding. Many social systems have an authority system consisting of several levels, such as president, vice presidents, managers, and workers. Most of the members are both high and low power, depending on whether they are interacting with their superiors or subordinates. *Authority* is power vested in a particular position and viewed as legitimate by the powerholder and by subordinates. Compliance with authoritative requests is a generalized role expectation in organizations. There is no more pervasive law of organization than the occupants of certain roles shall obey certain kinds of requests from occupants of certain other roles. Authority is usually backed by the power to reward and punish. Thus, it is no surprise that compared to high-power individuals, low-power individuals tend to be more cooperative (e.g., Lindskold & Aronoff, 1980), to make more concessions (e.g., Lawler & Yoon, 1993), to be more compliant in response to threat while negotiating (e.g., Lawler & Yoon, 1993), to yield to superiors when interpersonal conflicts arise (e.g., Kramer, 1996), and to behave less aggressively (e.g., Epstein & Taylor, 1967; Ohbuchi & Saito, 1986). Low-power individuals, furthermore, tend to use ingratiation, conformity, flattery, and effacing self-presentation to induce the high-power members to like and to reward them (Tjosvold, 1978). All of these behaviors are appropriate within an authority hierarchy and help the social system function effectively.

LOW-POWER STRATEGIES TO CHANGE THE STATUS QUO

C   *Cooperative, compliant*, yielding in interactions with high-power members
O   Attribution of causes of group successes to *own* efforts
R   *Resistance*, psychological reactance, obstruction of high-power members' efforts
E   Negative *evaluations* of high-power individuals

The O stands for attributing the success of joint efforts with high-power individuals to one's (i.e., the low-power individual's) *own* efforts. Attributions of the cause of successful goal accomplishment tend to be self-serving and, therefore, low-power members tend to devalue the performances of high-power members and take responsibility for the group's success.

The R stands for *resistance*, psychological *reactance*, and obstruction. When the legitimacy of the powerholders is not accepted by low-power group members, low-power individuals tend to resist attempts by powerholders to control them. The resistance is reflected in low-power members defying threats, counter-threatening, and refusing to comply with an influence attempt, even when resistance is costly (Tjosvold, 1978). Low-power individuals generally find their relationships with high-power people threatening and debilitating, as low-power individuals cannot be certain about their success in achieving their goals because of the unpredictability of high-power members. These feelings of uncertainty and anxiety tend to result in (1) increased vigilance and attempts to understand and predict high-power members' behavior, (2) stifling of criticism of high-power members, (3) unwillingness to clarify one's position to high-power members, and (4) a mixture of fear of and attraction to high-power members (Tjosvold, 1978). Low-power members tend to believe that because they have no retaliatory capability, they are vulnerable and helpless and will be exploited. As a consequence, low-power members have been found to direct much of their communication and attention to high-power members and to keep on good terms with them. In addition, low-power individuals often experience psychological reactance, which motivates them to take actions that will help them regain their freedom and control.

The E stands for negative *evaluation* of high-power individuals. Low-power group members tend to express dislike for high-power members, have distorted perceptions that underestimate the positive intent of high-power members toward them, and see high-power members as competitors (Tjosvold, 1978).

What can the research on group dynamics recommend to low-power group members? The first recommendation is to apply the dynamic interdependence strategy of

(1) clarifying low-power members' goals and increasing their positive interdependence, (2) clarifying and developing low-power members' resources, so that, if necessary, they can function independently of the high-power members (this not only makes low-power members less vulnerable to exploitation but also reduces dependence on high-power members), (3) identifying the goals that are important to high-power members but cannot be accomplished without the cooperation of low-power members (thus increasing the positive interdependence between low- and high-power individuals), and (4) negotiating a new and better contract with the high-power members. The increased positive interdependence and the experience of working together will tend to increase the high-power individuals' positive feelings toward low-power individuals.

The second recommendation is to use education and moral persuasion to change those in high power. As Scrooge showed in Dickens's *A Christmas Carol,* even the most recalcitrant person can change under certain circumstances. Both education and increased positive interdependence will tend to increase the high-power individuals' positive feelings toward low-power individuals.

The third recommendation involves bringing the high-power group members to the negotiating table. One strategy for doing so is to use existing legal procedures to bring pressures for change to bear on high-power members. Another strategy is to use obstruction or harassment to increase the high-power members' costs of staying with the status quo. In both of these cases, the low-power members may be successful, but potentially at the cost of creating negative feelings by high-power individuals toward the low-power individuals. Perhaps the most extreme strategy for influencing high-power individuals and groups is terrorism.

Terrorism. The U.S. State Department defines *terrorism* as politically motivated violence perpetrated against noncombatant targets. Others have defined terrorism as violent, often unpredictable strategies designed to kill innocent people with the goal of politically intimidating and controlling a group or nation (Gurwitch, Sitterle, Young, & Pfefferbaum, 2002). At one level, terrorism is aimed at achieving perceived justice, calling attention to one's cause, protecting one's identity and values, creating communal meaning through sacrifice, and fulfilling a spiritual obligation. At another level, terrorism is aimed at inflicting pain on the high-power group, striking back from a position of weakness, and venting rage, frustration, humiliation, and hatred. One problem with discussing terrorism is that it is defined differently by high- and low-power groups. A violent political act may be "terrorism" from a high-power perspective but a "humanitarian attempt at liberation" from a low-power perspective. The low-power group's revolutionary hero is the high-power group's terrorist. From the high-power perspective, it makes strategic sense to define any act of political rebellion as terrorism in order to weaken the low-power opposition. There is little research on the effectiveness of terrorism, but it is clear that terroristic acts can significantly change and reduce the quality of life of high-power individuals and groups. The suffering caused by terrorism is beyond calculation. There are, however, examples of terrorism that derived from desperation and a desire for social justice, and leaders such as Nelson Mandela have succeeded in changing their societies for the better through terrorism. Especially for young people, engaging in terroristic acts may result from a quest for identity and a crisis of meaning an hope (Wessells, 2002).

The Metamorphic Effects of Low Power. Having low power in a situation can change a person. In the Stanford prison experiment, for example, the students randomly assigned to the role of prisoner mostly became withdrawn and depressed and even pressured their fellow prisoners to follow the rules, even though the rules became increasingly tyrannical and arbitrary (such as standing at attention for hours and cleaning toilets with their bare hands) (Zimbardo, 1975). These "prisoners" were young male students at Stanford University who were highly intelligent, psychologically healthy, and from middle- to upper-class backgrounds. Yet they still broke down and became passive acceptors of brutal treatment.

Relationships Among Low-Power Groups. While there has been considerable examination of relationships between high- and low-power groups, there has been little research on how low-power groups relate to each other. There are two views of the way low-power groups relate to one another. Based on the similarity-attraction hypothesis (Brown, 1984; Byrne, 1971) and on the common-enemy position (Sherif Harvey, White, Hood, & Sherif, 1988), it can be argued that low-power group members will be attracted to one another. The similarity-attraction hypothesis says that two low-power groups may be attracted to one another because of their similar circumstance. The common-enemy position argues that two low-power groups might join together to fight their common, high-power enemy. On the other hand, disadvantaged groups may perceive their similar status as a threat to their distinctiveness, which may decrease the integrity of their identity and self-esteem, thus motivating the group to derogate other low-power outgroups to enhance differentiation (Brown, 1984; Turner, 1978). There is evidence that low-power groups tend to react negatively to the good fortune of other low-power groups but react positively to the good fortune of high-power groups (Rothgerber & Worchel, 1997). Thus, when a low-power group begins to succeed and increase its power, other low-power groups may try to restrain the group's progress and keep the group's members from bettering themselves. This, of course, helps the high-power group keep its power advantage.

Revenge. Interaction between high- and low-power individuals often results in the low-power person feeling abused and mistreated. Power asymmetry between parties affects whether revenge will be carried out or suppressed (Heider, 1958; Raven & Kruglanski, 1970). In general, people of low power are unlikely to take revenge against a more powerful harm-doer out of fear of the high-power person's counter-revenge. In the presence of a third party concerned with justice issues, however, upward revenge by low-power participants has been found to be greater than downward revenge (Kim, Smith, & Brigham, 1998).

Power and Conflict

Power and conflict are interrelated. While power is always present in interpersonal and group interaction, conflict occurs only when a person wants other group members to do something they do not want to do and the person does not have enough power to overcome their unwillingness. No conflict exits when (1) a person wants group members to do something and they want to do it (even when the person does not have the power to influence them to do so) and (2) a person wants group members to do something and has the power to influence them do it. Conflict often ends when the use of power is successful but is escalated when influence attempts are unsuccessful—that is, when the desire to influence is not matched by the capacity to influence. Most conflicts concern power directly (such as conflicts between the "haves" and the "have-nots") or indirectly as leverage for achieving one's goals, or as a symbolic expression of one's identity. The destructive management of conflict, furthermore, results in fewer and fewer bases of power being effective. Informational power and expertise power are apt to be rejected because each participant sees the other as being untrustworthy and as trying to use expertise for personal gain. Hostility and distrust undermine legitimate power and mutual referent power. Reward power can arouse suspicions of bribery or suggest that one is attempting to increase another's dependence. Only coercive power is left and thus is relied on more and more.

Coercion and threats can sometimes shorten or control a conflict through inducing compliance or withdrawal. Typically, however, the use of coercive power is destructive. Coercion decreases the frequency and reliability of communication. It exacerbates the conflict, thereby increasing hostility, resentment, lies, threats, retaliation, revenge, and distrust. Coercion often includes the threat of violence, which may lead to aggression and counterthreats by low-power individuals. For these and many other reasons, the use of coercive power is counterproductive and should be avoided in conflicts.

GROUP NORMS: INDIRECT POWER

"What's it to be? Pizza or hamburgers?" Six friends who had just exited a movie theater were trying to decide what to eat. "Pizza!" immediately said five. "Hamburgers!" Keith answered. In rapid fire everyone talked to Keith. "We always get pizza." "Pizza is our group's official food." "You can have hamburger on your pizza." "We never eat hamburgers; hamburgers are for kids!" "Don't be a killjoy!" "OK," said Keith. "Let's get pizza." This scenario occurs many times a day. The majority members of a group decide on a particular course of action that another member prefers not to follow. The majority then remind the dissenter of group norms designed to pressure and persuade the member to adopt the group's perspective. The incident concludes when the holdout member gives in and conforms to the group's norms.

Group norms often serve as substitutes for the direct use of power among group members. **Norms** are prescribed modes of conduct and belief that guide the behavior of group members. Conformity to group norms is usually a requirement for continued membership in the group. Norms introduce regularity and control into group members' interactions without making direct interpersonal application of power necessary. Indirect influence through group norms saves the group considerable energy and resources and avoids the resistance and lack of wholehearted cooperation that may result from the direct application of power. Group norms control the behavior of high-power members as well as low-power members and set limits on the use of power. Group members give up part of their personal power to the norms to protect themselves from the capricious or inconsistent use of power and save the surveillance costs of checking to make sure everyone is behaving appropriately. Individuals let themselves be influenced by norms in ways that they would never permit themselves to be influenced by others, for norms often take on the characteristics of moral obligations (they have a specific "ought to" and "must" quality).

Conforming to Group Norms

As for conforming outwardly, and living your own life inwardly,
I do not think much of that.

Henry David Thoreau

A man stands up and faces the group. "My name is Dale," he says. "I am an alcoholic. I have not had a drink for three years, two months, and six days." The group applauds. This is a typical exchange at a meeting of Alcoholics Anonymous. One AA group norm is to take the "first step" and admit that you are an alcoholic. Another group norm is to stay sober, one day at a time. Dale just testified he is conforming to these normative expectations. In return, the group gives him support and recognition. This sequence occurs countless times daily in families, businesses, schools, churches, and all other groups. A group cannot exist, cannot survive, cannot function, and cannot be productive unless most members conform to its norms most of the time.

Conformity is defined as changes in behavior that result from group influences. The changes include **compliance** (behavioral change without internal acceptance) and *private acceptance* (changes in both behavior and attitudes). Many people think of conformity as a blind, unreasoning, spineless, weak, slavish adherence to the demands of the majority of peers or authority figures. Even among social psychologists, a common conception of conformity is agreement with the majority or authority figure for the sake of agreement, even when doing so involves lying about one's perceptions or beliefs. Under most conditions, however, these pejorative connotations of conformity are inaccurate. Under some conditions, conformity to group norms may violate an individual's values and principles, and under other conditions, conforming may support these values and beliefs. Conforming to group norms frequently improves the functioning of a group at no expense to the individual's principles or beliefs. Conforming to a classroom norm that one should provide help and assistance to classmates, for example, is beneficial for the group and the students involved.

The classic studies on conformity under group pressures were conducted by Solomon Asch (1956). Asch was born in 1907 in Poland. He arrived in the United States at age thirteen. In 1928 he received a bachelor's degree from City College of New York. In 1932 he received a doctorate from Columbia University. He was an unusually independent person and of him it often has been said that it took the least conformant of social psychologists to defend conformity and to point out that an essential feature of social life is the willingness to trust the observations of others.

In his experimental studies on conformity, Asch placed participants in groups and asked them to choose which of several lines came closest in length to a line they had just seen. There was an obvious correct answer. Yet each participant found himself or herself faced with most or all fellow group members (the group size ranged from three to fifteen) agreeing on an obviously wrong answer. The participant thus was faced with a conflict: accepting the evidence of his or her own eyes or going along with the group's perception. Sixty-eight percent of the individual estimates remained independent; 32% were deflected part or all of the way to the unanimous judgment of the fellow group members. One-fourth of the participants made no concessions to the unanimous majority, and one-third conformed on half or more of the trials. Whether the majority consisted of three or fifteen members made little difference as long as it was unanimous. If one other member agreed with the participant, the tendency to follow the majority opinion dropped from 32% to 10%. If the participant reported his estimates secretly, furthermore, the pro-majority errors were fewer. The results of the Asch experiments were somewhat shocking, as they seemed to indicate that many people go along with an erroneous group judgment even when they know it is false.

Conformity to group norms can be differentiated along two dimensions: conformity versus anticonformity and independence versus dependence (Allen, 1965; Hollander & Willis, 1967). The conformers and anticonformers both react to the group norm and base their behavior on it: the conformers agree with the norm, the anticonformers disagree with the norm, and both behave accordingly. An independent person, on the other hand, does not give undue importance to the group norm in making her judgment.

Not all behaviors are covered by group norms. Few groups care what foods members eat or whether members prefer one type of drink to another. Group norms deal primarily with the behavior affecting the completion of the group's tasks and the ability of the group to maintain itself over time. In general, the more relevant the individual's behavior is to the accomplishment of the group's goals and the maintenance of the group, the greater are the pressures to conform. Many years ago, observers in industrial organizations noted that members of work groups typically established production standards (norms) that were adhered to by most members (Homans, 1950; Roethlisberger & Dickson, 1939). When a worker deviated too much from the standard, he or she was subjected to ridicule and other sanctions. If the worker produced too much, he was referred to as a "speed king" or a "rate-buster"; if he produced too little, the worker was a "chiseler." Schachter (1951; Schacter et al., 1954) and Emerson (1954) found in their studies of deviation from group norms that the more relevant the deviation was to the purposes of the group, the greater the rejection of the deviant by the other group members. Festinger (1950) and Allen (1965) concluded there are greater pressures to conform to task-related norms if goal attainment depends on the coordinated behavior of the group members. Raven and Rietsema (1957) found that the clearer the group goal and the path to the goal are to the group members, the stronger are the pressures toward uniformity in task behavior. In general, nonconforming behaviors are accepted if they are perceived by the group's members as potentially improving the group's ability to accomplish its goals and maintain itself; they are not accepted if they interfere with group maintenance and goal accomplishment.

Implementing Group Norms

Norms can be initiated in several ways (Johnson, 1970). A member may state the norm directly and tell other members to accept it, such as, "I think we should express our feelings openly about this topic." Norms can be initiated through modeling; members learn to conform to a group norm by watching others conform. Norms can be imported from other groups. Many norms of *social responsibility* (you should help someone who is in need of help), *fair play* (don't kick someone when he's down), and *reciprocity* (if someone does you a favor, you should do her a favor in return) are imported from the broader culture. Finally, perhaps the most effective way of establishing group norms is through group discussion.

Johnson (1970) has presented a set of general guidelines for the establishment and support of group norms. Group members accept and internalize group norms when they:

1. Recognize that the norms exist, see the other members accepting and following the norms, and feel some commitment to the norms.
2. See the norms as helping accomplish the goals to which members are committed. It is helpful, therefore, for a group to clarify how conformity to a norm can help goal accomplishment.
3. Feel a sense of ownership for the norms. Ownership is usually established through involvement in establishing the norms.
4. Enforce the norms to one another immediately after a violation. Consistent enforcement enhances both understanding of the norms and commitment to them.
5. See appropriate models and examples of conforming to the norms and have a chance to practice the desired behaviors.
6. Import cultural norms that promote goal accomplishment, group maintenance, and growth.
7. Perceive that the norms are flexible, so at any time, more appropriate norms can be substituted to increase group effectiveness.

 ## THE GROUP MIND

In 1212, bands of children and young people in Germany and France responded to the Church's call to reconquer Jerusalem. They began the Children's Crusade, convinced that only the pure in spirit could succeed in taking the Holy Land from the Muslims. In Germany, a boy named Nicholas led the children from town to town, gathering increasing numbers. They walked across the Alps into Italy and then to the sea. The children expected the sea to divide so they could walk to the Holy Land. It did not. Confused, some returned home, and merchants sold some into slavery. No one knows if any reached the Holy Land. Why did thousands of children join the Crusade? Why did their parents let them?

Group members sometimes engage in *collective behavior*, in which they spontaneously perform atypical actions such as riots, panics, and mass hysteria (the spontaneous outbreak of atypical thoughts, feelings, or actions in a group, including psychogenic illness, common hallucinations, and bizarre actions [Pennebaker, 1982; Phoon, 1982]). In 1903, for example, there was a panic at Chicago's Iroquois Theater. A small fire broke out backstage, and the management tried to calm the audience. When the fire became visible to the crowd, however, the audience stampeded for the exits. Some died by jumping from the fire escapes to the pavement. Many more were trampled by fleeing patrons. Some were burned. Nearly 600 people were killed.

A number of explanations have been proposed to account for such group behavior. The first was the concept of *group mind,* proposed by Le Bon. In 1895, Gustave Le Bon published his classic study *The Crowd* to explain why people in a mob lose their sense of responsibility. Le Bon argued that people in crowds show "impulsiveness, irritability, incapacity to reason," and "exaggeration of sentiments" (p. 40). No matter what the individual qualities of the people in the group, once they fall under the "law of the mental unity of crowds," they all act in ways that are impulsive, unreasonable, and extreme. Le Bon believed crowd behavior resulted from three mechanisms. The first is *anonymity:* People feel less responsible for their behavior when they cannot be identified. Since crowds create relative anonymity, individual responsibility tends to be reduced, and people then commit acts for which they believe they cannot be held responsible. The second is *contagion:* Emotional states tend to spread from person to person in the same way that diseases spread. Le Bon was a physician who viewed the collective mind as a kind of disease that began at one point and then spread throughout the rest of the crowd, causing people to behave in very similar ways. The third is *suggestibility:* Crowd members tend to completely accept suggestions, just as if they were hypnotized.

A second possible explanation for collective behavior is convergence theory. According to *convergence theory,* crowd behavior represents the convergence of people with compatible needs, desires, motivations, and emotions, whose membership in the crowd triggers the spontaneous release of previously controlled behaviors (Freud, 1922; Turner & Killian, 1987). A specific event brings together people who share similar convictions and predispositions. Members bring a common mood to the crowd (as in a protest demonstration). The crowd eventually acts out this mood. Convergence theory seeks to identify the latent tendencies in people that cause them to act alike, the circumstances that bring people with such tendencies together, and the kinds of events that will cause these tendencies to be released. Sigmund Freud (1922) believed that people join collectives to satisfy repressed unconscious desires that otherwise never would be fulfilled. In a group situation, control over behavior is transferred to the leader or the other group members, and each person is thus freed from the bonds of restraint and guilt. As a result, formerly repressed needs come to motivate behavior, and atypical actions become more likely.

A third explanation is *emergent norm theory.* Ralph Turner and Lewis Killian (1987) argue that crowds are quite heterogeneous and do not have a "mental unity." Rather, the members all adhere to norms that are relevant to the given situation. They hypothesized that all crowds share a number of common elements. Crowds form in ambiguous situations in which the participants' behaviors are unplanned. A sense of urgency characterizes the feelings of the crowd members. As the crowd gets larger, norms emerge and are communicated throughout the crowd about appropriate moods, imagery, and actions. Individuals become highly susceptible to suggestions consistent with the emergent norm. As a result, they engage in actions they ordinarily would inhibit.

The fourth explanation is *deindividuation theory.* **Deindividuation** is a state of relative anonymity, in which group members do not feel singled out or identifiable (Festinger, Pepitone, & Newcomb, 1952). When people cannot be identified, they are more likely to perform antisocial acts. Festinger, Pepitone, and Newcomb (1952) argued that people in groups feel themselves to be "submerged in the group" and lose their personal identity, which creates a "reduction of inner restraints" and, in the extreme case, atypical actions. Philip Zimbardo (1970) explained the reduction of inner constraints by dividing deindividuation into the conditions of deindividuation (inputs), the state of deindividuation (internal changes), and deindividuated behaviors (outputs).

The *conditions of deindividuation* (inputs) include anonymity, reduced responsibility, membership in a large group, and arousal. Anonymity exists when others cannot identify or single out a person for evaluation, criticism, judgment, or punishment. Personal responsibility is reduced by the demands for compliance by an authority figure, the separation of the consequences from the act itself, and a diffusion of responsibility among group members. As the size of the crowd increases, so does the deindividuation. Finally, arousal is increased through altered temporal perspective, sensory overload, heightened involvement, and the lack of situational structure.

The *state of deindividuation* (internal changes) is characterized by profound changes in emotions, memory, and **self-regulation.** Deindividuation is experienced as (1) a loss of self-awareness (minimal self-consciousness, lack of conscious planning, uninhibited speech, and performing uninhibited tasks) and (2) altered experiencing (disturbances in concentration and judgment, the feeling that time is moving slowly or rapidly, extreme emotions, a sense of unreality, and perceptual distortions). Members

REVIEW OF IMPORTANT CONCEPTS

Match the following concepts with their definitions. Find a partner and compare answers.

_____ 1. Power

_____ 2. High power

_____ 3. Low power

_____ 4. Power majority

_____ 5. Power minority

_____ 6. Norms

_____ 7. Conformity

_____ 8. Compliance

_____ 9. Collective behavior

_____ 10. Deindividuation

a. Prescribed modes of conduct and belief that guide the behavior of group members.

b. Changes in behavior that result from group influences.

c. Behavioral change without internal acceptance.

d. Capacity to affect another person's goal accomplishment.

e. State of relative anonymity in which group members do not feel singled out or identifiable.

f. Spontaneous performance by individuals of atypical actions, such as in riots, panics, and mass hysteria episodes.

g. Capacity to have considerable influence on another person's goal accomplishment.

h. Capacity to have little influence on another person's goal accomplishment.

i. Group that has the most control over how important resources are distributed (this group may be a numerical minority).

j. Group that has little control over the distribution of important resources (the group may be a numerical majority).

lower the threshold of behavior they normally restrain because of low self-awareness and altered experiencing. People who are deindividuated have lost self-awareness and their personal identity in the group situation. They experience cognitive and emotional changes, including disturbances in concentration and judgment, the feeling that time is moving slowly or rapidly, extreme emotions, a sense of unreality, perceptual distortions, and intense pleasure.

Finally, *deindividuated behaviors* (outputs) replace reason and order with impulse and chaos. Members engage in extreme, atypical, or polarized actions such as violence and destruction. Zimbardo (1975) states that the conditions that reduce a person's sense of uniqueness and individuality are the wellsprings of antisocial behaviors, such as aggression, vandalism, stealing, cheating, and rudeness, as well as a general loss of concern for others. The deindividuated person reacts strongly to emotions and situational cues that may lead to uninhibited behaviors and is less concerned with norms, personal punishment, or long-term consequences.

As research and theory on the group mind demonstrate, power can be exercised by the group as a whole and not only by individuals within the group. Collective behavior, such as riots and mass hysteria, may be explained by the group mind, the convergence of people who share similar convictions and predispositions, following norms that emerge in the crowd, or deindividuation. It should be remembered, however, that collective behavior and other group influences can also encourage members to behave altruistically and in other positive ways.

EXERCISE 6.5

YOUR POWER BEHAVIOR

Having completed this chapter, it may be helpful to focus again on your behavior in exercising power. Form a group of three with two persons who know you well and who have participated with you in some of the exercises in this book. Then complete the following tasks, taking at least two hours to do so.

1. Reflect silently on how each member uses power. Give one another feedback about the animal, song, or book that each member reminds the others of on the basis of how he or she deals with power. Each person explains why he or she chose the animal, song, or book that he or she did.
2. Write down your individual strengths in using power constructively and effectively. Share your lists. Members should add to one another's lists.
3. Write down the individual skills you need to develop in order to use power more constructively and effectively. Share your lists. Members should add to one another's lists.
4. Discuss the feelings each member has in using power and why he or she reacts that way. Help one another think of alternative ways of reacting to the use of power.
5. From magazine pictures and any other materials, build a collage about the way in which you exercise power. Share the collage with the other members. Add ideas to one another's collages.

INDIVIDUAL VERSUS RELATIONSHIP PERSPECTIVES

There is a division within the field of group dynamics between social scientists who focus on individual variables and those who focus on relationship variables. The individual orientation to human behavior results in social scientists searching for laws governing the behavior of a single individual and looking at the individual's attitudes, personality traits, skills, aptitudes, genes, and other causes of behavior. These causes are often assumed to be static, to be present at any one moment, and to have a physical, often neuropsychological, representation of some kind.

In contrast, relationship scholars seek laws governing the nature of individuals' interactions with one another. By looking inside relationships, they identify dynamics such as power, conflict, love, and cooperation. There is a rhythm displayed in regularities in interaction patterns, and the relationship perspective seeks to identify the causal conditions responsible for that rhythm. The rhythm of relationships is revealed over time in specific situations; relationships are inherently temporal rather than static and are influenced by the situational context. A relationship's rhythm is not presumed to have a direct representation. Rather, like gravity and electricity, its existence can be discerned only by observing its effects.

SUMMARY

Power is the capacity to affect the outcomes of oneself, others, and the environment. Power is constructive when it enhances group effectiveness and destructive when it interferes with group effectiveness. Although the dominant view of power focuses on its potential destructiveness, exerting power offers many potential positive outcomes. In fact, the positive use of power is essential for group effectiveness.

The dynamic interdependence approach to influence posits that who is influencing whom to what degree changes constantly as members strive to achieve the group's goals. Power is thus an attribute of an interpersonal relationship in which people are dependent on one another for outcomes and resources. In any relationship, the use of power is inevitable, essential, constantly changing, and pervades all aspects of the relationship. The use of power is greatly affected by the context in which it takes place. In a competitive context, power tends to be viewed as a limited zero-sum resource that should be accumulated and hoarded, being unidirectional, and being inherently coercive. The coercive use of power creates resistance, psychological reactance, and resentment toward and dislike of the powerholder. In a cooperative context, power is viewed as expandable, something to be shared, by acting in a bidirectional way and being inherently noncoercive. The key to power in a cooperative context is inducibility, the openness to influencing and being influenced by other group members.

The trait factor approach to influence views power as an attribute of a person. The assumption is that certain individuals are born with an inherent capacity to influence others. Two of the trait factor approaches to power are persuasion and social dominance. The persuasion position states that a person exerts power by (1) being credible and attractive, (2) phrasing messages so that they are two-sided, action-oriented, and discrepant with members' current beliefs, and (3) playing on others' low self-esteem and low intelligence, giving them no forewarning of the influence attempt, distracting them during the influence attempt, convincing them the attitudes under modification are peripheral to them, and having them role play positions counter to their beliefs. Social dominance theory assumes that resources are limited and, therefore, resource acquisition compels competition among group members. A person's ability to successfully compete for limited resources defines his or her position in the social hierarchy.

Power may be based on the ability to deliver rewards, the ability to deliver punishments, a legitimate position of authority, being a referent for others, being an expert, or having needed information. When the distribution of power is unequal, both the high- and low-power person experience difficulties. Although the use of power is ever present in relationships, it is during conflicts that individuals become most conscious of its use.

Besides the direct use of power, power may be exerted indirectly through group norms. Collective behavior, in addition, may have its origins in the group mind, converging with people who share similar convictions and predispositions, following norms that emerge in the group, or members becoming deindividuated.

You now should have a good understanding of what power is and how it can help or hinder a group. You have experienced high- and low-power situations. In the next chapter, you will learn how to make effective group decisions.

CHAPTER SEVEN

Decision Making

BASIC CONCEPTS TO BE COVERED IN THIS CHAPTER

In this chapter a number of concepts are defined and discussed. The major ones are in the following list. Divide into heterogeneous pairs. Each pair is to (1) define each concept, noting the page on which it is defined and discussed, and (2) ensure that both members of the pair understand the meaning of each concept. Then combine into groups of four. Compare the answers of the two pairs. If there is disagreement, look up the concept in the chapter and clarify it until all members agree on and understand the definition.

CONCEPTS

1. Decision
2. Effective group decision
3. Consensus
4. Majority vote
5. Minority control
6. Averaging opinions
7. Defensive avoidance
8. Groupthink
9. Concurrence seeking
10. Dissonance reduction
11. Vigilance

MAKING EFFECTIVE DECISIONS

Imagine you are driving down the street. A police officer stops you for a minor traffic violation and then notices that your appearance matches the description of a person who has just robbed a nearby bank. He arrests you and, to your horror, no fewer than six eyewitnesses identify you as the bank robber. You cannot provide a good alibi for the time of the robbery (you were driving around by yourself), and no one pays any attention to your protestations of innocence. The ordeal drags on until the day you go to court and face your accusers. As the trial begins, you realize the only barrier between you and a prison sentence is a small group of your peers. The jury members are strangers to one another, chosen randomly from your community, unschooled in legal principles, and unpracticed in group decision making. They hold your fate, your future, and your well-being in their hands.

Trial by a jury of peers to determine guilt and innocence has formed the foundation of judicial systems for hundreds of years. As far back as the eleventh century, juries were used both to provide information about the actions of the accused and to weigh the evidence. Gradually, juries evolved into finders of fact that weigh the testimony of each person before deciding if a law has been broken.

A jury is only one of the small groups in our society that have to make vital decisions. Many groups exist to make decisions for our society. Governments, large corporations, military units, and virtually all other social entities entrust their key decisions to groups. As a result, most of the laws, policies, and practices that affect our daily lives, as well as the future course of society, are determined by teams, committees, boards of directors, and similar groups, *not* by single individuals. How good the decisions are depends on how effective the group is.

The purpose of group decision making is to decide on well-considered, well-understood, realistic action toward goals every member wishes to achieve. A **group decision** implies that some agreement prevails among group members as to which of several courses of action is most desirable for achieving the group's goals. Making a **decision** is just one step in the more general problem-solving process of goal-directed groups. After defining a problem or issue, thinking over alternative courses of action, and weighing the advantages and disadvantages of each, a group will decide which course is the most desirable to implement.

Typically, groups try to make their decisions as effective as possible. There are five major characteristics of an **effective group decision:**

1. The resources of group members are fully utilized.
2. Time is well used.
3. The decision is correct or of high quality.
4. The decision is implemented fully by all the required group members.
5. The problem-solving ability of the group is improved, or at least not lessened.

A decision is effective to the extent that these five criteria are met; if all five are not met, the decision has not been made effectively.

Not everyone agrees that group decision making is a good idea. For decades, social scientists have disagreed over whether individuals or groups make better decisions. The first issue examined in this chapter, therefore, is the comparative effectiveness of individual and group decision making. Next, the different methods a group can use to arrive at a decision are explained. After that, the factors that facilitate and hinder an effective group decision are discussed. Finally, a process that groups can use to ensure effective decision making is outlined. Figure 7.1 contains an overview to delineate further how these issues are developed in the chapter.

Individual versus Group Decision Making

Process gain	Involvement and commitment
Correct one another's errors	Changed behavior and attitudes
Social facilitation	Type of task
Risk taking	Potential group productivity

Methods of Decision Making

Decision by authority without group discussion	Decision by minority
Decision by expert	Decision by majority vote
Decision by averaging individuals' opinions	Decision by consensus
Decision by authority after group discussion	Time and decision making

Essential Components	Hindering Factors	
Positive interdependence	Lack of group maturity	Homogeneity
Face-to-face promotive interaction	Dominant response	Production blocking
Individual accountability	Social loafing	Inappropriate size
Social skills	Free riding	Dissonance reduction
Group processing	Not being a sucker	Lack of skills
	Groupthink	Lack of incentives
	Conflicting goals	for and barriers
	Egocentrism of	to contributing
	group members	

Considered and Thoughtful Decision Making

Identifying and defining problem	Deciding on a solution
Gathering information about problem	Second-chance meeting
Forming alternative solutions	Presenting recommendation to organization
Force field analysis	Evaluating success of implementation
Vigilant analysis	
Barriers	

Problems with Theorizing on Decision Making

Figure 7.1 Overview of the chapter.

EXERCISE 7.1

INDIVIDUAL VERSUS GROUP DECISION MAKING

There has been some controversy over whether individual or group decision making is more effective. The purpose of this exercise is to structure a critical discussion of the issue.

1. **Assignment to Groups:** Assign participants to groups of four. Each group is to write a short statement summarizing and explaining its position on whether individual or group decision making is more effective.
2. **Assignment to Pairs and Positions:** Divide each group into two pairs. Pair 1 is assigned the position that individuals are superior to groups in making decisions and given Briefing Sheet One. Pair 2 is assigned the position that groups are superior to individuals in making decisions and given Briefing Sheet Two. The procedure and guidelines for constructive controversy may be reviewed (p. 32).
3. **Preparation of Positions:** The pairs meet separately. They have ten minutes to prepare a forceful and persuasive three-minute presentation of their position. Anything in this chapter or in the field of decision making may be included in the presentation. Both members of the pair have to be ready to give the presentation.
4. **Presentation of Positions:** New pairs are formed consisting of one person from pair 1 and one person from pair 2. Each person presents his or her assigned position. The listener takes notes and asks for clarification of anything that is not fully understood. Each person can present for only three minutes.
5. **Attack and Defend Discussion:** A ten-minute discussion of the issue is conducted. Each person critically analyzes the opposing position and points out its shortcomings. Each person defends his or her position from the attacks of the opponent. The discussion should focus on theory, research, and facts, not on opinions and impressions.
6. **Reverse Perspectives:** Each person has two minutes to summarize the opponent's position and best reasoning. The summary should be complete and accurate.
7. **Joint Report:** The pair writes one statement summarizing and explaining its conclusions on whether individual or group decision making is more effective. The best reasoning from both sides should be synthesized or integrated into a position both members of the pair believe is valid. The statement should include theory, research, and facts.
8. **Conclusions and Processing:** The pairs join together into a group of four and compare the two statements, then write down three conclusions about what they have learned concerning the relative advantages of individual and group decision making. Finally, each person tells one other group member one thing the person liked about working with him or her.

BRIEFING SHEET ONE: INDIVIDUALS MAKE SUPERIOR DECISIONS

Your position is that individuals make higher-quality decisions than do groups. To support your position, use the two quotations below, any material from this chapter that is applicable, and what you know from your outside reading.

> If anything, group membership blunts ethical perception and fetters moral imagination, because we then uncritically and possibly let others think for us. (Labarre, 1972, p. 14)

> When a hundred clever heads join a group, one big nincompoop is the result, because every individual is trammeled by the otherness of others. (Jung, cited in Illing, 1957, p. 80)

BRIEFING SHEET TWO: GROUPS MAKE SUPERIOR DECISIONS

Your position is that groups make higher-quality decisions than do individuals. To support your position, use the quotation below, any material from this chapter that is applicable, and what you know from your outside reading.

> Group operations have two kinds of potential advantage over action by a single individual. One is the caliber of thinking, the range of resources, and the critical scrutiny which enter the problem solving. The other is the willingness with which people carry out decisions they have helped to make.... Groups may sometimes be more sane, moderate, well-balanced and wise than their average member.... A thoughtful group may make its members more rational, more self-critical, and more ready to revise personal prejudices in the light of objective evidence, than these members would be if they were studying alone. (Watson & Johnson, 1972, pp. 130–131)

INDIVIDUAL VERSUS GROUP DECISION MAKING

Which is more productive, groups or individuals? One of the earliest studies to compare individual and group decision making was conducted by Goodwin Watson (1931). Watson received his bachelor of arts degree from the University of Wisconsin and his master's and doctorate from Columbia University. He taught at Columbia University from 1925 to 1962. A vigorous, dedicated psychologist, Watson fought against all types of discrimination and challenged the value of standardized intelligence tests. In his 1931 study, he used three equivalent forms of an intelligence test, each consisting of nine tasks suited to bright adults. Sixty-eight graduate students participated in the study. The first and third tests were given to individual students to complete while working by themselves; each student's performance on the tests was averaged. For the second test, however, students were put into groups of four or five to take the test cooperatively. Groups had no previous practice in working together and were allowed only ten minutes per task. Eleven of the fifteen groups scored higher than their average member and six of the fifteen groups scored higher than their best individual performer. The typical group attained a level of intellectual performance of about the seventieth percentile of its members working alone. Numerous other studies have found that after a group discussion, decisions surpassed both the average of the decisions of individual members and the best individual member's answers (e.g., Barnlund, 1959; Watson, Michaelsen, & Sharp, 1991). The superiority of group over individual decision making was also demonstrated by Marvin Shaw (1932), who conducted a study in which individuals and four-person groups attempted to solve a series of intellectual puzzles called *eureka tasks:* If the correct solution is proposed, it is clear that it is correct (Lorge, Fox, Davitz, & Brenner, 1958). One puzzle had three married couples trying to cross a river in a boat that could hold only three passengers. Only the husbands could row, and no husband would allow his wife to be in the presence of any of the other husbands unless he was present. Only 14% of the individuals were able to solve the husbands-and-wives puzzle, whereas 60% of the groups were able to do so.

As a result of studies such as these, Thorndike (1938) concluded that the superiority of group to individual problem solving and decision making was proved. More recent reviews have also concluded that groups generally learn faster, make fewer errors, recall information better, make better decisions, and produce a higher-quality product than do individuals (Baron, Kerr, & Miller, 1992; Davis, 1969; Johnson & Johnson, 1989; Laughlin, 1980).

Why are groups superior to individuals? One reason (based on the results of Goodwin Watson's study) is *process gain:* The interaction among group members results in ideas, insights, and strategies that no one member previously had thought of on his or her own. Group discussions tend to lead to decisions that none of the participants had thought of before the discussion (Falk & Johnson, 1977; Hall & Williams, 1966), and groups discussing problems have been found to derive more crucial insights into how best to solve the problems than individuals working alone (Johnson, Skon, & Johnson, 1980; Skon, Johnson, & Johnson, 1981). Ames and Murray (1982) even demonstrated that when two young children who did not know the basic principles of conservation worked on conservation problems together, they tended to gain the critical insight and solve the problems correctly. While only 6% of the children working alone gave conservation answers and explanations on the posttest, 42% of the children in the cooperative condition did so. Overall, it may be concluded that process gain often occurs in groups, as the discussion usually stimulates ideas that might not occur to the individual working alone (Figure 7.2).

Another reason is that in groups, incorrect solutions are more likely to be recognized and rejected (Shaw, 1932). In groups, for example, chance errors and blind spots may be corrected (because it is usually easier to see others' mistakes than one's own), and members can remedy one another's mistakes (Ziller, 1957).

A third reason is that groups have a more accurate memory of facts and events than do individuals. Bekhterev and DeLange (1924) briefly showed a picture to groups and asked members to write down all the details they could remember from the picture. A discussion period followed in which the group tried to reach a consensus about each item. The group decision corrected many of the mistaken recollections of the members. Villasenor (1977) notes that the jurors in the Juan Corona trial remembered far more of the evidence and the testimony collectively than they did individually. This is known as *transactive memory*, which is the knowledge of each individual member and the ways to exchange it through communication (Wegner, 1995). The transactive memory of two or more people is more efficient than the memory of either individual alone. Most groups have transactive memories, possessing more knowledge as a group than any individual member has alone (e.g., Hollingshead, Fulk, & Monge, 2002).

A fourth reason is that group members may share unique information that other members did not know. In group decision making, some information is known to all members and some information is known to only one or a few members. When

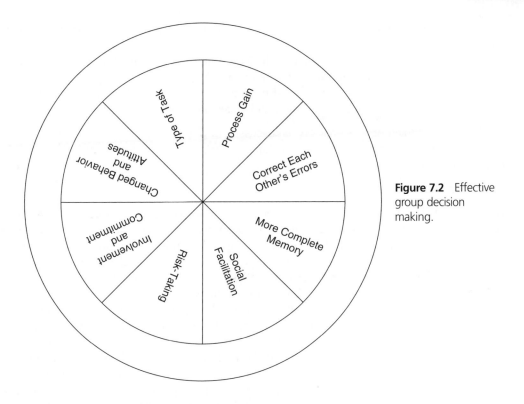

Figure 7.2 Effective group decision making.

group members freely share information, they tend to make better decisions than do individuals (Thompson, Levine, & Messick, 1999). If every member has the same information, however, the group has no advantage over individuals. The quality of the decision making is dependent on members sharing their unique information as well as summarizing information that is shared by all. Kelly and Karau (1999) found that groups are more likely to focus on unshared information. Unique information is more likely to be brought up later over time, suggesting that group discussions should last long enough to get beyond what everyone already knows (Larson, Christensen, Franz, & Abbott, 1998; Larson, Foster-Fishman, & Franz, 1998). Different group members may be assigned to specific areas of expertise so that they know that they alone are responsible for certain types of information. The tendency in ineffective groups of members to fail to share important unique information may be overcome if members learn who is responsible for what kinds of information and take the time to discuss the unique information (Stasser, 2000).

Other reasons why groups may make better decisions than individuals include the following:

1. Groups facilitate higher motivation to achieve.
2. Groups make riskier, more polarized decisions.

3. Involvement in decision making increases members' commitment to implement the decision.
4. Involvement in group decision making facilitates the changes in behavior and attitudes required to implement the decision.
5. Diversity of membership increases the variety of resources available.
6. Face-to-face discussion enhances the quality of reasoning and creativity.

Each of these reasons is discussed in the following sections. The issue of whether decision-making groups work up to their potential is then examined.

Social Facilitation

Does the presence of others facilitate or impair one's performance? Working in the presence of others has been found to improve performance on a variety of tasks, such as fishing-reel winding (Triplett, 1898), dressing in familiar clothes (Markus, 1978), recognition of salient stimuli (Cottrell, Wack, Sekerak, & Rittle, 1968), negotiating simple mazes (Hunt & Hillery, 1973), and copying simple material (Sanders & Baron, 1975). On the other hand, working in the presence of others has been found to impair performance on other tasks, such as solving difficult anagrams (Green, 1977), dressing in unfamiliar clothes (Markus, 1978), recognizing novel stimuli (Cottrell et al., 1968), negotiating difficult mazes (Hunt & Hillery, 1973), and copying difficult material (Sanders & Baron, 1975). Thus, as long as the task is relatively a simple, well-learned one, having others around us appears to facilitate performance, but when the task is difficult, complex, or new, the presence of others tends to impair our performance. Social facilitation and impairment effects, furthermore, seem to occur across a wide range of species.

There are several theoretical explanations for why social facilitation and social impairment take place. In an influential article, Zajonc (1965) proposed that the presence of others increases physiological arousal and this arousal increases the likelihood that our dominant or most probable response will occur. If the well-learned, dominant response includes behaviors that lead to successful performance (as in the case of simple tasks), then people do better. If the well-learned, dominant response primarily includes behaviors that lead to poor performance (as in the case of difficult tasks), then people do worse. Robert Baron and his associates (1978) proposed that social facilitation occurs because audiences, co-actors, and even bystanders often lead performers into "attentional temptation" in which they are placed in conflict regarding whether to attend to other people or to the ongoing task. Since the performer wishes to pay attention to more than he or she can manage, the resulting conflict leads to drive arousal and stress, which in turn produces the social facilitation or impairment effects. Distraction during a simple task will actually improve performance if it triggers attentional conflict (Baron, 1986; Sanders, 1981). Duval and Wicklund (1972) proposed that social facilitation occurs because (1) audiences or co-actors heighten self-consciousness and (2) self-aware individuals will try harder. Social impairment occurs on difficult tasks because when self-aware people see that they are not succeeding, their motivation drops, and they stop trying. Bond (1982) argues that audiences and co-actors affect performance by increasing our concerns about projecting a positive self-image to onlookers. From this self-presentation perspective, social impairment occurs on difficult tasks because initial failures produce embarrassment, which then disrupts performance. Finally, social facilitation may be created by **evaluation apprehension** (concern over being judged). It may not be the presence of others but the presence of others who are evaluating our performance that causes arousal and subsequent social facilitation (Blascovich, Mendes, Hunter, & Salomon, 1999; Bond, Atoum, & Van Leeuwen, 1996; Jackson & Williams, 1985). When other people are evaluating your performance, the stakes are raised in that you will feel embarrassed if you do poorly and pleased if you do well.

From the social facilitation research it may be concluded that group decision making will be more effective than individual decision making because in groups, the co-operation and social support among group members will moderate arousal and reduce competitiveness and evaluation apprehension. In other words, the stronger the positive interdependence and social support, the greater the social facilitation and the less the social impairment.

Group Polarization

A group discussion can polarize decisions by causing the group to adopt a position more extreme than the positions individual members held beforehand. **Group polarization** is the tendency for groups to make decisions that are more extreme than the initial inclination of its members (Brauer, Judd, & Jacquelin, 2001; Moscovici & Zavalloni, 1969). If members' initial tendency was to be risky, the group decision may be even more risky; if members were initially cautious, the group decision may be even more cautious (Friedkin, 1999). When a group faces a situation that requires creative thinking and new perspectives, such risk taking enhances the quality of group decisions.

In 1961, James Stoner, then an MIT graduate student in industrial management, compared risk taking by individuals and groups for his master's thesis. He wanted to test the commonly held belief that groups were more conservative in their decisions than were individuals. Stoner's procedure, which was followed in dozens of later experiments, posed some decision dilemmas to individuals. Each problem described a decision faced by a fictitious person. The subject's task was to advise the person how much risk to take. For example, what advice would you give the person in the following situation?

> Henry is a writer who is said to have considerable creative talent but who so far has been earning a comfortable living by writing cheap westerns. Recently he has come up with an idea for a potentially significant novel. If it could be written and accepted, it might have considerable literary impact and give a big boost to his career. On the other hand, if he is not able to work out his idea or if the novel is a flop, he will have expended considerable time and energy without remuneration.

Imagine that you are advising Henry. Please check the *lowest* probability that you would consider acceptable for Henry to attempt to write the novel.

Henry should attempt to write the novel if the chances that the novel will be a success are at least:

____ 1 in 10	____ 4 in 10	____ 7 in 10
____ 2 in 10	____ 5 in 10	____ 8 in 10
____ 3 in 10	____ 6 in 10	____ 9 in 10

____ 10 in 10 (Place a check here if you think Henry should attempt the novel only if it is certain that the novel will be a success.)

After marking their advice on a dozen items similar to this one, subjects were placed in groups of five or so to discuss each item and reach a unanimous decision on how much risk the person should take. Much to everyone's surprise, the decisions chosen by the group were by and large riskier than those selected before discussion. The finding was immediately dubbed the "risky shift" phenomenon. Over 300 research studies have since been conducted on this issue. Most of these studies used Stoner's method and found that group decisions were indeed riskier. Other research indicates that group discussion intensifies all sorts of attitudes, beliefs, values, judgments, and perceptions (Myers, 1982; Figure 7.3).

More recently, researchers have realized that although group discussion often produces a shift in individual opinions, such a shift is not necessarily in the direction of greater risk. It could be in the direction of greater cautiousness (a *caution shift*; Fraser,

---

Mr. A., an electrical engineer who is married and has one child, has been working for a large electronics corporation since graduating from college five years ago. He is assured of a lifetime job with a modest, though adequate, salary and liberal pension benefits on retirement. On the other hand, it is very unlikely that his salary will increase much before he retires. While attending a convention, Mr. A. is offered a job with a small, newly founded company that has a highly uncertain future. The new job would pay more to start and would offer the possibility of a share in the ownership if the company survived the competition of the larger firms.

Imagine that you are advising Mr. A. Following are several probabilities or odds of the new company proving financially sound.

Please check the lowest probability that you would consider acceptable to make it worthwhile for Mr. A. to take the new job.

_____ The chances are 1 in 10 that the company will prove financially sound.

_____ The chances are 3 in 10 that the company will prove financially sound.

_____ The chances are 5 in 10 that the company will prove financially sound.

_____ The chances are 7 in 10 that the company will prove financially sound.

_____ The chances are 9 in 10 that the company will prove financially sound.

_____ Place a check here if you think Mr. A. should not take the new job no matter what the probabilities.

Figure 7.3 A choice-dilemma questionnaire item.
Source: M. Wallach, N. Kogan, and D. Bem, Group influence on individual risk taking. *Journal of Abnormal and Social Psychology, 65* (1962), 75–86.

1971; Myers & Bishop, 1970). Group members' positions become more polarized after discussion, and therefore the term *group polarization* has replaced the term **risky shift.** Discussion tends to exaggerate and enhance group members' prediscussion views (Figure 7.4). At least three explanations have been given for the group polarization effect:

1. *Normative influences.* Groups may polarize because members want to create a favorable impression on others, and therefore (a) they compare their opinions with those of other group members, and (b) they modify their opinions to be a strong advocate of the group's position. Such normative influence is more likely when the topic concerns values, tastes, and preferences as opposed to factual issues (Laughlin & Early, 1982) or when the situation or topic is ambiguous.

2. *Informational influences.* Groups may polarize because members learn new information that causes them to modify their opinions (Kaplan & Miller, 1987) and members are confronted with persuasive arguments that are (a) compelling (logical and well thought out) and (b) new to some of the group members (Burnstein & Vinokur, 1977; Isenberg, 1986).

3. *Social identification.* Groups may polarize because individuals want to identify with the group and be considered members (Isenberg, 1986; Kaplan & Miller, 1987).

The group polarization effect is limited and even reversed when groups make decisions that have real, binding, costly consequences for all group members (Baron, Roper, & Baron, 1974).

Involvement in Decision Making

All group members should be involved in the group's decision making, for at least two reasons. The first reason is to increase the quality of the decision by fully utilizing the resources of each member. The more group members that participate in the making of a decision, the more resources are available, and consequently the higher the quality of the decision. The members responsible for implementing the decision should be especially knowledgeable about what the decision should be; that knowledge is best obtained through being involved in making the decision.

The second reason is to increase members' commitment to implement the decision. Involvement in decision making tends to increase members' allegiance to the group and commitment to seeing the decision through to fruition. One of the most famous research studies of the 1940s dealt with involving workers in

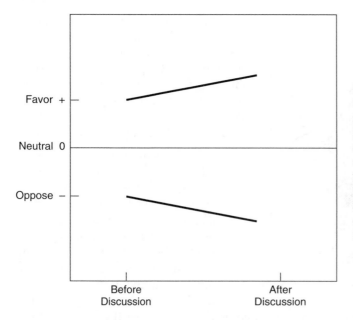

Favor +

Neutral 0

Oppose −

Before
Discussion

After
Discussion

Figure 7.4 The group polarization hypothesis predicts that an attitude shared by group members will usually be strengthened by discussion. For example, if people initially tend to favor risk on a life dilemma question (such as that in the previous example concerning Henry), they tend to favor it even more after discussion. If initially they tend to oppose risk, they tend to oppose it even more after discussion.

decisions about how their work should be conducted. An associate of Kurt Lewin and the personnel manager of a clothing factory teamed up to do a study on overcoming workers' resistance to changes in their work activities (French & Coch, 1948). The workers in question resisted management's changes in work activities by quitting their jobs, lowering their level of production, and expressing verbal hostility toward the plant and coworkers. French and Coch decided to try out three methods of instituting changes in job duties. One group of workers was told about the planned changes in their jobs and what was expected of them; they did not participate in the decision making. The second group appointed representatives to meet with management to consider problems involved in changing work methods. All members of the third group met with management, participated actively in discussions, shared many suggestions, and helped plan the most efficient methods for mastering the new jobs.

The differences in outcome were dramatic. Average production in the nonparticipating group dropped 20% immediately and did not regain the prechange level. Nine percent of the group quit. Morale fell sharply, as evidenced by marked hostility toward the supervisor, slowdowns, complaints to the union, and other instances of aggressive behavior. The group that participated through representatives required two weeks to recover its prechange output. Their attitude was cooperative, and none of the members quit their jobs. The consequences in the total-participation group were even more positive. Members of this group regained the prechange output after only two days, and output then climbed steadily until it reached a level about 14% higher than the earlier average. No one quit, all members of the group worked well with their supervisors, and there were no signs of aggression. In a related study, Zander and Armstrong (1972) found that when work groups in a slipper factory were asked to set their own daily production goals, they tended to aim for goals higher than the standard set by the manager.

Perhaps the only times decisions should be made by one or a few group members are (1) when the decisions are about matters that do not need committed action by most group members, (2) when the decisions are so simple that coordination among group members and understanding of what to do are easy, and (3) when the decisions have to be made quickly.

Changing Behavioral Patterns and Attitudes

It is easier to change individuals formed into a group than to change any of them separately.

Kurt Lewin (1951, p. 228)

Participating in a decision-making discussion within a group can affect a person's subsequent behavior and attitudes. During World War II, the U.S. government was concerned about the reactions of the public to food rationing and the need to promote the use of foods not ordinarily eaten by its citizens. Kurt Lewin was persuaded to come to Washington and help. He and his associates conducted a series of experiments to determine what procedures were most effective in changing behavior and attitudes (i.e., eating foods they considered undesirable). In the first study, Lewin (1943) attempted to encourage housewives to use less-popular meat products, such as kidneys and sweetbreads. The subjects were six groups of Red Cross volunteers ranging from thirteen to seventeen members each. Half of the groups were given an interesting lecture arguing for greater use of these meat products, and the other half were led through a group discussion that developed the same arguments as those presented in the lecture. At the end of the group discussion, the group leader asked for a show of hands by those willing to try one of the undesirable meat products. A follow-up survey revealed that only 3% of those in the lecture groups had served one of these meats, whereas 32% of those in the group-decision groups had served them. Similar results were found by Radke and Klishurich (1947) in a study contrasting lecture and group discussion on the increased consumption of milk. A third study contrasted the reading of interesting materials on the use of orange juice and cod liver oil by babies or participating in a group discussion covering the same information (Radke & Klishurich, 1947). Participants were farm mothers with their first baby. Again, the group decision procedure was more effective in getting the mothers to actually use more orange juice and cod liver oil.

Numerous studies have confirmed the findings of Lewin and his associates (e.g., Kostick, 1957; Levine & Butler, 1952). Two causes of the success of group discussion have been studied: public commitment to peers and the degree of perceived consensus in the group (Bennett, 1955; Pelz, 1958; Pennington, Haravey, & Bass, 1958). When people participate in a group decision to change an attitude or behavior, they are more likely to implement the decision when they are committed to the group and they believe the rest of the group members are implementing the decision. The nature of group leadership has also been examined. Participatory leaders (who encourage all members to take part in the discussion, consider each member's ideas, discourage chance methods of decision making, and urge members to complete the group's assigned work in the allotted time) were more effective in changing members' attitudes than were supervisory leaders (who did not participate in the discussion and limited their responsibility to seeing that the work was done in the allotted time) (Preston & Heintz, 1949). Participatory group members also were more satisfied with their group's decision than were members of the supervisory groups, found the task more interesting and meaningful, and rated their group discussions as more friendly and enjoyable.

Type of Task

Whether groups or individuals are more productive may depend on the type of task. If the task is one that allows group members to pool their efforts (such as pulling on a rope in a tug-of-war), groups should do better than individuals (with comparable abilities). But if the task requires extremely precise coordination of action (such as splitting a diamond, driving a car), a well-trained individual will outperform a group. Steiner (1966, 1972) proposed that tasks can be (1) divisible (split into parts) or unitary (done as a whole) and (2) maximizing (amount and speed of work) or optimizing (quality of work). On divisible, maximizing, and optimizing tasks, groups tend to do better than individuals. On **unitary tasks,** comparisons between groups and individuals are more complex. Steiner proposed that there are four types of unitary tasks: **disjunctive** (the group score is that of the best individual member), **conjunctive** (the group score is that of the worst individual member), **additive** (the group score is the sum of group member contributions), and **discretionary** (the group score is any combination of individual efforts the group wants to put together). Baron, Kerr, and Miller (1992) present an interesting illustration of this task taxonomy. Imagine three track groups, each with four runners, competing in the 400-meter run. The finishing times of group A are 46 seconds, 47 seconds, 47 seconds, and 49 seconds. For group B, the finishing times are 44 seconds, 45 seconds, 49 seconds, and 53 seconds. For group C, the finishing times are 45 seconds, 45 seconds, 46 seconds, and 51 seconds. Which group wins? It depends on how group performance is defined. If the winning group is the group with the first runner to cross the finish line (disjunctive task demands), then group B wins. If every member of the group must cross the finish line before the group is considered to have finished the race (conjunctive task demands), then group A is the winner. And if the group score is the simple sum of the times of its four runners (additive task demands), then group C wins. In short, while groups may outperform individuals on almost all tasks, under some conditions individuals may do better on some unitary tasks.

Potential Group Productivity

A number of psychologists believe there is one way in which groups are typically inferior to individuals—productivity per person. If, for example, instead of simply comparing groups and individuals on the time needed for a solution (an approach that tends to favor groups in most studies), the number of *person-minutes* required were compared (i.e., solution time × size of the group), then individuals might solve the problem in fewer person-minutes than groups. If, for example, a group of six people took 42 minutes to make a decision, then 252 person-minutes were spent making the decision. Even if a single individual needed twice as long as the group took to make a decision, the person-minutes involved would be only 84. Person-minutes, however, do not reflect the quality of the decision.

Looking strictly at person-minutes, however, ignores other factors involved in group decision making. Steiner (1966, 1972) proposed that the most important question is not whether groups are more productive than individuals, but whether groups are as productive as they should be. He defined a group's *potential productivity* as the group's maximum possible level of productivity at a task and suggested that it depends on two factors: member resources and task demands. He proposed that groups rarely achieve to their potential because of *process loss* due to *coordination losses* that occur when group members do not organize their efforts optimally and *motivation losses* that occur when members are not optimally motivated. In other words:

$$\text{Actual Productivity} = \text{Potential Productivity} - \text{Process Loss}$$

Problems exist with Steiner's model. First, it implies that there exists a single, unique potential productivity baseline that constitutes an upper boundary on group performance. This is true for certain very simple tasks, but on more complex tasks there is more than one way to define a group's potential productivity. Second, Steiner assumes that individuals cannot be any more motivated in groups than they are when working individually. Frequently, however, people are more motivated in group settings (Hackman & Morris, 1975). It is possible that groups exhibit motivational gains as well as motivational losses (the social facilitation research is an example). Finally, Steiner seems to assume that individuals are always performing up to their potential. Individuals rarely achieve up to their potential. An individual's potential also depends on the person's resources and the demands of the task. And individuals can suffer process loss due to lack of motivation.

Member Diversity

Heterogeneous groups may have advantages over homogeneous groups (e.g., Jackson, 1992; Levine & Moreland, 1998; Schulz-Hardt, Jochims, & Frey, 2002). Most problem-solving groups require at least one member who is achievement motivated and energetic (otherwise the group does not do any work), one member who is curious and imaginative (otherwise the group does not generate any good or novel ideas), and one member who is agreeable and supportive (otherwise the group members do not get along) (Morrison, 1993). Productive groups tend to have members who complement one another. Heterogeneous membership is especially helpful on tasks in which a group needs only one member to get the correct answer and on tasks requiring new solutions, flexibility, and quick adjustments to changing conditions (e.g., Nemeth, 1992). Scientists, for example, perform better when they work in groups in which members span a wider range of scientific disciplines (Pelz, 1956), and management teams whose members have different areas of expertise and educational backgrounds are more innovative (Bantel & Jackson, 1989; Wiersema & Bantel, 1992).

There are costs to diversity. Diversity in experience may hurt performance on tasks in which groups succeed only if each member performs his or her role well. Business teams varying widely in personalities, values, or backgrounds often have high turnover (Cohen & Bailey, 1997; McCain, O'Reilly, & Pfeffer, 1983), and communication in highly diverse groups tends to be less frequent and more formal (Zenger & Lawrence, 1989). The benefits of heterogeneous groups must be weighed, then, against their costs.

Online Decision Making

People communicate with one another through e-mail, live chat rooms, and instant messaging more and more each day. Computer-mediated communication is not only used for communication; it is used to bring groups of people together to make important decisions in organizations all over the world. The benefits of doing so seem obvious. Having group members who live and work in different offices, cities, or even countries interact electronically and make decisions saves the organization the considerable money and time it would take to bring them together face-to-face. These savings, however, may come at the cost of effective decisions. A meta-analytic review concluded that groups communicating via computers generally make lower-quality decisions than when they speak face to face (Baltes, Dickson, Sherman, Bauer, & LaGanke, 2002). When groups had unlimited time to discuss the issues and were able to do so anonymously, computer-mediation decision making was as effective as face-to-face decision making. These conditions, however, almost never occur in the real world. Face-to-face interaction may be superior to electronic interaction for a number of reasons. There is a vitality and richness in getting together face to face; group members come to trust and understand one another through face-to-face interaction (Prusak & Cohen, 2001). This is true in formal meetings, but it is especially true if the meetings include opportunities for causal and personal conversations during coffee breaks and other informal moments. Telephones, video conferencing, e-mail, and other innovations all share a similar problem: They tend not to produce intense human relationships. Personal relationships, group cohesion, and member commitment to the group tend to be built through face-to-face interaction. Members of electronic groups tend to miss the friendships, helpful tips, and attention that come from face-to-face interaction. Ingenuity and innovation thrive more on face-to-face interaction. All nonverbal communication is eliminated in electronic interaction. The physical spaces within which groups work are often designed to include nooks, niches, and residual spaces to foster incidental face-to-face contact and exchange. The more group members communicate electronically, the more they may need to meet face to face, and face-to-face meetings may make subsequent electronic interaction more effective. "Out of sight, out of mind" seems to be an important aspect of effective decision making.

Digital Decision-Making Skills

In addition to the skills that individuals need to be productive and responsible group members, they also need to develop digital skills. Digital skills enable online users to use technology in safe and responsible ways to participate in online decision making and groupwork. Like all skills, there are corresponding attitudes involving commitment to the group, cooperativeness, and the avoidance of competitiveness. In many ways, being a good group member on the Internet is the same as being a good collaborator. Most technology is used to achieve mutual goals and is, therefore, a cooperative endeavor. Technology makes the resources and shared spaces available to complete group tasks and achieve group goals even when the group members are separated geographically. Technology also gives group members access to needed resources even when the resources are distributed across the world. Group members' behavior online, furthermore, can define their identity as a group member. Social networking allows groups to form and function when members live in different cities and even in different countries. Digital decision-making skills thus have become an essential aspect of individuals' lives in the twenty-first century.

When Group Decision Making Fails

Groups do not always make better decisions than do individuals. Sometimes groups just do not possess accurate or relevant information. Sometimes the relevant information is not shared effectively, even when someone in the group has it (Sargis & Larson, 2002). Even when knowledge is effectively shared in a group, that information may still be processed in a biased manner. Like individuals thinking alone, groups may favor information confirming their initial views (Brownstein, 2003; Frey & Schulz-Hardt, 2001; Kray & Gallinsky, 2003). In addition, groups with diverse membership may initially have difficulty working together until the necessary social skills are learned and accommodations to each other's cultures are made (Watson, Kumar, & Michaelsen, 1993). Thus, a group may need to develop before its superiority over individual decision making is clear.

For many reasons, groups generally make better decisions than do individuals, even if the groups do not always work up to their potential. A variety of decision-making methods exist, and there are factors that enhance the effectiveness of group decision making and other factors that inhibit groups from making good decisions. These methods and factors are discussed in the following sections.

EXERCISE 7.2

THE BEAN JAR (I)

The purpose of this exercise is to compare the reactions of group members to the seven methods of decision making discussed in the next section of this chapter. A large jar containing a known quantity of beans is required for the exercise. The procedure for the coordinator is as follows:

1. Set a large jar of beans in front of the participants. You need to know exactly how many beans are in the jar. Inform the participants that they will be asked to estimate how many beans the jar contains.
2. Divide the participants into groups of six. Seven groups are ideal for this exercise. Appoint one member of the group to be the recorder. After the group has made its decision and all group members have completed the postdecision questionnaire (at the end of this exercise), the recorder collects the results and computes a group average for each question by totaling the individual scores for each question and dividing the sum by the number of members in the group.

continued on next page

continued from previous page

3. State that each group has to estimate the number of beans the jar contains. Assign one method of decision making to each group. The instructions for each method are as follows:

   a. The member with the most authority makes the decision. One member is appointed leader by the coordinator. This person should exercise control by such means as telling the group how to sit while waiting for the decision to be made and how to use their time while she is deciding. The leader then estimates how many beans are in the jar and announces her decision to the group. All members of the group then complete the postdecision questionnaire.

   b. The member with the most expertise makes the decision. The coordinator appoints the member with the most training in mathematics to be the leader. The expert then considers how many beans are in the jar, makes a decision, and announces it to the group. All group members then complete the postdecision questionnaire.

   c. The opinions of the individual members are averaged. Each member of the group backs away from the group so that he cannot see the answers of other group members and they cannot see his answer. Each member independently estimates the number of beans in the jar without interacting with the other group members. The recorder then asks each member for his estimate, adds the estimates, and divides the sum by the number of members. The resulting number is announced as the group's decision. All group members then complete the postdecision questionnaire.

   d. The member with the most authority makes the decision following a group discussion. One member is appointed leader by the coordinator, and she calls the meeting to order. She asks the group to discuss how many beans are in the jar. When she thinks she knows how many beans are in the jar, she announces her decision to the group. This is not consensus or majority vote; the leader has full responsibility and makes the decision she thinks is best. All members of the group then complete the postdecision questionnaire.

   e. A minority of group members make the decision. The coordinator appoints an executive committee of two members. The committee meets away from the group to decide how many beans are in the jar. They announce their decision to the group. All group members then complete the postdecision questionnaire.

   f. Majority vote. Each group member estimates the number of beans in the jar, and the group then votes on which estimate is to be its decision. When the majority of members agree on an estimate, the group decision is made. All group members then complete the postdecision questionnaire.

   g. Consensus. All members of the group participate in a discussion of how many beans are in the jar. Discuss the issue until all members of the group can live with and support the group's estimate. Follow the basic guidelines for consensual decision making given on page 265. When an estimate is agreed on, all members of the group complete the postdecision questionnaire.

4. Collect the results from the postdecision questionnaires and enter them in the summary table. Instruct each group to make four conclusions as to what can be learned from these results. Each group shares its conclusions with the class. Then conduct a class discussion on how the conclusions agree or disagree with the material presented in this chapter. Point out the following relationships:

   a. The extent to which a member feels understood and influential in the group is related to how well his or her resources are utilized.

   b. The extent to which a member is committed to the decision and responsible for its implementation is related to his or her commitment to implement the decision.

   c. The extent to which a member is satisfied with his or her participation and the positiveness of the group atmosphere is related to the future problem-solving ability of the group.

5. Note how accurate each group's estimate was. Usually, the more group members are directly involved in the decision making, the better the decision is.

POSTDECISION QUESTIONNAIRE

On a sheet of paper record your answers to the following questions. Then hand the paper to the recorder in your group.

1. How well do you feel your group understood and listened to you?

   Not at all   1 : 2 : 3 : 4 : 5 : 6 : 7 : 8 : 9   Completely

2. How much influence do you feel you had in your group's decision making?

   None   1 : 2 : 3 : 4 : 5 : 6 : 7 : 8 : 9   A great deal

3. How committed do you feel to the decision your group made?

   Very uncommitted   1 : 2 : 3 : 4 : 5 : 6 : 7 : 8 : 9   Very committed

4. How much responsibility do you feel for making the decision work?

   None   1 : 2 : 3 : 4 : 5 : 6 : 7 : 8 : 9   A great deal

5. How satisfied do you feel with the amount and quality of your participation in your group's decision making?

   Very dissatisfied   1 : 2 : 3 : 4 : 5 : 6 : 7 : 8 : 9   Very satisfied

6. Write one adjective that describes the atmosphere in your group during the decision making. _____

Results of Postdecision Questionnaire

Method of Decision Making	Understanding	Influence	Commitment	Responsibility	Satisfaction	Atmosphere
Decision by authority without discussion						
Expert member						
Average member						
Decision by authority after discussion						
Minority rule						
Majority rule						
Consensus						

METHODS OF DECISION MAKING

Groups can use a variety of ways to make decisions, from flipping a coin to thoughtful discussion followed by a vote in which the majority wins. Seven of the major methods of group decision making are discussed in this chapter. Each decision-making method has its uses and is appropriate under certain circumstances. Each also has its particular consequences for the group's future operation. An effective group member understands each method of decision making well enough to choose the method that best suits the following conditions:

1. The type of decision to be made
2. The amount of time and resources available
3. The history of the group
4. The nature of the task being worked on
5. The kind of climate the group wishes to establish
6. The type of setting in which the group is working

Table 7.1 lists the advantages and disadvantages of the seven decision-making methods discussed in this section.

Method 1: Decision by Authority Without Group Discussion

In this method the designated leader makes all the decisions without consulting the group members in any way. This method is quite common in organizations. It is an efficient method, as it takes a short time to execute, but it is not very effective. Even if the designated leader is a good listener who sorts out the correct information on which to base a decision, it is still the group members who have to act on the decision. They may not understand what the decision is or how they are supposed to implement it; they may disagree with the decision and not want to implement it; and, even if they agree with the decision, they may lack commitment to implementing the decision. Under this method, how well the decision is implemented is particularly crucial.

Method 2: Decision by Expert

Group decisions can be made by letting the most expert member in the group decide what the group should do. The procedure for this method is to select the expert, let him or her consider the issues, and then have that person tell the group what the decision is. The group does not discuss the issue.

A major problem with this method is determining which member has the most expertise. On most complex issues, individuals disagree as to what the best approach is, and this makes it difficult for them to identify the expert among them. Personal popularity and the amount of power a person has over the group members often interfere with the selection of the most expert member. The classic illustration of this point is the story of the general with a college education and several captains with Ph.D.s in engineering discussing how a bridge should be built. Needless to say, the general designs the bridge, simply because he has the most power. Individuals with a great

TABLE 7.1   **Advantages and Disadvantages of Decision-Making Methods**

METHOD OF DECISION MAKING	DISADVANTAGES	ADVANTAGES
1. Decision by authority without discussion	One person is not a good resource for every decision; advantages of group interaction are lost; no commitment to implement the decision is developed among other group members; resentment and disagreement may result in sabotage and deterioration of group effectiveness; resources of other members are not used.	Applies more to administrative needs; useful for simple, routine decisions; should be used when very little time is available to make the decision, when group members expect the designated leader to make the decision, and when group members lack the skills and information to make the decision any other way.
2. Expert member	It is difficult to determine who the expert is; no commitment to implement the decision is built; advantages of group interaction are lost; resentment and disagreement may result in sabotage and deterioration of group effectiveness; resources of other members are not used.	Useful when the expertise of one person is so far superior to that of all other group members that little is to be gained by discussion; should be used when little membership action is needed to implement the decision.
3. Average of members' opinions	There is not enough interaction among group members for them to gain from each other's resources and from the benefits of group discussion; no commitment to implement the decision is built; unresolved conflict and controversy may damage group effectiveness in the future.	Useful when it is difficult to get group members together to talk, when the decision is so urgent that there is no time for group discussion, when member commitment is not necessary for implementing the decision, and when group members lack the skills and information to make the decision any other way; applicable to simple, routine decisions.
4. Decision by authority after discussion	Does not develop commitment to implement the decision; does not resolve the controversies and conflicts among group members; tends to create situations in which group members either compete to impress the designated leader or tell the leader what they think he or she wants to hear.	Uses the resources of the group members more than previous methods; gains some of the benefits of group discussion.
5. Minority control	Does not utilize the resources of many group members; does not establish widespread commitment to implement the decision; unresolved conflict and controversy may damage future group effectiveness; not much benefit from group interaction.	Can be used when not everyone can meet to make a decision, when the group is under such time pressure that it must delegate responsibility to a committee, when only a few members have any relevant resources, and when broad member commitment is not needed to implement the decision; useful for simple, routine decisions.

(continued)

TABLE 7.1 **Advantages and Disadvantages of Decision-Making Methods** (*Continued*)

METHOD OF DECISION MAKING	DISADVANTAGES	ADVANTAGES
6. Majority control	Usually leaves an alienated minority, which damages future group effectiveness; relevant resources of many group members may be lost; full commitment to implement the decision is absent; full benefit of group interaction is not obtained.	Can be used when there is not sufficient time for decision by consensus or when the decision is not so important that consensus needs to be used and when complete member commitment is not necessary for implementing the decision; closes discussion on issues that are not highly important for the group.
7. Consensus	Takes a great deal of time and psychological energy and a high level of member skill; time pressure must be minimal, and there must be no emergency in progress.	Produces an innovative, creative, and high-quality decision; elicits commitment by all members to implement the decision; uses the resources of all members; the future decision-making ability of the group is enhanced; useful in making serious, important, and complex decisions to which all members are to be committed.

deal of power are notorious for overestimating their expertise while underestimating the expertise of others. Unless there is a clear and effective way to determine who the expert is, this method does not work very well. Moreover, it too fails to involve group members, which affects the implementation of the decision.

Method 3: Decision by Averaging Individuals' Opinions

This method consists of separately asking each group member his or her opinion and then averaging the results. When the chair of a group, for example, calls each member on the telephone, asks what the member's opinion is, and then takes the most popular opinion as the group's decision, the chair is using the averaging method. This method is similar to majority voting, except that the group's decision may be determined by less than 50% of the members (the most common opinion is not necessarily the opinion of more than half of the members) and no direct discussion is held among members.

Because individual errors and extreme opinions tend to cancel themselves out under this method, it usually is a better procedure to follow than the designated leader method (without a group discussion). At least members are consulted. The disadvantage of averaging is that the opinions of the least knowledgeable members may annul the opinions of the most knowledgeable members. Letting the most expert member make the decision is always better than using a group average to decide. And although group members are consulted before the decision is made, they are still relatively uninvolved in the decision making itself. Consequently, their commitment to the decision may not be strong. If implementation of a decision made by this method requires the efforts of all group members, the effectiveness of the decision probably will be slight.

Group decision-making procedures have been created to average group opinions while eliminating or controlling members' interaction with one another. The *Delphi technique* was developed by Dalkey, Helmer, and their colleagues at the RAND Corporation (Dalkey, 1969, 1975) to improve judgmental forecasting (e.g., economic forecasts and the cost of fringe benefits) by providing practical procedures for eliciting expert opinions. First, members are asked to provide individual estimates for the focal quality, and their opinions are collected and summarized in a way that ensures the anonymity of each member. Then a summary of the members' opinions is circulated among the members. The members are then provided with an opportunity to revise their earlier forecasts. This procedure is repeated several times until individual opinions stabilize—that is, members change no more. The median or mean of the set of individual estimates is taken as the final group forecast. Dalkey (1969) claimed that the procedure avoided the "biasing effects of dominant individuals, or irrelevant communications, and of group pressure toward conformity" (p. 408).

A *nominal group technique* meeting begins with individual assessment of the problem; individuals first generate ideas concerning the issue without any discussion. Each participant then presents personal ideas in a face-to-face group meeting, and these ideas are recorded. After all the ideas are recorded, group discussion begins, and is primarily focused on clarifying the stated ideas. Finally, each member evaluates the ideas by ranking them, and these rankings are combined mathematically to yield a group judgment (Delbecq, Van de Ven, & Gustafson, 1975). Both of these methods are based on the assumption that groups are so poorly structured and members are so unskilled that interaction among members is better avoided. They should be used only as a last resort when other decision-making methods have failed.

Method 4: Decision by Authority After Group Discussion

Many groups have an authority structure that clearly indicates that the designated leader makes the decisions. Groups that function within organizations such as businesses and government agencies usually employ this method of decision making. The designated leader calls a meeting of the group, presents the issues, listens to the discussion until he or she is sure of what the decision should be, and then announces the decision to the group.

Listening to a group discussion will usually improve the accuracy of a decision made by the group's leader. The greater the leader's skill as a listener, the greater will be the benefits of the group discussion. But although members can become involved in the discussion, they have no part in the decision making, which tends not to help the decision's effectiveness. As a result, during the group discussion members may tend to either compete to impress the leader or tell the leader what they think he or she wants to hear.

Method 5: Decision by Minority

A minority—two or more members who constitute less than 50% of the group—can make the group's decisions in several ways, some legitimate and some illegitimate. This form of decision making is known as **minority control.** One legitimate method is for the minority to act as an executive committee to make decisions for the group. Another is for the minority to act as a temporary committee that considers special problems and decides what action the group should take. An illegitimate method is railroading. Railroading occurs when two or more members come to a quick agreement on a course of action, challenge the rest of the group with a sudden "Does anyone object?" and, if no one replies fast enough, proceed with a "Let's go ahead, then." Or a minority may forcibly recommend a course of action—implying that anyone who disagrees is in for a fight—and then move ahead before other members can consider the issue carefully. They assume that anyone who is silent agrees. But silence may mean that members need more time to organize their thoughts or are afraid to be the only one who disagrees.

The minority members who make the decision may be committed to implementing it, but the majority may not only be uncommitted, they may even want to prevent the decision from being implemented. When a group has a large number of decisions to be made and not enough time to deal with them all, decision-making committees can be efficient. This method also may be effective if a large number of decisions do not require the involvement and support of the rest of the group in order to be implemented. In general, however, decision by minority is not a good method of decision making.

Method 6: Decision by Majority Vote

Majority vote is the method of group decision making most commonly used in the United States, so much so, it is almost a ritual. The procedure is to discuss an issue only as long as it takes 51% of the members to agree on a course of action. On the surface, majority voting resembles our election system, but critical differences exist between elections and the use of majority vote in most groups. In our political system, minority rights are carefully protected through the Bill of Rights and the Constitution, and political minorities always have the right to compete on equal terms in the next election in order to become a majority. In most groups, however, minority opinions are not always safeguarded, and in retaliation, members holding the minority position may refuse to contribute their resources in implementing the decision. Minority opinion members tend to support the majority position only when they believe their views have been fairly considered and will be considered again in the future. If majority voting is to be used, the group must be sure that it has created a climate in which members feel they have had their day in court and will feel obliged to support the majority decision. Where commitment by everyone is not essential, of course, a majority vote can serve very well.

Method 7: Decision by Consensus

Consensus is the most effective method of group decision making, but it also requires the most time and resources. **Consensus** means that everyone agrees on the same course of action. It typically requires sufficient open communication and social support that all members believe they have had a fair chance to influence the decision.

When a decision is made by consensus, all members understand the decision and are prepared to support it. Members who have doubts nevertheless say publicly that they are willing to give the decision a try for a period of time. Decisions made by consensus sometimes are referred to as synergistic decisions.

To achieve consensus, members must have enough time to discuss their views thoroughly. Members should believe that their views have been listened to, considered, and understood. Members need to see differences of opinion as a way of (1) gathering additional information, (2) clarifying issues, and (3) motivating the group to seek better alternative courses of action. The basic guidelines for consensual decision making are as follows:

1. *Seek out differences of opinion.* They are natural and expected. Try to involve everyone in the decision because doing so will access a wide range of information and opinions, thereby creating a better chance for the group to create more adequate solutions.

2. *Present your position as clearly and logically as possible.* Be persuasive. Make sure you present the best case possible for what you believe. Listen carefully to other members' reactions, and consider them carefully before you press your point.

3. *Critically analyze the other positions.* Give them a "trial by fire" by pointing out their shortcomings and listening to their advocates responses.

4. *Encourage all group members to present the best case possible for what they believe.*

5. *Change your mind* when you are logically persuaded to do so. Do not simply agree to reach agreement and avoid conflict. Yield only to positions that have objective and logically sound foundations.

6. *Avoid conflict-reducing procedures* such as majority voting, tossing a coin, averaging, and bargaining.

7. *Keep the goal of reaching the best decision possible salient.* Do not assume that someone must win and someone must lose when discussion reaches a stalemate. Instead, look for the next most acceptable alternative for all members.

Consensus is the best method for producing an innovative, creative, and high-quality decision that (1) all members will be committed to implementing, (2) uses the resources of all group members, and (3) increases the future decision-making effectiveness of the group. It is often difficult to reach (Kerr et al., 1976). Striving for consensus is characterized by more conflict among members, more shifts of opinion, a longer time to reach a conclusion, and more confidence by members in the correctness of their decision (Nemeth, 1977). To reach consensus, group leaders should encourage all members to participate, encourage differences of opinions to be expressed, and express acceptance of different positions and perspectives (Torrance, 1957). Group leaders also should encourage minority opinions and conflict among members (Maier & Solem, 1952).

Relation Between Time and Decision Making

Every method of decision making takes a different amount of time. The more persons involved in the decision making, the longer it will tend to take to reach a decision. Figure 7.5 summarizes the relationship among the number of persons involved, the

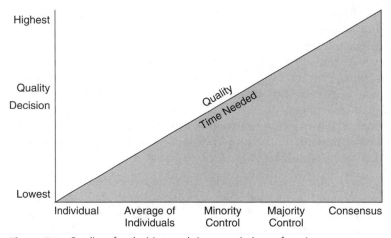

Figure 7.5 Quality of a decision and time needed as a function of the number of decision makers.

type of method used, the quality of the decision, and the time needed to arrive at a decision. If the time needed for both making and implementing a decision is considered, however, the time factor becomes less clear. Often the extra time taken to make a consensual decision will greatly reduce the time needed to implement it. Thus, many group authorities insist that if the whole process of decision making and implementation is considered, consensus is the least time-consuming method.

Generally, you are better off making important decisions in groups than you are having one person make the decision. This does not mean, however, that group decision making is easy or always effective. Some groups have a difficult time making decisions. Groups can make bad decisions as well as good ones. To help ensure their group will make an effective decision, members not only must take advantage of factors that facilitate effective decision making but also must pay attention to factors that may block effective decision making.

FACTORS THAT AFFECT GROUP DECISION MAKING

Whether a group decision is effective or ineffective depends on how the group is structured. When you want to maximize the likelihood that the group will make a good decision, you need to structure five essential elements into group life: positive interdependence, face-to-face promotive interaction, individual accountability, social skills, and group processing (see Chapter 1). Because we have discussed in previous chapters many of the factors that promote effective group decision making, we now turn our attention to factors that get in the way of effective decision making.

Although groups tend to make higher-quality decisions than individuals working alone, there is nothing magical about groups. There are conditions under which groups function inefficiently and conditions under which group function ineffectively. Many of the potential barriers to effective group decision making are discussed in this section.

Lack of Group Maturity

In many of the studies on group decision making, college students were randomly assigned to groups in which they worked with strangers for a few minutes to an hour or so. Such random, temporary, ad hoc groups did not have time to develop enough maturity to function with full effectiveness. Group members need time and experience working together to develop into a mature decision-making group. Even if all the group members possess group skills and previously have participated in effective groups, it takes time and experience to adapt their behavior to the dynamics of the new group. *Group maturity* may be defined as members working with one another long enough that they coordinate their behavior and complement one another's efforts auto matically, without conscious planning or thought. For some groups, maturing takes years.

Uncritically Giving One's Dominant Response

Poor decisions often are made because group members quickly decide on an alternative course of action based on their *dominant response* (i.e., the initial majority opinion of group members). Doing so shortcuts the process of identifying possible alternative courses of action and closes down the process of evaluating and choosing among the alternatives initially suggested (Maier & Thurber, 1969). Both Berlyne (1965) and Maier (1970) have theorized that responses are arranged hierarchically and that when a problem arises, the dominant response may result in the correct solution receiving little consideration. Dominant responses can be based on (1) physical states such as hunger that affect which stimuli a person attends to (Levine, Chein, & Murphy, 1942; McClelland & Atkinson, 1948), (2) psychological states such as attitudes and beliefs that affect what a person perceives (Allport & Postman, 1945; Iverson & Schwab, 1967), (3) general cultural perspectives that lead to distortions in information perceived (Bartlett, 1932), (4) mental sets that cause the same words to have different meanings for different persons (Foley & MacMillan, 1943), (5) expectations that bias how ambiguous events are interpreted (Bruner & Minturn, 1955) and create a sensitivity to perceiving some stimuli and not others (Neisser, 1954), (6) fixation on the first reasonable solution thought of (Simon, 1976), (7) laziness that results in available information not being cognitively processed and alternative ways of understanding such information not being fully considered (Langer, Blank, & Chanowitz, 1978; Taylor, 1980), and (8) adoption of previously useful solutions (Luchins, 1942). In group decision-making situations, each member may have his or her own dominant response, which collectively make up the group's hierarchy of responses.

Social Loafing: Hiding in the Crowd

In certain groups (such as sports groups and combat units), factors exist (such as contagious excitement, strong norms favoring maximal effort, and intense feelings of commitment, loyalty, and obligation) that cause group members to demonstrate levels of motivation and effort far beyond what would be expected from an individual acting alone. During a college basketball game in 1989, for example, Jay Burson, a player on The Ohio State University team, continued to play in a game after he suffered a broken neck. Many other examples exist in which people double their efforts or place themselves in great jeopardy because of their devotion and loyalty to other group members. In addition, when group members believe that the group will fail due to the poor performance of its weaker members, the members who know they are not among the best often experience a motivation gain and increase their efforts to contribute (e.g., Hertel, Kerr, & Messe, 2000). The members do not want to be seen (or to see themselves) as the "weakest link" in the group. Most of the research, however, has focused on how being a group member can lower motivation.

Max Ringelmann, a French professor of agricultural engineering, wanted to assess the relative efficiency of humans, oxen, and machinery in pulling and pushing loads. In the course of his investigations, he studied additive tasks by having individuals and groups of two, three, and eight men pull on a rope attached to a pressure gauge (reported in Moede, 1927). Two people, of course, pulled harder than one person. And three people pulled harder than two people. Individuals, on the average, exerted 63 kilograms of pressure, dyads about 118 kg, triads about 160 kg, and groups of eight about 248 kg of pressure. The intriguing aspect of these findings was that each person added did not increase the performance by 63 kg. Triads, for example, only performed at 2.5 times as much as the performance of one individual. On four-person teams, each man was only 77% as productive, and on eight-person teams, each man was merely 49% as productive. The inverse relationship between the number of people in a group and the quality and/or magnitude of individual performance on additive tasks was dubbed the *Ringelmann effect*. Similar results have been observed for groups working on intellectual puzzles (Taylor & Faust, 1952), creativity tasks (Gibb, 1951), and perceptual judgments and complex reasoning (Ziller, 1957). Ingham, Levinger, Graves, and Peckham (1974) replicated Ringelmann's study to determine if the loss of effort was due to group process problems, such as difficulty in coordinating the efforts of group members (on pulling a rope, for example, people have to position themselves to get a good

hold on the rope, and then they have to pull and pause at the same time), or to some group members loafing. They demonstrated that as groups got larger, members pulled less hard, at least partly because they were less motivated. A similar replication conducted a few years later used a new task, cheering as loudly as possible (Latané, Williams, & Harkins, 1979). Latané called the decline in motivation social loafing. **Social loafing** is a reduction of individual effort when working with others on an additive group task. *Additive tasks* require the summing together of individual group members' inputs to maximize the group product. Social loafing has been demonstrated on a variety of additive tasks, such as rope pulling, shouting, clapping, evaluation of poems and editorials, cheering, cycling, pumping air or water, producing ideas, typing, and detecting signals. It has also been demonstrated in the cultures of many different countries, including India (Weiner, Pandy, & Latané, 1981), Japan (Williams & Williams, 1984), and Taiwan (Gabrenya, Wang, & Latané, 1983).

There are tasks on which social loafing is perfectly sensible. If it only takes the effort of three individuals to lift a weight, and if six individuals are lifting, they do not have to use their full strength to get the job done. In most situations, however, the full effort of all group members is needed and expected. Several situational and social factors appear to have an important impact on the magnitude of the effect. For instance, social loafing has been shown to occur especially when group members lack identifiable contributions (Williams, Harkins, & Latané, 1981), when there is an increased likelihood of redundant efforts (Harkins & Petty, 1982), when there is a lack of cohesiveness among group members (Williams, 1981), when there is lessened responsibility for the final outcome (Petty, Harkins, Williams, & Latané, 1977), when the task is boring (as opposed to challenging, appealing, or involving; Brickner, Harkins, & Ostrom, 1986), when there is no spirit of commitment to the group (Hackman, 1987), and when group members believe that others are loafing (Zaccaro, 1984). Studies show that when individuals working on additive tasks believe they are lost in the crowd and therefore are not accountable and cannot evaluate their own efforts, responsibility is diffused across all group members.

Based on a meta-analysis of almost eighty studies, Karau and Williams (1993, 2001) suggest that social loafing may be reduced or avoided altogether when (1) each group member's contributions are identifiable, (2) the task and performance goals are personally meaningful, challenging, important, involving, attractive, and intrinsically interesting, (3) there is be a strong incentive for doing well on the task, (4) members understand that their personal efforts will lead to a better group performance, (5) group cohesiveness is high, and (6) the performance of each member is evaluated by groupmates and authorities (such as their boss or teacher).

Free Riding: Getting Something for Nothing

When you work alone, success or failure is entirely your own responsibility. When you work in a group, however, the responsibility for the group's success or failure usually is shared among group members. In an emergency, for example, the responsibility for helping appears to be spread among bystanders. In fact, the larger the group, the less likely it is that any one particular individual will be required to provide help (Darley & Latané, 1968; Latané & Nida, 1981). Similarly, if you are sharing an apartment with several other people, if one person cooks dinner for everyone, no one else has to do so at that time. Tasks that require only one person to complete but that benefit everyone in the group are called *disjunctive tasks.*

Although disjunctive tasks allow individuals to bear less responsibility for completing a task, they also present the possibility that some group members may take a *free ride* (Olson, 1965). A free ride is defined as one person benefiting from the work of other group members while doing no work him- or herself. Usually, the main cause of group members taking a free ride is that they believe their efforts are not needed; they believe they are dispensable (Kerr, 1983; Kerr & Bruun, 1983). When group members perceive their contributions to be dispensable, such that group success or failure depends little on whether or not they exert effort, they are less likely to exert themselves on the group's behalf. Furthermore, the more costly the effort to help is to the individual, the more sensitive he or she is to feeling dispensable, resulting in even less effort being put forth. The opportunity to free ride—to get something for nothing—is not the same as the opportunity to socially loaf.

Motivation Losses Due to Perceived Inequity: Not Being a Sucker

What would you do if you were sharing an apartment and found that you were the only person who cleaned it—that is, everyone else was enjoying the benefits of your cleaning but was making no attempt to help keep the apartment clean? Kerr (1983) labeled the tendency to reduce your efforts when other group members are engaging in free riding the *sucker effect.* He demonstrated that people are willing to reduce their efforts (and thereby their rewards) rather than "play the sucker" and be exploited by a free-riding partner. This does not mean that everyone has to contribute the same amount to the group's efforts. People generally do not feel like a sucker when another group is trying hard to contribute but unable to do so (Kerr, 1983; Tjosvold, Johnson, & Johnson, 1981).

Groupthink and Defensive Avoidance

Its wing badly damaged, the space shuttle *Columbia* disintegrated on re-entry into Earth's atmosphere. All seven astronauts aboard were killed. The investigation included the failures of the decision-making culture at NASA. Effective decision making requires a serious consideration of alternative views. Yet, when the chairwoman of the mission management team, who overruled the request for satellite photos of the wing that a group of lower level engineers suspected had been damaged during lift-off, was asked what procedures were used to seek out dissenting opinions, she had no answer (Langewiesche, 2003, p. 82). The exchange went like this:

Investigator: "As a manager, how do you seek out dissenting opinions?"
Manager: "Well, when I hear about them...."
Investigator: "By their very nature you may not hear about them ... what techniques do you use to get them?"
Manager: [No answer.]

Decision makers often are reluctant to take action. They are beset by conflict, doubts, and worry, and they struggle with conflicting longings, antipathies, and loyalties. In response to these difficulties, they sometimes seek relief in **defensive avoidance**—procrastinating, rationalizing, or denying responsibility for their own choices. When group decision making is dominated by defensive avoidance, bad decisions usually are the result. Social psychologist Irving Janis (1971, 1982) analyzed the decision-making procedures that led to several major fiascoes, among them the following:

1. *Pearl Harbor:* In the weeks preceding the 1941 Pearl Harbor attack, military commanders in Hawaii were fed a steady stream of information about Japan's preparations for attack—somewhere. Then military intelligence lost radio contact with Japanese aircraft carriers, which had begun moving full-steam straight for Hawaii. Air reconnaissance could have spotted the carriers, or at least provided a few minutes of warning of the impending attack, but the commanders decided against such precautions.

2. *Bay of Pigs Invasion:* "How could we have been so stupid?" asked President John Kennedy after the 1961 invasion of Cuba by 1,400 CIA-trained Cuban exiles. Nearly all the invaders were soon killed or captured, the United States was humiliated, and Cuba allied itself even closer to the USSR.

3. *Vietnam War:* From 1964 to 1967 President Lyndon Johnson and his "Tuesday lunch group" of policy advisers escalated the Vietnam War on the assumption that the escalations (U.S. aerial bombardment, defoliation, and search-and-destroy missions) were likely to bring North Vietnam to the negotiating table. The escalation decisions were made despite warnings from government intelligence experts, as well as from leaders of nearly all U.S. allies. The resulting disaster cost 56,500 Americans and more than one million Vietnamese their lives, drove Lyndon Johnson from office, and created huge budget deficits that helped fuel inflation in the 1970s.

Janis (1972, 1982) coined the term *groupthink* to describe the decision-making process in these fiascoes. **Groupthink** is the collective striving for unanimity that overrides group members' motivation to appraise alternative courses of action realistically and thereby leads to (1) a deterioration of mental efficiency, reality testing, and moral judgment and (2) the ignoring of external information inconsistent with the favored alternative course of action. Groupthink leads to **concurrence seeking,** characterized by group members inhibiting discussion in order to avoid any disagreement or arguments, emphasize agreement, and avoid realistic appraisal of alternative ideas and courses of action. Quick compromises and censorship of disagreement are characteristic of groups dominated by concurrence seeking. When group members feel strong pressure to agree with one another, they often fail to engage in effective discussion (e.g., Postemes, Spears, & Cihangir, 2001; Quinn & Schlenker, 2002).

Groupthink is promoted when the group is highly cohesive, when it is insulated from outside criticism, when the leader is directive and dynamic, and when the group does not search for and critically evaluate alternatives (Figure 7.6). Group members rely on shared illusions and rationalizations to bolster whatever option is preferred by the

```
┌─────────────────────────────────────────────────────────────────────────┐
│                         Antecedent Conditions                             │
│                                                                           │
│  1. High cohesiveness                                                     │
│  2. Insulation of the group                                               │
│  3. Lack of methodical procedures for search and appraisal                │
│  4. Directive leadership                                                  │
│  5. High stress with a low degree of hope for finding a better solution   │
│     than the one favored by the leader or other influential persons       │
└─────────────────────────────────────────────────────────────────────────┘
                                    │
                                    ▼
┌─────────────────────────────────────────────────────────────────────────┐
│                      Concurrence-Seeking Tendency                         │
└─────────────────────────────────────────────────────────────────────────┘
                                    │
                                    ▼
┌─────────────────────────────────────────────────────────────────────────┐
│                         Symptoms of Groupthink                            │
│                                                                           │
│  1. Illusion of invulnerability                                           │
│  2. Collective rationalization                                            │
│  3. Belief in inherent morality of the group                              │
│  4. Stereotypes of outgroups                                              │
│  5. Direct pressure on dissenters                                         │
│  6. Self-censorship                                                       │
│  7. Illusion of unanimity                                                 │
│  8. Self-appointed mind guards                                            │
└─────────────────────────────────────────────────────────────────────────┘
                                    │
                                    ▼
┌─────────────────────────────────────────────────────────────────────────┐
│                 Symptoms of Defective Decision Making                     │
│                                                                           │
│  1. Incomplete survey of alternatives                                     │
│  2. Incomplete survey of objectives                                       │
│  3. Failure to examine risks of preferred choice                          │
│  4. Poor information search                                               │
│  5. Selective bias in processing information at hand                      │
│  6. Failure to reappraise alternatives                                    │
│  7. Failure to work out contingency plans                                 │
└─────────────────────────────────────────────────────────────────────────┘
```

Figure 7.6   A model of groupthink.

leader. In seeking concurrence and avoiding disagreement, members become trapped in the dynamics of groupthink:

1. *Self-censorship:* Each member minimizes any doubts about the apparent group consensus.
2. *Illusion of unanimity:* Each member assumes that everyone (except oneself) is in agreement. There is a state of pluralistic ignorance where members falsely assume that the silence of other members implies consent and agreement.
3. *Direct pressure on dissenters:* Anyone expressing doubts is pressured to conform.
4. *Mind guards:* Certain group members try to prevent dissenters from raising objections.
5. *Illusion of invulnerability:* Members develop an illusion of invulnerability, characterized by unwarranted optimism and excessive risk taking. They often believe that the group is above attack and reproach.

6. *Rationalization:* Group members invent justifications for whatever action is about to be undertaken, thus preventing misgivings and appropriate reconsideration.
7. *Illusion of morality:* Members ignore the ethical consequences of the favored alternative and assume that the group's actions are morally justified.
8. *Stereotyping and moral exclusion:* Group members dismiss competitors, rivals, and potential critics as too weak or stupid to react effectively or as too evil to warrant genuine attempts at negotiation.

These aspects of groupthink lead to a number of defects in the decision-making process. They include an incomplete survey of alternatives and objectives, failure to examine risks of the preferred choice, poor information search, selective bias in processing information, failing to reappraise alternatives, and making no contingency plans.

Aldag and Fuller (1993) conducted an extensive review of literature and concluded that most support for groupthink has come from retrospective case studies focused on decision fiascoes rather than from comparing the decision-making processes associated with good versus bad decisions. Overall, the research does not provide convincing support for the validity of the groupthink phenomenon or for the suggestion that groupthink characteristics lead to negative outcomes. Controlled experimental research on the groupthink process has been sparse. Some laboratory research indicates that high cohesion generally does not produce the poor discussion quality Janis's theory predicts (e.g., Flowers, 1977; Leana, 1985), but directive leadership does result in low-quality group problem solving (e.g., Flowers, 1977).

The historical examples that Janis presents have to be viewed with caution because we cannot be certain that contradictory examples were not overlooked (Longley & Pruitt, 1980). Tetlock (1979), however, did a quantitative content analysis of public statements made by key decision makers and found that for policy decisions Janis had categorized as exemplifying groupthink, decision makers' perceptions of the issue were much more simplistic than was true for decisions that Janis had categorized as non-groupthink. Herek, Janis, and Huth (1987) reported a negative correlation between the number of groupthink symptoms and the quality of the decision: The greater the groupthink, the more negative was the outcome of the decision. McCauley (1989) did a historical analysis and found that two key groupthink decisions discussed by Janis were made under pressure despite decision makers' serious reservations regarding the decision. McCauley's analysis also suggests that stating the leader's views early (directive leadership), homogeneity among group members, and insulation of the group from outside influence are crucial factors in the groupthink process.

Poor Conflict Management by Group Members

Conflicts occur continually in groups and, when managed constructively, they enhance group effectiveness. But when members manage conflicts ineptly, group effectiveness decreases. In some cases, conflict among members' goals may result in some members wishing, consciously or unconsciously, to sabotage the group effort. Others have self-oriented needs that may interfere with attention to making an effective decision. Members may be competing with one another in ways that reduce their effectiveness in working together. Even when members are genuinely work-oriented and anxious to achieve results, they may have different ideas about how to proceed and may not be able to manage such conflicts constructively.

Egocentrism of Group Members

A critical aspect of effective decision making is the ability to view the issues being discussed from a variety of points of view. When members egocentrically present their opinions and coldly evaluate the extent to which the information and conclusions of other members agree with their own, a competition develops over whose ideas are going to dominate. An egocentric approach to decision making tends to result in lower-quality decisions than does an approach that emphasizes understanding of other members' perspectives (Falk & Johnson, 1977; Johnson, 1972, 1977). The more members are embedded in their own perspective and the more they refuse to consider the perspectives of others, the lower the quality of the group's decisions will tend to be.

Lack of Sufficient Heterogeneity

Whether a group will be optimally productive depends on how fully the necessary information, skills, and viewpoints are represented. The more homogeneous the participants, the less each member adds to the resources present in the others. In general, homogeneous groups make less effective decisions than do heterogeneous groups. The more heterogeneous the group, the more frequent the conflict among group members (Hoffman, 1959), the less willing members are to accept incorrect responses from one another (Goldman, Dietz, & McGlynn, 1968), and the greater the group productivity (Goldman, Dietz, et al., 1968; Hoffman & Maier, 1961).

Interference or Production Blocking

Because only one person can talk (and be heard) at any one time, participants in a discussion often have to wait to make their point. Sometimes the delay is so long that the whole course of the discussion has changed before the would-be speaker gets a chance to be heard. He or she may then drop the idea entirely, which deprives the group; or bring the idea belatedly, which causes the group to backtrack to a prior issue. *Production blocking* exists when the participation of one member interferes with the participation of other members. The result is a decrease in decision-making effectiveness. When groups are given the task to generate as many ideas as possible, for example, they usually produce fewer (sometimes more than 50% fewer) ideas than do nominal groups (Diehl & Stroebe, 1987; Lamm & Trommsdorff, 1973). One of the reasons for this process loss is production blocking: Only one group member can talk at any one time.

Inappropriate Group Size

Some decisions require that a large number of persons participate; other decisions need only one or two individuals. Inappropriate group size may interfere with effective group decision making in a number of ways:

1. *The greater the discrepancy between functional and actual group size, the more ineffective the group will be.* Stephan and Mishler (1952) found that the proportion of active speakers in discussion groups declined with group size. That is, as groups get larger, fewer members actively try to solve the problem. The functional size of the group, then, could be much smaller than the actual group size. Bray, Kerr, and Atkin (1978), for example, found that in most instances, groups were solving problems about as quickly as the fastest participant when the group size was two. In groups with more than eight or nine members, a few participants were likely to dominate and others were likely to remain passive (Watson & Johnson, 1972).

2. *The less group members see their individual efforts as essential to group success, the less effective the group will be.* Generally, as the group gets larger and larger, members are less likely to see their own contribution as being important to the group's chances of success (Kerr, 1989; Olson, 1965). As noted previously, social loafing increases as the size of the group increases. Even in smaller groups, Morgan, Coates, and Rebbin (1970) found that team performance actually improved when one member was missing from five-person teams, perhaps because members believed their contributions were more necessary. Finally, as group size increases, so does the likelihood that individuals will alter their statements to conform to the perceived beliefs of the group (Gerard, et al., 1968; Rosenberg, 1961).

3. *Generally, the greater the complexity of the group structure and the more time it takes to organize joint efforts, the less effective the group will be.* A certain amount of time is needed to organize a group that is unnecessary for individuals (Bales & Strodtbeck, 1951). In general, when the task assigned to a group is complex or involves many steps, and when the group consists of many people on subgroups and committees, one can expect the decision-making process to take a great deal of time. One also should expect the decisions made by this type of group to be less effective and less cohesive than decisions made by smaller, more streamlined groups.

4. *The less members identify with the group, the less effective the group will be.* Kramer and Brewer (1986) have shown that a strong sense of belonging or social identity leads to cooperative behavior. They suggest that the more you feel part of the group, the less strongly you distinguish between your personal welfare and the group's welfare. Small groups typically are easier to identify with than large groups.

5. *The less members follow the group's norms, the less effective the group will be.* Enforcement of group norms requires the ability to monitor members' behavior so that norm violations are detected. It also requires that the social sanctions the group uses to punish norm violation carry weight for the individuals. Reducing

group size makes it easier to monitor members' behavior and increases members' attachment to the group, thereby making rejection by the group more punishing (Fox, 1985).

Premature Closure and Dissonance Reduction

Making a decision prematurely and then reducing any dissonance felt by group members can contribute to ineffective decision making. According to the dissonance theory (Festinger, 1957), any time someone is forced to choose between two attractive options, postdecision cognitive dissonance is present. **Cognitive dissonance** exists when a person possesses two cognitions that contradict one another. Dissonance exists, for example, if a group member knows the group selected one alternative as the most desirable option when other attractive alternatives also existed. Group members are generally motivated to reduce or eliminate it. One way to reduce the dissonance is to increase the perceived desirability of the decision made and decrease the perceived desirability of the alternatives that were not chosen. The more difficult or important the decision, the more likely group members are to find reasons that support the choice that was made and to minimize the attractive qualities of the forgone choice. This spreads apart the alternatives so that the one chosen is viewed as more attractive (in comparison with the other alternatives) after the decision than before it. If the group needs to reconsider the decision or reopen the decision making, **dissonance reduction** may interfere with their doing so.

Members Not Having Relevant Skills

If group members do not have the needed skills to complete the task and work together effectively, the decisions they make will not be effective. There are two types of relevant skills—those required to complete the task (task-work skills) and those required to work as part of a group (group-work skills). Groups with incapable members may often underperform a skilled individual. A skilled lumberjack, for example, could undoubtedly cut, trim, split, and load more timber on his own than any given group of college professors. It is not enough for a group member to know the correct answer to the problem. The member must be able to share the solution with the rest of the group and persuade them to accept it. Factors that may interfere with doing so include the member's status in the group (Torrance, 1954), the confidence the member has in his or her solution, and the amount of his or her participation in the discussion (Thomas & Fink, 1961). In other words, when the most capable members of a problem-solving group are not confident, have low status, or are not talkative, the group is likely to underutilize its resources. If task-work and group-work skills are low, the quality of the group's decision making will suffer.

Lack of Individual Incentives for and Barriers to Contributing

After completing a meta-analysis of the relevant research, Shepperd (1993) concluded that when incentives for contributing are low, members make little effort to achieve group goals. Correspondingly, there may be barriers that undermine the value of contributing or that provide a motive to withhold contributions. When contributing to the group takes time and energy that would better be spent elsewhere or when a person believes others are exploiting his or her contributions, the person may feel an incentive not to contribute to a group effort.

EXERCISE 7.3

WINTER SURVIVAL

The purpose of this exercise is to compare the effectiveness of five different methods of making decisions. Three of the methods do not utilize group discussion; the others do. The methods compared are (1) decision by a designated leader before a discussion, (2) decision by averaging members' opinions, (3) decision by an expert member, (4) decision by a designated leader after a discussion, and (5) decision by consensus. At least four groups of eight to twelve members each should take part. Inasmuch as the results are predictable, however, fewer groups with fewer members may be used if necessary. The exercise takes approximately two hours. The materials needed are as follows:

> Instructions for observers
> A description of the situation and a decision form
> A group summary sheet
> Instructions for groups that decide by consensus
> Instructions for groups whose leader decides
> A summary table

The coordinator for the exercise should use the following procedure:

1. State that the purpose of the exercise is to compare several different methods of decision making. Set the stage by pointing out that group decision making is one of the most significant aspects of group functioning, that most consequential decisions are made by groups rather than by individuals, that although many decisions are routine, others are extremely crucial, and that participants in this exercise are now in a situation where the decisions they make as a group may determine whether or not they survive.
2. Divide the participants into groups of approximately eight members—six participants and two observers. Give each group a number or name for purposes of identification, ask the observers to meet at a central place to be briefed, and then distribute the description and decision forms to the participants. Review the situation with the participants, again emphasizing that their survival depends on the quality of their decision. In half of the groups, designate one person as the leader; in the other groups, make no mention of leadership. Then instruct the participants to complete the decision form quietly and by themselves so that the results indicate their own decisions. They have fifteen minutes to complete the decision form and make a duplicate copy of their ranking. The designated group leaders should write "leader" on their duplicate copy, and all participants must write their group designation on their duplicate copy. At the end of the fifteen minutes, collect the duplicate copies.
3. While the participants are completing their decision forms, brief the observers. Give each a copy of the instructions for observers and copies of the description and the decision form (to orient them to the group task). Review the instructions to make sure the observers understand their task.

continued on next page

continued from previous page

4. Distribute one copy of the group summary sheet and the appropriate instruction sheet to each participant. (The groups with a leader receive one instruction sheet and the groups without a leader receive the other instruction sheet.) Observers also should receive a copy of the instructions for their group. The groups should be placed far enough apart so that they cannot hear one another's discussions or be aware that they have different instructions. The groups have forty-five minutes to decide on a group ranking of the items on the decision form. They are to make a copy of their group ranking with their group designation clearly written on the top.

5. While the groups are working on their rankings, score the individual decision forms in the following way:
   a. Score the net difference between the participant's answer and the correct answer. For example, if the participant's answer was 9 and the correct answer is 12, the net difference is 3. Disregard all plus or minus signs; find only the net difference for each item. (The correct ranking appears in the Appendix.)
   b. Total these scores; the result is the participant's score. The lower the score, the more accurate the ranking.
   c. To arrive at an average member's score, total all members' scores for each group and divide by the number of members.
   d. Put the scores in order from best to worst for each group. This ranking will be used to compare how many members, if any, had more accurate scores than the group's score.
   e. In the summary table that follows the instruction sheets for the groups, enter the average member's score for each group and the score of the most accurate group member. Then, for the groups with a designated leader, enter the score of that person.

6. At the end of forty minutes, give a five-minute warning. After forty-five minutes, instruct the groups to complete their ranking in the next thirty seconds and, with the group number or name clearly marked on the paper, to turn in their group ranking. Quickly score the groups' rankings and enter them in the appropriate place in the summary table. Recruit one or two observers to help if you need them.

7. In a session with all the participants, give the correct ranking and the rationale for each item. The correct ranking and the rationale appear on pages 537–539 in the Appendix. Then explain how the rankings are scored so that each person can determine his or her score.

INSTRUCTION TO OBSERVERS

This exercise looks at the process by which groups make decisions. Crucial issues are how well the group uses the resources of its members, how much commitment to implement the decision is mustered, how the future decision-making ability of the group is affected, and how members feel about and react to what is taking place. As an observer, you may wish to focus on the following issues:

1. Who does and does not participate in the discussion? Who participates the most?
2. Who influences the decision and who does not? How is influence determined (expertise, gender, loudness of voice)?
3. Who is involved and who is uninvolved?
4. What are the dominant feelings of the group members? How would you describe the group atmosphere during the meeting?
5. What leadership behaviors are present and absent in the group? You may wish to use the task behavior and maintenance behavior observation sheets on pages 000–000.
6. Why were the members' resources used or not used?

WINTER SURVIVAL EXERCISE: THE SITUATION

You have just crash-landed in the woods of northern Minnesota and southern Manitoba. It is 11:32 A.M. in mid-January. The light plane in which you were traveling crashed in a lake. The pilot and copilot were killed. Shortly after the crash the plane sank completely into the lake, with the pilot's and copilot's bodies inside. None of you is seriously injured, and you are all dry.

The crash came suddenly, before the pilot had time to radio for help or inform anyone of your position. Because the pilot was trying to avoid a storm, you know the plane was considerably off course. The pilot announced shortly before the crash that you were 20 miles northwest of a small town that is the nearest known habitation.

You are in a wilderness area made up of thick woods broken by many lakes and streams. The snow depth varies from above the ankles in windswept areas to knee-deep where it has drifted. The last weather report indicated that the temperature would reach −25°F in the daytime and −40°F at night. There is plenty of dead wood and twigs in the immediate area. You are dressed in winter clothing appropriate for city wear—suits, pantsuits, street shoes, and overcoats.

While escaping from the plane, several members of your group salvaged twelve items. Your task is to rank these items according to their importance to your survival, starting with 1 for the most important item and ending with 12 for the least important one.

You may assume that the number of passengers is the same as the number of persons in your group and that the group has agreed to stick together.

WINTER SURVIVAL DECISION FORM

Rank the following items according to their importance to your survival, starting with 1 for the most important and proceeding to 12 for the least important.

____ ball of steel wool	____ sectional air map made of plastic
____ newspapers (one per person)	____ 20 × 20-ft piece of heavy-duty canvas
____ compass	____ extra shirt and pants for each survivor
____ hand ax	____ can of shortening
____ cigarette lighter (without fluid)	____ quart of 100-proof whiskey
____ loaded .45-caliber pistol	____ family-size chocolate bar (one per person)

INSTRUCTIONS FOR GROUPS WITHOUT A LEADER

This is an exercise in group decision making. Your group is to employ the method of group consensus in reaching its decision. This means that each group member must agree on the ranking for each of the twelve survival items before it becomes a part of the group decision. Consensus is difficult to reach. Therefore, not every ranking will meet with everyone's complete approval. Try, as a group, to make each ranking one with which all group members can at least partially agree. Here are some guidelines to use in reaching a consensus:

1. Avoid arguing blindly for your own opinions. Present your position as clearly and logically as possible, but listen to other members' reactions and consider them carefully before you press your point.
2. Avoid changing your mind simply to reach agreement and avoid conflict. Support only solutions with which you are able to agree to at least some degree. Yield only to positions that have objective and logically sound foundations.
3. Avoid conflict-reducing procedures such as majority voting, tossing a coin, averaging, and bargaining.
4. Seek out differences of opinion. They are natural and expected. Try to involve everyone in the decision process. Disagreements can improve the group's decision, because a wide

continued on next page

continued from previous page

range of information and opinions improves the group's chance to hit on more adequate solutions.

5. Do not assume that someone must win and someone must lose when discussion reaches a stalemate. Instead, look for the next most acceptable alternative for all members.

6. Discuss underlying assumptions, listen carefully to one another, and encourage the participation of all members—the crucial factors in reaching decisions by consensus.

Winter Survival: Group Summary Sheet

Item	Members						Summary
	1	2	3	4	5	6	
Ball of steel wool							
Newspapers							
Compass							
Hand ax							
Cigarette lighter							
.45-caliber pistol							
Sectional air map							
Canvas							
Shirt and pants							
Shortening							
Whiskey							
Chocolate bars							

INSTRUCTIONS FOR GROUPS WITH A LEADER

This is an exercise in how a leader makes decisions after participating in a group discussion. Your group is to discuss what the ranking of the survival items should be, but the final decision rests with the designated leader of your group. At the end of forty-five minutes, your group's leader will hand in what he or she considers to be the best ranking of the items. The role of the group members is to provide as much help as the leader wants in trying to determine how the items should be ranked.

Summary Table: Accuracy of Decisions

Group	Before Group Discussion			After Group Discussion		Gain or Loss Over Designated Leader's Score	Gain or Loss Over Average Member's Score	Gain or Loss Over Accurate Member's Score	Number of Members Superior to Group Score
	Designated Leader's Score	Average Member's Score	Most Accurate Member's Score	Leader-Group Score	Consensus-Group Score				
1									
2									
3									
4									

EXERCISE 7.4

THEY'LL NEVER TAKE US ALIVE

This exercise uses the same procedure as Winter Survival Exercise 7.3.

THEY'LL NEVER TAKE US ALIVE RANKING SHEET

In a recent survey, *Dun's Review* lists the most perilous products or activities in the United States based on annual death statistics. Following are fifteen of these death-causing hazards. Your task is to rank them in order of dangerousness according to the number of deaths caused each year. Place 1 by the most dangerous hazard, 2 by the next most dangerous one, and so forth. See page 539 for correct ranking.

____ swimming	____ nuclear power	____ bicycles
____ railroads	____ smoking	____ firefighting
____ police work	____ motor vehicles	____ mountain climbing
____ home appliances	____ pesticides	____ vaccinations
____ alcohol	____ handguns	____ surgery

CONSIDERED AND THOUGHTFUL DECISION MAKING

Making a considered and thoughtful decision that everyone is committed to implementing is harder to do than it sounds. Decision making occurs within the context of problem solving. In order to consider the steps involved in making considered and thoughtful decisions, the whole problem-solving procedure must be discussed (Johnson & Johnson, 1989).

Identifying and Defining the Problem or Issue

The first step a decision-making group needs to take is to identify and define the problem. A **problem** is a discrepancy or difference between an actual state of affairs and a desired state of affairs. Problem solving requires both an idea about where the group should be and valid information about where it is now. The more clear and accurate the definition of the problem, the easier it is to complete the other steps in the problem-solving processes. There are three steps in defining the problem:

1. Reaching agreement on what the desired state of affairs is (that is, the group's purposes, goals, and objectives).
2. Obtaining valid, reliable, directly verifiable, descriptive (not inferential or evaluative), and correct information about the existing state of affairs.

3. Discussing thoroughly the difference between the desired and actual state of affairs; awareness of this discrepancy creates the commitment and motivation to solve the problem.

Because problem-solving groups often progress too quickly toward a solution to the problem without first getting a clear, consensual definition of the problem itself, members of the group should see to it that everyone understands what the problem is before trying to assess its magnitude. The nature of the problem can be clarified by:

1. Listing a series of statements about the problem. Describe it as concretely as possible by mentioning people, places, and resources. There should be as many different statements of the problem as the members are willing to give. Write them on a chalkboard where everyone can see them. Avoid arguing about whether the problem is stated perfectly.
2. Restating each problem statement so it includes a description of both the desired and the actual state of affairs. Eliminate alternative definitions that are beyond the resources of the group to solve. Choose the definition the group members agree is most correct. *The problem should be important, solvable, and urgent.*
3. Writing out a detailed description of what group life will be like when the problem is solved. The more detailed and specific the scenario is, the better.

Gathering Information About the Existence of the Problem

The second step in the problem-solving process is diagnosing the occurrence, magnitude, and nature of the problem. Valid information must be gathered. Then the information must be thoroughly discussed and analyzed to ensure that all group members understand it. The actual frequency of occurrence of the problem, the magnitude of the forces helping the group to move toward the desired state of affairs, and the forces hindering this movement need to be documented. Determining what forces are acting on the problem situation is called **force field analysis** (Lewin, 1935; Myrdal, 1944). In force field analysis, the problem is seen as a balance between forces working in opposite directions, some helping the movement toward the desired state of affairs and others restraining such movement. The balance that results between the helping and restraining forces is the actual state of affairs—a *quasi-stationary equilibrium* that can be altered through changes in the forces. In Figure 7.7, the ideal state of affairs toward which the group is working is on the right side and is represented by a plus sign. The worst state of affairs, on the left side of the figure, is represented by a minus sign. The vertical line in the middle signifies the current state of affairs—a middle ground. On any problem numerous forces are at work, some restraining change and others helping change.

There are two basic steps for a group to follow in doing a force field analysis:

1. Make up lists of forces by first brainstorming all the helping forces and then all the restraining forces. The list should include all possible forces, whether psychological, interpersonal, organizational, or societal. If a force seems to be

a complex of variables, each variable should be listed separately. Evaluation of suggestions should be avoided; it is essential that every member's ideas be publicly requested and aired.

2. Rank the forces according to their importance in affecting the present situation. Agree on the most important helping and restraining forces, which may total from three to six each. Rate the important forces according to how easily they can be resolved, and avoid spending time discussing those that the group cannot influence with their current resources.

For example, the implementation of cooperative learning within a school may be seen as a balance between forces helping teachers implement cooperative learning and forces restraining teachers from using cooperative learning. The use of cooperative learning is promoted by the teachers' awareness that it will increase student achievement, higher-level reasoning, social skills, self-esteem, and social support. The use of cooperative learning is restrained by teachers habitually using other instructional procedures, not being willing to commit the time to learn how to use cooperative learning, inherent fear of change, lack of willingness to revise their standard lessons, and incomplete understanding of what cooperative learning is (Figure 7.8).

There are two major barriers to gathering valid information about the nature and magnitude of the problem. The first is not getting the needed information. When

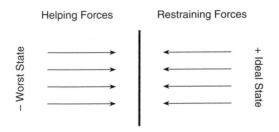

Figure 7.7 Force field analysis.

HELPING FORCES   RESTRAINING FORCES

Achievement increases ▷   ◁ Habit of status quo
Higher-level reasoning ▷   ◁ Time needed to learn how
Improved social skills ▷   ◁ Fear of change
Increased self-esteem ▷   ◁ Time to revise lessons
More social support ▷   ◁ Lack of understanding
Liking for school ▷   ◁ Teacher isolation

− No Use   + Skilled Use

Current Level of Use

Figure 7.8 Implementing cooperative learning.

information is minimal, the definition of the problem will be inadequate, fewer alternative strategies for the solution will be generated, and potential consequences of those alternatives will not be properly explored. The result is relatively inadequate solutions. The second barrier is poor communication within the group. Poor communication among group members has the same effect as lack of information, with the added problem that it makes difficult the implementation of any action that requires coordination among group members.

Formulating and Considering Alternative Solutions

The third step in problem solving is identifying and analyzing alternative ways to solve the problem. Groups often make poor decisions because they do not think of the proper alternative solutions or they do a poor job of evaluating and choosing among the alternatives considered. Systematically analyzing the advantages and disadvantages of each alternative before making a final decision may be the most important factor in effective decision making. To reduce the likelihood that an alternative is overlooked or rationalized away, an explicit and systematic *critical evaluation* process should be used. If decision makers do know what the alternatives are and have correctly diagnosed each alternative's inherent advantages and disadvantages, they will not choose a certain course of action unless its advantages are expected to exceed its disadvantages.

Identifying and analyzing alternative ways to solve the problem requires creative, divergent, and inventive reasoning. Such "higher-level" thinking and analysis comes primarily from intellectual disagreement and challenge (i.e., controversy). Controversy is discussed in Chapter 8. By definition, all decisions involve controversy, as decision making is a choice among alternative courses of action. Controversy is structured within problem-solving groups through the use of advocacy subgroups. In order to participate competently in the controversy process, group members must be able to prepare a position, advocate it, defend it from criticism, critically evaluate the alternative positions, be able to view the problem from all perspectives, and be able to synthesize and integrate the best parts of all solutions.

Force Field Analysis. Force field analysis is a particularly useful way of specifying alternative strategies for solving a problem. It is based on the assumption that changes in the present situation will occur only as the helpful and restraining forces are changed so that the level where they balance (equilibrium point) is adjusted. There are two basic methods for changing the equilibrium point between the two sets of forces: increasing the strength or number of the helping forces and decreasing the strength or number of the restraining forces. Of the two, the preferable strategy is to reduce the strength of or eliminate the restraining forces. Increasing the pressure for change in the present situation by strengthening the helping forces also increases natural resistance to change, reducing the strategy's effectiveness. Restraining forces may be reduced or eliminated without creating resistance. Reducing the restraining forces, therefore, is usually the more effective of the two strategies. The fewer the forces acting on the present situation, furthermore, the lower the tension level of the people in the situation.

The two methods of changing the equilibrium point are not mutually exclusive. Often you will need to reduce restraining forces and increase helping forces at the same time. When this can be done, it is very effective. One way of intervening simultaneously with both types of forces is to modify a restraining force so that it becomes a helping force. One of the most successful strategies for changing the direction of a restraining force is to involve the group members who are resisting the desired changes in diagnosing the problem situation and in planning the solutions (Watson & Johnson, 1972). *People enjoy and affirm the changes they make themselves, and they resist changes imposed on them by others.* Involvement of resisters in the diagnosing and planning of change often means a more difficult planning process, but it virtually guarantees that they are committed to the proposed changes. It also helps clear up any misunderstandings and differences of opinion before the strategies are implemented, and it uses the resources of the "opposition." Force field analysis is useful at this stage of the problem-solving process, because it allows group members to identify several points at which they may intervene in their attempt to produce a change. Because any change is the result of a number of factors, an effective change strategy involves multiple actions directed toward several of those factors. When the group works to modify several factors at the same time, the possibility is increased that the improvement will be permanent.

In specifying alternative strategies for change, group members should think of as many ways as possible to reduce the forces that keep the group from moving toward the desired state. They should obtain ideas from everyone in the group. If group members do not have many ideas, outside consultants can be invited to lend assistance. Bringing in an expert who knows a lot about the substance of the problem is often extremely helpful at this point. Group members should try to take each restraining force in turn and think up ways to reduce its strength or to eliminate it altogether. Divergent thinking should be encouraged.

Vigilant Analysis. Janis and Mann (1977) recommend a procedure they believe eliminates the possibility of defensive avoidance and ensures that vigilant consideration of each alternative solution takes place. The group systematically evaluates each alternative solution on the basis of four factors:

1. The tangible gains and losses for the group members
2. The tangible gains and losses for significant others, such as other members of the organization
3. Member self-approval or self-disapproval (Will we feel proud or ashamed if we choose this alternative?)
4. The approval or disapproval of the group by significant others (Will important people we are connected with think we made the right decision?)

The group uses these four factors to analyze each alternative in the following way:

1. A balance sheet is completed for each course of action considered. A balance sheet consists of listing the tangible gains from adopting the alternative on one side and the tangible losses on the other.

2. Each gain or loss is rated in terms of its importance on a ten-point scale, where 1 is "no importance" and 10 is "extremely important."

3. After a balance sheet is completed for each alternative course of action, the balance sheets are compared and the alternatives are ranked from "most desirable" to "least desirable."

Using a balance sheet to ensure systematic evaluation has been found to be related to level of satisfaction with a decision, commitment to a decision, and security about the correctness of a decision (Janis & Mann, 1977).

Other procedures can be followed for ensuring that high-quality decisions are made. Such procedures specifically focus on preventing groupthink and structuring systematic evaluation. They include the following procedures (Janis & Mann, 1977; Mann & Janis, 1983).

1. *Impartial leadership.* The leader abstains from communicating his or her position at the outset so that members cannot adopt it uncritically. By not stating preferences and expectations at the outset and by not advocating specific proposals, the leader allows members to develop an atmosphere of open inquiry and to explore impartially a wide range of policy alternatives.

2. *Critical evaluator role for every member.* Group members are encouraged to express doubts and objections freely. The leader assigns each member the role of critical evaluator, giving high priority to the airing of objections and doubts and accepting criticism of judgments in order to discourage group members from soft-pedaling their disagreements.

3. *Devil's advocate.* One or more group members are assigned the role of challenging the testimony of all those who support the majority opinion. Members are chosen to represent unpopular positions in the group.

4. *Outside experts.* Outside experts are invited to group meetings and asked to challenge the views of group members.

Barriers. There are a number of barriers to formulating and considering alternative solutions to the problem. The first is *a failure to identify the proper alternative courses of action.* If a course of action is not identified, it cannot be considered and evaluated. The second is *premature elimination of courses of action* without proper analysis and evaluation, or uninformed and premature choice. Groups often make poor decisions, not because they did not think of the proper alternatives, but because they did a poor job of evaluating and choosing among the alternatives they considered (Maier & Thurber, 1969). For most people, ideas are fragile creations, easily blighted by a chill, easily blighted by a chilly reception. As groups proceed in their problem-solving activities, they must avoid all tendencies to squelch each idea as it comes along; instead, they should create an atmosphere that supports the presentation and the pooling of a wide assortment of ideas. All alternative solutions should receive a fair hearing. Only then can the group avoid becoming fixated on the first reasonable solution suggested and critically evaluate the worth of all alternatives. The third barrier is *pressures for conformity.* Pressures for conformity and compliance slow down the development of different and diverse ideas. Divergent thinking as well as convergent thinking are necessary for sound problem solving.

The fourth barrier is *a lack of inquiry and problem-solving skills.* Some groups may need special training in how to use inquiry and problem-solving methods to their advantage. An expert member of the group may provide training, or the group may wish to call in an outside consultant. The fifth barrier is *a lack of procedures to aid analysis and synthesis.* The forces creating the problem must be understood and analyzed systematically in order for new alternatives to be created.

Deciding on a Solution

Once all the possible solutions have been identified and formulated in specific terms, the group needs to select the solution to implement. Making a decision involves considering possible alternatives and choosing one. The purpose of group decision making is to decide on well-considered, well-understood, realistic action toward goals every member wishes to achieve. Whenever possible, decisions by task forces should be made by consensus. As previously discussed in this chapter, consensus is not easy to achieve, as it is characterized by more conflict among members, more shifts of opinion, and a longer time to reach a conclusion. It is, however, worth the time and trouble, and it leads to group members' increased confidence in the correctness of their decision.

Second-Chance Meeting. Even when decisions are made by consensus, there are times when members fixate on an alternative without thinking through all its consequences. One procedure for ensuring that a decision is not made too hastily is *second-chance meetings.* Alfred Sloan, when he was Chairman of General Motors, once called an executive meeting to consider a major decision. He concluded

the meeting by saying, "Gentlemen, I take it we are all in complete agreement on the decision here.... Then I propose we postpone further discussion until our next meeting to give ourselves time to develop disagreement and perhaps gain some understanding of what the decision is all about." After a preliminary consensus on the best alternative, a *second-chance meeting* can be held at which all members are encouraged to express any remaining doubts and criticisms. Second-chance meetings help prevent premature consensus and concurrence seeking.

A number of societies have assumed that under the influence of alcohol, there would be fewer inhibitions against expressing residual doubts about a preliminary decision made when everyone was sober. According to Herodotus, the ancient Persians would make important decisions twice—first sober, then drunk. According to Tacitus, the Germans in Roman times also followed this practice. In Japan, where an emphasis is placed on harmony and politeness, a decision is frequently reconsidered after work in a bar. "Sake talk" takes place after each person has had a couple of cups of sake and therefore is no longer required to be polite. How group members really feel about the decision is then revealed. Although it's not necessary to bring alcohol into the decision-making process, groups should consider second-chance meetings as opportunities to make sure people are expressing themselves fully and truthfully. For example, a group may decide to meet a week after the decision initially is made for another, more casual follow-up discussion.

Evaluating the Extent and Success of Implementation

The responsibilities of the group members do not end when the group makes a decision. The group still has to implement the decision. *Decision implementation* is a process of taking the necessary actions that result in the execution of the decision. Decision implementation requires internal commitment by relevant group members to the decisions made. No decision is worthwhile unless it is implemented.

To evaluate the success of the solution the group has decided to implement, members must determine whether the solution was successfully implemented and what the effects were. The first activity is sometimes called *process evaluation* because it deals with the process of implementing a strategy. The second is called *outcome evaluation* because it involves assessing or judging the consequences of implementing the strategy. Planners should establish criteria for judging the effectiveness of their implementation. The major criterion for assessing the outcome of an implemented strategy is whether the actual state of affairs is closer to the desired state of affairs than it was before the strategy was carried out. The group documents the extent to which implementation takes place, notes barriers to implementation, and evaluates the success of the decision. For example, the outcome evaluation would consider the extent to which company communications improved once the new software was in place: Are more people using e-mail to document conversations? Does the scheduling feature allow people to organize meetings more efficiently? Did some employees resist learning the new programs?

If the group finds that its solution has been implemented successfully but has failed to change the current situation into the ideal state of affairs, a new solution must be chosen and implemented. The overall job of the group is to improve the situation and solve the problem, no matter how many times they need to make a decision and implement it. Solving one set of problems, however, often brings other problems into the open. In trying out various strategies, the group may discover it has not been working to solve the most critical problem in the situation. The final result of the evaluation stage, therefore, should be to show the group what problems have been solved and to what extent, what problems still need to be solved, and what new problems have developed. Evaluation should result in a new definition of a problem, a rediagnosis of the situation, and the beginning of a new problem-solving sequence.

POTENTIAL PROBLEMS IN DECISION MAKING

When two men in business always agree, one of them is unnecessary.

William Wrigley, Jr.

Decision making in groups does not always go smoothly. Although groups generally make more effective decisions than do individuals, it is also true that group decision making can take more time and involve different pitfalls than does individual decision making. The problems with group decision making include the following:

1. Group members tend to have an initial preference for which course of action to adopt, and they tend to argue in favor of their preference, resist changing their minds, and come to a final decision that reflects their initial preferences (Brodbeck, Kerschreiter, Mojzisch, Frey, & Schulz-Hardt,, 2002; Greitemeyer & Schulz-Hardt, 2003; Henningsen & Henningsen, 2003).

2. Similar to those who exhibit initial preference bias, group members tend to seek out information that confirms their initial opinions and beliefs, accepting the information uncritically at face value, and either ignore disconfirming information or subject it to a highly critical evaluation (Hart et. al., 2009; Lord, Ross, & Lepper, 1979). Group members frequently adjust their position instead of challenging their current point of view (i.e., they often look for confirming information and ignore disconfirming information). The bias toward confirming information tends to strengthen group members' attitudes, beliefs, values, judgments, and perceptions, especially when it comes to those beliefs that are based on prejudice, faith, or tradition rather than on empirical evidence (Hart et. al., 2009; Myers, 1982; Sunstein, 2002). It also impairs a group's ability to discover novel solutions or test minority positions against reality (Schulz-Hardt, Jachims, & Frey, 2002). Highly prejudiced individuals, for example, became even more prejudiced when they discussed racial issues with other prejudiced individuals. The confirmation bias is lessened, however, when one dissenter is included in the group and almost eliminated when two dissenters are included in the group (Schulz-Hardt, Frey, Luethgens, & Moscovici., 2000; Schulz-Hardt, Jochims, & Frey, 2002). The more sincerely and confidently the dissent is expressed, the more influence it tends to have on the other group members. Thus, there is value in including members who have a range of experiences and opinions and who disagree with each other.

3. The bias toward seeking out confirming information means that not all options are presented at equal strength (Johnson & Johnson, 2007). There is a bias toward presenting favored options with more conviction and confidence. The initially preferred option, and the confirming information supporting it, are presented and advocated strongly and receive uncritical consideration. The less-preferred options tend to be presented weakly and receive highly critical consideration. To overcome this bias, it is necessary to ensure that all options are strongly advocated and receive a complete and fair hearing.

4. There is a tendency for group members to discuss shared information (i.e., facts that two or more group members know in common) rather than unshared information (Wittenbaum, Hollingshead, & Botero, 2004). This pattern of behavior is less pronounced when groups are striving to make the best decision, meetings

last a long time (because shared information tends to be discussed first), the diversity of opinions in the group increases, an advocacy approach to discussion is used, the importance of dissent is emphasized, or the decision is first being discussed (rather than a return to a previously discussed decision) (Greitemeyer, Schulz-Hardt, Brodbeck, & Frey, 2006; Kloche, 2007; Larson, Foster-Fishman, & Keys, 1994; Reimer, Reimer, & Hinsz, 2008; Scholten, van Knippenberg, Nijstad, & De Dreu, 2007; Smith, 2008; Winquist & Larson, 1998).

5. There is a conformity bias, wherein group members tend to change their view and attitudes toward the view and attitudes of the majority of group members, even if doing so goes against their own judgment (Haslam, 2004; Sanders & Baron, 1977). Sometimes group members overdo it and become slightly more extreme than the rest of the group members (Weigold & Schlenker, 1991). This shift decreases the diversity of opinions in the group and can result in pluralistic ignorance, which occurs when a member of a group assumes that other group members are all in agreement and he or she is the only one who disagrees, when in fact almost all members disagree with the proposed course of action. What results is a decision that everyone votes for but no one wants. There may be some benefits to the conformity bias, such as greater cooperation and efficiency in reaching a common goal (Peterson & Nemeth, 1996). The costs, however, include the loss of divergent points of view and creativity (Gruenfeld, 1995; Nemeth, 1986; Nemeth & Wachtler, 1973). The more people are controlled by conformity pressure, the less willing they will be to suggest novel, dissenting, and creative ideas (Nemeth & Staw, 1989).

6. Group members tend to generate more arguments supporting the position endorsed by the majority of group, or the position that is most consistent with dominant social values (Burnstein & Vinokur, 1973, 1977; Vinokur & Burnstein, 1974, 1978). Because group members tend to change their opinions in response to others' arguments, this means that they will tend to be more convinced that the dominant position is valid. Group members may also engage in a process of self-persuasion by advocating the majority position. In addition, group members tend to remember the popular arguments more accurately and longer than the unpopular arguments (Brauer, Judd, & Gliner, 1995).

7. Under certain conditions, such as time pressure, noise, fatigue, or considerable ambiguity, group members may seek quick agreement to maintain group unity and view disagreement and conflict as disruptive to group unity (Kruglanski, Pierro, Mannetti, & DeGrada, 2006). The group strives for **cognitive closure**, through a quick, definite decision to end uncertainty, confusion, or ambiguity. Focusing on group unity at the expense of the quality of the decision is known as **group centrism**.

8. Finally, there is a blindness that comes with expertise. Most important group decisions involve more than one expert and, as Tversky and Kahneman (1981) note, most decision makers are normally unaware of alternative perspectives and frames of reference and of their potential effects on the relative attractiveness of options. Thus, two different experts, with different information and perspectives, can make directly opposing decisions without recognizing the limitations of their frames of reference. Experts do not see the "whole world"; they see only the part they specialize in, and they tend to overestimate the importance of their

expertise for making the decision and examine relevant information in a biased manner. Conflict and disagreement result. The conflicts are often difficult to resolve, as most decisions have to be made under the condition of uncertainty (the probability of desired outcomes resulting from the alternative course of action are unknown).

Most of the problems in making group decisions can be solved through the use of the constructive controversy procedure, in which group members have a structured process for disagreeing with each other and challenging each other's reasoning and conclusions. Constructive controversy is discussed in the next chapter.

PROBLEMS WITH THEORIZING ON DECISION MAKING

There are at least two major problems with theorizing and research on decision making in small groups. The first is that much of the research has focused on whether the decisions made by groups are of high or low quality. In the real world, many decisions cannot be objectively evaluated in terms of success or failure because their long-term effects cannot be fully measured. To evaluate long-term success or failure, one would need to take into account the negative consequences of the decision made, the positive consequences that would have resulted if each of the other alternatives had been adopted as the decision, the positive consequences of the decision, and the negative consequences that would have resulted if each of the other alternatives had been adopted. Obviously, it is difficult if not impossible to quantify these factors.

The second problem is that much of the theorizing and research on decision making has assumed that decision makers are completely informed (they know all the possible courses of action and the potential outcomes of each), infinitely sensitive (they see each alternative in all its complexity), and always rational (they always maximize the outcomes of their action). Real-life decision makers, however, are not always completely informed (they do not or cannot know all courses of action and their potential outcomes), do not understand fully the intricacies of various alternatives, and are rarely completely rational. Real-life decision makers often seem beset by conflicts, doubts, and worries; they struggle with conflicting loyalties, antipathies, and longings and engage in procrastination, rationalization, and denial of responsibility for their decisions. Instead of determining the solution that maximizes their outcomes, many decision makers look only for the alternative that meets a minimal set of requirements (this is called *satisficing*) and make quick decisions (Hoffman, 1961; Simon, 1976). Ineffective groups seem to operate under a variety of decision-making rules, such as "Tell a qualified expert about the problem and do whatever he or she says—that will be good enough" or "Do what we did last time if it worked, and the opposite if it didn't work." Real-life decision makers also realize how expensive it is in time, effort, and money to collect and dissect the huge amounts of information a group needs in order to use an ideal form of decision making.

Researchers can alleviate these two problems by studying the process of decision making rather than focusing on quality, and by specifying procedures that encourage real-life decision makers to become more systematic and rational in their decision making.

EXERCISE 7.5

A PROBLEM DIAGNOSIS PROGRAM

This program is designed to help you in diagnosing a problem that involves people working together in a group. In this program eleven separate steps are presented, each of which contains a complete and separate idea, question, or instruction. Be sure that you understand and complete each step before going on to the next one.

1. Identify the problem you wish to work on. Describe the problem as you now see it.

_____

_____

_____

2. Most problem statements can be rephrased so that they describe two things:
   a. The situation as it is now.
   b. The situation as you would like it to be (the ideal).
   Restate your problem situation in these terms. _____

   _____

   _____

   _____

3. Most problem situations can be understood in terms of the forces that push toward and against change—in other words, helping forces and restraining forces. It is useful to analyze a problem by making lists of the helping and restraining forces affecting a situation. Think about these now and list them. Be sure to list as many as you can, not worrying at this point about how important each one is. Use additional paper if you need to.

Helping	Restraining

4. Review the two lists. Underline those forces that seem to be most important right now and that you think you might be able to influence constructively. Depending on the problem, there may be one specific force that stands out, or there may be two or three helping forces and two or three restraining forces that are particularly important.

5. Now, for each restraining force you have underlined, list some possible courses of action you might be able to plan and carry out to reduce the effect of the force or to eliminate it completely. Brainstorm. List as many action steps as possible, without worrying about how effective or practical they would be. Later on, you will have a chance to decide which are the most appropriate.

   Restraining force A. Possible action steps to reduce this force

   _____

   _____

Restraining force B. Possible action steps to reduce this force

_____

_____

Restraining force C. Possible action steps to reduce this force

_____

_____

6. Now do the same with each helping force you underlined. List all the action steps that come to mind that would increase the effect of each helping force.
Helping force A. Possible action steps to increase this force

_____

_____

Helping force B. Possible action steps to increase this force

_____

_____

Helping force C. Possible action steps to increase this force

_____

_____

7. You now have listed action steps to change the key forces affecting your problem situation. Review these possible action steps and underline those that seem promising.

8. List the steps you have underlined. Then for each action step list the materials, people, and other resources available to you for carrying out the action.

Action Steps	Resources Available

9. Review the list of action steps and resources and think about how each might fit into a comprehensive action plan. Take out those items that do not seem to fit into the overall plan, add any new steps and resources that will round out the plan, and think about a possible sequence of action.

_____

_____

_____

_____

10. Plan a way of evaluating the effectiveness of your action program as it is implemented. Think about this now, and list the evaluation procedures you will use.

_____

_____

_____

_____

11. You now have a plan of action to deal with the problem situation. The next step is for you to implement it.

EXERCISE 7.6

YOUR DECISION-MAKING BEHAVIOR

Before this chapter ends, it might be useful for you to consider your decision-making behavior. How do you usually behave in a decision-making group? How would you like to behave? Here is a closing exercise for you to do in a group with two of your classmates:

1. Throw all your loose change into the center of the group. Decide (using consensus) how to use the money. Then look at the group decision in terms of the behaviors of each member. How did each of you behave? What task and maintenance functions did you yourself fulfill? How did you feel about your participation? How did your usual behavior reveal itself in the group decision making?

2. Review as a group the task and maintenance functions listed in Chapter 5. Discuss what other functions could be added. Examples are:

   a. *Clarification or elaboration.* Interpret or reflect on ideas or suggestions; clear up confusion; bring up alternatives and new issues before the group; give examples.

   b. *Summarization.* Pull together related ideas; restate suggestions after the group has discussed them.

   c. *Consensus testing.* Check with the group to see how much agreement has been reached; test to see if the group is nearing a decision.

   d. *Communication of feelings.* Express your feelings about the issues the group is discussing and the way in which it is functioning.

   e. *Verification of feelings.* Ask other members how they are feeling; check to see if your perception of their feelings is correct.

   Pick the task and maintenance functions you usually engage in; pick those you would like to perform better. Give one another feedback about each member's behavior.

3. Have you received any feedback on your behavior that has increased your awareness of how you behave? How would you now describe your behavior in decision-making situations?

4. Decide as a group when to end this exercise.

HOW I BEHAVE QUESTIONNAIRE

The purpose of this questionnaire is to help you look at how you behave in a group that is making a decision. Different persons act in different ways when they are members of groups that are making decisions. Moreover, the same person may act differently at different times, depending on the group, the decision to be made, and the circumstances. But, in general, how do you act when a group of which you are a member is making a decision? For each of the following three statements, choose the best description of the way you behave when a group to which you belong is making a decision. Be as objective and honest as you can; the results are for your use only.

1. When my group is making a decision, I:

   _____ Passively defer to others.

   _____ Work for a decision that satisfies everyone without worrying about how good it is.

   _____ Look entirely at the merits of the alternatives, without thinking about how the members of the group feel or how satisfied they are.

   _____ Look for alternatives that work, though I might not personally think they are the best.

   _____ Work for a strong, creative decision having a common basis of understanding among group members.

2. When my group is facing a decision, I:

____ Show little interest in the decision or the other group members.

____ Think mostly about how the members of the group are getting along, without worrying about what the decision will be.

____ Push for a really good decision and view the other members only as contributors of resources that will help make a better decision.

____ Work for good relations among the members and a good solution, though I am willing to sacrifice a little of each to get the job done.

____ Avoid compromise and try to get everyone to agree to and be satisfied with a decision that is based on looking at the situation in a realistic way.

3. When my group is making a decision, I:

____ Wait for the group to tell me what to do and accept what they recommend for me.

____ Help others participate by giving them moral support and by testing to see if members can agree.

____ Give information, evaluate how well the group is working toward completing the task, set ground rules for behavior, and see that everyone stays at the task.

____ Summarize periodically what has been discussed, call for things to be made clearer, and encourage members to compromise.

____ Help the groupthink of alternatives, discuss how practical the alternatives are, and work out ways in which the group can come to an agreement.

You can plot this self-assessment using the task maintenance grid in Exercise 5.3 (p. 183). Each of the preceding statements can be completed in five possible ways. The first alternative for each statement is a (6, 6) response; it shows that this person has little or no interest in either maintaining the group or helping it accomplish its task of making a decision. The second alternative is a (6, 30) response, showing that this member emphasizes group maintenance while ignoring the task. The third alternative is a (30, 6) response; here the person focuses on getting the task done but ignores group maintenance. The fourth alternative is an (18, 18) response, indicating a member who compromises on both task and maintenance in order to reach a decision. The fifth alternative for each question is a (30, 30) response; this person tries to achieve a creative, consensual decision and emphasizes both the task and maintenance functions of the group.

Look at your three responses. Locate each on the task maintenance grid. Then discuss the results in groups of three, comparing your responses here with those you gave on the leadership surveys in the previous chapter and with the way you would like to act in groups.

SUMMARY

Typically, groups rather than individuals make more effective decisions, because groups create the possibility for social facilitation, risk taking, member commitment to the group, appropriate behavioral and attitudinal patterns being adopted, and the likelihood that the task is better done in a group. Once a group is given the responsibility for making the decision, it can follow any of seven methods, ranging from letting the member with the highest authority decide to averaging individual opinions to group consensus. In using the decision-making methods, components such as positive interdependence, promotive interaction, individual accountability, social skills, and group processing must be structured carefully.

Groups will run into factors that hinder their decision-making efforts. The hindering factors include lack of group maturity, taking the dominant response, social loafing, free riding, fear of being a sucker, groupthink, conflicting goals, members' egocentrism, homogeneity, production blocking, inappropriate size, dissonance reduction, and the lack of necessary task-work and teamwork skills. In order to structure the essential components and avoid the hindering factors, the group has to engage in considered and thoughtful decision making. The steps for doing so are to identify and define the problem, gather the information needed to diagnose it, formulate alternative solutions, decide on the solution to implement, present the group's recommendations to the larger organization (if appropriate), and evaluate the success of the implementation to determine if the problem has been solved.

An essential aspect of decision making is deciding among alternative solutions. To do so effectively, conflict among members' preferences, analyses, conclusions, and theories must be encouraged and resolved constructively. The next chapter focuses on structuring decision-making controversies and ensuring that it leads to creative problem solving.

CHAPTER EIGHT

Controversy and Creativity

BASIC CONCEPTS TO BE COVERED IN THIS CHAPTER

In this chapter a number of concepts are defined and discussed. The major ones are in the following list. Divide into heterogeneous pairs. Each pair is to (1) define each concept, noting the page on which it is defined and discussed, and (2) ensure that both members of the pair understand the meaning of each concept. Then combine into groups of four. Compare the answers of the two pairs. If there is disagreement, look up the concept in the chapter and clarify it until all members agree on and understand the definition.

CONCEPTS

1. Controversy
2. Debate
3. Conceptual conflict
4. Concurrence seeking
5. Cognitive perspective
6. Differentiation of positions
7. Integration of positions
8. Epistemic curiosity
9. Perspective taking
10. Creativity
11. Open-mindedness
12. Dogmatism
13. Analytic phase
14. Brainstorming

CONTROVERSY AND DECISION MAKING

Since the general or prevailing opinion on any subject is rarely or never the whole truth, it is only by the collision of adverse opinion that the remainder of the truth has any chance of being supplied.

John Stuart Mill

To be effective over time, most groups need to improve continuously, innovate, and find creative solutions to challenges they face. Creative ideas are the lifeblood of the most successful groups (Amabile, 1996; Collins & Porras, 1994). Creative ideas are the raw material necessary for innovation, and a strong competitive advantage is conferred upon organizations that are adept at eliciting creative solutions from their employees (Kanter, 1988). A single creative idea may be hugely profitable, such as one employee's idea for a "failed" adhesive that gave rise to the Post-It Note by the 3M Corporation (Collins & Porras, 1994), which resulted in untold millions of dollars to the company's bottom line (Von Hippel, Thomke, & Sonnack, 1999). The need for creativity and creative decision making is noted in groups stating that they need to "reinvent themselves" periodically. Motorola calls this "self-renewal," Philip Morris calls it "individual initiative," and Sony calls it "being a pioneer." The reinvention results in **innovation,** the process through which new practices and procedures are successfully implemented at the organization level. There is, therefore, considerable pressure in many groups to generate new ideas that suggest productive new directions (Amabile, 1996). Many creative ideas, however, are rejected outright because they are either perceived to be too risky or threatening to the status quo (Staw, 1995). Pressure to conform to the status quo is a serious impediment to creativity and innovation, and to implement creative innovations it is necessary to reduce or eliminate any pressure to conform (Nemeth, 1977). Desiring, expecting, and even rewarding creativity and innovation, furthermore, does not necessarily increase it. Increased motivation and effort may result in variations on a theme, but they are unlikely to create major changes in perspective or reformulation. Creative problem solving and decision making is most likely to occur when the group culture permits, encourages, and welcomes dissent and independence of thought (Nemeth & Staw, 1989). Group creativity is stimulated by the free expression of dissenting opinions because, even when they are wrong, they cause group members to think and solve problems more creatively (Gruenfeld, 1995; Nemeth, 1986). What groups need is an institutionalized procedure that ensures that decision making optimizes creativity and potential innovation. Constructive controversy is such a procedure.

NATURE OF CONTROVERSY

In reorganizing, a company specializing in providing residential services for people with special needs had to decide whether or not to collapse two departments into one. The CEO and eight managers were involved in making the decision. To ensure that the best decision was made, the CEO established two advocacy teams, assigning four managers to the "collapse the two departments into one" team and four managers to the "keep two separate departments" team. They were given ten days to develop the best case possible for their assigned position, detailing the relative long-term costs, gains, and efficacy. They then were given three hours to present their position. The two sides discussed the future of the two departments, challenging one another's information, reasoning, and conclusions. After several hours of discussion, the two sides summarized the best case possible for the opposing position, ensuring that all members could see the issue from both perspectives. After further consideration, it became clear that two departments were still needed, but the makeup of each department needed to be considerably modified. Through the use of the constructive controversy procedure, the CEO ensured that the management team made a high-quality decision.

By definition, decisions involve conflict, as several alternative courses of action are identified and considered before agreement is reached. As members discuss the decision to be made, different ideas, opinions, beliefs, and information can surface and clash. The result is **controversy**—the conflict that arises when one person's ideas, information, conclusions, theories, and opinions are incompatible with those of another person, and the two seek to reach an agreement. Figure 8.1 summarizes this process. The word is derived from the Latin *controversia*, as a composite of *controversus* (turned in an opposite direction) from *contra* ("against") and *vertere* (to turn) or *versus*, hence, "to turn against." Controversies are resolved by engaging in what Aristotle called **deliberate discourse** (i.e., the discussion of the advantages and disadvantages of proposed actions) aimed at synthesizing novel solutions (i.e., **creative problem solving**). A procedure for managing the controversy consists of the following steps (Johnson, 1970; Johnson, F. Johnson, & Johnson, 1976; Johnson & R. Johnson, 1979, 1989, 2007, 2009):

1. **Research and prepare a position.** Each alternative course of action is assigned to a two-person advocacy team. The advocacy teams are given time to (a) research their assigned alternative course of action and find all the supporting evidence available, (b) organize their findings into a coherent and reasoned position, and (c) plan how to present their case so that all group members give it a fair and complete hearing, understand it, and are convinced of its validity.
2. **Present and advocate their position.** Each advocacy pair presents its position forcefully, sincerely, and persuasively. Other group members listen carefully and critically, but with an open mind.
3. **Engage in an open discussion.** Each advocacy pair (a) continues to advocate its position, (b) attempts to refute opposing positions, and (c) rebuts attacks on its position. Each alternative course of action is thus given a "trial by fire."
4. **Reverse perspectives:** Advocacy pairs reverse perspectives and present one another's positions. In arguing for the opposing position, group members summarize it in a forceful, sincere, and persuasive way. They add any new information that the opposing pairs did not think to present. They strive to see the issue from all perspectives simultaneously.
5. **Reach a decision through consensus as to which course of action to implement.** Group members drop all advocacy and integrate what they know

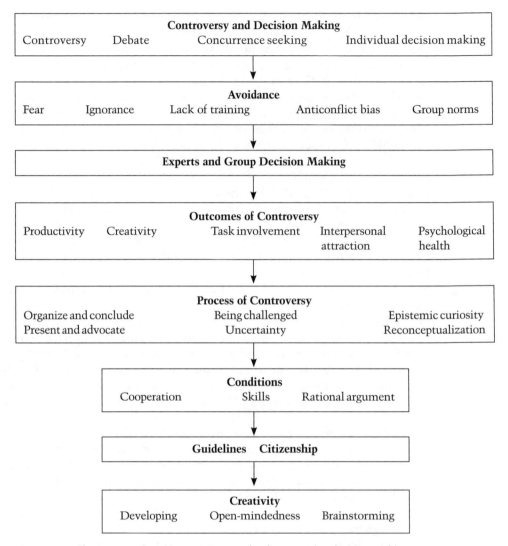

Figure 8.1 Chapter overview. How controversy leads to creative decision making.

into a reasoned decision to which all members agree. This requires reconceptualizing the issue by synthesizing and integrating the best information and reasoning from all sides. The group's decision then reflects their best reasoned judgment.

Structured controversies most commonly are compared to and contrasted with concurrence-seeking, debate, and individualistic decision making. **Concurrence seeking** occurs when members of a group inhibit discussion to avoid any disagreement or arguments, emphasize agreement, and avoid realistic appraisal of alternative

ideas and courses of action. If the group is concurrence seeking, it would stipulate that group members are not to argue but instead must compromise quickly whenever opposing opinions are expressed. Most group decision-making situations are dominated by concurrence seeking (Walton, 1987). Concurrence seeking is close to the **groupthink** concept of Janis (1982) in which members of a decision-making group set aside their doubts and misgivings about whatever policy is favored by the emerging consensus so as to be able to concur with the other members. The underlying motivation of groupthink and concurrence seeking is the strong desire to preserve the harmonious atmosphere of the group on which each member has become dependent for coping with the stresses of external crises and for maintaining self- esteem.

Debate exists when two or more individuals argue positions that are incompatible with one another and a judge declares a winner on the basis of who presented their position the best. An example would be a group in which each member is assigned a position on whether more or fewer regulations are needed to control hazardous wastes. After each member presents, an authority declares as the winner the person who made the best presentation of his or her position to the group.

Individualistic decision making occurs when isolated individuals independently decide on a course of action without talking with one another. Each decision maker comes to his or her decision without interacting with others or discussing the information upon which the decision is being made. The processes generated by controversy, debate, concurrence seeking, and individual decision making are summarized in Table 8.1.

Closely related to the concept of controversy are the concepts of dissent and argumentation. **Dissent** can be defined as differences in opinion or conclusion, especially from the majority. Dissent often results in an argument. An **argument** is a thesis statement or claim supported by at least one reason and **arguing** is a social process in which two or more individuals engage in a dialogue where arguments are constructed, presented, and critiqued. Arguing is often called *dialectical argumentation* because a thesis and supporting reasons can be contradicted by an antithesis and its supporting reasons. A distinction has also been made between collaborative argumentation (the goal to work cooperatively to explore and critique different ideas, positions, and conclusions) and adversarial argumentation (the goal is to "win" an argument, as in a debate) (Brown & Renshaw, 2000; Gilbert, 1997; see Table 8.2).

TABLE 8.1   **Controversy, Debate, Concurrence-Seeking, and Individualistic Processes**

CONTROVERSY	DEBATE	CONCURRENCE SEEKING	INDIVIDUALISTIC
Categorizing and organizing information to derive conclusions	Categorizing and organizing information to derive conclusions	Categorizing and organizing information to derive conclusions	Categorizing and organizing information to derive conclusions
Presenting, advocating, and elaborating position and rationale	Presenting, advocating, and elaborating position and rationale	Presenting, advocating, and elaborating position and rationale	No oral statement of position
Being challenged by opposing views results in **conceptual conflict** and uncertainty about correctness of own views	Being challenged by opposing views results in conceptual conflict and uncertainty about correctness of own views	Being challenged by opposing views results in conceptual conflict and uncertainty about correctness of own view	Presence of only one view results in high certainty about the correctness of own view
Epistemic curiosity motivates active search for new information and perspectives	Closed-minded rejection of opposing information and perspectives	Apprehension about differences and closed-minded adherence to own point of view	Continued high certainty about the correctness of own view
Reconceptualization, synthesis, integration	Closed-minded adherence to own point of view	Quick compromise to dominant view	Adherence to own point of view
High achievement, positive relationships, psychological health	Moderate achievement, relationships, psychological health	Low achievement, relationships, psychological health	Low achievement, relationships, psychological health

Source: Adapted with permission from D. W. Johnson and R. Johnson. *Constructive controversy: Intellectual challenge in the class-room* (4th ed.) (Edina, MN: Interaction Book Company, 2007).

TABLE 8.2   **Nature of Decision-Making Procedures**

	CONTROVERSY	DEBATE	CONCURRENCE SEEKING	INDIVIDUALISTIC
Positive goal interdependence	Yes	No	Yes	No
Resource interdependence	Yes	Yes	No	No
Negative goal interdependence	No	Yes	No	No
Conflict	Yes	Yes	No	No

Source: Johnson, D. W., & Johnson, R. T. (2007). *Creative controversy: Intellectual challenge in the classroom* (4th ed.). Edina, MN: Interaction Book Company.

Controversies are common within decision-making situations. In the mining industry, for example, engineers are accustomed to addressing issues such as land use, air and water pollution, and health and safety. The complexity of the design of production processes, the balancing of environmental and manufacturing interests, and numerous other factors often create controversy. Every effective decision-making situation thrives on what controversy has to offer. Decisions are by their very nature controversial, as alternative solutions are suggested and considered before agreement is reached. When a decision is made, the controversy ends and participants commit themselves to a common course of action.

EXERCISE 8.1

CONTROVERSY: WAS PETER PAN RIGHT OR WRONG?

Task: In the book *Peter Pan,* a case is made for staying young forever in Never-Never Land. Is this a good idea? Would you like to live in Never-Never Land and never grow up? Write a report presenting your conclusion and the reasons why it is valid on the issue, "Was Peter Pan right or wrong? Should you grow up or stay a child?" There are two positions on this issue:

1. It is better to stay young and never grow up.
2. It is better to grow up and leave childhood behind.

    Cooperative: Write one report for the group—everyone has to agree and everyone has to be able to explain the choice made and the reasons why the choice is a good one.

PROCEDURE

1. Review the rules for constructive controversy in chapter 1, page 32.
2. **Research and Prepare Your Position:** Your group of four has been divided into two pairs. One pair has been assigned the pro position and the other pair has been assigned the con position. With your partner, plan how to present to the other pair the best case possible for your assigned position in order to make sure it receives a fair and complete hearing. Research your position and get as much information to support it as possible. Make sure both you and your partner are ready to present.
3. **Present and Advocate Your Position:** Forcefully and persuasively present the best case for your position to the opposing pair. Be as convincing as possible. Take notes and clarify anything you do not understand when the opposing pair presents.
4. **Open Discussion:** Argue forcefully and persuasively for your position, presenting as many supporting facts as you can. Critically evaluate the opposing pair's arguments, challenge their information and reasoning, and defend your position from their attacks. Keep in mind that you need to know both sides to write a good report.
5. **Reverse Perspectives:** Reverse perspectives and present the best case for the opposing position. The opposing pair will do the same. Strive to see the issue from both perspectives simultaneously.
6. **Synthesis:** Drop all advocacy. Synthesize and integrate the best evidence and reasoning from both sides into a joint position to which all members can agree. Then (a) finalize the group report, (b) present your conclusions to the class, (c) individually take the test covering both sides of the issue, and (d) process how well you worked together as a group and how you could be even more effective next time.

EXERCISE 8.2

HOW I BEHAVE IN CONTROVERSIES

This exercise should make you more aware of your typical actions when you are involved in a controversy, and make your group more aware of the pattern of members' actions when they are involved in a controversy. The procedure is as follows:

1. Working by yourself, complete the following questionnaire.
2. Using the scoring table, determine (a) your scores and (b) the average of all group members' scores.
3. Engage in a group discussion of (a) the strategies used most frequently during a controversy and (b) how controversies may be managed more constructively.

Each of the following questions describes an action taken during a controversy. For each question write a "5" if you always behave that way, "4" if you frequently behave that way, "3" if you occasionally behave that way, "2" if you seldom behave that way, and "1" if you never behave that way.

_____ 1. I try to avoid individuals who argue with me.
_____ 2. When I disagree with other group members, I insist that they change their opinions to match mine.
_____ 3. When I do not care about the decision, I agree with the person who cares the most about what the decision should be.
_____ 4. I only discuss an issue as long as it takes 51% of the members to agree on a course of action.
_____ 5. When others disagree with me, I view it as an interesting opportunity to learn and to improve the quality of my ideas and reasoning.
_____ 6. When others disagree with me, I generally keep my ideas and opinions to myself.
_____ 7. When I get involved in an argument with others, I become more and more certain that I am correct and argue more and more strongly for my own point of view.
_____ 8. When I have nothing at stake in the decision, I try to support the person who has the soundest logic and information.
_____ 9. Once the majority has decided, the decision is made.
_____ 10. When others disagree with me, I encourage them to express their ideas and opinions fully, seek to clarify the differences between their position and perspective and mine, and seek to find a new position that incorporates the best ideas from both sides.
_____ 11. I am careful not to share my ideas and opinions when I think others may disagree with them.
_____ 12. I view my disagreements with others as opportunities to see who "wins" and who "loses."
_____ 13. Sometimes the decision does not affect me in any way, and then I support the person with the most persuasive reasoning and rationale.
_____ 14. Even if I do not agree, I go along with the majority opinion.
_____ 15. When I disagree with others, I listen carefully to their ideas and opinions and change my mind when doing so is warranted by their information and reasoning.
_____ 16. I refuse to get into an argument with anyone.
_____ 17. When others and I disagree, I try to overpower them with my facts and reasoning.
_____ 18. When none of the alternative courses of action appeal to me, I defer to the most interested party.

_____ 19. I believe that the majority should rule.

_____ 20. When others disagree with me, I try to clarify the differences among our ideas and opinions, clarify the points of agreement, and seek a creative integration of all our ideas and information.

_____ 21. When others disagree with me, I stay very quiet and try to avoid them in the future.

_____ 22. When others and I disagree, I have to convince them that I am right and they are wrong.

_____ 23. If I have no opinion about what is the best course of action, I agree with the person with whom I have the best relationship.

_____ 24. I tend to agree with the majority whenever a decision is to be made.

_____ 25. When I am involved in an argument, I never forget that we are trying to make the best decision possible by combining the best of all our facts and reasoning.

HOW I BEHAVE IN CONTROVERSIES: SCORING

Avoiding	Winning	Agreeing	Majority Rules	Synthesis, Integration
_____ 1	_____ 2	_____ 3	_____ 4	_____ 5
_____ 6	_____ 7	_____ 8	_____ 9	_____ 10
_____ 11	_____ 12	_____ 13	_____ 14	_____ 15
_____ 16	_____ 17	_____ 18	_____ 19	_____ 20
_____ 21	_____ 22	_____ 23	_____ 24	_____ 25
_____ Total	_____ Total	_____ Total	_____ Total	_____ Total

The higher your total score for each decision-making procedure, the more frequently you tend to use that procedure. The lower the total score for each decision-making procedure, the less frequently you tend to use that procedure.

CONTROVERSY/DECISION-MAKING PROCEDURES: WHAT ARE YOU LIKE?

Different people use different strategies for making decisions and managing the inherent conflicts in doing so. Usually, we overlearn these strategies and they seem to function as automatic habit patterns. But now that you have learned our preferred procedures for decision making, you can change them. When engaging in a controversy, you should take two concerns into account:

1. **Reaching a decision that incorporates the best reasoning and information from all points of view.** The decision requires choosing among alternative courses of action usually based on differing perspectives. The goal of making the best decision possible can be placed on a continuum ranging from unimportant to highly important.
2. **Maintaining an effective working relationship with other members.** Some relationships are temporary whereas some are permanent. Relationships with the other group members can be placed on a continuum between being of little importance to being highly important.

The procedure used to make the decision depends on how important the goal of making the best decision possible is to the involved parties and how important they perceive their relationships with each other to be. Given these two concerns, five basic strategies are used to make decisions.

continued on next page

continued from previous page

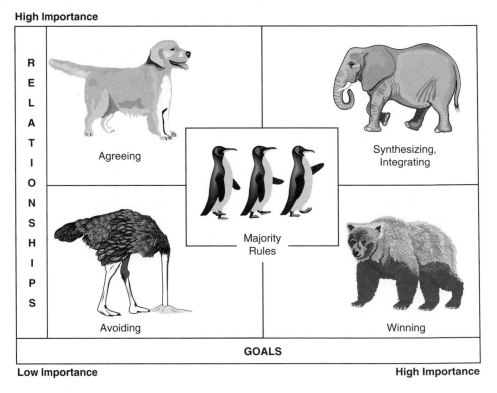

1. **The Elephant (Synthesizing, Integrating):** Elephants highly value the goal and the relationship. When both the goal and the relationship are highly important, you seek a synthesis or an integration of the various alternative courses of action. A decision is sought that ensures both you and the other parties fully achieve your goals and resolve any tensions and negative feelings among you. This strategy requires high trust, fully explaining the rationale for your position and learning the rationales for the other positions.
2. **The Golden Retriever (Agreeing).** To golden retrievers, the relationship is of great importance while the decision to be made is of little importance. They, therefore, emphasize agreeing with the other parties in order to maintain the relationship at the highest quality possible. When other parties care much more about the decision, golden retrievers tend to just agree with the other parties.
3. **The Bear (Winning):** Bears see the relationship as of no importance but having their desired alternative course of action adopted as very important. When the nature of the decision is very important but the relationship is not, group members seek to dictate the nature of the decision. The decision making situation is seen as a competition in which the most powerful or persuasive person wins.
4. **The Penguin (Majority Rules):** Penguins are moderately concerned with the nature of the decision and the relationship with the other group members. When both the decision

and the relationship are moderately important, and it appears that no one can get what he or she wants, a vote can be taken and the majority opinion is adopted. Majority rule is often used when group members wish to synthesize or integrate the best points from all positions, but do not have the time to do so.

5. **The Ostrich (Avoiding):** Ostriches bury their heads in the sand to avoid making decisions, valuing neither relationships nor the nature of the decision. When the decision is not important and the relationships with the other parties are of no consequence, individuals may wish to bury their heads in the sand and avoid the issue and the other person.

How I Behave in Controversies: Group Scoring

	1	2	3	4	5	Total
Synthesizing, Integrating						
Majority Rule						
Agreeing						
Winning						
Avoiding						

Procedure

1. Rank your total responses for each procedure from "1" for most frequently preferred to "5" for least frequently preferred.
2. In the table above, record the ranking given each procedure by each group member.
3. Total each row by multiplying the frequency by the rank. For example, if three group members ranked avoiding as "4," you multiple the frequency, 3, by the rank, 4, and get a score of 12 for that cell in the table.
4. Total the scores for each cell in the row to get a total score for each row (i.e., each procedure).
5. The lower the score for the row (i.e., procedure), the more frequently the procedure tends to be preferred by group members.

EXERCISE 8.3

WHO SHOULD GET THE PENICILLIN?

The purpose of this exercise is to examine the dynamics of controversy within a social studies lesson. The materials needed for the exercise are a description of the situation, a briefing sheet for the medical point of view, a briefing sheet for the military point of view, a postdecision questionnaire, a summary table, a constructive controversy checklist, and a controversy observation form. The last four items are also used in Exercises 8.4, 8.5, and 8.6. Approximately ninety minutes are needed for the exercise. The procedure for the coordinator is as follows:

1. Introduce the exercise by stating its objective and reviewing the overall procedure.
2. Form groups of five members. One member from each group should volunteer to be an observer. The observer's role is to record the nature of each member's participation in the group, using the controversy observation form.

continued on next page

continued from previous page

3. Divide the remaining four members of each group into two pairs. Give one pair a copy of the medical viewpoint briefing sheet and the other pair a copy of the military viewpoint briefing sheet.
4. Introduce the situation. Instruct the pairs to build as good a rationale for their assigned position as they can in fifteen or twenty minutes, using the information on the briefing sheet as a guide.
5. Instruct the pairs to meet together as a group of four. The group is to come to a decision on which all four members can agree. The decision should reflect the best reasoning of the entire group. The group discussion should follow these steps:
   a. Each pair presents its position as forcefully and persuasively as it can while the opposing pair takes notes and clarifies anything the two members do not fully understand.
   b. Have an open discussion in which the members of each pair (1) argue forcefully and persuasively for their position, presenting as many facts as they can to support it, and (2) listen critically to the members of the opposing pair, asking them for the facts that support their point of view. This is a complex issue, and members need to know both sides in order to come to a thoughtful decision.
6. Instruct the pairs to reverse their perspectives by switching sides and arguing for the opposite point of view as forcefully and persuasively as possible. Members should see if they can think of any new facts that the opposing pair did not present in support of its position and should elaborate on that position.
7. Instruct the groups to come to a joint decision by:
   a. Summarizing the best arguments for both points of view.
   b. Detailing the facts they know about World War II and the African campaign.
   c. Achieving consensus among the members.
   d. Organizing the rationale supporting the decision they will present to the rest of the class. They should be ready to defend the validity of their decision to groups who may have come to the opposite decision.
8. Instruct participants to complete the postdecision questionnaire. Then have the observers determine the group mean for each question.
9. Summarize the decision of each group in front of the entire class. Then summarize the results of the postdecision questionnaire, using the summary table.
10. Instruct each group to discuss their experience, using:
    a. The decision and questionnaire results
    b. The information collected by the observers
    c. The impressions of the group members
    d. The constructive controversy checklist
11. The following questions may help the groups discuss how they managed the controversy:
    a. How did the group manage disagreements among its members? (Use the checklist for constructive controversy as a guide.)
    b. From its experience, what conclusions can the group reach about the constructive handling of controversies?
    c. Did the opinions of the group members change as a result of the group's discussion? Did members gain insight into the other point of view through the perspective reversal procedure? Did members learn anything new about World War II?
    d. What did members learn about themselves and other group members? How did each member react to the controversy?
12. Have each group share its conclusions about the constructive management of controversy with the rest of the class.

WHO SHOULD GET THE PENICILLIN EXERCISE SITUATION

In 1943, penicillin, which is used for the prevention of infection, was in short supply among the U.S. armed forces in North Africa. Decisions had to be made on whether to use this meager supply for the thousands of hospitalized victims of venereal disease or for the thousands of victims of battle wounds at the front. If you were a member of a team of medical and military personnel, for whom would you use the penicillin?

_____ victims of venereal disease
_____ victims of battle wounds

Share your position and rationale with your group. Stick to your guns unless logically persuaded otherwise. At the same time, help your group achieve consensus on this issue.

BRIEFING SHEET: THE MEDICAL VIEWPOINT—
WHO SHOULD GET THE PENICILLIN EXERCISE

Your position is to give the penicillin to the battle-wounded. Whether or not you agree with this position, argue for it as strongly and honestly as you can, using arguments that make sense and are rational. Be creative and invent new supporting arguments. Seek out information; ask members of other groups who may know the answers to your questions. Remember to learn the rationale for both your position and the military position. Challenge the military position; think of loopholes in its logic; demand facts and information that back up its arguments.

1. Our responsibility is to treat the wounded and save as many lives as possible. Without the penicillin, many of the wounded will die needlessly. Minor wounds will get infected and become major, life-threatening wounds.
2. Our strategies must be based on the premise that human life is sacred. If one person dies needlessly, we have failed in our responsibility. The soldiers who have sacrificed so much to help us win the war must be treated with all the care, concern, and resources we can muster. Our soldiers must be able to fight harder than the German soldiers.
3. Troop morale is vital. Nothing raises troop morale as much as the men's knowledge that if they are wounded they will receive top-notch medical treatment.
4. Morale at home is vital. People must make sacrifices to produce the goods and materials we need to win the war. Nothing raises morale at home more than knowing that husbands, sons, and brothers are receiving the most effective medical care that is humanly possible. It would be devastating for word to reach the United States that we were needlessly letting soldiers die for lack of medical care.
5. Even though we are at war, we must not lose our humanity. It will do no good to defeat Germany if we become Nazis in the process.
6. At this point the war is going badly in North Africa. Rommel and the German army are cutting through our lines like butter. We are on the verge of being pushed out of Africa, in which case we will lose the war. Rommel must be stopped.
7. Fresh troops and supplies are unavailable. The German submarines control the Atlantic, and we cannot get troop ships or supply ships into African ports. We have to make do with what we have.
8. Penicillin is a wonder drug that will save countless lives if it is used to treat the wounded.

BRIEFING SHEET: THE MILITARY VIEWPOINT—
WHO SHOULD GET THE PENICILLIN EXERCISE

Your position is to give the penicillin to the VD patients. Whether or not you agree with this position, argue for it as strongly and honestly as you can, using arguments that make sense and are

continued on next page

continued from previous page

rational. Be creative and invent new supporting arguments. Seek out information that supports your position. If you do not have needed information, ask members of other groups who may. Remember to learn the rationale for both your position and the medical position. Challenge the medical position; think of loopholes in its logic; demand facts and information that back up its arguments.

1. Our responsibility is to win the war for our country at all costs. If we lose Africa, we will lose Europe to Hitler, and eventually we will be fighting in the United States.
2. Our strategies to win must be based on the premise of the greatest good for the greatest number. We may have to sacrifice soldiers in order to win the war, save our democracy, and free Europe.
3. Troop morale is vital. Our soldiers must be able to fight harder than the German soldiers. Nothing raises troop morale like seeing fresh troops arrive at the front.
4. Morale at home is vital. People must make sacrifices to produce the goods and materials we need to fight the war. Nothing raises morale at home like hearing of battles won and progress being made in winning the war. Victories give our people at home more dedication.
5. At this point, the war is going badly in North Africa. Rommel and the German army are cutting through our lines like butter. We are on the verge of being pushed out of Africa, in which case we will lose the war. Rommel must be stopped at all costs!
6. Penicillin is a wonder drug that will send VD into remission, and within twenty-four hours the VD patients will be free from pain and able to function effectively on the battlefield.

THEORY OF CONSTRUCTIVE CONTROVERSY

How conflict is structured in decision-making situations determines how group members interact with each other, which in turn determines the quality of the decision and other relevant outcomes. Conflict among group members over which course of action to take can be structured along a continuum. At one end of the continuum is constructive controversy and at the other end is concurrence seeking. Each way of structuring conflict in decision-making situations leads to a different process of interaction among group members.

PROCESS OF CONTROVERSY

Difference of opinion leads to inquiry, and inquiry to truth.

Thomas Jefferson

The process by which controversy sparks high-quality decision making, productivity, positive relationships, psychological health, and other positive outcomes is outlined in Figure 8.2. During a constructive controversy, decision makers proceed through the following process (Johnson & Johnson, 1979, 1989, 2000, 2003a, 2005b; Johnson, Johnson, & Tjosvold, 2000):

1. When individuals are presented with a problem or decision, they form an initial conclusion based on categorizing and organizing their current (but usually

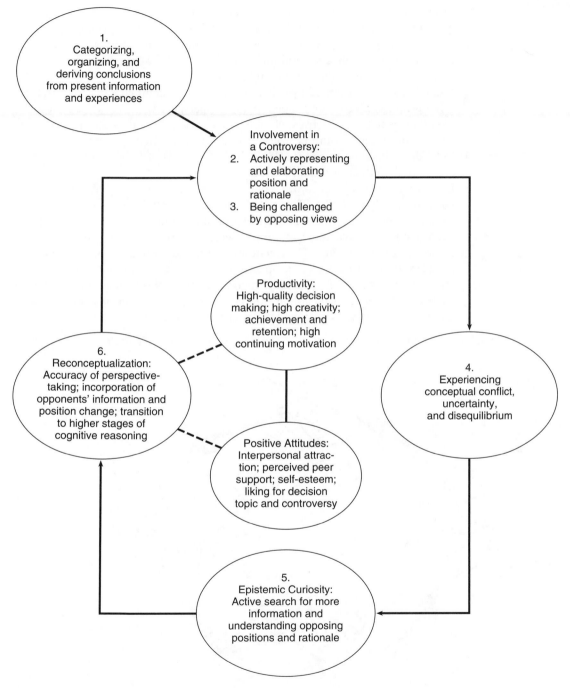

Figure 8.2 Process of controversy.

Source: D. W. Johnson and R. T. Johnson, (2007), Creative controversy: Intellectual challenge in the classroom. Edina, MN: Interaction Book Company.

limited) information, experience, and perspectives. They tend to have a high de-gree of confidence in their initial conclusion (they freeze the epistemic process).

2. When individuals present their conclusion and its rationale to others, they en-gage in cognitive rehearsal and higher-level reasoning strategies, thereby deep-ening their understanding of the problem or decision.

3. Individuals are confronted by other people with different conclusions based on other people's information, experiences, and perspectives. They tend to become uncertain as to the correctness of their own conclusion, and a state of conceptual conflict or disequilibrium is aroused. They unfreeze their epistemic process.

4. Individuals become uncertain as to the correctness of their views. A state of conceptual conflict or disequilibrium is aroused.

5. Uncertainty, conceptual conflict, or disequilibrium tends to motivate *epistemic curiosity* (Berlyne, 1965). The result is an active search for (a) more informa-tion and new experiences (increased specific content) and (b) a more adequate **cognitive perspective** and reasoning process (increased validity) in the hope of resolving the uncertainty. Divergent attention and thought are stimulated.

6. By adapting their cognitive perspective and reasoning through understanding and accommodating the perspective and reasoning of others, a new, reconcep-tualized, and reorganized conclusion is derived. Novel solutions and decisions are detected that are, on balance, qualitatively better and tend to be detected.

Each of these premises is discussed in the following sections (Figure 8.3).

Figure 8.3 Illustration of controversy.
Source: D. W. Johnson and R. T. Johnson, (2007), Creative controversy: Intellectual challenge in the classroom. Edina, MN: Interaction Book Company.

Step 1: Organizing Information and Deriving Conclusions

In order to make high-quality decisions, individuals have to think of the proper alternatives, do a good job of evaluating them, and choose the most promising one. When individuals are presented with a problem or decision, they have an initial conclusion based on current knowledge, perspective, dominant response, expectations, and past experiences.

Step 2: Presenting and Advocating Positions

Edward R. Murrow, the noted journalist, said, *"To be persuasive we must be believable; to be believable we must be credible; to be credible, we must be truthful."* In a controversy, individuals present and advocate positions to others who, in turn, are advocating opposing positions. The intent is to convert the other group members to one's position. Conversion requires that other group members become convinced that the dissenter is correct. **Advocacy** occurs when an individual presents a position and provides reasons why others should adopt it. Decisions and conclusions are then reached through a process of argument and counter-argument aimed at persuading others to adopt, modify, or drop positions. Other group members, knowing that the presenting group member is trying to convert them, scrutinize the person's position and critically analyze it, as part of their resistance to being converted (Baker & Petty, 1994; Erb, Bohner, Rank, & Einwiller, 2002; Hewstone & Martin, 2008). Advocating a position and defending it against refutation require engaging in considerable cognitive rehearsal and elaboration, which results in increased understanding of the position, discovery of higher-level reasoning processes, discovery of a greater amount of information and variety of facts, and changes in the salience of known information. Individuals' commitment to their position tends to increase as they advocate it. They tend to have a high degree of confidence in their initial conclusion (they freeze the epistemic process).

Step 3: Being Challenged by Opposing Views

"Has anything escaped me?" I asked with some self-importance.
"I trust there is nothing of consequence that I have overlooked?"
"I'm afraid, my dear Watson, that most of your conclusions were
erroneous. When I said that you stimulated me I meant, to be frank, that
in noting your fallacies I was occasionally guided towards the truth."

From **The Hound of the Baskervilles** by Sir Arthur Conan Doyle

In controversy, advocates of one position challenge the positions of opposing advocates. Members critically analyze one another's positions in attempts to discern weaknesses and strengths. They attempt to refute opposing positions while rebutting attacks on their own position. At the same time, they are aware that they need to learn the information being presented and understand the perspective of the other group members. Individuals engaged in controversy are motivated to know the others' positions and to develop understanding and appreciation of them (see Johnson & Johnson, 1979, 1989, 2000, 2003a, 2005b,). When members hear opposing views being advocated, furthermore, it stimulates new cognitive analysis and frees them to create alternative and original conclusions. Even being confronted with an erroneous point of view can result in more divergent thinking and the generation of novel and more cognitively advanced solutions—it unfreezes the epistemic process.

On nonroutine tasks, conflict over the nature of the decision may cause the group to evaluate information more critically (Postmes, Spears, & Cihangir, 2001) and break the tendency of groups to try to achieve consensus before all available alternatives have been thoroughly considered (Janis, 1971, 1972). Dissenters tend to stimulate divergent thinking and the consideration of multiple perspectives. Members start with the assumption that the dissenter is not correct. If a dissenter persists, however, it suggests a complexity that stimulates a reappraisal of the issue. The reappraisal involves divergent thinking and a consideration of multiple sources of information and ways of thinking about the issue. On balance, this increases the quality of decision making and the likelihood of finding creative solutions to problems (Nemeth, 1986, 1995).

Step 4: Conceptual Conflict and Uncertainty

Conceptual conflict, disequilibrium, and uncertainty often result when members hear their groupmates advocate alternatives to their position, when their position is criticized and refuted, and when they are challenged by information that is incompatible with their conclusions. The greater the disagreement among group members, the more frequently disagreement occurs. The greater the number of people disagreeing with a person's position, the more competitive the context of the controversy. The more affronted the person feels, the greater the conceptual conflict, disequilibrium, and uncertainty the person experiences (see Johnson & Johnson, 1979, 1989, 2000, 2003a, 2005b).

Step 5: Epistemic Curiosity and Perspective Taking

Macbeth said, *"Stay, you imperfect speakers, tell me more."* When faced with intellectual oppositional within a cooperative context, individuals tend to ask one another for more information, seek to view the information from all sides of the issue, and utilize more ways of looking at facts (Nemeth & Goncalo, 2005; Nemeth & Rogers, 1996). Conceptual conflict motivates an active search for more information (called **epistemic curiosity**) in hopes of resolving the uncertainty. Indices of epistemic curiosity in an individual include actively (a) searching for more information, (b) seeking to understand opposing positions and rationales, and (c) attempting to view the situation from opposing perspectives.

Step 6: Reconceptualization, Synthesis, and Integration

Andre Gide said, *"One completely overcomes only what one assimilates."* Nothing could be truer of controversy. When overt controversy is structured by identifying alternatives and assigning members to advocate the best case for each alternative, the purpose is not to choose one of the alternatives. The purpose is to create a synthesis of the best reasoning and conclusions from all the various alternatives. **Synthesizing** occurs when individuals integrate a number of different ideas and facts into a single position. They intellectually bring together ideas and facts and engage in inductive reasoning by restating a large amount of information into a conclusion or summary. Synthesizing is a creative process in which individuals see new patterns within a body of evidence, view the issue from a variety of perspectives, and generate a number of optional ways of integrating the evidence. This requires **probabilistic** (i.e., knowledge is available only in degrees of certainty) rather than **dualistic** (i.e., there is only right and wrong and authority should not be questioned) or **relativistic thinking** (i.e., authorities are seen as sometimes right, but right and wrong depend on your perspective). The dual purposes of synthesis are to arrive at the best possible decision and find a position that all group members can commit themselves to implement. When consensus is required for decision making, the dissenting members tend to maintain their position longer, the deliberation tends to be more "robust," and group members tend to feel that justice has been better served (Nemeth, 1977).

Process of Concurrence Seeking

When groups seek concurrence among group members' conclusions to make a quick decision, members avoid any disagreement or dissent, emphasize agreement, and avoid realistic appraisal of alternative ideas and courses of action, see Table 8.3. In other words, there is pressure for everyone to conform to the dominant, majority opinion in the group. Conformity promotes the domination of majority thought so that there is a false consensus—members agree to a decision they do not really believe is the most desirable course of action to take. More specifically, the steps of concurrence seeking are as follows.

Step 1 *The Dominant Position Is Derived* When faced with a problem to be solved or a decision to be made, the group member with the most power (i.e., the boss) or the majority of the members derive an initial position from their analysis

TABLE 8.3 **Process of Controversy and Concurrence Seeking**

CONTROVERSY	CONCURRENCE-SEEKING
Organizing what is known into an initial conclusion	Organizing what is known into an initial conclusion
Presenting, advocating, elaborating position and rationale	Presenting, advocating, elaborating dominant position and rationale
Being challenged by opposing views results in conceptual conflict and uncertainty about correctness of own views	Majority pressures dissenting group members to conform to majority position and perspective, creating a conflict between public compliance and private belief
Conceptual conflict, uncertainty, disequilibrium result	Conflict between public and private position
Epistemic curiosity motivates active search for new information and perspectives	Seeking confirming information that strengthens and supports the dominant position and perspective
Reconceptualization, synthesis, integration resulting in consensus consisting of best joint reasoned judgment reflecting all points of view	Consensus on majority position, often false consensus due to members publicly agreeing while privately disagreeing

of the situation based on their current knowledge, perspective, dominant re-sponse, expectations, and past experiences. They tend to have a high degree of confidence in their initial conclusion (they freeze the epistemic process).

Step 2   *The Dominant Position Is Presented and Advocated* The dominant position is presented and advocated by the most powerful member in the group or a representative of the majority. It may be explained in detail or briefly, as it is expected that all group members will quickly agree and adopt the recom-mended position. When individuals present their conclusion and its rationale to others, they engage in cognitive rehearsal and reconceptualize their position as they speak, deepening their understanding of their position, and discovering higher-level reasoning strategies. In addition, their commitment to their posi-tion increases, making them more closed-minded toward other positions.

Step 3   *Being Confronted with the Demand to Concur and Conform* Members are faced with the implicit or explicit demand to concur with the recommended position. The pressure to conform creates evaluation apprehension that implies that members who disagree will be perceived negatively and rejected (Diehl & Stroebe, 1987). Conformity pressure is also used to prevent members from sug-gesting new ideas, thereby stifling creativity (Moscovici, 1985). The dominant person or the majority of the members tend to impose their perspective on the issue onto the other group members, so that all members view the issue from the dominant frame of reference, resulting in a convergence of thought and a narrowing of focus in members' thinking.

Step 4   *Conflict Between Public and Private Positions* Members who do not agree with the recommended position have a choice: concur with the majority opin-ion or voice their dissent and face possible ridicule, rejection, ostracism, and being disliked (Freese & Fay, 2001; Nemeth & Goncalo, 2011). The advocacy by the most powerful person in the group or by the majority of members cre-ates a conflict between public compliance and private belief. This conflict can create considerable distress when the dissenter keeps silent, and perhaps even more stress when the dissenter voices his or her opinion (Van Dyne & Saavadra, 1996). Dissenters realize that if they persist in their disagreement, (a) they may be viewed negatively and will be disliked and isolated by both their peers and their supervisors and/or (b) a destructively managed conflict may result that will split the group into hostile factions. Because of these potential penalties, many potential dissenters find it easier to remain silent and suppress their true opinions.

Step 5   *Seeking Confirming Information* Members concur publicly with the dominant position and its rationale without critical analysis. In addition, they seek out supporting evidence to strengthen the dominant position and they view the issue only from the dominant perspective (thus eliminating the possible con-sideration of divergent points of view). Thus, there is a convergence of thought and a narrowing of focus in members' thinking. Dissenters adopt the majority position basically for two reasons: They assume that truth lies in numbers and so the majority is probably correct, or they fear that disagreeing openly would result in ridicule and rejection and therefore pretend to accept the majority posi-tion to be liked and accepted. In addition to adopting the majority's perspective and position, they also search for information in a biased manner to confirm the majority position and they even adopt the majority strategy for solving problems to the exclusion of other strategies. As a result, they are relatively unable to detect original solutions to problems (Nemeth & Wachtler (1983).

Step 6 *Public Consensus* All members agree about the course of action the group is to take while privately some members may believe that other courses of action would be more effective.

OUTCOMES OF CONTROVERSY

Have you learned lessons only of those who admired you, and were tender with you, and stood aside for you?
*   Have you not learned great lessons from those who brace themselves against you, and disputed the passage with you?*

Walt Whitman (1860)

When controversy is suppressed and concurrence seeking is emphasized, several defects in making decisions appear. When NASA, for example, decided to launch the space shuttle Challenger, engineers at the Morton Thiokal Company (which made the shuttle's rocket boosters) and at Rockwell International (which manufactured the orbiter) opposed the launch because of dangers posed by the subfreezing temperatures. The Thiokol engineers feared the cold would make the rubber seals at the joints between the rocket's four main segments too brittle to contain the rocket's superhot gases. Several months before the doomed mission, the company's top expert had warned in a memo that it was a "jump ball" as to whether the seal would hold, and that if it failed, "the result would be a catastrophe of the highest order" (Magnuson, 1986). In a group discussion the night before the launch, the engineers argued for a delay with their uncertain managers and the NASA officials who wanted to launch on schedule. Since the engineers could not prove there was danger, they were silenced (illusion of invulnerability). Conformity pressures were aimed at the engineers, such as when one of the NASA officials complained, "My God, Thiokol, when do you want me to launch, next April?" The NASA managers made a coalition with the Thiokol managers to shut the engineers out of the decision making (illusion of unanimity). Finally, the top NASA executive who made the final decision to launch was never told about the engineers' concerns, nor about the reservations of the Rockwell officials. Protected from the disagreeable information, he confidently gave the go-ahead to launch the Challenger on its tragic flight. On January 28, 1986, seven astronauts were killed when the *Challenger* exploded minutes after launching.

How could such faulty decision making take place? Because of the lack of controversy. NASA officials never gave the alternative of delaying the launch a fair and complete hearing. Disagreement was stifled rather than utilized. Often in group discussions, if a margin of support for one alternative develops, then better ideas have little chance of being accepted. Group discussions can exacerbate tendencies toward overconfidence, thereby heightening an illusion of judgmental accuracy (Dunning & Ross, 1988). Minority opinions can be suppressed. In one study, only one member of a six-member group knew the correct answer to a question. The single member failed to convince the others almost 75% of the time because the answer was not given a fair and complete hearing (Laughlin, 1980; Laughlin & Adamopoulos, 1980). Group decision making often goes wrong because alternatives are not considered carefully, minority opinions are silenced, and disagreement among members' conclusions is suppressed.

Without controversy, group decisions may always be less than optimal. More than twenty-five experimental studies on controversy have been conducted. The nature and results of those and related studies form a solid body of evidence that controversy promotes high productivity and quality of decision making, creativity, task involvement, positive interpersonal relationships, and psychological health (Johnson & Johnson, 1979, 1989, 2000, 2003a, 2005b; Johnson, Johnson, & Tjosvold, 2000).

Quality of Decision Making and Problem Solving

The results of a meta-analysis of the research indicate that controversy tended to result in greater mastery and retention of the material and of the skills being learned than did concurrence seeking (effect size [ES] = 0.70), debate (ES = 0.62), or individualistic efforts (ES = 0.76) (Johnson & Johnson, 2009a). More specifically, participation in a constructive controversy—in comparison with concurrence seeking, debate, and individualistic efforts—tended to result in (a) significantly greater ability to recall the information and reasoning contained in one's own and others' positions, (b) more skillful transferring of such efforts to new situations, and (c) greater generalization of principles learned to a wider variety of situations. In addition, constructive controversy tended to result in higher-quality decisions (including decisions that involved ethical dilemmas) and higher-quality solutions to complex problems for which different viewpoints could plausibly be developed (Glidewell, 1953; Hall & Williams, 1966, 1970; Hoffman, Harburg, & Maier, 1962a; Hoffman & Maier, 1961; Maier & Hoffman, 1964; Maier & Solem, 1952). Disagreeing for mutual benefit tended to result in integrated, high-quality solutions to problems (Lovelace, Shapiro, & Weingart, 2001; Nauta, DeDreu, & Van Der Vaart, 2002). Finally, controversy promoted cognitive rehearsal and accurate understanding of both perspectives (Smith, Johnson, & Johnson, 1981) and enhanced elaboration in oral interactions (Smith, Johnson, & Johnson, 1984). Finally, group members tend to exert more physical and psychological energy in working on the decision when controversy occurs.

These findings are corroborated by the research on dissent, which indicates it facilitates the quality of group decision making (Nemeth, 1995). Dooley and Fryxell (1999), in a study of American hospitals, found that dissent was positively associated with high-quality decision-making teams when the teams preserved dissent while at the same time building toward a consensus. Dissent tends to increase overall group performance (Jehn, Northcraft, & Neale, 1999), partly because it promotes a deeper understanding of the task (Amason & Schweiger, 1994) and stimulating the consideration of new ideas (Baron, 1991).

An interesting question concerning controversy and problem solving is, "Can the advocacy of two conflicting but wrong solutions to a problem create a correct one?" A number of studies with both adults and children have found significant gains in decision making, level of reasoning, and learning even when erroneous information is presented by one or both sides in a controversy. Ames and Murray (1982) compared the impact of controversy, modeling, and nonsocial presentation of information on the performance of nonconserving, cognitively immature children on conservation tasks. The cognitive immature children were presented with erroneous information that conflicted with their initial position. Ames and Murray found modest but significant gains in conservation performance. Three children with scores of 0 out of 18 later scored between 16 and 18 out of 18 on the posttest, and 11 children with initial scores of 0 later scored between 5 and 15. They conclude that conflict **qua** is not only cognitively motivating, but that the resolution of the conflict is likely to be in the direction of correct performance. In this limited way, two wrongs came to make a right. Nemeth and Wachtler (1983) found that participants exposed to a credible minority view generated more solutions to a problem and more correct solutions than did participants exposed to a consistent single view, even if the minority view was incorrect. For example, a number of studies on cognitive reasoning have focused on how nonconserving, cognitively immature children can be influenced to gain critical insights into conservation. Presenting immature children with erroneous information that conflicts with their initial position has been found to promote some cognitive growth, although not as much growth as when they receive correct information (Cook & Murray, 1973; Doise, Mugny, & Perret-Clermont, 1976; Murray, 1972). On subsequent posttests taken individually after controversy, the children recorded significant gains in performance. Doise and Mugny (1979) found that when children faced a partner at the same cognitive level who proposed an erroneous response, both partners showed progress on an individual posttest. The same results were found using confrontations with an incorrect response (Mugny et al., 1975–1976), and even when a more erroneous response was proposed (Mugny, Levy, & Doise, 1978). Schwartz, Neuman, and Biezuner (2000) found that paired children who had systematic mistakes on math problems and disagreed and argued tended to end up with the correct answer, even when both were initially incorrect. The value of the controversy process lies not so much in the correctness of an opposing position as in the attention and thought processes it induces. More cognitive processing may take place when individuals are exposed to more than one point of view, even if the point of view is incorrect. In other words, a better and more effective course of action can result when there are two, less-than-optimal, alternative courses of action argued and challenged.

Creativity

By blending the breath of the sun and the shade,
true harmony comes into the world.

                    Tao Te Ching

Disagreements and arguments among individuals with diverse information and ideas are important aspects of gaining creative insight. From the research, we can conclude that controversy tends to promote creative insight by influencing individuals to (a) view problems from different perspectives and (b) reformulate problems in ways that allow the emergence of new orientations to a solution. There is evidence that controversy increases the number of ideas, the quality of ideas, feelings of stimulation and enjoyment, and originality of expression in creative problem solving (Bahn, 1964; Bolen & Torrance, 1978; Dunnette, Campbell, & Jaastad, 1963; Falk & Johnson, 1977; Gruber, 2006; Maier, 1970; Peters & Torrance, 1972; Torrance, 1970, 1971, 1973; Triandis,

Bass, Ewen, & Mikesele, 1963). Being confronted with credible alternative views has resulted in the generation of more novel solutions (Nemeth & Wachtler, 1983), varied strategies (Nemeth & Kwan, 1987), and original ideas (Nemeth & Kwan, 1985). A cooperative orientation produces more creative syntheses than do individualistic (Gruber, 2006) or competitive orientations (Carnevale & Probst, 1998). Competition, especially, leads to restricted judgment, reduced awareness of complexity, inability to consider alternative perspectives, and less creativity (Carnevale & Probst, 1998). Gruber (2006) notes that some problems absolutely require the synthesis of disparate points of view. And there is evidence that controversy results in more creative solutions to problems, with more satisfaction among group members, than do group efforts that do not include controversy (Glidewell, 1953; Hall & Williams, 1966, 1970; Hoffman, Harburg, & Maier, 1962a; Maier & Hoffman, 1964; Rogers, 1970a). Allowing people to disagree, criticize each other's ideas, and engage in dissent in order to come up with new ideas, leads to creativity (Nemeth et al., 2004; Postmes, Spears, & Cihangir, 2001). The greater the heterogeneity of group members (i.e., personality, gender, attitudes, background, social class, reasoning strategies, cognitive perspectives, information, ability levels, and skills), furthermore, the greater the amount of time spent in argumentation (Nijhof & Kommers, 1982) and the greater the achievement and productivity (Fiedler, Meuwese, & Conk, 1961; Frick, 1973; Johnson, 1977; Torrance, 1961; Webb, 1977). Studies further demonstrate that controversy encourages group members to dig into a problem, raise issues, and settle them. Groups benefit when a wide range of ideas are used and show a high degree of emotional involvement in and commitment to solving the problems the group is working on.

There is corroborating research that disagreement stimulates more originality than does concurring with the dominant or majority opinion (which stimulates conventionality of thought) (Nemeth & Kwan, 1985). Those exposed to dissenting views come up with more creative solutions to problems (Nemeth, Brown, & Rogers, 2001). Dissent, even when wrong, can stimulate creativity (De Dreu & West, 2001; Gruenfeld, 1995; Simons & Peterson, 2000). Van Dyne and Saavadra (1996), in a field study of natural work groups, found that groups in which one person took the role of dissenter engaged in more divergent thinking and came up with more original product ideas than did groups in which no one dissented. Peterson, Owens, Tetlock, Fan, & Martorana (1998) found that the most successful top management teams of seven "Fortune 500" companies encouraged dissent in private meetings.

Because the connection between controversy and creativity is so strong, we will return to the topic of creativity later in this chapter.

Higher-Level Reasoning

Group members who have participated in constructive controversies progress to using higher-level reasoning and metacognitive thought more frequently than do individuals participating in concurrence seeking ($ES = 0.84$), debate ($ES = 1.38$), or individualistic efforts ($ES = 1.10$). Several studies have demonstrated that pairing a conserver with a nonconserver, giving the pair conservation problems to solve, and instructing them to argue until reaching agreement or stalemate resulted in the conserver's answer prevailing in the great majority of trials and in the nonconservers learning how to conserve (Ames & Murray, 1982). Change tended to be unidirectional and nonreversible. Children who understood conservation did not adopt erroneous strategies, whereas nonconservers tended to advance toward a greater understanding of conservation. Walker (1983) found that students progressed in their stage of reasoning when confronted with explanations that opposed their own views and that were one stage ahead of their own reasoning or even at the same stage of reasoning. Tichy, Johnson, Johnson, and Roseth (2010) examined the impact of controversy compared with individualistic efforts on the four components of moral development (Rest, Narvaez, Bebeau, & Thoma, 1999). Controversy tended to produce significantly higher levels of moral motivation, moral judgment, and moral character, as well as the more frequent mastery of a number of ethical skills.

Task Involvement

Task involvement refers to the quality and quantity of the physical and psychological energy that individuals invest in their efforts to achieve. Task involvement is reflected in the attitudes participants have toward the task and toward the controversy experience. Individuals who engaged in controversies tended to like the task and procedure more and generally had more positive attitudes toward the experience than did individuals who engaged in concurrence-seeking discussions, individualistic efforts, or debate. Controversy, furthermore, tends to result in greater task involvement reflected in greater emotional commitment to solving the problem, more feelings of stimulation, and greater enjoyment of the process (see Johnson & Johnson, 1979, 1989, 2000, 2003a, 2005b; Johnson, Johnson, & Tjosvold, 2000). As Samuel Johnson once stated, "*I dogmatize and am contradicted, and in this conflict of opinions and sentiments I find delight.*"

Motivation to Improve Understanding

Participants in a controversy tend to have more continuing motivation to learn about the issue and to come to the best reasoned judgment possible than do participants in concurrence seeking ($ES = 0.68$), debate ($ES = 0.73$), or individualistic efforts ($ES = 0.65$; see Table 8.4). Participants in a controversy tend to search for (a) more information and new experiences (increased specific content), and (b) a more adequate cognitive perspective and reasoning process (increased validity) in hopes of resolving the uncertainty. There is also an active interest in learning others' positions and developing an understanding and appreciation of them. Lowry and Johnson (1981), for example, found that students involved in a controversy, as compared with students involved in concurrence seeking, read more library materials, reviewed more classroom materials, more frequently watched an optional movie shown during recess, and more frequently requested information from others.

Attitude Change on the Issue

Participating in a controversy tends to result in greater attitude change on the issue under discussion than does participating in concurrence seeking, no controversy, or individualistic efforts (Johnson & Johnson, 1985; R. Johnson, Johnson, Scott, & Ramolae, 1985). Correspondingly, conflicting perspectives about goals between the majority of members and a persistent minority tend to lead to attitude change (Nemeth & Owens, 1996). Disagreements within a group have been found to provide a greater amount of

TABLE 8.4   **Mean Effect Sizes of Controversy on Productivity**

DEPENDENT VARIABLE	CONTROVERSY/ CONCURRENCE SEEKING	CONTROVERSY/ DEBATE	CONTROVERSY/ INDIVIDUALISTIC EFFORTS
Achievement	0.70	0.62	0.76
Cognitive Reasoning	0.84	1.38	1.10
Perspective Taking	0.97	0.20	0.59
Motivation	0.68	0.73	0.65
Attitudes Toward Task	0.35	0.84	0.72
Interpersonal Attraction	0.32	0.67	0.80
Social Support	0.50	0.83	2.18
Self-Esteem	0.56	0.58	0.85

Reprinted with permission from: Johnson, D. W., & Johnson, R. (2007). *Creative controversy: Intellectual conflict in the classroom*. Edina, MN: Interaction Book Company.

information and greater variety of facts, and a change in the salience of known information, which, in turn, resulted in shifts of judgment (Anderson & Graesser, 1976; Kaplan, 1977; Kaplan & Miller, 1977; Nijhof & Kommers, 1982; Vinokur & Burnstein, 1974). Participants in a controversy tend to reevaluate their attitudes about the issue and incorporate opponents' arguments. The attitude change resulting from controversy tends to be relatively stable over time (not merely a response to the controversy experience itself).

Interpersonal Attraction Among Participants

Within controversy and debate there are elements of disagreement, argumentation, and rebuttal that can result in individuals disliking one another and can create difficulties in establishing good relationships. The research indicates otherwise (1979, 1989, 2000, 2003a, 2005b; Johnson, Johnson, & Tjosvold, 2000). Constructive controversy was found to promote greater liking among participants than did concurrence seeking (*ES* = 0.32), debate (*ES* = 0.67), or individualistic efforts (*ES* = 0.80; see Table 8.4). Debate tended to promote greater interpersonal attraction among participants than did individualistic efforts (*ES* = 0.46). Spirited disagreement and intellectual challenge can bind people into deeper and more meaningful relationships.

Social Support

Constructive controversy tended to promote greater social support among participants than did concurrence seeking (*ES* = 0.50), debate (*ES* = 0.83), or individualistic effort (*ES* = 2.18; see Table 8.4). Debate tended to promote greater social support among participants than did individualistic efforts (*ES* = 0.85). Constructive controversy has been found to be significantly correlated with both task support and personal support (Tjosvold, XueHuang, Johnson, & Johnson, 2008).

Psychological Health and Social Competence

There are a number of components of psychological health that are strengthened by participating in constructive controversies (see Johnson & Johnson, 1979, 1989, 2000, 2003a, 2005b; Johnson, Johnson, & Tjosvold, 2000). Compared with concurrence-seeking, debate, and individualistic efforts, controversy tends to result in such aspects of psychological health as higher levels of task-oriented self-esteem, cognitive and moral reasoning, and perspective-taking accuracy.

Self-Esteem. Participation in future controversies may be enhanced when participants feel good about themselves as a result of being involved in the current controversy, whether or not they agree with it. Constructive controversy tended to promote higher self-esteem than did concurrence seeking ($ES = 0.56$), debate ($ES = 0.58$), or individualistic effort ($ES = 0.85$; see Table 8.4). Debate tended to promote higher self-esteem than did individualistic effort ($ES = 0.45$). Constructive controversy has been found to be significantly correlated with task self-esteem (Tjosvold et al., in press).

Perspective Taking. To discuss difficult issues, make joint reasoned judgments, and increase commitment to implement a decision, it is helpful to understand and consider all perspectives. Most group members are usually unaware of their groupmates' alternative perspectives and frames of reference and of their potential effects on the accumulation and understanding of information (Tversky & Kahneman, 1981). Group members interpret information using different perspectives and can draw directly opposing conclusions without recognizing the limitations of their thinking. In addition, group members are apt to process information in a biased manner, accepting confirming evidence at face value and subjecting disconfirming evidence to highly critical evaluation (Lord, Ross, & Lepper, 1979). Constructive controversy tends to promote more accurate and complete understanding of opposing perspectives than do concurrence seeking ($ES = 0.97$), debate ($ES = 0.20$), and individualistic efforts ($ES = 0.59$; see Table 8.4). Engaging in controversy tends to result in greater understanding of another person's cognitive perspective than does avoiding controversy. In the studies reviewed, individuals who engaged in a controversy tended to be more accurate in subsequently predicting what line of reasoning their opponent would use in solving a future problem than were individuals who interacted without any controversy. Increased understanding of opposing perspectives tends to result from engaging in controversy (as opposed to engaging in concurrence-seeking discussions or individualistic efforts), regardless of whether one is a high-, medium-, or low-achieving group member. Increased perspective taking tends to enhance individuals' ability to discover beneficial agreements in conflicts (Galinsky, Maddux, Gilin, & White, 2008). Finally, when group members make comments that transform, extend, or summarize the reasoning of another person, more effective moral discussions tend to occur (Berkowitz & Gibbs, 1983; Berkowitz, Gibbs, & Broughton, 1980).

Open-Mindedness. Individuals participating in controversies in a cooperative context tend to be more open-minded in listening to the opposing position than do individuals participating in controversies in a competitive context (Tjosvold & Johnson,

1978). Tjosvold and Johnson note that when the context was competitive, there was a closed-minded orientation in which participants felt comparatively unwilling to make concessions to the opponent's viewpoint and closed-mindedly refused to incorporate any of that viewpoint into their own position. In a competitive context, the increased understanding resulting from controversy tended to be ignored in favor of a defensive adherence to one's own position (Tjosvold & Johnson, 1978).

CONDITIONS DETERMINING THE CONSTRUCTIVENESS OF CONTROVERSY

He that wrestles with us strengthens our nerves, and sharpens our skill.
Our antagonist is our helper.

Edmund Burke, *Reflection of the Revolution in France*

Although controversies can create beneficial outcomes, they will not do so under all conditions. As with all types of conflicts, the potential for either constructive or destructive outcomes is present in a controversy. Whether there are positive or negative consequences depends on the conditions under which controversy occurs and the way in which it is managed. These key elements include the context within which the controversy takes place, the heterogeneity of participants, the distribution of information among group members, the level of group members' social skills, and group members' ability to engage in rational argument (Johnson & Johnson, 1979, 1989, 2005b, 2000, 2003a; Johnson, Johnson, & Tjosvold, 2000).

Cooperative Goal Structure

The context in which conflicts occur has important effects on whether the conflict turns out to be constructive or destructive (Deutsch, 1973). There are two possible contexts for controversy: cooperative and competitive. Compared with a competitive context, a cooperative context promotes (Johnson & Johnson, 1979, 1989, 2000, 2003a, 2005b) (a) more frequent, accurate, and complete communication in which one another's information is utilized and incorporated in participants' thinking, (b) a supportive climate in which group members feel safe enough to challenge one another's ideas, (c) beliefs that controversy is valid and valuable, (d) accurate perspective-taking in which participants are able to understand what others are feeling and why they are feeling that way, (e) the definition of conflicts as problems to be solved (rather than as win-lose situations), and (f) the identification of more similarities between participants' positions.

In a series of studies, Dean Tjosvold and his associates studied the impact of cooperative and competitive contexts on controversy (Tjosvold, 1995a). They found that controversy within a competitive context promoted closed-minded disinterest and rejection of the opponent's ideas and information, a refusal to incorporate any of the opponents' viewpoints into one's own position, and a defensive adherence to one's own position. When competitors were unsure of the correctness of their position, they selected to be exposed to disconfirming information when it could be easily refuted, presumably because such refutation affirmed their own beliefs. Avoidance of controversy resulted in little interest in or actual knowledge of opposing ideas and information and the making of a decision that reflected one's own views only. Within a cooperative context, controversy induced feelings of comfort, pleasure, and helpfulness in discussing opposing positions, an open-minded listening to the opposing positions, motivation to hear more about the opponent's arguments, more accurate understanding of the opponent's position, and the reaching of more integrated positions where both one's own and one's opponent's conclusions and reasoning are synthesized into a final position.

Skilled Disagreement

Effectively engaging in the controversy procedures requires several important social skills (Johnson, 1991, 2006; Johnson & Johnson, 1989, 2000, 2003a, 2005b). One of the most important skills is disagreeing with another person's ideas while confirming the person's competence. When you disagree with a person's ideas while imputing that he or she is incompetent, the other person tends to become more committed to his or her own ideas and more rejecting of your information and reasoning. When you disagree with a person's ideas while confirming the person's competence, the other person will tend to like you more, be less critical of your ideas, be more interested in learning more about your ideas, and be more willing to incorporate your information and reasoning into his or her own analysis of the problem.

To obtain a creative synthesis of all positions in a controversy, group members need an accurate assessment of the validity and relative merits of each position. Doing

so requires "standing in the other person's shoes" and viewing the situation from the other person's perspective. Perspective-taking is essential to ensure relevant information is presented in ways that other group members can understand and that other members' messages are comprehended accurately (Johnson, 1971a). Perspective-taking facilitates the achievement of creative, high-quality problem solving (Falk & Johnson, 1977; Johnson, 1977). Perspective-taking also promotes more positive perceptions of the information-exchange process, fellow group members, and the group's work.

A third set of skills involves the cycle of differentiating the various positions (i.e., bringing out differences in positions) and then seeking an integration that incorporates the best information and reasoning from all sides (i.e., combining several positions into one new, creative position). Differentiation must precede integration. Differentiation involves seeking out and clarifying differences among members' ideas, information, conclusions, theories, and opinions. All different points of view should be presented and explored thoroughly before new, creative solutions are sought. Integration involves combining the information, reasoning, theories, and conclusions of the various group members so that all members are satisfied. The potential for integration is never greater than the adequacy of the differentiation already achieved. Most controversies go through a series of differentiations and integrations before reaching a final decision.

Rational Argument

During a controversy, group members follow the canons of rational argumentation. Members present their position and its rationale while asking other members for proof their analyses and conclusions are valid. Rational argumentation includes generating ideas, collecting and organizing relevant information, using inductive and deductive logic, and making tentative conclusions based on current understanding. It requires that group members keep an open mind, changing their conclusions and positions when others' information, rationale, proof, and logical reasoning are persuasive and convincing. The abilities to gather, organize, and present information, to challenge and disagree, and to engage in logical reasoning are essential for the constructive management of controversies.

ELEMENTS FACILITATING CONSTRUCTIVE CONTROVERSY

1. **A cooperative context.** Communication of information is more complete, accurate, encouraged, and utilized in a cooperative context than in a competitive context. Controversy in a cooperative context promotes open-minded listening to the opposing position, while in a competitive context controversy promotes a closed-minded orientation in which individuals were unwilling to make concessions to the opponent's viewpoint and refuse to incorporate other viewpoints into their position.

2. **Heterogeneous participants.** Heterogeneity among individuals leads to potential controversy, and to more diverse interaction patterns and resources for decision making.

3. **Relevant information distributed among participants.** The more information individuals have about an issue, the more successful their decision making.

4. **Social skills.** In order for controversies to be managed constructively, individuals need a number of conflict management skills, such as disagreeing with one another's ideas while confirming one another's competence, and seeing the issue from a number of perspectives.

5. **Rational argument.** Rational argumentation includes generating ideas, collecting and organizing relevant information, using inductive and deductive logic, and making tentative conclusions based on current understanding.

![] INQUIRY-BASED ADVOCACY

In decision-making situations, truth is more likely to be approximated if opposing views can be freely and openly expressed. Rooted in the ancient Athenian tradition of the democratic, open society, group members need to encourage rather than suppress the expression of opposing views. In other words, through the use of constructive controversy, group members engage inquiry-based advocacy. **Advocacy** is presenting a position and providing reasons why others should adopt it. **Inquiry** is investigating an issue to establish the best answer or course of action; it involves asking questions and seeking to learn the necessary facts to answer the questions. Inquiry usually begins with a focal point, something that captures the participants' attention, holds it, and motivates them to investigate. Disinterested people do not inquire. When group members define the problem to be solved and then present alternative courses of action to solve the problem, it creates the focal point of the inquiry. **Inquiry-based advocacy**, therefore, is two or more parties presenting opposing positions in order to investigate an issue and establish the underlying facts and logic needed to reach a reasoned judgment about the most desirable course of action.

![] MINORITY INFLUENCE, CONTROVERSY, AND DECISION MAKING

The beliefs and attitudes of the majority influence the judgments of the other group members. Members in the minority usually conform to the beliefs of the majority and, under certain conditions, even distort their perceptions so that they see what the majority sees (Asch, 1952, 1956, 1957). Majority opinion members sometimes silence disagreement, reject those who dissent, and persuade all group members to go along with the majority view. So do members who are in the minority ever influence the majority?

Minority influence occurs when group members who are in the opinion minority persuade members in the opinion majority to change their opinion and agree with the minority (Moscovici, 1985a, 1985b; Moscovici, Mucchi-Faina, & Maass, 1994; Wood, Lundgren, Ouelletter, Busceme, & Blackstone, 1994). This is difficult to accomplish because (a) opinion minorities usually can exert little social or normative pressure on members of the opinion majority, and (b) opinions expressed by a member gain credibility and validity the more other members also express the opinion. Because members who hold minority views are less able to rely on the powers of social reward and punishment, they face an uphill battle. They must have strong arguments, present them credibly, and have groupmates motivated to make the best decision. Opinion minorities are most persuasive when:

1. They hold steadily in their views—that is, they are consistent over time. By consistently expressing their opinion, minorities demonstrate they their views are clearly convincing to them and should be to others as well.
2. They once held the majority position. A person adds to the credibility of a position when he or she becomes a convert.

3. They are willing to compromise a bit. Members who are willing to negotiate often come across as reasonable and nonrigid. Members who seem rigid in their views tend to be less credible.

4. They have at least some support from others. Two or more individuals holding a minority opinion are viewed as more credible.

5. They present their views as compatible with the majority view, but just a bit ahead of the curve. This makes it easier for opinion majority members to switch to the minority position.

6. All group members want to make an accurate decision and, therefore, pay close attention to the quality of the arguments.

There is a difference between majority and minority influence (Moscovici, 1980). Majorities induce compliance, especially public compliance. Minorities induce a conversion process. The majority creates a conflict of "responses" between public compliance and private belief. Compliance means that no scrutiny is required. Majorities may stimulate thinking about the issue from the majority's perspective, so there is a narrowing of focus, a convergence of thought (Nemeth, 1976, 1986). People tend to assume that truth lies in numbers and they agree with the majority so that they will be liked and accepted.

The minority creates a conflict between what the majority believes and what the minority believes. This may result in the minority's position being carefully scrutinized, opening the way for majority members to be converted (although there is also evidence of systematic processing of majority positions) (Baker & Petty, 1994; Erb, Bohner, Rank, & Einwiller, 2002; Mackie, 1987). Majority members start with the assumption that the minority is not correct, but the minority's persistence suggests a complexity that stimulates a reappraisal of the situation, divergent thinking, the consideration of multiple perspectives, and a consideration of multiple sources of information and ways of thinking about the issue (Nemeth, 1976, 1986). On balance, this increases the quality of decision making and the finding of creative solutions to problems (Nemeth, 1986, 1995). Even when minority opinion members are persuasive, their influence may be indirect or hidden. Some members of the majority may privately agree, but be unwilling to say so in public. Well-presented minority arguments may not be immediately convincing, but may cause people to reassess their views and think harder and more creatively about the issue (e.g., DeDreu & West, 2001; Martin, Gardikiotis, & Hewstone, 2002). Over time, this reevaluation may lead people to shift their opinions. Hewstone and Martin (2008) concluded that on balance, the research supports conversion theory—that there is message processing only in a minority. Processing of the majority's message seems to occur when there is a motivation to carefully attend to the content of the majority's arguments.

One of the purposes of the controversy procedure is to ensure that opinion minorities have an equal opportunity to influence the group's decision. When all alternative courses of action are assigned an advocacy subgroup, those alternatives supported by opinion minorities have their day in court. In addition, because the purpose is to integrate the best information and reasoning from all positions, the stress is on informational influence rather than on conformity to the opinion majority.

STRUCTURING CONSTRUCTIVE CONTROVERSIES

Effective decision making largely depends on the constructive use of controversy. There is more to creating constructive controversy, however, than just saying, "let's argue." To help make sure the group engages in controversy that leads to these positive outcomes rather than one that dissolves into bickering, defensiveness, and noncommunication, the following steps should be followed:

1. Propose several courses of action that will solve the problem under consideration.
2. Form advocacy teams: To ensure that each course of action receives a fair and complete hearing, assign two or three group members to be an advocacy team to present the best case possible for the assigned position. Highlight the goal of making the best decision possible.
3. Engage in the controversy procedure:
   a. Each advocacy team researches its position and prepares a persuasive presentation to convince other group members of its validity.
   b. Each advocacy team presents without interruption the best case possible for its assigned alternative course of action to the entire group. Other advocacy teams listen carefully, taking notes and striving to learn the information provided.
   c. There is an open discussion characterized by advocacy, refutation, and rebuttal. The advocacy teams give opposing positions, a "trial by fire," seeking to refute them by challenging the validity of their information and logic. They defend their own position while continuing to attempt to persuade other group members of its validity. Members are encouraged to engage in spirited arguing and play devil's advocate.
   d. Advocacy teams reverse perspectives by sincerely and forcefully presenting the best case for the opposing position.
   e. Group members drop their advocacy and reach a decision by consensus based on their best reasoned judgment about the issue. Often the decision represents a synthesis.
   f. Group members process how well the group functioned and how their performance can be improved during the next controversy.
4. Implement the decision: Once the decision is made, all members commit themselves to implement it.

BEING A CITIZEN IN A DEMOCRACY

The word "democracy" comes from the Greek word *demokratia*, which is a combination of *demos* (the Greek word for "people") and *kratos* (the Greek word for "rule"). Thomas Jefferson believed that rule by the people required free and open discussion. He further believed that knowledge—not the social rank within which a person was born—is the basis of influence within society. American democracy was thus founded on the premise that "truth" will result from free and open discussion in which opposing points of view are advocated and vigorously argued. Before a decision is made, every citizen is given the opportunity to advocate for his or her ideas. A vote is then taken and the majority rules. The minority is then expected to willingly go along with the majority because they know (a) they received a fair and complete hearing and (b) they will have another chance in two or four years.

For individuals to be good citizens, they need to learn how to engage in collective decision making about community and societal issues (Dalton, 2007). Such decision making is known as political discourse (Johnson & Johnson, 2000). Thomas Jefferson, James Madison, and the other founders of the American Republic considered political discourse to be the heart of democracy. The clash of opposing positions was expected to increase citizens' understanding of the issues and the quality of decision making, given that citizens would keep open minds and change their opinions when logically persuaded to do so. Generally, political education in U.S. schools is insufficient (Parker, 2006). Students need to be educated for a "culture of argument" (Walzer, 2004, p. 107). When students participate in a controversy, they are also learning the procedures necessary to being an effective citizen in a democracy. The combination of cooperative learning and constructive controversy has been used to teach elementary and secondary students in Armenia how to be citizens in a democracy (Hovhannisyan, Varrella, Johnson, & Johnson, 2003a, 2005a; 2005b). Constructive controversy was used in Azerbaijan, the Czech Republic, Lithuania, and the United States (in Chicago, the District of Columbia, and Los Angeles) by secondary school teachers with 1,109 students as part of the Deliberating in a Democracy Project (Avery, Freeman, Greenwalt, & Trout, 2006).

IN CONCLUSION

Decision making typically involves considering possible alternatives and choosing one. By definition, all decision-making situations involve some conflict as to which of the several alternatives should be chosen. Within decision-making groups, conflict takes the form of controversy. Controversy begins when a group assigns the major alternatives to advocacy subgroups and has each subgroup develop the best case possible for its assigned alternative and plan how to present its alternative to the rest of the group. Each subgroup then presents and advocates its position to the rest of the group. An open discussion follows in which members attempt to refute opposing positions while rebutting the attacks on their position. Advocacy subgroups then reverse perspectives, sincerely and forcefully presenting the best case possible to the opposing positions. Finally, group members drop all advocacy and reach consensus on their best reasoned judgment, integrating the best information and reasoning from all positions.

This procedure is based on a theoretical framework in which group members initially have a conclusion about an issue, present it to the group, are faced with opposing views, feel uncertain and are in a state of conceptual conflict or disequilibrium, experience epistemic curiosity and search for more information and a better perspective, and come to a new conclusion based on the reorganization and reconceptualization of what they know. Controversies tend to be constructive when the situational context is cooperative, when there is some heterogeneity among group members, when information and expertise are distributed within the group, when members have the necessary conflict skills, and if the canons of rational argumentation are followed. An essential aspect of controversy is the creativity that is derived from the collision of adverse opinions.

TEST YOUR UNDERSTANDING

In the following table, match the correct definition with the correct concept. Find a partner and compare answers and explain your reasoning for each answer.

Rating	Concept	Definitions
_____	Constructive controversy	a. Two or more individuals argue positions that are incompatible and a judge declares a winner on the basis of who best presented their position.
_____	Deliberate discourse	b. Members of a decision-making group set aside their doubts and misgivings about whatever policy is favored by the emerging consensus so as to be able to agree with the other members.
_____	Creative problem solving	c. Group members inhibit discussion to avoid any arguments, emphasize agreement, and avoid realistic appraisal of alternative ideas and courses of action.
_____	Debate	d. Individuals work alone at their own pace and with their set of materials without interacting with one another.
_____	Concurrence seeking	e. Discussion that generates novel solutions to a problem.
_____	Individualistic effort	f. One group member's ideas, information, conclusions, theories, and opinions are incompatible with those of another, and the two seek to reach an agreement.
_____	Groupthink	g. The discussion of the advantages and disadvantages of proposed actions.

EXERCISE 8.4

THE JOHNSON SCHOOL

Form groups of six. Give one set of cards to each group. Each member should take one of the cards. The cards should contain the following statements, one on each card.

1. The strongest coach coached wrestling second.
   Track was a sport coached at the Johnson School.
   Dale offered to recruit cheerleaders for the school.
2. Members of your group have all the information needed to find the answer to the following question (only one answer is correct): *In what sequence did the Johnsons coach the sports taught at their school?* Some of the information your group has is not relevant and will not help your group solve the problem.
3. Frank coached wrestling third.
   The strongest coach had been coaching longer than the other coaches.
   Edye's favorite sport was eating.

continued on next page

continued from previous page

4. The strongest coach coached first the sport that David liked the best.
   All coaches coached all the sports.
   Keith preferred telling others what to do rather than doing it himself.
5. Helen had been coaching longer than any of the other coaches.
   David coached basketball third.
   Each coach coached the sport he or she liked best second.
6. Roger preferred to coach golf more than the other sports.
   All coaches preferred or liked one sport above the others.
   All coaches coached at the same time.

Give the following instructions: You have all the information you need to define a problem and solve it. You have twenty to forty minutes. One rule you must follow: Although you may tell your group what is on your card, you may not pass it around for others to read. All communication in the group is to be verbal. I repeat, you may not let others read what is on your card; you may only tell them what it says.

EXERCISE 8.5

AVOIDING CONTROVERSIES

People often find ingenious methods to keep from having to deal directly with controversies. How do you behave when you want to avoid a dispute? How do the other members of your group behave?

The following exercise is designed to produce feedback about how other group members see your behavior when you want to avoid a controversy. Its objective is for participants to examine their own behavior in controversies and disagreements. Understanding avoidance behavior, or how people avoid responding, can be as helpful as increasing their awareness of constructive behaviors. The procedure for the coordinator is as follows:

1. Introduce the exercise as a chance for each group member to get feedback from other group members on his or her behavior.
2. Tell each group member to place a sheet of paper on the wall with his or her name clearly written at the top.
3. Have group members walk around the room writing down their impressions of how each of the others behaves when he or she wants to avoid a controversy. You may wish to use the checklist below to trigger ideas.
4. All members should classify themselves according to the checklist below and then read the remarks other group members have written on their sheet.
5. Divide the participants into groups of three and have them discuss the content of the remarks written on their sheets, their own perceptions of their behavior, and the feelings generated by the exercise. Although the defenses against directly facing controversy are not helpful to the group and will promote destructive outcomes, they are at times very helpful and have constructive value for the individual. Participants should ask themselves whether there are ways to protect themselves without being harmful to the group.

DEFENSES AGAINST CONTROVERSY

1. *Ostrich:* Deny that the controversy exists; refuse to see the potential or actual disagreement.
2. *Turtle:* Withdraw from the issue and the persons disagreeing with you.
3. *Lemming:* Give in and accept the other person's point of view or ideas.
4. *Weasel:* Rationalize by stating that the issue is not important, that you really don't hold an opposing opinion, that the issue is one on which you have no expertise, and so on.
5. *Gorilla:* Overpower the other members by forcing them to accept your ideas and point of view.
6. *Owl:* Intellectualize about the issue and ideas so that all feelings and emotions are hidden.
7. *Sheep:* Formulate, support, and conform to group norms forbidding the expression of opposition and disagreement in the group.

EXERCISE 8.6

BELIEFS ABOUT CREATIVITY

The purpose of this exercise is to provoke a discussion concerning the nature of creativity. The procedure is as follows:

1. Working by yourself, react to the following statements about creativity.
   a. Creativity and intelligence are (1) unrelated, (2) highly related to each other in the sense that creativity promotes cognitive development.
   b. Creativity is (1) a stable trait that some persons are born with and others lack, (2) a process of problem solving characterized by an interaction between group members and the challenges of their environment.
   c. Creativity (1) is at the same level across situations—a creative person is creative in every situation, or (2) varies a great deal from situation to situation, depending on the problem-solving process being used.
   d. Creativity is something that (1) cannot be taught because it is an inborn trait, (2) can be taught because it is a problem-solving process.
   e. The role of the school is (1) to discover or identify creative group members and place them in accelerated programs so that their creativity is utilized, (2) to develop creative competencies in all group members by providing the needed challenges and teaching them the problem-solving skills necessary for a creative response.
2. Form groups of six and arrive at a group consensus for each question.
3. Compare your group's answers with those of the other groups in the class.

 ## CREATIVITY

The myth of the creative individual is deeply embedded in Western society. Our creative heroes— Michelangelo, Picasso, Charles Dickens, Walt Disney, and countless others— are seen as extraordinary individuals who, working alone, created great works of art. But even as the lone creative genius gallops through our imagined history, the truth is that it is groups of people, not only individuals, who successfully create new and wonderful things. Creativity tends to be social, interpersonal, not individual. The accomplishment of important goals requires the coordinated contributions of many talented people. One person cannot create a global business or map the mysteries of the human brain, no matter how intelligent or creative he or she is. Most problems facing individuals, groups, and societies are just too large. Yet, even in the social sciences, the case for the social nature of creativity is resisted and ignored. Our mythology and our reality are out of step. Despite all evidence, we cling to "The Great Man or Women" theory of creativity and ignore "The Great Group" theory of creativity. In Great Groups, creativity comes alive.

Creativity is the process of bringing something new into existence. An example of the social nature of creativity is the collaboration between Pablo Picasso and Georges Braque (which resulted in the birth of Cubism). The two men dressed alike, in mechanics' clothes, and jokingly compared themselves to the Wright brothers (Picasso called Braque, "Wilbur"). For several years, they saw each other almost every day, talked constantly about their revolutionary new style, and painted as similarly as possible. They would have intense discussions about what they planned to paint, then spent all day painting separately. Each evening, they would rush to the other's apartment to view what the other had done, which they proceeded to criticize intensely. A painting was not finished until both said it was finished.

*Almost every evening, either I went to Braque's studio or Braque came to mine. Each of us **had** to see what the other had done during the day. We criticized each other's work. A canvas wasn't finished unless both of us felt it was.*

Pablo Picasso (in a letter to Francoise Gilot)

The things Picasso and I said to one another during those years will never be said again, and even if they were, no one would understand them anymore. It was like being roped together on a mountain.

Georges Braque

Despite this and many other examples of the social nature of creativity, early research was conducted primarily at the individual level; especially on the traits that distinguish highly creative individuals from their peers (Helson, 1996). This large body of research on personality traits supports the widespread opinion that creative insights are most likely to emerge from the mind of a lone genius working in isolation (Perry-Smith & Shalley, 2003). In the 1990s, however, research on creativity reduced its focus on individual traits (Helson, 1996), and began focusing on the impact social situations have on creativity (Amabile, 1996), and on groups of people who collaborate to generate creative ideas (Bennis, 1998; Paulus & Nijstad, 2003; Perry-Smith, 2006). The social nature of creativity and the creative process began to be more widely recognized.

The Creative Process

The creative process consists of a sequence of overlapping phases (Johnson, 1979):

1. Group members must recognize that a problem exists and it is challenging enough to motivate them to solve it. For the possibility of creativity to

exist, group members need to be aroused to a level of motivation sufficient to sustain problem-solving efforts despite frustrations and dead ends (Deutsch, 1969). This level of motivation, however, cannot be so intense that it overwhelms members or keeps them too close to the problem (Johnson, 1979). Intrinsic motivation has been considered to be a driver of creativity (Amabile, 1996). When individuals enjoy working on the group's task, they tend to process information flexibly, experience positive affect, take more risks, and are more persistent in their efforts to achieve (Eisbach & Hargadon, 2006; Shalley, Zhou, & Oldham, 2004). The motivation to persist is increased by both controversy and a group tradition supporting the view that with time and effort, constructive solutions can be discovered or invented for seemingly insoluble problems.

2. Group members must gather the necessary knowledge and resources and plan an intense, long-term effort to solve the problem. The more members are immersed in and focused on the problem and the relevant information and circumstances, the greater the likelihood they will achieve a creative insight.

3. Cooperative context must be highlighted in order for the necessary level of social support to be achieved within the group. Members must not feel threatened or under too much pressure (Deutsch, 1969; Rokeach, 1960; Stein, 1968). Feeling threatened prompts defensiveness in group members and reduces their tolerance of ambiguity and receptiveness to new and unfamiliar ideas. Too much tension leads to stereotyping of thought processes. Feeling threatened and under pressure prevents group members from becoming sufficiently detached from their original viewpoint to be able to see the problem from new perspectives.

4. One's initial ideas and conclusions need to be challenged and disputed by other group members with different perspectives and conclusions. The intellectual disputed passage results in uncertainty and leads to a search for more information, a new perspective, and insights into the problem being solved. Creative insight usually depends on (a) the availability of diverse information and viewpoints and (b) group members disagreeing and challenging one another's reasoning and perspectives. The more varied and diverse the members of a group, the more likely the group will arrive at a creative solution. Members with diverging ideas and perspectives must disagree and challenge one another's reasoning and perspectives in order to understand each other's positions, ensure the positions are valid, and

put the ideas and perspectives together into new and varied patterns. Controversy among group members tends to spark new ideas and approaches, broaden the range of available solutions, and produce moments of insight or inspiration by one or more group members. Creative insight often is accompanied by intense emotional experiences of illumination and excitement and leads to the formulation of a tentative solution.

5. Group members need to seek out different perspectives and different ways of viewing the problem so they can reformulate it in a way that lets new orientations to a solution emerge. To generate useful and novel ideas it is necessary to take others' perspectives; the desire to do so comes from prosocial motivation—the desire to benefit others (De Dreu & Nauta, 2009; De Dreu, Weingart, & Kwon, 2000). The combination of intrinsic and prosocial motivation tends to generate the most perspective taking (Grant & Berry, 2011). It often takes an outside person to help us realize the limitations of our analyses, lines of thought, and conclusions, and an intellectual challenge to motivate us to reconsider our conclusions and reopen our perspective.

6. Group members need to experience an incubation period during which they feel frustration, tension, and discomfort due to their failure to produce an adequate solution to the problem and temporarily withdraw from the issue. In order for group members to derive creative answers to problems they are working on, they must be allowed time to reflect. Instant answers should not be demanded. Creative thinking *"is commonly typified by periods of intense application and periods of inactivity"* (Treffinger, Speedie, & Brunner, 1974, p. 21). After all sides of a controversy have been presented, group members should be allowed to think about solutions for a day or so before trying to put things together in new and varied patterns.

7. Finally, group members formulate a new and unique solution to the problem, work out the details of implementing it, and test it against reality. After group members have had time to reflect on the alternatives, they need to come back together and decide on a final solution. The decision then needs to be implemented in a real-world environment to see if it does indeed solve the problem. If the implementation is successful, group members then give the validated solution to relevant audiences.

DEVELOPING AND FOSTERING CREATIVITY

How do you increase group members' creative thinking? There are no easy answers to this question. Here is a set of procedures that can be used to promote creativity:

1. Reaffirm the cooperative goal of making the best decision possible.
2. Promote controversy among ideas, opinions, information, theories, and perspectives of group members. Members should promote different points of view, critically analyze one another's information and reasoning, serve as devil's advocates

to challenge other members' positions and create diversity of opinion, and re-combine already known facts into new combinations and relationships. Members should be enthusiastic about originality in thinking and become immersed in solving the problem.

3. Set aside time for members to reflect on the diverse ideas and perspectives generated by the controversy process. Encourage persistence in solving the problem, no matter how difficult it is. Creative insights come out of struggle, not quick reflection. Creative individuals such as Einstein and Picasso experienced great difficulties before achieving insight.

4. Meet to make final decision, but do not rush to judgment. Creative insights cannot be hurried.

David and Houtman (1968) are the authors of *Think Creatively: A Guide to Training Imagination*, a book intended to teach creativity. They suggest four learnable methods of generating novel ideas: part changing, using a checkerboard figure, using a checklist, and finding something similar. The *part-changing method* involves group members in identifying the parts or attributes of something that might be changed. For example:

> Four qualities of a chair are color, shape, size, and hardness. Invent a new kind of chair by listing fifteen different colors, ten different shapes, five sizes, and five grades of hardness. Try to think of different ideas, and do not worry about whether they are any good. Think of different ways to change each part of the chair. Use your imagination.

The *checkerboard method* involves making a checkerboard figure with spaces for entering words or phrases on the vertical and horizontal axes. Different sets of properties or attributes are listed on the axes. Then group members examine the interaction or combination of each pair of things or attributes. For example:

> Your group is to invent a new sport. Place materials and equipment along the top, horizontal axis and place the things the players do (such as running, batting, kicking, hanging from their knees) down the side or vertical axis. Then examine the combination of each item on each axis with all the other items on the other axis.

The *checklist method* involves developing and using checklists to make sure that something is not left out or forgotten. A group can apply this checklist to any object or problem. David and Houtman suggest a checklist that includes the following procedures:

1. Change color.
2. Change size.
3. Change shape.
4. Use new or different material.
5. Add or subtract something.
6. Rearrange things.
7. Identify a new design.

The *find-something-similar method* involves encouraging group members to come up with new ideas by thinking of other persons, animals, or social units in the world that perform the same acts the group wants to perform. For example:

Imagine your city has a parking problem. Find ideas for solving this problem by thinking of how bees, squirrels, ants, shoe stores, clothing stores, and so on store things.

Another technique designed to enhance the creativity of group members is *synectics,* developed by William J. Gordon (1961). Gordon stresses the importance of psychological states in achieving creativity and the use of metaphor in achieving the proper psychological state. He suggests using three interrelated techniques for making the strange appear familiar and the familiar strange:

1. *Personal analogy,* in which individuals imagine how it feels to be part of the phenomenon being studied. Asking them how they would feel if they were an incomplete sentence or if they were Paul Revere's horse are examples.
2. *Direct analogy,* in which group members are asked to think about a parallel situation in order to gain insight into what they are studying. Asking them to describe how a book is like a light bulb or how a beaver chewing on a log resembles a typewriter are examples.
3. *Compressed conflict,* in which group members are forced to perceive an object or concept from two frames of reference. Asking them to give examples of repulsive attraction or cooperative competition are illustrations.

EXERCISE 8.7

CREATIVITY

This problem requires creativity on the part of the group attempting to solve it. The class should divide into groups of three. Each group's assignment is to connect all nine dots with only four straight and connected lines (answer is on p. 540 in the Appendix).

EXERCISE 8.8

JOE DOODLEBUG

This problem is taken from Rokeach (1960) and solving it requires group creativity. The procedure for the coordinator is as follows:

1. Have the class divide into groups of three.
2. Hand out copies of the problem sheet and state that it contains all the necessary information. The problem is why Joe has to take four jumps to reach the food, which is only 3 feet away. The groups have thirty minutes to come up with an answer. Explain that you will give hints after fifteen, twenty, and twenty-five minutes if the groups have not solved the problem.
3. After fifteen minutes give the first hint, after twenty minutes the second, and after twenty-five minutes the third (see p. 540 in the Appendix).
4. At the end of thirty minutes, stop the groups and give them the answer (it appears on p. 540 in the Appendix). After clarifying the answer, conduct a discussion of moving outside one's belief system to solve a problem. Then ask the group to discuss how they worked together, listened to each other, handled controversies, and so on.

THE PROBLEM

Joe Doodlebug has been jumping all over the place getting some exercise when his master places a pile of food 3 feet directly west of him. Joe notices that the pile of food is a little larger than he. As soon as Joe sees all this food, he stops dead in his tracks, facing north. After all his exercise Joe is hungry, and he wants to get the food as quickly as possible. Joe examines the situation and then says, "I'll have to jump four times to get the food." Why does Joe have to take four jumps to get to the food?

Joe Doodlebug, a strange sort of imaginary bug, can and cannot do the following things: (1) He can jump only in four different directions: north, south, east, and west (he cannot jump diagonally, such as southwest); (2) once he starts in any direction, he must jump four times in that direction before he can change direction; (3) he can only jump, not crawl, fly, or walk; (4) he cannot jump less than 1 inch per jump or more than 10 feet per jump; (5) Joe cannot turn around.

OPEN VERSUS CLOSED BELIEF SYSTEMS

A key element of creative problem solving is having the open-mindedness to view the problem from diverse perspectives. Group members are *open-minded* when they are willing to attend to, comprehend, and gain insight into information, ideas, perspectives, assumptions, beliefs, conclusions, and opinions different from their own. When group members resist such opportunities, they are *closed-minded* and dogmatic. The extent to which a group member can receive, evaluate, and act on relevant information on its own merits—as opposed to viewing it only from his or her own perspective—defines the extent to which the member is open-minded (Rokeach, 1960). Without seeing the problem from a variety of perspectives, members are not able to analyze it fully and synthesize various positions so as to produce creative solutions. Controversy is an essential ingredient in discovering new perspectives on the problem being solved.

How do you tell if a group is open- or closed-minded? *Closed-minded groups* (1) emphasize the differences between what they believe and what they do not believe, (2) deny information that is contrary to what they believe, (3) have contradictory beliefs that go unquestioned, (4) discard as irrelevant similarities between what they believe and what they reject, (5) avoid exploring and considering differences in beliefs, and (6) distort information that does not fit their beliefs. *Open-minded groups* (1) seek out opposing and differing beliefs, (2) discover new beliefs, (3) remember and consider information that disagrees with currently held beliefs, and (4) organize new beliefs to solve the problem. **Open-mindedness** is an important requirement for creative problem solving.

Rokeach (1954, 1960) has developed the concept of dogmatism to categorize people in terms of the openness or closedness of their belief systems. **Dogmatism** is a relatively closed organization of beliefs and disbeliefs about reality that is organized around a central set of beliefs about absolute authority, which in turn provides a framework for intolerance toward others. Compared with open-minded individuals, closed-minded people (Ehrlich & Lee, 1969; Vacchiano, Strauss, & Hochman, 1968):

1. Are less able to learn new beliefs and to change old beliefs.
2. Are less able to organize new beliefs and integrate them into their existing cognitive systems during problem solving, and thus take longer to solve problems involving new beliefs.
3. Are less accepting of belief-discrepant information.
4. Are more resistant to changing their beliefs.
5. Reject information that is potentially threatening to their perceptual and attitudinal organization more frequently.
6. Have less recall of information inconsistent with their beliefs.
7. Evaluate information consistent with their beliefs more positively.
8. Have more difficulty in discriminating between the information received and its source, so that the status of an authority is confused with the validity of what the authority is stating. In other words, dogmatic persons tend to accept what authorities say as the truth and discount what low-status individuals say as invalid.
9. Resolve fewer issues in conflict situations, are more resistant to compromise, and are more likely to view compromise as defeat.

The creative solution of problems requires open-mindedness. In being open-minded, group members must be willing to give up their current beliefs about the situation and adopt new ones. The new beliefs help them synthesize an unforeseen but effective solution. The replacement of old beliefs with new beliefs is called the *analytic phase* of the problem-solving process. Once new beliefs have superseded the old ones, group members must organize their new beliefs in a way that leads them to the solution of the problem. This organizational step is called the *synthesizing phase* of the problem-solving process.

In solving the Joe Doodlebug problem in Exercise 8.8, for example, group members must first overcome three beliefs, one by one, and replace them with three new beliefs.

The *first* belief to be replaced is the facing belief. In everyday life we have to face the food we are to eat. But Joe does not have to face the food in order to eat it; he can land on top of it. The *second* is the direction belief. In everyday life we can change direction at will. But Joe is not able to do this because he must forever face north. The only way Joe can change direction is by jumping sideways and backward. The *third* belief that must be replaced is the movement belief. When we wish to change direction in everyday life, there is nothing to stop us from doing so immediately. But Joe's freedom of movement is restricted by the fact that once he moves in a particular direction (north, south, east, or west), he has to continue four times in that direction before he can change it. Many group members assume that Joe is at the end rather than possibly in the middle of a jumping sequence.

The replacement of old beliefs that limit a group's thinking with new beliefs that enable whole new orientations and perspectives depends on the old beliefs being challenged and disconfirmed. It is conflict that sparks the cognitive changes that enable creative insight. If group members are to engage in creative problem solving, they must be open-minded and be challenged with opposing positions, which results in seeing the issue from a variety of perspectives, which leads to developing a creative synthesis that solves the problem.

BRAINSTORMING

Problem solving depends on developing divergent views that conflict with one another. Often groups suffer by members not producing a wide variety of diverse ideas that can be contrasted with one another. Brainstorming was invented to (1) encourage divergent thinking, (2) produce many different ideas in a short period of time, and (3) ensure the full participation of all group members. **Brainstorming** is a procedure in which group members are asked to produce as many, and as uninhibited, ideas as they possibly can and to withhold criticism in order to optimize creativity. All criticism is withheld in order to reduce evaluation apprehension. The engaging of free association of ideas is supposed to open new avenues of thought. Brainstorming tends to increase member participation and involvement, generate lots of ideas in a relatively short period of time, and reduce the need to look for the "right" idea in order to impress authority figures in the group. During brainstorming, the ground rules are as follows:

1. *Rule out all criticism or evaluation of ideas.* Ideas are simply placed before the group.
2. *Expect wild ideas* in the spontaneity that evolves when the group suspends judgment. Practical considerations are not important at this point. The session is to be freewheeling.
3. *Value the quantity of ideas,* not their quality. All ideas should be expressed, and none should be screened out by any individual. A great number of ideas will increase the likelihood of the group discovering good ones.
4. *Build on the ideas of other group members when possible.* Pool your creativity. Everyone should be free to build onto ideas and to make interesting combinations from the various suggestions.

5. *Focus on a single problem or issue.* Don't skip around to various problems or try to brainstorm a complex, multipart problem.
6. *Promote a congenial, relaxed, cooperative atmosphere.*
7. *Make sure that all members, no matter how shy and reluctant to contribute, get their ideas heard.*
8. *Record all ideas.*

After the period of brainstorming, all the ideas are categorized, and the group critically evaluates them for possible use or application. Priorities are selected, and the best ideas are applied. The rationale for brainstorming is the belief that many ideas are never born or are quickly stifled due to domineering members, stereotypes of one another's expertise and intelligence, interpersonal conflicts, habitual patterns of uninvolvement and silence, fear of ridicule or evaluation. It is like a vice president in charge of a group of managers saying, "Those opposed will signify by clearing out their desks, putting on their hats, and saying 'I resign.'"

There is only one problem with brainstorming. Most research suggests that it is less effective than allowing the same number of people to generate ideas on their own, independent of any group experience (Diehl & Stroebe, 1987; Mullen, Johnson, & Salas, 1991). The primary reason for the lack of effectiveness of brainstorming may be production blocking. *Production blocking* reflects the group norm that only one person is to speak at a given time. This prevents members from blurting out their ideas the moment they think of them and thereby the ideas may be forgotten or censored. Groups (compared to isolated individuals) are at a definite disadvantage for generating lots of ideas in a short period of time. Yet the use of brainstorming remains widespread. The reasons may include that (1) people enjoy working in groups and are therefore more motivated to produce ideas in a group setting (Stroebe, Diehl, & Abukoumkin, 1992) and (2) the dynamics of group brainstorming create better analysis, adoption, and implementation in later stages of group problem solving.

Attention has shifted to the generation of ideas by retrieving relevant information from one's long-term conceptual memory (Brown & Paulus, 2002). It seems individuals do not brainstorm effectively on topics they know nothing about. Concepts that are closely connected to those that are currently active should be more accessible than concepts than are less strongly connected to currently active ideas. There is a tendency, therefore, for convergent thinking, in which a person thinks of ideas from one category and keeps generating ideas from that category. Divergent thinkers, on the other hand, tend to jump around between categories in generating ideas. More ideas tend to be generated by divergent than by convergent thinking. In promoting divergent thinking, two critical factors are priming, to make a wide variety of categories accessible, and attention.

Priming is presenting a brainstormer with ideas from low-accessible categories. *Accessible categories* are categories that reflect a person's experiences, whereas *inaccessible categories* deal with concepts unrelated to a person's experiences. In order to generate ideas from a conceptual category, the category must be accessible (Brown & Paulus, 2002). When brainstorming ways to improve the quality of life, for example, a wealthy person from the United States is unlikely to start generating ideas for preventing starvation. But if another brainstormer from an agrarian country mentions starvation, the wealthy American might have relevant ideas, perhaps based on reading or travel. Presenting a brainstormer with ideas from low-accessible categories increases the number of ideas generated from those categories and also increases the total number of ideas generated overall. In other words, priming categories unlikely to be utilized by someone brainstorming on his or her own increases the group productivity.

Priming by other members is effective only to the extent that group members pay attention to each other's ideas. *Attention* is the probability that an individual group member will use the current speaker's ideas as the basis for generating his or her next idea (as opposed to continuing his or her own internal train of thought). Generally, the more attention each individual pays to fellow group members, the better the performance of the group on brainstorming tasks, presumably because the member is primed to consider ideas from his or her own low-accessible categories (Brown & Paulus, 2002). This is especially true when the group members are heterogeneous, with differing knowledge of and perspectives on the problem.

There is reason to believe that there is no such thing as a creative person, only creative groups. The way we all think is highly influenced by the thinking of those with whom we talk and otherwise interact. It is almost always possible to be part of a group process that encourages, supports, and rewards our potential for creativity. The ideas of others spark our own. The theory of one group member may help build a much more creative theory by touching off all sorts of new ideas among the rest of the members. Untold amounts of creative problem solving may occur when diversity and controversy are sought and used.

EXERCISE 8.9

BRAINSTORMING

The objective of this exercise is to come up with a large number of ideas or solutions to a problem by temporarily suspending criticism and evaluation—in other words, to experience the process of brainstorming. The procedure follows.

1. The group reviews the ground rules for brainstorming.
2. The group is presented with a problem: One of the authors of this book has been cast ashore nude on a desert island, with nothing but a glass peace symbol on a leather strap.
3. The group has fifteen minutes to generate ideas as to what can be done with this object.
4. The group has another fifteen minutes to critically select its best ideas.
5. The group discusses how well it applied the rules of brainstorming and what its results were. Was creativity enhanced? Did it help the group to discover interesting ways of using the object?

After initial exposure to brainstorming, a group should pick a specific problem it is working on and apply brainstorming to it to see if new, creative perspectives can be gained. If, however, a second practice session is desired, the following story can be used:

> A small wholesaler in the hinterland of New Mexico called his buyer in Santa Fe and asked him to obtain a large order of pipe cleaners from Mexico. The buyer agreed. He also agreed to advance the wholesaler the money to finance the deal. A month later, as the shipment of pipe cleaners was arriving, the buyer received a phone call from the wholesaler: His warehouse and outlet store had burned down, and there simply was no more business. The buyer was suddenly faced with the prospect of trying to sell 20,000 pipe cleaners.

continued on next page

continued from previous page

In one minute, group members should generate as many ideas as possible (with a recorder counting the number of different ideas) for selling pipe cleaners. (A relatively spontaneous group will create approximately twenty-five ideas in little more than a minute. If the group creates fifteen or fewer ideas, it should be given more training in brainstorming.)

In brainstorming a group problem, it is important that the problem be well defined and specific. It also must be a problem that the group has the power to do something about. If possible, the group members should be notified in advance about the issue to be explored so they can give it some thought.

EXERCISE 8.10

CREATIVITY WARM-UP

Have you ever felt in a rut? Have you ever felt embarrassed about sharing new or wild ideas? Have you ever ignored your thinking because you felt it was too far out? Do you ever enjoy letting your imagination and thoughts run wild? Have you ever been so critical of your own thoughts that you could not get started?

Here are six short, enjoyable exercises to loosen up group thinking and warm up group creativity:

1. The group sits in a circle (group size should be limited to eight members or so). The person nearest the window says the first thing that comes to his mind. The statement should be short, no more than a sentence or two. Without pause, the person to his left says what comes to her mind. Her statement must be relevant to something the first person said. The relevance may be of any kind—an association, a contrast, an alternative, a continuation, and so on. The process continues at high speed until at least three rounds have been completed. Members critique the process by discussing the feelings they had during the exercise.

2. The group sits in a circle and identifies a problem or issue. The person nearest the door states his solution. Each subsequent group member (to his left) states her's, using as many ideas of previous speakers as possible. The process continues until a plan generally acceptable to all the group members is arrived at. When a member cannot add anything new, he or she passes. Finally, members' reactions to and feelings about the experience are discussed.

3. The group sits in a circle, and a group problem or issue is identified. The first person states her solution to the problem. The next person immediately states what his opposition to the first person's solution is. The third person immediately states her opposition to the second person's opposition. The process continues until everyone in the group has spoken at least three times. The emphasis is on generating creative ideas in arguments. Members' reactions to and feelings about the experience are discussed.

4. The group lies on the floor, members' heads toward the center of the room. The first person begins with a fantasy about what the group could be like. After no more than two or three minutes, the fantasy is passed on to the next group member, who continues it, adding his or her own associations and fantasies. The process continues until everyone has spoken at least three times. Members' reactions to and feelings about the exercise are examined.

5. The group has before it a number of assorted materials, such as clay, waterpaints, Tinker Toys, magazines, newspapers, and so on. It then creates something out of the materials—a mural, a collage, a design. If more than one group participates, they end the exercise by discussing one another's creations.
6. The group acts out a walk through the woods. Each member takes the leadership role for a while and directs the walk, indicating what he or she is experiencing and seeing. What the members learn about one another, the group, and walking through the woods should be discussed.

EXERCISE 8.11

YOUR BEHAVIOR IN CONTROVERSIES (II)

How do you behave in controversies? Has your behavior changed as a result of your experiences connected with this chapter? How would you now describe your behavior?

1. When a difficult decision is to be made:
   _____ I seek out people who agree with me and see the situation the same way I do.
   _____ I seek out people who disagree with me and see the situation much differently than I do.
2. When I disagree with other members of my group, I:
   _____ Become more and more certain I am right and try to overpower any opposition so that I "win" by having the final decision reflect what I want to do.
   _____ Present my point of view but listen carefully to everyone else's ideas and change my mind when I am logically persuaded to do so.
3. When other members of the group disagree with my ideas, I:
   _____ Feel hurt and rejected.
   _____ Believe they may have important information and insights that my help me better understand the situation.
4. When other group members disagree with me, I:
   _____ Try to stand in their shoes and see the situation from their point of view.
   _____ Am puzzled that they cannot see the situation as accurately and completely as I do.
5. When other members of my group disagree with me, I:
   _____ State my position and my feelings so that everything is out in the open.
   _____ Keep quiet and "sit the discussion out."
6. When I get involved in an argument, I:
   _____ Incorporate other members' ideas into my thinking, try to see the situation from all perspectives, and search for a creative synthesis that is better than my original position.
   _____ Become more and more certain that I am correct and argue more and more strongly for my point of view.
7. Disagreement and arguments among group members are:
   _____ Constructive because they clear the air and enhance involvement and commitment of group members while improving the creativity and quality of decision making.
   _____ Destructive because they lead to dislike, rejection, and defeat.

continued on next page

continued from previous page

Compare your answers with the answers you gave to the questionnaire at the beginning of the chapter. Have you changed? How would you now describe your behavior in controversy situations? Write a description of your controversy behavior and share it with two people who know you well and who have participated in some of the controversy exercises with you. Ask them to add to and modify your self-description.

 # SUMMARY

A large pharmaceutical company faced the decision of whether to buy or build a chemical plant (*The Wall Street Journal*, October 22, 1975). To maximize the likelihood that the best decision was made, the president established two advocacy teams to ensure that each both the "buy" and the "build" alternatives received a fair and complete hearing. An **advocacy team** is a subgroup that prepares and presents a particular policy alternative to the decision-making group. The "buy" team was instructed to prepare and present the best case for purchasing a chemical plant, and the "build" team was told to prepare and present the best case for constructing a new chemical plant near the company's national headquarters. The "buy" team identified over 100 existing plants that would meet the company's needs, narrowed the field down to twenty, further narrowed the field down to three, and then selected one plant as the ideal plant to buy. The "build" team contacted dozens of engineering firms and, after four months of consideration, selected a design for the ideal plant to build. Nine months after they were established, the two teams, armed with all the details about cost, convenience, and efficacy (a) presented their best case and (b) challenged one another's information, reasoning, and conclusions. From the spirited discussion, it became apparent that the two options would cost about the same amount of money. The group, therefore, chose the "build" option because it allowed the plant to be conveniently located near company headquarters. This procedure represents the structured use of controversy to ensure high quality decision making.

By definition, all decision-making situations involve some conflict as to which of several alternatives should be chosen. Within decision-making groups, that conflict takes the form of controversy. Controversy exists when one individual's ideas, information, conclusions, theories, and opinions are incompatible with those of another, and the two seek to reach an agreement. Such intellectual conflict among individuals can be avoided and suppressed or it can be structured and encouraged.

Conflicts among ideas, conclusions, theories, information, perspectives, opinions, and preferences are inevitable. The controversy procedure, when used in the proper way in a cooperative environment, can help the group make a better decision. The controversy procedure begins when a group faced with a decision assigns the major alternatives to advocacy subgroups. Each subgroup develops its alternative in depth and plans how to present the best case possible to the rest of the group. High-quality decisions and conclusions are reached through a process of argument and counterargument aimed at persuading others to adopt, modify, or drop positions. When faced with opposing positions, criticisms of positions, and information that is incompatible with their conclusions, group members enter a state of conceptual conflict. This conceptual conflict leads members into epistemic curiosity, where divergent attention and thought are stimulated. Members then reorganize and reconceptualize their conclusions.

Controversies tend to be constructive when the situational context is cooperative, there is some heterogeneity among group members, information and expertise are distributed within the group, members have the necessary conflict skills, and the canons of rational argumentation are followed.

An essential aspect of controversy is the creativity that is derived from the collision of adverse opinions. Creativity is the process of bringing something new into existence. To encourage creative thinking, group members need to create a cooperative atmosphere in which different opinions and perspectives are valued and time is provided during which members consider the diversity of ideas available. Possible methods for generating creative ideas include part changing, using a checkerboard figure, using a checklist, and finding something similar. Another method for encouraging creativity is synectics, which connects metaphor and psychological state in such a way that new ideas generate from changing perspectives.

Key to the successful use of controversy and creativity in problem solving is how open-minded or closed-minded the group is. Finding creative solutions depends on a group having an open mind to new ideas, different perspectives, conflicting opinions, and opposing beliefs. Brainstorming, a process in which group members produce as many ideas as possible in a given period of time, also helps a group access its creativity. Brainstorming requires open-mindedness, because ideas are not judged during a brainstorming session. Instead, brainstorming is about members throwing out ideas, playing off someone else's idea, and taking processes in new directions.

This chapter focused on the use of the controversy procedure to increase the creativeness and quality of group decision making. The next chapter focuses on the related topic of the constructive resolution of conflicts of interest.

CHAPTER NINE

Managing Conflicts of Interest

BASIC CONCEPTS TO BE COVERED IN THIS CHAPTER

In this chapter a number of concepts are defined and discussed. The major ones are in the following list. Divide into heterogeneous pairs. Each pair is to (1) define each concept, noting the page on which it is defined and discussed, and (2) ensure that both members of the pair understand the meaning of each concept. Then combine into groups of four. Compare the answers of the two pairs. If there is disagreement, look up the concept in the chapter and clarify it until all members agree on and understand the definition.

CONCEPTS

1. Conflict-positive group
2. Conflicts of interest
3. Negotiation
4. Smoothing
5. Forcing
6. Compromise
7. Withdrawal
8. Distributive, win–lose negotiations
9. Integrative, problem-solving negotiations
10. Dilemma of trust
11. Dilemma of openness and honesty
12. Norm of reciprocity
13. Goal dilemma
14. Steps of integrative negotiating
15. Psychological reactance
16. Attribution theory
17. Fundamental attribution error
18. Self-fulfilling prophecy
19. Superordinate goal
20. Mediation

CONFLICT-POSITIVE GROUP

If groups are to be effective, they must resolve the conflicts of interests among members constructively. Groups can be either conflict negative or conflict positive (Tjosvold, 1991b; Table 9.1). In a **conflict-negative group,** conflicts are suppressed and avoided and, when they occur, are managed in destructive ways. In a **conflict-positive group,** conflicts are encouraged and managed constructively to maximize their potential in enhancing the quality of decision making and problem solving and group life in general. Group members create, encourage, and support the possibility of conflict.

In order to create a conflict-positive group, you must understand:

1. The nature of conflicts of interest
2. The five strategies most commonly used to manage conflicts of interest
3. The nature of distributive and integrative negotiations
4. The steps for using integrative negotiations
5. The nature of intergroup conflict
6. How to apply constructive procedures to intergroup conflict

NATURE OF CONFLICTS OF INTEREST

According to the *World Book Dictionary,* a **conflict** is a fight, struggle, battle, disagreement, dispute, or quarrel. A conflict can be as small as a disagreement or as large as a war. The word *conflict* is derived from the Latin *conflictus,* meaning a "striking together with force." There are times when group members' wants and goals "strike together" and produce disruptive effects. To understand what a conflict of interest is, however, it is first necessary to define *interest.*

We are all unique individuals with separate wants, needs, and goals. Therefore, within joint efforts, conflicts of interest inevitably result. To understand conflicts of interest, you must first understand what wants, needs, goals, and interests are (Johnson & Johnson, 2005b; Table 9.2). There are many things each of us want. A **want** is a desire for something. Each person basically has a unique set of wants. A **need** is a necessity

TABLE 9.1   **Conflict-Negative and Conflict-Positive Groups**

CONFLICT-NEGATIVE GROUP	**CONFLICT-POSITIVE GROUP**
Sees conflict as unitary	Recognizes different types of conflicts
Sees conflict as the problem	Sees conflict as part of the solution
Avoids, suppresses, contains conflicts	Seeks out and encourages conflicts
Believes conflict is inherently destructive	Believes conflict is potentially constructive
Sees no value in conflict	Sees many values in conflict
Believes conflicts create anxiety and defensiveness	Believes conflicts create excitement, interest, focus
Individuals go for a "win"	Individuals try to "solve the problem"

TABLE 9.2   **Understanding Conflicts of Interest**

CONCEPT	DEFINITION
Want	Desire for something
Need	Universal necessity for survival
Goal	Desired ideal state of future affairs
Interests	Potential benefits to be gained by achieving goals
Conflicts of interest	Actions taken by person A to achieve goals that prevent, block, or interfere with actions taken by person B to achieve goals
Negotiation	Process by which persons who have shared and opposed interests want to come to an agreement to try to work out a settlement

for survival. Needs are more universal. Every person needs to survive and reproduce (have access to water, food, shelter, and sex), belong (experience loving, sharing, and cooperating), have power, have freedom, and have fun (Glasser, 1984). On the basis of our wants and needs, we set goals. A **goal** is an ideal state of affairs that we value and are working to achieve. Our goals are related through social interdependence. When we have mutual goals we are in a *cooperative* relationship; when our goals are opposed we are in a *competitive* relationship. Our **interests** are the potential benefits to be gained by achieving our goals.

A **conflict of interest** exists when the actions of one person attempting to maximize his or her benefits prevent, block, interfere with, injure, or in some way make less effective the actions of another person attempting to maximize his or her benefits (Deutsch, 1973). Conflict among interests can be based on (1) differences in wants, needs, goals, and values, (2) scarcities of certain resources, such as power, influence, money, time, space, popularity, and position, or (3) rivalry. Conflicts of interest both occur naturally and are deliberately created, and so are common. The management of conflicts of interest is an important aspect of group effectiveness (Figure 9.1).

CONFLICTS CAN BE DESTRUCTIVE OR CONSTRUCTIVE

Inherent in any conflict is the potential for destructive or constructive outcomes (Deutsch, 1973; Johnson, 1970; Johnson & Johnson, 2007). On the *destructive* side, conflicts can create anger, hostility, lasting animosity, and even violence. Conflicts can result in pain and sadness. Conflicts can end in lawsuits, divorce, and war. Destructively managed conflicts are highly costly to a group, destroying the group's effectiveness, ripping apart relationships, sabotaging work, delaying and decreasing teaching and learning efforts, and devastating individuals' commitment to the group's goals, sense of security, and personal feelings (Janz & Tjosvold, 1985).

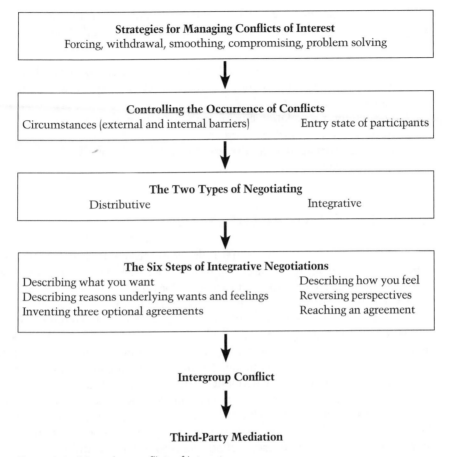

Figure 9.1 Managing conflicts of interest.

Poorly managed conflicts result in group members spending time brooding and fighting rather than working to achieve the group's goals.

Conflicts, however, carry the potential for many important *positive outcomes*. Conflicts can focus attention on problems that need to be solved, and can energize and motivate group members to solve them. Conflicts can clarify how members of the group need to change. Patterns of behavior that are dysfunctional are highlighted and clarified by conflicts. Conflicts can clarify what group members care about and to whom they are committed. Conflicts clarify group members' identity and values. Conflicts help group members understand the values and identities of groupmates. Conflicts keep the relationships among members clear of irritations and resentments and strengthen members' confidence that they can resolve conflicts constructively. Conflicts can release anger, anxiety, insecurity, and sadness that, if kept inside, make a person mentally and physically ill. Conflicts can be fun. Life would be boring if there were no conflict.

It is not the presence of conflicts but the way in which they are managed that determines whether they are destructive or constructive. Conflicts are *constructive* to the extent that they:

1. Result in an agreement that allows all participants to achieve their goals. The agreement maximizes joint outcomes, benefits everyone, and is in all participants' best interests.
2. Strengthen the relationship among participants by increasing their liking, respect, and trust for one another.
3. Increase participants' ability to resolve future conflicts with one another constructively.

CONFLICT AND AGGRESSION

There is a considerable literature that links destructively managed conflicts with interpersonal aggression. *Aggression* is physical (e.g., striking, kicking, shoving) or verbal (e.g., insulting, cursing, threatening) behavior intended to injure another (Baron & Richardson, 1994; Bushman & Anderson, 2001). Three important aspects of this definition are that aggression is behavior (as opposed to thoughts), it is intended or purposeful (as opposed to accidental), and it is aimed at hurting another person. Aggression can be distinguished from *assertiveness*, which is behavior intended to express confidence or dominance. Aggression with malicious intent is also distinguished from playful aggression (which is characterized by frequent smiling and laughter).

A further distinction is made between indirect and direct aggression. *Indirect aggression* involves an attempt to hurt another person without obvious face-to-face conflict, such as through malicious gossip. *Direct aggression* is behavior aimed at hurting another person to his or her face. *Emotional aggression*, hurtful behavior that stems from out-of-control anger, can be distinguished from *instrumental aggression*, hurting another person to accomplish a goal (Berkowitz, 1993). Finally, *displaced aggression* refers to instances in which people behave aggressively toward a person who is not the causal agent of the instigating provocation (Dollard, Doob, Miller, Mowrer, & Sears, 1939; Marcus-Newhall, Pedersen, Carlson, & Miller, 2000). A meta-analysis of the research indicates that the magnitude of displaced aggression is strongly moderated by the similarity between the provocateur and the target of the displaced aggression (Marcus-Newhall, Pedersen, Carlson, & Miller, 2000).

Aggression tends to be related to a variety of factors, including depersonalization (e.g., Zimbardo, 1970), the existence of primes for aggression (e.g., Anderson, Benjamin, & Bartholomew, 1998; Berkowitz & LePage, 1967), temperature and other environmental triggers (e.g., Anderson, Anderson, Dorr, DeNeve, & Flanagan, 2000), the utilitarian need to achieve desired goals (Berkowitz, 1993), and provocations (Bettencourt & Miller, 1996). Having a weapon in sight, for example, intensifies aggression, especially against members of outgroups (Carlson, Marcus-Newhall, & Miller, 1990). In conflict situations, aggression usually provokes counteraggression, as well as feelings such as fear, anger, and a desire for revenge. It is therefore typically a sign of destructive conflict management.

The link between frustration and aggression is one of the oldest social psychological explanations of hostility and physical violence (Dollard, Doob, Miller, Mowrer, &

Sears, 1939). The **frustration-aggression process** can be summarized in the following way (Berkowitz, 1978): Individuals who are unable to attain the goals they desire because of personal limitations or external influences sometimes experience frustration. This frustration produces a readiness to respond in an aggressive manner, which may boil over into hostility and violence if situational cues that serve as "releasers" are present. Negotiators can become frustrated and, at any sign of belligerence or hostility by others, release verbal and, in some cases, physical violence.

An interesting aspect of intergroup aggression is that group members often aggress against outgroup members who have never done them any harm. Lickel, Schmader, and Miller (2003) define such vicarious aggression as a member of a group committing an act of aggression toward outgroup members for a provocation that had no personal consequences for him or her but did harm a fellow ingroup member. Mob violence is an example of vicarious aggression, as most if not all members of a mob have not been harmed by the actions of the victims.

EXERCISE 9.1

YOUR CONFLICT MANAGEMENT STRATEGIES

Different people learn different ways of managing conflicts. The strategies you use to manage conflicts may be quite different from those used by your friends and acquaintances. This exercise gives you an opportunity to increase your awareness of what conflict strategies you use and how they compare with the strategies used by others. The procedure is as follows:

1. Form groups of six. Make sure you know the other group members. Do not join a group of strangers.
2. Working by yourself, complete the following questionnaire.
3. Working by yourself, read the accompanying discussion of conflict strategies. Then make five slips of paper. Write the names of the other five members of your group on the slips of paper, one name to a slip.
4. On each slip of paper write the conflict strategy that best fits the actions of the person named.
5. After all group members are finished, pass out your slips of paper to the persons whose names are on them. In turn, you should end up with five slips of paper, each containing a description of your conflict style as seen by another group member. Likewise, each member of your group should end up with five slips of paper describing his or her conflict strategy.
6. Score your questionnaire, using the table that follows the discussion of conflict strategies. Rank the five conflict strategies from the one you use the most to the one you use the least. This will give you an indication of how you see your own conflict strategy. The second most frequently used strategy is your backup strategy, the one you use if your first one fails.
7. After drawing names to see who goes first, one member describes the results of his or her questionnaire. This is the member's view of his or her own conflict strategies. The member then reads each of the five slips of paper on which are written the views of the group members about his or her conflict strategy. Next the member asks the group members to give specific examples of how they have seen him or her act in conflicts. The group members should use the rules for constructive feedback. The person to the left of the first member repeats this procedure, and so on around the group.
8. Each group discusses the strengths and weaknesses of each of the conflict strategies.

continued on next page

continued from previous page

HOW YOU ACT IN CONFLICTS

The following proverbs can be thought of as descriptions of some of the different strategies for resolving conflicts. Proverbs state traditional wisdom; these reflect traditional wisdom for resolving conflicts. Read each carefully, and using the following scale, indicate how typical each proverb is of your actions in a conflict.

> 5 = very typical of the way I act in a conflict
> 4 = frequently typical of the way I act in a conflict
> 3 = sometimes typical of the way I act in a conflict
> 2 = seldom typical of the way I act in a conflict
> 1 = never typical of the way I act in a conflict

_____ 1. It is easier to refrain than to retreat from a quarrel.
_____ 2. If you cannot make a person think as you do, make him or her do as you think.
_____ 3. Soft words win hard hearts.
_____ 4. You scratch my back, I'll scratch yours.
_____ 5. Come now and let us reason together.
_____ 6. When two quarrel, the person who keeps silent first is the most praiseworthy.
_____ 7. Might overcomes right.
_____ 8. Smooth words make smooth ways.
_____ 9. Better half a loaf than no bread at all.
_____ 10. Truth lies in knowledge, not in majority opinion.
_____ 11. He who fights and runs away lives to fight another day.
_____ 12. He hath conquered well that hath made his enemies flee.
_____ 13. Kill your enemies with kindness.
_____ 14. A fair exchange brings no quarrel.
_____ 15. No person has the final answer, but every person has a piece to contribute.
_____ 16. Stay away from people who disagree with you.
_____ 17. Fields are won by those who believe in winning.
_____ 18. Kind words are worth much and cost little.
_____ 19. Tit for tat is fair play.
_____ 20. Only the person who is willing to give up his or her monopoly on truth can ever profit from the truths that others hold.
_____ 21. Avoid quarrelsome people, as they will only make your life miserable.
_____ 22. A person who will not flee will make others flee.
_____ 23. Soft words ensure harmony.
_____ 24. One gift for another makes good friends.
_____ 25. Bring your conflicts into the open and face them directly; only then will the best solution be discovered.
_____ 26. The best way of handling conflicts is to avoid them.
_____ 27. Put your foot down where you mean to stand.
_____ 28. Gentleness will triumph over anger.
_____ 29. Getting part of what you want is better than not getting anything at all.
_____ 30. Frankness, honesty, and trust will move mountains.
_____ 31. There is nothing so important you have to fight for it.
_____ 32. There are two kinds of people in the world, the winners and the losers.
_____ 33. When one hits you with a stone, hit him or her with a piece of cotton.
_____ 34. When both give in halfway, a fair settlement is achieved.
_____ 35. By digging and digging, the truth is discovered.

Scoring

Withdrawing	Forcing	Smoothing	Compromising	Problem Solving
_____ 1.	_____ 2.	_____ 3.	_____ 4.	_____ 5.
_____ 6.	_____ 7.	_____ 8.	_____ 9.	_____ 10.
_____ 11.	_____ 12.	_____ 13.	_____ 14.	_____ 15.
_____ 16.	_____ 17.	_____ 18.	_____ 19.	_____ 20.
_____ 21.	_____ 22.	_____ 23.	_____ 24.	_____ 25.
_____ 26.	_____ 27.	_____ 28.	_____ 29.	_____ 30.
_____ 31.	_____ 32.	_____ 33.	_____ 34.	_____ 35.
_____ Total	_____ Total	_____ Total	_____ Total	_____ Total

The higher the total score for each conflict management strategy, the more frequently you tend to use that strategy. The lower the total score for each conflict management strategy, the less frequently you tend to use that strategy.

CONFLICT MANAGEMENT STRATEGIES: WHAT ARE YOU LIKE?

Dealing with conflicts of interest is like going swimming in a cold lake. Some people like to test the water, stick a foot in, and enter slowly so that they can get used to the cold gradually. Other people like to take a running start and leap in so that they can get the cold shock over quickly. Similarly, different people use different strategies for managing conflicts. Usually, we learn these strategies in childhood, so that later they seem to function automatically on a preconscious level—we just do whatever seems to come naturally. But we do have a personal strategy, and because it was learned, we can change it by learning new and more effective ways of managing conflicts.

When we become engaged in a conflict, we have to take two major concerns into account (Johnson & Johnson, 2005b):

1. *Reaching an agreement that satisfies our wants and meets our goals.* We are in conflict because we have a goal or interest that conflicts with another person's goal or interest. Our goal can be placed on a continuum ranging from unimportant to highly important.
2. *Maintaining an appropriate relationship with the other person.* Some relationships are temporary; some are permanent. Our relationship with the other person can be placed on a continuum between being of little importance to being highly important.

The dual-concern model of conflict resolution has its origins in Blake and Mouton's (1964) managerial grid and has been articulated by several theorists (Cosier & Ruble, 1981; Filley, 1975; Johnson, 1978; Pruitt & Rubin, 1986; Rahim, 1983; Thomas, 1976). Other labels are sometimes given to the two concerns, such as *concern for self* and *concern for other*. In conflicts of interest, how you behave

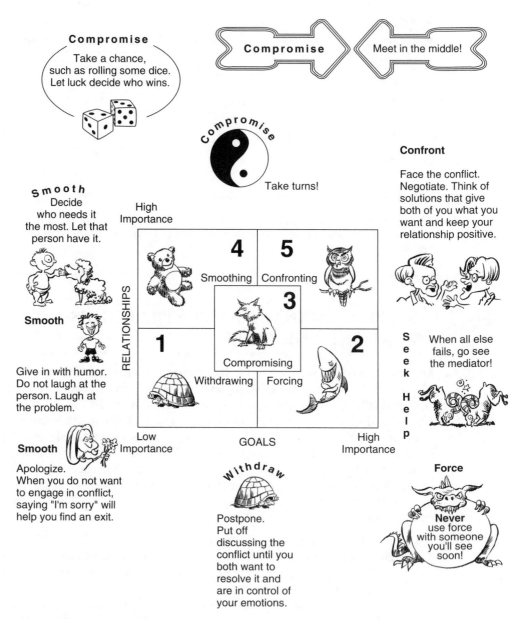

Figure 9.2 Conflict strategies game.
Source: D. W. Johnson and R. Johnson, *Teaching students to be peacemakers* (3rd ed.). (Edina, MN: Interactive Book Company, 2005b). Reprinted with permission of the authors.

depends on how important your goals are to you and how important you perceive the relationship to be. Given these two concerns, five basic strategies are used to manage conflicts (Figure 9.2):

1. *The owl (problem-solving negotiations):* Owls highly value the goal and the relationship. When both the goal and the relationship are highly important to

you, you initiate problem-solving negotiations to resolve the conflict. Solutions are sought that ensure that both you and the other group member fully achieve your goals and resolve any tensions and negative feelings between the two of you. This strategy requires risky moves, such as revealing your underlying interests while expecting the other to do the same.

2. *The teddy bear (smoothing):* To teddy bears the relationship is of great importance, whereas the goal is of little importance. When the goal is of little importance to you but the relationship is of high importance, you give up your goal in order to maintain the relationship at the highest quality possible. When you think the other person's interests are much stronger or more important than yours, you smooth and assist the other person in achieving his or her goal.

3. *The shark (forcing or win–lose negotiations):* Sharks see the relationship as of no importance and try to overpower opponents by forcing them to give in so the shark can achieve his or her goal. When the goal is very important but the relationship is not, you seek to achieve your goal by forcing or persuading the other to yield. Tactics used to win include making **threats,** physical and verbal aggression, imposing penalties that will be withdrawn if the other concedes, and taking preemptive actions designed to resolve the conflict without the other's consent (such as taking a book home that the other insists is his). Tactics to persuade the other to yield include presenting persuasive arguments, imposing a deadline, committing oneself to an "unalterable" position, or making demands that far exceed what is actually acceptable.

4. *The fox (compromising):* Foxes are moderately concerned with the goal and the relationship with the other member. When both the goal and the relationship are moderately important to you, and it appears that both you and the other person cannot get what you want, you may need to give up part of your goals and sacrifice part of the relationship in order to reach an agreement. Compromising may be meeting in the middle so each gets half, or flipping a coin to let chance decide who will get his or her way. Compromising is often used when **disputants** wish to engage in problem-solving negotiations but do not have the time to do so.

5. *The turtle (withdrawing):* Turtles withdraw into their shells to avoid conflicts, valuing neither the relationship nor the goal. When the goal is not important and you do not need to keep a relationship with the other person, you may wish to give up both your goal and the relationship and avoid the issue and the other person. Avoiding a hostile stranger, for example, may be the best thing to do. Sometimes you may wish to withdraw from a conflict until you and the other person have calmed down and are in control of your feelings.

In using these strategies, there are five important points to consider. *First,* to be competent in managing conflicts, you must be able to engage competently in each strategy. You need to practice all five strategies until they are thoroughly mastered. You do not want to be an overspecialized dinosaur that can deal with conflict in only one way. Each strategy is appropriate under a certain set of conditions and, based on the dual concerns of one's goals and the relationship with the other person, you choose the conflict strategy appropriate to the situation.

Second, some of the strategies require the participation of the other disputant and some may be enacted alone. You can give up your goals by using withdrawing and smoothing no matter what the other disputant does. When you try to achieve your goals by using forcing, compromising, and problem solving, the other disputant has to participate in the process.

Third, the strategies tend to be incompatible in the sense that using one of them makes using the others less possible. For example, although withdrawing is sometimes used in combination—say, temporarily withdrawing before initiating problem-solving negotiations—withdrawing implies lack of commitment to one's goals. Negotiating, on the other hand, implies high commitment to one's goals. Forcing implies low commitment to the relationship, whereas smoothing implies high commitment to the relationship. Essentially, the five strategies are independent of one another, and when you engage in one, it is hard if not impossible to switch effectively to another strategy.

Fourth, certain strategies may deteriorate into other strategies. When you try to withdraw and the other disputant pursues you and does not allow you to withdraw, you may respond with forcing. When you try to initiate problem-solving negotiations and the other disputant responds with forcing, you may reciprocate by engaging in win–lose tactics. When time is short, problem-solving negotiations may deteriorate into compromising.

Fifth, whether problem-solving or win–lose negotiations are initiated depends on your perception of the future of the relationship. When conflicts arise, the potential short-term gains must be weighed against potential long-term losses. When you perceive the relationship as being unimportant, you may go for the "win" by attempting to force the other person to capitulate or give in. The relationship may be perceived as unimportant because there will be only one or a few interactions, or perhaps because you are so angry at the other person that only the present matters. When you perceive the relationship as important, then you will try to solve the problem in a way that achieves the other person's goals as well as your own. The relationship is perceived to be important because it is ongoing and long-term, or because there are strong, positive emotions (such as liking and respect) that bond you to the other person.

The shadow of the future looms largest when interactions among individuals are durable and frequent. *Durability* ensures that individuals will not easily forget how they have treated and been treated by others. *Frequency* promotes stability by making the consequences of today's actions more salient for tomorrow's dealings. When individuals realize they will work with one another frequently and for a long period of time, they see that the long-term benefits of cooperation outweigh the short-term benefits of taking advantage of the other person. In ongoing relationships, the future outweighs the present, so that the quality of the relationship is more important than the outcome of any particular negotiation.

Field studies have found problem solving to be strongly associated with constructive resolution of conflicts and high organizational performance, whereas forcing the other person to accept one's position is associated with ineffective conflict management (Burke, 1969, 1970; Lawrence & Lorsch, 1967). Experimental studies have found that high concern about one's own and others' outcomes produces high joint outcomes. High concern about one's own outcomes but low concern about others' outcomes tends to result in attempts to dominate and persuade. Finally, low concern about one's own outcomes but high concern about others' outcomes results in low joint benefit (Ben-Yoav & Pruitt, 1984a, 1984b; Carnevale & Keenan, 1990; Pruitt & Syna, 1983).

CONTROLLING THE OCCURRENCE OF CONFLICTS

Not everything that is faced can be changed but nothing can be changed until it is faced.

James Baldwin

When a conflict of interest arises, usually the best course of action is to face the conflict and resolve it. You can control the occurrence of a conflict when you understand the circumstances that brought about the conflict and the entry state of the participants. The circumstances that surround the conflict include both the *barriers* to the beginning of negotiations and the *events that trigger* the conflict (Walton, 1987). *Barriers* that prevent the conflict from being expressed can be internal or external. **Internal barriers** include negative attitudes, values, fears, anxieties, and habitual patterns of avoiding conflict. **External barriers** may include task requirements, group norms for avoiding conflict, pressure to maintain a congenial public image, and perceptions of one's vulnerability and others' strength. Physical separation is a frequently used barrier to the expression of conflicts of interest. Placing members in different locations, avoiding being in the same room with certain other members, and removing a member from the group can all suppress a conflict of interest. A **triggering event** may be as simple as two group members being physically near one another or as complex as two members being in competition. Negative remarks, sarcasm, and criticism on sensitive points are common triggering events, as is the feeling of being deprived, neglected, or ignored. Some events may trigger a destructive cycle of conflict and others may trigger problem solving; group members should try to maximize the occurrence of the latter type of triggering event.

From discovering the barriers to negotiation and what triggers open expression of the conflict, group members can choose the time and place to deal with the conflict. If an appropriate time is not immediately available, the conflict may be avoided by increasing the barriers to expressing the conflict and removing the triggering events. If the time seems appropriate, the conflict may be faced by strengthening the triggering events and decreasing the barriers.

The second factor in controlling the occurrence of a conflict is the entry state of the disputants. *Entry state* is the person's ability to deal constructively with the conflict. Important aspects of a group member's entry state include the member's level of self-awareness, ability to control one's behavior, skills in communicating, and general interpersonal effectiveness (see Johnson, 2006). A group member may be too anxious, defensive, psychologically unstable, or unmotivated to resolve a conflict effectively. The entry state of a group member may be improved by support from and consultation with groupmates.

Not every conflict of interest is resolvable. It is a mistake to assume that you can always openly resolve a conflict. There are times when conflicts are better avoided.

Usually, however, through careful attention to the entry state of participants and the circumstances that trigger or prevent a conflict, a time optimal for constructive resolution can be chosen.

THE NATURE OF NEGOTIATIONS

Negotiation is woven into the daily fabric of our lives. Negotiating with skill and grace, however, is not easy. It must be learned. **Negotiation** is a process by which people with shared and opposed interests attempt to reach an agreement that specifies what each gives to and receives from one another (Johnson & Johnson, 2005b). Negotiation may involve *distributive issues,* where one member benefits only if the other member agrees to make a concession, or *integrative issues,* where two people work together to seek a solution that will benefit both (Figure 9.3). You spend a great deal of time negotiating even when you do not think of yourself as doing so. You can tell you are negotiating by using the following checklist:

_____ Is there another person involved, and are you dependent on one another for information (about what is a reasonable agreement) and an agreement (you get what you want only if the other person agrees, and vice versa)?

_____ Are both cooperative elements (we both wish to reach an agreement) and competitive elements (we both wish the agreement to be as favorable to ourselves as possible) present in this situation?

_____ Are both primary and secondary gains a concern?

_____ Are there contractual norms on how negotiation should be conducted?

_____ Is there a beginning, a middle, and an end?

_____ Do you wish to propose an agreement that is favorable to yourself but not so one-sided that it drives the other away from negotiations?

Each of the items in the checklist needs to be discussed. *First,* three types of interdependence are inherent in any negotiation: participation interdependence, outcome interdependence, and **information interdependence. Participation interdependence** exists because it takes at least two to negotiate, whether it is two individuals, two groups, two organizations, or two nations. **Outcome interdependence** exists because an agreement can be reached only if the other disputant agrees. To resolve a conflict, disputants must commit themselves to an agreement, and therefore, each is dependent on the other for the outcome. *Information dependence* exists because negotiators depend on one another for information about a possible agreement. Such information can be secured in one of two ways: negotiators can openly and honestly share their expectations, or they can induce what the other expects from his or her behavior during the negotiations. This is a complicated issue, because negotiators often do not know what their own expectations should be until they learn what the other negotiator's expectations are. To the point that negotiators know both what the other wants and what is the least the other will accept, they will be able to develop an effective negotiating position.

Information dependence sets up two dilemmas: the dilemma of trust and the dilemma of honesty and openness. The **dilemma of trust** involves a choice between believing or

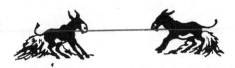

Figure 9.3 Integrative negotiations.

not believing the other negotiator. To believe the other negotiator is to risk potential exploitation. Disbelieving the other negotiator reduces the possibility of any agreement being reached. The **dilemma of honesty and openness** involves the risk of either being exploited for disclosing too much too quickly or seriously damaging the negotiating relationship by refusing to disclose information and thereby seeming deceitful or distrusting.

Second, in negotiations there are both cooperative and competitive elements. The mixed-motive situation is created by the desire to reach an agreement and the desire to make that agreement as favorable to oneself as possible. The two motives can seriously interfere with one another. The balance between the cooperative and competitive elements determines how negotiations are conducted.

Third, both primary and secondary gains must be attended to in negotiations. The *primary gain* is the main benefit each party gains from the agreement. The more favorable the agreement is to a member's interests, the greater his or her primary gain. The *secondary gain* is determined by the impact of the agreement on the negotiator's future well-being, the well-being of relevant third parties, and the factors influencing the effectiveness of the group, such as the member's relationships with groupmates and important third parties' reactions to the agreement.

Fourth, during negotiations, **contractual norms** are developed that spell out the ground rules for conducting the negotiations and managing the difficulties involved in reaching an agreement. Two common norms are the **norm of reciprocity** (a negotiator should return the same benefit or harm given him or her by the other negotiator) and the **norm of equity** (the benefits received or the costs assessed by the negotiators should be equal).

Fifth, negotiations have important time dimensions. There is a beginning, middle, and end. The strategies and tactics used to initiate negotiations, exchange proposals and information, and precipitate an agreement can be quite different and sometimes contradictory.

Sixth, in negotiations disputants face a **goal dilemma:** how to reach an agreement favorable to oneself but not so one-sided that the other negotiator refuses to agree. In resolving the goal dilemma, negotiators must decide on a reasonable proposal, one that will not only get the most for themselves but will also have a good chance of being acceptable to the other. Inasmuch as there is rarely any obviously correct agreement, each negotiator must decide during the negotiations what a reasonable outcome is for self and for the other negotiator.

EXERCISE 9.2

MAKING A PROFIT

The purpose of this exercise is to give participants an opportunity to negotiate a profit–loss situation so that they can examine the dynamics of bargaining. The exercise can be conducted in less than an hour. The procedure for the coordinator is as follows:

1. Introduce the exercise as an opportunity to study the dynamics of negotiation between two persons with different interests. The negotiation is between a buyer and a seller in a wholesale market. Explain that the exercise has three parts: (a) preparing for negotiations, (b) negotiating, and (c) discussing what happened in negotiations.

2. Divide the class into heterogeneous groups of four. Divide each group into two pairs. Assign one pair the role of buyers and the other pair the role of sellers. Give each pair the appropriate profit schedule (see p. 000 in the Appendix). *Their first task is to prepare for negotiations.* Both pair members need to (a) understand the profit schedule so that they know which agreements are most and least profitable for them and (b) be ready to negotiate an agreement that is beneficial to them. On the profit schedule are three commodities (oil, gas, coal). The nine prices for each commodity are represented by the letters A to I. Next to each price is the profit the person would make. The following questions may clarify whether pair members understand the profit schedule:

   a. What is your most important commodity? _____

   b. What is your least important commodity? _____

   c. For price B for coal, what would your profit be? _____

   d. For price D for gas, what would your profit be? _____

   Make sure participants understand that all communication during negotiations will be verbal only. They cannot show their profit schedules to the opposing negotiator.

3. One member of each pair switches chairs so that a buyer is facing a seller. *The second task is to negotiate one agreement that includes a price for each of the three commodities (oil, gas, coal),* such as AAA, III, or BDC. Each person is expected to make and respond to proposed agreements. Participants can say anything they want to one another, but they may not show one another their profit schedule. When an agreement is reached, the parties write it down and sign it. Each negotiator then writes down (without asking one another) (a) which commodity was most important to the opponent and (b) which commodity was least important to the opponent.

4. The two pairs combine into a group of four and complete the *third task* by discussing the following questions:

   a. What were the agreements reached by the members of the group? Each person writes down: (1) the buyer's total profit, (2) the seller's total profit, and (3) the joint profit (the buyer's and seller's profits added together).

   b. How did negotiators communicate information about their profit schedule, and how did they learn about the profit schedule of their opponent? Were their perceptions of what commodities were most and least important to their opponent correct? Was information exchange direct (did buyer and seller accurately tell one another their profit schedules)? Or was it indirect (did they deduce one another's profit schedule by comparing one another's responses to different package offers)?

   c. Did negotiators try to win (maximize their own profit at the other's expense) or solve the problem (maximize their joint profit)?

   d. Did the negotiators make package deals or did they negotiate the commodities one at a time?

   e. What conclusions can the group make about negotiations on the basis of their experience and discussion?

5. Have each group share its conclusions with the rest of the class.

TWO TYPES OF NEGOTIATING

When you use negotiations to resolve a conflict of interest, you have a choice. You can go for a win by acting like a shark and using **forcing** or distributive procedures, or you can go for solving the problem in a mutually beneficial way by acting like an owl and

TABLE 9.3 **The Two Types of Negotiating Strategies**

DISTRIBUTIVE (WIN–LOSE)	INTEGRATIVE (PROBLEM SOLVING)
Presenting an opening offer very favorable to oneself and refusing to modify that position.	Describing what you want.
Gathering information about what the other considers a reasonable agreement from the other's opening offer and proposals.	Describing how you feel.
Continually pointing out the validity of one's own position and the incorrectness of the other person's.	Describing the reasons underlying your wants and feelings.
Using a combination of threats and promises to convince the other person that he or she has to accept one's offer.	Reversing perspectives.
Committing oneself to a position in such a way that if an agreement is to be reached, the other person has to agree to one's terms.	Inventing at least three optional agreements that maximize joint outcomes.
Agreeing if one's benefits are greater than the other's or if no better outcome is available elsewhere.	Choosing one alternative and agreeing to it.

using integrative or problem-solving procedures (Table 9.3). Both are appropriate under certain circumstances.

Distributive Negotiations: Win–Lose Negotiations

People...are trying to either shun conflict or crush it. Neither strategy is working. Avoidance and force only raise the level of conflict.... They have become parts of the problem rather than the solution.

DeCecco and Richards (1974)

When the negotiation is with a person whose continued goodwill and cooperation are not necessary (such as a car salesperson), then you negotiate to win, which means the other person loses. In **distributive negotiations**, the goal is to maximize your outcomes while minimizing the other person's outcomes. You try to reach an agreement more favorable to you than to the other person. You go for the win when your wants, needs, and goals are important and you have a temporary, ad hoc relationship with the other person. In some cultures, where **bargaining** is a way of life, this type of negotiating is both recreation and an art form.

In distributive negotiations, a sequence of behavior occurs in which one party presents a proposal, the other evaluates it and presents a counterproposal, the first party replies with a modified proposal, and so on until a settlement is reached (Chertkoff & Esser, 1976; Johnson, 1974; Johnson & Johnson, 2005b; Rubin, Pruitt, & Kim, 1994; Walton & McKersie, 1965). The negotiators use this sequence of behaviors to obtain information that helps resolve the dilemma of goals. On the basis of the other party's opening offer, the proposals one receives, and the counterproposals one offers, a negotiator can obtain an idea as to what sort of settlement the other person might accept.

A common win–lose negotiating pattern is for both negotiators to set a relatively high but tentative goal at first; they then change their positions on the basis of the other person's reactions and counterproposals.

This sequence of behaviors, which allows one negotiator to assess the second negotiator's points of potential settlement, also can be used to influence the second negotiator's assessment of the first's points. Through their opening offers and their counterproposals negotiators can influence the other's expectations of what they consider a reasonable agreement. Ideally, a win–lose negotiator would like to obtain the maximal information about the other's preferences while disclosing the minimal, or misleading, information about the negotiator's own preferences. Helpful hints for engaging in distributive negotiations, therefore, are:

1. *Identify triggering events and barriers to negotiations.* Trigger the conflict at a moment when it is most advantageous to you and least advantageous to your opponent.

2. *Make an extreme opening offer* (if you are willing to pay $1,500, offer $500) to (a) establish a negotiating range skewed in your favor, (b) influence the other's expectations about one's anticipated minimal terms (do not let the other person know how much you are willing to pay), (c) change the other's beliefs about his or her minimum terms, and (d) create an impression of "toughness." Perceptions of toughness have considerable influence on determining how far a negotiator thinks he can push an opposing negotiator (that is, what terms the opponent will finally agree to).

3. *Compromise slowly* (try to get the other person to compromise first). A slow rate of compromise is aimed at creating an image of toughness and influencing the opponent's expectations as to (a) what a reasonable outcome is for him or her and (b) what one's expectations of a reasonable outcome are. As the opponent reconnoiters the negotiating range for possible points of agreement, he or she seeks information to reduce the uncertainty as to what the agreement might be. Every action a negotiator undertakes affects the opponent's conclusions about what to propose next.

4. *Use threats, promises, sticking doggedly to a committed position, and arguments* to (a) coerce and entice the opponent to accept one's proposal, (b) convince the other person what he or she wants is unreasonable and unattainable, and (c) change the other's evaluation of how many concessions are required to reach an agreement. A *threat* states that if the other negotiator performs an undesired act, you will harm him or her. A *promise* states that if the other negotiator performs a desired act, you will provide benefits. A **preemptive action** is designed to resolve the conflict without the other's consent (such as taking up residence on a disputed piece of land). A **persuasive argument** is pointing out the validity of your position and the incorrectness of the other's. *Committing oneself to an unalterable position* makes it clear that the other negotiator is the one who has the last chance of avoiding no agreement. Plugging up your ears until the other negotiator says "yes" is an example.

5. *Be ready to walk away with no agreement.* Every negotiator is faced with a continual threefold choice of (a) accepting the available terms for agreement,

(b) trying to improve the available terms through further negotiation, and (c) discontinuing negotiations without agreement and with no intention of resuming them. If you cannot walk away with no agreement, you must accept what the opponent is willing to give.

For a goal-oriented group, a win–lose strategy of negotiation has some fundamental shortcomings. Although it often results in more favorable primary gains for some group members, the damage it can cause to future cooperation among group members significantly reduces its secondary gains. Because a win–lose strategy emphasizes power inequalities, it undermines trust, inhibits dialogue and communication, and diminishes the likelihood that the conflict will be resolved constructively. Attempts to create cooperative relations between negotiators are more effective if their power is equal (Deutsch, 1973). Walton (1987) notes that when power is unequally distributed, the low-power person will automatically distrust the high-power person because he or she knows that those with power have a tendency to use it for their own interests. Usually, the greater the difference in power, the more negative the attitudes toward the high-power person and the less likely the low-power person is to present his or her views in a clear and forceful way. The high-power person, on the other hand, tends to underestimate the low-power person's positive intent and reacts with hostility whenever the low-power person tries to reduce his or her power. Even when an agreement is reached, losers have little motivation to carry out the actions agreed on, resent the winner, and often try to sabotage the agreement. The winner finds it hard to enforce the agreement. Damage to interpersonal relationships results as winners and losers are often hostile toward one another.

In going for the win, you assume that the relationship is unimportant and has no future. This is often a mistake. There are very few times in your life when you negotiate with someone you will never interact with again. If you go for a win and then face the person the next day, sooner or later the other person gets revenge! In most situations, therefore, you want to try to resolve the conflict by maximizing joint outcomes. A famous example is the dispute between Israel and Egypt. When Egypt and Israel sat down to negotiate at Camp David in October 1978, it appeared that they had before them an intractable conflict. Egypt demanded the immediate return of the entire Sinai peninsula; Israel, which had occupied the Sinai since the 1967 Middle East war, refused to return an inch of this land. Efforts to reach agreement, including the proposal of a compromise in which each nation would retain half of the Sinai, proved completely unacceptable to both sides. As long as the dispute was defined in terms of what percentage of the land each side would control, no agreement could be reached. Once both realized that what Israel really cared about was the security that the land offered, while Egypt was primarily interested in sovereignty over it, the stalemate was broken. The two countries were then able to reach an integrative solution: Israel would return the Sinai to Egypt in exchange for assurances of a demilitarized zone and Israeli air bases in the Sinai.

Integrative Negotiations: Negotiating to Solve the Problem

Imagine that you and another person are rowing a boat across the ocean and you cannot row the boat by yourself. While the two of you may have conflicts about how to row, how much to row, what direction to row, and so forth, you seek food and water for the other person as well as for yourself. Otherwise, you may perish. Your conflicts become mutual problems that must be solved to both persons' satisfaction. In **integrative negotiations,** the goal is to maximize joint benefits. Maintaining a high-quality relationship with other group members usually is more important than is getting your way on any one issue. In a family, for example, ensuring the survival of the family is almost always more important than winning on any one issue. Integrative negotiations, therefore, consist of a hard-headed, side-by-side search for an agreement that is advantageous to both sides.

In ongoing relationships, conflicts are often resolved by a procedure known as the *one-step negotiation.* Each person (1) assesses the strength of his or her interests, (2) assesses the strength of the other person's interests, and (3) agrees that whoever has the greatest need gets his or her way. Marital satisfaction, for example, has been found to be higher when couples allocate decision-making power such that each person exercises more power on decisions that matter to that individual (Beach & Tesser, 1993). The one-step negotiation procedure only works if it is reciprocal. Each should get his or her way half the time. Ongoing relationships are guided by a *norm of mutual responsiveness* (you help them reach their goals and they help you reach your goals). One-way relationships never last long.

When disputants have to achieve their goals, so that the one-step procedure is not appropriate, they engage in integrative negotiations. There are six basic steps in negotiating a workable solution to a problem that maximizes joint outcomes:

1. Each person explains what he or she wants in a descriptive, nonevaluative way.
2. Each person explains how he or she feels in a descriptive, nonevaluative way.
3. Each person explains his or her reasons for wanting what he or she wants and feeling the way he or she does.
4. Each person reverses perspectives by summarizing what the other person wants and feels and the reasons underlying those wants and feelings.
5. The participants invent at least three good optional agreements that would maximize joint outcomes.
6. The participants choose the agreement that seems the wisest and agree to abide by its conditions.

EXERCISE 9.3

NEGOTIATING RESOLUTIONS TO CONFLICTS OF INTEREST

The purpose of this exercise is to stimulate a discussion on how to negotiate constructive resolutions to conflicts of interest. The procedure is as follows:

1. Form groups of four. Divide each group into two pairs. Assign one pair the role of Chris and the other pair the role of Pat or the instructor. Brief descriptions of several conflicts of interest appear below. Taking one at a time, the pair prepares to role play its assigned

continued on next page

continued from previous page

character by reading the description of the situation and writing out the answers to the following questions:

a. What do you want?

b. How do you feel?

c. What are your reasons for wanting what you want and feeling as you do?

2. One person from each pair changes chairs. A Chris and a Pat should now be seated together. They role play negotiating an agreement that resolves the conflict. The role play will be more interesting if you overdramatize somewhat.

3. Combine both pairs into a group of four. Each group is to share the agreements negotiated, discuss what made the conflict difficult to resolve, come to a consensus how it could be managed most constructively, and write out the ideal agreement to be negotiated. Each group shares its solution with the rest of the class.

CONFLICT DESCRIPTIONS

1. Chris enters a large lecture class and takes an aisle chair. Before the class begins, Chris places his or her books on the table to get a drink of water. On returning, Chris finds the books sitting in the aisle and Pat in the chair. What do you do? Role play the exchange.

2. Chris tells Pat (a friend) in confidence about someone Chris would like to date. The next day several people comment on it. Chris gets Pat alone to talk about it. What do you do? Role play the exchange.

3. Chris has been sick for several weeks. The science instructor refuses to extend the deadline for Chris's final project. Since Chris cannot finish the project in time, this means that Chris will receive a low grade in the class. Chris believes the instructor is being very unfair. Chris decides to try talking to the instructor again. Role play the exchange.

4. Chris borrows Pat's history book. The next day, when Chris returns the book, it is muddy and the cover is torn. Pat believes that when you borrow something, you are responsible for taking care of it. Pat spends twenty minutes cleaning the book and taping the cover back together. Chris laughs and calls Pat a "neatness freak." What do you do? Role play the exchange.

HAMLET AND HIS FATHER'S GHOST

Using the preceding instructions, role play the negotiations between Hamlet and his father's ghost.

Situation

The scene is the battlements of the castle of the King of Denmark. It is midnight, the witching hour. The ghost of Hamlet's father appears and beckons Hamlet to follow the ghost for a private talk. They have a conflict that must be resolved.

Find a partner. Flip a coin to see who will be Hamlet and who will be his father's ghost. Then resolve the conflict using the problem-solving negotiation procedure.

Ghost

I am your father's spirit. Listen to me. If you ever loved me you must avenge my foul, strange, and most unnatural murder. I was not bitten by a poisonous snake. The serpent that bit me now wears my crown. He is an incestuous beast. He seduced your mother, a seemingly virtuous queen. Then, when I was asleep in the garden, he poured poison into my ear. My own brother, your uncle, killed me to gain both my crown and my wife. This is horrible! Horrible! You must kill him! You are my son, and it is your duty to avenge my death. I cannot rest in my grave until my murder is avenged. You must fulfill your obligation and put me to rest. Denmark will not prosper with such a man on the throne. The king must be committed to the welfare of Denmark, not himself. And besides, if he has a son, you will lose your birthright.

Hamlet

I did not know you were murdered. This is surprising. I thought you died of a snake bite. The fact that my uncle murdered you is even more a surprise, as he is very friendly and nice to me. I certainly want justice, but let us not be hasty. Asking me to kill him is a serious request. First, I may be too young and inexperienced to do it right. You would do better to ask one of your generals to do it. Second, killing my uncle could seriously damage my future career options and quality of life. Don't be so blood-thirsty. Think of my future! Third, this is not the time for me to kill someone. I am a carefree youth! I am in love. I'm still in school. I have years of learning and maturing left before I may be ready to kill someone. Fourth, I might go to hell if I killed my uncle. Finally, killing my uncle is a complex task. I have to catch him alone doing something wicked so his soul will go to hell. What use is it if I kill him when he is doing something virtuous and he goes to heaven? This is not one of the usual "walk into the room and stab him" killing. I'm not sure I want to do that much work.

THE INTEGRATIVE NEGOTIATING PROCEDURE

Step One: Describe What You Want (Your Interests)

In describing what you want, you assert your wants and listen carefully to the other person's wants. Describing your wants and goals includes describing (not evaluating) the other person's actions and defining the conflict as a mutual problem and in as small and specific a way as possible.

Negotiating begins when you describe what you want. Everyone has a perfect right to express what his or her wants, needs, and goals are (Alberti & Emmons, 1978; Table 9.4). You have a perfect right to assert what you want, and the other person has a perfect right to assert what he or she wants. Being *assertive* is stating your wants, needs, and goals directly to another person in an honest and appropriate way that respects both yourself and the other person. Assertiveness is often contrasted with aggressive and nonassertive. Being *aggressive* is similar to forcing, where you try to dominate the other person by trying to hurt him or her psychologically or physically to force him or her to concede. Being *nonassertive* is similar to inappropriate smoothing, where you say nothing, give up your interests, and keep your wants to yourself, letting the other person have his or her way. Assertiveness is related to such positive interpersonal behavior as self-regulation, making personal choices, being expressive, being self-enhancing, and achieving desired goals (Eisenberg & Mussen, 1995). Assertiveness skills enable one to solve problems, resolve conflicts, and help prevent depression (Seligman, 1995).

TABLE 9.4 **Respect for Self and Others**

MY RESPECT FOR ME	MY RESPECT FOR YOU
I HAVE A PERFECT RIGHT TO:	**YOU HAVE A PERFECT RIGHT TO:**
My needs and wants	Your wants and needs
Tell you what I want	Tell me what you want
Tell you how I feel	Tell me how you feel
Refuse to give you what you want	Refuse to give me what I want

We Have a Perfect Right to Negotiate with Each Other

Just as everyone has a perfect right to assert what he or she wants, everyone has a perfect right to refuse to give you what you want. When someone wants something that is detrimental to your interests or well-being, you have a perfect right to say no. After asserting your wants and goals, therefore, do not expect the other person to do exactly as you wish. Do not confuse letting others know what you want with demanding that they act as you think they should.

Communicating what you want involves taking ownership of your interests by making personal statements that describe your wants and goals. To clearly communicate your wants and goals to the other person (Johnson, 2006; Johnson & Johnson, 2005b):

1. *Make personal statements* that refer to *I, me, my,* or *mine.*
2. *Be specific about your wants, needs, and goals* and establish their legitimacy.
3. *Acknowledge the other person's goals as part of the problem.* Describe how the other person's actions are blocking what you want. In doing so, separate the behavior from the person. More specifically, a *behavior description* includes
   a. A *personal statement* that refers to *I, me, my,* or *mine.*
   b. A *description statement* of the specific behaviors you have observed and does *not* include any judgment or evaluation or any inferences about the person's motives, personality, or attitudes.
4. *Focus on the long-term cooperative relationship.* Negotiations within a long-term cooperative relationship include discussing how the relationship can be changed so the two of you can work together better. During such conversations, you need to make relationship statements. A *relationship statement* describes some aspect of the way the two of you are interacting with one another. A good relationship statement indicates clear ownership (refers to *I, me, my,* or *mine*) and describes how you see the relationship. "I think we need to talk about our disagreement yesterday" is a good relationship statement.

In presenting a proposed agreement, group members may overemphasize the factors that favor their position, and this overattention to positive arguments tends to result in selective retention of position-consistent information. Although arguing for their position tends to increase their commitment to it (Hovland, Janis, & Kelley, 1953), if they are too demanding, the attempt to persuade may boomerang. Jack Brehm (1976;

Brehm & Brehm, 1981) demonstrated that persuasive attempts that are viewed as co-ercive or biased often cause others to reject what is being presented and increase their commitment to their original positions. This intensification is called **psychological reactance**—the need to reestablish your freedom whenever it is threatened. In one of Brehm's studies, for example, two teammates had to choose between two alternatives marked 1-A and 1-B. When the partner stated, "I prefer 1-A," 73% chose 1-A, but when the partner stated, "I think we should both do 1-A," only 40% chose 1-A (Brehm & Sensenig, 1966). Similarly, 83% of the members of a group refused to go along with a member who stated, "I think it's pretty obvious all of us are going to work on task A" (Worchel & Brehm, 1971).

Listening to the Other Person's Wants. Your success as a negotiator largely depends on showing the other person how his or her wants and goals can be met through ac-cepting your proposals. In order to make a persuasive case for your position, you have to understand clearly what the other person's interests and feelings are. This requires careful listening and being able to see the situation from the other person's perspective. To listen to another person you must face the person, stay quiet (until your turn), think about what the person is *saying, and show* you understand. The keystone to careful listening is *paraphrasing—paraphrasing is* restating, in your own words, what the per-son says, feels, and means. This improves communication by helping avoid judging and evaluating (when restating, you are not passing judgment), giving the sender feedback on how well you understand the messages (if you do not fully understand, the sender can clarify), communicating to the sender that you want to understand what he is saying, and helping you see the issue from the sender's perspective. The **paraphrasing rule** is that before you can reply to a statement, you must restate what the sender says, feels, and means correctly and to the sender's satisfaction (Johnson, 1971b). When you use paraphrasing, there is a rhythm to your statements. The rhythm is, *"You said...; I say...."* First you say what the sender said ("You said"). Then you reply ("I say"). Paraphrasing is often essential in defining a conflict so that a constructive resolution can be negotiated.

Describing the Other Person's Actions. Imagine you and a close friend are in a con-flict. Your friend believes you have behaved in a very destructive way. You believe your behavior was caused by extenuating circumstances, the actions of other people, and a desire to do the right thing. You conclude that your friend should understand and for-give you. Your friend, however, insists that your behavior was caused by your negative personal characteristics such as poor judgment, irresponsibility, selfishness, a lack of concern, a tendency to show off, and incompetence. You are deeply hurt and counterat-tack, accusing your friend of being a person of low moral character who is irresponsible and selfish, has poor judgment, and lacks any concern for you. Both you and your friend consider the other's attributions to be unfair and unreasonable and, therefore, the con-flict is escalated. Harold Kelley and his associates (Kelley, 1979; Orvis, Kelley, & Butler, 1976) found just such a cycle in a study of 700 conflicts in forty-one marriages.

Conflicts are created and escalated when individuals engage in destructive acts. The harm destructive acts do cannot be easily repaired, no matter how considerate and thoughtful a person is later. Destructive acts are exceptionally detrimental to relationships, whereas constructive acts do not yield commensurately positive consequences (e.g., Gottman, 1993; Jacobson & Margolin, 1979; Markman, 1981; Rusbult & Van Lange, 1996). In conflicts, there are two general classes of destructive acts:

1. Directly hurting the other person
2. Inferring that the other person's actions are the result of dispositional (personality, beliefs, attitudes, and values) factors

Avoiding directly hurtful actions is always a good idea. More difficult to control, however, are the inferences you make about other people's behavior. Especially in conflicts, there is a tendency to attribute the causes of the opponent's behavior to his or her inner psychological states (Blake & Mouton, 1962; Chesler & Franklin, 1968; Sherif & Sherif, 1969) while at the same time attributing the causes of your own behavior to situational (environmental) factors. This is known as the **fundamental attribution error** (Ross, 1977; Ross & Nisbett, 1991). Inferences about the causes of behaviors and events are known as *attributions*. **Attribution theory** posits that people continually formulate intuitive causal hypotheses so that they can understand and predict events that transpire (Heider, 1958). Attributions are especially important in conflicts, since attributions influence perceptions of groupmates' motives and intentions (Steiner, 1959) and mediate reactions to groupmates' behaviors (Horai, 1977; Messe, Stollak, Larson, & Michaels, 1979). If attributions are accurate, they help group members understand one another. If attributions are inaccurate, they tend to alienate group members from one another and make conflicts more difficult to resolve. If group members believe you are trying to label them as sick, weak, incompetent, or ineffective, they will refuse to negotiate flexibly (Brown, 1968; Pruitt & Johnson, 1970; Tjosvold, 1974, 1977).

DEFINING THE CONFLICT AS A MUTUAL PROBLEM

A house divided against itself cannot stand.

Abraham Lincoln

Two drivers, coming from different directions, are roaring down a one-lane road. Soon they will crash head-on. If the two drivers define the situation as a competition to see who will "chicken out," they will probably crash and probably die. If the two drivers define the situation as a problem to be solved, they will tend to see a solution in which they alternate giving one another the right-of-way. Even simple and small conflicts become major and difficult to resolve when they are defined in a competitive, win–lose way; even major and difficult conflicts become resolvable when they are defined as problems to be solved.

A conflict defined as a problem to be solved is much easier to resolve constructively than a conflict defined as a win–lose situation (Blake & Mouton, 1962; Deutsch & Lewicki, 1970). The total benefits for all sides in negotiations are higher when problem-solving strategies are used (Lewis & Pruitt, 1971). Defining the conflict as a mutual problem to be solved tends to increase communication, trust, liking for one another, and cooperation.

Defining the Conflict as Being Small and Specific. In defining a conflict, the smaller and more specific it is defined, the easier it is to resolve (Deutsch, Canavan, & Rubin, 1971). The more global, general, and vague the definition of the conflict, the harder the conflict is to resolve. Defining a conflict as, "She always lies" makes it more difficult to resolve than defining it as "Her statement was not true."

Step Two: Describe Your Feelings

Many of us in business, especially if we are very sure of our ideas, have hot tempers. My father knew he had to keep the damage from his own temper to a minimum.

Thomas Watson, Jr., Chairman Emeritus, IBM

The second step of negotiating to solve a problem is describing how you feel. In order to communicate your feelings you must be aware of them, accept them, and be skillful in expressing them constructively. Expressing and controlling your feelings is one of the most difficult aspects of resolving conflicts. For several reasons, it is also one of the most important (Johnson, 2006; Johnson & Johnson, 2005b). *First,* many conflicts cannot be resolved unless feelings are recognized and expressed openly. If individuals hide or suppress their anger, for example, they may make an agreement but keep their resentment and hostility toward the other person. Not only is their ability to work effectively with the other person and resolve future conflicts constructively damaged, the conflict tends to reoccur. *Second,* it is through experiencing and sharing feelings that close relationships are built and maintained. Feelings are the cement that holds relationships together, as well as the means for deepening relationships and making them more effective and personal. *Third,* feelings that are not accepted and recognized can bias judgments, create insecurities that make it more difficult to manage conflicts constructively, and reduce control over your behavior. *Fourth,* the only way other people can know how you are feeling and reacting is for you to tell them. The more you practice telling people how you feel, the more skillful you will be at expressing those feelings constructively.

Step Three: Exchange Reasons for Positions

Once both you and the other person have expressed what you want and how you feel, listened carefully to one another, and defined the conflict as a small and specific mutual problem, you must exchange the reasons for your respective positions on the conflict. To do so, negotiators have to:

1. Express cooperative intentions.
2. Present your reasons and listen to the other person's reasons.
3. Focus on wants and interests, not positions.
4. Clarify the differences between your and the other's interests before trying to integrate them into an agreement.
5. Empower the other person.

Express Cooperative Intentions: Enlarging the Shadow of the Future. One of the most constructive things you can do in resolving a conflict is to highlight the long-term cooperative relationships. This is done in three ways. (1) Stress dealing with the conflict in a problem-solving way. You want to say such things as, *"This situation means that we will have to work together,"* or *"Let's cooperate in reaching an agreement,"* or *"Let's try to reach an agreement that is good for both of us."* (2) State that you are committed to maximizing the joint outcomes. Successful negotiation requires finding out what the other person really wants, and showing him or her a way to get it while you get what you want. (3) Enlarge the shadow of the future by stating that you are committed to the continuation and success of the joint cooperative efforts. In doing so, you must wish to point out the long-term mutual goals and the ways the two of you are interdependent for the foreseeable future.

The clear and unambiguous expression of cooperative intentions in negotiations results in higher-quality agreements being reached in a shorter amount of time (i.e., better agreements faster). The other person becomes less defensive, more willing to change his or her position, less concerned about who is right and who is wrong, and more understanding of your views and ideas (Johnson, 1971b, 1974; Johnson, McCarty, & Allen, 1976). The other person also tends to see you as an understanding and trustworthy person in whom he or she can confide.

The expression of competitive intentions, such as threats and punishments, tends to escalate the conflict (Deutsch & Krauss, 1960, 1962). Imagine you own a trucking company that carries merchandise from point A to point B. Each time your truck reaches its destination, you earn 60 cents minus the operating cost of 1 cent for each second it takes. A part of the road is one-way. If you encounter a truck going the opposite way, one of you has to reverse to let the other through. If the other person refuses to back up, you can close a gate at the other end, and then he or she must back up and take the alternative route. You can then open the gate for yourself and proceed rapidly to your destination. Describe how you would behave.

Morton Deutsch and Robert Krauss (1960, 1962) used this situation to determine how the use of threats affects hostility, counterthreats, and unwillingness to compromise. In the unilateral-threat condition, only one participant had a gate. In the bilateral-threat condition, both sides had gates. In the control condition, no gates were present. When no gate was present, the participants learned to alternate in their use of the one-way road, and both made a profit of about $1.00. When one participant had a gate, participants lost an average of $2.03 per person, although the participant with the gate lost less than the participant without the gate. When both participants had a gate, participants lost an average of $4.38 per person. Thus, the use of threats was counterproductive, intensifying the destructive aspects of the conflict. In considering the use of threats, you may want to remember the advice of Niccolo Machiavelli, an adviser to sixteenth-century Florentine princes:

> I hold it be a proof of great prudence for men to abstain from threats and insulting words toward anyone, for neither ... diminishes the strength of the enemy; but the one makes him more cautious and the other increases his hatred of you and makes him more persevering in his efforts to injure you.

Presenting Your Reasons and Listening to the Other Person's Reasons. Simply saying what you want and how you feel is not enough when you are in an integrative negotiation. You also must give your reasons for wanting what you want and feeling as you do. It is not enough to say, "I want to use the computer now and I'm angry at you for not letting me have it." You must elaborate, "I have an important homework assignment due today and this is my only chance to get it done." Your reasons are aimed at informing the other person and persuading him or her to agree with you.

Many times you will have to ask the other person why he or she has taken a certain position. You ask a friend to study with you. She might reply "no." Until you understand the reasons for the answer, you will not be able to think creatively of ways for both of you to get what you want. The statement in doing so is, "May I ask why?" If the answer is vague, you add, "Could you be more specific? What do you mean when you say … ? I'm not sure I understand." Your tone of voice is as important as the words you use when you ask these questions. If you sound sarcastic, your attempt to understand the other person will backfire.

Once both of you have explained your reasons, either of you may agree or disagree to help the other person to reach his or her goals. The decision to help the other person reach his or her goals or keep negotiating is based on two factors:

1. How important your goal is to you
2. How important the other person's goal is to him or her (based on the reasons presented)

You must listen carefully to the reasons given and decide whether they are valid. If you decide that the other person's goals are far more important to him or her than yours are to you, you may wish to agree at this point. Keep in mind, though, that giving up your goals to help the other person reach his or her goals works only if he or she does the same for you about 50% of the time. This is the one-step negotiation procedure discussed earlier in this chapter.

If the other person's reasons are not valid, you need to point that out so he or she may see the inadequacies of his or her proposals. If neither you nor the other person is convinced to give up your goals for the goals of the other person, then the two of you must reaffirm your cooperative relationship and explore one another's reasons on a deeper level.

Focus on Wants and Interests, Not Positions. In order to negotiate successfully and reach an agreement that satisfies both people, you have to approach the other person on the basis of his or her wants and goals. The classic example of the need to separate interests from positions is that of two sisters, each of whom wanted the only orange available. One sister wanted the peel of the orange to make a cake; the other wanted the inner pulp to make orange juice. Their positions ("I want the orange!") were opposed, but their interests were not. Often, when conflicting parties reveal their underlying interests, it is possible to find a solution that suits them both.

The success of integrative negotiations depends on finding out what the other person really wants, and showing him or her a way to get it while you get what you want. Reaching a wise decision, therefore, requires reconciling wants and goals, not positions. Usually, several possible positions can be found that satisfy various wants or goals. A common mistake is to assume that because the other person's position is opposed to yours, his or her goals also must be opposed. Behind opposed positions lie shared and compatible goals, as well as conflicting ones. To identify the other person's wants and goals, ask "Why?" or "Why not?" and think about his or her choice. Realize that the other person has many different wants and goals.

Focusing on wants and goals rather than positions eliminates many of the traps that cause conflicts to become destructive. One such trap is the aggression that arises from being frustrated by the opponent's refusal to agree with your position. Negotiators can become frustrated and, at any sign of belligerence or hostility by others, release verbal and, in some cases, physical violence. What often prevents high levels of frustration is the continual clarification of wants and goals and the search from new positions that let all members reach their goals.

Differentiate Before Integrating. Conflicts cannot be resolved unless you understand what you and the other person are disagreeing about. If you do not know what you are disagreeing about, you cannot find a way to reach an agreement. The more you differentiate between your interests and those of the other person, the better you will be able to integrate them into a mutually satisfying agreement. In discussing a conflict, try to find the answers to these questions: (1) What are the differences between my wants and goals and yours? (2) Where are our wants and goals the same? (3) What actions of the other person do I find unacceptable? (4) What actions of mine does the other person find unacceptable?

Empower the Other Person. During negotiations it is important that you not let the other person feel powerless. Shared power and wise agreements go hand in hand. There are two ways to empower the other person. The first is by being open to negotiations and flexible about potential agreements. If you refuse to negotiate, the other person is powerless. Willingness to negotiate is based on being open to the possibility that a better option may be available. Staying tentative and flexible means that you do not become overcommitted to any one potential agreement until negotiations have ended. The second is to provide choice among options. Generate a variety of possible solutions before deciding what to do.

The psychological costs of being helpless to resolve conflicts include frustration, anxiety, and friction. When a person is powerless, he or she becomes either hostile or apathetic. We all need to believe that we have been granted a fair hearing and that we should have the power and the right to gain justice when we have been wronged. If it becomes evident that we cannot gain justice, frustration, anger, depression, and anxiety may result (Deutsch, 1985).

Stay Flexible. Negotiating is a rational process. You are seeking a way to satisfy your wants and reach your goals and the other person is doing the same. How successful you are in reaching an agreement depends on how creatively you can think of alternatives that are good for both you and the other person. This requires flexibility and a willingness to change your mind when you are persuaded that it is rational to do so. It is easy to become entrapped in your commitment to a position and close your mind to alternative agreements. Allan Teger (1980), for example, studied the entrapment process through conducting "dollar auctions." A dollar is auctioned off to the highest bidder with the rule that although the highest bidder gets to keep the dollar, the second highest bidder must pay the amount he or she bid. Thus, if a person bid eighty cents for the dollar and someone else bid ninety cents, the person is entrapped in bidding higher to avoid losing the eighty cents. Negotiators need to be vigilant against being entrapped by their commitment to old proposals and positions.

Coordinate Motivation to Negotiate in Good Faith. Differences in motivation to resolve a conflict often can be found among negotiators. You may want to resolve a conflict, but other group members could care less. A groupmate may be very concerned about resolving a conflict with you, but you may want to avoid the whole thing.

Usually, a conflict cannot be resolved until both persons are motivated to resolve it at the same time. The motivation to resolve a conflict based on the costs and gains of continuing the conflict for each person. The costs of continuing a conflict may be the loss of a friendship, loss of enjoyment from work, the loss of job productivity, or the loss of a friend. The gains from continuing the conflict may be satisfaction in expressing your anger or resentment and protection of the status quo. By protecting the status quo, you avoid the possibility that things might get worse when the conflict is resolved. Answering the following questions may help you clarify your motivation and the motivation of the other person to resolve the conflict:

1. What do I gain from continuing the conflict?
2. What does the other person gain from continuing the conflict?
3. What do I lose from continuing the conflict?
4. What does the other person lose from continuing the conflict?

A person's motivation to resolve a conflict can be changed. By increasing the costs of continuing the conflict or by increasing the gains for resolving it, the other person's motivation to resolve may be increased. Your own motivations can be changed in the same manner.

When the outcomes of negotiations are presented as gains more concessions are made than when the outcomes are presented as losses. Negotiators who think in terms of losses or costs are more likely to take the risk of losing all by holding out in an attempt to force further concessions from the opponent.

The dilemmas of trust and openness arise when negotiators begin to exchange proposals and feelings. When negotiating, a person faces the dilemmas of whether (1) to trust opponents to tell the truth about their interests and (2) to tell the truth about his or her own interests to the opposing negotiators. Deutsch (1958, 1960, 1973) used the **Prisoner's Dilemma** game to study the issue of trust within conflict situations. The Prisoner's Dilemma derives its name from a hypothetical situation studied by mathematical game theorists (Luce & Raiffa, 1957). Imagine that you and your partner have just robbed a bank, hidden the money, and are arrested by police, who are sure you are guilty but have no proof. The officers' only hope of convicting you is for you to confess. They take you and your partner into separate rooms to question you (Figure 9.4). You are both presented with two alternatives: Either you can confess to the crime or you can remain silent. If neither of you confesses, you will both be tried on a minor charge that carries a light sentence of one year in prison. If you both confess, then each will spend five years in prison. If your partner confesses and you do not, your partner will go free but you will get ten years in prison. Conversely, if you confess and your partner does not, you will go free and your partner will go to prison for ten years. The dilemma

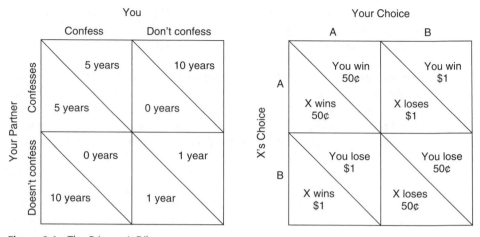

Figure 9.4   The Prisoner's Dilemma game.

for you and your partner is whether to trust the other to remain silent and not exploit your silence if you remain silent. If both you and your partner trust the other to keep silent, both of you benefit.

To conduct research on trust, Deutsch used the Prisoner's Dilemma situation in a game format in which pairs of participants were paid according to the combination of their choices (see Figure 9.4). If both choose A, both would receive 50 cents. If both choose B, both would lose fifty cents. If one chooses A and the other chooses B, the person choosing B wins $1.00 and the person choosing A loses $1.00. The use of the Prisoner's Dilemma game was a remarkable methodological breakthrough for research on conflict and trust. The results of the research demonstrated that the pursuit of self-interest by each group member leads to a poor outcome for all. In the long run, only cooperative behavior based on trust ensures the well-being and productiveness of the group.

Potential Problems. There are three problems in analyzing underlying interests. *First,* sometimes a person does not understand the interests underlying his or her position and preferences and, therefore, cannot describe them to others. *Second,* disputants may not wish to reveal their interests out of fear that the other might use this information for personal advantage. Revealing one's wants, goals, and interests always carries the risk of having one's vulnerability exploited. *Third,* a person's interests often are organized into hierarchical trees, with the initial interests discussed being the tip of the iceberg. With more and more discussion, deeper and deeper interests may be revealed.

Step Four: Understand the Other Person's Perspective

The test of a first-rate intelligence is the ability to hold two opposed ideas in the mind at the same time, and still retain the ability to function.

F. Scott Fitzgerald

To reach a wise agreement, you must have a clear understanding of all sides of the issue, an accurate assessment of their validity and relative merits, and the ability to think creatively to come up with potential solutions that maximize joint outcomes and fulfill the interests of all disputants. To do all this, you must be able to (1) see the conflict from both your own and the other person's perspective and (2) keep both perspectives in mind at the same time. A *perspective* is a way of viewing the world (as well as specific situations) and one's relation to it. *Social perspective taking* is the ability to understand how a situation appears to another person and how that person is reacting cognitively and emotionally to the situation. The opposite of perspective taking is *egocentrism,* or being unaware that other perspectives exist and that one's own view of the conflict is incomplete and limited.

To see the situation from another person's shoes, you need to understand several aspects of perspectives:

1. Each person has a unique perspective (a way of viewing the world and his or her relation to it) that is different from the perspectives of others. As a result of their life experiences, no two people will see a problem in exactly the same way. Each person will view an event somewhat differently.

2. A person's perspective selects and organizes what the person attends to and experiences. All experiences are interpreted and understood within the perspective in which they are viewed. People also tend to see only what they want to see. Out of a mass of detailed information, people tend to pick out and focus on those facts that confirm their prior perceptions, and to disregard or misinterpret those that call their perceptions into question. Each side in a negotiation tends to see only the merits of its case, and only the faults of the other side.

3. Each person can have different perspectives at different times. If you have been lifting 100-pound bags of cement and someone tosses you a 40-pound bag, it will seem very light. But if you have been lifting 20-pound bags, the 40-pound bag will seem very heavy. When you are hungry, you notice all the food in a room. When you are not hungry, the food does not attract your attention. As your job role, experiences, assumptions, physiological states, and values change, your perspective will also change.

4. The same message can mean two entirely different things from two different perspectives. If you provoke your coworker, she may laugh. But if you provoke your boss, she may get angry and fire you! Different perspectives mean the message will be given different meanings. From one perspective, the same message may be interpreted as friendly teasing or as hostile insubordination. A person's perspective determines how a message will be interpreted.

5. Misunderstandings often occur because we assume that everyone sees things from the same perspective as we do. If we like Italian food, we assume that all our friends like Italian food. Accurate perspective taking is one of the most difficult aspects of conflict resolution. It is also one of the most important (see Johnson & Johnson [1989] for a complete review of the research). Perspective-taking improves communication and reduces misunderstandings and distortions by influencing how messages are phrased and received. The better you understand the other person's perspective, the more able you are to phrase messages so the

other person can easily understand them. If a person does not know what snow is, for example, you do not refer to "corn snow" or "fresh powder." In addition, understanding the other person's perspective helps you accurately understand the messages you are receiving from that person. If the other person says, "That's just great!" for example, the meaning reverses if you know the person is frustrated. You must be able to stand in the sender's shoes to understand accurately the meaning of the messages that person is sending you.

Engaging in perspective taking tends to improve the relationship with the other person. You are more liked and respected when the other person realizes that you are seeing his or her perspective accurately and using it to create potential agreements that benefit both sides equally.

Seeing a situation from a variety of points of view demonstrates membership in the broader moral community. By seeing the situation from the opponent's perspective, students (1) remain moral persons who are caring and just and (2) realize that the other person is someone who is entitled to caring and justice.

Failure to understand the other's perspective increases the likelihood of the conflict being managed destructively. In their study of conflict in schools, DeCecco and Richards (1974) found that inability to take the perspectives of others seriously impeded negotiations as a means of conflict resolution.

Taking the other person's perspective transforms a disputant's motivation from immediate self-interest to long-term concerns about joint outcome and the well-being of the relationship. Being locked in one's own perspective results in acting on the basis of immediate self-interest (Dehue, McClintock, & Liebrand, 1993; Yovetich & Rusbult, 1994). Adopting the other person's perspective activates broader concerns, including joint outcomes and the well-being of the other person and relationship (Davis, Conklin, Smith, & Luce, 1996; Johnson, 1971b). Adopting the other person's perspective results in more positive and less negative emotion and cognition, such as situationally based, less blameful construals of the partner's seemingly destructive acts (Johnson, 1971b; Jones & Nesbett, 1972; Regan & Totten, 1975; Storms, 1973). Adopting the perspective of the other person both increases positive emotional reactions (caring, affectionate), relationship-enhancing attributions, and constructive behavior preferences and reduces negative emotions, blaming attributions, and destructive and passive behavioral preferences (Arriaga & Rusbult, 1998).

You ensure that you accurately see the situation from the other person's perspective by (1) asking for clarification or correction to make sure your understanding is accurate (this is called *perception checking*), (2) stating your understanding of the other's wants and goals (i.e., paraphrasing), and (3) presenting the other's position from his or her perspective (i.e., role playing).

The most effective way to gain insight into the other person's perspective is to role play that you are the other person and present the other person's position and reasoning as if you were he or she. Then have the other person do the same. The more involved the two of you get in arguing for the other's position, the more you will understand how the conflict appears from the other person's viewpoint. Such role playing is invaluable in finding solutions that are mutually acceptable.

A systematic series of studies on the impact of perspective reversal on the resolution of conflicts has been conducted (Johnson, 1971b). The results indicate that skillful perspective reversal increases cooperative behavior between negotiators, clarifies misunderstanding of the other's position, increases understanding of the other's position, and aids one's ability to perceive the issue from the other's perspective. The skillful use of perspective reversal results in a reevaluation of the issue and a change of attitude toward it, as well as the perspective reverser being perceived as a person who tries to understand the other's position and the other person in general, who is willing to compromise, and who is a cooperative and trustworthy person. Temporarily arguing for the other person's position results in insight into his or her perspective and changes your attitudes about the issues being negotiated.

There is nothing more important to resolving conflicts constructively than understanding how the conflict appears from the other person's perspective. Once you can view the conflict both from your own perspective and from the other person's perspective, you are more likely to find mutually beneficial solutions and communicate to the other person that you really understand his or her wants, feelings, and goals. The more skilled you are in seeing things from other people's shoes, the more skilled you will be in resolving conflicts constructively.

Step Five: Inventing Options for Mutual Gain

The *fifth* step of negotiating is to identify several possible agreements. People have a tendency to agree to the first reasonable solution proposed, thereby shutting off consideration of even more advantageous agreements. Disputants, therefore, should generate at least three good alternative agreements before deciding on which one to adopt. To invent a number of potential agreements, you must avoid a number of obstacles and you must think creatively.

Avoiding Obstacles. In most negotiations there are five major obstacles that inhibit the inventing of a number of options:

1. *Judging prematurely.* Nothing is so harmful to inventing options as a critical attitude waiting to pounce on the drawbacks of any new idea. Premature criticism is the first impediment to creative thinking.
2. *Searching for the single answer.* Premature closure and fixation on the first proposal formulated as the single best answer is a sure short-circuit of wise decision making.
3. *Assuming a fixed pie.* Do not assume that the pie is fixed, so the less for you, the more for me. Rarely, if ever, is this assumption true. Expanding the pie is key to flexible problem solving.
4. *Being concerned only with your own immediate wants and goals.* In a relationship, to meet your wants you also have to meet the other person's wants. Shortsighted self-concern leads to partisan positions, partisan arguments, and one-sided solutions.
5. *Defensively sticking with the status quo to avoid the fear of the unknown inherent in change.* Changing creates anxiety about potential new and unknown problems and guilt over ineffective or inappropriate behavior in the past. Many times people try to justify their past actions by refusing to change.

Invent Creative Options. Follett (1940) gives an example of a conflict between two people reading in a library room. One asks, "Is it OK if I open the window?" The other replies, "No, I want the window closed." Their conflict could escalate at this point, but the first person asks, "Why do you want the window closed?" After some discussion, it is determined that one wants to open the window for ventilation, the other wants to keep it closed in order not to catch a cold. To resolve their conflict they search for creative options. They finally agree to open a window in the next room, thereby letting in fresh air while avoiding a draft.

Finding potential agreements that will maximize joint outcomes often takes creative problem solving. To invent creative options, you need to:

1. *Think of as many options as possible.* The more options there are, the greater room for negotiations.
2. *Separate the act of inventing options from the act of judging them.* Invent first, judge later.
3. *Gather as much information as possible about the problem.* The more you know about the problem, the easier it is to find solutions.
4. *See the problem from different perspectives and reformulate it in a way that lets new orientations to a solution emerge.* Such a reformulation often produces a moment of insight by one or both participants. The insight is often accompanied by intense emotional experiences of illumination and excitement and leads to the reformulation of the problem so that solutions emerge.
5. *Search for mutual gains.* There always exists the possibility of joint gain. Look for solutions that satisfy the other person as well as yourself. Try to maximize joint outcomes.
6. *Invent ways of making decisions easily.* If you want a horse to jump a fence, do not raise the fence. Propose "yesable" agreements.
7. *Test each proposed agreement against reality.* What are its strengths and weaknesses? What does each person gain and lose? How does it maximize joint outcomes?

The types of agreements that help maximize joint outcomes include the following:

1. *Expanding the pie* by finding ways to increase the resources available: Many conflicts arise from a perceived resource shortage. In such circumstances, integrative agreements can be devised by increasing the available resources.
2. *Package deals,* in which parties include in one agreement several related issues.
3. *Trade-offs,* in which two different things of comparable value are exchanged.
4. *Tie-ins,* in which an issue considered extraneous by the other person is introduced and you offer to accept a certain settlement provided this extraneous issue will also be settled to one's satisfaction.
5. *Carve-outs,* in which an issue is carved out of a larger context, leaving the related issues unsettled. This is the opposite of a tie-in.
6. *Logrolling,* in which each party concedes on his or her low-priority issues that are of high priority to the other person.
7. *Cost cutting,* in which one person gets what he or she wants and the other's cost of conceding on those issues is reduced or eliminated.

8. *Bridging the initial positions* by creating a new option that satisfies both parties' interests that is different from each originally thought they wanted. Rubin, Pruitt, and Kim (1994), for example, discuss a married couple in conflict over whether to vacation at the seashore or in the mountains. After some discussion, they identified their respective interests as swimming and fishing. They then agreed to visit a lake region that was neither at the seashore nor in the mountains, but offered excellent swimming and fishing.

After inventing a number of options, you and the other person will have to agree on which one to try out first. Some realistic assessment of the alternatives then takes place. In trying to decide which alternative to try first it may help to remember Aesop's fable about the mice in trouble. The mice were saying, "It's terrible! Just terrible! We really must do something about it! But what?" The mice were talking about the cat. One by one they were falling into her claws. She would steal up softly, spring suddenly, and there would be one less mouse. At last, the mice held a meeting to decide what to do. After some discussion a young mouse jumped up. "I know what we should do! Tie a bell around the cat's neck! Then we would hear her coming and we could run away fast!" The mice clapped their little paws for joy. What a good idea! Why hadn't they thought of it before? And what a very clever little fellow this young mouse was! But now a very old mouse, who hadn't opened his mouth during the whole meeting, got up to speak. "Friends, I agree that the plan of the young mouse is very clever indeed. But I should like to ask one question. Which of us is going to tie the bell around the cat's neck?" The moral is there is no use adopting an option that cannot be implemented by one or both persons. Once a variety of optional agreements are invented that maximize mutual gain and fulfill the interests of all parties, one of the options is selected to be the initial agreement.

Step Six: Reaching a Wise Agreement

I never let the sun set on a disagreement with anybody who means a lot to me.

Thomas Watson, Sr., founder, IBM

Given that we are separate individuals with unique wants and goals, whenever we interact with others, some of our interests are congruent and other interests are in conflict. It takes wisdom to manage the combination of shared and opposed interests and reach an agreement. *Wise agreements* are those that are fair to all participants, are based on principles, strengthen participants' abilities to work together cooperatively, and improve participants' ability to resolve future conflicts constructively. In other words, wise agreements are those that meet the following criteria.

The first requirement for a wise agreement is that the agreement must meet the legitimate goals of all participants and be viewed as fair by everyone involved. In deciding which option to adopt, keep in mind the importance of preserving mutual interests and maximizing joint benefits. Avoid having either side "win."

The second requirement is that the agreement should clearly specify the responsibilities and rights of everyone involved in implementing the agreement. This includes:

1. *The ways each person will act differently in the future.* These responsibilities should be stated in a specific (tells who does what when, where, and how), realistic (each can do what he or she is agreeing to do), and shared (everyone agrees to do something different) way.

2. *How the agreement will be reviewed and renegotiated if it turns out to be unworkable.* This includes (a) the ways in which cooperation will be restored if one person slips and acts inappropriately and (b) the times participants will meet to discuss whether the agreement is working and what further steps can be taken to improve cooperation with one another. You cannot be sure the agreement will work until you try it out. After you have tested it for a while, it is a good idea to set aside some time to talk over how things are going. You may find that you need to make some changes or even rethink the whole problem. The idea is to keep on top of the problem so that the two of you may creatively solve it.

The third requirement for a wise agreement is that the agreement maintain or even improve the relationship among disputants. In deciding on which option to adopt, keep in mind the importance of shared good feelings and preserving your shared history. Focus on the long-term relationship to ensure that the agreement is durable. Point out that the long-term survival and quality of the relationship should not be jeopardized by any agreement reached. The agreement and the process of reaching the agreement strengthen participants' ability to work together cooperatively in the future (the trust, respect, and liking among participants should be increased). The more committed individuals are to their relationship, the more they inhibit negative emotions (annoyance, bitterness), negative attributions (it is all the other person's fault), and negative behaviors (passiveness, destructive acts) (Arriaga & Rusbult, 1998). Commitment appears to involve the inhibition of destructive processes rather than the activation of constructive processes. Individuals inhibit destructive patterns of thinking (e.g., do not think bad things about us [Rusbult Yovetich, & Verette, 1996]), drive away thoughts of tempting alternatives relationships (D. Johnson & Rusbult, 1989), and think in collective terms (e.g., "we, us, our" rather than "I, me, mine") (Agnew, Van Lange, Rusbult, & Langston, 1998). Improving the relationship also involves participants remaining moral persons who are caring and just as they resolve the conflict and the perception that the other disputants are entitled to caring and justice.

The fourth requirement for a wise agreement is that the agreement and the process of reaching the agreement strengthen participants' ability to resolve future conflicts constructively. Conflicts of interests will reoccur frequently, and each time one is faced and resolved, the procedures and skills used should be strengthened and validated.

The fifth requirement for a wise agreement is that it be based on principles that can be justified on some objective criteria (Fisher & Ury, 1981). The objective criteria may be:

1. Everyone has an *equal chance* of benefiting (for example, determined by flipping a coin; one cutting, the other choosing; or letting a third-party arbitrator decide).

2. *Fairness* (taking turns, sharing, equal use). One way to assess fairness is to list the gains and losses for each person if the agreement is adopted and then see if they balance.

3. *Scientific merit* (based on theory and evidence indicating it will work).
4. *Community values* (those most in need are taken care of first).

Evaluate each of the proposed options on the basis of these objective criteria. Using objective criteria to evaluate a possible agreement may result in clarifying what is fair and just from both sides of the issue. Think through which standards are most appropriate to evaluate the options, and make a decision based on principle. The more you do so, the more likely you are to produce a final agreement that is wise and fair.

Using objective criteria to evaluate a possible agreement may result in clarifying what is fair and just from both sides of the issue. Remember King Solomon. One of the first problems the new King Solomon was presented with involved two women who both claimed the same baby. They wanted him to decide whose it was. Sitting on his throne, Solomon listened carefully. The two women lived together in the same house. Their babies had been born only three days apart. Then one of the babies died. The first woman said, "This woman's child died in the night. She then arose and took my son from beside me and placed the dead child next to me. When I woke to feed my baby, I found her dead child in my arms." "No!" the other woman cried frantically. "The living child is my son!" Solomon calmly said, "Bring me a sword and bring me the baby. Divide the living child in two and give half to the one and half to the other." Everyone was shocked. "No! Please don't!" screamed the real mother. "She can have the child. Don't kill it!" "No," the other woman said, "let the child be neither mine nor yours, but divide it." "Aha!" said Solomon. "Now I know to whom the child belongs." Then, pointing to the woman who had asked that the baby's life be spared, he said, "Give her the living child. She is its mother."

One way to understand how constructive agreements may be reached is to look at a few examples.

1. Miguel was a coin collector; his wife, Ann, loved to raise and show championship rabbits. Their income did not leave enough money for both to practice their hobbies, and splitting the cash they did have would not have left enough for either. Solution: Put all the first year's money into the rabbits, and then, after they were grown, use the income from their litters and show prizes to pay for Miguel's coins.

2. Edythe and Buddy shared an office but had different work habits. Edythe liked to do her work in silence, whereas Buddy liked to socialize in the office and have the radio on. Solution: On Mondays and Wednesdays, Buddy would help keep silence in the office; on Tuesdays and Thursdays, Edythe would work in a conference room that was free. On Fridays, the two worked together on joint projects.

3. Roberto loved to spend his evenings talking to people all over the world on the Internet. His wife, Simone, felt cheated out of the few hours of each day they could spend together. Roberto did not want to give up his computer time and Simone was not willing to forgo the time they had together. Solution: Four nights each week, Roberto stayed up late and talked to his Internet friends after spending the evening with Simone. On the following mornings, Simone drove Roberto to work instead of having him go with a carpool, which allowed him to sleep later.

TRY, TRY AGAIN

When you fail at negotiating an integrative agreement that is wise, the next step is to start over. To be successful at negotiating in a problem-solving way, you must remember to try, try again. No matter how far apart the two sides seem, no matter how opposed your interests seem to be, keep talking. With persistent discussion, a viable and wise decision will eventually become clear.

EXERCISE 9.4

NEGOTIATING WITHIN AN ORGANIZATION

This exercise consists of two situations in which members of the same organization or group have to negotiate a resolution to a conflict of interest. In each situation the basic procedure for the coordinator is the same. The exercise takes less than one hour to complete.

1. Introduce the exercise as one in which the dynamics of negotiation among members of a group become apparent. Divide the class into groups of three (two participants and one observer) for case studies 1 and 2. You need at least two groups. Distribute the accompanying background sheets and role-playing sheets to the participants and observers. Give each observer one copy of the observers' instructions used in the previous exercise. Without letting the groups know that they are getting different instructions, give half of them copies of the accompanying bargaining instructions and the other half copies of the role reversal instructions.
2. Meet with the observers to make sure they understand what they are expected to do.
3. Give them the signal to begin. Groups have up to twenty-five minutes to negotiate an agreement. If they finish before their time is up, note how long it took them to negotiate an agreement and what type of negotiation instructions they had.
4. At the end of twenty-five minutes announce that the time is up and the negotiations must end. Ask each participant to write on a sheet of paper two adjectives describing his feelings during the negotiations and hand it to you. Record how many groups negotiated an agreement and which type of instructions (bargaining or role reversal) they had.
5. Ask each group to discuss its experience with its observer. The main topics of the discussion should be the negotiation strategies used, how members reacted to one another's strategies, and how successful the different strategies were. Then, on a sheet of newsprint, have each group summarize its strategies, how successful they were, how members reacted to them, and any conclusions members can make about their effectiveness.
6. In a general session have each group share its instructions for negotiation, the strategies its members used, and its conclusions about their effectiveness. You can then reveal how participants with bargaining instructions reacted to the negotiations compared with participants with role reversal instructions, how many groups with each type of instructions completed the negotiations successfully, and how long it took these groups to do so. Summarize the main points of the discussion.
7. Have the participants read the subsequent sections on negotiation and compare their conclusions with the material in those sections.

NEGOTIATION EXERCISE: CASE STUDY 1

Background

Jim and Terry (a female) both work for a research firm but in different divisions. Terry has been assigned project leader of a study, and Jim has been assigned from the other division to work on it. This does not necessarily imply that Terry is Jim's boss. This arrangement has been in effect for about a year and is relatively unsatisfactory to Terry, who would like to have Jim taken off the project. Meetings of the project team are often dominated by arguments between Terry and Jim. As a result, Terry has often held meetings without notifying Jim. Jim and Terry are meeting to see if the conflict between them can be resolved.

Terry

Jim is a know-it-all who is always trying to tell you how to run your project. You do not agree with his approach. Jim comes into meetings, slumps down in a chair, and demands that everyone pay attention to him, even if he is late and they have already started. What he wants to study is not the subject of the research. You cannot stand Jim's voice. He has an extremely grating voice that he uses with imperious overtones. He is generally obnoxious. Jim doesn't give others a chance to talk, and always interrupts if they do get a chance.

Jim does not care about the project. If he finds something else to do that he likes better, he simply ignores his responsibilities for completing work on the project. The group has already missed one deadline because he chose to do something else, and in the report before, you had to rewrite an entire section because what he turned in was not adequate. He was busy working on something for the director of the organization just to make a name for himself. Meanwhile, he sacrificed your reputation by causing your project to be late and your group to produce inferior work.

Jim

You do not agree with Terry's approach to the project. Working with her is difficult because her main emphasis is on something that is not relevant to the real problems. She is ignoring the immediate problems that need to be solved and focusing on future issues that are not yet relevant. You believe you cannot tell her this, because Terry thinks she is better than anyone else around her and only the research *she* is doing is any good. She is a prima donna who thinks all the other work in the organization is trash except for hers. Consequently, you do not really feel involved in the project, especially because Terry accepts what everyone else on the project is doing but criticizes your area. Occasionally you have worked on other projects. The director, for example, had you working on something more important for the organization for a while. But Terry is not willing to agree that anyone except herself can do anything well.

NEGOTIATION EXERCISE: CASE STUDY 2

Background

Juanita and Richard both work for a research organization. Originally the director of the organization was the leader of a project. Richard was interviewed for a position on that project and hired by the director. Juanita also interviewed Richard, and strongly opposed his being hired for the project. Juanita thought Richard wasn't competent to do the job. Five or six months after work on the project began, the director decided she wanted to be relieved and proposed that

continued on next page

continued from previous page

Richard and Juanita conduct it jointly. Juanita agreed only reluctantly, and with the stipulation that it be made clear she was not working for Richard. The director consented. They were to have a shared directorship. Within a month Juanita was angry because Richard was acting toward others as though he were the director of the entire project and she were working for him. Juanita and Richard are meeting to see if the conflict between them can be resolved.

Juanita

Right after the joint-leadership arrangement was reached with the director, Richard called a meeting of the project team without even consulting you about the time or content. He just told you when it was being held and said you should be there. At the meeting Richard reviewed everyone's paper line by line—including yours, thus treating you as just another team member working for him. He sends out letters and signs himself as project director, which obviously implies to others that you are working for him. You are hurt, angry, and determined to re-establish your position as joint director of the project.

Richard

You think Juanita is all hung up with feelings of power and titles. Just because you are project director, or sign yourself that way, doesn't mean that she is working for you. You do not see anything to get excited about. What difference does it make? She is too sensitive about every-thing. You call a meeting and right away she thinks you are trying to run everything. Juanita has other things to do and other projects to run, so she does not pay too much attention to this one. She mostly lets things slide. But when you take the initiative to set up a meeting, she starts jumping up and down about how you are trying to make her work for you.

NEGOTIATION EXERCISE: WIN–LOSE NEGOTIATING INSTRUCTIONS

Win–lose negotiations exist when each person attempts to reach an agreement as more favor-able to oneself than to the other person. Strategies used to be successful include:

1. Presenting an opening offer very favorable to oneself and refusing to modify that position.
2. Gathering information about what the other considers a reasonable agreement from the other's opening offer and proposals.
3. Continually pointing out the validity of one's own position and the incorrectness of the other person's.
4. Using a combination of threats and promises to convince the other person that he or she has to accept one's offer.
5. Committing oneself to a position in such a way that if an agreement is to be reached, the other person has to agree to one's terms.

NEGOTIATION EXERCISE: ROLE REVERSAL INSTRUCTIONS

Role reversal is defined as a negotiating action in which one person accurately and completely paraphrases, in a warm and involved way, the feelings and position of another. It is the ex-pression of a sincere interest in understanding other person's position and feelings. The basic rule for role reversal is this: Each person speaks up for her- or himself only after restating the ideas and feelings of the other person accurately and to the other's satisfaction. In other words, before one person presents his point of view, it is necessary for him to achieve the other person's perspective or frame of reference and to understand her position and feelings so well that he can paraphrase them accurately and completely. General guidelines for role reversal are as follows:

1. Restate the other person's expressed ideas and feelings in your own words rather than parroting the words of the other person.
2. Preface your reflected remarks with "You think . . . ," "Your position is . . . ," "You feel . . . ," "It seems to you that . . . ," and so on.
3. Avoid any indication of approval or disapproval in paraphrasing the other person's statements. It is important to refrain from interpreting, blaming, persuading, or advising.
4. Make your nonverbal messages congruent with your verbal paraphrasing. Look attentive, be interested in and open to the other's ideas and feelings, and show that you are concentrating on what the other person is trying to communicate.

In this exercise you are to engage in role reversal during the entire negotiating session and use it to arrive at the solution to the problems you and the other person are facing.

NEGOTIATING IN GOOD FAITH

You can bring your credibility down in a second. It takes a million acts to build it up, but one act can bring it down …We try very hard not to do things that will create distrust.

Howard K. Sperlich, president, Chrysler Corporation

Everyone has a negotiating reputation. The promises of some people are to be believed; other people rarely keep their commitments. You want to build a reputation as a person who is honest, truthful, trustworthy, and keeps your promises. When you have failed to keep agreements in the past, there are at least three strategies you can use to increase your credibility:

1. *Pay your debts.* Whatever you have agreed to do in the past and not yet done, do it. Once you have fulfilled past promises, your current promise is more credible.
2. *Use collateral.* The collateral should be something of value, something the other person does not expect you to give up. While being significant enough to be meaningful, the collateral should not be something so outrageous that it is not believable. Promising to give someone $1,000 if you break your word is not believable.
3. *Have a "cosigner" who guarantees your word.* Find someone who trusts you that the other person trusts, and have that person guarantee that you will keep your word.

REFUSAL SKILLS: THIS ISSUE IS NON-NEGOTIABLE

Not all issues are negotiable. Group members must be able to know when an issue is or is not negotiable and be able to say "no" or "I refuse to negotiate this issue," such as when the issue involves illegal or inappropriate behavior, when other people will be

TABLE 9.5   **Reasons for Saying "No"**

CLEAR	UNCLEAR
It is illegal.	My intuition tells me to say "no."
It is inappropriate.	I am not sure.
It will hurt other people.	The right option is not there.
I will not be able to keep my word.	I have changed my mind.

hurt, or when you do not think you can keep your word. Unclear reasons for saying "no" also exist, such as intuition, being uncertain, not seeing the right option, or having changed your mind. You can save considerable time and trouble by not negotiating on issues that are non-negotiable (Table 9.5).

EXERCISE 9.5

BREAKING BALLOONS

This exercise seeks to demonstrate a nonverbal conflict, which is a complete change from the previous highly verbal activities. The procedure is as follows:

> Each participant is to blow up a balloon and tie it to his or her ankle with a string. Then when the coordinator gives the signal, the participants are to try to break one another's balloons by stepping on them. The person whose balloon is broken is "out," and must sit and watch from the sidelines; the last person to have an unbroken balloon is the winner. The participants can then discuss their feelings of aggression, defense, defeat, and victory. Strategies for protecting one's balloon while attacking others should be noted. A variation on the exercise is to have teams with different-colored balloons competing against one another.

EXERCISE 9.6

INTERGROUP CONFLICT

This exercise studies the dynamics of intergroup conflict and negotiation among groups with conflicting positions. It takes two hours. The procedure for the coordinator is as follows:

1. Introduce the exercise as an experience in intergroup conflict and negotiation. Divide the participants into four groups of not less than six members each and distribute a copy of one of the accompanying instruction sheets to each group. Emphasize that the exercise will determine which group is best.
2. Have each group meet separately to select a negotiator and to develop proposals on the issue. They have half an hour to do this. At the end of this period give them the accompanying reaction form and ask them to answer only questions 1, 2, and 5 and to write the name of their group at the top.

3. Have the negotiators meet in the center of the room, each with her group sitting behind her. Give each group representative five minutes to present her group's proposals. After each representative has completed her presentation, have all participants complete the reaction form, answering all questions.

4. Tell the groups to reconvene separately and brief their negotiator on the best way to proceed in a second presentation of their position. The groups have fifteen minutes to confer. At the end of this period they again answer questions 1, 2, and 5 on the reaction form.

5. Have the negotiators again meet in the center of the room with their groups seated behind them. They have up to half an hour to reach an agreement. Group members can communicate with their negotiator through written notes. At the end of fifteen minutes stop the negotiations and have everyone again complete the questionnaire. Negotiations then resume, and at the end of the thirty-minute period, everyone answers the reaction form for the last time.

6. Conduct a general session in which the results of the questionnaire are presented and discussed. Ask group members how they feel about the experience and then focus upon the experience of the negotiators.

7. Have the groups meet separately to discuss how well they worked together and what the experience was like for them. Develop a list of conclusions about intergroup conflict and place it on newsprint.

8. Again conduct a general session, this time to discuss the conclusions reached by each group.

INSTRUCTIONS TO COORDINATOR FOR USE OF THE REACTION FORMS

1. Pick one person in each group—as many assistants as you need—to hand out and collect the reaction forms and to compute the group mean for each question each time the forms are used.

2. Copy the four accompanying charts on a blackboard or large sheets of newsprint. After each use of the reaction forms, calculate the group means and place them on the charts, using a different color for each group. The response to question 5 should be listed for use in the discussion sessions. Do not let the participants see the results until the general session in which the results are discussed.

3. In discussing the results of each question, look for certain trends. The response to question 1 should be somewhat high in the beginning, increase after comparison with other group's proposals, and drop off if agreement is reached. If no agreement is reached it should not drop off. For question 2, look for the "hero-traitor" dynamic: Satisfaction goes up if the negotiator convinces other groups that her proposals are best, and goes down if she compromises the group's position. It is often helpful to look at the notes passed to the negotiator to see how the group is reacting. The responses to question 3 should be the reverse of the responses to question 1 (if satisfaction with one's own group's proposal is high, satisfaction with the other groups' proposals is low, and vice versa). This usually amounts to devaluing the other group's proposals and a loss of objectivity in evaluation. Question 4 usually demonstrates overconfidence in one's own group's proposal, though this sense of superiority gradually slips from an initial high as negotiations progress.

ADMINISTRATOR-TEACHER GROUP

You are residents of Ravenville, a town of about 15,000 residents. Your town has one high school, which was built thirty-five years ago to house 800 students. Because of steady growth, the school has exceeded its limit and now has over 950 students. The extra students have been accommodated in portable buildings that are aging, and these buildings and the entire

continued on next page

continued from previous page

school are a target for vandals and thieves. Students have to go back and forth in bad weather, which is not healthy for them. In addition, the science labs are sadly out-of-date, the cafeteria and library are too small, and the building is not adequately wired for the computers that are needed to help students learn and do online research in this digital age.

Four opposing groups in the community, yours among them, have suggested various solutions to some of these problems. The school board has asked the four groups to get together and settle on a single set of four to six proposals, which it will then implement.

As a member of an administrator and teacher group, you think the school board should plan to build a new school that will house all the students comfortably with updated science labs and adequate wiring for computers. You think updated facilities will boost the morale of current teachers and help attract good new teachers.

Your group is to submit four to six recommendations for dealing with the problems at a meeting at which your representative and one from each of the other three groups will be present. You and your groupmates may prepare a simple chart of the main points you wish to emphasize. Try to make your recommendations original and creative, because it will be to your advantage if the other groups accept your proposals. After the representatives have presented their proposals, they will negotiate a composite proposal of four to six points to be presented to the school board.

TAXPAYERS' GROUP

As a member of a taxpayers' group, you think that school taxes are already too high. Any bond issues floated to pay for building a new high school will add to the current debt and raise the tax burden on the townspeople. You are opposed to the expense of building a new school and feel that the school is good enough as it is.

PARENTS OF STUDENTS' GROUP

As a member of the parents' group, you feel that the building is outdated and that your children deserve a better learning environment. You feel that building a new school is not necessary but you see the shabbiness of the current building interfering with school pride and student effort. You believe that a complete renovation of the current building will create the necessary positive and updated learning environment.

You are members of an alumni group of graduates from the current high school. You are greatly attached to the building—it was the place of many fond memories from your school days. Because your group collects donations from alumni to use for student scholarships, you are afraid that any substantial change in the building will diminish alumni school loyalty and cause donations to drop off. While you acknowledge that the building may need a few repairs, you are in favor of making whatever minimal repairs are needed to keep up with new technology but not changing the current building in any substantial way.

INTERGROUP CONFLICT

The first half of this chapter discussed the nature of conflicts among individuals within groups and ways to manage them. The groups to which we belong interact with other groups and sometimes conflicts arise. Knowing how to manage conflicts among groups is equally as important as knowing how to deal with conflicts among individuals.

About 1260 B.C., one of the great intergroup conflicts in history occurred between the powerful Greek king of Sparta (Menelaus) and his allies and Paris from the city of Troy. During the ten-year war, Troy was destroyed and Greece lost some of its greatest warriors and kings. It took another ten years for one of the Greek heroes (Odysseus) to get home. The conflict was over Helen (the most beautiful woman in the world at the time). It began at the wedding of Peleus, a mortal king, and Thetis, an immortal sea-nymph. During the ceremony the goddess Eris (goddess of strife and discord) appeared. Angered that she was not invited to the wedding, Eris left a golden apple that she proclaimed would go to the most beautiful goddess. This understandably created a conflict. Hera (supreme goddess of heaven), Athena (goddess of wisdom), and Aphrodite (goddess of love) all were convinced that they were the most beautiful goddess. They began to argue, and the argument raged until Zeus stepped in and ordered that Paris, the son of Priam, the king of Troy, decide. Each of the three goddesses offered Paris a bribe. Hera promised to make him ruler of the entire world if he named her the most beautiful, Athena offered him glory in war, and Aphrodite offered him the most beautiful woman in the world, Helen. Paris chose Aphrodite's offer and named her the most beautiful of the goddesses.

Paris then set sail for Greece to claim his prize. The problem was that Helen was already married to the powerful Greek king of Sparta, Menelaus. Because of Helen's beauty, when Menelaus was courting her, virtually every unmarried Greek male wanted her for his wife. Helen's father, realizing that no matter whom he chose to wed his daughter the others would feel slighted and would very likely seek revenge, consulted the advice of Odysseus (who was famed for his cleverness) and made each of Helen's suitors swear an oath that he would defend the marriage, no matter who won her hand, and that if she was ever carried off, he would aid in getting her back. When Paris arrived at the palace of Menelaus he was given food, shelter, and gifts according the rules of hospitality. When Menelaus left, however, Paris and Helen—who was irresistibly attracted to him, thanks to Aphrodite—eloped to Troy. When Menelaus returned to find his wife taken he invoked the suitors' oaths, and began preparations for a huge invasion force to win back Helen. The Trojan War was the result.

The classic studies on intergroup conflict were conducted by Muzafer Sherif and Robert Blake. Intergroup conflict is based on a distinction between "us" and "them." Perhaps the most famous intergroup conflict theory, however, is contact theory. In order to resolve intergroup conflicts, furthermore, it may be necessary to awaken a sense of injustice or to seek mediation. Each of these topics is discussed in this chapter.

Sherif's Studies of Intergroup Conflict

Among the social scientists who have worked to develop an intergroup conflict theory, the two most successful historically are Muzafer Sherif and Robert Blake. Perhaps the best-known studies of intergroup conflict were performed under the direction of Muzafer Sherif (Sherif, Harvey, White, Hood, & Sherif, 1988). Sherif was born in 1906 in Izmir, Turkey. After attending Izmir International College, he studied at the University of Istanbul, receiving a master's degree in 1928. Awarded a fellowship in national competition for study abroad, he went to Harvard University in 1929, receiving another master's degree in 1932, and then traveled to Germany, where he attended Kohler's lectures at the University of Berlin. He then taught in Turkey, returned to Harvard to conduct research, and subsequently studied at Columbia University (1934–1936), where he received a PhD in 1935. His dissertation was published as a book, *The Psychology of Group Norms* (discussed in Chapter 1). He studied in Paris, then taught in Turkey until January 1945, when he returned to the United States. After teaching at both Princeton and Yale, he became director of the Institute of Group Relations at the University of Oklahoma, a position he held from 1949 to 1966. In 1966 he moved to Pennsylvania State University. It was during the years he spent at Oklahoma that he conducted his famous research on intergroup conflict and superordinate goals.

To study intergroup conflict and its resolution, Sherif and his students and colleagues ran a summer camp in the early 1950s. Initially, they selected twenty-two well-adjusted, white, fifth-grade (twelve-year-old) boys, with above-average intelligence, average to good school performance, and Protestant, middle-class, two-parent family backgrounds. All the boys attended different schools in the Oklahoma City area and did not know one another prior to the study. The researchers then split the boys into two essentially identical groups and sent them to camp at Robbers Cave State Park in rural Oklahoma. The camp setting, isolated from outside influences, afforded the experimenters a unique opportunity to control the interaction among the camp members.

For the first few days, each group engaged in typical camp activities, such as sports, hiking, and swimming. Daily activities were structured so that the group members had to work together to achieve desired goals (the food, for example, needed to be cooked over a campfire and distributed among the group members). The groups quickly developed leaders, norms, favorite activities, and even names (the Rattlers and the Eagles).

The researchers began a four-day tournament of baseball games, tug-of-war, touch football, tent pitching, a treasure hunt, and cabin inspections. The winning group received a trophy, individual medals, and highly appealing camping knives. The losing group got nothing. Animosity between the two groups began during the first baseball game and escalated throughout the competition. The Eagles burned the Rattlers' flag; the Rattlers raided the Eagles' cabin, turning over beds and scattering possessions. Derogatory name-calling became frequent and intense. There were several fistfights. Eventually the two groups were having food fights, throwing mashed potatoes, leftovers, bottle caps, and the like in the dining hall. The Eagles won, and while they were celebrating, the Rattlers raided their cabin and stole the camping knives. The researchers then had to physically separate the groups to avoid a full-scale fight. After a cooling-off period in which the groups were kept apart for two days, the boys rated the characteristics of each group. Campers rated members of their own group as brave, tough, and friendly, and members of the other group as sneaky, smart-alecky stinkers.

Several different methods of reducing the conflict between the groups were then tested. To find out the effects of social contact between groups on intergroup conflict, Sherif devised several pleasant situations in which members of the rival groups interacted with one another. These situations included eating together in the same dining room, watching a movie together, and shooting firecrackers in the same area. These contact situations had no effect in reducing intergroup conflict. If anything, they were utilized by members of both groups as opportunities for further name-calling and other forms of conflict. Sherif concluded that contact between groups in pleasant situations does not in itself decrease existing intergroup tension.

The next strategy was the establishment of a common enemy. A softball game was arranged in which the two groups joined together to play against a group of boys from a nearby town. The experience did reduce some of the hostility between the two camp groups, but the conflict was simply transferred to the town team. Sherif concluded that bringing some groups together against a common enemy results in larger and more devastating conflicts in the long run.

Sherif hypothesized that contact between the rival groups would resolve the conflict only when the groups came together to work cooperatively toward goals that were more important to the groups than the continuation of their conflict. Since cooperation toward common goals had been effective in forming the two ingroups, Sherif reasoned, it would be effective in reducing the conflict between the groups. Sherif therefore arranged a series of superordinate-goal situations for the two antagonistic groups of campers to engage in. He defined **superordinate goals** as goals that cannot be easily ignored by members of two antagonistic groups, but whose attainment is beyond the resources and efforts of either group alone; the two groups, therefore, must join in a cooperative effort in order to attain the goals. One such goal was to repair the water supply system, which the experimenters had earlier sabotaged. Another was to obtain money to rent a movie that both groups wanted to see. Still another was to push a truck to get it started after it had suddenly broken down on its way to a camp-out with food. After the campers had participated in a series of such activities their attitude toward members of the outgroup changed; several friendships among members of different groups were formed, members of the rival group were no longer disliked, and the friction between the groups disappeared.

The characteristics of the superordinate goals introduced by Sherif and his associates in their studies were as follows:

1. They were introduced by a more powerful third party (the experimenters).
2. They were perceived by campers to be natural events in no way identified with the third party.
3. They were not perceived by the two groups of campers as being aimed at resolving the conflict.
4. They transcended the conflict situation and restructured the competitive relationship between the groups into a cooperative one.

In most conflict situations such superordinate goals are not feasible alternatives. A third party, for example, rarely had the power to initiate goals with the above characteristics. Nor could a participant in a conflict easily initiate such a goal in an attempt to resolve the conflict. Sherif's (1966) studies provide clear documentation that compelling cooperative goals will resolve intergroup conflict and produce friendly relationships among members of the previously conflicting groups. The cooperative goals in Sherif's studies, however, were presented to the campers as acts of God or natural disasters (the truck just happened to break down, the water system just happened to stop working). Johnson and Lewicki (1969) compared the effects of two types of superordinate cooperative goals on the resolution of intergroup conflict. In one condition, the superordinate goal appeared to be an act of God, and in the other condition the superordinate goal was introduced by one of the groups engaged in the conflict as a means of resolving the conflict. The act-of-God cooperative goal did in fact resolve the intergroup conflict. In the second condition, however, the opposing group refused to accept the superordinate cooperative goal; they perceived it as part of a competitive strategy aimed at furthering the initiating group's vested interests. Thus, to be effective in resolving intergroup conflict, cooperative goals may have to be presented by a third-party or appear to be natural disasters independent of the parties involved in the conflict.

Blake and Mouton Studies of Intergroup Conflict

Following up on Sherif's work with children, Robert Blake and Jane Mouton (1962, 1983) conducted a series of studies with adult businessmen on the nature of intergroup conflicts and ways in which they can be managed effectively. They focused on the dynamics of intergroup conflict within and between groups before, during, and after the conflict. The results of their many studies can be summarized as follows.

Within groups, intergroup conflict tends to increase group cohesion as members join together to defend their group. Members become more loyal and put aside their conflicts with one another. Militant leaders take control, and group members become more willing to accept autocratic leadership. Maintenance needs become secondary to task needs, and the group becomes more tightly structured and organized. Conformity is demanded; a "solid front" must be presented.

Between groups, hostility tends to develop. The opposing group and its positions are belittled and devalued. Each sees the other as the enemy. Inaccurate and uncomplimentary stereotypes form. Each group sees only the best parts of itself and the worst parts of the other group. Interaction and communication decrease between members of the conflicting groups. They misperceive and fail to listen carefully to the other group's position. Group members tend to listen only to what supports their own position and stereotypes.

During negotiations, a win–lose approach tends to be taken. The result is distortions of judgment about the merits of the positions; one's position is seen more favorably than the opposing group's position. Negotiators tend to be blind to points of agreement between their own and the other side's positions, and they tend to emphasize the differences. The win–lose approach to negotiations results in the **hero–traitor dynamic**—the negotiator who wins is seen as a hero and the one who loses is viewed as a traitor. When a neutral third party decides who is right and who is wrong, the winner considers the third party to be impartial and objective; the loser views the third party as biased and thoughtless. Each side sees itself as objective and rational and the other side as unjust and irrational. The common result of win–lose negotiations is deadlock.

After negotiations, the group that wins tends to become even more cohesive and self-satisfied. The leadership that was responsible for the victory is consolidated. Winning confirms members' positive stereotype of their own group and negative stereotype of the other group. There is little motivation to improve group effectiveness. The losing group frequently splinters (bringing unresolved conflicts among members to the surface), seeks the reasons for its defeat, reorganizes, and works even harder. The group often seeks someone to blame for the defeat and replaces the leadership responsible for the loss. If future victories seem impossible, members may become completely demoralized and assume a defeatist, apathetic attitude toward the group. The losing group is likely to reorganize and become more cohesive and effective once it has accepted the loss realistically.

IMPORTANT CONCEPTS

Demonstrate your understanding of the following concepts by matching the definitions with the appropriate concept. Find a partner. Compare answers.

	Concept	Definitions
_____	1. Psycho-dynamic fallacy	a. Seeing every action of members of other groups as a move to dominate, create an advantage, or win.
_____	2. Win–lose dynamic	b. The capacity to affect another person's goal accomplishment.
_____	3. Hero–traitor dynamic	c. Feelings of discontent aroused by the belief that one fares poorly compared to others.
_____	4. Superordinate goals	d. Seeing the motivation for the behavior of members of other groups in terms of personality factors rather than the dynamics of inter-group conflict.
_____	5. Power	e. When a person is frustrated but cannot attack the source because of fear or simple unavailability, the person attacks an innocent third party because the party is available and has less power.
_____	6. Relative deprivation	f. Goals that cannot be easily ignored by members of two antagonistic groups, but whose attainment is beyond the resources and efforts of either group alone.
_____	7. Displaced aggression	g. Antagonism between groups arises from real conflicts of interest and the frustrations these conflicts produce.
_____	8. Authoritarian personality	h. Your expectations cause you to behave in a way that provokes behavior from others that confirms your expectations.
_____	9. Realistic group conflict	i. Prejudice arises when one group frustrates the other group's goal achievement and the frustrated group reacts with aggression.
_____	10. Self-fulfilling prophecy	j. Conflict over basic values occurring among individuals from different cultures.
_____	11. Culture clash	k. The negotiator who *wins* is seen as a *hero* and the one who *loses* is seen as a *traitor.*
_____	12. Frustration- aggression theory	l. Person characterized by exaggerated submission to authority, rigid conformity to conventional norms, self-righteous hostility, and harsh punitiveness toward anyone considered different.

Blake and Mouton (1983) emphasize that those who use this procedure must avoid three traps that tend to escalate the conflict: (1) the **win–lose dynamic** of seeing every action of the other group as a move to dominate, create an advantage, or win, (2) the **psycho dynamic fallacy** of seeing the motivation for the behavior of another group in terms of personality factors rather than the dynamics of intergroup conflict, and (3) the **self-fulfilling prophecy** of seeing the other group as belligerent, engaging in hostile behavior in an attempt to defend itself by mounting a good offense, thereby provoking belligerence on the part of the other group, which confirms the original assumption.

Distinction Between "Us" and "Them"

Humans tend to see the world in an "us-versus-them" framework. If you selected ten people at random and randomly divided them into two groups of five, they would quickly begin to compete with the other group, value their own group more than other groups and discriminate in favor of it, and depersonalize the members of other groups.

Intergroup Competition. When two groups are placed in the same room and given unrelated tasks, they often quickly begin to compete with one another (Johnson & Johnson, 1989). One explanation for this effect is *social dominance orientation*, which is the extent to which a person wants his or her own group to dominate and be superior to other groups (Pratto, Sidanius, Stallworth, & Malle, 1994; Sidanius & Pratto, 1999). Individuals with a strong dominance orientation believe that superior groups (very often their own) ought to be healthier and more powerful. Being a member of a dominant group, or even being temporarily assigned a position of power over others, tends to create or enhance the belief that those who are better off deserve more than those who are not (e.g., Guimond, Dambrun, Michinov, & Duarte, 2003). Social dominance orientation, furthermore, is related to increased ethnic, gender, social class, and cultural prejudices (Pratto, Lio, Levin, Sidanius, Shih, & Bachrach, 1998; Pratto, Sidanius, Stallworth, & Malle, 1994). Intergroup competition and social dominance orientation may be especially strong during economic rough times. When economic times were difficult, white Southerners in the United States lynched more blacks (Hepworth & West, 1988; Hovland & Sears, 1940), and whites in the North engaged in more violence toward blacks and immigrant Chinese (Olzak, 1992). Indeed, people direct their hostilities toward those groups they see themselves competing with at the moment (Pettigrew & Meertens, 1995). Because economic competition in different countries and localities involves different groups, each society possesses a somewhat distinct set of cultural stereotypes and prejudices.

Unfortunately, competition and hostility breed increased competition and hostility. Competition can become a *self-fulfilling prophecy*. As people view others as competitors, they themselves begin to compete, inadvertently bringing about or amplifying the competition they initially feared (Kelley & Stahelski, 1970). The competition may spiral into more and more intense situations as those involved become more and more convinced of the malicious intent of the competing group. Intergroup competition may be especially self-fulfilling, since groups compete more intensely against one another for resources than do individuals (Schopler et al., 2001).

Ingroup–Outgroup Bias. Intergroup contact often produces an *ingroup–outgroup bias*, in which we hold more-favorable views of groups to which we belong and less-favorable opinions of groups to which we do not belong (Lindeman, 1997; Mullen, Brown, & Smith, 1992; Perdue, Dovidio, Gutman, & Tyler, 1990; Tajfel, 1982a, 1982b). People tend to reward members of their own group at the expense of members of other groups and attribute more positive personality traits to members of the ingroup. Ingroup bias often is accompanied by the *outgroup homogeneity bias*, or the belief that there is less variability among the members of outgroups than within one's own ingroup (Linville, Fisher, & Salovey, 1989). In other words, we all are unique individuals in this group; in that group they are all the same. Outgroup homogeneity bias depersonalizes the members of the outgroup and lumps them all in the same category.

The bias against outgroups tends to be even stronger when outgroups have very obvious and salient differences from ingroups. Ingroup bias, however, may be created by either antipathy ("hate") toward outgroups or affinity ("love") for the ingroup (Brewer, 2001). Love of the ingroup does not necessarily promote derogation of outgroups. It may be that it is only when the groups see themselves as competing for common resources that the ingroup–outgroup bias results.

Social Identity and Social Categorization Theories. Two theories focus on intergroup competition, ingroup bias, and outgroup homogeneity: social identity and social categorization theories. *Social identity theory*, formulated by Henri Tajfel (1982a) and John Turner (1987), is based on the hypothesis that individuals seek a positively valued distinctiveness for their own groups compared with other groups to achieve a positive social identity (Figure 9.5). *Social identity* is the individual's knowledge that he or she belongs to social groups that have significance to the individual (Tajfel, 1982a). According to social identity theory, people strive to enhance their self-esteem, which has two components: a personal identity and the various social identities derived from the

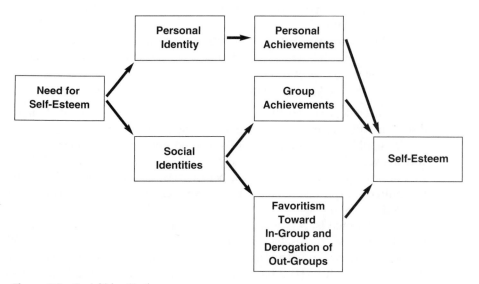

Figure 9.5   Social identity theory.

groups to which they belong (Tajfel, 1974; Tajfel & Turner, 1986; Turner, Pratkanis, Probasco, & Leve, 1992). Thus, people may boost their self-esteem by viewing their ingroups more favorably than they view outgroups to which they do not belong. In other words, our quest for a positive social identity leads us to inflate the positive aspects of the group to which we belong and belittle groups to which we do not belong (Tajfel, 1974; Tajfel & Turner, 1986; Turner, Pratkanis, Probasco, & Leve, 1992). When a group is successful, members' self-esteem can rise, and conversely, when members' self-esteem is threatened, they feel a heightened need for ingroup favoritism, which in turn enhances their self-esteem (Crocker & Luhranen, 1990).

The differentiation between ingroup and outgroups is based on *social categorization*. Social categories function as cognitive "labor-saving devices" by helping you place other people into meaningful categories. Although you may use a wide range of categories for classifying people (for example, male, friend, stranger, Christian, neighbor, political, athlete), two very basic social categorizations are (1) member of my group and (2) member of another group (Hamilton, 1979). *Social categorization theory* is based on the hypothesis that personal and social identities are self-categorizations (Turner & Oakes, 1989) that, in and of themselves, are sufficient to create discriminatory intergroup behavior. Social identity is based on differentiating among groups (I am American, male, and Protestant, as opposed to Canadian, female, and Catholic) and is assumed to be a more inclusive, superordinate level of abstraction than personal identity in the categorization of the self.

A premise of social identity and social categorization theories is that the process of making categorical distinctions to understand the social world involves minimizing perceived differences within categories and accentuating differences between categories (Tajfel, 1969). This results in three principles:

1. The *intergroup accentuation principle* (there is assimilation within category boundaries and contrast between categories, such that all members of the ingroup are perceived to be more similar to the self than to members of the outgroup).
2. The *ingroup favoritism principle* (positive affect [trust, liking] is selectively generalized to fellow ingroup members but not to outgroup members).
3. The *social competition principle* (intergroup social comparison is based on perceived negative interdependence [competition] between ingroup and outgroup).

Some evidence exists that the desire to see oneself as fair-minded can work against discriminating against outgroup members (Singh, Choo, & Poh, 1998).

It should be remembered that people do not categorize themselves in the same way in every situation. When in Indiana, a person may say, "I'm from Muncie"; when in California or Singapore, the same person may say, "I'm from Indiana," or "I'm from the United States," respectively. As situations change, so do the ways people categorize themselves and others.

Another premise of social identity and social categorization theories is since individual persons are themselves members of some social categories and not others, social categorization carries with it implicit ingroup–outgroup (we–they) distinctions. These distinctions result in (1) intergroup competition, (2) ingroup members receiving preferred treatment, and (3) depersonalization of outgroup members (Turner, 1985). Even when social categorizations are imposed on people (given the acceptance and internalization of the categories), members of the ingroup are liked more and treated better than members of outgroups. In order to overcome these effects, a process of decategorization and then recategorization must take place.

Decategorization: Personalizing Interaction. Primary consequences of categorization are ingroup bias and the depersonalization of members of outgroups. Individual members of outgroups tend to be treated as undifferentiated representatives, not as unique individuals. In order to reduce ingroup bias and the depersonalization of outgroup members, contact among members of the different groups is required. These intergroup interactions should be structured so as to reduce the salience of category distinctions and to promote opportunities to get to know outgroup members as individuals (Miller, Brewer, & Edwards, 1985). Contact will be most effective when interactions are highly personalized rather than category based (Miller, 2002). Attending to personal characteristics of outgroup members tends to disconfirm category stereotypes and decrease the perception of outgroups as homogeneous units.

Recategorization: Building a Common Ingroup Identity. Johnson and Johnson (1992a) and Gaertner and his associates (1993) posited that ingroup bias and the depersonalization of outgroup members can be reduced through building a new, common group identity. The contact among members of different groups needs to be structured so that attention is focused on a superordinate category that encompasses both ingroup and outgroup in a single social group. Although there may be white Americans, black Americans, Asian Americans, and Hispanic Americans, for example, highlighting the **superordinate identity** of *American* can place all citizens into a single social category and identification. Attention to category differences is superseded by a new inclusive group identity. It should be noted that decategorization and recategorization are not mutually exclusive. When groups work together to accomplish cooperation goals, they begin to see one another in multidimensional ways (i.e., they decategorize) and form a common identity (i.e., recategorize).

The classic work on intergroup conflict was conducted by Muzafer Sherif and Robert Blake. More recent work, however, notes that intergroup conflict begins with a distinction between "us" and "them." Once that distinction is made, groups are quick to compete with one another, value their own group more than other groups, and depersonalize the members of other groups, which may lead to discrimination against outgroup members. These dynamics involve the importance of social identity and social categorization. Social identity theory posits that people seek to enhance their self-esteem by viewing the groups to which they belong more positively than they do the groups to which they do not belong. Social categorization theory posits that defining oneself and others as members of groups saves time and effort in dealing with the world. Simply categorizing a person as an outgroup member is sufficient to create discriminatory behavior. Such negative aspects of categorization may be ended by decategorizing and/or recategorizing into a common ingroup.

Whereas Sherif's research indicates that the resolution of intergroup conflict requires compelling cooperative goals, and the cognitive view points toward decategorization and recategorization, the broadest approach to resolving intergroup conflict is contact theory. Other procedures include awakening a sense of injustice in the high-power group and mediation.

Resolving Intergroup Conflict: Contact Theory

Resolving intergroup conflict is based on the assumption that contact between members of different groups will result in positive relationships and a reduction of stereotyping and prejudice. One of the most studied intergroup conflicts is that between white and black Americans. Historically, social scientists believed that sheer ignorance about African Americans and their lives contributed to erroneous and oversimplified racial stereotypes (Myrdal, 1944). Contact was seen as the solution. A wide variety of studies conducted in the 1930s, 1940s, and 1950s indicated that such contact was not a straightforward matter. The nature of the contact between members of different ethnic groups, not the frequency, seemed to determine whether favorable intergroup attitudes resulted. Researchers studied the effects of actual contact between blacks and whites, utilizing visiting black lecturers in classrooms (Young, 1932), meetings with black professionals (F. Smith, 1943), school integration (Horowitz, 1936), joint recreational activities in integrated summer camps (Williams, 1948; Yarrow, Campbel, & Yarrow, 1958), voyages of white merchant seamen serving with black seamen (Brophy, 1945), and contact within combat infantry platoons (Mannheimer & Williams, 1949; Star, Williams, & Stouffer, 1965). Many of the earliest research studies used questionnaires in which respondents were asked to note their attitudes toward members of an ethnic group and then to describe the nature and frequency of their contact with members of that group (Allport & Kramer, 1946; Harlan, 1942; MacKenzie, 1948; Rosenblith, 1949). Somewhat later studies were based on postwar occupational and educational desegregation (Gray & Thompson, 1953; Gundlach, 1950; Harding & Hogerge, 1952; Minard, 1952; Reed, 1947; Rose, 1948; Williams & Ryan, 1954) and desegregated residential settings (Deutsch & Collins, 1951; Irish, 1952; Jahoda & West, 1951; Kramer, 1951; Wilner, Walkey, & Cook, 1952; Winder, 1952). These latter studies indicated that the greater the degree of cooperation growing out of involuntary residential proximity between white and black residents, the more likely the development of friendly ethnic relationships.

Years later, we realize that the issue is not so simple. Sometimes intergroup contact is associated with less prejudice. According to national surveys, having more black friends or more contact with gay men and lesbians is associated with less prejudice (Herek & Capitanio, 1996; Jackman & Crane, 1986). Contact, however, is also correlated with more prejudice. Whites who have had the most contact with illegal immigrants (Espenshade & Calhoun, 1993) and whites living in areas of the South with the largest concentration of African Americans have the most prejudiced political attitudes (Giles & Buckner, 1993; Key, 1949). Thus, contact can either increase or decrease prejudice and discrimination.

Based on these early studies, in 1947 Goodwin Watson published a review of the previous research and writings on intergroup relations. He concluded that contact between members of different ethnic groups was likely to be more effective in changing behavior and attitudes than were such alternative experiences as exposure to correct information or persuasive communication, given that the contact met a number of conditions. The conditions included the following:

1. Cooperative action to achieve mutual goals (the diverse individuals have to engage in cooperative activities together)
2. Personal interactions among individuals from the different groups
3. Social norms and authorities favoring equalitarian cross-ethnic contact
4. Equal status contact

In the same year, Williams (1947) published a similar list of conditions for constructive cross-ethnic contact, as did Kenneth Clark in 1953. In 1954 Gordon Allport published his famous book, *The Nature of Prejudice*, in which he identified a similar list of conditions. Stuart Cook followed with a review in 1957.

Between 1950 and 1970, approximately forty studies were conducted on cross-ethnic interaction (Amir, 1969; Cook, 1969; Stephan, 1978). The reviewers of this research concluded that the evidence was inconclusive as to whether cross-ethnic contact resulted in more favorable cross-ethnic attitudes and relationships. Under favorable conditions, contact seemed to reduce prejudice, and under unfavorable conditions, contact seemed to increase prejudice. The major determinant of whether cross-ethnic contact produced positive attitudes and relationships was cooperative interaction among the individuals involved.

The most recent formulations of contact theory specify that the following conditions must exist for contact to result in a reduction of prejudice, stereotyping, and racism:

1. *Cooperative action to achieve mutual goals.* What largely determines whether interaction results in positive or negative relationships is the context within which the interaction takes place. Rather than requiring members of different groups to compete or work individualistically on their own, they must work together to achieve mutual goals. Two meta-analyses indicated that cooperative experiences promote more positive relationships among heterogeneous individuals (Johnson & Johnson, 1989; Johnson, Johnson, & Maruyama, 1983). When people cooperate, they tend to like one another more, trust one another more, be more candid with one another, and be more willing to listen to and be influenced by one another than are people competing or working individualistically. In addition, cooperative experiences promote more positive, committed, and caring relationships regardless of differences in ethnic, cultural, language, social class, gender, ability, or other differences.
2. *Personal interactions among individuals from the different groups.* Ingroup members tend to assume that outgroup members are all alike. Through intimate, one-on-one interaction, those categories should break down and outgroup members should be perceived in more individualized terms (Brewer & Miller, 1984; Marcus-Newhall Miller, Holtz, & Brewer, 1993; Miller, 2002; Urban & Miller, 1998; Wilder, 1986).
3. *Support from social norms and authorities.* The social norms, defined in part by relevant authorities, should favor intergroup contact. Greenberg and Pyszczynski (1985) demonstrated that participants expressed more prejudice after they overheard a confederate utter a racial slur. College students being interviewed about a racial incident on campus conveyed more racist sentiment

after they heard a fellow student do the same (Blanchard, Lilly, & Vaughn, 1991). Participants were more likely to rate an outgroup member as "typical" when they were with fellow ingroup members than when they were alone (Wilder & Shapiro, 1991).

4. *Equal status of the two groups in the contact situation.* Desegregation situations that provided equal status contact, as in the army and public housing projects, have been successful (Pettigrew, 1969).

In addition to these four conditions, researchers have suggested additional conditions that may be required for contact between diverse groups to have constructive rather than destructive effects. One is the salience of social categories. When category distinctions are highly salient in an intergroup contact situation, group members are more apt to respond in ways that are category based (Brewer & Miller, 1984; Hong & Harrod, 1988; Miller, 2002; Oakes, 1987; Tajfel, 1978; Wilder & Shapiro, 1989a, 1989b) and are more biased in their intergroup attitudes (Haunschild, Moreland, & Murrell, 1994; Hong & Harrod, 1988). Three ways to reduce the salience of social categories are:

1. *Making shared categories salient.* Ingroup bias is higher when people differ on two real social categories (such as ethnicity and gender) than when they differ on one category but share another (Brewer, Ho, Lee, & Miller, 1987; Islam & Hewstone, 1993; Urban & Miller, 1998). Similar results have been found in laboratory studies on nominal group categories (Des champs, 1977; Deschamps & Doise, 1978; Vanbeselaere, 1987, 1991).

2. *Have equal representation of majority and minority members* in cooperative groups (M. Rogers, Hennigan, Bosman, & Miller, 1984; Worchel, Andreoli, & Folger, 1977). Members of numerical minorities are more aware of their social category than are members of numerical majorities (McGuire, McGuire, Child, & Fujioka, 1978; McGuire, McGuire, & Winton, 1979; Mullen, 1983), express more ingroup bias than do numerical majorities (Brewer, Manzi, & Shaw, 1993; Gerard & Hoyt, 1974; Mullen, Brown, & Smith, 1992; Sachdev & Bourhis, 1984, 1991), and are less accepting of members of other groups (Miller & Davidson-Podgorny, 1987). Groups for whom category salience is high are more biased in their intergroup attitudes (Haunschild, Moreland, & Murrell, 1994; Hong & Harrod, 1988).

3. *Create a common identity among majority and minority members* (Johnson & Johnson, 1999b). When majority and minority members are assigned the same role, for example, they perceive themselves as sharing a common identity (Bettencourt, Charlton, & Kernahan, 1997; Bettencourt & Dorr, 1998).

The second potential addition to contact theory is the role of intergroup friendship. Having outgroup friends creates a strong negative relationship to prejudice and a positive relationship to favorable intergroup attitudes (Herek & Capitanio, 1996; Wright, Aron, McLaughlin-Volpe, & Ropp, 1997). In a 1988 survey of 3,806 respondents in seven national probability samples conducted in France, Great Britain, the Netherlands, and West Germany, Pettigrew (1997) found that intergroup friendship is a strong and consistent predictor of reduced prejudice and pro-immigrant policy preferences. The reduction of prejudice among those with diverse friends generalized to more positive feelings about a wide variety of outgroups. There seems to be a benevolent spiral in which intergroup friendship reduces prejudice, and reduced prejudice in turn increases the likelihood of further intergroup friendships. Similar effects were not found when the individual had an outgroup coworker or neighbor (but not a friend).

Since its original formulation fifty years ago, extensive research has been inspired by contact theory. The research has generally confirmed the theory across a variety of societies, situations, and groups. These include German children in school with Turkish children (Wagner, Hewstone, & Machleit, 1989), the elderly (Caspi, 1984), and the mentally ill (Desforges et al., 1991). The theory has been confirmed by laboratory (e.g., Cook, 1978; Johnson & Johnson, 1989), survey (e.g., Sigelman & Welch, 1993), field (e.g., Meer & Freedman, 1966; Johnson & Johnson, 1989), and archival (e.g., Fine, 1979) research.

There are problems with contact theory. The *first* is that the proliferation of required conditions renders the theory meaningless. As a result of all the diverse research, many social scientists have suggested revisions to contact theory. Some of the revisions have been situational (such as intimacy [Amir, 1976] or salience of social categories [Brewer & Miller, 1984]) and some have been individual (such as low authoritarianism [Weigel & Howes, 1985]). The danger is that contact theory may become a "grocery list" of necessary conditions rather than a coherent model of attitude and behavior change. The proliferation of conditions may result from social scientists' confusing facilitating with essential conditions. Some of the conditions suggested for optimal contact may be catalytic (not essential for harmonious relationships but related to underlying mediating processes). Pettigrew (1997) suggests four broad, encompassing processes: (1) learning about the outgroup, (2) empathizing with the outgroup, (3) identifying with the outgroup, and (4) reappraising the ingroup. Some of the conditions proposed as requirements for constructive contact may actually be facilitators of one or more of these processes.

The *second* problem is the need to specify more precisely the variables that mediate contact effects. Social judgment theory, which is discussed in the next chapter, is an attempt to be more specific about the mediators of contact and positive relationships.

The *third* problem is that while contact theory is about interaction among diverse groups, it focuses on interpersonal interaction. It needs to refocus on the contact of group with group (Hewstone & Brown, 1986) rather than on the contact of individuals from two groups. There is evidence that the perceived collective other is a qualitatively different kind of actor than a perceived individual other. Groups evoke stronger reactions than an individual engaging in the same behavior and actions by groups, and individuals elicit differing preferences for redress (Abelson, Dasgupta, Park, & Banaji, 1998). When observers perceive individuals as part of a cohesive group (as opposed to an aggregate of unrelated individuals), the observers express stereotypic judgments about the individuals and infer that their behavior was shaped by the presence of others (Oakes & Turner, 1986; Oakes, Turner, & Haslam, 1991; Wilder, 1977, 1978b). A racial slur by an individual, for example, provokes a different reaction than a racial slur delivered by a group. Considerably more research is needed on intergroup (as opposed to interpersonal) contact.

THIRD-PARTY MEDIATION

William Ury often tells a tale of an old gentleman who in his will requests that his estate be divided among his three sons in the following manner: one-half to his eldest son, one-third to his middle son, and one-ninth to his youngest son. When the loving father died, his estate consisted of seventeen camels. The three sons attempted to divide up the estate according to their father's wishes but quickly found that they could not do so without cutting some of the camels into pieces. They argued and argued without agreeing on how to divide the camels. Eventually, a village elder rode up on his own dusty camel and inquired about their problem. The three brothers explained the situation. The elder then offered to make his own camel available if that might help. It did. With eighteen camels, the brothers could solve the problem. The oldest soon took nine camels (one-half of eighteen), the middle son choose six more (one-third of eighteen), and the youngest son extracted two camels (one-ninth of eighteen). Nine plus six plus two equals seventeen. Almost before the three brothers knew what had happened, the wise man climbed back onto his own camel and rode off into the setting desert sun.

This story illustrates what a clever and creative mediator can do. A **mediator** is a neutral person who helps two or more people reach an agreement that both believe is fair, just, and workable. A mediator does *not* tell disputants what to do, decide who is right and who is wrong, or talk about what he or she would do in such a situation. The mediator is simply a facilitator with no formal power over either disputant. **Mediation** exists, therefore, when a neutral and impartial third party assists two or more people in negotiating a constructive resolution to their conflict. Mediation is unlikely to be effective when the relationship between the two parties is poor and when resources are scarce. Conversely, mediation is most likely to be successful when both parties are highly motivated to engage in the mediation process. Most studies show satisfaction rates of 75% or higher with the mediation process (Kressel & Pruitt, 1985). Mediation facilitates conflict resolution in the following ways (Raven & Rubin, 1976, p. 462):

1. By reducing emotional upset by giving parties an opportunity to vent their feelings
2. By presenting alternative solutions by recasting the issues in different or more acceptable terms
3. By providing opportunities for graceful retreat or face-saving in the eyes of one's adversary, one's constituency, the public, or oneself
4. By facilitating constructive communication among parties
5. By controlling contact between the parties, including aspects such as the neutrality of the meeting site, the formality of the setting, the time constraints, and the number and kinds of people at the meeting

To be successful, mediators need to be perceived as trustworthy and able (Rubin, Pruitt, & Kim, 1994). Mediators also need to convey an impression of legitimacy, social position, and expertise in order to gain the confidence of both parties and to win acceptance for the proposed solution (Kolb, 1985). Mediators tailor tactics to particular situations. Mediators may lower hostility by being very directive and using humor with people experienced in **integrative negotiating,** but by being nondirective with inexperienced parties who lack expertise in negotiating (Carnevale & Pegnetter, 1985). When mediation fails, an arbitrator may be brought in. **Arbitration** is a binding settlement of a conflict determined by a disinterested third party.

Restorative Justice

There are times when negotiations take place to repair the past harm that a perpetrator has caused a victim to experience. The goal of such negotiations is restorative justice. There are several types of justice. Justice may involve ensuring that benefits are distributed justly (i.e., distributive justice), the same procedures are applied fairly to all members (i.e., procedural justice), everyone is perceived to be part of the same moral community (i.e., moral inclusion), and any wrongs suffered are righted (restorative justice) (Deutsch, 2006; Johnson & R. Johnson, 2011).

Distributive Justice. Distributive justice is the method used to grant benefits (and sometimes costs) to group or organizational members (Deutsch, 1985). There are three major ways in which benefits can be distributed: (1) The **equity (or merit) view** is that a person's rewards should be in proportion to his or her contributions to the group's effort. This view is inherent in competitive situations. (2) The *equality view* is that all group members should benefit equally. It is inherent in cooperative situations. (3) The *need view* is that group members' benefits should be awarded in proportion to their need. Cooperators typically ensure that all participants receive the social minimum needed for their well-being. Whatever system is used, it has to be perceived as *"just."* When rewards are distributed unjustly, the group may be characterized by low morale, high conflict, and low productivity (Johnson & Johnson, 2011).

Procedural Justice. Procedural justice involves fairness of the procedures that determine the benefits and outcomes that a person receives (Deutsch, 2006; Johnson & Johnson, 2011). Fair procedures are those that are applied equally to everyone and implemented with polite, dignified, and respectful behavior. Typically, fairness of procedures and treatment is a more pervasive concern to most people than are fair outcomes (Deutsch, 2006). The more cooperative the group, the more members tend to believe that everyone who tried has an equal chance to succeed, that members get the benefits they deserve, and that the evaluation system is fair (Johnson & Johnson, 2005a, 2009a). Even when their task performances are markedly discrepant, members of cooperative groups tend to view themselves and their groupmates as being equally deserving of benefits and rewards.

Scope of Justice. Justice tends to be given only to individuals who are perceived to be included in one's moral community—that is, those who fall within the scope of justice. Individuals and groups who are outside the boundary of one's moral community may be treated in ways that would be considered immoral if people within the moral community were so treated. The **scope of justice** is the extent to which a person's concepts of justice apply to specific others (Deutsch, 1985, 2006; Opotow, 1990). Moral considerations guide our behavior with those individuals and groups who are inside our scope of justice. **Moral inclusion**, therefore, is applying considerations of fairness and justice to others, seeing them as entitled to a share of the community's resources, and seeing them as entitled to help, even at a cost to oneself (Opotow, 1990, 1993). Moral inclusion includes the values of fairness, equality, and humanitarianism. **Moral exclusion** occurs when a person excludes groups or individuals from his or her scope of justice, a share of the community's resources, and the right to be helped. When moral exclusion exists, moral values and rules that apply in relations with insiders are not applicable. Perpetrators, and often bystanders, tend to morally exclude victims and consider them outside the scope of justice.

Restorative Justice. While distributive justice focuses on the perceived fairness of the distribution of benefits and rewards, and procedural justice focuses on the perceived fairness of the procedures used to determine outcomes, restorative justice focuses on righting the wrongs suffered in a destructively managed conflict. It becomes a concern after a conflict has taken place in which one party was harmed by another or another type of justice was violated. **Restorative justice** involves bringing together all parties affected by harm or wrongdoing (e.g., offenders and their families, victims and their families, other members of the community, and professionals), discussing what happened and how they were affected, and agreeing on what should be done to right any wrongs suffered (Morrison & Ahmed, 2006; Umbreit, 1995). It is a form of justice that emphasizes repairing the harm done in interpersonal, intragroup, and intergroup relationships. Restorative justice deals with at least two issues: (1) resolving past conflicts to restore cooperation among parties and within the community as a whole; and (2) creating the conditions for maintaining long-term, ongoing cooperation among parties in the future. Restorative justice is aimed both at the present and the future. The shadow of the future is always present in establishing restorative justice, as it re-establishes the membership of the offender and victim in a moral community in which they will continue to interact in an on-going, long-term relationship. There are a number of characteristics necessary for restorative justice to be created: (1) there must be identifiable victims and offenders, (2) the participation of victims and offenders must be voluntary, (3) victims and offenders must have the capacity to engage fully and safely in dialogue and integrative negotiation, and (4) a facilitator must be present to provide the help and support that the victims and offenders need.

Three important aspects of restorative justice are remorse, forgiveness, and reconciliation. *Remorse* is an emotional expression of personal regret felt by persons after they have committed an act that they deem to be shameful, hurtful, or violent. *Forgiveness* occurs when the victim pardons the offender and lets go of any grudge, desire for revenge, or resentment toward the offender for the wrongdoing (Enright, Gassin, & Knutson, 2003). *Reconciliation* is an emotional reattachment and affiliation between former opponents after conflict-induced separation (de Waal, 2000; Roseth, et al., 2010). It reaffirms and restores the positive, cooperative relationship among the parties in a conflict. Reconciliation usually includes an apology, communicates that justice has prevailed, recognizes the negativity of the acts perpetuated, restores respect for the social identity of those formerly demeaned, validates and recognizes the suffering undergone by the victim and relevant community members, establishes trust between victim and offender, and removes the reasons for either party to use violence to "right" the wrongs of the past.

There are at least four places where restorative justice has been established. In some schools, a "just" community has been established in which restoration must take place when one student harms another. Students are taught the norms, values, and procedures needed for restorative justice to work. The emphasis is on long-term prevention. In the aftermath of criminal acts, offender and victims meet in order to repair some of the damage done by the crime. There are national reconciliations, such as Australia's efforts to reconcile with its aborigines. Finally, there are National Truth and Reconciliation Commissions, such as the one in South Africa, in which aggrieved parties voice their anger, describe injustices experienced, and sometimes face those who have oppressed them.

Restorative justice involves a process in which individuals meet, engage in a problem-solving dialogue, and negotiate with each other. The victim is given the opportunity to express their needs and feelings and help determine the best way for the offender to repair the harm he or she has created. The offender is expected to take responsibility for his or her actions and realize that the actions had real consequences for the victim and the community. The community is given the opportunity to participate in the process because the responsibility for reconciliation is partially theirs. The process is based on a set of values that emphasize the importance of healing, repairing, restoring, and preventing harm to others, as well as reintegrating the relationships among the relevant parties.

The outcomes of restorative justice include an integrative agreement reflecting (a) reparation (i.e., restitution agreed on by offender, victim, and community) and (b) the reestablishment of constructive relationships among offender, victim, and the community as a whole. Restorative justice takes place under the shadow of the future as well as the pain of the past. Restoration should reestablish the membership of the offender and the victim in a moral community where they will continue to interact in an ongoing, long-term relationship. In many ways, the process of restoring justice is more important than the outcomes.

Awakening A Sense of Injustice. In order for restorative justice to take place, and for an offender to feel remorse, the offender needs to feel a sense of injustice. A **sense of injustice** is awakened in majority members about their treatment of minority and low-power group members (Deutsch, 1985). Deutsch posits that no change in discriminatory practices is possible until a sense of injustice is awakened by following six steps:

1. Remove the majority's ignorance of the injustices experienced by minorities. Often the majority "insulates" itself from the victims by avoiding contact (living in all-white suburbs) or structuring the contact in ways that prevent the possibility of becoming aware of the discrimination (such as *"employee of the month"* celebrations). This **insulated ignorance** protects majority group members from being aware of the consequences of their behavior (Hornstein & Johnson, 1966).

2. Delegitimize the officially sanctioned ideologies and myths that "justify" the injustices (i.e., *"the cream rises to the top"*). Majority group members are largely content and tend to have a vested interest in preserving the status quo (which ensures their superior roles and privileges). Awaking a sense of injustice requires

that majority group members become aware of their ideologies, question the ideologies, and decide that the ideologies are no longer legitimate.

3. Expose the majority to new ideologies, models, and reference groups that support action to undo the disadvantages of the minorities. Majority group members must interact with minority group members, come to understand their perspective and experience, and form a new reference group that includes both majority and minority individuals. The new reference group must support change. The action steps must be clear.

4. Stimulate the hope of the majority that it can effectively reduce injustice. Once victimization has become deeply embedded in social institutions, individual action to overcome it is frequently viewed as futile and costly. There must be hope of success in order for majority group members to take action.

5. Increase the majority's belief it will benefit from reducing injustice. This involves (a) reducing the fear of the majority that its new actions will have costly, harmful consequences and (b) enhancing the majority's prospect of material and psychic gains from a positive change in its relationships with the minority. Both the majority and the minorities must be seen as being better off as a result of decreasing discrimination.

6. Increase the majority's belief that continuation of the old relationship will no longer produce the material benefits and gains the majority has experienced in the past. Thus, continuing the status quo may have costly, harmful consequences for the majority.

EXERCISE 9.7

YOUR CONFLICT MANAGEMENT BEHAVIOR

Having completed this chapter, it may be helpful to focus again on your behavior in conflict situations. Form a group of three with two persons who know you well and who have participated with you in some of the exercises in this book. Then complete the following tasks, taking at least two hours to do so.

1. Reflect silently on how each member deals with conflict. Give one another feedback about the animal, song, or book that each member reminds the others of on the basis of how he or she deals with conflict. Each person explains why he or she chose the animal, song, or book that he or she did.

2. Write down your individual strengths in managing conflicts constructively. Share your lists. Members should add to one another's lists.

3. Write down the individual skills you need to develop in order to manage conflict more constructively. Share your lists. Members should add to one another's lists.

4. Discuss the feelings each member has in conflict situations and why he or she reacts that way. Help one another think of alternative ways of reacting to conflict situations.

5. From magazine pictures and any other materials, build a collage about the way in which you behave in conflict situations. Share the collage with the other members. Add ideas to one another's collages.

SUMMARY

Conflicts of interest will occur frequently among members of effective groups. Conflicts often, but not always, involve indirect or direct aggression. They may have constructive or destructive effects on the group, depending on how members manage them. There are five basic strategies for managing conflicts of interest: withdrawal, forcing (distributive negotiations), smoothing, compromise, and problem solving (integrative negotiations). The occurrence of conflicts may be controlled through controlling triggering events and the entry states of disputants. Negotiations involve participation, information, and outcome interdependence and result in both primary and secondary gains. Distributive negotiations involve procedures such as an extreme opening offer and a slow rate of compromise. Integrative negotiations involve a six-step procedure of describing what you want, describing what you feel, exchanging reasons for holding the positions you do, understanding the other's perspective, inventing options for mutual gain, and reaching a wise decision.

Conflicts of interest occur between groups as well as between group members. Intergroup conflict has been studied in children's camps and among adult businessmen. It may develop through ingroup–outgroup bias. Two of the cognitive theories attempting to explain intergroup conflict are social identity and social categorization theories. They posit that intergroup conflict is resolved through recategorization. Contact theory may be the most widely known theory of resolving intergroup conflict. It posits that conflicts among groups are resolved through members engaging in cooperative actions, in which personal relationships may develop, supported by social norms and authorities, and equal status among everyone involved. Intergroup conflicts may also be developed through awakening a sense of injustice in high-power group members and through mediation.

Now that you are acquainted with the dynamics involved in resolving conflicts of interest and have practiced resolving them, you are ready to encounter diversity as it exists in society and in the groups to which you belong. You will do so in the next chapter.

CHAPTER TEN

Valuing Diversity

BASIC CONCEPTS TO BE COVERED IN THIS CHAPTER

In this chapter a number of concepts are defined and discussed. The major ones are in the following list. Divide into pairs. Each pair is to (1) define each concept, noting the page on which it is defined and discussed, and (2) ensure that both members of the pair understand the meaning of each concept. Then join with another pair to make a group of four. Compare the answers of the two pairs. If there is disagreement, look up the concept in the chapter and clarify it until all members agree on and understand the definition.

CONCEPTS

 1. Ability and skill diversity
 2. Demographic diversity
 3. Stereotype
 4. Prejudice
 5. Ethnocentrism
 6. Discrimination
 7. Blaming the victim
 8. Causal attribution
 9. Culture clash
10. Personal identity
11. Personal diversity

INTRODUCTION

In the story *Beauty and the Beast*, Beauty, to save her father's life, agrees to live in an enchanted castle with the Beast. Although initially fearful of the Beast and horrified by his appearance, she later is able to see beyond his monstrous appearance and into his heart. Her perception of his appearance changes; she no longer is repelled by the way he looks but instead is drawn to his kind and generous nature. At the end of the story, finding him dying of a broken heart, she reveals her love for him, which transforms the Beast into a handsome prince. Beauty and the Beast not only live happily ever after, but all those who stumble into their domain in despair change, finding on their departure that their hearts are filled with goodness and beauty.

One reason *Beauty and the Beast* retains its popularity is because it strikes a familiar chord in many people. Many times we are repelled by those we do not know. But after we come to know them and they have become our friends, we cannot understand how they once seemed so foreign to us. The moral of *Beauty and the Beast* is applicable especially in small groups. Small groups almost always contain a diverse selection of individuals, and in order for a group to be successful and effective, diversity must be faced and eventually valued.

The diversity that exists among individuals creates an opportunity for both positive and negative outcomes when these individuals come together in groups to achieve a goal or complete a task (Johnson & Johnson, 1989). More specifically, *diversity among group members can result in beneficial consequences,* such as increased achievement and productivity, creative problem solving, growth in cognitive and moral reasoning, increased perspective-taking ability, improved relationships, and general sophistication in interacting and working with peers from a variety of cultural and ethnic backgrounds. On the other hand, *diversity among group members can result in harmful consequences,* such as lower achievement and productivity, closed-minded rejection of new information, increased egocentrism, and negative relationships characterized by hostility, rejection, divisiveness, scapegoating, bullying, stereotyping, prejudice, and racism. Both the positive and negative consequences of diversity on group life are discussed in this chapter.

Whether diversity leads to positive or negative outcomes in a group largely depends on group members' abilities and their willingness to understand and appreciate the diversity that exists in the group. Specifically, the outcomes of diversity depend on your abilities to (Johnson & Johnson, 1989, 1995, 1999b):

1. Recognize that diversity exists and is a valuable resource.
2. Build a coherent personal identity that includes (a) your own cultural/ethnic heritage and (b) a view of yourself as an individual who respects and values differences among individuals.
3. Understand the internal cognitive barriers (such as stereotyping and prejudice) to building relationships with diverse peers, and work to reduce the barriers.
4. Understand the dynamics of intergroup conflict (see Chapter 9).
5. Understand the social judgment process, and know how to create the process of acceptance while avoiding the process of rejection (see Chapter 3).
6. Create a cooperative context in which positive relationships among diverse individuals can be built (see Chapter 3). This requires building cooperation as

opposed to a competitive or individualistic effort. It is within a cooperative context that diverse individuals develop personal (as opposed to impersonal) relationships.

7. Manage conflicts in constructive ways. This includes (a) intellectual conflicts that are part of decision-making and learning situations (controversy) (see Chapter 8) and (b) conflicts of interest that are resolved by problem-solving negotiations and mediation (see Chapter 9).

8. Learn and internalize pluralistic, democratic values.

EXERCISE 10.1

DIVERSITY: BENEFICIAL OR HARMFUL?

Task: Your tasks are to (1) write a group report on the question, "Is diversity beneficial or harmful?" and (2) individually pass a test on the information from both sides of the issue. Your report should provide details of the advantages and disadvantages of diversity. Review the rules for constructive controversy on page 00 in Chapter 1.

A controversy about the value of diversity is raging. Imagine that you are a committee of the top four officials who are trying to decide whether diversity should be encouraged or discouraged. To ensure that both sides get a complete and fair hearing, you have divided the committee into two groups to present the best case possible for each side of the issue. Your thesis will be either of the following two choices:

_____ Diversity is a resource that has many beneficial influences.
_____ Diversity is a problem that has many harmful influences.

Cooperative: Write one report for the group of four. All members have to agree. Everyone has to be able to explain the choice made and the reasons why the choice is a good one. To help you write the best report possible, your group of four has been divided into two pairs. One pair has been assigned the position that diversity is beneficial, and the other pair has been assigned the position that diversity is harmful.

PROCEDURE

1. **Research and Prepare Your Positions:** Your group of four has been divided into two pairs. Each pair is to (a) research its assigned position, (b) organize it into a persuasive argument (thesis, rationale, conclusion), and (c) plan how to present the best case for its position to the other pair.

2. **Present and Advocate Your Position:** Make sure your assigned position receives a fair and complete hearing. Forcefully and persuasively present the best case for your position to the opposing pair. Be as convincing as possible. Take notes and clarify anything you do not understand when the opposing pair presents.

3. **Open Discussion (Advocate, Refute, Rebut):** Argue forcefully and persuasively for your position. Critically evaluate and challenge the opposing pair's information and reasoning. Defend your position from attack.

4. **Reverse Perspectives:** Reverse perspectives and present the best case for the opposing position. The opposing pair will present your position. Strive to see the issue from both perspectives simultaneously.

5. **Synthesis:** Drop all advocacy. Synthesize and integrate the best information and reasoning from both sides into a joint position on which all group members can agree. Then (a) finalize the group report, (b) plan how to present your conclusions to the class, (c) ensure that all group members are prepared to take the test, and (d) analyze how well you worked together as a group and how you could be even more effective next time.

DIVERSITY IS BENEFICIAL

You represent the prodiversity perspective. Your position is: *Diversity is a resource that has many beneficial influences.* Arguments that support your position follow. Summarize the evidence given. Research your position and find as much additional information to support it as possible. Arrange your information into a compelling, convincing, and persuasive argument showing that your position is valid and correct. Plan how best to present your assigned position to ensure that it receives a fair and complete hearing. Make at least one visual aid to help you present a persuasive case for your position.

1. **Diversity decreases stereotyping and prejudice.** It is only through direct contact and interaction with diverse individuals that stereotypes can be disconfirmed, personal relationships can be built, and prejudice can be reduced.
2. **Diversity increases the positiveness of relationships.** There is evidence that we want people we work with to achieve mutual goals. Positive relationships can lead to acceptance, respect, appreciation, and a commitment to equality.
3. **Diversity renews the vitality of society** by providing a source of energy and creativity. Music, dance, art, literature, and other aspects of culture are enriched and advanced by the mixture of different cultural traditions and ways of perceiving the world.
4. **Diversity increases achievement and productivity.** Diverse groups have a wider range of resources available for completing the task and therefore tend to have higher achievement and to be more productive than homogeneous groups.
5. **Diversity increases creative problem solving.** Diverse groups tend to be more creative in their problem solving than are homogeneous groups. The conflicts and disagreements that arise from the different perspectives and conclusions generate more creativity than is available in homogeneous groups.
6. **Diversity fosters growth in cognitive and moral reasoning.** Cognitive and moral growth depend on applying at least two different perspectives to the same issue. Without such diversity, cognitive and moral growth cannot take place.
7. **Diversity fosters perspective taking** and a broader, more sophisticated view of the world and what happens in it. Without exposure to other perspectives, perspective-taking ability cannot develop. The more able a person is to take a wide variety of perspectives, the more sophisticated the person is. Being sophisticated means that one can see the world, events, and issues from a variety of perspectives. It is through diversity that sophistication is created.
8. **Diversity builds a commitment to American democracy.** It is not possible to value a fully American democracy in a homogeneous environment. The values advocated in the Constitution and the Declaration of Independence can best be understood through the protection of minority rights and the ability of minorities to influence the decisions of the majority.

DIVERSITY IS HARMFUL

You represent the antidiversity perspective. Your position is: *Diversity is a problem that has many harmful influences.* Arguments that support your position follow. Summarize the
continued on next page

continued from previous page

evidence given. Research your position and find as much additional information to support it as possible. Arrange your information into a compelling, convincing, and persuasive argument showing that your position is valid and correct. Plan how best to present your assigned position to ensure that it receives a fair and complete hearing. Make at least one visual aid to help you present a persuasive case for your position.

1. **Diversity increases stereotyping and prejudice.** Before actual contact takes place, only vague impressions of members of other groups may exist. With actual contact with diverse individuals, stereotypes can be confirmed and prejudice can be strengthened.
2. **Diversity creates interaction strain** (feeling discomfort and uncertainty as to how to behave). Interaction strain inhibits interaction, creates ambivalence, and fosters atypical behavior, such as overfriendliness, followed by withdrawal and avoidance.
3. **Diversity increases the negativity of relationships.** There is evidence that we like people we see as similar to ourselves and dislike people who seem different. Dislike can lead to rejection, scapegoating, bullying, hostility, and even prejudice.
4. **Diversity lowers productivity.** Diversity creates difficulties in communication, coordination, and decision making. These difficulties result in spending more time trying to communicate and less time completing the task. Productivity suffers.
5. **Diversity makes life more complex and difficult.** It is easy to relate to similar people. You never have to stop and think about what to say or do. The more diverse the group, the more you have to monitor your statements and behavior to ensure that you do not inadvertently insult or hurt someone's feelings.
6. **Diversity requires more effort to relate to others.** Even talking to a person from another culture takes more concentration and effort. Accents can be distracting. Phrases can be unusual. Communicating effectively with diverse individuals takes more effort than communicating with individuals like yourself.
7. **Diversity can be threatening,** which creates defensiveness, egocentrism, and closed-minded rejection of new information. The more defensive a person is, the more closed-minded and less receptive to new information the person becomes.
8. **Diversity creates internal dissonance and anxiety** by challenging the standard ways of thinking and doing things. Strange new ways of perceiving the world and completing tasks can create dissonance about one's traditional behavior, and anxiety results. People are calmer and happier when they are with homogeneous peers.

SOURCES OF DIVERSITY

Three major sources of diversity can be identified: demographic characteristics, personality characteristics, and abilities and skills. On their own and in conjunction, these sources of diversity affect how people interact with one another. **Demographic diversity** includes culture, ethnicity, language, handicapping conditions, age, gender, social class, religion, and regional differences. North America, for example, is becoming more multicultural and multilingual. Historically, the United States always has been pluralistic, with citizens coming here from all over the world. In the 1980s alone, over 7.8 million people from over 150 different countries and speaking dozens of different languages immigrated to the United States (Table 10.1). Our common culture has been formed

TABLE 10.1   **Waves of Immigration**

ORIGIN	1820–1860	1901–1921	1970–1986
Northern, Western Europe	95%	41%	6%
Southern, Eastern Europe		44	9
Latin America			37
Asia		4	41
North America	3	6	3
Other	2	1	4

Sources: Population Reference Bureau, Bureau of the Census, Immigration and Naturalization Service.

by the interaction of various cultures and has been influenced over time by a wide variety of willing (and sometimes unwilling) European, African, and Asian immigrants as well as Native Americans. What we call American music, art, literature, language, food, and customs all show the effects of the integration of diverse cultures into one nation by representing all of these backgrounds.

In addition to demographic diversity, individuals have different personal characteristics, such as age, gender, communication style, economic background, and so on. Some people may be introverts whereas others are extroverts; some people approach problems randomly and others take a sequential approach. People from the same age group may have similar attitudes toward economic conditions and war but find that those attitudes differ greatly from the attitudes of people in a different age group. Males and females often have different opinions about interpersonal relationships. A person's education level may inform his or her attitudes toward innovation. In terms of group dynamics, group members usually have different values, attitudes, opinions, lifestyles, styles of interaction, and commitments—all of which determine the course of the group's life.

Finally, individuals differ in the **abilities and skills**—both social and technical—they bring to the group. Experts from a variety of fields, for example, may be brought together to solve a problem or conduct a project. Representatives from design, manufacturing, distribution, and sales departments may form a team to bring a new product to market. Accountants and creative artists may work together to revitalize a neighborhood. It is difficult, if not impossible, to find a productive group whose members do not have a wide variety of abilities and skills.

THE IMPORTANCE OF MANAGING DIVERSITY

The more voices we allow to speak about one thing, the more eyes, different eyes we can use to observe one thing, the more complete will our concept of this thing, our objectivity, be.

Nietzsche

Utilizing diversity in ways that produce many positive outcomes and few negative outcomes is one of the major challenges facing modern societies. Finding ways to deal with diversity is becoming increasingly important, for several reasons. *First, we increasingly live in one world.* The problems that face each person, each community, and each country cannot be solved without global cooperation and joint action. Changes in the world economy, transportation, and communication are resulting in increased interdependence among individuals, groups, organizations, communities, and societies. The more interdependent the world becomes, the more diverse the membership of any one group is likely to be. In the global village model used to speak of this world community, highly diverse individuals are interdependent and must find ways to interact and work together.

Second, diversity in most settings is inevitable; therefore, individuals need the skills to interact effectively with people from a wide variety of backgrounds. For 200,000 years humans lived in small hunting-and-gathering groups, interacting only infrequently with other nearby small groups. It is only with the recent development of worldwide interdependence and communication and transportation systems that diverse types of individuals have begun to interact with, work with, and live next to one another. In North America, Europe, and throughout the world, individuals increasingly interact with people who come from different cultures and ethnic backgrounds, speak different languages, and have grown up in markedly different conditions. In addition, people of different genders, age groups, and economic groups have more opportunities to interact with one another in modern society than they did in the past. These days, diversity among acquaintances, classmates, coworkers, neighbors, and friends is increasingly inevitable.

Third, economically there has been a globalization of business, as reflected in the increase in multinational companies, coproduction agreements, and offshore operations. More and more companies must translate their local and national perspectives into a worldview. Companies staffed by individuals skilled in building relationships with diverse types of persons have an advantage in the global market.

With increasing interdependence among people throughout the world, diversity in small groups cannot and should not be avoided or bypassed. Any group may consist of members who are diverse on a large number of personal characteristics and the abilities and skills they contribute to the group's efforts. *Tomorrow's effective groups (including large groups such as organizations and nations) will be those that have learned to be productive with a diverse membership.* The rest of this chapter, therefore, focuses on the ways groups can take full advantage of the positive consequences of diversity and can minimize the potentially negative consequences. The remainder of this chapter is divided into three sections. First, evidence is reviewed that indicates diversity in **group composition** increases productivity on a variety of tasks. Second, the difficulties with diversity that have to be faced, such as stereotypes, prejudice, racism, blaming the victim, and culture clash, are discussed. Finally, the practical procedures that groups can use to ensure that diversity is a resource and not a hindrance are presented.

THE VALUE OF DIVERSITY

Research documenting the value of diversity has focused primarily on a group's performance on a variety of tasks. Some research examines the impact of diversity on group cohesion and group conflict, which are determinants of overall group absenteeism, turnover, and satisfaction.

Group Composition and Performance on Tasks

How does heterogeneity of group membership affect group performance? Researchers have studied the degree of homogeneity–heterogeneity among members' demographic attributes, personal attributes, and abilities and skills. Three types of tasks have been studied: (1) performance on clearly defined production tasks, (2) performance on cognitive or intellective tasks, and (3) creative idea generation and decision making related to ambiguous judgmental tasks (Jackson, 1992; Johnson & Johnson, 1989; McGrath, 1984).

Production tasks have objective standards for performance evaluation and require the proficient use of perceptual and motor skills (McGrath, 1984). Haythorn (1968) conducted a comprehensive review of research on group composition and **performance tasks,** covering studies conducted primarily between 1940 and 1968. Shaw (1981), McGrath (1984), and Driskell, Hogan, and Salas (1987) have conducted subsequent reviews. These reviews indicate that relatively few studies, with mixed results, have assessed the impact of personal attribute composition on performance tasks. Two studies found performance to be higher in groups whose members were homogeneous in personal attributes (Clement & Schiereck, 1973; Fenelon & Megaree, 1971). Terborg, Castore, and DeNinno (1976), however, found attitude heterogeneity–homogeneity to be unrelated to performance in a longitudinal study of student groups working on land-surveying tasks.

To summarize this research, we can say that groups composed of members with heterogeneous technical abilities may do better on production tasks than groups composed of members with homogeneous technical abilities (Jackson, 1992). Pelz (1956) found that more productive scientists and engineers tended to create informal communication networks with dissimilar peers. The productivity among scientists and engineers correlated positively with their frequency of contact with colleagues whose training and expertise were dissimilar to their own. Such networks resemble loosely structured heterogeneous groups. Voiers (1956) found that heterogeneous abilities facilitated the performance of B-29 bomber crews when the crews could take advantage of the ability heterogeneity by assigning members to tasks for which they were best suited. In addition, athletic teams with more diverse skills, such as good offensive and defensive units, have been found to outperform teams with less diverse skills.

Intellective tasks are problem-solving tasks with correct answers (McGrath, 1984). Wood (1987) reviewed the research on the impact of gender differences on group performance. He found twelve studies in which objective performance results (accuracy and speed) could be compared for same- versus mixed-sex groups. He found weak support for the conclusion that mixed-sex groups tend to outperform same-sex groups, whether male or female. Similar findings have been reported in studies of more complex learning tasks (R. Johnson, Johnson, Scott, & Ramolae, 1985; Peterson, Johnson, & Johnson, 1991). Laughlin and colleagues (see Laughlin, 1980), for example, have demonstrated that in problem-solving groups, "truth supported wins." Furthermore, when heterogeneity increases the probability that the group contains some members who are capable of determining the correct answer to the problems being solved, mixed-attribute groups should outperform homogeneous groups. Other studies have demonstrated that groups made up of individuals with different ability levels (high, medium, low) outperform individuals on intellective tasks (Johnson & Johnson, 1989).

Decision-making tasks involve reaching a consensus about the best solution to a problem when the "correct" answer is not known (McGrath, 1984). Research reviews indicate that heterogeneous groups are more likely than homogeneous groups to be creative and to reach high-quality decisions (Fiedler, Meuwese, & Conk, 1961; Filley, House, & Kerr, 1976; Frick, 1973; Hoffman, 1979; Johnson, 1977; Johnson & Johnson, 1989; McGrath, 1984; Shaw, 1981; Torrance, 1961; Webb, 1977). The conclusion holds for a variety of personal attributes, including personality (Hoffman & Maier, 1961), leadership abilities (Ghiselli & Lodahl, 1958), types of training (Pelz, 1956), and attitudes (Hoffman, Harburg, & Maier, 1962b; Triandis, Hall, & Ewen, 1965; Willems & Clark, 1971).

In one decision-making task study, Ziller, Behringer, and Goodchilds (1962) created heterogeneity in some groups by changing the group members (open groups); other groups maintained the same members (closed groups). The researchers asked the groups to write cartoon captions. Captions written by the heterogeneous (open) groups were judged to have greater fluency and originality. Pelz and Andrews (1966) also found that groups with fluid membership are likely to be more creative, even when the groups are interdisciplinary. They concluded that when scientists from interdisciplinary teams worked closely together on a daily basis, within three years they became homogeneous in their perspectives and approach to solving problems.

Although diverse perspectives are potentially advantageous, heterogeneous groups may not always function at an optimal level. Hill (1982) reviewed several studies whose results indicated that on creative and decision-making tasks, the performance of interacting groups was less than their potential, as estimated by statistical pooling. Hall and Williams (1966), however, found exactly the opposite. Furthermore, in a field study of 119 top management teams in the banking industry in six Midwestern states, Bantel and Jackson (1989) found that the more heterogeneous (in terms of job expertise) the decision-making teams, the more frequently the bank adopted new, innovative practices.

Overall, whether for better or worse, the range of skills and abilities a group can access in its diverse members affects its performance on creative and decision-making tasks. Laughlin and Bitz (1975) used a word-association task to compare the performance of groups composed of members with dissimilar ability levels with the performance of individuals whose ability was equivalent to that of the highest-ability group member. They found that the groups outperformed the high-ability individuals. Their findings suggest that high-ability members can benefit from interaction with others who have less ability, perhaps because the high-ability individuals take on the role of teacher, which leads them to sharpen their own thinking. Or perhaps the questions and input of more naive members encourage the more expert members to re-examine the assumptions and rules they automatically use when dealing with issues and problems in which they are experts (Simon, 1979). This re-examination increases the likelihood that unwarranted assumptions are reconsidered and rules are re-examined for exceptions.

Overall, the evidence indicates that when working on complex, nonroutine problems (a situation that requires some degree of creativity), groups are more effective when composed of individuals with diverse types of skills, knowledge, abilities, and perspectives. The results of the research on group composition and task performance are summarized in Table 10.2.

Other Outcomes

Other group outcomes affected by diversity among group members include absenteeism, turnover, and satisfaction. Often, these other outcomes are nearly as important as group performance to groups and organizations (Nadler, Hackman, & Lawler, 1979; Schmidt, 1974). Absenteeism, turnover, and satisfaction levels largely are determined

TABLE 10.2 **Impact of Group Composition on Outcomes**

TYPES OF OUTCOMES	PERSONAL ATTRIBUTES	ABILITIES AND SKILLS
Production tasks	The few studies found mixed results, so no clear effect of group composition on performance is proved.	The few studies found that heterogeneity of types and levels of ability increases productivity.
Intellective tasks	Overall, there are not enough studies to allow a conclusion to be drawn. Mixed-sex groups may outperform same-sex groups	Almost no directly relevant research
Decision-making tasks	Heterogeneous groups outperform homogeneous groups.	Heterogeneity of ability levels is beneficial.
Cohesion	Heterogeneous groups are somewhat less cohesive and have higher turnover rates.	Almost no direct research
Conflict	More conflicts tend to occur in heterogeneous groups.	Almost no direct research

by the levels of cohesion and conflict that exist in a group. A group that does not handle diversity well may not achieve the necessary level of cohesion that keeps a group together. It also may not handle other types of conflict well, leading to higher levels of absenteeism and turnover and lower levels of satisfaction among group members.

Research on the topic of how group diversity affects levels of group cohesion and conflict has come to a variety of conclusions. Haythorn (1968), for one, reviewed evidence and concluded that the effects of *personality heterogeneity–homogeneity* on cohesion depended on a number of factors, including personality characteristics, task characteristics, and extent of interpersonal contact. Bantel and Jackson (1989), in their field study of decision-making teams at 119 banks in six states, found no relationship between team heterogeneity and cohesiveness. Jackson, Brett, Sessa, Cooper, Julin, and Peyronnin (1991), in a follow-up study, found that the demographically homogeneous teams had lower turnover and were more likely to fill vacancies with employees from inside the firm, both of which may indicate higher cohesion.

Turnover tends to be higher in work groups composed of members who are more diverse with respect to their *ages* and *years of organizational tenure* (e.g., Jackson et al., 1991; McCain, O'Reilly, & Pfeffer, 1983; O'Reilly, Caldwell, & Barnett, 1989). Turnover also is higher in groups whose members are heterogeneous in terms of college alma mater, curriculum studied, and industry experiences (Jackson et al., 1991).

Attitude similarity has been found to be related mildly to group cohesion. Some evidence exists that people are attracted to others with similar attitudes (Byrne, 1971; Heider, 1958; Newcomb, 1961) and that group members tend to become more similar in their attitudes as they interact over time (Newcomb, 1956). Terborg, Castore, and DeNinno (1976), however, conducted one of the few studies in which attitudes were assessed directly and then used to assemble groups. In their longitudinal investigation of student groups, cohesiveness was assessed at six points in time. At each assessment, cohesiveness was greater in the groups composed of members who had similar attitudes. The magnitude of the effect of attitude similarity on cohesiveness did not approach statistical significance, however, until the last three assessments.

Finally, heterogeneity among group members promotes increased argumentation and more conflict (Nijhof & Kommers, 1982). Such conflicts can be beneficial for completing complex problem-solving tasks (Cosier, 1981; Janis, 1972; Johnson & Johnson, 1979, 1989, 1992a; Schweiger, Sandberg, & Rechner, 1989; Schwenk, 1983). Review Chapter 8 for a discussion of how conflict and controversy can lead to improved group performance and effectiveness.

Disadvantages of Homogeneity of Membership

The alternative to having groups with diverse members is to build a homogeneous group. Although this option may sound like a good way to improve group performance, group homogeneity has a number of disadvantages. *First,* homogeneous groups may lack the controversy and clash of perspectives so essential to high-quality decision making and creative thinking. Too many members who think alike and see the world the same way make for a dull and mediocre group. *Second,* such groups tend to avoid taking risks (Bantel & Jackson, 1989) and therefore, may miss opportunities to increase their productivity. *Third,* they more frequently engage in groupthink (Janis, 1972).

Fourth, they tend to function best in static situations; they have trouble adapting to changing conditions.

Bringing diverse individuals together does not result automatically in positive outcomes, however (Johnson & Johnson, 1989). Proximity is a necessary condition for the positive potential of diversity to be realized, but it is not sufficient in itself. What proximity does create is visibility and initial contact. The initial contact often is dominated by *interaction strain* (individuals feel discomfort and uncertainty as to how to behave). Interaction strain inhibits interaction, creates ambivalence, and fosters atypical behavior such as overfriendliness followed by withdrawal and avoidance.

Under competitive and individualistic conditions, furthermore, pluralism and diversity may cause problems. Diversity can result in lower achievement due to increased difficulties in communication and coordination. It can create threat, defensiveness, increased egocentrism, and closed-minded rejection of new information. Direct interaction among diverse individuals in competitive situations also can create negative relationships characterized by hostility, rejection, divisiveness, scapegoating, bullying, stereotyping, and prejudice, all of which are discussed in the next section.

Conclusions

A number of problems can be found with the existing research on group composition and how it affects groups' interactions and outcomes. *First, in considering member heterogeneity, it is difficult to determine what attributes are important.* The research has focused on personal attributes (such as personality, attitudes, gender, ethnicity) and skills and abilities. These two categories have been focused on because they can be measured and group members can be selected based on them. It is not clear that they are the variables that affect team performance, however.

Second, no one attribute is likely to make much difference in the complexity of real work. Thus, multiattribute research may be more important. Instead of studying the impact of gender, ethnicity, age, or cognitive style, studies that track composition along all of these dimensions simultaneously are needed.

Third, organizations employ people to perform a wide variety of both simple and complex tasks that involve perceptual and motor performance, intellective performance, creativity, and judgmental decision making. Groups may be working on a variety of tasks simultaneously, and the tasks they are doing today may not be the same as those they will work on tomorrow. Over time, the tasks a group faces are unpredictable; therefore, the safest thing to do is to maximize the heterogeneity in the group.

Fourth, it is difficult to determine what is and is not diversity. What outsiders may define as heterogeneity may not be perceived as such by insiders. Turner (1987), in his discussion of self-categorization theory, argues that many group phenomena (including cohesiveness and cooperation) are influenced by the self-categorizations of group members. Specifically, psychological ingroups form when people perceive themselves to be relatively similar to one another in some way(s) and relatively different from others, who are viewed as the outgroup. Thus, in order to judge whether a group is heterogeneous or homogeneous with respect to an attribute, it is important to consider how the group defines diversity in that regard.

Fifth, little is known about precisely how group composition and tasks interact to affect performance. Thus, recommendations cannot be made about the procedures and strategies group members should use to make their diversity work for them and improve their productivity. If not enough is known to make recommendations about specific, limited, artificial situations, then in the complex real world, recommendations about using heterogeneous groups are impossible.

Finally, group members simultaneously are both heterogeneous and homogeneous. Each person has hundreds of characteristics and abilities. Members who are homogeneous on one or two attributes are heterogeneous with respect to others. Conversely, members who are heterogeneous with respect to several attributes still share other common attributes. In truth, it is nearly impossible to create a completely homogeneous group. *Clearly, it is unrealistic to cope with the diversity of people by attempting to completely control the composition of groups.* Instead, we need to find ways to manage groups to ensure that the positive consequences of heterogeneity are maximized and the potentially negative consequences of heterogeneity are minimized.

Because diversity is inevitable and ever increasing, the choice to avoid diversity does not exist for most people. In school, on the job, and in the community, you interact with people who are different from you in many ways, whether or not you wish to do so. The promise of diversity far outweighs the problems as long as the individuals involved understand how to capitalize on the benefits while avoiding the pitfalls. The greater the understanding of human relations, for example, the more constructive the results of diversity will be.

BARRIERS TO INTERACTING WITH DIVERSE PEERS

We know that diversity among group members is an important resource that can be utilized to improve the group's productivity. We also know that doing so may not be easy. A number of barriers exist to interacting effectively with diverse peers (Johnson, 2003; Johnson & Johnson, 1999b). They include stereotyping, prejudice, the tendency to blame the victim, and cultural clashes.

Stereotypes

Stereotypes can be found everywhere, and everyone makes and uses them. Stereotypes are a product of the way the mind stores, organizes, and recalls information. They are used to describe differences among groups and to predict how others will behave. They reduce complexity, help us make quick decisions, fill in the gaps in what we know, help us make sense out of who we are and what has happened to us, and help us create and recognize the patterns needed to draw conclusions. In and of themselves, stereotypes do not necessarily have to be bad. Unfortunately, stereotypes often are the basis for unfairness and injustice in the way people deal with one another.

The term *stereotype* was first used in the eighteenth century to describe a printing process designed to duplicate pages of type. In the nineteenth century, psychiatrists used the term *stereotypy* to describe a behavior of persistent repetitiveness and unchanging mode of expression. Modern use of the term *stereotype* originated with Lippmann (1922) in his book, *Public Opinion*. He argued, "there is neither time nor opportunity for intimate acquaintance. Instead we notice a trait which marks a well known type, and fill in the rest of the picture by means of the stereotypes we carry about in our heads" (p. 59).

In modern usage, a **stereotype** is defined as a belief that associates a whole group of people with certain traits. Stereotypes (1) are cognitive; (2) reflect a set of related beliefs rather than an isolated bit of information; (3) describe attributes, personalities, and characters so that groups can be compared and differentiated; and (4) are shared by individuals and groups holding them (Ashmore & Del Boca, 1979). In these ways, stereotypes function as simplifiers and organizers of social information. They reduce the complexity of the social environment and make it more manageable.

People form stereotypes in two ways. First, they categorize by sorting single objects into groups rather than thinking of each one as unique. Second, they differentiate between ingroups and outgroups. People commonly assume that the members of outgroups are quite similar but recognize that the members of the ingroup they identify with are quite diverse (*outgroup homogeneity effect*). The failure to notice differences among outgroup members may result from lack of personal contact with people from these outgroups. A white person, for example, may see all Hispanics as being alike, but someone with a wide variety of Hispanic friends may see little similarity among Puerto Ricans, Cubans, Mexicans, and Argentineans.

An efficient cognitive system, which stereotyping can be, does more than simply make cognition easy for people at all costs. It also helps people in ways that maximize the informational value they can gain for the effort they expend. In this regard, stereotyping is efficient, for several reasons. First, the social categorization that precedes stereotyping reduces the amount of information that must be attended to each time an individual is encountered. In other words, when you view a certain group in one light, you reduce the need to form individualized impressions of each category member (Allport, 1954; Brewer, 1988; Fiske & Neuberg, 1990; Hamilton & Sherman, 1994; Lippmann, 1922). Second, stereotypes expand your base of knowledge by allowing you to infer a person's attributes without having to attend carefully to the person's behavior (Brewer, 1988; Fiske & Neuberg, 1990; Hamilton & Sherman, 1994; Medin, 1988; Sherman, 1996). Through the relatively simple act of social categorization, stereotypes allow you to gain a large amount of "functionally accurate" information (Swann, 1984), thus resulting in a beneficial ratio of information gained to effort expended.

Although stereotypes do allow people to make assumptions about individuals in a relatively efficient manner, stereotypes also have the power to cause harm. When taken to extremes, the above-mentioned benefits instead become a crutch that allows people to avoid interacting with others on their own merits. Stereotyping can become a kind of shorthand that unfairly defines individuals, because the person holding the stereotype does not take the time to interact with the individual as his or her own person. When this happens, we end up with stereotypes such as men are more competitive than women, black people are better athletes than white people, Asian people work harder than Americans, and so on. In short, stereotypes can lead to false generalizations aimed at an entire group of people, generalizations that prevent that group from being seen as individuals within a group.

People who hold strong stereotypes often are prone to the *fundamental attribution error*. That is, they attribute negative behavior on the part of a minority-group member to dispositional characteristics. Positive behavior by a minority-group member, on the other hand, is believed to be the result of situational factors. When it comes to judging their own behavior, however, negative behavior is attributed to situational causes and positive behavior is viewed as dispositional. When a minority-group member acts in an undesirable way, the attribution is "That's the way those people are" or "Those people are born like that." If the minority-group member is seen engaging in desirable behavior, the person holding the stereotype might view that individual as "an exception to the rule."

Stereotypes are perpetuated and protected in four ways. *First*, stereotypes influence what we perceive and remember about the actions of outgroup members. The social categories we use to process information about the world control what we tend to perceive and not perceive. Our prejudice makes us notice the negative traits we ascribe to the groups we are prejudiced against. Furthermore, when individuals expect members of an outgroup to behave in a certain way, they tend to recall more accurately instances that confirm rather than disconfirm their expectations. Hence, if an outgroup is perceived to be of low intelligence, individuals tend to remember instances in which an outgroup member was confused in class or failed a test. But they tend to forget instances in which an outgroup member achieved a 4.0 grade point average or became class valedictorian (Rothbart, Evans, & Fulero, 1979).

Second, stereotypes create an oversimplified picture of outgroup members. The act of categorization itself leads people to assume similarity among the members of a category. Even when the distinctions between groups are arbitrary, people tend to minimize the differences they see among members of the same group and to accentuate the differences between members of two different groups. When processing information about their ingroups and outgroups, people develop relatively simplistic and nonspecific pictures of outgroups. The larger the outgroup, the more likely it is that oversimplifications occur. Individuals, furthermore, do more than simply note the differences between their ingroup and the outgroups. They often attempt to emphasize the differences and take actions that discriminate in favor of their own group.

Third, individuals tend to overestimate the similarity of behavior among outgroup members. Because outgroups are perceived to be homogeneous, the actions of one member can be generalized to all. If an older person witnesses one teenager driving recklessly, it may be a short jump for the older person to stereotype that all teenage drivers are reckless.

Fourth, stereotypes can lead to scapegoating. A **scapegoat** is a guiltless but defenseless group that is attacked to provide an outlet for another group's pent-up anger and frustration. The term *scapegoat* comes from a biblical guilt-transference ritual in which a group's sins are conveyed to a goat, which then is sent out into the wilderness, taking the sins along.

Scapegoating might look like this in action: Group 1 interferes with group 2, and group 2 should respond by retaliating against group 1. If, however, group 1 is extremely powerful, too distant, or too difficult to locate, group 2 may respond by turning its aggression on group 3. Group 3, although in no way responsible for the difficulties group 2 experienced, nonetheless would be blamed and thereby become the target of group 2's aggressive actions. Stereotypes of certain outgroups can create a continual scapegoat that is blamed for all problems and difficulties, no matter what their origins.

People who are stereotyped are affected not only by the increased possibility of being treated unfairly by those holding the stereotypes, but also by the possibility of accepting the stereotype themselves. In other words, people who are stereotyped might come to accept the stereotype and believe it, modifying their behaviors and actions to fit the stereotype. When a widely known negative stereotype (e.g., poor intellectual ability)

WHY DO STEREOTYPES ENDURE?

Following are several reasons why stereotypes persist. Rank them from most important (1) to least important (7). Write down the rationale for your ranking. Find a partner and share your ranking and rationale, listen to his or her ranking and rationale, and cooperatively create a new, improved ranking and rationale. Then find another pair and repeat the procedure in a group of four.

Rank	Reason
_____	The tendency for people to overestimate the association between variables that are only slightly correlated or not correlated at all (i.e., **illusionary correlation**). Many people, for example, perceive that being poor and being lazy are associated. Any poor person who is not hard at work the moment you notice him or her may be perceived as lazy. Low-power groups can acquire negative traits easily and, once acquired, the stereotype is hard to lose.
_____	Your prejudice makes you notice the negative traits you ascribe to the groups you are prejudiced against, and you more readily believe information that confirms your stereotypes than evidence that challenges them. People tend to process information in ways that verify existing beliefs. This is known as the *confirmation bias* (the tendency to seek, interpret, and create information that verifies existing beliefs).
_____	You tend to have a **false consensus bias** by believing that most other people share your stereotypes (see poor people as being lazy). You tend to see your own behavior and judgments as quite common and appropriate, and to view alternative responses as uncommon and often inappropriate.
_____	Your stereotypes tend to be *self-fulfilling*. Stereotypes can subtly influence intergroup interactions in such a way that the stereotype is behaviorally confirmed. You can behave in ways that elicit the actions you expect from outgroup members, thus confirming your stereotype.
_____	You dismiss individuals who do not match your stereotype as exceptions to the rule or representatives of a subcategory.
_____	Your stereotypes often operate at an implicit level without your conscious awareness.
_____	You often develop a rationale and explanation to justify your stereotypes and prejudices.

exists about a group, it creates for its members a burden of suspicion that acts as a threat. This threat arises whenever individuals' behavior can be interpreted in terms of a stereotype—that is, whenever group members run the risk of confirming the stereotype.

Steele and Aronson (1995), in studying *stereotype threat,* found that negative stereotypes about blacks' intellectual ability created a "situational pressure" that distracted black students and depressed their academic performance. They suggest that stereotype threat is the reason for the underachievement of black students. Seventy percent of black college students drop out of college (as opposed to about 35% of white students), and the dropout rate is the highest among black students ranked in the top third by SAT scores. In addition, black students with the highest SAT scores fail more frequently than black students with lower scores and at a rate more than three times that of whites with similar scores. When blacks are placed in achievement situations, the negative stereotypes are activated and black students become more self-conscious and work less efficiently. Similar findings were reported on a study of lower-class individuals (Croizet & Claire, 1998). Stereotype threat is eliminated in programs such as the University of Michigan's Twenty-First Century Program, where black and white students are randomly recruited, live together, study together cooperatively, and have personal discussions on social issues.

As the program at the University of Michigan suggests, stereotypes can be changed. The more personal information you have about someone, the less likely you are to stereotype him or her. The more time and energy you have to consider the person's characteristics and behavior, the less you stereotype. The more motivated you are to form an accurate impression of someone, the less you stereotype. The more you perceive that individualized person to be typical of the stereotyped group, the more your interaction changes your stereotypes. What these factors indicate is that in order for stereotypes to change, members of different groups need to interact for prolonged periods of time under conditions in which they get to know one another personally and see one another as being typical members of their group.

Prejudice and Discrimination

To know one's self is wisdom, but to know one's neighbor is genius.

Minna Antrim

To be prejudiced means, literally, to prejudge. **Prejudice** can be defined as an unjustified negative attitude toward a person based solely on that individual's membership in a group other than one's own. Stereotypes taken to extremes, prejudices are judgments made about others that establish a superiority/inferiority belief system. If one person dislikes another simply because that other person is a member of a different ethnic group, sex, religion, or other group, we are dealing with prejudice.

Ethnocentrism is the tendency to regard one's own ethnic group, nation, religion, or culture as better or more "correct" than others. The word is derived from *ethnic,* meaning a group united by similar customs, characteristics, race, or other common factors, and *center.* When ethnocentrism is present, the standards and values of our culture are used as a yardstick to measure the worth of other ethnic groups. Ethnocentrism often is perpetuated by *cultural conditioning.* As children we are raised to fit into a particular culture. We are conditioned to respond to various situations as we see others in our culture react. Based on that conditioning, when we encounter someone from outside that culture, we may react negatively to his or her ways of doing things.

Related to ethnocentrism, **racism** is prejudice directed at people because of their race or ethnic membership. Science indicates that only one human race exists, with many variations, but many people assume biological differences exist as evidenced by physical appearances. Although race has dubious value as a scientific classification system, it has had real consequences for the life experiences and life opportunities of many nonwhite groups. Race has taken on social meaning suggesting one's status within the social system. This status structure introduces power differences as people of different races interact with one another.

Overall, prejudices deal with the formation of unfounded and often inaccurate opinions about a group, leading to biased behavior against members of that group. Other common forms of prejudice are **sexism,** prejudice directed at someone because of his or her gender, and **ageism,** prejudice against the elderly. Many other types of "isms" can be located in our society; they can be based on anything from physical appearance to religious beliefs.

Traditionally, in the United States, racism, sexism, and other prejudices were expressed through statements that indicated such views merely reflected the "natural world order." Examples include, "Blacks are not as smart as whites" and "Women are too emotional to be good managers." The negative evaluations these types of statements represented were the foundation of institutional and societal measures that preserved separation of groups and social injustice.

Beginning with the civil rights movement in the 1960s, however, much work has been put into making people see one another as individuals, not as members of an ethnic, gender, or other type of group. To a certain extent, much progress has been made on this front. On the other hand, the concept of **modern racism** posits that if we scratch the apparently nonracist surface of many people, we often find bigotry lurking beneath. Modern racism and sexism camouflage prejudices within more sophisticated language, but the basic beliefs are the same, as evidenced by such statements as "Blacks and women have gone too far; they are pushing for jobs they do not deserve" (Swim, Aikin, Hall, & Hunter, 1995). Racism arises in the modern era because people can see themselves as being fair, humanitarian, and egalitarian while at the same time holding a somewhat negative view of members of groups other than their own.

Having prejudiced thoughts, however, does not necessarily make you a racist (Devine, Monteith, Zuwerink, & Elliot, 1991). Even those who completely reject prejudice may sometimes experience unintentional prejudice, including thoughts and feelings based on prior learning or experiences. In this case, racism is like a lingering bad habit that surfaces despite people's best efforts to avoid it. As with all bad habits, with enough commitment and support, racism can be eradicated.

When prejudice is acted on, it is discrimination. **Discrimination** is an action taken to harm a group or any of its members. It is a negative, often aggressive action aimed at the target of prejudice. Discrimination is aimed at denying members of the targeted groups treatment and opportunities equal to those afforded to the dominant group.

To reduce your prejudices, use of stereotypes, and potential to discriminate, the following steps may be helpful (Johnson & Johnson, 1999b):

1. Admit that you have prejudices (everyone does; you are no exception) and commit yourself to reducing them.
2. Identify the stereotypes that reflect your prejudices and modify them.
3. Identify the actions that reflect your prejudices and modify them.
4. Seek feedback from diverse friends and colleagues about how well you are valuing and communicating respect for diversity.

Blaming the Victim and Attribution Theory

Many people believe the world is a just place where people generally get what they deserve. If you win the lottery, it must be because you are a nice person who deserves some good luck. If you are robbed, it must be because you were careless and wanted to be punished for past misdeeds. Any person who is mugged in a dark alley while carrying a great deal of cash may be seen as "asking to be robbed." Relatedly, most people tend to believe that they deserve what happens to them. Victims of violence, for example, often believe they "deserved" to be attacked because of some misdeed on their part. It is all too easy to forget that victims do not have the benefit of hindsight to guide their actions in the moment, however.

Errors in Making Decisions About Diverse Others

Making a decision requires gathering information on each major alternative action and inferring from the information which alternative will maximize gain and minimize costs.

Errors in Making Inferences

Relying on small samples	Small samples are highly unreliable.
Relying on biased samples	People often ignore clear information about how typical and representative a sample is.
Underutilization of base-rate information	People tend to pay more attention to a single concrete instance than to valid base-rate information, perhaps because the single concrete instance is vivid and salient and thus more compelling.

Errors from Cognitive Heuristics

Availability heuristic	Estimating the frequency of some event by the ease with which you can bring instances to mind. People tend to overestimate the frequency of events that are easy to remember.
Representativeness heuristic	Seeing how well the information matches some imagined average or typical person in the category; the closer the person is to the prototype, the more likely we are to judge the person to be in the category.

Weighing Information

Positive frame	People avoid risks and opt for the "sure thing."
Negative frame	People take risks to avoid costs.
Postdecision rationalization	The alternative chosen becomes more attractive and the alternatives not chosen become less desirable.

So what happens when situations appear to be unjust? One method is to blame the victim by convincing ourselves that no injustice has occurred. When someone is a victim of prejudice, stereotyping, and discrimination, all too often he or she is seen as "doing *something* wrong." **Blaming the victim** occurs when we attribute the cause of discrimination or misfortune to the personal characteristics and actions of the victim. The situation is examined for potential causes that enable us to maintain our belief in a just world. If the victim can be blamed for causing the discrimination, then we can believe the future is predictable and controllable because everyone gets what he or she deserves.

Blaming the victim occurs as we try to attribute a cause to events. We constantly interpret the meaning of our behavior and events that occur in our lives. Many times we want to figure out why we acted in a particular way or why a certain outcome occurred. If we get angry when someone infers we are stupid but not when someone calls us "clumsy," we want to know why we are so sensitive about our intelligence. When we are standing on a street corner after a rainstorm and a car splashes us with water, we want to know whether it was caused by our carelessness, the driver's meanness, or just bad luck.

This process of explaining or inferring the causes of events has been termed *causal attribution*. An attribution is an inference drawn about the causes of a behavior or event. Any behavior or event can have a variety of possible causes. We observe the behavior or event and then infer the cause. When our boss criticizes our work, for example, we can attribute his or her behavior to a grouchy mood, being under too much pressure, disliking us, or the sloppiness of our work.

Causal attribution begins early in childhood, when we begin observing our own behavior and drawing conclusions about ourselves. We seem to have a fundamental need to understand both our own behavior and the behavior of others. In trying to understand why a behavior or event occurred, we generally choose to attribute causes either to internal personal factors or external situational factors. Internal personal factors are such things as effort and ability, while external situational factors include luck, task difficulty, or the behavior/personality of other people. For example, if you do well on a test, you can attribute it to your hard work and great intelligence (an internal attribution) or to the fact that the test was incredibly easy (an external attribution). When a friend drops out of school, you can attribute it to a lack of motivation (an internal attribution) or a lack of money (an external attribution).

Dimensions of Attributions				**Success Orientation**		
	Stable	**Unstable**			**Stable**	**Unstable**
Internal	Ability	Effort	**Success**		Ability	Effort
External	Task difficulty	Luck	**Failure**		Task difficulty	Luck

People make causal attributions to explain their successes and failures. Frequently such attributions are *self-serving,* designed to permit us to take credit for positive outcomes and to avoid blame for negative ones. We have a systematic tendency to claim that our successes are due to our ability and efforts, whereas our failures are due to bad luck, obstructive people, or task difficulty. We also have a systematic tendency to claim responsibility for the success of group efforts ("It was all my idea in the first place, and I did most of the work") and avoid responsibility for group failures ("If the other members had tried harder, this would not have happened").

Culture Clash

Another common barrier to interacting effectively with diverse groupmates is a cultural clash. A **culture clash** is a conflict over basic values that occurs among individuals from different cultures. The most common form occurs when members of minority groups question the values of the majority. Common reactions by majority-group members when their values are being questioned are feeling:

1. *Threatened:* Their responses include avoidance, denial, and defensiveness.
2. *Confused:* Their responses include seeking more information in an attempt to redefine the problem.
3. *Enhanced:* Their responses include heightened anticipation, awareness, and positive actions that lead to solving the problem.

GUIDELINES FOR DEALING WITH DIVERSITY

1. Recognize that diversity among members is ever present and unavoidable.
2. Recognize that the more interdependent the world becomes, the more important it is to be able to work effectively with diverse groupmates.
3. Maximize heterogeneity among members in both personal characteristics and abilities in order to maximize the group's productivity and success.
4. With heterogeneous membership comes increased conflict. Structure constructive procedures for managing conflicts among group members.
5. Identify and eliminate barriers to the utilization of diversity (stereotyping, prejudice, blaming the victim, cultural clashes).
6. Ensure that diversity is utilized as a resource by strengthening the positive interdependence within the group in order to create a context in which diversity is a resource, not a hindrance.
7. Ensure that diversity is utilized as a strength by uniting the personal identities of members of diverse groups. Create a superordinate identity based on a pluralistic set of values. Encourage individuals to develop:
   a. An appreciation for their own gender, religious, ethnic, and cultural backgrounds.
   b. An appreciation for the gender, religious, ethnic, and cultural backgrounds of other group members.
   c. A strong superordinate identity of "group member" that transcends the differences among members.
   d. A pluralistic set of values concerning equality, freedom, the rights of individual members, and the responsibilities of group membership.
8. Ensure that diversity is utilized as a strength by fostering personal relationships among members that allow for candid discussions that increase members' sophistication about their differences.
9. Ensure that diversity is utilized as a strength by clarifying miscommunications among diverse group members.

Many cultural clashes develop in and between groups. These clashes range from threatening to confusing to enhancing. When handled properly, cultural clashes are another form of conflict; they can serve as learning experiences rather than barriers.

As prejudice, stereotyping, and discrimination are reduced, the tendency to blame the victim is avoided, and cultural clashes become enhancing rather than threatening experiences. At this point, the stage is set for everyone to recognize and value diversity.

MAKING MEMBER DIVERSITY A STRENGTH

Diversity among members in any group is a potential source of creativity and productivity. For group members to capitalize on their differences, they must:

1. Ensure that a high level of positive interdependence exists among group members.
2. Create a superordinate group identity that (a) unites the diverse personal identities of group members and (b) is based on a pluralistic set of values.
3. Gain sophistication about the differences among members through personal relationships that allow for candid discussions.
4. Clarify miscommunications among group members from different cultures, ethnic and historical backgrounds, social classes, genders, age cohorts, and so forth.

Structuring and strengthening positive interdependence is discussed thoroughly in Chapter 3, so here we discuss the subsequent steps a group must take to make diversity work for rather than against them.

Creating a Superordinate Group Identity

Diverse individuals from different gender, religious, social class, ethnic, and cultural backgrounds come together in small-group settings. The results can be positive if group members get to know one another, appreciate and value the vitality of diversity, and learn how to use their diversity for creative problem solving and enhanced productivity. In order for these measures to be taken, group members must internalize a common superordinate identity that binds them all together. That is, they must arrive at a single group identity that, while larger than any individual member, also encompasses all of the diversity present in the group. It is the creation of one from many.

Creating an *unum* (one) from *pluribus* (many) is done in four steps. *First, group members must have an appreciation for their own historic, cultural, ethnic, and religious backgrounds as well as their other important personal characteristics.* Members should value and recognize the culture, history, and homeland of their ancestors as part of their personal identities. A *personal identity* is a consistent set of attitudes that defines "who you are" (see Johnson [1999] for a full discussion on developing a personal identity). An identity helps a person cope with stress, provides stability and consistency to the person's life, and directs what information is attended to, how it is organized, and how it is remembered. A personal identity consists of multiple subidentities that are organized into a coherent, stable, and integrated whole. The subidentities include a *gender identity* (fundamental sense of maleness or femaleness), a *cultural identity*

BEING AN AMERICAN

Being an American is creedal rather than racial or ancestral. It is our belief that "all [humans] are created equal and endowed by their creator with certain inalienable rights" (i.e., our commitment to the Constitution, Bill of Rights, and Declaration of Independence of the United States) that provide our superordinate identity as Americans. To be an American is to adopt a set of values concerning democracy, freedom, liberty, equality, justice, the rights of individuals, and the responsibilities of citizenship (Johnson & Johnson, 1994). It is these values that form the American creed. The common commitment to equality, justice, and liberty for all unites us as one people, even though we are the descendants of many cultures, races, religions, and ethnic groups. Each cultural group is part of the whole, and members of each new immigrant group, while modifying and enriching our national identity, learn that they are first and foremost Americans. America is one of the few successful examples of a pluralistic society where different groups clashed but ultimately learned to live together by achieving a sense of common nationhood. In our diversity, there has always been a broad recognition that we are one people. Whatever our origins, we are all Americans. It is from the following four steps that the United States creates an *unum* from *pluribus*.

1. I respect, appreciate, and value my religious, ethnic, and cultural background.

2. I respect, appreciate, and value the religious, ethnic, and cultural backgrounds of others.

3. I have a strong superordinate identity as an "American." Being an American is creedal. I believe in the American creed.

4. I have pluralistic values. I value democracy, freedom, liberty, equality, justice, the rights of individuals, and the responsibilities of citizenship.

(sense of origins and membership in a culture), an *ethnic identity* (sense of belonging to one particular ethnic group), a *religious identity* (sense of belonging to one particular religious group), and so forth. Each of these subidentities should be recognized and valued, and they need to be organized into a coherent, stable, and integrated overall sense of self. Respect for one's subidentities may be the basis for self-respect.

Second, group members develop an appreciation for the historic, cultural, ethnic, and religious backgrounds and other important personal characteristics of other group members. A critical aspect of developing a historical, cultural, and ethnic identity is whether ethnocentricity is inherent in one's definition of oneself. A personal identity that includes one's heritage must be developed in a way that does not lead to rejecting the heritages of other people. The degree to which a group member's identity leads to respect for and valuing of other members' diversity depends on developing a superordinate identity that subsumes both one's own heritage and the heritage of all other group members. Members need to learn how to express respect for diverse backgrounds and value them as a resource that increases the quality of life and adds to the viability of the group.

Third, encourage members to develop a strong superordinate identity of "group member" that transcends the differences among members. Being a member of a work group is decided by circumstance rather than by ancestry or religion. The work group unites widely diverse people. In essence, the work group has its own culture that supersedes the individual cultures of members. Members need to learn how to highlight the group's super ordinate identity and use it to resolve conflicts based on members' differences.

Fourth, group members adopt a pluralistic set of values concerning democracy, freedom, liberty, equality, justice, the rights of individuals, and the responsibilities of citizenship. All members have a say in how the group operates. All members are free to speak their minds and give their opinions. All members are considered to be of equal value. Every member has the right and responsibility to contribute his or her resources and efforts toward achieving the group's goals. Each member has a right to expect the group to be considerate of his or her needs and wants. All members must at times put the good of the group above their own needs and desires. It is these values that form the group or organizational culture. In the group, members must respect basic human rights, listen to dissenters instead of rejecting them, have freedom of speech, and have open discussion of differences. It is these values that bind group members together. Most groups are or will become a multicultural unit knitted together by a common set of values.

Gaining Sophistication Through Intergroup Relationships

Some people are *sophisticated* about how to act appropriately within many different cultures and perspectives; they are courteous, well-mannered, and refined. Other people are quite *provincial*, knowing how to act appropriately only within their narrow perspective. To become sophisticated, a person must be able to see the situation from the cultural perspective of the other people involved. Much of the information available about different cultural and ethnic heritages and perspectives cannot be attained by reading books and listening to lectures. Only by knowing, working with, and personally interacting with members of diverse groups can individuals really learn to value diversity, utilize diversity for creative problem solving, and work effectively with diverse peers.

To gain the sophistication and skills required to build relationships with diverse peers, you need to develop relationships with people from a wide variety of cultural, ethnic, social class, and historical backgrounds. Many aspects of relating to individuals different from you are learned only from friends who are candid about misunderstandings you inadvertently are creating. To gain the necessary *sophistication* and skills to relate to, work with, and become friends with diverse peers, you need:

1. *Actual interaction:* Seek opportunities to interact with a wide variety of peers. You do so because you value diversity, recognize the importance of relating effectively to diverse peers, and recognize the importance of increasing your knowledge of multicultural issues.
2. *Trust:* Build trust by being open about yourself and your commitment to cross-cultural relationships and by being trustworthy when others share their opinions and reactions with you. Being trustworthy includes expressing respect for diverse backgrounds and valuing them as a resource that increases the quality of your life and adds to the viability of your society.

3. *Candor:* Persuade your peers to be candid by openly discussing their personal opinions, feelings, and reactions with you. Sometimes events or individuals' use of words or expressions that seem neutral to you are offensive and hurtful to individuals from backgrounds different from yours. In order to understand what is and is not disrespectful and hurtful, your peers must be candid about their reactions and explain them to you.

If you are not sophisticated and skilled in building relationships with diverse peers, you are in danger of colluding with current patterns of discrimination. **Collusion** is conscious and unconscious reinforcement of stereotypic attitudes, behaviors, and prevailing norms. People collude with discriminatory practices and prejudiced actions through ignorance, silence, denial, and active support. Perhaps the only way not to collude with existing discriminatory practices is to build friendships with diverse peers that allow you to understand when discrimination and prejudice occur.

Clarifying Miscommunications

Imagine that you and several friends went to hear a speaker. Although the content was good and the delivery entertaining, two of your friends walked out in protest. When you asked them why, they called your attention to the facts that the speaker continually used "you guys" even though half the audience was women, used only sports and military examples, quoted only men, and joked about senility and old age. Your friends were insulted.

Communication is one of the most complex aspects of managing relationships with diverse peers. To communicate effectively with people from different cultural, ethnic, social class, and historical backgrounds, you must increase your:

1. *Language sensitivity.* Knowledge of words and expressions appropriate and inappropriate for communicating with diverse groups. The use of language can play a powerful role in reinforcing stereotypes and garbling communication. To avoid this, individuals need to heighten their sensitivity and avoid using terms and expressions that ignore or devalue others.

2. *Awareness of stylistic elements of communication.* Knowledge of the key elements of communication style and how diverse

cultures use these elements to communicate. Without awareness of nuances in language and differences in style, the potential for garbled communication is enormous when interacting with diverse peers.

Your ability to communicate with credibility to diverse peers is closely linked to your use of language. You must be sophisticated enough to anticipate how your messages will be interpreted by the listener. If you are unaware of nuances and innuendoes contained in your message, then you are more likely to miscommunicate. The words you choose often tell other people more about your values, attitudes, and socialization than you intend to reveal. Receivers react to the subtleties conveyed and interpret the implied messages behind your words. The first step in establishing relationships with diverse peers, therefore, is to understand how language reinforces stereotypes and to adjust your usage accordingly.

You never can predict with certainty how every person is going to react to what you say. You can, however, minimize the possibility of miscommunicating by following some basic guidelines:

1. Use all the communication skills discussed in this book and in Johnson (2006).
2. Negotiate for meaning whenever you think the other person you are talking with misinterpreted what you said.
3. Use words that are inclusive (e.g., women, men, participants) rather than exclusive.
4. Avoid adjectives that spotlight specific groups and imply that the individual is an exception, such as *black doctor, woman pilot, older teacher,* or *blind lawyer.*
5. Use quotations, references, metaphors, and analogies that reflect diversity and are from diverse sources—for example, from Asian and African as well as European and American sources.
6. Avoid terms that define, demean, or devalue others, such as *cripple, girl, boy,* or *agitator.*
7. Be aware of the genealogy of words viewed as inappropriate by others. The connotations the receiver places on your words are what count, not your own connotations. These connotations change over time, so continual clarification is needed. Some words that seem neutral to one person may be "loaded" or highly judgmental to people of diverse backgrounds. The word *lady,* for example, was a compliment some years ago, but today it fails to take into account women's independence and equal status in society and, therefore, is offensive to many women. Words such as *girls* and *gals* are just as offensive.

SUMMARY

In our increasingly global community, highly diverse individuals interact daily, studying, working, and playing together in small groups. Rapidly growing global interdependence and the increasing emphasis on teamwork result in groups with quite diverse membership. Diversity among members is no longer exceptional or optional; it is the everyday rule. You will be expected to interact effectively with people with a wide variety of characteristics and backgrounds. Doing so has many advantages, including

IMPORTANT CONCEPTS

Demonstrate your understanding of the following concepts by matching the definitions with the appropriate concept. Find a partner. Compare answers.

	Concept		Definition
_____	1. Prejudice	a.	Belief that associates a whole group of people with certain traits
_____	2. Ethnocentrism	b.	An action taken to harm a group or any of its members
_____	3. Stereotype	c.	Unjustified negative attitude toward a person based solely on that individual's membership in a group other than one's own
_____	4. Illusionary correlation	d.	Attribute the cause of discrimination or misfortune to the personal characteristics and actions of the victim
_____	5. Discrimination	e.	Conflict over basic values that occurs among individuals from different cultures
_____	6. Blaming the victim	f.	Conscious or unconscious reinforcement of stereotypic attitudes, behaviors, and prevailing norms
_____	7. Collusion	g.	Tendency to overestimate the association between variables that are only slightly correlated or not correlated at all
_____	8. Scapegoat	h.	Prejudice directed at people because of their ethnic membership
_____	9. Racism	i.	Believing that most other people share their stereotypes
_____	10. Modern racism	j.	Guiltless but defenseless group that is attacked to provide an outlet for pent-up anger and frustration caused by another group
_____	11. False consensus bias	k.	Subtle forms of prejudice in which people appear, on the surface, not to harbor prejudice but actually do hold prejudiced attitudes
_____	12. Stereotype threat	l.	Tendency to regard one's own ethnic group, nation, religion, culture, or gender as being more correct than others
_____	13. Culture clash	m.	Whenever group members run the risk of confirming the stereotype

increased group productivity on a variety of tasks. Heterogeneity in groups also increases the difficulty of developing cohesive relationships among members and increases the potential for conflicts among members. Diversity among members is advantageous, but it is not easy to manage.

Accepting others begins with accepting yourself (see Johnson [1999] for a thorough discussion of self-acceptance). But even for individuals who are quite accepting of themselves and others, there are barriers to building positive relationships with diverse peers. The most notable barriers are prejudice, blaming the victim, and culture clash. Minimizing these barriers makes it easier to recognize that diversity exists and that fundamental differences among people are to be both respected and valued.

For group members to capitalize on their differences, they must ensure that a high level of positive interdependence exists among group members, highlight important mutual goals that require cooperative action, and develop a common ground on which everyone is co-oriented. They also must create a superordinate group identity that unites the diverse personal identities of group members. The superordinate group identity should be based on a pluralistic set of values, and it should enable members to gain sophistication about the differences among members through personal relationships that have sufficient trust to allow for candid discussions. Finally, the superordinate identity should help clarify miscommunications that arise when group members from different cultures, ethnic and historical backgrounds, social classes, genders, age cohorts, and so forth work together.

EXERCISE 10.2

STEREOTYPING

Once you realize that everyone is socialized to be prejudiced and to stereotype others, you need to clarify exactly what stereotypes you hold. This exercise is aimed at clarifying (1) what stereotypes you have been taught about other groups, (2) what stereotypes they have been taught about you, and (3) how the process of stereotyping works.

1. Post each word from the following list on sheets of paper around the room:

Male	Roman Catholic	Hispanic American
Teenager	Southern	Deaf
Asian American	Female	Middle income
Native American	Over age 70	Protestant
Blind	African American	Midwestern
Lower income		

2. Each participant is to circulate around the room, read the various words, and write one stereotype he or she has heard under each heading. Participants are told not to repeat anything already written down. They are not to make anything up. They are to write down *all* the stereotypes they have heard about each of the groups listed.
3. After everyone has finished writing, participants are to read all the stereotypes under each category.

continued on next page

continued from previous page

4. Participants discuss:
    a. Their personal reactions.
    b. How accurate the stereotypes of the identities are.
    c. What they have learned about stereotyping others.

EXERCISE 10.3

INTERACTING ON THE BASIS OF STEREOTYPES

Stereotypes are rigid judgments made about other groups that ignore individual differences. The purpose of this exercise is to demonstrate how stereotypes are associated with primary and secondary dimensions of diversity.

1. Divide participants into groups of five. The groups are to role play a discussion of employees of a large corporation about the ways in which the percentage of people of color and women in higher-level executive positions may be increased from 10% to 50%.
2. Give each member of each group a headband to wear with a particular identity written on it for other group members to see. **Group members are not to look at their own headbands.** The five identities are

    Single mother of two young children, receptionist
    Employee with physical disability   Woman, age 72
    White male, company president   Black female, union official

3. Stop the discussion after ten minutes or so. Then have the groups discuss
    a. What each person thinks the label on his or her headband was.
    b. Their personal reactions.
    c. The participation pattern of each member—who dominated, who withdrew, who was interrupted, who was influential.
    d. What they have learned about stereotyping others.

EXERCISE 10.4

GREETINGS AND GOODBYES

This exercise increases awareness of how different cultural patterns of greetings and goodbyes can create communication problems. The procedure is as follows:

1. Divide the class into groups of four. Divide each group into two pairs, Americans and Lakians (from a fictitious country named Lake). If possible, give each pair something such as colored ribbons or armbands that visually distinguish them from each other.
2. Ask all American pairs to go to one end of the room and all Lakian pairs to go to the other. They receive separate briefings.

3. The participants are to role play that they are business associates who are to engage in an informal discussion of general economic conditions in their countries.
   a. The **American pairs** are instructed to greet their Lakian business associates in the traditional North American fashion. They are to shake hands, say "Good to see you again," talk about the economic conditions of North America for a while, and then say goodbye by shaking hands and waving.
   b. The **Lakian pairs** are instructed to greet their American business associates in the traditional Lakian fashion. They are to give the Americans a warm embrace and then to take and hold their hands for at least thirty seconds. They are to talk about the economic condition of Lake for a while. Then they are to say goodbye by giving the Americans a warm embrace, holding their hands for at least thirty seconds, and telling them how great it was to talk to them.
4. The group of four meets. If they finish the conversation before other groups in the room do, each pair should find another pair from the other country and repeat the experience.
5. The group of four discusses the experience:
   a. What were the cultural differences?
   b. What communication barriers did the cultural differences create?
   c. How did the participants feel during the interchange between the Americans and Lakians?
   d. What are three conclusions about cross-cultural communication that can be drawn from the experience?

The English and their North American counterparts are sometimes seen as being impoverished when it comes to kinesic communication, using words to denote what gesture or tone would express in other cultures. In North America, for example, people often are reserved when greeting others. Body contact is avoided. Yet in some Arab countries, men kiss each other on the street when they meet. Nigerian men often walk hand in hand. Italian men embrace warmly and remain touching when engaged in conversation. In some African countries, handshakes may be extended for long periods of time, and a hand on the knee among males is not an offense. All of these differences create potential communication problems when members of different cultures meet.

EXERCISE 10.5

CROSS-CULTURAL COMMUNICATION

The purpose of this exercise is to increase awareness of how cultural differences can create barriers to communication among group members. The procedure is as follows:

1. Form groups of six and divide each group into three pairs.
2. Each pair is assigned a particular cultural identity based on being a citizen of the country of Winkin, Blinkin, or Nod. Their task is to plan how they will act during the exercise based on the information about their country given on their briefing sheet. The pair is to work together cooperatively to ensure that both members understand how to act appropriately as a citizen of their country. They have ten minutes to prepare.
3. Two triads are formed, one member from each country. Each triad is assigned the task of identifying the ten most important principles of cross-cultural communication. They have fifteen minutes to do so.

continued on next page

continued from previous page

4. The group of six discusses the following questions:
    a. How are the two lists different? How are they the same?
    b. How did members react to their assigned roles? Were there any difficulties in enacting them?
    c. What were the communication barriers among the citizens of the three countries? Why did they occur?
    d. How could the communication barriers be avoided or overcome?
    e. What conclusions can be drawn from the exercise?
    f. What applications does the exercise have for everyday life?

CONFIDENTIAL: TO BE SEEN BY WINKIN CITIZENS ONLY

Behavioral Characteristics of the Country of Winkin

1. **Orientation Toward Touch:** Touch as much as possible, stand and sit close to people, and give a long handshake (about fifteen to thirty seconds) when you greet a person.

2. **Orientation Toward Eye Contact:** Look other people in the eyes when you talk to them.

3. **Orientation Toward Disclosure:** You are interested only in yourself, and you love to share yourself with other people. Talk only about yourself and what interests you. Do not listen to other people—they are boring. You do not want to understand other people better; you want them to understand you. Whenever they start talking, you interrupt them and refocus the conversation on yourself.

4. **Orientation Toward Conflict:** You like to argue for the sake of arguing so that people will pay attention to you.

5. **Orientation Toward Helping Others:** You avoid helping people under any circumstances.

CONFIDENTIAL: TO BE SEEN BY BLINKIN CITIZENS ONLY

Behavioral Characteristics of the Country of Blinkin

1. **Orientation Toward Touch:** Do not touch other people. Stand and sit far away from other people. Greet other people by nodding your head—do not shake hands.

2. **Orientation Toward Eye Contact:** Do not look other people in the eyes when you talk to them. If you happen to look a person in the eyes, look for only a split second.

3. **Orientation Toward Disclosure:** You are genuinely interested in other people. You are inquisitive. You get to know other people by asking them questions about what they are interested in. You listen carefully and let other people finish what they are saying before you speak. You never interrupt. You never talk about yourself.

4. **Orientation Toward Conflict:** You are very uncomfortable with conflict and want to avoid it at all costs. You never argue about a point with which you disagree. Instead you change the subject and try to find something else to talk about.

5. **Orientation Toward Helping Others:** You try to help other people (especially in solving a problem) as much as possible.

CONFIDENTIAL: TO BE SEEN BY NOD CITIZENS ONLY

Behavioral Characteristics of the Country of Nod

1. **Orientation Toward Touch:** Touch people only occasionally when you are talking. Stand and sit about an arm's length from a person. Give a short handshake when you are greeting a person.

2. **Orientation Toward Eye Contact:** Look other people in the eyes for only about three seconds at a time when you talk to them.

3. **Orientation Toward Disclosure:** You want to exchange ideas and thoughts. You share your interests and opinions, and you want other people to share theirs with you. You want to talk *with* other people instead of *to* them.

4. **Orientation Toward Conflict:** You seek reasoned judgments. You ignore who is right and who is wrong. You focus on the quality of ideas, seeking a synthesis or integration of different points of view. You listen carefully, add what you want to say, and make an informed judgment based on all positions and perspectives.

5. **Orientation Toward Helping Others:** You help other people only when it benefits you, that is, when it is rational to do so.

EXERCISE 10.6

MERGING DIFFERENT CULTURES

This exercise merges individuals from two different cultures into one group. The procedure for the exercise is as follows:

1. The materials you need to assemble for the exercise are:
   a. Using poster board, construct ten sets of Figure 10.1 for each participant in Atlantis and one set of Figure 10.2 for every participant taking part in the exercise.
   b. One envelope per participant.
   c. One die for each group in Atlantis.
2. Divide the class into citizens of Atlantis and Mu. Assign participants to the society of Mu for every participant assigned to Atlantis. The citizens of Atlantis meet at one end of the room, and the citizens of Mu meet at the other end.
3. At the Atlantis end of the room, assign participants to groups of four and seat each group around a table.
   a. Place enough pieces for ten complete Ts per member in the center of each group (pieces for forty Ts).
   b. Tell the participants

   You are a worker in Atlantis who earns his or her living by constructing Ts. A T is formed using four triangles and three squares. Life is hard in Atlantis, so everyone looks out for "number one." You build your Ts by taking pieces from the center of the table. You will take turns in acquiring the shapes. When it is your turn, you acquire shapes by either (a) taking two pieces from the pile or (b) rolling the

   continued on next page

continued from previous page

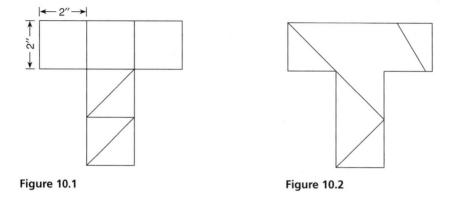

Figure 10.1   **Figure 10.2**

die (if you roll an even number [2, 4, 6] you can select that number of pieces, but if you roll an odd number [1, 3, 5] you lose that number of pieces from those you have accumulated thus far, including those composing complete Ts). The member with the greatest number of Ts will be declared the wealthiest and will survive. The poorest will perish. You can begin.

4. At the Mu end of the room, a second instructor divides the citizens into groups of four members and seats each group around a table. Their task is to earn their livelihood by constructing Ts. Each citizen of Mu is to form a T using the five pieces as shown in Figure 10.2. The instructor takes the pieces to make up the four Ts for each group and randomly divides the pieces into four envelopes (five pieces in each), making sure that no one envelope contains the correct five pieces for completing a T. One envelope is given to each group member. The instructor tells the participants

> You are a worker in Mu who earns his or her living by constructing Ts. Life is hard in Mu, so everyone looks out for everyone else. There are enough pieces among the members of your group to form one complete T for each member, but no one member has the right combination of pieces to complete his or her T. Mu, however, is a heterogeneous society that does not have a common language. The members of your group, therefore, will not speak to each other. **No verbal communication is allowed.**
>
> Group members must share pieces in order to be successful. You may offer pieces to another group member and accept pieces offered to you by another group member. You cannot offer pieces to more than one person at the same time. You may not ask for a particular piece by pointing, talking, nudging, grimacing, or any other method. When you give a piece to another member, simply hand it to the person without demonstrating how the piece fits into his or her T. You have five minutes to complete this task. You may open your envelopes.

After five minutes, the instructor collects each group's pieces and again places the pieces randomly in the envelopes.

5. The Mu groups repeat the task, except that this time they may use any form of communication they wish. All other rules remain in effect. They have five minutes to complete the task.
6. Bring the Atlantis citizens to join the Mu society. Evenly distribute the citizens of Atlantis among the Mu groups. Add to each group's Ts one additional T for each new member. Take the combined pieces and randomly distribute them in envelopes, one for each member of the integrated groups. Tell the participants

> The citizens of Atlantis are immigrants to Mu. They are to have a part in the work of Mu, and the sooner they learn to earn a livelihood, the better off Mu will be. Members of Atlantis, however, do not

speak Mu's language and the meaning of nonverbal gestures in the two societies is quite different. *There will, therefore, be no talking and no nonverbal signaling such as pointing or gesturing.* Your task is to build Ts. The Ts are formed differently from those made in Atlantis. You can begin work.

Stop the groups when all groups have built their Ts or after ten minutes, whichever comes first.

7. Have the groups discuss
   a. How did the members of each society feel about working in integrated units?
   b. How did the two societies differ?
   c. Why was your group successful or unsuccessful in integrating the two societies?
   d. What conclusions can be drawn about work groups consisting of members from more than one society?

CHAPTER ELEVEN

Cooperative Learning in the Classroom

BASIC CONCEPTS TO BE COVERED IN THIS CHAPTER

In this chapter a number of concepts are defined and discussed. The major ones are listed below. Students should divide into pairs. Each pair is to (a) define each concept, noting the page on which it is defined and discussed and (b) ensure that both members understand its meaning. Then combine into groups of four. Compare the answers of the two pairs. If there is disagreement, look up the concept in the chapter and clarify it until all members agree on and understand the definition.

CONCEPTS

1. Cooperative learning
2. Competitive learning
3. Individualistic learning
4. Formal cooperative learning
5. Informal cooperative learning
6. Cooperative base groups
7. Individual accountability
8. Promotive interaction
9. Group processing
10. Cooperative school

NATURE OF COOPERATIVE LEARNING

Groups have existed for as long as life forms have been around, from the earliest plant and animal life to modern humans. Every human society has used groups to accomplish its goals and celebrated when the groups were successful. Groups built the pyramids, constructed the Temple of Artemis at Ephesus, and created the Colossus of Rhodes and the hanging gardens of Babylon. The bulk of this book has shown the many ways in which groups outperform individuals, especially when performance requires multiple skills, judgments, and experiences. Many educators, however, overlook opportunities to use groups to enhance student learning and increase their own success. In this chapter, we present the concept of cooperative learning in the classroom setting. This information can help you in your own classroom experiences, as a student and perhaps even as a teacher.

History of Cooperative Learning

Cooperative learning is an old idea. The Talmud clearly states that in order to learn, you must have a learning partner. In the first century, Quintilian argued that students could benefit from teaching one another. The Roman philosopher Seneca advocated cooperative learning through such statements as *Qui docet discet* (When you teach, you learn twice). Johann Amos Comenius (1592–1679) believed that students would benefit from both teaching and being taught by other students. In the late 1700s, Joseph Lancaster and Andrew Bell made extensive use of cooperative learning groups in England, and the idea was brought to America when a Lancastrian school was opened in New York City in 1806.

The Common School movement in the United States in the early 1800s placed a strong emphasis on cooperative learning. In the last three decades of the nineteenth century, Colonel Francis Parker brought to his advocacy of cooperative learning enthusiasm, idealism, practicality, and an intense devotion to freedom, democracy, and individuality in the public schools. His fame and success rested on his power to create a classroom atmosphere that truly was cooperative and democratic. Parker's advocacy of cooperation among students dominated American education through the turn of the century. Following Parker, John Dewey promoted the use of cooperative learning groups as part of his famous project method in instruction. In the late 1930s, however, interpersonal competition began to be emphasized in schools, and in the late 1960s, individualistic learning began to be used extensively. In the 1980s, schools once again began to use cooperative learning.

Capitalizing on the Power of Groups

The opportunity to capitalize on the power of groups in schools begins with understanding the answers to the following questions (see Table 11.1):

1. What is cooperative learning?
2. Why use cooperative learning?
3. What are the expected outcomes resulting from cooperative efforts?

TABLE 11.1 **Overview of Chapter: Cooperative Learning**

SOCIAL INTERDEPENDENCE				
Cooperative		Competitive		Individualistic

RESEARCH: WHY USE COOPERATIVE LEARNING				
Effort to achieve		Positive relationships		Psychological health

FIVE BASIC ELEMENTS				
Positive interdependence	Individual accountability	Promotive interaction	Social skills	Group processing

COOPERATIVE LEARNING		
FORMAL COOPERATIVE LEARNING	**INFORMAL COOPERATIVE LEARNING**	**COOPERATIVE BASE GROUPS**
Make preinstructional decisions.	Conduct introductory focused discussion.	Structure opening class meeting to check homework, ensure that members understand academic material, complete routine tasks such as taking attendance.
Explain task and cooperative structure.	Conduct intermittent pair discussions every ten or fifteen minutes.	Structure ending class meeting to ensure that members understand academic material, homework assignment.
Monitor learning groups and intervene to improve task work and teamwork.	Conduct closure-focused discussion.	Members help each other learn between classes.
Assess student learning and process group effectiveness.		Conduct semester- or year-long school or class service projects.

COOPERATIVE SCHOOL		
Teaching teams	Site-based decision making	Faculty meetings

CONSTRUCTIVE CONFLICT			
STUDENTS		**FACULTY**	
Academic controversy	Negotiating, mediating	Decision-making controversy	Negotiating, mediating

CIVIC VALUES				
Work for mutual benefit, common good	Equality of all members	Trusting, caring relationships	View situations from all perspectives	Unconditional worth of self, diverse others

4. How do you structure formal cooperative learning?
5. How do you structure informal cooperative learning?
6. How do you structure cooperative base groups?
7. How do you use the three types of cooperative learning in an integrated way?
8. What are the basic elements of cooperative learning that make it work?
9. How do you structure cooperation among faculty and staff to ensure that cooperative efforts are institutionalized throughout school life?

What Is Cooperative Learning?

To understand the nature of cooperative learning, it is necessary to place it within the broader context of social interdependence. In Chapter 3, *social interdependence* was defined as each individual's outcomes being affected by the actions of others. Interdependence among individuals' goals can be positive (e.g., cooperation) or negative (e.g., competition). Social independence, on the other hand, is characterized by individualistic action where the outcomes of each person are unaffected by others' actions.

Cooperation is working together to accomplish shared goals. **Cooperative learning** is the instructional use of small groups so that students work together to maximize everyone's learning. Within cooperative learning groups, students discuss the material to be learned with one another, help one another to understand it, and encourage one another to work hard. **Competitive learning** is students working to achieve a goal, such as a grade of A, that only one or a few students can attain. Striving to achieve higher than other students involves obstructing each other's attempts to achieve. **Individualistic learning** is students working by themselves to accomplish learning goals unrelated to those of the other students.

In cooperative and individualistic learning, students' efforts are evaluated on a criteria-referenced basis. In competitive learning, students are graded on a norm-referenced basis. Although there are limitations on when and where competitive and individualistic learning may be used appropriately, any learning task in any subject area with any curriculum can be structured cooperatively.

There are three types of cooperative learning (see Table 11.2). Cooperative learning groups can be used to teach specific content (formal cooperative learning groups), to ensure active cognitive processing of information during a lecture or demonstration (informal cooperative learning groups), and to provide long-term support and assistance for academic progress (cooperative base groups) (Johnson, Johnson, & Holubec, 2008; Johnson, Johnson, & Smith, 2006).

FORMAL COOPERATIVE LEARNING: BEING "A GUIDE ON THE SIDE"

At age fifty-five, after his defeat by Woodrow Wilson for president of the United States, Teddy Roosevelt took a journey to South America. The Brazilian government suggested that he lead an expedition to explore a vast, unmapped river deep in the jungle. Known as the River of Doubt, it was believed to be a tributary to the Amazon.

WHAT TYPE OF SITUATION IS IT?

Following are twelve statements. Form a pair and agree on whether each statement reflects a cooperative, competitive, or individualistic situation. Place each statement in the appropriate column in the table.

Statements

1. Strive for everyone's success.

2. Strive to be better than others.

3. Strive for one's own success only.

4. What benefits oneself does not affect others.

5. Joint success is celebrated.

6. What benefits oneself benefits others.

7. Only one's own success is celebrated.

8. Motivated to help others.

9. What benefits oneself deprives/hurts others.

10. Motivated only to maximize one's own productivity.

11. One's own success and others' failure are celebrated.

12. Motivated to ensure that no one else does better than oneself.

Cooperative	Competitive	Individualistic

Roosevelt accepted instantly. "We will go down the unknown river," he declared, and the Brazilian government organized an expedition for the trip. "I had to go," he said later. "It was my last chance to be a boy." Accompanied by his son Kermit and a party of eighteen, Roosevelt headed into the jungle. "On February 27, 1914, shortly after midday, we started down the River of Doubt into the unknown," Roosevelt wrote. The journey was an ordeal. Natives harassed them, they lost canoes, food supplies ran low, and equipment was lost. One man drowned; another went berserk, killed a member of the expedition, and then disappeared into the wilderness. Roosevelt became ill with fever and badly injured his leg. Lying in a tent with an infected leg and a temperature of 105°F, he asked to be left behind. Ignoring his pleas, Kermit brought his father to safety with the help of the other members of the expedition. Teddy Roosevelt barely survived, but he and his companions accomplished their mission. The party mapped

TABLE 11.2 **Types of Cooperative Learning**

FORMAL COOPERATIVE LEARNING	INFORMAL COOPERATIVE LEARNING	COOPERATIVE BASE GROUPS
Complete assignment, lesson, unit, project to maximize own and groupmates' learning.	Discuss assigned questions for a few minutes to focus attention, organize knowledge, set expectations, create mood, ensure cognitive processing and rehearsal, summarize, precue next session, provide closure.	Permanent; lasts for one semester, one year, or several years to ensure that all members make academic progress and develop cognitively and socially in healthy ways.
TEACHER PROCEDURE	**TEACHER PROCEDURE**	**TEACHER PROCEDURE**
Make preinstructional decisions.	Conduct introductory-focused discussion.	Structure opening class meeting to check homework, ensure that members understand academic material, complete routine tasks such as taking attendance, and prepare members for the day.
Explain task and cooperative structure.	Conduct intermittent-pair discussions every ten or fifteen minutes.	Structure ending class meeting to ensure that all members understand academic material, know what homework to do, and are making progress on long-term assignments.
Monitor learning groups and intervene to improve task work and teamwork.	Conduct closure-focused discussion.	Members help and assist each other learn between classes.
Assess learning and monitor group effectiveness.		Conduct semester- or year-long school or class service projects.

the 1,000-mile River of Doubt and collected priceless specimens for the Museum of Natural History. The river was renamed in his honor, the Rio Theodore.

A cooperative expedition such as Roosevelt's trip down the River of Doubt consists of four phases:

1. Make a series of prejourney decisions about the number of people needed, the materials and equipment required, and the route to be taken.
2. Brief all participants on the goals and objectives of the journey, emphasize that members' survival depends on the joint efforts of all, and describe the expected behaviors of members of the expedition.
3. Make the journey, carefully mapping the area traveled and collecting the targeted specimens.
4. Report the findings to interested parties, reflect on what went right and wrong with fellow members, and write memoirs.

Conducting a formal cooperative lesson is done in the same way. The teacher (1) makes a number of preinstructional decisions, (2) explains to students the instructional task and the cooperative nature of the lesson, (3) conducts the lesson, and (4) evaluates and processes the results. To help you as teachers, group leaders, and students take full advantage of the benefits of cooperative learning experiences, the following sections provide in-depth details on what is involved in each of these four steps.

In each class session, teachers must make the choice of being the center of the session, "a sage on the stage"; or being an assistant, "a guide on the side." In doing so, they should remember the challenge in teaching is not covering the material *for* the students, it's uncovering the material *with* the students.

PREINSTRUCTIONAL DECISIONS

Before a cooperative group can begin an assignment or task, a series of preinstructional decisions must be made. For every lesson, instructors (a) formulate objectives, (b) decide on the size of groups, (c) choose a method for assigning students to groups, (d) decide which roles to assign to group members, (e) arrange the room, and (f) arrange the materials students need to complete the assignment.

Specifying the Instructional Objectives

To plan for a lesson, you must know what the lesson is aimed at accomplishing. You need to specify *academic objectives* (based on a conceptual or task analysis) and *social-skills objectives* that detail what interpersonal and small-group skills you wish to emphasize during the lesson (Johnson, Johnson, & Holubec, 2008).

Deciding on the Size of the Group

To assign students to groups, you must decide (a) how large a group should be, (b) how students should be assigned to a group, (c) how long the groups will exist, and (d) what combination of groups will be used in the lesson.

Although cooperative learning groups typically range in size from two to four, the basic rule is: *The smaller the better.* There is, however, no ideal size for a cooperative learning group. A common mistake is to have students work in groups of four or five before they have the skills to do so competently. In selecting the size of a cooperative learning group, remember this advice:

GROUP SIZE DEPENDS ON "TEAM"

T	= **T**ime limits
E	= **E**xperience working in groups
A	= **A**ge
M	= **M**aterials and equipment available

1. **With the addition of each group member, the resources to help the group succeed increase.** As the size of the learning group increases, so do

(a) the range of abilities, expertise, and skills; (b) the number of minds available for acquiring and processing information; and (c) the diversity of viewpoints.

2. **The shorter the period of time available, the smaller the learning group should be.** If only a brief period of time is available for the lesson, then smaller groups, such as pairs, are more effective. Smaller groups take less time to organize, they operate faster, and there is more "air time" per member.

3. **The smaller the group, the more difficult it is for students to hide and not do their share of the work.** Small groups increase the visibility of students' efforts and thereby make them more accountable.

4. **The larger the group, the more skillful group members must be.** In a pair, students have to manage two interactions. In a group of three, there are six interactions to manage. In a group of four, there are twelve interactions to manage. As the size of the group increases, the interpersonal and small-group skills required to manage the interactions among group members become far more complex and sophisticated.

5. **The larger the group, the less the interaction among members.** The result is less group cohesion, fewer friendships, and less personal support.

6. **The materials available or the specific nature of the task may dictate a group's size.** When you have ten computers and thirty students, you may wish to assign students to groups of three. When the task is to practice tennis, a group size of two seems natural.

7. **The smaller the group, the easier it is to identify any difficulties students have in working together.** Problems in leadership, unresolved conflicts among group members, issues over power and control, tendencies such as sitting back and waiting for others to do the work, and other problems students have in working together are more visible when groups are small. Groups need to be small enough to ensure that all students are actively involved and participating equally.

Assigning Students to Groups

There may be times when you use cooperative learning groups that are homogeneous in ability to teach specific skills or to achieve certain instructional objectives. Generally, however, there are advantages to heterogeneous groups in which students come from diverse backgrounds and have different abilities, experiences, and interests:

1. Students are exposed to a variety of ideas, multiple perspectives, and different problem-solving methods.

2. Students generate more cognitive disequilibrium, which stimulates learning, creativity, and cognitive and social development.

3. Students engage in more elaborative thinking, give and receive more explanations, and engage in more frequent perspective-taking in discussing material, all of which increase the depth of understanding, the quality of reasoning, and the accuracy of long-term retention.

The easiest and most effective way to assign students to a group is randomly. You divide the number of students in your class by the size of the group desired. If you wish to have groups of three and you have thirty students in your class, you divide thirty by three. You have students number off by the result (e.g., ten). Students with the same number find each other (all ones get together, all twos get together, and so forth).

A related procedure for assigning students to groups is *stratified random assignment*. This is the same as random assignment except that you choose one or two characteristics of students (such as reading level, task orientation, or personal interest) and make sure that one or more students in each group have that characteristic. One modified stratified random procedure is to assign students to groups by *preferences*. Have students write their favorite sport on a slip of paper, and then have them find groupmates who like to participate in the same sport. Variations include favorite food, celebrity, skill, car, president, animal, vegetable, fairy tale character, and so forth.

Length of Group Life. A common question is, "How long should cooperative learning groups stay together?" The type of cooperative learning group you use determines one answer to this question. Base groups (discussed later in this chapter) last for at least one semester or one year. Informal cooperative learning groups last for only a few minutes or, at most, one class period. Formal cooperative learning groups usually stay together to complete a task, unit, or chapter. During a course, every student should eventually work with every other classmate.

Assigning Roles to Ensure Interdependence

In planning the lesson, think through the actions that need to occur to maximize student learning. Roles prescribe what other group members expect from a student and therefore what the student is obligated to do. Roles also indicate what that person has a right to expect from other group members who have complementary roles. There is a progression for using roles to structure cooperative efforts:

1. Do not assign roles until students get used to working together.
2. At first, assign simple roles to students, such as reader, recorder, and encourager of participation. Rotate the roles so that each group member plays each one several times.
3. Add to the rotation a new role that is slightly more sophisticated, such as that of a checker for understanding (e.g., asking groupmates to explain what they are learning).
4. Over time, add roles that do not occur naturally in the group, such as that of an elaborator of ideas (e.g., relating what is being learned to previous learnings). Students typically do not relate what they are learning to what they already know until you specifically train them to do so.

Solving and Preventing Problems in Working Together. At times, some students refuse to participate in a cooperative group or do not understand how to help the group succeed. You can solve and prevent such problems when you give each group member a specific role to play. Assigning appropriate roles may be used to:

1. Reduce problems such as one or more members' making no contribution or one member dominating the group.

2. Ensure that vital group skills are enacted in the group and that group members learn targeted skills.
3. Create interdependence among group members. You structure **role inter-dependence** by assigning each member complementary and interconnected roles.

Arranging the Room

The design and arrangement of classroom space and furniture communicate what is appropriate behavior and what learning activities are going to take place. Desks in a row communicate a different message and expectation than do desks grouped in small circles. Spatial design also defines the circulation patterns in the classroom. *Circulation* is the flow of movement into, out of, and within the classroom. It is movement through space. You determine what students see, when they see it, and with whom students interact by the way you arrange your classroom.

No single classroom arrangement meets the requirements of all lessons. Reference points and well-defined boundaries of work spaces are needed to move students from rows to triads to pairs to fours to rows. Color, form, and lighting also are important because they focus students' visual attention on points of emphasis in the classroom—the learning group, you, instructional materials. These elements also define the territorial boundaries of work spaces—where students do small-group work, where they present to the class, and so on. You define boundaries by:

1. **Using labels and signs** that designate areas.
2. **Using colors** to attract visual attention and define group and individual spaces, as well as different storage areas and resource centers.
3. **Taping lines** on the floor or wall to define the different work areas.
4. **Using mobiles and forms** (such as arrows) taped on the wall or hanging from the ceiling to direct attention or designate work areas.
5. **Using lighting** to define specific work areas. Directed light (illuminating part of the room while leaving other areas dim) intensifies and directs students' attention. Brightly lit areas can draw people to the areas and suggest activity. More dimly lit areas surrounding the lighted ones become area boundaries. As the activity in the classroom changes, the lighting also could change.
6. **Moving furniture** to define work and resource areas. Even tall plants, when placed in pots with wheels, can be moved to provide spatial boundaries.
7. **Displaying group work** to designate work spaces. If a cooperative group is to remain together for a period of several days or weeks, members may wish to build a poster or collage that designates their work area.

You can use many of these same procedures to control the level of noise in the classroom.

Planning the Instructional Materials

The types of tasks students are required to complete determine what materials are needed for the lesson. You, the teacher, decide how materials are to be arranged and distributed among group members to maximize their participation and achievement. Usually, you should distribute materials in a way that communicates that the assignment is a joint effort, not an individual one. You establish a group-work atmosphere by creating:

1. **Materials interdependence.** Give each group only one copy of the materials. The students then have to work together in order to be successful. This is especially effective the first few times the group meets. After students are accustomed to working cooperatively, teachers can give a copy of the materials to each student.

2. **Information interdependence (i.e., jigsaw).** Arrange materials like a jigsaw puzzle so that each student has part of the materials needed to complete the assignment. Each group member can receive different books or resource materials that need to be synthesized. Such procedures require that every member participate in order for the group to be successful.

IMPORTANCE OF CLASSROOM DESIGN

Form a pair. Rank order the following outcomes of classroom design from most important (1) to least important (9).

_____ Students' academic achievement. The way in which interior space is designed influences the amount of time students spend on task and other variables affecting achievement.

_____ Students' visual and auditory focus. The way in which interior space is designed creates overall visual order, focuses visual attention, and controls acoustics.

_____ Students' participation in learning groups and activities. Classroom design influences the patterns of student (and teacher) participation in instructional activities, the emergence of leadership in learning groups, and the patterns of communication among students and between students and teacher.

_____ Opportunities for social contact and friendships among students.

_____ Learning climate. The design of interior space affects students' and teachers' feelings (such as comfort, enjoyment, well-being, anger, depression) and general morale. Good spatial definition helps students feel secure by delineating structured learning areas.

_____ Classroom management. Spatial definition prevents discipline problems by defining how and where students work, how to interact with others, and how to move through the classroom.

_____ Students' ease of access to each other, teachers, learning materials.

_____ Students' ability to make quick transitions from one group to another.

_____ Teacher's movement from group to group to monitor student interaction carefully during the lesson.

3. **Intergroup tournament.** Structure materials into an intergroup tournament format and have groups compete to see who has learned the most, a procedure introduced by DeVries and Edwards (1973). In the Teams-Games-Tournament format, students are divided into heterogeneous cooperative learning teams to prepare members for a tournament in which they compete with the other teams. During the intergroup competition, the students individually compete against members with about the same achievement level from other teams. The team whose members do the best in the competition is pronounced the winner by the teacher.

EXPLAINING THE TASK AND COOPERATIVE STRUCTURE

Once you have completed your preinstructional planning, you are ready to explain the task and the cooperative structure to the students (Johnson, Johnson, & Holubec, 1994, 2008). For every lesson, you need to (a) explain the academic assignment, (b) explain the criteria for success, (c) structure positive interdependence at the group and the intergroup levels, (d) explain individual accountability, and (e) explain the behaviors you expect to see during the lesson.

Explaining the Academic Task

When explaining the task to the class, you need to define three things: what the assignment is, what to do to complete the assignment, and how to do it.

Explaining Criteria for Success

While explaining to students the academic task they are to complete, you need to communicate the level of performance you expect. Cooperative learning requires criterion-based evaluation. *Criterion-referenced* or *categorical judgments* are made by adopting a fixed set of standards and judging the achievement of each student against these standards. A common version of criterion-referenced grading involves assigning letter grades on the basis of the percentage of test items answered correctly. Alternatively, you might say, "The group is not finished until every member has demonstrated mastery." Sometimes improvement—doing better this week than one did last week—may be set as the criterion of excellence. To promote intergroup cooperation, you also may want to set criteria for the whole class to reach. "If we as a class can score over 520 words correct on our vocabulary test, each student will receive 2 bonus points."

Grade	Percent Correct
A	95–100
B	85–94
C	75–84
D	65–74
F	Less than 64

Structuring Positive Interdependence

Positive interdependence among students is the heart of cooperative learning. As defined in Chapter 3, positive goal interdependence exists when a mutual or joint goal is established so that individuals perceive that they can attain their goals if and only if their groupmates attain their goals. Members know that they cannot succeed unless all other members of their group succeed. Without positive goal interdependence, cooperation does not exist. Students must believe that they are in a "sink or swim together" learning situation.

To create this cooperative environment, you first structure positive goal interdependence. To ensure that students think **"We, not me,"** you (the teacher) say to students:

> You have two responsibilities. You are responsible for learning the assigned material. You are responsible for making sure that all other members of your group learn the assigned material.

Second, you supplement positive goal interdependence with other types of positive interdependence, such as reward (if all group members achieve above the criteria, each will receive bonus points), resource (members have different information or expertise), role (summarizer, encourager of participation, elaborator), or identity (group name, motto, symbol) interdependence. Positive reward interdependence, for example, may be structured by providing group rewards—"If all members of your group score above 90% on the test, each of you will receive 5 bonus points." Usually, the more ways positive interdependence is structured in a lesson, the better.

Structuring Individual Accountability

In cooperative groups, everyone has to do his or her fair share of the work. *An underlying purpose of cooperative learning is to make each group member a stronger individual in his or her own right.* This is accomplished by holding each individual accountable for his or her progress as well as for the progress of his or her groupmates. Individual accountability is established by:

1. Assessing the performance of each member.
2. Giving the results to the individual and the group to compare to preset criteria.

The feedback enables members to (a) recognize and celebrate efforts to learn and contributions to groupmates' learning, (b) provide immediate remediation and any needed assistance or encouragement, and (c) reassign responsibilities to avoid any redundant efforts by members.

Individual accountability results in group members knowing that they cannot "hitchhike" on the work of others, loaf, or get a free ride. Ways of ensuring individual accountability include keeping the group size small, giving an individual test to each student, giving random individual oral examinations, observing and recording the frequency with which each member contributes to the group's work, having students teach what they know to someone else, and having students use what they have learned on different problems.

Specifying Desired Behaviors

When you use cooperative learning, you must teach students the small-group and interpersonal skills they need to work effectively with one another. In cooperative learning groups, students must learn both academic subject matter (taskwork) and the interpersonal and small group skills required to work as part of a group (teamwork). Cooperative learning is inherently more complex than competitive or individualistic learning because students have to engage simultaneously in taskwork and teamwork. If students do not learn the teamwork skills, then they cannot complete the taskwork. The greater the members' teamwork skills, the higher will be the quality and quantity of their learning.

Three rules of thumb in teaching social skills are as follows: (1) **Be specific.** Operationally define each social skill by specifying the required behaviors to engage in the skill. (2) **Start small.** Do not overload your students with more social skills than they can learn at one time. One or two skills for a few lessons are enough. (3) **Emphasize overlearning.** Having students practice skills once or twice is not enough. Keep emphasizing a skill until the students have integrated it into their behavioral repertoires and do it automatically and habitually.

Structuring Intergroup Cooperation

You can extend the positive outcomes resulting from cooperative learning to the entire class by structuring intergroup cooperation. This is done by establishing class goals as well as group and individual goals. When a group finishes its work, for example, encourage members to find other groups that are not finished and help them understand how to complete the assignment successfully. Groups that are finished with a task can find other finished groups and compare answers and strategies. If the whole class is made to understand that the ultimate class goal is for every student to master a skill or complete a task, cooperation among all students is necessary.

MONITORING AND INTERVENING

The only thing that endures over time is the law of the farm: I must
prepare the ground, put in the seed, cultivate it, water it, then gradually
nurture growth and development to full maturity—there is no quick fix.

Stephen Covey

Now that students have the assignment and a cooperative structure has been introduced, it is time for the students to complete the task. Your job as teacher is not over, however, simply because students are at work on a lesson. Rather, you must (a) conduct the lesson, (b) monitor each learning group, (c) intervene when needed to improve taskwork and teamwork, and (d) bring closure to the lesson. Your job now is to monitor students' interactions and to help students learn and interact more skillfully (Johnson, Johnson, & Holubec, 2008).

Monitoring Students' Behavior

An instructor's job begins in earnest when the cooperative learning groups start working. Instructors observe the interaction among group members to assess students' academic progress and appropriate use of interpersonal and small-group skills.

Observations can be formal with the use of an observation schedule on which frequencies are tallied. Or, observations can take the anecdotal form of informal descriptions of students' statements and actions. Based on your observations, you then can intervene to improve students' academic learning and/or interpersonal and small group skills. Remember, *students respect what we inspect*. If students know that you are monitoring their behaviors and interactions, they are more likely to stay on task and work together.

To monitor means to check continuously. It can be done by you, the teacher, and/ or by selected students within each group. Monitoring has four stages:

1. **Preparing to observe** the learning groups by deciding who will be the observers, what observation forms to use, and training the observers.
2. **Observing** to assess the quality of cooperative efforts in the learning groups.
3. **Intervening when necessary** to improve a group's taskwork or teamwork.
4. **Having students engage in group processing.** They do so by assessing the quality of their own participation in the learning groups (to encourage self-monitoring), assessing the effectiveness of the group, and setting both individual and group growth goals.

In monitoring cooperative learning groups, there are a number of guidelines for teachers to follow:

1. Plan a route through the classroom. Note the length of time you spend observing each group so that you can observe all groups during a lesson.
2. Use a formal observation sheet to count the number of times you observe appropriate behaviors being used by students. The more concrete the data, the more useful the data are to you and to students.
3. Initially, do not try to count too many different behaviors. At first you may wish simply to keep track of who talks. Your observations should focus on positive behaviors.
4. Supplement and extend the frequency data with notes on specific student actions. Especially useful are descriptions of skillful interchanges that can be shared with students later and with parents in conferences or telephone conversations.
5. Train and utilize student observers. Student observers tend to obtain more complete data on each group's functioning (since they do not move from group to group) and may learn important lessons about appropriate and inappropriate behavior.
6. Allocate sufficient time at the end of each group session for discussion of the data gathered by the observers. Observations have little purpose if they are not shared with the people being observed.

Providing Task Assistance

Cooperative learning groups provide teachers with a window into students' minds. When working cooperatively, students make hidden thinking processes overt and subject to observation and commentary. From carefully listening to students explain to one another what they are learning, you can determine what students do and do not understand. Consequently, you may wish to intervene to clarify instructions, review important procedures and strategies for completing the assignment, answer questions, and teach task skills as necessary.

In discussing the concepts and information to be learned, you should make specific statements. Say, "Yes, that is one way to find the main idea of a paragraph," not "Yes, that is right." The more specific statement reinforces the desired learning and promotes positive transfer by helping the students associate a term with their learning. Metacognitive thought may be encouraged by asking students (a) "What are you doing?" (b) "Why are you doing it?" and (c) "How will it help you?"

Intervening to Teach Social Skills

Cooperative learning groups provide teachers with a picture of students' social skills. The social skills required for productive group work are discussed in detail, along with activities that may be used in teaching them, in Johnson (1991, 2009). While monitoring the learning groups, you may intervene to suggest more effective procedures for working together or reinforce particularly effective and skillful behaviors.

Choosing when to intervene is part of the art of teaching. Stepping in too soon prevents students from finding their own path to an answer or a skill. Wait too long, however, and students may get off track or become discouraged and give up. As a rule of thumb, intervene when students are off task whether because of a communication problem or a lack of knowledge. When you do intervene, ask group members to follow the steps of Figure 11.1.

Providing Closure to the Lesson

You provide closure to a lesson by having students summarize the major points in the lesson, recall ideas, and identify final questions for the teacher. Students should be able to summarize what they have learned and to understand how they will use it in the future.

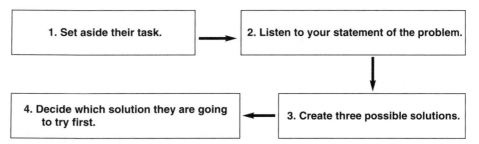

Figure 11.1 When to intervene.

EVALUATING LEARNING AND PROCESSING INTERACTION

When the lesson has been completed, it is time for you to assess and evaluate the quality and quantity of student achievement. In doing so, you need to ensure that students carefully process the effectiveness of their learning groups. You also should have students make a plan for future improvement and celebrate the hard work of group members.

Assessing the Quality and Quantity of Learning

The quality and quantity of student learning should be assessed regularly and evaluated occasionally using a criterion-referenced system. This is covered in depth in *Meaningful and Manageable Assessment Through Cooperative Learning* (Johnson & Johnson, 2002). Cooperative learning, furthermore, provides an arena in which three forms of assessment can take place. First, teachers can make *performance-based assessments* by requiring students to demonstrate what they can do with what they know by performing a procedure or skill. Second, teachers can make *authentic assessments* by requiring students to demonstrate the desired procedure or skill in a real-life context. Third, teachers can make *total quality learning assessments* by measuring the continuous improvement of the process of students helping teammates learn.

A wide variety of other assessment formats may be used, and students may be directly involved in assessing one another's level of learning. Students then can provide immediate remediation to ensure that all group members' learning is maximized.

ASSESSMENT PROCEDURES

Form a pair. Rank order each of the following columns from most important to you (1) to least important to you.

What Is Assessed	Procedures	Ways Cooperative Learning Helps
_____ Academic learning	_____ Goal setting	_____ Additional sources of labor
_____ Reasoning strategies	_____ Testing	_____ More modalities in assessment
_____ Skills, competencies	_____ Compositions	_____ More diverse outcomes
_____ Attitudes	_____ Presentations	_____ More sources of information
_____ Work habits	_____ Projects	_____ Reduction of bias
	_____ Portfolios	_____ Development of rubrics
	_____ Logs, journals	_____ Implement improvement plan

Processing How Well the Group Functioned

When students have completed the assignment or at the end of each class session, they describe what member actions were helpful and unhelpful in completing the group's work. They also make decisions about what behaviors to continue and which ones to change. Group processing occurs at two levels—in each learning group and in the class as a whole. There are five parts to processing:

1. **Feedback.** Ensure that each student, each group, and the class as a whole gives and receives feedback on the effectiveness of taskwork and teamwork. Feedback given to students should be descriptive and specific, not evaluative and general (Johnson, 2009).
2. **Reflection.** Have students analyze and reflect on the feedback they receive. Avoid questions that can be answered "yes" or "no." Instead of asking, "Did everyone help one another learn?" you should ask, "How frequently did each member explain how to solve a problem and correct or clarify other members' explanations?"
3. **Analysis.** Have students describe the actions each member engaged in that contributed to the group effectively completing the assignment.
4. **Improvement goals.** Help individuals and groups set goals for improving the quality of their work.
5. **Celebration.** Encourage the celebration of members' hard work and the group's success.

INFORMAL COOPERATIVE LEARNING GROUPS

Sometimes teachers need to lecture, show a movie or DVD, give a demonstration, or have a guest speaker in the classroom. In such cases, informal cooperative learning may be used to ensure that students are active cognitively (Johnson, Johnson, & Holubec, 2008). Informal cooperative learning (Figure 11.2) consists of having students

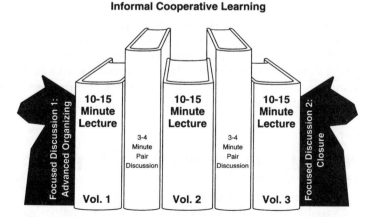

Figure 11.2   Informal cooperative learning.

PURPOSES OF INFORMAL COOPERATIVE LEARNING

Form a pair. Rank order the following purposes of informal cooperative learning from most important (1) to least important (7).

_____ Focuses student attention on the material to be learned.

_____ Sets a mood conducive to learning.

_____ Helps cognitively organize in advance the material to be covered in a class session.

_____ Ensures that students cognitively process the material being taught.

_____ Provides closure to an instructional session.

_____ Allows for identifying and correcting misconceptions, incorrect understanding, and gaps in comprehension.

_____ Personalizes learning experiences.

work together to achieve a joint learning goal in temporary, ad hoc groups on tasks that last for a few minutes to one class period. The *purposes* of these groups are to focus student attention on the material to be learned, set a mood conducive to learning, help organize in advance the material to be covered in a class session, ensure that students cognitively process the material being taught, and provide closure to an instructional session. Informal cooperative learning groups also ensure that misconceptions, incorrect understanding, and gaps in understanding are identified and corrected and that learning experiences are personalized.

During lecturing and direct teaching, the instructional challenge for the instructor is to ensure that students do the intellectual work of organizing material, explaining it, summarizing it, and integrating it into existing conceptual networks. This may be achieved by having students engage in advanced organizing discussion, cognitively rehearse and organize the material being presented, and provide closure to the lesson in a wrap-up session. Engaging in these activities actively engages students in what is going on in the classroom at the time, even when the lesson is delivered in a one-way stream such as a lecture or video. Breaking up lectures with short cooperative processing periods gives teachers slightly less lecture time but helps counter what is proclaimed as the main problem of lectures: "The information passes from the notes of the professor to the notes of the student without passing through the mind of either one."

USING INFORMAL COOPERATIVE LEARNING

The following procedure is designed to help you plan a lecture that keeps students more actively engaged intellectually through the use of informal cooperative learning groups (Johnson & Johnson, 1999a; Johnson, Johnson, & Holubec, 2008). It entails having *focused discussions* before and after the lecture (i.e., bookends) and interspersing *pair discussions* throughout the lecture. Two important aspects of using informal cooperative learning groups are to (a) make the task and the instructions explicit and precise and (b) require the groups to produce a specific product, such as a written answer. The procedure is as follows.

First, structure an introductory-focused discussion. Assign students to pairs. The person nearest them will do. You may wish to require different seating arrangements for each class period so that students can meet and interact with a number of classmates. Give the pairs the cooperative assignment of completing the initial (advance organizer) task. Give them only four or five minutes to do so. The discussion task is aimed at promoting *advance organizing* of what the students know about the topic to be presented and *establishing expectations* about what the lecture will cover.

Second, structure intermittent-focused discussions. Deliver the first segment of the lecture. This segment should last for ten to fifteen minutes. This is about the length of time a motivated adult can concentrate on a lecture. For unmotivated children and adolescents, the time may be shorter. At the end of the segment, give the students a two- to four-minute discussion task focused on the material you presented. This short discussion ensures that students are actively cognitively processing the material being presented. The discussion task may be to (a) give an answer to a question posed by the instructor; (b) give a reaction to the theory, concepts, or information being presented; or (c) relate the material to past learning so that it is integrated into existing conceptual frameworks (i.e., elaborate the material being presented). The structure for the pair discussion is (a) each student formulates what he or she is going to say, (b) students share their answer with their partner, (c) students listen carefully to their partner's answer, and (d) pairs create a new answer that is superior to each member's initial formulation through the process of association, building on each other's thoughts, and synthesizing. Randomly choose two or three students to give thirty-second summaries of their discussions. It is important that students are called on randomly to share their answers after each discussion task. Such individual accountability ensures that the pairs take the tasks seriously and check each other to ensure that both are prepared to answer. Instructors repeat this sequence of lecture segment following by a pair discussion until the presentation is over.

Third, structure a closure-focused discussion. Give students an ending discussion task lasting for three to five minutes to summarize what students have learned from the lecture. The discussion should result in students integrating what they have just learned into existing conceptual frameworks. The task also may point students toward what the homework will cover or what will be presented in the next class session. This provides closure to the lecture.

Informal cooperative learning ensures that students actively are involved in understanding what they are learning. It also provides time for instructors to gather their wits, reorganize notes, take a deep breath, and move around the class listening to what students are saying. Listening to student discussions can give instructors direction and insight into how well students understand the concepts and material being taught. Instructors can pick up on points that should be covered again because students have not grasped the full idea or are not applying it correctly.

BASE GROUPS

Committed group relationships do not develop in a few hours or even a few days. They develop from spending many hours working together during which group members come to depend on and support one another. In schools, therefore, it is important that some of the relationships built through cooperative learning groups are long term. School has to be more than a series of temporary encounters that last for only a few minutes, a class period, an instructional unit, or a semester. To help students foster more committed long-term group relationships, they can be assigned to permanent cooperative base groups (Johnson & Johnson, 1999a; Johnson, Johnson, & Holubec, 2008).

Cooperative base groups are long-term, heterogeneous cooperative learning groups with stable membership. Members' primary responsibilities are to (a) provide one another with support, encouragement, and assistance in completing assignments; (b) hold one another accountable for striving to learn; and (c) ensure that all members are making good academic progress. Typically, cooperative base groups are heterogeneous in membership, especially in terms of achievement motivation and task orientation. They meet regularly—daily or biweekly—for the duration of the class (a semester or a year) or, preferably, longer.

Types of Base Groups

Base group can be used in two ways. The *first* is to have a base group in each class. Class base groups stay together only for the duration of the course. The *second* is to organize all students within the school into base groups and have the groups function as an essential component of school life. School base groups stay together for at least a year and preferably for four years, or until all members graduate.

1. **Academic support tasks:** Base group members encourage one another to master course content and complete all assignments. Members check to see what help if any is needed to complete his or her assignments. The group discusses assignments; answers any questions about assignments; provides information about what a member may have missed; and plans, reviews, and edits papers. Members can prepare one another to take tests and go over the questions missed afterward. Members also share their areas of expertise, such as art or computers, with one another. Above all, members monitor one another's academic progress and make sure that all members are achieving.

2. **Personal support tasks:** Base group members may listen sympathetically when a member has problems with parents or friends, have general discussions about life, give advice about relationships, and help solve nonacademic problems. Base groups provide interpersonal relationships that personalize the course.

3. **Routine tasks:** The base group provides a structure for managing course procedures such as taking attendance and homework.

BASE GROUPS

Types	Functions	Nature
Class (meet at the beginning and ending of each session or week)	Provide academic support to members	Heterogeneous in membership
School (meet at the beginning and ending of each day or week)	Provide personal support to members	Meet regularly (daily, biweekly)
	Manage class routines and administrative requirements	Last for duration of class, year, or until graduation
	Personalize class and school experience	Ensure all members are making good academic progress

4. **Assessment and evaluation tasks:** The base group provides a structure for assessing and evaluating student academic learning. Many of the more complex and important assessment procedures can be used best in the context of cooperative learning groups.

Forming Base Groups

Group size: Four (or three)
Assigning students: Random assignment to ensure heterogeneity
Arranging the room: Providing a permanent place for each group to meet
Preparing materials: Standard forms students use at each meeting; group file folders
Assigning roles: Runner, explainer, accuracy checker, encourager

TYPES OF COOPERATIVE LEARNING

Form a pair. In the spaces provided, write out the definition of each type of cooperative learning in your own words.

Formal	Informal	Base Groups

INTEGRATED USE OF ALL THREE GOAL STRUCTURES

The third step in increasing your expertise in using cooperative learning is to use all three goal structures—cooperation, competition, and individual work—in an integrated way. Although the dominant goal structure within any classroom should be cooperation (which ideally would be most of the time), competitive and individualistic efforts are useful supplements. Competition may be used for an enjoyable change of pace during an instructional unit that predominantly is structured cooperatively. Individualistic learning often is productive when the information learned is used subsequently in a cooperative activity. The integrated use of cooperative, competitive, and individualistic learning is described in more detail in Johnson and Johnson (1999a) and in Johnson, Johnson, and Holubec (2008).

An example of the integrated use of cooperative learning procedures is as follows. Students arrive at class and meet in their base groups to welcome one another, complete a self-disclosure task, check each other's homework to make sure all members understand the academic material and are prepared for the class session, and tell one another to have a great day.

The teacher then begins a lesson on the limitations of being human. To help students cognitively organize in advance what they know about the advantages and disadvantages of being human, the teacher uses informal cooperative learning groups. The teacher asks students to form a triad and ponder the question, "What are five things you cannot do with your human limitations that a Billion-Dollar Being might be designed to do?" Students have four minutes to do so. In the next ten minutes, the teacher explains that although the human body is a marvelous system, we have very specific limitations. We cannot see bacteria in a drop of water or the rings of Saturn unaided. We cannot hear as well as a deer can or fly like an eagle. Humans never have been satisfied in being limited, however, so we have invented microscopes, telescopes, and our own wings. The teacher then instructs students to turn to the person next to them and answer the questions, "What are three limitations of humans?" "What have we invented to overcome them?" and "What other human limitations might we be able to overcome?"

Formal cooperative learning also is used in this lesson. (For the Billion-Dollar Being lesson, see *Topics in Applied Science*, Jefferson County Schools, Golden, Colorado.) The teacher has the thirty-two students count off from one to eight to form groups of four randomly. Group members sit so they can face one another and the teacher. Each member is assigned a role: researcher/runner, summarizer/timekeeper, collector/recorder, and technical adviser (role interdependence). Every group gets one large 2×3-foot piece of paper, a marking pen, a rough draft sheet for designing the Being, an assignment sheet explaining the task and the cooperative goal structure, and four student self-evaluation checklists (resource interdependence). The task is to design a Billion-Dollar Being that overcomes the human limitations thought of by the class and the group. The group members are to draw a diagram of the Being on the scratch paper and, when they have something they like, transfer it to the larger paper.

The teacher establishes positive goal interdependence in this lesson by asking for one drawing from the group that all group members contribute to and can explain. The criterion for success is to complete the diagram in the thirty-minute time limit. The teacher ensures individual accountability by observing each group to ensure that members are fulfilling their roles and that any one member can explain any part of the Being at any time. The teacher informs students that the expected social skills to be used by all students are encouraging everyone's participation, contributing ideas, and summarizing. He or she defines the skill of encouraging participation and has each student practice it twice before the lesson begins.

While students work in their groups, the teacher monitors by systematically observing each group and intervening to provide (a) academic assistance and (b) help in using the interpersonal and small-group skills required to work together effectively.

Integrated Use of All Types of Cooperative Learning for Fifty-Minute Session

Step	Activity	Time (in minutes)
1	Welcome and opening base group meeting	10
2	Choice 1: Direct teaching, informal cooperative learning	35
3	Choice 2: Work in formal cooperative learning groups	35
4	Choice 3: Direct teaching, formal cooperative learning groups	35
5	Choice 4: Academic controversy	35
6	Closing base group meeting	5

Weekly Schedule for Fifty-Minute Class Sessions

Session 1		Session 2		Session 3	
Time	Activity	Time	Activity	Time	Activity
15	Base group meeting	5	Base group meeting	5	Base group meeting
30	Lecture with informal CL	35	Formal CL groups work on assignment or controversy	15	Formal CL groups work on assignment
5	Base group meeting	5	Base group meeting	10	Lecture with informal CL
				15	Base group meeting

Integrated Use of All Types of Cooperative Learning for Ninety-Minute Session

Step	Activity	Time
1	Opening base group meeting	10
2	Direct teaching with informal cooperative learning	25
3	Work on assignment in formal cooperative learning	40
4	Direct teaching with informal cooperative learning	10
5	Closing base group meeting	5

At the end of the lesson, the groups hand in their diagrams of the Billion-Dollar Being to be assessed and evaluated. Group members then process how well they worked together by identifying actions each member engaged in that helped the group succeed and one thing that could be added to improve their group next time.

The teacher then returns to informal cooperative learning to provide closure to the lesson by asking students to meet in new triads and write out six conclusions about the limitations of human beings and what we have done to overcome them.

At the end of the class session, the cooperative base groups meet to review what students believe is the most important thing they have learned during the lesson, what homework has been assigned, what help each member needs to complete the homework, and to wish one another a good rest of the day.

THE COOPERATIVE SCHOOL

W. Edwards Deming, Joseph Juran, and other founders of the quality movement have stated that over 85% of the behavior of members of an organization is directly attributable to the organization's structure, not the nature of the individuals involved. Your classroom is no exception. If competitive or individualistic learning dominates your classroom, your students behave accordingly, regardless of whether you have put them temporarily in cooperative groups. If cooperative learning dominates your classroom, on the other hand, your students behave accordingly and a true learning community can develop.

The issue of cooperation among students is part of a larger issue of the organizational structure of schools (Johnson & Johnson, 1994). For decades, schools have functioned as mass-production organizations that divided work into component parts (first grade, second grade, English, social studies, science) to be performed by teachers who are isolated from their colleagues and work alone, in their own room, with their own set of students, and with their own set of curriculum materials. Students can be assigned to any teacher because students are considered to be interchangeable parts in the education machine. When you use cooperative learning, however, the majority of the time you are changing the basic organizational structure of your classroom to one that is a team-based. In other words, cooperation is more than an instructional procedure. It is a basic shift in organizational structure that affects all aspects of classroom life.

In a cooperative school, students work primarily in cooperative learning groups, teachers and building staff work in cooperative teams, and district administrators work in cooperative teams (Johnson & Johnson, 1994). The organizational structures of the classroom, school, and district then are congruent. Each level of cooperative teams supports and enhances the other levels.

A cooperative school structure begins in the classroom with the predominant use of cooperative learning (Johnson & Johnson, 1994). Work teams are the heart of the team-based organizational structure, and cooperative learning groups are the primary work teams.

The second level in creating a cooperative school is to create faculty-based cooperative teams and a school-based decision-making procedure. Creating this level of cooperative work involves establishing collegial teaching teams, task forces, and ad hoc decision-making groups within the school (Johnson & Johnson, 1994). Collegial teaching teams are small, cooperative groups (two to five teachers) whose purpose is to increase teachers' instructional expertise and success (Johnson & Johnson, 1994). A task force considers a school problem and proposes a solution to the faculty as a whole. The faculty then is divided into ad hoc decision-making groups and considers whether to accept or modify the proposal. The decisions made by the ad hoc groups are summarized, and the entire faculty then decides on the action to be taken to solve the problem. Teacher teams can be equally as effective as student teams. Just as the heart of the classroom is cooperative learning, the heart of the school is the collegial teaching team.

The third level in creating a cooperative school is to implement administrative cooperative teams within the district (Johnson & Johnson, 1994). Administrators are organized into collegial teams to increase their administrative expertise, as well as task forces and ad hoc decision-making groups. Working as a cooperative group, they make decisions that affect every teacher and student within the school district.

Willi Unsoeld, a mountain climber and philosopher, gave this advice as the secret to survival to all those who set off to climb a mountain: "Take care of each other and share your energies with the group. No one must feel alone, cut off, for that is when you do not make it." The same may be said for everyone entering a school.

SUMMARY

Cooperative learning is a very old idea. It may be defined as students working together to achieve mutual learning goals. It is most often contrasted with competitive and individualistic learning. There are three types of cooperative learning. Formal cooperative learning is having students work together to achieve a mutual learning goal on tasks that may last for one to several class periods. The instructor's role in using formal cooperative learning consists of making preinstructional decisions, explaining the instructional task and cooperative structure, monitoring student learning groups and intervening when needed to improve both taskwork and teamwork, and assessing student learning and having students process how effectively they are working together.

Informal cooperative learning is having students work together in temporary, ad hoc groups to achieve a mutual learning goal on a task that lasts for a few minutes. The instructor's role involves having students form temporary pairs to answer a set of questions that serve as advance organizers for a lecture, video, or demonstration. The lecture or demonstration is then presented in segments, each of which is followed by an intermittent pair discussion to ensure students' process the material being presented. Finally, a pair discussion is used to provide closure to the presentation.

Cooperative base groups is having students work together in groups with stable membership to achieve mutual learning goals on long-term tasks that last for a semester or year. They typically begin and end each class session (or each week). Students are responsible for ensuring all group members are making good academic progress by providing academic and personal support, managing routine tasks, and assessing each other's work.

All three types of cooperative learning tend to be used during a lesson. The lesson begins with a base group meeting, the instructor may present new material while using informal cooperative learning, a formal cooperative learning lesson is conducted, the instructor summarizes using informal cooperative learning, and the class ends with a base group meeting.

Cooperative learning forms the basis for creating an organizational context that is team-based and focused on high performance. In a high-performance school, teaching teams, faculty meetings, and site-based decision making are structured cooperatively. The organizational context of learning is then congruent with instructional practice, enhancing the effectiveness of both.

CHAPTER TWELVE

Leading Growth and Counseling Groups

BASIC CONCEPTS TO BE COVERED IN THIS CHAPTER

A number of concepts are defined and discussed in this chapter. The major ones are listed below. Students should divide into pairs. Each pair is to (a) define each concept, noting the page on which it is defined and discussed, and (b) ensure that both members of the pair understand the meaning of each concept. Then combine into groups of four, and compare the answers of the two pairs. If there is disagreement, look up the concept in the chapter and clarify it until all members agree on and understand the definition.

CONCEPTS

1. Counseling and therapy groups
2. Growth groups
3. Interpersonal effectiveness
4. Intuition
5. Psychological health
6. Reactance
7. Self-actualization
8. Self-help groups

INTRODUCTION

In addition to solving a problem or completing an assignment, groups also can function as a means of helping individuals grow and change in constructive ways. A wide variety of therapeutic groups aim at achieving many different personal growth goals. What they have in common is an emphasis on members improving their psychological health, happiness, effectiveness, and competence.

A number of therapeutic events promote the achievement of these personal growth goals. Individuals may change by themselves in isolation from others; by working one on one with a counselor, therapist, minister, or friend; or by participating in small groups, such as growth, counseling, or therapy groups. Groups, however, have several unique powers that make them the ideal setting for personal change. In this chapter the therapeutic power of groups will be discussed, along with the conditions under which therapeutic events may be promoted.

TYPES OF THERAPEUTIC GROUPS

Millions of Americans have participated or are participating in groups aimed at personal growth, therapeutic change, or self-help (Figure 12.1). **Growth groups** focus on emotional growth, improved interpersonal relationships, and group skills. They include T-groups, encounter groups, human relations training groups, and structured growth groups. **Counseling** and **therapy groups** focus on increased psychological adjustment and health. They include psychoanalytic groups, Adlerian groups, psychodrama groups, Gestalt groups, cognitive-behavioral groups, existential groups, person-centered groups, rational-emotive groups, reality groups, and interpersonal therapy groups. **Self-help groups** focus on overcoming or coping with life stresses, such as addiction or illness. An enormous number of self-help groups can be found in our society.

Goals

Growth, counseling, and self-help groups have similar, overlapping goals. Although the diversity of groups in each area precludes a complete listing of goals applicable to all, generally these groups seek goals such as:

1. Decreasing self-defeating patterns and increasing self-enhancing patterns of behavior and attitudes. Many individuals have developed behavior patterns and attitudes that create and sustain negative and self-destructive consequences and ultimately lead to a more painful and troubled life. They may join groups to identify these self-defeating and self-destructive patterns and change them to patterns that promote the ability to maintain themselves, grow, and flourish.
2. Increasing psychological health and decreasing psychological pathology. **Psychological health** is the ability to be aware of and manage effectively one's interdependent interactions with others (Johnson, 1980b; Johnson & Johnson, 1989). Feelings such as depression, anxiety, or anger and problems interacting

Types of Therapy Groups	
Growth Groups	Self-Help Groups
Unique power of groups	Importance of disclosing emotions
Leading growth and therapy groups	Conceptualizing, feelings, intuition
Becoming a facilitator	Growth groups and anxiety, costs
Costs of participating in groups	Comparative effectiveness

Figure 12.1 Growth and therapy groups.

appropriately with others in family or work situations may drive people to seek help in groups.

3. Increasing the ability to build and maintain humanizing relationships. **Humanizing relationships** reflect the qualities of empathy, kindness, compassion, consideration, mercy, love, responsiveness, and friendship.

4. Increasing self-actualization. **Self-actualization** is the psychological need for growth, development, and utilization of potential (Maslow, 1954). A self-actualizing person moves toward the full use of his or her talents, capacities, and potentialities. Self-actualization involves both self-development and self-utilization: One develops potentialities and then uses them in order to actualize oneself.

5. Increasing interpersonal effectiveness. **Interpersonal effectiveness** is the extent to which the consequences of a person's behavior match his or her intentions (Johnson, 2006). When two participants interact, for example, they are seeking to achieve certain consequences. When their behavior results in the consequences they want, their interpersonal effectiveness is high; when the consequences are not what they want, their interpersonal effectiveness is low. Interpersonal effectiveness depends on mastering interpersonal and small group skills. All the group skills discussed in this book and the interpersonal skills discussed in Johnson (2006) are relevant to interpersonal effectiveness.

Participants in growth, therapy, or self-help groups, and the group's facilitator have a set of goals for the group. If the goals of the participants and those of the group facilitator do not completely overlap, the two must negotiate a set of goals they can mutually commit themselves to achieving.

Growth Groups

Growth groups take advantage of the benefits of small groups by bringing people into contact with one another in order to develop interpersonal skills and personal insights that lead to more satisfactory relationships in all parts of the participants' lives. The improvement of the group skills discussed throughout this book is an example of a goal of growth groups.

T-Groups. Broadly speaking, the term *T-group* (sometimes known as *laboratory-training* or *sensitivity-training* group) refers to groups whose primary emphasis is on studying the development of the group and the relationships among group members (Watson & Johnson, 1972). The primary source of information for learning is the behavior of the group members themselves. The discussions focus on what is happening in the group. T-groups are associated with the National Training Laboratories for Applied Behavioral Science in Bethel, Maine, and Washington, D.C.

T-groups originated from an accident that occurred in the presence of Kurt Lewin, who was quick to appreciate the potential utility of what was taking place (Marrow, 1969). In 1946, Lewin was asked to conduct a workshop to explore the use of small groups to train community facilitators to strengthen democracy at the grassroots level. The participants were educators, public officials, and social scientists. They met in small groups focused on the development of democratic facilitators. The small groups were observed by several of Lewin's graduate students (one of whom was **Morton Deutsch**), who met in the evenings to discuss the dynamics of the group discussions they had observed during the day. One evening, two of the participants asked if they could sit in and listen while the graduate students discussed their observations. Much to everyone's surprise, Lewin said, "Yes." By chance, the observers were discussing an episode that involved one of these participants. As the discussion progressed, the participant became more and more agitated until she interrupted and disagreed with the observers' interpretations. She then proceeded to give her version of the episode, which led to a discussion that proved to be both involving and enlightening. The next night, all fifty of the participants showed up and enthusiastically joined in the discussion, frequently disagreeing with and clarifying the interpretations of the trained observers. The participants had sources of information not available to the observers—namely, the participants' intentions.

Lewin and his students grasped the significance of the evening discussions. They concluded that a group engaged in a problem-solving discussion can benefit enormously by taking time out to discuss its own dynamics, or *group process*. After a time, what evolved was a group whose purpose was to study its own development and dynamics. The initial name, *sensitivity-training* (as the experience sensitized participants to the impact of their behavior on others), or *laboratory-training* groups, was eventually shortened to *training group* and then to *T-group*. After Lewin's death in 1947, the National Training Laboratory of Applied Behavioral Science (NTL) was organized by Lewin's colleagues and students at the Research Center for Group Dynamics, the National Education Association, and the Office of Naval Research.

Generally, participants in a T-group learn about the way they interact with others while providing leadership, making group decisions, striving to influence what the group does, resolving conflicts, setting group norms, and so forth. They also learn how others see them, how their behavior affects the other participants, and how they are affected by other participants' actions. They learn how to communicate more effectively, how to understand their own feelings and the feelings of other people, and how to build and maintain relationships with others. Many times participants seek answers to specific questions: "Why do I have difficulties getting along with other people?" "Why is it so hard for me to make friends?" "How can I handle my anger?" "Why do I have such difficulty trusting people?" "Why am I so powerless in most groups?" and so forth.

The use of T-groups has proved popular for several reasons: They use an inductive method of teaching group dynamics, they involve learning through experience, and they generate personal learning and emotional experiences by examining the interaction among members. T-groups probably were used most frequently in the 1960s, and today, T-groups are a key component of many companies and organizations' human resources departments (Burke & Day, 1986).

The traditional difference between T-groups and counseling groups (discussed in the next section) is that in a T-group the facilitator and the other participants do not attempt to interpret participants' motives or probe their past experiences. Instead, they focus on behavior in the group and reactions of the other participants to the behavior.

Encounter Groups. The distinction between T-groups and counseling groups became blurred in the 1960s with the advent of encounter groups. Promoted by psychotherapists such as Carl Rogers (1970b), encounter groups emphasized participants accepting and trusting their feelings, accepting their most personal qualities, and being more open in interacting with others. Participants are encouraged to encounter one another "authentically" by displaying their true emotions, thoughts, and worries. The facilitator displays unconditional positive regard and helps participants experience and express their intense feelings. Role playing and other exercises may be used to help participants experience and express feelings such as caring, loneliness, helplessness, and anger. In encounter groups, individuals are encouraged to explain their present behavior in terms of past experiences and to seek healing for past hurts.

Human Relations Training Groups. Human relations training groups focus on increasing members' competence in interacting effectively with individuals from diverse ethnic and cultural backgrounds. Small groups with members from diverse backgrounds study their own interactions and work to build effective relationships with one another. In human relations training groups, interactions among diverse individuals may be experienced and studied simultaneously. Group members tend to develop insights into cultural differences and the ways in which constructive relationships among diverse individuals may be built and maintained.

Structured Growth Groups. Structured growth groups focus on specific interpersonal problems or skills. Exercises may be used to help participants practice the targeted behaviors and skills. Assertiveness training, which focuses on teaching individuals the difference between being aggressive, passive, and assertive, is an example. All of the exercises in this book are examples of structured growth exercises. Countless organizations all over the world use structured growth groups in their workshops and seminars. They usually follow the format of skills training discussed in Chapter 2.

Counseling and Therapy Groups

Psychoanalytic Groups. Psychoanalytic groups focus on the inner conflicts underlying psychological problems. Sigmund Freud, one of the originators of the psychoanalytic method, believed that most people avoid confronting their conflicts by repressing them. During psychoanalytic group sessions, therefore, participants are encouraged to discuss their memories, fears, fantasies, and dreams in order to gain insight into their unconscious. The group facilitator may offer interpretations of the participants' free associations to promote insights. Facilitators also may take advantage of transference, the tendency of participants to transfer the emotions they feel for their parents to the therapist, to determine the root cause of a particular issue or problem.

Various schools of psychoanalytical thought exist, based on the specific theories of various psychotherapists and theorists. In Freudian groups, for example, the therapist dominates, working with each participant while the other group members observe. Jungian groups, on the other hand, may focus more on dreams.

Adlerian Group Psychotherapy. Alfred Adler contended that people often feel inferior in regard to others because of children's early recognition of their dependence on adults. That feeling of inferiority motivates them to strive for mastery, superiority, power, and, ultimately, perfection. He believed that social forces primarily motivate people as they search for significance in their lives. Thus, people's neuroses are determined by social factors and are best cured in social contexts, such as therapy groups. Striving to overcome inferiority results in a move toward cooperative social living to overcome aloneness and weakness (Richardson & Manaster, 1997).

Other Adlerian theorists have outlined four stages of group counseling to help people overcome their feelings of inferiority. The steps are building cohesion, assessing each member's psychological health and functioning, helping each member increase self-understanding and gain insights, and helping each member reorient him- or herself by seeing new ways of behaving and new choices that may be made (Sonstegard, Dreikurs, & Bitter, 1982; Sonstegard & Bitter, 1998).

Psychodrama. Moreno (1932/1953) developed therapy groups in which participants acted out past emotional experiences as psychodramas. His psychodrama theory is based on two assumptions. First, he believed physically acting out traumatic past events is more involving than a passive discussion of them. Second, he believed that the dramatic enactment helps group members overcome their reluctance to discuss intimate and upsetting issues.

Gestalt Group Therapy. Fritz Perls (1969), who generally is recognized as the founder of Gestalt therapy, emphasized (a) the integration of mind and body; (b) increased clarity about one's wants, values, and goals; (c) greater awareness of oneself, especially one's feelings and one's impact on others; and (d) the resolution or completion of unfinished business. A person is not fully functioning until past experiences are resolved in some way. These experiences could include interpersonal conflicts that still upset, the death of a relative or friend that still hurts, or a past failure that still sparks regret. Generally, the problems are unresolved because individuals repress their emotions. For people to reach their potential, they have to complete their unfinished business by getting in touch with their feelings and resolving their interpersonal problems.

In many cases, resolving a problem is difficult because the other person (such as a parent) has died. To solve such problems and to uncover repressed feelings, Perls recommends procedures such as the *empty-chair method*, in which the participant imagines his or her parent sitting in the empty chair and has a conversation with the imagined person. Another procedure is the *reversal experiment*, in which a person role plays a side of him- or herself rarely or never expressed.

Perls viewed therapy as a process by which negative identifications with significant others are replaced with positive identification with the therapist. The facilitator of a Gestalt therapy group works with one member at a time, with the other members observing the process. One by one, each participant is placed in the "hot seat" and works through his or her unfinished business.

Cognitive-Behavioral Group Psychotherapy. Cognitive-behavioral group psychotherapy applies the behavior theories of Skinner (1953, 1971) and the social learning theories of Bandura (1976, 2006) to engineer changes in behavior without concern for the origins of the ineffective actions or the psychodynamics of the person. Individuals decide how they wish to change, and through procedures such as modeling, rehearsal, feedback, and reinforcement, they develop more effective behavioral patterns. Group members learn self-management skills to control their lives and deal effectively with problems (Watson & Tharp, 1997).

Existential Group Psychotherapy. Existential group psychotherapy helps participants confront the basic "givens" or ultimate concerns of existence: death (conflict between the awareness of the inevitability of death and the wish to continue to be), freedom (conflict between groundlessness and desire for structure), existential isolation (conflict between awareness of one's absolute isolation and the wish for protection, closeness, and desire to be a part of the larger whole), and meaninglessness (conflict between the apparent meaninglessness of life and the desire for a life with meaning).

Existential therapy assumes that all individuals are free to choose what to make of their circumstances and, therefore, are responsible for their choices and actions. Each person is the architect of his or her life. Group members are encouraged to take responsibility for their lives, rather than being passive victims of circumstances. They are helped to discover alternative ways of dealing with their problems so they can choose the path they wish to follow, thus becoming the authors of their lives. In doing so, they resolve their concerns about death, freedom, isolation, and meaning.

Person-Centered Group Psychotherapy. Developed by Carl Rogers, the person-centered approach to group psychotherapy assumes that human beings tend to move toward wholeness and self-actualization and that they can find their way without much direction from the group facilitator. The facilitator creates a healing climate in the group by being caring, empathetic, understanding, accepting, warm, and genuine. In such an environment, group members are able to drop their defenses and work toward meaningful goals. There is a basic trust in the person's ability to move forward if the appropriate conditions for fostering growth are present.

Rational-Emotive Behavior Group Psychotherapy. Rational-emotive behavior group psychotherapy is based on the assumption that at an early age individuals learn "shoulds," "oughts," and "musts" that are translated into irrational assumptions held on a preconscious level. These assumptions then lead to self-defeating beliefs and behaviors (Ellis, 1996, 1997). An irrational assumption is a belief that makes you depressed, anxious, or upset most of the time. An example of such an irrational assumption is "I must be loved, liked, and approved of by everyone all the time or I will be absolutely miserable and will feel totally worthless." Obviously, everyone will not love you all the time, and therefore, this assumption inevitably results in depression and disappointment. To combat such an irrational assumption, a person must (a) become aware of the irrational assumption being made and (b) engage in an internal debate to replace it with a new, more constructive one.

Reality Group Psychotherapy. Reality therapy is based on the assumptions that (a) humans are motivated to fulfill their basic needs for survival, love and belonging, power, freedom, and fun and (b) each person chooses how to fulfill these needs in his or her current relationships (Glasser, 1998). The emphasis is on controlling one's own behavior to better meet one's needs in one's current relationships. Thus, in the group, members talk about their current behavior and how to become more effective. Group members explore their needs, examine the effectiveness of their current behavior in meeting their needs, identify the aspects of their behavior they wish to change, and plan how to do so.

Interpersonal Group Psychotherapy. Interpersonal group psychotherapy is based on the assumption that many psychological problems result from problems in relationships (Johnson & Matross, 1977; Yalom & Leszoz, 2005). Depression, anxiety, and personality disorders may be due to problems in relationships with romantic partners, friends, or family members. Individuals need to correct self-defeating, unsuccessful, and ineffective patterns of behavior. The group is used as a social microcosm in which members interact similarly to how they generally behave outside the group. Self-defeating patterns of behavior become apparent in the group, are identified, and are corrected within the group. The new, self-enhancing patterns of behavior then are generalized to relationships outside of the group.

Self-Help, Mutual-Support Groups

Self-help or mutual-support groups are voluntary groups whose members meet to exchange social support and aid in order to solve or deal with a common problem or condition (Goodman & Jacobs, 1994). Individuals join self-help groups because they face a common predicament, problem, or concern that causes them to bond psychologically. The price for membership usually is not money, but rather (a) admitting that one shares the common problem, (b) reciprocal helping, and (c) commitment to follow the recovery or treatment program advocated by the group, such as the 12-Step Program advocated by Alcoholics Anonymous.

Although many differences exist among support groups, most are self-governing, with members, not "experts," determining the group's procedures. In order to conduct an Alcoholics Anonymous group, for example, one must be an alcoholic. An academic researcher on addiction who had never been an alcoholic would not be accepted as a facilitator. This is so because the members believe they, the people actually living with the problem or affliction, are the best resource for finding ways of coping, managing, and solving the problem.

The variety of self-help groups available is enormous and they are proliferating, primarily because members believe that their needs are not being met by existing educational, social, or health agencies. Goodman and Jacobs (1994) estimate that as many as 8 million people in the United States alone belong to self-help groups. Self-help groups exist for almost every major stress-related, psychological, and medical problem. If you have an addiction to alcohol, other drugs, sex, shopping, or any other activity, support groups are available. If you have lost a child or a spouse or a friend, there is a grief-oriented support group for you. If you have cancer, heart problems, diabetes, or any other major medical condition, support groups exist. If you are dying, support groups are available.

THE UNIQUE POWER OF GROUP EXPERIENCES

Some people seek isolation and privacy while they try to think through their problems and decide how to improve their relationships. Others seek out a friend or a counselor and discuss their problems and plans in a dyad. Groups, however, have several unique advantages over solitary contemplation and dyadic discussion for those who want to grow, develop, change, and heal. Their unique capacities are due largely to the more heterogeneous, complex social setting that groups provide. The greater number of relationships available in the group provides richness and potential for learning, growth, change, and healing that are not possible in a dyad or a solitary situation.

Supportive Community

Groups generate a sense of community, belonging, caring, support, acceptance, and assistance. So many benefits come from being part of a supportive community that encourages change and growth that it would take an entire book to discuss them. To list a few, though, membership in a supportive group strengthens one's identity as a person who is growing and changing, eases the pain associated with therapeutic exploration, and encourages risk taking in achieving growth goals. It also reduces neurotic distress, increases hope, reduces depression and loneliness, increases self-esteem, improves one's problem-solving ability, and increases feelings of validation (Cline, 1999; Johnson & Johnson, 1989). Each member's confidence in his or her ability to grow and change tends to increase as the other group members commit themselves to assisting and supporting the member in doing so. The power of authenticating affirmations from diverse peers gives groups far more influence over individuals' growth and health than do solitary contemplation or dyad interactions.

Hope

Supportive groups also have the power to inculcate hope and decrease demoralization in their members. A person's sense of hope may be one of the best predictors of mental health and adjustment, and a person's sense of demoralization may be an accurate predictor of psychological problems (Snyder, Cheavens, & Sympson, 1997). To be *demoralized* is to be disheartened, bewildered, confused, disordered, and deprived of courage. The demoralized person feels isolated, hopeless, and helpless. Group situations can generate events that inspire hope, the feeling that one can change, and the belief that one can influence the causes of one's problems. Seeing other group members who have successfully grappled with problems or who have changed as a result of their participation in the group is one such event. The more hope an individual has, the more ways the individual can identify to reach personal goals and the more confident the person is that he or she can engage in the actions necessary to reach those goals.

Microcosm of the Real World

Groups also function as a microcosm of the real world. Participants eventually create in a growth or therapy group the same interpersonal dynamics they always have been involved in by behaving as they do in their relationships outside of the group. The benefit of this happening in a supportive group is that maladaptive interpersonal behavior is revealed in a setting where it can be changed. In other words, groups provide a remedial environment for the solution of personal and interpersonal problems.

In general, people originally learn their maladaptive patterns of behaving and thinking by participating in relationships with others. Within supportive groups, however, people have the opportunity to learn constructive patterns of behaving and reasoning. Growth and therapy groups enable participants to work on their problems immediately by taking corrective steps in their relationships with other group members. In addition, strengths and positive interpersonal behavior are revealed in a setting in which they can be enhanced. In creating a microcosm of the outside world, groups provide an arena for participants to interact freely with others, help them to identify and understand what goes wrong and right in their interactions, and ultimately enable them to change maladaptive patterns and refine constructive patterns.

Induce and Reduce Powerful Feelings

Groups have the ability to induce and then reduce powerful feelings. Not only may the relationship with the facilitator re-create emotions felt toward authority figures, but relationships with other group members also may re-create emotions felt toward siblings and schoolmates. The wider variety of people and the more diverse interpersonal events that take place within a group enable the group to induce a wide range of powerful emotions.

One specific way in which groups induce and reduce powerful feelings is by providing an environment in which participants may experience previously deeply upsetting feelings with a new sense of acceptance. In therapy groups, participants may encounter their worst fears head-on in order to understand and overcome them. By finding that the previously feared feelings are not overwhelming or that the feared consequences do not occur, participants may have a corrective emotional experience. Experiencing and discussing emotions in a supportive and caring environment usually reduces the emotions and decreases their influence on participants' future behavior and thinking.

Perspective Taking

With psychological problems comes egocentrism. A depressed or panicked person is focused on him- or herself. Growth and support groups, however, provide a setting in which participants' egocentrism may be decreased and their perspective-taking ability and empathy increased. The individual's egocentrism is reduced when group members focus on other members' problems and experience a variety of responses to their own actions. Through exchanges of ideas about problems and solutions within a supportive context where group members feel understood and accepted, members become more aware of and open to other perspectives.

Group facilitators also may structure perspective-reversal situations in which participants switch positions and argue one another's point of view or take the perspective of a significant person outside of the group, such as a mother, boss, or spouse. As the ability of a group member to understand the other members' perspectives and feel empathy for their plights grows, his or her egocentrism decreases and the ability to solve personal problems increases.

Multiple Sources of Feedback

Another benefit inherent in groups is they provide multiple sources of feedback. The availability of immediate information about how one is perceived by peers is unique to the group situation. Each group member uses the other members as a mirror to reflect reactions to his or her actions. Although people usually have an accurate view of themselves (they see themselves as others see them), there are times when others see them quite differently from how they see themselves. The other group members thus become a resource that a group member uses to understand him- or herself. The other group members, due to their differing perspectives, perceive the actions and experiences of each member in a variety of ways. The resulting reactions and feedback provide a rich source for understanding oneself and reframing one's experiences.

Multiple Sources of Social Comparison

Groups provide multiple sources of social comparison for participants. Such comparisons cause members to recognize that their problems are universal. Each group member realizes that his or her problems are not unique, but rather a common human experience shared by other members. Yalom and Leszoz (2005) note that many people secretly believe that they are unique in their wretchedness, that they alone have certain frightening or unacceptable problems, thoughts, impulses, and fantasies. Finding out, in reality, that many other people feel the same way is a powerful source of relief.

When individuals feel threatened, confused, or stressed, they often affiliate with others who face similar problems or troubling events (Schachter, 1959), and they tend to feel better about themselves and have a more positive mood after doing so (Frable, Platt, & Hoey, 1998). Group members often compare their feelings, perceptions, attitudes, and behavior with those of their groupmates. Such comparisons occur naturally within a group and facilitate the discovery of possible new ways of feeling, perceiving, and behaving. In a growth or therapy group, members may make *downward social comparisons* (comparing themselves with someone who has even more severe problems) to raise self-esteem and reduce stress (Gibbons & Gerrard, 1989; Wood, Taylor, & Lichtman, 1985). Alternatively, they may make *upward social comparisons* (comparing themselves with someone who is coping effectively with the problem) to identify ways to improve their own coping skills (Blanton, Buunk, Gibbons, & Kuyper, 1999; Collins, 1996; Vrugt & Koenis, 2002).

Vicarious Learning

Groups provide the opportunity for vicarious learning, which is the ability to learn based on what others around you are saying and doing. Social learning theory posits that people can acquire new attitudes and behaviors by observing others' actions (Bandura, 1976, 2006). Within growth and support groups, individuals can witness their groupmates modeling constructive behavior and attitudes that they themselves wish to master. Observing other group members resolve conflicts, build trust, and provide assistance to one another can offer clear guidelines for how the member should behave in the future. Evidence suggests that members of groups that emphasize explicit modeling of constructive behavior improve more than do members of groups that discuss only the problematic behavior (Falloon, Lindley, McDonald, & Marks, 1977).

Require Wide Variety of Social Skills

Groups promote the learning and use of a wide variety of social skills and competencies. A group is the ideal setting in which to increase a person's expertise in using interpersonal and small-group skills. People can read books and study research all they want, but true expertise is built by engaging in an action, receiving feedback on its effectiveness, engaging in a modified action, receiving feedback, and so on. Having experimented with new behavior patterns in the group, the participants feel able to engage in the new behaviors in the outside world.

Groups provide a setting in which problem areas can be identified, new patterns of behavior can be tried out under low-risk conditions, feedback can be attained from others, and the effectiveness of the new behaviors can be determined. Listening to others discuss their problems and helping them experiment with more constructive ways of behaving and thinking, for example, requires social skills and competencies that may never be required in a dyadic relationship. Participants in therapeutic groups stress interpersonal learning as being one of the most helpful results of their participation (Kivlighan & Mullison, 1988; Kivlighan, Multon, & Brossart, 1996).

Influence Behaviors and Attitudes

Groups are powerful influences on the behavioral and attitudinal patterns of members. Factors that have been demonstrated to impact patterns of behavior and attitudes include internalizing group norms, publicly committing oneself to engage in new behaviors, viewing credible models, identifying with other group members, being confronted with personalized information, discussing information with peers, and teaching what one has learned to others (see Chapter 6). In a growth or therapy group, the emphasis is on the mastery and adoption of more constructive ways of behaving and thinking.

Helping Others

Groups provide opportunities for participants to understand and help their peers. By working to understand others in the group and by caring for the personal struggles that other members are going through, group members gain in a variety of ways. *First*, helping others reduces egocentrism and focuses attention and energy on others rather than away from others. *Second*, helping others results in personal change. Alcoholics Anonymous, for example, states that the best way to remain sober is to target one's energy outward by helping others remain sober. *Third*, in helping other group members, participants build self-esteem, self-insight, and increased interpersonal competence. Participants may feel needed and helpful. *Fourth*, helping others provides an important opportunity for engaging in altruistic behavior that may be absent from members' daily lives. *Fifth*, a person who can help others is psychologically healthy. Helping others in itself is a sign of health and self-actualization. *Finally*, change is promoted by accepting the help and support of others. In some cases, the help is from external sources such as a higher being (12-Step Program). In other cases, the help is from other group members. While being helped, members benefit from personalized learning, social approval in a supportive climate, and observing others struggle with similar problems.

Resources for Gaining Self-Insight

Groups provide greater resources for obtaining insight into oneself than do dyads or isolated thought. Change is promoted by reframing past experiences and current problems so that a new social reality emerges. Group members gain a deeper understanding of themselves through other members' reactions to their behavior and disclosures, revealing their problems for the group to analyze, the feedback they receive from groupmates, and their reactions to other members' actions and problems. Groups provide a variety of perspectives and reactions that stimulate insight into and understanding of one's problems and behavior. The other group members become an avenue used by the individual to understand him- or herself. In addition, a group adds to any insight achieved by a member through its consensual validation of the insight. By providing labels for the member's thoughts, feelings, and experiences, and by helping the member reflect on his or her interactions with them, the other group members help the member understand his or her actions.

Cognitive Learning

Groups increase the quantity and quality of cognitive learning (Johnson, Johnson, & Holubec, 2002). Many types of growth, therapy, and self-help groups emphasize the learning of specific cognitive frameworks as part of positive change. Both increased understanding of oneself and the conscious implementation of increased competencies depend on cognitive learning. In their classic study of growth groups, Lieberman, Yalom, and Miles (1973) found that self-disclosure involving some sort of cognitive mastery or understanding, not self-disclosure in itself, was related to positive change. That is, self-discovery that leads to some sort of real change in thought process is more important than merely stating the problem.

IMPORTANCE OF DISCLOSING EMOTIONS

Change is promoted by experiencing and expressing positive and negative emotions about the actions of other group members and about important life events. The therapeutic and growth value of such self-disclosure depends, of course, on group members responding with acceptance, support, and caring feelings. *First*, change is promoted by experiencing intense positive and negative emotions, whether or not they are expressed. Events within the group may unleash emotions that participants previously have been unable or unwilling to experience. In many instances, participants find that such feelings are not overwhelming or that the feared consequences do not occur. Participants may learn to accept the feelings they previously were afraid of, and a corrective emotional experience may result even when the feelings are not expressed overtly.

Second, change is promoted by expressing emotions and describing emotional experiences tends to unify group members and increase their commitment to one another and to the group (Corey & Corey, 2005; Leichtentritt & Shechtman, 1998). Self-disclosure to a group of peers is quite different from self-disclosure to one other person. It feels less dramatic and is less anxiety-laden to reveal private information to a single person than to a group. Taking the risk of making a self-disclosure to a group is more meaningful, then, because it deepens the group's intimacy and trust, which in turn makes further self-disclosures possible (Kaul & Bednar, 2003; Johnson & Noonan, 1972; Roark & Sharah, 1989; Tschuschke & Dies, 1994).

The significance of self-disclosure is not the content of what is disclosed but, rather, the response of other members to what one has said. In getting to the response, a group may move through several stages of self-disclosure (Altman & Taylor, 1973). In the *orientation stage*, members focus on superficial topics and avoid disclosing anything too personal or provocative. They form general impressions of one another and strive to present a good impression of themselves. In the *exploratory affective stage*, members discuss their personal attitudes and opinions on a moderate level but avoid disclosing strongly held emotions or intimate details about themselves. In the *affective stage*,

only a few topics are avoided. Positive and negative feelings are expressed toward one another's actions. In the *stable exchange stage*, all personal feelings are shared. Members express feelings they had blocked previously and thereby unburden themselves of emotional restraint.

Third, change is promoted by expressing previously hidden strong emotions. Venting strong emotions can be cathartic and free individuals from the tension and strain of keeping the emotions suppressed.

Fourth, beneficial change is promoted by observing other group members having significant emotional experiences. Other members' emotional experiences may clarify issues for a participant, who then may use the experiences in his or her own problematic areas.

Fifth, disclosing strong emotional experiences to a supportive and caring group can have considerable therapeutic effects, not the least of which is the realization that one's problems are shared by others and that there is hope of feeling better. Secrets often promote dysfunctional patterns of behavior and feeling. As long as strong emotional experiences are hidden, a person may believe that he or she is uniquely troubled or that no one else could possibly understand what he or she is going through. Revealing one's secrets can result in the discovery that one's problems are universal and that other group members have struggled with similar experiences. Self-disclosure can be therapeutic when participants discover that no one is shocked by their deeply hidden secrets that have always made them feel ashamed, guilty, depressed, or angry. They are freed from anxiety-producing feelings when no one is shocked or horrified by their problems.

Sixth, in self-help groups especially, disclosure change is promoted by more senior members, which may result in identification and reduced isolation for newer group members (Mullan, 1992).

Finally, self-disclosure provides participants with insight into their problems. To communicate their emotions and experiences to other group members, they first must organize and think through their experiences. New insights into one's problems and the dynamics of the situations being discussed tend to emerge from such reconceptualizations. The experience of listening to oneself communicate one's emotions and experiences to others can help one see a new side or dimension to the problem or make a previously unrecognized connection between events and feelings.

LEADING A GROWTH GROUP

Participation in a growth, therapy, or self-help group may result in significant health-producing experiences, but skilled group facilitation is needed to guide the process. Group facilitators must possess several sets of complex skills:

1. Establishing the conditions for experiencing and disclosing emotions and for modifying participants' patterns of behavior and attitudes.
2. Being a resource expert on group dynamics, experiential learning, and the approach to growth being emphasized. Must be able to define and diagnose participants' problems.
3. Teaching needed interpersonal and small-group skills.
4. Modeling the constructive use of small-group and interpersonal skills.
5. Ensuring that members have opportunities for self-disclosure and experimentation with new attitude and behavior patterns.
6. Ensuring that members are provided with constructive confrontations and feedback.
7. Promoting corrective or reparative emotional experiences within the group.
8. Guiding problem solving within which participants can address their concerns.
9. Establishing and enforcing a contract with participants.
10. Carrying out the executive functions of the group.

Establishing Conditions for Participant Change

This set of skills consists of establishing the conditions for change in order for group members to (a) become aware of their ineffective and self-destructive patterns of behavior and attitudes, (b) change to more effective and self-enhancing patterns of behavior and attitudes, and (c) stabilize the new patterns of behavior and attitudes so that they become automatic habit patterns. Establishing the conditions for change is discussed in detail in Johnson (1980b). Examples include the following:

The group leader first needs to establish a supportive group climate characterized by empathy, acceptance, genuineness, spontaneity, and egalitarianism. A supportive climate tends to promote personal disclosures, self-awareness, experiencing and disclosing emotions, experimentation with new patterns of behaving and thinking, and giving and receiving feedback. Disclosing how one is feeling and reacting tends to result in feeling validated, confirmed as a person, better understood, helped, satisfied, and less isolated.

Second, the group facilitator creates a strong sense of positive interdependence and commitment to the group's goals, whether the goals are for self-actualization or for psychological healing (see Chapter 3). The mutual goals focus on three levels of activity:

maximizing one's own growth, maximizing the growth of the other group members, and contributing to the common good. Self-help groups in particular have a strong sense of shared identity, often creating a sense of shared suffering among members (Lieberman, 1993). Meetings of Alcoholics Anonymous, for example, begin with each member publicly stating, "I am an alcoholic." This ritual asserts the group identity and focuses on their shared problem.

Third, the group leader promotes a sufficient level of trust among group members to ensure that participants feel free to take risks (see Chapter 3). Trust is built by (a) openness and sharing (being trusting) and (b) acceptance, support, and cooperativeness (being trustworthy). A group facilitator models both and ensures that group members behave similarly.

Fourth, the group facilitator promotes participants' hope and optimism, positive identification with groupmates who have the skills and competencies the participants need in order to solve the problems they are experiencing, and ability to view problems from a variety of perspectives (thereby reducing their egocentrism).

Being a Resource Expert

The resource expertise a facilitator needs varies with the type of group with which he or she is involved. Almost universally, however, facilitators need expertise in (a) group dynamics, (b) experiential and inquiry learning methods, (c) the approach to growth and therapy being used in the group (T-group, encounter group, psychoanalytic, Adlerian, Gestalt, and so forth), and (d) the diagnoses of personal and interpersonal problems.

Expertise in Group Dynamics. Group facilitators need to be experts in group dynamics. First and foremost, a growth or therapy group needs to be an effective group (see Chapter 1), and therefore, facilitators need a thorough understanding of group dynamics and a mastery of all the group skills discussed in this book. In a growth or therapy group, the facilitator must be able to create clear, operational, mutual goals that members are committed to achieving, promote clear and accurate communication of ideas and feelings among group members, and ensure that participation and leadership are distributed among group members. In addition, the facilitator needs to ensure that all members have equal access to power based on expertise and access to information. He or she must flexibly match decision procedures with situational needs, promote constructive controversy to promote creative problem solving and critical thinking, and ensure that conflicts are faced and resolved constructively. Regardless of the type of growth or therapy group, the group has to be effective if members are to learn, change, and actualize.

Expertise in Experiential Learning. Group facilitators need to be experts in experiential and inquiry methods of learning (see Chapter 2). Almost all types of growth and therapy groups emphasize inquiry into the experiences of the group members. Group facilitators need expertise in helping participants become aware of their action theories, engage in behavior aimed at improving their own and other group members' effectiveness, assess the consequences of and obtain feedback on their behavior, reflect, and modify and refine their action theories and patterns of behavior and attitudes.

Expertise in the Approach to Health and Growth. Group facilitators need to be experts in the approach to growth or to the therapy being used in the group. The resulting conceptual frameworks are used to interpret events within the group and to reinterpret life events. Wide diversity can be found among facilitators in terms of the theories being used to promote growth and health. For some it may be the literature on skill training and for others it may be the theories of Freud, Adler, or Rogers.

Whatever approach is being used, the facilitator presents conceptual frameworks that enable group members to understand more fully the personal and interpersonal dynamics they are involved in as well as to gain insight into their own behavior and attitudes. In their classic study on growth groups, Lieberman, Yalom, and Miles (1973) found that the most effective facilitators had a great ability to present conceptualizations that gave meaning to the members' experiences. Thus, a facilitator should have a solid knowledge of one of the social sciences (such as psychology or sociology) and the ability to use his or her knowledge and expertise to help the members understand what they are experiencing.

Expertise in Diagnosis. Group facilitators need to be able to diagnose the personal and interpersonal problems experienced by group members. To make such diagnoses, the facilitator applies a conceptual framework based on theory and research to the behavior of the group members. Such conceptualizations are especially useful to members after the group experience has ended, when they are able to use them to understand more fully their day-to-day interpersonal and group situations.

A fundamental activity of growth and therapy group facilitators is creating meaning for participants. A facilitator creates meaning by (a) labeling feelings and events that participants undergo, (b) influencing the attributions of causation made by group members, (c) influencing perceived personal control of one's life, and (d) influencing perceived freedom in solving problems. Comfort may be given when the facilitator can help a participant label a physiological reaction as "anxiety" or a reaction as a "defense mechanism." Such labeling not only increases members' self-understanding, it also reduces their fear and anxiety concerning emotional and interpersonal experiences; they aren't abnormal if what they are experiencing has a name. This labeling and accompanying information also provides individuals with cognitive tools they can use in future situations.

In helping participants understand their feelings and experiences, the facilitator must be careful about the way in which he or she attributes the causes of their problems and must pay attention to the resulting sense of personal control experienced by participants (Johnson & Matross, 1977). A participant's problems may be attributed to something within the participant (internal causation) or something outside of the participant (external causation). Causes also may be viewed as stable (incapable of change) or unstable (capable of change). Depending on the problem and the situation, a facilitator may wish to help the participant view a problem as having stable, external causes or unstable, internal causes. When a person is deeply depressed about a perceived failure, for example, the facilitator may wish to help that person focus on the external unstable causes of the failure. But when a group member succeeds, the facilitator may wish to emphasize the internal stable causes of the success in order to improve the person's self-esteem.

In discussing events that take place within the group, facilitators may wish to define members' actions as reflecting high personal control and sense of freedom. A belief that one is in control of one's life makes the world seem more predictable and one's experiences more positive. One of the reasons for severe depression following a major illness such as a heart attack is assumed to be the feeling that one has lost control over one's life (Glass, 1977). A belief in one's control over events affects performance on tasks (Glass & Singer, 1973), judgments of the pleasantness of one's surroundings and mood (Rodin, Solomon, & Metcalf, 1978), the positiveness of one's reactions (Glass, 1977), how active, sociable, and vigorous a person is (Langer & Rodin, 1976), and general health and length of life (Rodin & Langer, 1977). The group facilitator usually should define and diagnose participants' problems in ways that maximize their sense of control over their lives.

Group facilitators also should define participants' problems in ways that maximize their sense of freedom in solving them. The loss of control or of freedom of choice tends to result in psychological reactance (Brehm, 1966; Brehm & Brehm, 1981). **Reactance** is a motivational state aroused whenever individuals feel their freedom has been abridged or threatened. Threats to personal freedom motivate individuals to take actions that help them regain their freedom and control. This motivation to regain freedom can be used to change self-defeating attitudes and behaviors to self-enhancing ones. Being placed in a dependent position, on the other hand, can lead to a significant drop in later performance when one is asked to behave independently on one's own.

Teaching Social Skills and Constructive Patterns of Behavior and Reasoning

One of the major keys to decreasing self-defeating behavior and increasing self-enhancing behavior is improving participants' group and interpersonal skills. Group members' problems often exist because the members lack social skills or are unable to utilize them effectively. Social skills may be taught experientially by recognizing what works and does not work in interacting with other group members. Interpersonal and group skills also may be taught directly through exercises like the ones contained in this book.

Leading growth groups requires the capacity to facilitate the social-skill learning of the participants. Group facilitators need to be able to explain what the skill is and why it is important, create opportunities for members to practice the skill, ensure that feedback is received on how well the skill was enacted, and create ongoing opportunities for members to practice the skill until they perfect it.

Modeling Social Skills and Constructive Behavior

To explain the nature of a social skill, it always is helpful to demonstrate it. To encourage group members to self-disclose and experiment with new behavior, it is helpful for facilitators to model such actions. Social-learning theory (Bandura, 1976, 2006) emphasizes the importance of modeling desired behaviors and then reinforcing group members for imitating the model. Modeling often is followed by rehearsal, where group members practice the targeted skills themselves, either through role playing or with one another. A willingness to model targeted skills means that the facilitator actively participates in the group and interacts with other group members. Activeness on the part of the facilitator is preferable to passiveness, which, when it pertains to members, is associated with anxiety, dissatisfaction, silence, poor attendance, discontinuance, and lack of learning. Care should be taken, however, to make sure activeness does not turn into domination of the group by the facilitator (Bierman, 1969).

Ensuring Opportunities for Self-Disclosure and Experimentation

Many of the important experiences in growth groups come directly from participants' self-disclosures and experimentation with new patterns of thinking and behaving. An important function of the group facilitator, therefore, is to ensure that opportunities to self-disclose and experiment with new behavior are present in the group.

Providing Constructive Feedback and Confrontations

The group facilitator must be able to make sure that members are provided with constructive feedback and that no destructive feedback is exchanged among members. **Helpful feedback** is the sharing, upon request, of a description of how one person sees another person's behavior and its consequences and a description of how the observer is reacting to the other person's behavior. In ensuring that feedback is constructive, it is helpful to differentiate among (a) the behavior being observed, (b) the conceptual framework the observer is using, and (c) the inferences and interpretations made about the person engaging in the behavior. A group facilitator should never let group members confuse these three elements. The actual behavior being observed should be the same for all group members (assuming that the observations are valid), but the conceptual frameworks used to understand the behavior and to make interpretations and inferences about it can be widely disparate. Not all feedback is helpful. **Destructive feedback** is an evaluation of the recipient's nature and worth as a person that is forced on the recipient.

Promoting Reparative Emotional Experiences

The facilitator needs to be able to promote corrective or reparative emotional experiences in the group. Highly personalized and relevant learning often arouses emotions in participants. High levels of caring, support, commitment, anger, frustration, and anxiety are found in most growth and therapy group experiences. A facilitator may stimulate emotional reactions by promoting feedback, supporting experimentation with alternative behaviors, encouraging problem solving, supporting self-disclosure, and expressing warmth and support for the members of the group.

The most effective facilitators in the Lieberman, Yalom, and Miles (1973) study engaged in a moderate amount of emotionally stimulating behavior. Although emotional experiences do not mean that learning is taking place, genuine learning often is accompanied by emotionality. The facilitator ensures that members not only experience emotions, but also reflect on and analyze their feelings.

Guiding Problem Solving

The group facilitator will wish to help participants clarify their self-defeating cycles of behavior and reasoning that cause such feelings as guilt, depression, anxiety, fear, anger, and resentment. Self-defeating cycles of behavior and reasoning are problems to be solved. Problem solving involves identifying a problem, diagnosing the causes of the problem, deciding on alternative ways of solving the problem, and implementing the alternative most likely to work. Communicating warmth and understanding, highlighting the conflict between desired consequences and actual behavior and thinking, initiating problem-solving discussions, and encouraging participants to take on the perspectives of others with whom they are involved, are all ways in which a group facilitator may promote participants' problem solving and mastery of more self-enhancing patterns of attitudes and behaviors (Johnson & Matross, 1977). In the problem-solving process, it may be important to bring in information about the person's past behavior and feelings as well as his or her behavior and feelings in the group (Lieberman, Yalom, & Miles, 1973).

Establishing and Maintaining a Contract

Sometimes it is useful for a facilitator to have a clear contract with participants concerning their responsibilities as group members. The contract might state, for example, that members are (a) to be completely open to the group about both past and current behavior, (b) to take responsibility for themselves once they enter the group and not blame others or circumstances for their predicaments, and (c) to get involved with the other group members and promote their learning. When an explicit contract is made, the facilitator becomes the "keeper of the contract" and should ensure that it is enforced.

Carrying out Executive Functions

A facilitator may have a variety of executive functions to carry out in addition to the therapeutic ones. These include organizing the group, arranging for facilities in which it is to meet, designing a schedule, providing it with needed materials, and evaluating its success. All of these tasks require that the facilitator possess a range of administrative and evaluative skills.

CONCEPTUAL FRAMEWORKS, FEELINGS, AND INTUITION

Effective facilitators utilize their conceptual frameworks, feelings, and intuition in an integrated way. A conceptual framework is a way of looking at members' behavior and connecting it to a pattern that makes the behavior understandable. They utilize conceptual frameworks to understand the dynamics of events taking place in the group, plan interventions, and give explanations of what has taken place. It is through conceptualizing what is happening within the group and among its members that the facilitator

usually finds effective interventions. It is through the facilitator's communication of his or her conceptualizations, furthermore, that much of members' learning takes place. The knowledge now available in the social sciences provides facilitators with explicit conceptual frameworks that can be used to help members learn from their experiences.

Feelings often are an important source of information about what is happening within the group and what sorts of problems are occurring among members. Feelings, however, are not infallible. They are susceptible to bias, distortion, and misunderstanding, especially in situations where the person is threatened, defensive, anxious, or tense. Moreover, all people have their blind spots, and in certain situations or under certain conditions, their feelings can be a reflection of their own fears and anxieties rather than of what actually is taking place in the group. It is important, therefore, for facilitators to "calibrate" themselves on the validity and reliability of their feelings in different situations and in response to different types of events.

Highly experienced facilitators also may intervene in a group on the basis of their intuition. **Intuition** is a preconscious process in which the person has a strong feeling about how something will turn out but does not know how the conclusions were determined. Intuitive thinking characteristically does not advance in careful, well-defined steps; the person has an emotional and cognitive reaction to the total situation and arrives at an answer. Intuition results from an immersion in the group process and from a strong identification with and empathy for what is occurring among group members. The more familiar facilitators are with the issues that concern the group, the greater the likelihood is that their intuitions are correct.

The overuse of intuition by facilitators may be problematic, however, for several reasons. First of all, intuitions are inferences that cannot be proven, and facilitators may overrate the validity of their personal observations. Second, the history of medicine and clinical psychology offers overwhelming evidence of the folly of treatments based on intuition. For example, for several centuries it was intuitively obvious that the insane were possessed by demons and that all diseases were in the blood; therefore, a sick person could be cured by being bled. Third, interventions based on intuitions can become self-fulfilling. That is, the actions of a facilitator whose intuition is wrong may set in motion certain dynamics that create the exact situation the facilitator is trying to correct. Fourth, usually there is little basis for determining if the intuition is right or wrong, because it is based on feelings and ideas more than on evidence. Even when the group does not manifest the behavior a facilitator intuits, it is hard to say that his or her intuition was "wrong" if the facilitator felt strongly about something. Finally, intuition represents an internal logic based on one's culture and frame of reference, and intuitive judgments about another culture or another frame of reference can be misleading. Experience in calibrating one's intuitive abilities is needed because one may find that one's intuition, like one's emotions, is sound on certain types of issues but misleading on others.

GROWTH GROUPS AND PARTICIPANT ANXIETY

Some people have expressed concern that growth groups may create levels of anxiety that have the potential to damage participants psychologically. To determine how anxious college students were before and after participating in a growth group, Johnson, Kavanagh, and Lubin (1973), in two separate studies, compared the anxiety level of participants in a growth group with their anxiety level before and after taking a final examination in a course in group dynamics. They found that participants' anxiety at the beginning of the growth group was less than that experienced before a final examination. In turn, participants' anxiety after the growth group was over was considerably less than that experienced after a final examination. Participating in a growth group, then, seems to be less stressful than taking course examinations.

COSTS OF GROWTH AND THERAPY GROUPS

Growth and therapy groups have costs as well as benefits. Groups usually require their members to commit considerable amounts of time and energy. Members may be expected to become involved with people they might not ordinarily seek out. A small percentage of participants may have negative experiences or find the groups unhelpful. Thus, some group members may drop out because the group does not seem beneficial enough, and a few individuals may feel like casualties and withdraw because they feel significantly harmed by the group experience. Both dropouts and casualties tend to be rare if the facilitator is skilled.

 COMPARATIVE EFFECTIVENESS

Groups are powerful tools that can be used to promote considerable positive growth and change, but there is little evidence to indicate that one type of group is more effective than another. In the classic study by Lieberman, Yalom, and Miles (1973), in which 206 students at Stanford University were assigned randomly to eighteen different types of growth and therapy groups, no one group approach was found to be superior to the others. Fuhriman and Burlingame (1994a), in a review of 700 group therapy studies and seven meta-analyses of the research, concluded that group methods are quite effective but that no one method is more effective than others. McRoberts, Burlingame, and Hoag (1998), in a review of twenty-three studies, concluded that group psychotherapy was quite effective, but no more so than was individual therapy. Bednar and Kaul (1994), however, concluded that group treatments were more effective than no treatment, placebo or nonspecific treatments, or other recognized psychological treatments. These research results are not definitive, however, due to the methodological difficulties of comparing one treatment with another.

SUMMARY

Millions of Americans participate in groups aimed at personal growth, therapeutic change, or self-help. These groups have similar overlapping goals of (a) decreasing self-defeating patterns of behavior and increasing self-enhancing ones, (b) increasing psychological health and decreasing psychological pathology, (c) increasing humanizing relationships, (d) increasing self-actualization, and (e) increasing interpersonal effectiveness. The types of growth groups include T-groups, encounter groups, human relations training groups, and structured growth groups. Counseling and therapy groups include psychoanalytic groups, Adlerian groups, psychodrama groups, Gestalt groups, cognitive-behavioral groups, person-centered groups, existential groups, rational-emotive groups, reality groups, and interpersonal therapy groups. There are an enormous number of self-help groups.

The greater number of relationships available in the group provides richness and potential for learning, growth, change, and healing not possible in a dyad or a solitary situation. The unique capacities of groups include (a) providing a supportive community within which to change, (b) increasing hope and decreasing demoralization, (c) creating a microcosm of the real world, (d) inducing and reducing powerful feelings, (e) increasing perspective-taking and decreasing egocentrism, (f) providing multiple sources of feedback, (g) providing multiple sources of social comparison, (h) providing multiple sources of vicarious learning, (i) requiring the use of a wide variety of social skills, (j) influencing behavioral and attitudinal patterns, (k) providing opportunities for helping others, (l) providing resources for self-insight, and (m) increasing cognitive learning.

One important influence on personal change is the experiencing and expression of positive and negative emotions toward the actions of other group members and about important life events. Both experiencing and expressing emotions can have therapeutic effects. Disclosing emotional experiences can decrease a sense of uniqueness and instill hope that one's problems can be solved. Expressing strong emotions can be cathartic. Observing other group members express their emotions can be beneficial. When more experienced group members disclose emotions, identification and imitation may result. Finally, emotional self-disclosure often provokes insights into one's problems.

Although participation in a growth, therapy, or self-help group may result in significant health-producing experiences, a skilled group facilitator is needed to guide the process. Evidence suggests that all sorts of growth and counseling groups are effective, but no one approach seems to be more effective than any others.

CHAPTER THIRTEEN

Team Development, Team Training

BASIC CONCEPTS TO BE COVERED IN THIS CHAPTER

In this chapter a number of concepts are defined and discussed. The major ones are listed below. Students should divide into pairs. Each pair is to (a) define each concept, noting the page on which it is defined and discussed and (b) ensure that both members understand its meaning. Then combine into groups of four. Compare the answers of the two pairs. If there is disagreement, look up the concept in the chapter and clarify it until all members agree on and understand the definition.

CONCEPTS

1. Team
2. Team building
3. Organizational development
4. Pareto chart
5. Mass-production organizational structure
6. High-performance organizational structure

INTRODUCTION

Productivity through people

Singapore Management Philosophy

The Killer Bees is a boys' high school basketball team from Bridgehampton, New York, a small, middle-class town on Long Island. Bridgehampton High School's total enrollment has steadily declined over the past twenty years, and recently fewer than twenty boys attended the school. There have never been more than seven players on the basketball team. Yet, since 1980 the Killer Bees have amassed a record of 164 wins and 32 losses, qualified for the state championship playoffs six times, won the state championship twice, and finished in the final four two other times. Not one of the Killer Bees went on to the pros, and the team was never tall. Although every Killer Bee graduated and most went on to college, few had the talent to play ball in college. To win against bigger, supposedly more talented opponents, the Killer Bees had to be the ultimate in versatility, flexibility, and speed. Their game was team basketball.

How did the Killer Bees become so successful with so few players and so little talent? A number of factors contributed to their success. The *first* is they had a richness and depth of purpose that eludes most teams. Their mission was more than winning basketball games. They were committed to bringing honor and recognition to their community, protecting and enhancing the team legacy, and one another. *Second*, the community backed the team. Fathers, brothers, and cousins had played on earlier teams, and mothers, sisters, and aunts cheered the team on relentlessly. *Third*, being a member of the Killer Bees was its own reward. No college scholarships awaited the players, and no high-paying pro position was coming along. All the reward came from membership in a unique, inspiring, high-performance team. The result was team members adopting an incredible work ethic and a focus on skill development (starting in preschool, they practiced 365 days a year), and a focus on playing as part of a team, not as individuals.

Teams such as the Killer Bees have been defined as a small group of people so committed to something larger than themselves that they will not be denied (Katzenbach & Smith, 2003). It is the potential for such high-level performance and success that makes teams the key to successful organizations.

Teams typically exist within an organizational context, and within organizations, many different types of teams are used. To improve the overall performance of the organization, the performance of each team must improve continuously. Continuous improvement depends on (a) understanding the nature of teams (including electronic teams and the research supporting the effectiveness of teams), (b) the impact of organizational context on team effectiveness (including the organizational development process), (c) implementing team-development programs (including selection of members, structuring positive interdependence, structuring individual and team accountability, building commitment to team goals, providing training in group skills, and providing administrative support), (d) assessing the quality of teams, (e) using teams for training, (f) implementing total quality management, and (g) dealing with problem members.

WHAT IS A TEAM?

*Never doubt that a small group of thoughtful, committed citizens can
change the world. Indeed, it is the only thing that ever has.*

Margaret Mead

To use teams and be a team member, you first need to know what is and is not a team. Just as aggregates are not groups, placing people in the same room and calling them a team does not make them one. To be a team, you first have to be a group. In many cases, the concepts *small group* and *team* are used interchangeably in the group dynamics literature, even within the same research study. But not all groups are teams, and teams are only one type of small group. Committees, task forces, departments, and councils are groups, but they are not necessarily teams. No matter how often it is called one, the entire membership of any large and complex organization is never a team.

So what is a team? A **team** is a set of interpersonal interactions structured to achieve established goals. More specifically, a team consists of two or more individuals who (a) are aware of their positive interdependence as they strive to achieve mutual goals, (b) interact while they do so, (c) are aware of who is and is not a member of the team, (d) have specific roles or functions to perform, and (e) have a limited life span of membership.

Teams can be placed along a continuum according to the amount of cooperation (integration and role differentiation) they require (Dyer, 1994). At one end of the continuum we would find golf teams, a team composed of a set of individual performers whose individual efforts are combined into a single team score. At the other end of the continuum are teams such as football teams, where the efforts of all team members combine in a single coordinated result and where the whole is more than and different from the sum of its parts.

In a field study conducted on actual ongoing work teams, Katzenbach and Smith (2003) distinguished between working groups and teams in organizations, see Table 13.1. They interviewed hundreds of people on more than fifty different teams in thirty different companies to discover what differentiates various levels

TABLE 13.1   **Working Groups Versus Teams**

WORKING GROUPS	TEAMS
A strong, clearly focused leader is appointed.	Shared leadership responsibilities exist among members.
The general organizational mission is the group's purpose.	A specific, well-defined purpose exists that is unique to the team.
Individual work provides the only products.	Team and individual work develop products.
Effectiveness is measured indirectly by the group's influence on others (e.g., financial performance of business, student scores on a standardized examination).	Effectiveness is measured directly by assessing team work products.
Individual accountability alone is evident.	Both team and individual accountability are evident.
Individual accomplishments are recognized and rewarded.	Team celebration occurs. Individual efforts that contribute to the team's success are also recognized and celebrated.
Meetings are efficiently run and last for short periods of time.	Meetings have open-ended discussions that include active problem solving.
In meetings members discuss, decide, and delegate.	In meetings, members discuss, decide, and perform real work together.

of team performance, where and how teams work best, and how to enhance the effectiveness of teams. The researchers found that in a *working group*, interdependence is low, and accountability focuses on individual members, not on the group as a whole. Each member has a task he or she completes, but members do not take responsibility for results other than their own. They also do not engage in tasks that require the combined work of two or more members. In meetings, members share information and make decisions that help each person do his or her job better, but the focus is always on individual performance.

A team, on the other hand, is more than the sum of its parts, that is, more than the sum of each person's individual effort (Katzenbach & Smith, 2003). For a team to exist, there must be a compelling team purpose that is distinctive and specific, and that requires the joint efforts of two or more members as well as individual work products. Teams not only meet to share information and perspectives and make decisions, they produce discrete work products through members' joint efforts and contributions.

Teams may be classified in an infinite number of ways. Three of the most common classifications are the setting in which teams are used, how teams are used within an organization, and what teams do. The first classification is useful because teams primarily are found in such places as work, sports, and learning situations. A second way to classify teams is by how they are used in an organization. Teams may be used to solve problems, complete special projects, and produce an entire product or service. A third way in which groups can be classified is by what they do. Teams can recommend things, make or do things, and run things.

Electronically Linked Teams

Historically, teams worked face-to-face. The Internet and modern electronic methods (such as e-mail, texting, social networking, groupware applications, and Web conferencing), have changed the way many teams work. In an electronically networked team, members can be separated geographically. The rise of wireless Internet connectivity allows people ever more freedom about where and when they work. Meetings require only that members be at their computers, iPads, or cell phones. With access to these technologies, all types of teams can be managed remotely, with team members living in various parts of the world.

Electronically linked teams offer many benefits. For one, communication between meetings can be asynchronous and extremely fast. For another, the participation of members of electronically linked teams tends to be more equalized and less affected by prestige and status (Johnson & Johnson, 2008). When people are not communicating face to face but over computer screens, they often feel freer to speak their minds, throw out new ideas, and disagree with someone in a higher job position. Another benefit is the ability to link teams between offices and locations as more organizations open international branches.

Electronic communication, however, relies almost entirely on plain text for conveying messages, text that is often ephemeral, appearing on and disappearing from a screen without any necessary tangible artifacts. Things are said and get dropped without full consideration. It becomes easy for a sender to be out of touch with his or her audience. It also is easy for the sender to be less constrained by conventional norms and rules for behavior in composing messages. The feeling of being freer to speak one's mind can lead to a greater sense of anonymity that allows team members to detect less individuality in others, feel less empathy, feel less guilt, be less concerned over how they compare with others, and be less influenced by social conventions (Johnson & Johnson, 2008). Such influences can lead to both more honesty and more "flaming" (name-calling and epithets).

Although electronic communication has many positive features, face-to-face communication has a richness that electronic communication may never match (Prusak & Cohen, 2001). There is evidence that up to 93% of people's intent is conveyed by facial expression and tone of voice, with the most important channel being facial expression (Druckman, Rozelle, & Baxter, 1982; Mehrabian, 1971). Harold Geneen, the former head of ITT, believed that his response to requests was different face-to-face than through electronic means, stating that it is easy to say "no" to an electronic request but face-to-face the answer may be "yes" because of the nonverbal cues attached to the request. He, therefore, made it company policy that problems are solved face-to-face (cited in Trevino, Lengel, & Draft, 1987). Office spaces are increasingly built to maximize face-to-face interaction. The biggest complaint of students in a virtual high school was that interactions with online students just did not measure up to face-to-face contact (Allen, 2001). On the other hand, Bonk and King (1998) suggest that promotive interaction in electronic environments has some advantages over live discussion in terms of engagement in learning, depth of discussion, time on task, and the promotion of higher-order thinking skills. Instructional programs, therefore, may be most effective when they include multiple ways for students to promote each other's success, both electronically and face-to-face whenever possible.

In order to understand how to make teams effective, it is necessary to understand the impact of organizational context on team performance, the nature of organizational development, how to build productive teams, the research specifically focused on team effectiveness, how to structure and nurture teams, how to build team commitment, individual and team accountability, the use of teams in training programs, team building, assessing the quality of work, the nature of total quality management, and dealing with problem behaviors in groups.

Research on Team Effectiveness

Hundreds of studies have been conducted on team effectiveness. Several meta-analyses have been done to summarize what we know from all this research. Johnson and Johnson (1992b) conducted a meta-analysis on the effectiveness of adults working in teams compared to individuals working competitively or individualistically. The studies used in this meta-analysis were divided into those using individual productivity as the measure of success and those using team productivity as the measure of success. Over 120 studies were found that compared team versus individual work on individual productivity. Overall, working in teams resulted in higher individual productivity than did working competitively or individualistically (effect sizes of 0.54 and 0.51, respectively). These results held true for verbal, mathematical, and procedural tasks. Over fifty studies compared team and individual work on team productivity. Overall, working in teams resulted in higher team productivity than did having team members work competitively or individualistically (effect sizes of 0.63 and 0.94, respectively). These results also held true for verbal, mathematical, and procedural tasks. Working in teams also was found to promote more positive relationships and social support among members as well as greater psychological health, self-esteem, and social competencies.

Another meta-analysis of 117 studies of team performance was conducted by Freeberg and Rock in 1987. To be included, a study had to measure team performance as a single entity rather than the individual performances of team members. An overall mean effect size of 0.42 (sd = –0.43, range = –0.48 to –0.99) was found. Almost all the studies were conducted in a laboratory, used college students as subjects, and used small groups (two to four members). The meta-analysis found a number of important influences on team productivity, including prior experience doing the task, practice, complexity of the task, the way the task was structured, task load, amount of interaction among team members, degree of coordination among team members, and amount of cooperation among team members. Cooperation was an especially important influence on team productivity, both in its direct effects and through mediating processes such as coordination and cohesion. These team variables were found to be more powerful influences on team productivity than were individual characteristics of members, such as their ability to do the task.

Zhining Qin (Qin, Johnson, & Johnson, 1995) identified sixty-three studies conducted between 1929 and 1989 examining the relative success of cooperative and competitive efforts on individual problem solving. She found that members of cooperative teams outperformed individuals who worked competitively on linguistic, nonlinguistic, well-defined, and ill-defined problems.

ORGANIZATIONAL CONTEXT

Most teams exist within an organizational context, and that context plays a large part in the success of the team and the actions of team members. W. Edwards Deming, J. Juran, and others have stated that over 85% of the behavior of members of an organization is attributable directly to the organization's structure, not the nature of the individuals involved (Walton, 1985). The organizational context in which teams work shapes the behavior of team members by presenting opportunities and constraints. One organizational context, for example, may offer members the opportunity to be included on a number of teams, whereas another organizational context may prevent members from interacting with anyone else.

Two basic organizational contexts can be identified—a mass-production organizational structure and a team-based, high-performance organizational structure (Johnson & Johnson, 1994). The **mass-production organizational structure** is designed to reduce the costs associated with making large quantities of the same products. In a mass-production organization, an authority hierarchy is imposed rigidly and work is divided into small component parts performed by individuals who work separately from and in competition with other members.

The **team-based, high-performance organizational structure** is designed to promote teams that focus on continuous improvement in quality. Organizations structured in this way may be conceptualized as a hierarchy of work teams or "families" tied together by linking individuals who are leaders in one team but peer-group members at the next highest organizational level (Figure 13.1). These individuals are known as *linking pins* (Likert, 1961).

Two important aspects of the organizational context are the degree of interdependence structured among members and social support. In general, when there is a high level of interdependence among organization members, the relations among divisions, departments, teams, and individuals in an organization are better than if the interdependence level is low (Brett & Rognes, 1986). Likewise, when social support in an organization is high, teams generally perform better (Baldwin & Ford, 1988; Sundstrom,

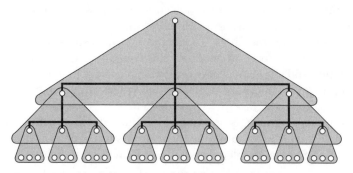

Figure 13.1 The linking-pin model of organizational structure.

Perkins, George, Futrell, & Hoffman, 1990). An atmosphere in which interdependence is encouraged and social support is high enables team members to focus on goals and tasks that benefit the entire organization. They do not have to fight for time to work on projects and make decisions; team members work together to meet mutual expectations; and the organization as a whole supports their work.

Although there is general agreement that organizational contexts greatly influence the behaviors of individuals and groups, few research studies articulate how contextual influences operate. One study that attempted to do so focused on the 1977 collision of a Pan Am 747 and a KLM 747 on the ground at Tenerife Airport that killed 583 people (Weick, 1990). Weick's analysis of the Tenerife air disaster emphasized contextual factors for cockpit and air-traffic-control crews that interrupted their routines and created stress. As a result of these interruptions and stress, both crews fell back on their most familiar and well-rehearsed response routines and acted as individuals rather than as a team. In doing so, the crews missed or did not share information and cues, leading to the deadly crash. Weick suggests that a major contributor to the wrong response patterns was that under a high level of stress, crew members ignored the need to coordinate their actions with fellow team members.

ORGANIZATIONAL DEVELOPMENT

Our people's hard work is our most important resource.

Japanese management philosophy

Organizational contexts are not static; they develop and change over time. Sometimes the changes are planned. One form of planned organizational change is organizational development. **Organizational development** is the use of diagnosis and intervention procedures to promote effective interpersonal, group, and intergroup behavior within the organization. **Organizational effectiveness** is the extent to which the organization achieves its goals with the use of minimal resources. In doing so the organization has to achieve its goals, maintain effective cooperation among members, and adapt to the external environment. Organizational effectiveness depends on members (a) having the *interpersonal* and *small-group skills* and *personal attitudes* and *technical competencies* needed to be effective contributors to the organization and (b) committing high levels of *psychological energy* to their work. The commitment of psychological energy and the use of teamwork and taskwork competencies may be encouraged by both the organizational structure and the organizational culture.

Typically referred to as simply OD, organizational development utilizes the action research methodology pioneered by Kurt Lewin to improve the effectiveness of organizations. First, the vision and goals of the organization are clarified and their cooperative nature is emphasized. Second, the action research methodology is implemented through the following steps:

1. *Diagnosis.* Diagnosis involves three steps:
   a. *Building a normative theory* of how the team or organization should be functioning. Normative theories focus on such factors as cooperation, communication, leadership, decision making, and conflict resolution. Each chapter

of this book presents such theories. Without knowledge of what effective leadership consists of, for example, a diagnosis of how effective the leadership of a group or organization is cannot take place.

   b. *Measuring current team or organizational functioning* by collecting data through interviews, observations, and questionnaires and by holding diagnostic group sessions.

   c. *Analyzing and organizing the data* so that discrepancies between observed and ideal performance and the causes for the discrepancies can be identified.

2. *Feedback.* The data are reported to those organizational members from whom the data were obtained to highlight the discrepancies between the ideal and actual functioning (i.e., problems) of various teams, work groups, departments, and the organization as a whole.

3. *Discussion and planning.* The problems identified by the data are analyzed, and the implications for improving the effectiveness of the relevant work groups and departments within the organization are discussed. A plan for improving organizational effectiveness is developed.

4. *Action.* The plan is implemented. Structural supports for the new behaviors and procedures are generated by changing role definitions and group norms. Interventions can be made on the individual (skill training or attitude change), group (modifying group structure and procedures), or intergroup (intergroup problem solving) levels.

5. *Rediagnosis.* New data are collected to determine if the plan was implemented and if it solved the problem. If not, the cycle is repeated.

This process should be continuous and ongoing within most teams and organizations.

EXERCISE 13.1

TEAM STRUCTURE

Task: Following are three ways of organizing a team. Describe the way team members would interact within each structure and predict the resulting productivity, morale, social support, and professional self-esteem.

   Cooperative: One answer from the three of you, everyone must agree, and everyone must be able to explain.

   Individual Accountability: One member of your group will be chosen randomly to explain the group's answers.

   Expected Behaviors: Everyone participates.

Criterion for Success: Thoughtful answers that have a clear supporting rationale spelled out in detail.

SITUATION 1: MERIT PAY FOR THE BEST TEAM MEMBER

Your organization has decided to implement a competitive merit pay system for employees. One hundred merit points are given to each team within the organization. You, the manager, are told to rank the team members from best to worst in job performance and divide the bonus points among the team members accordingly. A team member could receive all 100 points or no points, depending on how his or her job performance is rated for that year. The more merit points given to one team member, the fewer available for the other team members.

To implement this system, criteria on which the team members are to be evaluated have to be determined. On the basis of the selected criteria, team members are ranked from most successful to least successful. The most outstanding member of the team receives fifty merit points, the first runner-up receives thirty points, and the second runner-up receives twenty points. The rest of the team members receive no merit points.

SITUATION 2: MERIT PAY FOR OUTSTANDING INDIVIDUAL EFFORTS

Your organization has decided to implement an individualistic merit pay program for employees. You, the manager, are told to determine how many merit points each of your team members should receive. You decide to reward team members on the basis of how successful they have been this year. All team members who have demonstrated success will receive a merit bonus.

To implement this system, you set criteria for excellent, good, average, poor, and terrible performance. You evaluate the success of each team member. All excellent members are given twenty merit points, good members are given ten merit points, average members are given five merit points, poor members are given one merit point, and terrible members are given no merit points.

SITUATION 3: MERIT PAY FOR OUTSTANDING GROUP EFFORTS

Your organization decides to implement a cooperative merit pay program for employees. You, the manager, are told to determine how many merit points each of your team members should receive on the basis of how successful their team has been.

To implement the program, you organize all subordinates into teams. You then set criteria for excellent, good, average, poor, and terrible team performance. You evaluate the success of each team. Each member of the excellent teams is given twenty merit points, members of good teams are given ten merit points, members of average teams are given five merit points, members of poor teams are given one merit point, and members of terrible teams are given no merit points.

EXERCISE 13.2

THE COOPERATIVE TEAM SCENARIO

A responsibility of team leaders and members is to provide a vision of what the team will be like when the desired changes have been implemented. This vision must be clear and precise.

1. Working individually, write:
    a. Your personal vision of what you hope the team will be.
    b. Your perception of the team's mission.
    c. The immediate goals your team is working to achieve.
    d. The unique talents, skills, competencies, and perspectives you bring to the team's work.

continued on next page

continued from previous page

2. Form a triad. Working cooperatively, share your views of the team's mission and goals and come to a consensus as to what the mission and goals of the team should be.

3. In your triad:

   a. Write a detailed, behaviorally oriented scenario that describes what you would expect to see, hear, and feel if most team members acted cooperatively most of the time. Include how interaction and relationships among team members would be affected. This description should be a personal, realistic, and attainable description of what you are committed to achieving.

   b. It may be helpful to describe the team's mission, specify the environmental demands on your team, describe the current response to these demands, and then describe how cooperative efforts by team members will contribute to achieving the team's mission and responding to the current and future demands on your team.

   c. This is a cooperative effort. Form a group of three and write one description from the three of you. Everyone must contribute to the description, agree with it, and be able to explain it. Each will need his or her own copy of the scenario. Each will be accountable individually to present the group's scenario to another person. Plan how to do so effectively.

EXERCISE 13.3

DEGREE OF INTERDEPENDENCE

Task: Decide which team analogy best describes your team and why.

> **Cooperative:** Form groups of three. Agree on one answer and develop a rationale. Everyone must agree, and everyone must be able to explain the group's answer and reasoning.
> **Individual Accountability:** One member of your triad will be selected randomly to present the group's answer and rationale.

Criterion for Success: A reasoned answer backed up by examples and information.
Expected Behaviors: Everyone participates and contributes ideas, analyses, and examples.

TEAMS

1. **Golf Team:** Members all function independently of one another, working to achieve as high an individual score as possible, so that when individual scores are combined into team scores, their team wins.

2. **Baseball Team:** Members are relatively independent of one another, and although all members are required to be on the field together, they virtually never interact all at the same time.

3. **Football Team:** Members are divided into three subteams—offense, defense, and special teams. When the subteam is on the field, every player is involved in every play, but each has a set of specialized skills required by his or her individual position. The teamwork required is centered in the subteam, not the total team.

4. **Basketball Team:** All members play on the team as a whole. Every player is involved in all aspects of the game, offense and defense, and all must pass, run, guard, and shoot. When a substitute comes in, all must play with the new person. True teamwork is like a basketball team where division of effort is meshed into a single coordinated result—where the whole is more than, and different from, the sum of the individual parts.

BUILDING PRODUCTIVE TEAMS

The strength of the wolf is in the pack.

Rudyard Kipling

Team building is analyzing work procedures and activities to improve team productivity, the quality of the relationships among members, the level of members' social skills, and the ability of the team to adapt to changing conditions and demands. Team building is aimed at increasing long-term team effectiveness by improving the process of members working together.

Most team-building interventions typically are based on an **action research** model of data collection, feedback, and action planning. Team procedures and activities are analyzed, changes are planned to improve productivity and effectiveness, the changes are implemented, and their success is assessed to see if further changes are needed. Team members typically are involved in diagnosing and planning change. Action research interventions are commonly focused on (a) goal setting that clarifies the team's goals and the positive goal interdependence among members, (b) improving the interpersonal competence of members, (c) redefining and negotiating the role responsibilities of each member, and (d) identifying problems that interfere with effective teamwork and taskwork.

Team building consists of forming the team, establishing clear goals that create positive interdependence among members, ensuring individual and team accountability, building commitment to team goals, providing training in group skills, and providing administrative support.

Forming the Team

At least three issues should be considered when forming teams. First, keep the size of teams small. Small size is a pragmatic guide but not an absolute necessity for team success. The larger the group, however, (a) the smaller the percentage of individuals contributing to its efforts and (b) the more anonymous members feel, which often leads to less task involvement and less sense of responsibility for the team's success. Virtually all effective teams found by Katzenbach and Smith (2003) ranged between two and twenty-five people. The majority of the effective teams had fewer than ten members. Large numbers of people have trouble interacting constructively as a group, and doing real work together is even more difficult. Ten people are far more likely than fifty to work through their differences and develop a common set of goals specific enough for members to hold themselves jointly accountable for the results. Large groups face more obstacles to sharing the viewpoints needed to build a team. In addition, they also face difficult logistical issues, such as finding the physical space and time to meet that fits everyone's schedule.

Second, select team members on the basis of their (a) expertise and skills and (b) potential for developing new expertise and skills, not on the basis of their position or personality. No team succeeds without all the expertise and skills needed to meet its purpose and performance goals. As obvious as this sounds, it is a common failing in potential teams. Usually, teams are heterogeneous, with members who have expertise in different areas. The combination of unique individuals who combine into a team fuels productivity. Each individual brings something unique to the team that often combines into new strengths and talents that lead the team to higher levels of productivity. Selecting members with the right mix of teamwork and taskwork skills, however, is not easy. Most teams figure out the skills they need after they are formed. When team members are chosen for their current skills, the right mix may not be present because it is difficult to know in advance what skills the team will require to achieve its mission. Members' potential for improving existing skills and developing new ones, therefore, also should be considered.

Third, bring together the resources the team needs in order to function, such as space, materials, information, time lines, support personnel, and so forth. Careful planning and preparation are needed to form a team and give it the tools it needs in order to succeed. A team cannot be charged with the task of, say, creating a new cellular phone design and not be given access to computers, design software, meeting space, a budget, and a deadline. When forming a team, members should be asked for input on what resources the team requires. Giving a team a task without giving it resources is a recipe for failure.

Establishing Positive Interdependence

Team productivity depends on ensuring that a clear cooperative structure underlies team efforts. The team is presented with a compelling mission that can be achieved if and only if all members work together effectively. Either all team members succeed or no team member succeeds. Members sink or swim together. The members jointly redefine the mission into specific team goals and then translate the goals into measurable tasks they need to complete. Through this process members become committed to the team and accept ownership of its goals.

Besides goal interdependence, the selection of members with different expertise creates resource interdependence among group members. Members can be assigned complementary roles. A division of labor can be structured. A strong team identity can be formed. All of these procedures increase the positive interdependence among team members.

Finally, the team should have frequent celebrations in which members' contributions to team success are recognized. Celebrations and honest, positive feedback are powerful tools in helping to increase positive interdependence. Ultimately, the satisfaction shared by a team in its own performance becomes the most cherished reward.

Establishing Individual and Team Accountability

Two levels of accountability must be structured into teams: individual accountability and team accountability. The team must be accountable for achieving its goals, and each member must be accountable for contributing his or her share of the work. The team must succeed, and all team members must contribute in concrete ways to the team's success and do equivalent amounts of real work.

Mutual accountability cannot be coerced any more than people can be made to trust one another. Mutual accountability develops when the team is clear about its purpose and goals and is able to measure its progress toward achieving them.

Progress can be measured, however, only when the team and the individual team members know for what they are accountable. Once everyone understands the specifics of personal and team responsibilities, they are able to hold each other accountable for meeting those expectations. Accountability, however, is not about threats or fear of what will happen to members if they do not do their work. At its core, accountability is about the sincere promises members make to themselves and teammates. Accountability is experienced as a sense of personal responsibility to do one's best to help the team succeed.

There has to be a method of measuring both team performance and the contributions of each member. The team ensures that both individual and team accountability exists by directly measuring the progress the team is making in achieving its goals and plotting it on a quality chart. The results show the team's progress. This is especially true early in the team's life. Measuring results and establishing early successes are powerful interventions in building an effective team.

Although a team needs to know how well it is doing and what the contributions of each member are, team accountability may be more important than individual accountability. When Bell of Canada, for example, began monitoring the speed of its operators as a group rather than individually, not only did productivity remain high but the operators themselves also claimed both that their services improved and that they liked their job more (Bernstein, 1991). Teams that have a strong common purpose inevitably hold themselves responsible, both as individuals and as a team, for the team's performance.

Building Team Commitment

Ensuring that members jointly commit themselves to achieve the team's goals involves the following procedure. First, the team is assigned an initial mission and tasks. This provides the basic direction for the team's efforts. Second, the team reframes the mission into mutual goals to which all members can commit themselves. The team shapes its goals by putting its own "spin" on the demands, opportunities, timing, and approach specified by the assigned mission. Doing so increases the perceived positive interdependence among team members. Third, the mutual goals are put into operation as a series of distinctive, unique, and specific performance goals that are measurable. In going through this three-step process, team members get to know one another, unite their goals, and become a unified force.

Providing Training in Group Skills

Team building includes teaching team members the group skills they need to function effectively as contributing members. Training to enhance both taskwork and teamwork skills should be provided on a regular basis. As the team progresses in achieving its goals, new skills become relevant. Members need to sharpen their existing skills and gain new ones in order to keep the team progressing toward its goals. This book is about teaching such skills. Clear cooperative goals, effective communication, good leadership, effective decision making, constructive conflict management, and positive use of power all are essential to team productivity (see Figure 1.4).

Promoting Group Processing

To improve quality continuously, the process by which the work is completed should be examined and assessed carefully so that errors can be eliminated, the process can be streamlined, and the sources of variation can be reduced or eliminated. This is known as group processing. Time and procedures should be provided for group processing. Teams need to examine how effectively they are working and discuss ways to improve their effectiveness regularly. In order to do so, they must assess their current level of effectiveness, compare it with their desired level of effectiveness, and plan how to improve the processes being used to complete their work.

Conducting Administrative Tasks

To ensure that teams function effectively, there are a number of administrative tasks that need to be carried out. The team should have frequent and regular meetings that provide opportunities for team members to interact face-to-face and promote one another's success. Team members should spend a lot of time together, scheduled and unscheduled, especially in the beginning. Creative insights as well as personal bonding require impromptu and casual interactions as much as formal work time.

Particular attention should be focused on first meetings. When the team first gathers, members monitor the signals given by teammates to confirm, suspend, or dispel assumptions and concerns. In the initial meetings, clear rules of conduct need to be established. Some of the initial rules pertain to (a) attendance (no interruptions to take phone calls); (b) discussion (no sacred cows); (c) confidentiality (the only things to leave this room are what we agree on); (d) analytic approach (facts are friendly); (e) end-product orientation (everyone gets assignments and does them); (f) constructive confrontation (no finger pointing); and (g) contributions (everyone does real work).

Periodically, the team should be exposed to new facts and information that help it redefine and enrich its understanding of its mission, purpose, and goals. Teams err when they assume that all the information they need was known at the beginning of their work or exists in the collective experience and knowledge of their members. Organizational goals may change, a new direction may be taken, and new information comes to the surface—the team needs to be kept informed.

ASSESSING QUALITY OF WORK

To assess the quality of work, it is necessary to decide what to measure and how to measure it (measurement methods should be simple, realistic, and easy for everyone involved to use and understand). Once these questions have been answered, the resulting assessment allows the team to improve continuously the process by which it does its work. Continuous improvement is based on gathering data and communicating it so that informed decisions can be made. Data-based decision making requires practical tools. Seven of the most widely used tools are the flowchart, cause-and-effect diagram, check sheet, Pareto chart, run chart, scatter diagram, and histogram. Flowcharts, cause-and-effect diagrams, check sheets, and Pareto charts are most useful when the team is trying to learn about the process and narrow the focus of what it wants to improve. Later, tools such as run charts, scatter diagrams, and histograms can help provide a clearer picture of how the process is operating over time.

Flowchart

To understand how the team actually does its work, members need to draw a picture of the work process. The **flowchart** is a simple yet powerful visual tool to display all the steps in a process (Figure 13.2). Flowcharts are used when teams need to identify deviations between the actual and the ideal path for a given process. As such, the flowchart often is the first tool used to begin a process improvement project because it shows where the project is and where it should go. It also can be used to describe the flow of people, material, and information within a designated work space. The level of detail varies based on the needs of the team. Even without significant detail, flowcharts can help identify gaps, duplication, and other potential problems.

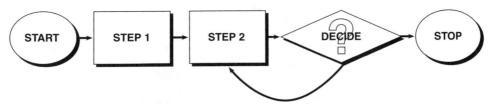

Figure 13.2 Flowchart.

A flowchart is created in several steps. First, clearly define the boundaries of the process—state exactly where the process starts and stops, what the inputs and outputs are, and who the customers are. Next, identify all the steps the process actually follows—what the key steps are, who is involved, and who does what and when. From here, draw the actual flowchart, plotting these steps in sequence. If the flowchart is being used in a process improvement project, the team now would draw a second flowchart that identifies all the steps the process should follow if everything worked properly. Compare the two charts.

Cause-and-Effect Diagram

A **cause-and-effect diagram** represents the relationship between some effect—the problem being studied—and its possible causes (Figure 13.3). It is used to explore systematically cause-and-effect relationships so that the most likely causes of a problem or effect can be identified. Developed by Kauru Ishikawa, this charting technique also is referred to as a *fishbone diagram* because it resembles a fish skeleton when completed. A cause-and-effect diagram usually is drawn with the effect or problem on the right side of the diagram. The major causes or influences are drawn to the left of the effect. For every effect there are likely to be several major categories of causes. Any category that helps team members think creatively can be used. Examples of common categories include person-power, machinery, methods, materials, and measurements.

A cause-and-effect diagram is created by (a) defining the problem or effect clearly, (b) drawing a horizontal line or arrow pointing to the effect (on the right), (c) determining the major categories of possible causes (use generic terms), (d) drawing a single line for each major category, that branches off from the horizontal line, (e) thinking of possible causes in each category, (f) adding each cause as a branch of the appropriate category (ask questions like "Why?" or "Why does this happen?"), (g) identifying and circling the root causes (start by looking for causes that appear repeatedly), and (h) using a check sheet to gather data to verify the most likely root cause(s). Use a Pareto chart to display the data collected.

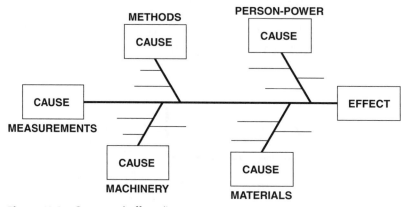

Figure 13.3 Cause-and-effect diagram.

EVENT	TIME PERIOD (days, weeks, months)			TOTAL
	1	2	3	
ERROR A	//	/	///	6
ERROR B	////	///	//	9
ERROR C		//	///	5
ERROR D	///////	////	////	14
ERROR E	///	///	/	7
TOTAL	15	13	13	41

Figure 13.4   Check sheet.

Check Sheet

A **check sheet** is an easy-to-understand form used to answer the question "How often are certain events happening?" (Figure 13.4). Check sheets help a team tally and count the number of times an event is observed in a specified time period or amount of product. Check sheets start the process of translating opinions into facts. They are simple to construct and interpret, and they can help identify patterns in the data, such as the number of errors made per day.

A check sheet is created by (a) defining exactly what event is being observed (everyone has to be looking for the same thing), (b) determining the time period during which the data will be collected (hours to weeks), (c) designing the form and making sure that all team members can use it, (d) collecting data consistently and honestly (ensure that sufficient time is made available to gather the data), and (e) looking for patterns both during and after the data-gathering effort. In constructing a check sheet, make sure all columns are labeled clearly and there is enough space to enter data.

Pareto Chart

The **Pareto chart** is a vertical bar chart that helps teams separate the few vital problems and causes from the many trivial ones. This type of chart takes its name from the Italian economist Vilfredo Frederico Damaso Pareto (1848–1923). While studying the unequal distribution of income, Pareto found that 80% of the wealth was controlled by only 20% of the population. His findings have been generalized into the *Pareto principle (80/20 rule)*, which states that 80% of the trouble comes from 20% of the problems. The Pareto chart is used to display the frequency and relative importance of problems, causes, or conditions in order to choose the starting point for process improvement, to monitor progress, or to identify root causes of a problem. Pareto analysis allows the team to take data from basic tools, such as check sheets and interviews, and present them in a simple bar-graph format.

TABLE 13.2   **Days Absent During June**

NAME	DAYS ABSENT	PERCENT OF TOTAL DAYS ABSENT
Shamus	10	40
Roberto	8	32
Helen	4	16
Edythe	2	8
Frank	1	4
Total	25	100

The steps in developing a Pareto chart are as follows:

1. List the condition(s) or cause(s) you wish to monitor. Absenteeism is the condition used in our example.
2. Collect the raw data on the number of times the condition occurred within a predetermined period of time. In our example, the data are the number of days absent during a thirty-day period and the names of the employees.
3. Rank the various conditions or causes from highest to lowest (most absent to least absent, see Table 13.2).
4. Under the horizontal axis, write the causes in descending order (the most important cause to the left and the least important to the right). In our example, we find David on the left, with ten absences, and Frank on the right, with only one absence (Figure 13.5).
5. On the left-hand vertical axis, list the measurement scale (total number of days absent).
6. On the right-hand vertical axis, note the percentage scale (the total number of absences must equal 100%).

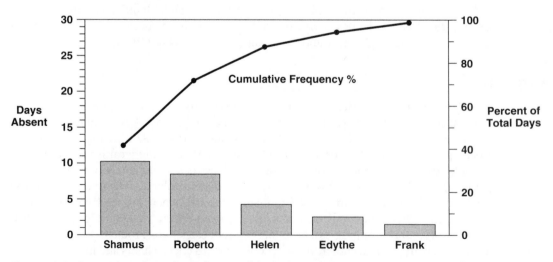

Figure 13.5   Pareto chart: Days absent from work in June per person.

7. Plot the quantitative data for each cause in a vertical bar graph. For our example, this data would be the number of times each employee was absent during June.

8. Draw a line for the cumulative frequencies. For our absenteeism example, Figure 13.5 shows that 88% of all absences are due to Shamus, Roberto, and Helen. An intervention may be planned for Shamus, Roberto, and perhaps also for Helen.

A Pareto diagram is an extension of the cause-and-effect diagram in that the causes are not only identified but also listed in order of their occurrence. The advantages of the Pareto diagram are it can be used to analyze almost anything, it is easy to do, and it is easy to understand. The disadvantage is that only quantifiable data can be used in constructing it.

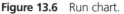 RUN CHART

A **run chart** is a line graph used to monitor the behavior of a selected characteristic over time (Figure 13.6). It provides teams with a method of identifying changes or shifts in the average performance of that characteristic. Run charts specifically are used to examine data for trends or patterns that occur over time.

A run chart is constructed by plotting data points on an x–y axis in chronological order. Measurement data are represented on the vertical (y) axis, and time or sequence is represented on the horizontal (x) axis. A marked point indicates the measurement taken at one point in time. A run chart is created by (a) marking off the time period to be used along the horizontal axis (i.e., hours, days, weeks), (b) entering the unit of measurement for the characteristic being studied along the left vertical axis, (c) entering the historical data as they become available (continue to update the chart and the average), and (d) looking for unusual patterns in the position of the data points relative to the average.

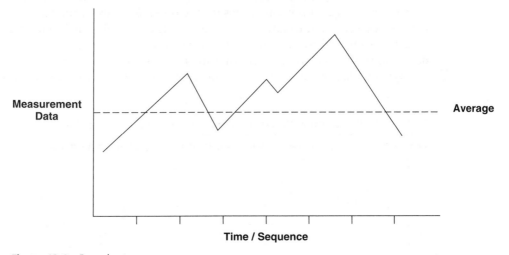

Figure 13.6 Run chart.

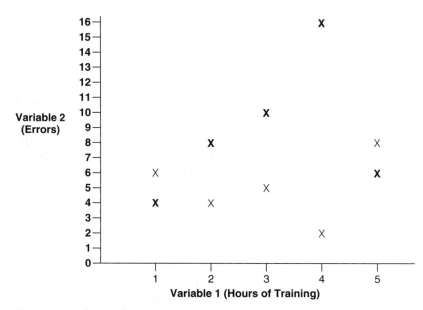

Figure 13.7   Scatter diagram.

Scatter Diagram

A **scatter diagram** displays the cause-and-effect relationship between two process variables or characteristics (Figure 13.7; Table 13.3). It is used to display what happens to one variable when another variable changes. Whereas a run chart lets you track one characteristic over time, a scatter diagram lets you observe the relationship between the two variables. A scatter diagram can indicate only the existence of a possible relationship and its strength; it cannot prove it. Its main use is to test the hypothesis that two variables are related, such as the amount of training received and error rates.

A scatter diagram usually is constructed as an x–y axis. The horizontal axis represents the measurement values for the possible-cause variable, and the vertical axis represents the measurement values for the possible-effect variable. A scatter diagram is created by (a) collecting paired samples that may be related (the more data points the better), (b) constructing a data sheet, and (c) plotting the data on the axis by placing an x on the axis at each point where the paired data intersect

TABLE 13.3   **Relationship Between Amount of Training and Error Rate**

SAMPLE	VARIABLE 1 (HOURS OF TRAINING)	VARIABLE 2 (ERRORS)
1	4	6
2	8	4
3	10	5
4	16	2
5	6	8

(circle repeated data points). The ways in which the points are scattered about the axis tell you if the two variables are related. A randomly scattered pattern suggests that they are unrelated. If the pattern moves from bottom left to top right, a positive correlation most likely exists. If the pattern moves from top left to bottom right, a negative correlation most likely exists. The more the cluster of data points resembles a straight line, the stronger the relationship.

Histogram

A **histogram** (history diagram) shows how continuous measurement data are clustered and dispersed (Figure 13.8). It is used when the distribution and spread of data need to be displayed. Histograms show the frequency of an occurrence and the dispersion between the highest and lowest values. By displaying measurement data across a range of values (spread), the team can learn about the process's ability to meet specifications, whether the distribution is centered in the right place, and whether the data points are balanced evenly or skewed. When large quantities of data are collected and simple tabulation does not provide easy analysis, histograms are useful.

A histogram consists of a series of equal-width columns of varying height. The horizontal axis represents the range of data, and the vertical axis represents the number of data points in each interval. Each column represents an interval within the range of data. Because interval size is constant, so are the column widths. Because column height represents the number of data points that occur within a given interval, column heights vary accordingly. The number of intervals (columns) determines how much of a pattern is visible. A histogram is created by:

1. Collecting the data to be analyzed.
2. Counting the number of data points to determine the size of the data set (n).
3. Determining the range (R) by subtracting the smallest values from the largest.
4. Determining the number of classes (K) to use (such as fewer than 50 data points = 5–7 classes, 50–100 data points = 6–10 classes, 100–250 data points = 7–12 classes, and more than 250 data points = 10–20 classes).
5. Determining class width or interval size (H) by dividing the range (R) by the number of classes (K) (H = R/K).

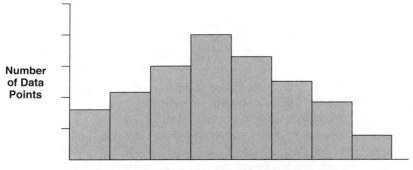

Number of Data Points

Interval / Range / Spread (Measurement Data)

Figure 13.8   Histogram.

6. Determining class boundaries for each interval by (a) finding the lowest-value data point (this is the start point for the first class boundary) and (b) finding the second class boundary by adding the class width (H) to the previous boundary's start point.

7. Making sure that each data point can fit in one and only one class (the endpoint of each interval always must be slightly less than the start point of the next class).

8. Counting and recording the number of data points that fall within each class or interval.

9. Drawing a column above each class (horizontal axis) reflecting the appropriate frequency of occurrences.

10. Analyzing the distribution and its implications.

USE OF TEAMS IN TRAINING PROGRAMS

Teams are the heart of effective training programs (Johnson & Johnson, 1994). Members of organizations have to be trained and continuously retrained throughout their career. The ultimate aim of training is procedural learning—that is, for trainees to be competent in performing a job such as operating and maintaining machines and equipment, conducting an interview, using a computer, piloting aircraft, or being an air-traffic controller. What is learned in a training program has to be transferred to the actual job situation and then maintained for years.

Teams are useful in training programs for a number of reasons. *First*, in order to be proficient at a job, individuals must understand conceptually what they are supposed to do. When team members explain to one another what they are learning, the material is learned better, retained longer, and transferred to actual job situations more frequently. In addition, team members develop shared mental models of how they are supposed to perform their jobs. *Second*, team members can provide one another with appropriate feedback that individuals learning alone cannot receive. *Third*, team members can encourage and motivate one another to try hard to learn. *Fourth*, doing a job well requires that trainees develop a number of relevant attitudes and values as well as learn how to do the job. Personal commitment to do the job well, liking for the job, and wanting to increase one's skills continuously are all attitudes that affect job performance. Such attitudes are better learned in groups than individually. *Finally*, learning how to do a job well affects one's view of oneself. A professional identity is adopted along with the job. This new identity is shared with other team members and with future colleagues, who make up a community of practice. Such socialization is facilitated when teammates enthusiastically adopt the new identity.

In order to maximize the performance of teams, individuals need to be trained to do their jobs and to function effectively as part of a team. This training can take place prior to their membership in the team or concurrently while they work as part of the team. In addition, a team as a whole can receive training through team-building procedures. The result of carefully structuring teams, training team members, and building team effectiveness is high-quality products and services delivered to customers.

TOTAL QUALITY MANAGEMENT

In a mass-production organizational structure, quality is determined by inspecting the final product to see if it is adequate or needs improvement. In a team-based, high-performance organizational structure, quality is determined by examining the process by which the product is created to determine if the process can be improved. A **process** is made up of all the tasks, organized in a sequence, that contribute to the accomplishment of one particular outcome, such as making a product or filling an order. Perhaps the most profound change that organizations have made in the past few decades to improve quality is to focus on processes rather than on products. **Total quality management (TQM)** refers to the use of teams to improve continuously the processes by which the product or service is produced. It requires the formation, training, and development of effective teams, a way to identify processes and measure their effectiveness, the creation of a continuous desire to improve the processes, and a focus on the customer. In other words, *where before companies sold a product, now they concentrate on being better at their processes than any other company in the world.*

The name most closely associated with TQM is W. Edwards Deming. A statistician by profession, he formed many of his theories during World War II, when he taught industries how to use statistical methods to improve the quality of military production. Deming taught the Japanese his theories of quality control and continuous improvement following the war, and he now is credited (along with J. Juran and others) with laying the groundwork for Japan's economic boom.

Deming's great insight was that management tends to look on what goes wrong in an organization as the fault of individual people, not the system itself. Deming (along with Juran) believes in the *85/15* rule, which states that 85% of problems can be corrected by changing systems (structures, practices, rules, expectations, and traditions largely determined by management) and less than 15% of the problems can be solved by individual workers. When problems arise, therefore, management should look for causes in the system and work to remove them before casting blame on workers.

To give some guidance to managers on how to eliminate systemic causes of problems, Deming formulated fourteen principles:

1. Create constancy of purpose for the improvement of products and services.
2. Adopt the new philosophy of total quality and continuous improvement.
3. Cease dependence on mass inspection.
4. End the practice of awarding business based on the price alone.
5. Improve constantly and forever the system of production and service.
6. Institute training on the job.
7. Institute leadership.
8. Drive out fear.
9. Break down barriers between staff areas.
10. Eliminate slogans, exhortations, and targets for the workforce.
11. Eliminate numerical quotas.
12. Remove barriers to pride of workmanship.
13. Institute a vigorous program of education and self-improvement.
14. Take action to accomplish the transformation.

TQM also is based on focusing on the customer and continuously improving organizational and team processes to serve the customer. Staying close to customers to satisfy their needs and anticipate their wants is a fundamental aspect of TQM. L. L. Bean is famous for its philosophy: "A customer is the most important person ever in this office, either in person, by mail, or over the phone. A customer is not dependent on us; we are dependent on him. A customer is not an interruption of our work; he is the purpose of it. We are not doing a favor by serving him; he is doing us a favor by giving us the chance to do so. Nobody ever won an argument with a customer." J. Juran stated that the customer should be the judge of the fitness of use of all products, goods, and services. The customer, thus, is not the point of sale; the customer is part of the design and production process.

A focus on quality begins with absolute commitment to meeting the needs of the customer by listening to customers and designing products and services that meet or exceed their expectations. Producing quality products, however, is not enough to stay competitive in today's world economy. Quality includes continuously improving all the organizational processes that lead to customer satisfaction. Continuous improvement demands examination of how the work gets done and leads to quality that is taken for granted. The major premise of continuous improvement is that everything an organization does can be improved by:

1. Involving everyone, from the boardroom to the mailroom, in a daily search for *incremental* improvements.
2. Providing everyone with the training, techniques, and authority they need to identify and fix problems.
3. Setting high-performance targets and measuring results.
4. Focusing the company's strategic vision on the needs of its customers.

TQM Procedure

How does TQM work? There are six steps. The first step in making TQM work is to form a team. Nothing can get done in TQM without a team. Teams have to be formed, trained, and developed. Teams are the primary units of performance in organizations. They are the most direct sources of continuous improvement. Kinlaw (1991), for example, concluded that (a) team development must precede all other kinds of improvement initiatives and (b) teams, more than executive leadership, cultural change, TQM training, or any other strategy, account for most major improvements in organizations. Team development must be placed strategically at the center of TQM and must form the hub around which other elements (customer satisfaction, supplier performance, measurement and assessment) revolve.

The second step is to select a process (subsystem) for improvement. The team needs a specific, definable process to work on. The team should ask four questions about the process selected: (1) How significant is the process (guard against investing more time and energy in a particular subsystem than makes sense), (2) what is the potential payoff for working on it, (3) is it a minor modification of the status quo or a meaningful change, and (4) is it of realistic size (can the team actually study and improve the process)?

The third step is to define the process clearly, using tools such as a flowchart and cause-and-effect diagram. The team cannot improve a process until the process has been defined. The best way to define the process is to draw a picture of it.

The fourth step is to develop a design for gathering information about the process to analyze its effectiveness. There are three parts to this step. First, quantifiable factors (such as time) have to be identified. If it cannot be counted, it cannot be improved. Second, a design for gathering the relevant data has to be developed. This includes specifying what data should be collected, who should collect it, when, and how. Finally, the data have to be analyzed and portrayed in a way that team members and other organizational members can understand easily.

The fifth step is to generate an improvement theory or plan based on the analysis of the data collected. The theory or plan specifies how the process has to be modified or replaced in order to improve the quality of the team's work. The plan then is implemented in a few settings. The implementation is evaluated, and more data are gathered. If the modified process works, it is adopted completely. If it does not work, it is redesigned and tried out again on a small basis.

The sixth step is to institutionalize the changes that work and the continuous improvement process. Ensure that there is no backsliding (reverting to the old practices) by always taking new data samples, analyzing them, revising the theory or plan, revising the process, and so forth.

DEALING WITH PROBLEM BEHAVIORS IN TEAMS

A General Electric (GE) Company plant in Salisbury, North Carolina, typically changes product models a dozen times a day by using a team system to produce lighting panel boards. This plant has increased productivity by a remarkable 250% compared with GE plants that produced the same products in 1985. The success of GE and other companies in using teams, however, does not mean that teams are problem free. Sooner or later, all teams have to deal with one or more members whose actions cause problems for the team.

Problem behaviors on teams may result from obstacles to effective team functioning. The first obstacle is lack of team maturity. Teams ordinarily require some time to develop and stabilize their patterns of working. The second obstacle is the team's history. Norms rooted in past practices sometimes can influence adversely team members' current behavior. The third obstacle is the mixed motives of team members. Individuals' motives are almost never purely cooperative. In varying degrees, members may desire team success as well as personal satisfaction. Each person may wish to be a star in order to secure individual rewards as well as contribute to the team's success. Finally, obstructive individual behaviors may interfere with team effectiveness. Despite good intentions, some people talk too much, argue too often, intimidate others, wander from the topic, become unnecessarily obsessed with details, acquiesce too soon, stubbornly resist, and generally behave in a very human fashion, complete with neurotic and nonneurotic foibles that obstruct group functioning.

When individuals first start working in teams, they sometimes engage in unhelpful behaviors. Whenever inappropriate member behavior occurs, the team leader's first move should be toward strengthening the perceived interdependence within the work situation. Four of the most common behavioral problems are passive uninvolvement, active uninvolvement, independence, and taking charge.

Passive Uninvolvement

When members are turning away from the team, not participating, not paying attention to the team's work, saying little or nothing, showing no enthusiasm, or not bringing their work or materials, group members can respond in a few ways. They may wish to:

1. Rearrange materials so that each team member has information the others need. If the passive and uninvolved member does not contribute his or her information voluntarily, the other team members need to involve the member actively by asking for the information.
2. Divide up roles and assign to the passive, uninvolved member a role that is essential to the team's success.
3. Reward the team on the basis of its average performance, which encourages other team members to derive strategies for increasing the problem member's involvement.

Active Uninvolvement

Sometimes a team member talks about everything but work, leaves the team, attempts to sabotage the team's work by giving wrong answers or destroying the team's product, refuses to do work, or refuses to work with another team member. When any of these situations arise, team leaders may wish to give a reward that this member or team finds especially attractive and then structure the task so that all members must work steadily and contribute in order for the team to succeed and attain the reward. Assigning the member a specific role to fulfill, making the member a team observer with high accountability for collecting data about team functioning, and sitting in on the team-processing session and confronting the member are other possibilities.

Independence

When you see a team member working alone and ignoring the team discussion, you can do a couple of things. You can:

1. Limit the materials for the team. If there is only one set of materials or one piece of equipment for the team, the member cannot work independently.
2. Rearrange resources so that the member cannot do the work without the other members' information. To complete the task, the independent member must interact and collaborate.

Taking Charge

When one team member is doing all the work, refusing to let other members participate, ordering other members around, bullying other members, or making decisions for the team without checking to see if the other members agree, team leaders have several options. They may wish to:

1. Rearrange resources so that the task cannot be completed without the team member encouraging others to participate and listening carefully to the other members' contributions.
2. Assign roles so that other team members have more powerful and dominant roles.
3. Reward the team on the basis of the lowest two performances by team members. This places pressure on the person taking charge to encourage and help other members learn the material and complete the task.

SUMMARY

A team is a set of interpersonal interactions structured to achieve established goals. Teams can be differentiated from working groups. A team's performance includes team work products that require the joint efforts of two or more members as well as individual work products. Teams can be classified in a number of ways, such as by the setting in which they are used (work, sports, learning), their use in an organization (problem solving, special purpose, self-managing), or what they do (recommend, make or do something, run things). Through the use of modern technology, teams can consist of individuals who are separated geographically.

A number of meta-analyses have found that under a wide range of conditions teams are more effective than individuals working by themselves. The productivity of teams is not a simple function of team members' technical competencies and task abilities, however. To be productive, teams (like all groups) must ensure that members perceive strong positive interdependence, interact in ways that promote one another's success and well-being, be individually accountable, employ their small team skills, and process how effectively the team has been working.

Teams exist within organizational contexts that greatly influence their effectiveness by presenting opportunities and constraints. A general estimate is that over 85% of the behavior of members of an organization is directly attributable to the organization's structure, not the nature of the individuals involved. There basically are two organizational contexts—a mass-production organizational structure and a team-based, high-performance organizational structure. The team-based organizational structure is considered to be the wave of the future because of the relationship between teams and productivity.

If high-quality products and services are to be created, organizations are well advised to use teams. Teams are the basic unit of performance for most organizations. Teams' effectiveness can be ensured by focusing on team development. This includes the selection of team members, structuring positive interdependence, structuring individual and team accountability, building commitment to team goals, providing training in group skills, giving the team the time and procedures for processing its effectiveness, and providing administrative support. The quality of the team's work needs to be assessed. Teams can be used for training. Finally, total quality management needs to be implemented to ensure that team effectiveness keeps improving.

The point of carefully structuring teams, training team members, and building team effectiveness is to deliver high-quality products and services to customers. Implementing TQM procedures involves focusing on the process by which work gets done rather than on inspecting the finished product or service. Teams have to be able to draw flowcharts of the way they work and measure their productiveness. Finally, no matter how carefully teams are formed and developed, problem behaviors arise that must be dealt with. Through progressively refining procedures and continuously improving members' teamwork skills and the team's procedures, the problems can be solved.

CHAPTER FOURTEEN

Epilogue

*I am cast upon a horrible, desolate island; void of all hope
of recovery. I am singled out and separated, as it were, from
all the world, to be miserable. I am divided from mankind,
a solitary; one banished from human society. I have no soul
to speak to or to relieve me.*

Daniel Defoe (1908, p. 51)

When Robinson Crusoe was cast up on the shore of a tropical island, the
lone survivor of a shipwreck, he had everything he needed for a comfortable
life. He had more than adequate food, the climate was ideal, and the setting
was beautiful. Although thankful he was alive, he cursed his solitary life.
He was emotionally miserable because he was no longer a member of any
human group.

Humans are small-group beings. We always have been and we always
will be. The ubiquitousness of groups and the inevitability of being in them
make groups one of the most important factors in our lives. As the effectiveness of our groups go, so goes the quality of our lives. Quite often groups
are not very effective. To create an effective group, we need to follow a set
of guidelines.

GUIDELINES FOR CREATING EFFECTIVE GROUPS

Guideline One

The first guideline is to establish clear, operational, relevant group goals that create positive interdependence and evoke a high level of commitment from every member. Groups exist for a reason. People join groups to achieve goals they are unable to achieve by themselves. To be effective, goals must be clear, so that all members understand the nature of the goals; the goals must be operational, so that members understand how to achieve the goals; the goals must be relevant to members' needs, so that they commit themselves to achieve the goals; and the goals must create positive interdependence among members. There are hundreds of studies indicating that group effectiveness, group cohesion, and the well-being of members depend on members believing that they "sink or swim together." If clear and operational positive goal interdependence is not established in a group, then all the following guidelines become meaningless.

Guideline Two

Once positive goal interdependence has been established, group members must communicate with each other to coordinate their efforts. The second guideline, therefore, is to establish an effective, two-way communication within which members communicate their ideas and feelings accurately and clearly. Communication is the basis for human interaction and group functioning. Members must send and receive messages effectively in order to exchange information and transmit meaning. Barriers to open and accurate communication, such as competition among members, must be minimized. Two-way communication is required for effective group work.

Guideline Three

The third guideline is to ensure that leadership and participation are distributed among all group members. All members are responsible for providing leadership. The equalization of participation and leadership ensures that all members are involved in the group's work, committed to implementing the group's decisions, and satisfied with their membership. It also (1) ensures that the resources of every member are fully utilized and (2) increases the cohesiveness of the group. Leadership is discussed in Chapter 5.

Guideline Four

The fourth guideline for creating an effective group is to ensure that the use of power is distributed among group members and that patterns of influence vary according to the needs of the group as members strive to achieve their mutual goals. Members' power is based on expertise, ability, and access to information, not on authority or personality characteristics. In order to implement this guideline, group members should remember two important principles: (1) power exists in relationships, not in individuals, and

(2) for power to be constructive, the context in which it is used has to be cooperative. This dynamic interdependent view of power assumes that (1) power inevitably exists in all relationships, (2) the use of power is essential to all aspects of group functioning, (3) the use of power is dynamic in that who is influencing whom, and to what degree, changes constantly as the group proceeds in working to achieve its goal, and (4) power is distributed among all group members. Power is discussed in Chapter 6.

Guideline Five

The fifth guideline is to be flexible in matching decision-making procedures with the needs of the situation. There are many different ways that groups can make decisions. There must be a balance between the availability of time and resources (such as members' skills) and the method of decision making used. Another balance must be struck among the size and seriousness of the decision, the commitment needed to put it into practice, and the method used for making the decision. The most effective way of making a decision is usually by consensus (unanimous agreement). Consensus promotes distributed participation, the equalization of power, productive controversy, cohesion, involvement, and commitment. Decision making is discussed in Chapter 7.

Guideline Six

The sixth guideline is for group members to engage in controversy by disagreeing and challenging each other's conclusions and reasoning, thus promoting creative decision making and problem solving. To make effective decisions, members must present the best case possible for each major alternative course of action and subject all other alternatives to critical analysis. Controversies (conflicts among opposing ideas and conclusions) promote involvement in the group's work, quality and creativity in decision making, and commitment to implementing the group's decisions. The controversy procedure ensures that minority opinions are accepted and used. Such intellectual conflict results in more creative, effective decisions. Controversy and creativity are discussed in Chapter 8.

Guideline Seven

The seventh guideline is for group members to face their conflicts of interest (conflicts promoted by incompatible needs or goals, scarce resources, and by competitiveness) and engage in problem-solving (integrative) negotiations to resolve them. There are five basic strategies to manage conflicts of interest: withdrawal, forcing (distributive, win–lose negotiations), smoothing, compromise, and problem-solving (integrative negotiations). The more effective the group, the more frequently conflicts of interest will be valued for their potential constructive outcomes and resolved through problem-solving negotiations. Where problem-solving negotiations fail, another group member needs to mediate. Even in intergroup and cross-ethnic conflicts, problem-solving negotiations need to be used. When they are resolved constructively, conflicts are an important and indispensable aspect of increasing group effectiveness. Conflicts of interest are discussed in Chapter 9.

LEARNING GROUP SKILLS

To ensure that groups are effective, members must be highly skilled in small-group skills. Humans are not born with these skills; they must be developed. You have now completed a variety of experiences aimed at increasing your group knowledge and skills. It is hoped that you are now a more effective group member. It is hoped that you are able to apply your increased skills and knowledge in a variety of groups and under a variety of conditions. You may wish to repeat many of the exercises in this book to reinforce your knowledge and to reread much of the material to gain a more complete understanding of how to utilize group skills. There are, however, two concluding exercises that you may find helpful in applying the material covered in this book to the memberships you hold in groups.

EXERCISE 14.1

TERMINATING A GROUP

The goals of this exercise are to (1) complete any unfinished business in a group, (2) relive and remember the positive group experiences the group has had, (3) synthesize what group members have received from being part of the group, and (4) describe and express constructively group members' feelings about the termination of the group. The theme of the exercise is that although every group ends, the things you as a member have given and received, the ways in which you have grown, and the skills you have learned all continue with you. Terminating relationships may be sad, but the ways in which you have grown within your relationships with other group members can be applied to group situations in the future. Here is the procedure for the group to follow in the exercise:

1. Discuss the topic "Is there anything that needs to be resolved, discussed, dealt with, or expressed before the group ends?"
2. Discuss these questions: "What have been the most significant experiences of the group?" "What have I gotten out of being a member of the group?" "How has being a part of this group facilitated my growth as a person?" and "What skills have I learned from being in this group?" As alternatives to a discussion, group members might make a painting, a collage, or a poem describing their experiences.
3. Discuss how you feel about the group's completing its activities and what feelings you want to express about the termination. Personal styles of handling the dissolution of a group may be discussed. If you cannot discuss this issue, the following alternatives may generate a productive discussion:
   a. Each of you in turn says goodbye to the group and leaves. Each of you then spends five minutes thinking about your feelings and returns to express anything you wanted to but did not express before.
   b. Each of you shows nonverbally how you felt when you first joined the group and then shows nonverbally how you feel now.
4. As a closing exercise, stand in a circle close together. You are all to imagine that you have the magical power to give anything you wish to another group member. You are then to give the person on your right a parting gift, each taking a turn so that everyone in the group can

hear what the gifts are. Examples of what individuals might give are moonbeams, a flower, a better self-concept, an ability to commit oneself to a relationship, comfort with conflict, more empathy with others, the perfect love affair, and so on. When giving the gift, extend your hands as if actually passing something to the other person.

5. Have a group hug.

EXERCISE 14.2

SELF-CONTRACT

Write a description of yourself as a group member. Mention all the strengths and skills you can think of, and mention the areas in which you need to increase your skills. Then make a contract with yourself to make some changes in your life; the contract can involve starting something new, stopping something old, or changing some present aspect of your life. It should involve applying your group skills to the actual group situations you are now facing, or working to develop certain skills further. It may involve joining new groups and terminating old group memberships. In making the contract, pick several group memberships you now have and set a series of goals concerning how you will behave to increase your effectiveness and satisfaction as a group member. Write the contract down, place it in an envelope, address the envelope to yourself, and open it three months later.

SUMMARY

Groups must have clear goals that highlight the positive interdependence among members. Cooperation among group members is so fundamental that it is part of the definition of what a group is. The more cooperative group members are, as opposed to competitive or individualistic, the more productive the group is, the more members like each other, and the more psychologically healthy group members tend to be. Effective two-way communication is the basis of all group functioning and interaction among group members. A group has to have shared leadership and the participation of all members. Groups need to balance their decision-making procedures with the time and resources available, the size and seriousness of the decision, and the commitment required to implement the decision. High-quality decisions require that all major alternatives are given a complete and fair hearing. That is ensured by the use of advocacy subgroups in the controversy process. The utilization of controversy enhances the quality and creativity of group decisions. There are, however, conflicts of interest among group members that must be resolved through negotiations. There are two types of negotiations: problem-solving and win–lose. Through the use of problem-solving negotiations, relationships among group members can be maintained while mutually acceptable agreements are worked out. Power needs to be used in positive ways to enhance mutual success. Group cohesion needs to be high.

Answers

1.4: Saving the World from Dracula: Answer Key

The following ranking was made on the basis of information in Bram Stoker's novel *Dracula* (New York: Tom Doherty Associates, 1989).

The first concern is to protect the parties in your group from Dracula. If you cannot stay alive, you cannot succeed. Therefore, the first two items are:

1. *The human ability to work together cooperatively.* Vampires are solitary creatures who cannot join forces with each other. The major advantage of humans is that they can cooperate in defending themselves and in carrying out coordinated attacks on a vampire. Humans have the power of cooperation. Vampires do not.

2. *The cross, holy water, communion wafer.* Vampires are made helpless by the power of Christianity. These three holy objects repel all vampires and protect the holder. An experienced and intelligent vampire such as Count Dracula, however, could find ways to get around holy objects in the hands of an isolated individual. These holy objects, therefore, are much more powerful when used by a group. Another use of the communion wafers (the host) is to seal a vampire in his or her coffin or prevent the vampire from returning to that coffin. Because they immobilize vampires, these holy objects have both a defensive and an offensive function.

There are other ways to protect yourself from vampires that are of little use in destroying Dracula. A vampire, for example, cannot enter your home unless invited. You could stay at home and not let anyone in. Vampires cannot pass swiftly running water. You could surround yourself with running water.

The second concern is to neutralize Dracula's strengths and exploit his weaknesses.

3. *Branch of wild rose:* The branch of the wild rose seals a vampire's coffin so that the vampire cannot leave or enter it. If the branch can be placed on Dracula's coffin before it is opened, it will neutralize all of Dracula's powers by confining him in the coffin. Since vampires have to return to their coffins every day, they are always vulnerable to being sealed in their graves.

4. *Table detailing sunrise and sunset in Transylvania:* The vampire's powers exist only at night. During the day Dracula loses all of his powers (except that he can change shape at exactly noon, sunrise, or sunset).

The third concern is to be able to destroy Dracula after he is neutralized. There are several ways to destroy Dracula (and any other vampire). Vampires can be destroyed only during the day. They must be denied access to their coffin (difficult, since any coffin that has earth from the vampire's grave works and since vampires tend to hide coffins in many different places in case one is found by their enemies) or confined in their coffin while one of two procedures is carried out. In this case, Dracula is already in his coffin, so the second way of destroying him is the best.

5. *Oak stake:* Vampires may be destroyed by driving an oak stake through their bodies and removing their hearts.

6. *Ax and garlic:* Vampires may be destroyed by cutting off their heads and filling their mouths with garlic.

The fourth concern is to find Count Dracula. When Dracula has been located and the scientists are protected against his attacks, they have the means to neutralize his powers. The next step is to destroy or contain him by resealing him in his coffin.

7. *Tickets to travel to Dracula's castle (plane to Budapest, train to Transylvania, car to castle):* In order to destroy Dracula, you must travel to his castle. While this is the first thing you would do, it is not the most important. Unless you are

protected, can immobilize Dracula and can destroy him, it makes no sense to travel to where he is.

8. *Map of Dracula's castle and key to his crypt:* Once you arrive at Dracula's castle, you cannot rely on the archaeologists to assist you. Since they do not believe in vampires, they will try to prevent you from destroying Dracula. You need to know all the ways to get to Dracula's crypt and be able to open it when you arrive.

9. High-intensity flashlights are needed to find your way through the castle and crypt.

There are a number of items that are useless or unneeded.

10. *44-magnum revolver:* This could be used to fight off wolves, bats, humans, and other creatures under Dracula's control. It will have no effect on Dracula and therefore is ranked very low.

11. *A collapsible steel cage:* This is of no use in containing or destroying Dracula and, therefore, is not needed.

12. *Herbs mixed by a witch at midnight under a full moon:* These have no effect on vampires. It is a waste of space to carry them.

3.5: Cooperative, Competitive, and Individualistic Goal Structures Exercise: Answers

Squares: 40
Biangles: 11
Triangles: 18

3.6: Subsistence Exercise: Hunting-and-Gathering Cards

You found no food today.

You made a beautiful shot at what looked like a deer, but it turned out to be a strangely shaped rock. You got no food today.

You shot a bird. You get one food card from the recorder.

Wild dogs chased you, and to get away you threw them one day's food. Give the recorder one food card. If you do not have a food card and if no one will give you one, you die of starvation.

You fell asleep and slept all day. You got no food today.

Excellent shot. You killed a deer worth two days' food. You get two food cards from the recorder.

You met a member of another group and fell in love. To impress your new love, you gave him or her one day's food. Give the recorder one food card. If you do not have a food card, and no one will give you one, you die of starvation.

You shot a snake. You get a food card from the recorder.

Army ants chased you, and to get away you threw them one day's food. Give the recorder one food card. If you do not have a food card and if no one will give you one, you die of starvation.

You shot a lizard. You get one food card from the recorder.

While running away from a lion, you took refuge in a peach tree. You receive one food card from the recorder.

You shot a deer but missed. You got no food today.

Lucky fluke! You shot at a deer and hit a rabbit. You get one food card from the recorder.

While you were hunting, a skunk broke into your hut and ate two days' worth of food. Give two food cards to the recorder. If you do not have two food cards and if no one will give you any, you die of starvation.

While you were hunting, a lion ate you and all your food. Give all your food cards to the recorder and drop out of the game. Since you did not starve, your group's points are not affected. You are reborn the next week.

You found a nest of field mice and hit each one over the head. You get one food card from the recorder.

You found no food today.

You shot a bird. You get one food card from the recorder.

You found a berry bush. Berries are in season. You get one food card from the recorder.

Lucky fluke! You shot at a wild pig and hit a rabbit. You get one food card from the recorder.

Excellent shot. You aimed at a bird you thought was standing on a rock. Your arrow hit the rock, which turned out to be a wild pig. You get two food cards from the recorder.

You found a deer, but a bear scared it away before you could shoot at it. You got no food today.

Excellent shot. Just as you shot at a deer, a wild pig ran in the way and got killed. You receive two food cards from the recorder.

You shot a rabbit. You get one food card from the recorder.

You found no food today. It was probably too hot for anything to be out and around.

You found some wild carrots. You get one food card from the recorder.

You found an apple tree. Birds had eaten almost all of the apples. You get one food card from the recorder.

Excellent shot. You killed a wild pig. You get two food cards from the recorder.

While hunting, you accidentally stepped on a snake and killed it. You receive one food card from the recorder.

On your way home you fell into a swamp. You lost two days' worth of food to a hungry crocodile. Give two food cards to the recorder. If you do not have them and if no one will give them to you, you die of starvation.

Excellent shot. You killed a deer. You get two food cards from the recorder.

You found some wild lettuce. You get one food card from the recorder.

You shot a rabbit. You get one food card from the recorder.

You shot a bird. You get one food card from the recorder.

You shot an aardvark. You get one food card from the recorder.

While hunting, you found a berry bush. Berries are in season. You get one food card from the recorder.

Best of luck! You found a deer with a broken leg. You killed it with your stone club. You get two food cards from the recorder.

You looked and looked and looked but found no food today.

You shot at a rabbit, but it zigged instead of zagged. You got no food today.

You walked for miles and found nothing to gather or shoot at. You got no food today.

4.2: Bewise College Problem: Solution

Name	Background	Education Degree	Teaching Experience	Public Relations Experience	Fund-Raising Experience	Administrative Experience
David Wolcott	African American	Master's	13 years	None	None	8 years
Roger Thornton	Upper-class family	B.A., master's	7 years	9 years; politician	None	16 years
Edythe Constable	Community center director	None	8 years	2 years	4 years	7 years
Frank Pierce	Neighborhood center worker; community relations	Master's	None	14 years	None	14 years
Helen Johnson	Childhood in slums	B.A., master's	4 years	5 years	2 years	15 years
Keith Clement	Volunteer work: author of book	B.A.	5 years	13 years	10 years	None

Andrews College is the smallest college in the state, and therefore, it had a completely black American student body in 1982.

As is evident from the table, all candidates but Helen Johnson are disqualified because they lack one of the qualifications outlined in the data sheets.

4.3: Solstice-Shenanigans Mystery: Solution

The Solstice-Shenanigans Mystery Exercise appears on pages 000–000. The painting by Artisimisso was stolen by Mr. Handsome, who took it with him when he left the party at 9:50. He took the painting because he was a kleptomaniac.

4.4: Square Arrangement I: One-Way Communication

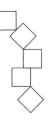

Instructions: Study the arrangement. With your back to the group members, instruct them on how to draw the squares. Begin with the top square and describe each in succession, taking particular note of the placement of each in relation to the preceding one. No questions allowed.

4.5: Square Arrangement II: Two-Way Communication

Instructions: Study the arrangement shown. Facing the group, instruct the members on how to draw the squares. Begin with the top square and describe each in succession, taking particular note of the placement of each in relation to the preceding one. Answer all questions from participants and repeat your description if necessary.

5.6: Hollow Square Exercise

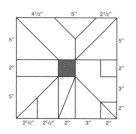

7.3: Winter Survival Exercise

Background Information for Coordinator

None of the information here should be given to participants until after they have completed the decision-making parts of the exercise. Mid-January is the coldest time of the year in Minnesota and Manitoba. The first problem the survivors face, therefore, is to preserve their body heat and protect themselves against its loss. This problem can be solved by building a fire, minimizing movement and exertion, using as much insulation as possible, and constructing a shelter.

The participants have just crash-landed. Many individuals tend to overlook the enormous shock reaction this has on the human body, and the death of the pilot and copilot increases the shock. Decision making under such conditions is extremely difficult. Such a situation requires a strong emphasis on the use of reasoning, not only for making decisions but also for reducing the fear and panic every survivor would naturally feel. Shock is manifested in feelings of helplessness, loneliness, and hopelessness as well as in fear. These feelings have brought about more fatalities than perhaps any other cause in survival situations. Through the use of reasoning, hope for survival and the will to live can be generated. Certainly the state of shock means that the movement of the survivors should be at a minimum and that an attempt to calm them should be made.

Before taking off, a pilot always has to file a flight plan. The flight plan contains the vital information regarding the flight, such as the course, speed, estimated time of arrival, type of aircraft, and number of persons on board. Search-and-rescue operations would begin shortly after the failure of the plane to appear at its destination at its estimated time of arrival.

The 20 miles to the nearest known town is a long walk even under ideal conditions, particularly if one is not used to walking such distances. Under the circumstances of being in shock, being dressed in city clothes, and having deep snow in the woods and a variety of water barriers to cross, to attempt to walk out would mean almost certain death from freezing and exhaustion. At temperatures of −25°F to −40°F, the loss of body heat through exertion is a very serious matter.

Once the survivors have found ways to keep warm, their immediate problem is to attract the attention of search planes and search parties. Thus, all the items the group has salvaged must be assessed for their value in signaling the group's whereabouts.

Winter Survival Exercise: Answer Key

Item	Experts' Ranking	Your Ranking	Difference Score
Ball of steel wool	2		
Newspapers (one per person)	8		
Compass	12		
Hand ax	6		
Cigarette lighter (without fluid)	1		
Loaded .45-caliber pistol	9		
Sectional air map made of plastic	11		
20 × 20-ft piece of heavy-duty canvas	5		
Extra shirt and pants for each survivor	3		
Can of shortening	4		
Quart of 100-proof whiskey	10		
Family-size chocolate bar (one per person)	7		
Total			_____

Explanation of Answer Key

The following ranking of the survivors' items was made on the basis of information provided by Mark Wanvig and Roger Johnson and supplemented by Rutstrum (1973). Wanvig was an instructor in survival training for three years in the reconnaissance school in the 101st Division of the U.S. Army and later an instructor in wilderness survival for four years at the Twin City Institute for Talented Youth. Johnson is a national expert on environmental education.

1. *Cigarette lighter (without fluid).* The gravest danger facing the group is exposure to the cold. The greatest need is for a source of warmth, and the second greatest need is for signaling devices. This makes building a fire the first order of business. Without matches, something is needed to produce sparks to start a fire. Even without fluid, the cigarette lighter can be used to produce sparks. The fire will provide not only warmth but also smoke for daytime signaling and firelight for nighttime signaling.

2. *Ball of steel wool.* To make a fire, the survivors need a means of catching the sparks made by the cigarette lighter. Steel wool is the best

substance with which to catch a spark and support a flame, even if it is a little wet.

3. *Extra shirt and pants for each survivor.* Clothes are probably the most versatile items one can have in a situation like this. Besides adding warmth to the body, they can be used for shelter, signaling, bedding, bandages, string when unraveled, and tinder to make fires. Even maps can be drawn on them. The versatility of clothes and the need for fires, signaling devices, and warmth make these items third in importance.

4. *Can of shortening.* This item has many uses— the most important being that a mirrorlike signaling device can be made from the lid. After shining the lid with the steel wool, the survivors can use it to produce an effective reflector of sunlight. A mirror is the most powerful tool they have for communicating their presence. In sunlight, a simple mirror can generate five to seven million candlepower. The reflected sunbeam can be seen beyond the horizon. Its effectiveness is somewhat limited by the trees, but one member of the group could climb a tree and use the mirror to signal search planes. If the survivors had no other means of signaling than this, they would still have a better than 80% chance of being rescued within the first twenty-four hours.

Other uses for this item are as follows: The shortening can be rubbed on exposed areas of the body, such as the face, lips, and hands, for protection from the cold. In extreme cases, it could be eaten in small amounts. When melted into an oil, the shortening is helpful in starting fires. When soaked into a piece of cloth, melted shortening will produce an effective candlewick. The can is useful in melting snow to produce drinking water. Even in winter, water is important, as the body loses water in many ways, such as through perspiration, respiration, and shock. This water must be replenished, because dehydration affects one's ability to make clear decisions. The can is also useful as a cup.

5. *20 by 20-foot piece of heavy-duty canvas.* The cold makes some form of shelter necessary. The canvas can be part of a shelter, protecting the survivors from the wind and possible snow. Spread on a frame and secured, it could make a good tent as well as a ground cover. Rigged as a wind screen, it could hold heat. Its squareness, contrasting with the surrounding terrain, might also be spotted in an air search, and this makes it an important signaling device.

6. *Hand ax.* The survivors need a continuous supply of wood in order to maintain the fire. The ax is useful for obtaining wood and for clearing a sheltered campsite, cutting boughs for ground insulation, and constructing a frame for the shelter.

7. *Family-size chocolate bars (one per person).* To gather wood for the fire and to set up signals, the survivors need energy. The chocolate will supply the energy to sustain them for some time. Because it contains mostly carbohydrates, it supplies energy without making digestive demands on the body.

8. *Newspapers (one per person).* The newspaper can be used for starting a fire. It will also serve as an insulator: When rolled up and placed under the clothes around a person's legs and arms, it provides dead-air space for extra protection from the cold. The survivors can use the paper for recreation by reading it, memorizing it, folding it, or tearing it. They can roll it into a cone and yell through it as a signal device. They can also spread it around an area to help signal a rescue party.

9. *Loaded .45-caliber pistol.* The pistol provides a sound-signaling device. (The international distress signal is three shots fired in rapid succession.) There have been numerous cases of survivors going undetected because they were too weak to make a loud enough noise to attract attention. The butt of the pistol can be used as a hammer. The powder from the shells will assist in fire building. By placing a small bit of cloth in a cartridge emptied of its bullet, one can start a fire by firing the gun at dry wood on the ground. At night the muzzle blast of the gun is visible, and this provides another means of signaling.

The pistol's advantages are counterbalanced by its dangerous disadvantages. Anger, frustration, impatience, irritability, and lapses of rationality may increase as the group waits to be rescued. The availability of a lethal weapon is a substantial danger to the group under these conditions. Although the pistol could be used for hunting, it would take a highly skilled marksman to kill an animal with it. Even then the animal would have to be transported through the snow to the crash area, which would probably consume more energy than would be advisable.

10. *Quart of 100-proof whiskey.* The only uses of the whiskey are as an aid in fire building and as a fuel. A torch could be made from a piece of clothing soaked in the whiskey and attached to an upright pole. The danger of whiskey is that someone might try to drink it when it is cold. Alcohol takes on the temperature it is exposed to, and a drink of it at −30°F would freeze a person's esophagus and stomach and do considerable damage to the mouth. Drinking it warm would cause dehydration. Alcohol, furthermore, mixes badly with cold because it dilates the blood vessels in the skin. This results in chilled blood being carried back to the heart, which in turn chills the heart and contributes to a rapid loss of body heat. An intoxicated person is much more likely to develop hypothermia than a nonintoxicated person. The bottle may be used to store heated water.

11. *Compass.* Because the compass may also encourage some survivors to try to walk to the nearest town, it too is a dangerous item. The only redeeming feature of the compass is the possible use of its glass top as a reflector of sunlight to signal search planes, but this would be the least effective of the potential signaling devices available. That it might tempt survivors to walk away from the crash site makes it the least desirable of the twelve items.

12. *Sectional air map made of plastic.* This item is dangerous because it will encourage individuals to attempt to walk to the nearest town—thereby condemning them to almost certain death.

7.4: They'll Never Take Us Alive Exercise: Answer Key

Item	Experts' Ranking	Your Ranking	Difference Score
Swimming	5		
Railroads	7		
Police work	11		
Home appliances	9		
Alcohol	2		
Nuclear power	12		
Smoking	1		
Motor vehicles	3		
Pesticides	15		
Handguns	4		
Bicycles	8		
Firefighting	10		
Mountain climbing	13		
Vaccinations	14		
Surgery	6		
Total			_____

8.4: The Johnson School Exercise: Solution

The following Johnsons coached the sports in the order listed.

1. Frank coached golf, basketball, wrestling, and track.
2. Roger coached basketball, golf, track, and wrestling.
3. David coached wrestling, track, basketball, and golf.
4. Helen coached track, wrestling, golf, and basketball.

8.7: Creativity Problem: Solution

The solution of this problem is based on the creative insight of going outside the obvious boundaries of the dots.

8.8: Joe Doodlebug Exercise: Hints

1. Joe does not always have to face the food in order to eat it.
2. Joe can jump sideways and backward as well as forward.
3. Read the problem again: Joe was moving east when the food was presented.

Joe Doodlebug Exercise: Solution

At the moment Joe's master set down the food, Joe had already jumped once to the east. He therefore has to jump sideways three times more to the east and once sideways back to the west, landing on top of the food. He can now eat.

9.2: Making a Profit Exercise: Buyer Profit Sheet

Oil			Gas			Coal	
Price	Profit		Price	Profit		Price	Profit
A	$4,000		A	$2,000		A	$1,000
B	3,500		B	1,750		B	875
C	3,000		C	1,500		C	750
D	2,500		D	1,250		D	625
E	2,000		E	1,000		E	500
F	1,500		F	750		F	375
G	1,000		G	500		G	250
H	500		H	250		H	125
I	0		I	0		I	0

The nine prices for each commodity are represented by the letters A to I. Next to each price is the profit you would make for each commodity if you sold it at that price.

You can say anything you wish during negotiations, but you may *not* show this profit sheet to the buyer you are negotiating with.

Making a Profit Exercise: Seller Profit Sheet

Oil Price	Oil Profit	Gas Price	Gas Profit	Coal Price	Coal Profit
A	$ 0	A	$ 0	A	$ 0
B	125	B	250	B	500
C	250	C	500	C	1,000
D	375	D	750	D	1,500
E	500	E	1,000	E	2,000
F	625	F	1,250	F	2,500
G	750	G	1,500	G	3,000
H	875	H	1,750	H	3,500
I	1,000	I	2,000	I	4,000

GLOSSARY

Ability and skill diversity: A measure of the variation within a group determined by the different abilities and skills that each individual brings to the group.

Acceptance: The communication of high regard toward others and their contributions to the group's work.

Action research: The use of the scientific method in solving research questions that have significant social value.

Action theory: Theory as to what actions are needed to achieve a desired consequence in a given situation.

Additive tasks: Tasks for which group productivity represents the sum of individual members' efforts.

Advocacy: Occurs when an individual presents a position and provides reasons why others should adopt it.

Advocacy team: A subgroup that prepares and presents a particular policy alternative to the decision-making group.

Ageism: Prejudice against the elderly.

Aggregate: Collection of individuals who do not interact with one another.

Arbitration: A form of third-party intervention in negotiations in which the recommendations of the person intervening are binding on the parties involved.

Arguing: A social process in which two or more individuals engage in a dialogue where arguments are constructed, presented, and critiqued.

Argument: A thesis statement or claim supported by at least one reason.

Assimilation: Changing a message to fit it into your own cognitive frameworks and perspective.

Attribution theory: A social-psychological explanation of how individuals make inferences about the causes of behaviors and events.

Authority: Legitimate power vested in a particular position to ensure that individuals in subordinate positions meet the requirements of their organizational role.

Autocratic leaders: Leaders that dictate orders and determine all policy without involving group members in decision making.

Bargaining: See **Negotiation.**

Blaming the victim: Attributing the cause of discrimination or misfortune to the personal characteristics and actions of the victim.

Brainstorming: A procedure in which group members are asked to produce as many, and as uninhibited, ideas as they possibly can and to withhold criticism in order to optimize creativity.

Cathexis: The investment of psychological energy in objects and events outside of oneself.

Cause-and-effect diagram: Visual representation of the relationship between some effect (the problem being studied) and its possible causes.

Channel: The means of sending a message to another person, such as sound and sight.

Charisma: An extraordinary power, as of working miracles.

Charismatic leader: A person who has (a) an extraordinary power or vision and is able to communicate it to others or (b) unusual powers of practical leadership that will enable him or her to achieve the goals that will alleviate followers' distress.

Check sheet: Form used to record the frequency with which certain events are happening.

Coercive power: The group leader's control over positive and negative consequences for other group members.

Cognitive closure: A quick, definite decision to end uncertainty, confusion, or ambiguity.

Cognitive dissonance: Possessing two cognitions that contradict each other. The theory developed by Leon Festinger predicts that dissonance is uncomfortable and that a person will seek to reduce it.

Cognitive perspective: An individual's mental interpretation of a situation based on his or her knowledge, understanding, and experiences.

Cognitive structure: A set of principles and processes that organizes cognitive experience.

Cohesion: All the forces (both positive and negative) that cause individuals to maintain their membership in specific groups. These include attraction to other group members and a close match between individuals' needs and the goals and activities of the group. The attractiveness that a group has for its members and that the members have for one another.

Collusion: The conscious and unconscious reinforcement of stereotypic attitudes, behaviors, and prevailing norms.

Communication: A message sent by a person to a receiver (or receivers) with the conscious intent of affecting the receiver's behavior.

Communication networks: Representations of the acceptable paths of communication between persons in a group or organization.

Competition: A negative correlation among group members' goal attainments; when group members perceive that they can obtain their goals if and only if the other members with whom they are competitively linked fail to obtain their goal.

Competitive learning: Students working to achieve a goal that only one or a few students can attain.

Compliance: Behavior in accordance with a direct request. Behavioral change without internal acceptance.

Compromise: The process of giving up part of the goal(s) and sacrificing part of a relationship in order to reach an agreement; employed when both the goal and relationship are of moderate importance.

Conceptual conflict: The uncertainty that results from having one's position criticized and refuted and being challenged by information and conclusions that are incompatible with one's own conclusions.

Concurrence seeking: Situation where members of a decision-making group inhibit discussion to avoid any disagreement or arguments and emphasize agreement; there is a suppression of different conclusions, an emphasis on quick compromise, and a lack of disagreement within the group.

Conflict: The occurrence of incompatible activities.

Conflict of interest: When the actions of one person attempting to maximize his or her needs and benefits prevent, block, interfere with, injure, or in some way make less effective the actions of another person attempting to maximize his or her needs and benefits.

Conflict-negative group: A group in which conflicts are suppressed and avoided and, when they occur, are managed in destructive ways.

Conflict-positive group: A group in which conflicts are encouraged and managed constructively in order to maximize their potential to enhance the quality of decision making, problem solving, and group life.

Conformity: Changes in behavior that result from group influences. Yielding to group pressures when no direct request to comply is made.

Confrontation: The direct expression of one's view of the conflict and one's feelings about it and, at the same time, an invitation to the opposition to do the same.

Conjunctive tasks: Tasks for which group productivity is determined by the effort or ability of the weakest member.

Consensus: A collective opinion arrived at by a group of individuals working together under conditions that permit communications to be sufficiently open and the group climate to be sufficiently supportive for everyone in the group to feel that he or she has had a fair chance to influence the decision.

Content: The subject that is being discussed within a group.

Contingency theory of leadership: A theory suggesting that effectiveness of leaders is determined both by characteristics of leaders and by several situational factors.

Contractual norms: Statements that spell out the rules to be observed and the penalties for violating them.

Control: When the person being influenced behaves in the way that the influencer intended.

Controversy: The situation that exists when one group member's ideas, information, conclusions, theories, and opinions are incompatible with those of another, and the two seek to reach an agreement.

Cooperation: A positive correlation among individuals' goal attainments.

Cooperative goal structure: A positive correlation among group members' goal attainments; when group members perceive that they can achieve their goal if and only if the other members with whom they are cooperatively linked obtain their goal.

Cooperative intentions: The expectations that you are going to behave cooperatively and that every group member will also cooperate in achieving the group's goals.

Cooperative learning: The instructional use of small groups so that students work together to maximize everyone's learning.

Counseling: Groups that focus on increased psychological adjustment and health. *Also see* Therapy groups.

Creativity: A process consisting of overlapping phases that brings something new into existence.

Credibility: The perceived ability and motivation of a communicator to know valid information and communicate this information without bias.

Critical path method: Identifying the final goal and working backward to detail what must happen (tasks and subgoals) before it is achieved, what resources must be allocated, what the timetable for accomplishing each subgoal should be, and who should have what responsibilities.

Culture clash: Conflict over basic values among individuals from different cultures.

Debate: Situation where group members present the best case for positions that are incompatible with one another and a winner is declared on the basis of who presented the best position.

Decision: The selection of one of multiple options.

Decision making: Obtaining some agreement among group members as to which of several courses of action is most desirable for achieving the group's goals. The process through which groups identify problems in achieving the group's goals and attain solutions to them.

Decision-making tasks: Tasks that require consensus about the best solution to a problem when the correct answer is not known.

Defensive avoidance: The process of procrastinating, rationalizing, or denying the responsibility for choices in order to deal with doubts, conflict, and worry regarding a decision.

Defensive behavior: Behavior that occurs when a person feels threatened or anticipates a threat.

Deindividuation: A psychological state characterized by reduced self-awareness and major shifts in perception. It is encouraged by certain external conditions (e.g., anonymity) and enhances the performance of wild, impulsive forms of behavior.

Deliberate discourse: When the advantages and disadvantages of proposed actions are discussed in order to resolve controversy.

Democratic leader: A leader who sets policies through group discussion and decision, encouraging and helping group members to interact, requesting the cooperation of others, and being considerate of members' feelings and needs.

Demographic diversity: A measure of the variation within a group determined by properties of the group members such as age, sex, culture, ethnicity, and language.

Destructive feedback: An evaluation of the recipient's nature and worth as a person that is forced on the recipient.

Deutsch, Morton: Social psychologist who theorized about cooperative, competitive, and individualistic goal structures.

Dilemma of honesty and openness: The risk of either being exploited for disclosing too much too quickly or seriously damaging the negotiating relationship by refusing to disclose information and thereby seeming to be deceitful or distrusting.

Dilemma of trust: Choice between believing the other negotiator and risking potential exploitation or disbelieving the other negotiator and risking no agreement.

Discretionary tasks: Tasks for which the group score is any combination of individual efforts the group wants to put together.

Discrimination: Action taken to harm a group or any of its members.

Disjunctive tasks: Tasks for which group performance is determined by the most competent or skilled member.

Disputants: The participants in the conflict who seek mediation.

Dissent: Exists when two or more individuals argue positions that are incompatible with one another and a judge declares a winner on the basis of two presented their position the best.

Dissonance reduction: The process by which an individual or group attempts to rationalize a decision.

Distributed-actions theory of leadership: The performance of acts that help the group to complete its task and to maintain effective working relationships among its members.

Distributive justice: The rewards of group success are distributed among group members in proportion to their contributions.

Distributive (win–lose) negotiations: In this type of negotiation the goal is to maximize your outcomes while minimizing the other person's outcomes.

Dogmatism: A relatively closed organization of beliefs centered around absolute authority that provide patterns of intolerance toward others.

Dualistic thinking: A type of thinking based on the premise that there is only one right and one wrong answer and that authority should not be questioned.

Dynamic interdependence view of power: Any two persons who interact constantly and are influenced by each other.

Effective communication: When the receiver interprets the sender's message in the same way the sender intended it.

Effective group: A group whose members commit themselves to the common purpose of maximizing their own and each other's success.

Effective group decision: A decision that is made when the group resources are fully utilized, time is well used, the decision is correct and of high quality, the decision is implemented fully by all required group members, and the problem-solving ability of the group is enhanced and maintained.

Egocentrism: Embeddedness in one's own viewpoint to the extent that one is unaware of other points of view and of the limitations of one's perspectives.

Epistemic curiosity: An active search for more information in hope of resolving the uncertainty caused by conceptual conflict.

Equality distribution of benefits: A system in which all group members benefit equally from success.

Equality system of distributive justice: All rewards are distributed equally among group members.

Equity or merit view of distributing rewards: A basic rule of distributive justice and equity theory: In a just distribution, rewards will be distributed among individuals in proportion to their contributions. In other words, those members who contribute the most to the group's success should receive the greatest benefits.

Ethnocentrism: Tendency to regard one's own ethnic group, nation, religion, culture, or gender as better or more correct than others.

Evaluation apprehension: Concern over being evaluated by others. Such concern may increase arousal and may play an important role in social facilitation.

Experiential learning: Generating an action theory from your own experiences and then continually modifying it to improve your effectiveness.

Expert power: When group members believe the leader has special knowledge or skill and is trustworthy.

Expertise: A person's proficiency, adroitness, competence, and skill.

External barriers: Task requirements, group norms for avoiding conflict, pressure to maintain a congenial public image, and faulty perceptions of one's vulnerability and others' strength.

False consensus bias: A belief (often false) that most other people think and feel very much as we do, such as sharing our stereotypes (e.g., believing that poor people are lazy).

Feedback: Information that allows individuals to compare their actual performance with standards of performance.

Flowchart: Visual tool to display all steps in a process.

Force field analysis: Portraying the problem as a balance between forces working in opposite directions—some helping the movement toward the desired state of affairs and others restraining such movement. The balance that results between the helping and restraining forces is the actual state of affairs—a *quasistationary equilibrium* that can be altered through changes in the forces.

Forcing: The process of attempting to achieve a goal by causing the other(s) to yield; employed when the goal is of much greater importance than a personal relationship.

Forewarning: Informing the audience of the communicator's intention of converting them to his or her point of view before the delivery of the message.

Frustration-aggression process: Frustration due to the inability to achieve one's goals produces a readiness to respond in an aggressive manner that may boil over into hostility and violence if situational cues that serve as releasers are present.

Fundamental attribution error: The attribution of the causes of others' behaviors to personal (disposition) factors and the causes of one's own behavior to situational (environmental) factors. In explaining the causes of the others' behavior, the attributor overestimates the causal importance of personality, beliefs, attitudes, and values and underestimates the causal importance of situational pressures. The opposite is done in explaining the causes of one's own behavior.

Gatekeeper: Person who translates and interprets messages, information, and new developments to groupmates. Also called *opinion leader.*

Goal: A desired situation toward which people are working; a state of affairs that people value.

Goal dilemma: The problem of reaching an agreement favorable to oneself but not so one-sided that the other negotiator will re fuse to agree.

Goal structure: The type of social interdependence specified among individuals as they strive to achieve their goals.

Great person theory of leadership: A theory suggesting that all great leaders share key traits that equip them for positions of power and authority.

Group: Two or more individuals in face-to-face interaction, each aware of his or her membership in the group, each aware of the others who belong to the group, and each aware of positive interdependence as they strive to achieve mutual goals.

Group accountability: Assessing the overall performance of the group and the results are given back to all group members to compare against a standard of performance.

Group centrism: Focusing on group unity at the expense of the quality of the decision.

Group cohesion: The mutual attraction among group members and the resulting desire to remain in the group.

Group communication: A message sent by a group member to one or more receivers with the intent of affecting the receivers' behavior.

Group composition: The demographic properties, personal traits, and abilities and skills that characterize a group.

Group decision: Agreement among group members as to which of several courses of action is most desirable for achieving group goals.

Group dynamics: The area of social science that focuses on advancing knowledge about the nature of group life. The scientific study of behavior in groups to advance our knowledge about the nature of groups, group development, and the interrelations between groups and individuals, other groups, and larger entities.

Group effectiveness: Success by the group in (a) achieving its goals, (b) maintaining good working relationships among members, and (c) developing and adapting to changing conditions to improve its ability to achieve (a) and (b).

Group goal: A future state of affairs desired by enough members of a group to motivate the group to work toward its achievement.

Group influence: The impact of groups on their members.

Group polarization: The tendency of group members to shift toward more extreme positions than those held initially as a function of group discussion. Formerly referred to as the *risky shift* phenomenon.

Group processing: Reflecting on a group session to (a) describe what member actions were helpful and unhelpful and (b) make decisions about what actions to continue or change.

Group structure: A stable pattern of interaction among group members created by a role structure and group norms.

Groupthink: The tendency of members of highly cohesive groups led by dynamic leaders to adhere to shared views so strongly that they totally ignore external information inconsistent with these views.

Group-to-individual transfer: When individuals who learned within a cooperative group demonstrate mastery on a subsequent test taken individually.

Growth groups: Groups that focus on emotional growth, improved interpersonal relationships, and group skills.

Hawthorne effect: A change in behavior that occurs when individuals know they are being observed by researchers.

Helpful feedback: The sharing, upon request, of a description of how one person sees another person's behavior and its consequences and a description of how the observer is reacting to the other person's behavior.

Hero–traitor dynamic: The negotiator who wins is seen as a hero, and the one who loses is perceived to be a traitor.

Hidden agendas: Personal goals that are unknown to all the other group members and are at cross-purposes with the dominant group goals.

High-performance group: A group that meets all effective group criteria and outperforms all reasonable expectations, given its membership. Most groups are unable to achieve this level of development.

Histogram: Visual representation of the frequency with which continuous measurement data are clustered and dispersed across a range of values.

Humanizing relationships: A relationship that reflects the qualities of empathy, kindness, compassion, consideration, mercy, love, responsiveness, and friendship.

Illusionary correlation: Association perceived between two unrelated factors, such as being poor and being lazy, usually leading to stereotypes.

Independent variable: The variable manipulated by the researcher in an experiment; the causal factor in a cause-and-effect relationship.

Individual accountability: Assessing the quality and quantity of each member's contributions and giving the results to all group members.

Individualistic decision making: When isolated individuals independently decide on a course of action without any interaction or consultation with each other.

Individualistic learning: Students working by themselves to accomplish learning goals unrelated to those of the other students.

Individualistic efforts: No correlation among individuals' goal attainments.

Individualistic goal structure: When group members perceive that obtaining their goal is unrelated to the goal achievement of other members.

Individualistic learning: Students working by themselves to accomplish learning goals unrelated to those of the other students.

Inducibility: Openness to influence.

Influence: Using power to change another person in a desired direction.

Information interdependence: Dependence on others for information about their preferences, needs, and expectations so that an agreement can be reached.

Informational power: When the group leader has informational resources that are useful in accomplishing the goal and are unavailable anywhere else.

Initiating group structure: Clearly defining one's role as leader and what one expects from the other members of the group.

Innovation: The process through which new practices and procedures are successfully implemented at the organization level.

Inquiry: Investigating an issue to establish the best answer or course of action; it involves asking questions and seeking to learn the necessary facts to answer the questions.

Inquiry-based advocacy: Two or more parties presenting opposing positions in order to investigate an issue and establish the underlying facts and logic needed to reach a reasoned judgment about the most desirable course of action.

Insulated ignorance: Protects majority group members from being aware of the consequences of their behavior. The majority "insulates" itself from the victims by avoiding contact or structuring the contact in ways that prevent the possibility of becoming aware of the discrimination.

Intellective tasks: Problem-solving tasks with correct answers.

Integrative negotiations: Negotiations in which the goal is to maximize joint benefits.

Interdependence: In a given set of individuals, an event that affects one member is likely to affect all.

Interest: Need, goal, benefit, profit, advantage, concern, right, or claim.

Internal barriers: Negative attitudes, values, fears, anxieties, and habitual patterns of avoiding conflict.

Interpersonal effectiveness: The extent to which the consequences of a person's behavior match his or her intentions.

Intuition: A preconscious process in which the person has a strong feeling about how something will turn out but does not know how the conclusions were determined.

Laissez-faire leader: A leader who does not participate in a group's decision making at all.

Leader: An individual in a group who exerts the greatest influence on other members.

Leadership: The process through which leaders exert their influence on other group members.

Leadership styles: The different ways in which a leader may operate.

Legitimate power: Power derived from group members' belief that leader should have influence over them because of special role responsibilities (such as police officer) or position in the group (such as employer).

Level of aspiration: The compromise between ideal goals and more realistic expectations. A concept developed primarily by Kurt Lewin to explain how people set and revise goals for themselves and their groups. Generally, individuals enter situations with an ideal outcome in mind but revise their goals upward after success and downward after failure.

Leveling: Making a message shorter, more concise, and more easily grasped and told. The reciprocal of sharpening.

Lewin, Kurt: Father of group dynamics; social psychologist who originated field theory, experimental group dynamics, and applied group dynamics.

Machiavellian leadership: Leadership based on the beliefs that (a) people are basically weak, fallible, and gullible, and not particularly trustworthy; (b) others are impersonal objects; and (c) one should manipulate others whenever it is necessary to achieve one's ends.

Majority vote: A method of group decision making in which an issue is discussed only as long as it takes at least 51% of group members to decide on a course of action.

Manipulation: The managing or controlling of others by a shrewd use of influence for one's own purposes and profit.

Mass-production organizational structure: An authority hierarchy is rigidly imposed and work is divided into small competent parts performed by individuals who work separately from and in competition with other members; designed to drive down the unit of costs of long runs of standardized products.

Means interdependence: The second major category of interdependence. The ways in which mutual group goals and rewards are to be accomplished (includes resource, role, and task interdependence).

Mediation: A form of third-party intervention in negotiations in which a neutral person recommends a nonbinding agreement.

Mediator: A neutral person who helps two or more people resolve their conflict by assisting them with problem-solving negotiations to reach an agreement that both parties believe is fair, just, and workable.

Merit distribution of benefits: A system in which the rewards of group success are contingent upon performance and contribution.

Message: Any verbal or nonverbal symbol that one person transmits to another; the subject matter being referred to in a symbolic way (all words are symbols).

Meta-analysis: A method of statistically combining the results of a set of independent studies that test the same hypothesis and using inferential statistics to draw conclusions about the overall result of the studies.

Minority control: A method of group decision making in which less than 50% of group members determine the group's course of action.

Minority influence: Occurs when group members who are in the opinion minority persuade members in the opinion majority to change their opinion and agree with the minority.

Modern racism: A more subtle form of prejudice in which people appear on the surface not to harbor prejudice, but who do in fact hold racist attitudes.

Moral exclusion: Occurs when a person excludes groups or individuals from his or her scope of justice, a share of the community's resources, and the right to be helped.

Moral inclusion: Applying considerations of fairness and justice to others, seeing them as entitled to a share of the community's resources, and seeing them as entitled to help, even at a cost to oneself.

Need: A necessity for survival.

Negotiation: A process by which persons who want to come to an agreement try to work out a settlement by exchanging proposals and counterproposals.

Noise: Any element that interferes with the communication process.

Nonoperational goals: Goals that are abstract in that the specific steps required to accomplish them are indiscernible; often used to describe broad, long-range goals.

Norm of equity: Norm specifying that the benefits received or the costs assessed by the negotiators should be equal.

Norm of reciprocity: Norm that a negotiator should return the same benefit or harm given him or her by the other negotiator; "an eye for an eye and a kiss for a kiss" is an example of a norm of reciprocity.

Norms: The rules or expectations that specify appropriate behavior in the group; the standards by which group members regulate their actions.

Observation procedures: Aimed at describing and recording behavior as it occurs. From the behavior of group members, an observer can make inferences about the way in which the group is functioning.

Observing: Describing and recording behavior as it occurs.

One-way communication: One group member giving instructions and making announcements to other group members who are not allowed to communicate with him or her.

Open-mindedness: The ability to listen to, comprehend, and gain insight from information, ideas, perspectives, assumptions, beliefs, conclusions, and opinions different from one's own.

Openness: The sharing of information, ideas, thoughts, feelings, and reactions to the issue the group is pursuing.

Operational goals: Goals for which specific steps to achievement are clear and identifiable.

Opinion leader: See **Gatekeeper.**

Oppositional interaction: Occurs as individuals discourage and obstruct each other's efforts to achieve.

Organizational development: The use of diagnosis and intervention procedures to promote effective interpersonal, group, and intergroup behavior within the organization.

Organizational effectiveness: The extent to which the organization achieves its goals with the use of minimal resources.

Outcome interdependence: When the goals and rewards directing individuals' actions are positively correlated; that is, if one person accomplishes his or her goal or receives a reward, all others with whom the person is cooperatively linked also achieve their goals or receive a reward.

Paraphrasing: Restating in your own words what the person says, feels, and means.

Pareto chart: Form of vertical bar chart that is used to display the frequency and relative importance of problems, causes, or conditions in order to choose the starting point for process improvement.

Participant–observer: A person who is skilled enough to both participate in group work and observe the group process at the same time; analysis of the group process and functioning by a participating member of the group.

Participation interdependence: The understanding that it takes two to negotiate—whether it is two group members, two organizations, or two nations.

Performance tasks: Tasks that can be completed only through the proficient use of perceptual and motor skills.

Personal diversity: A measure of the variation within a group determined by the differences in personalities and working and learning styles of group members.

Personal identity: One's perceptions of self, a function of a variety of factors such as age, sex, culture, ethnicity, language, abilities, skills, and so forth.

Perspective taking: The establishment of a position on an issue based on information, understanding, and experiences.

Persuasive argument: An attempt to point out the validity of your position and the incorrectness of the other's opinion.

Positive goal interdependence: When members perceive that they can achieve their goals if, and only if, all other members of their group also attain their goals.

Positive interdependence: The perception that one is linked with others in such a way that success is impossible without

them (and vice versa) and that the group effort must be coordinated in order to complete a task.

Power: The ability to influence and control others while resisting their influence and control.

Preemptive action: A type of conflict resolution designed to resolve the conflict without the other person's consent (such as taking up residence on a disputed piece of land).

Prejudice: An unjustified negative attitude toward a person based solely on that individual's membership in a group other than one's own.

Prisoner's Dilemma game: Non–zero sum game used by Deutsch and others to investigate trust and conflict.

Probabilistic thinking: A type of thinking based on the premise that knowledge is available only in degrees of certainty.

Problem: A discrepancy or difference between an actual state of affairs and a desired state of affairs.

Procedural justice: A form of justice that involves fairness of the procedures that determine the benefits and outcomes that a person receives.

Procedural learning: Learning conceptually what the skill is, when it should be used, how to engage in the skill, and practicing the skill while eliminating errors until an automatic level of mastery is attained.

Process: An identifiable sequence of events taking place over time.

Process consultation: An organizational-development procedure of analyzing group functioning by an observing expert.

Process gain: When new ideas, solutions, or efforts are generated through group interaction that are not generated when persons work individually.

Process goals: The sequence of events instrumental in achieving outcome goals.

Process loss: Losses in members' performance due to their participation in the group.

Process observation: The act of simultaneously participating in group work and observing group processes for the purpose of assessing group function.

Process of acceptance: Based on the individuals promoting mutual goal accomplishment as a result of their perceived positive interdependence.

Process of rejection: A result of oppositional or no interaction based on perceptions of negative or no interdependence.

Production tasks: Problem-solving tasks that have objective standards for performance evaluation and require the proficient use of perceptual and motor skills.

Promise: The statement that if you do as I want, I will engage in an act that will benefit you. A negotiator stating that if the other performs a desired act the negotiator will make sure the other receives benefits.

Promotive interaction: When individuals encourage and facilitate each other's efforts to complete tasks and achieve in order to reach the group's goals.

Pseudogroup: A group whose members have been assigned to work together but who have no interest in doing so.

Psychodynamic fallacy: Seeing the motivation for the other's behavior in terms of personality factors rather than the dynamics of intergroup conflict.

Psychological health: The ability to be aware of and manage effectively one's interdependent interactions with others.

Psychological health: The ability to develop, maintain, and appropriately modify interdependent relationships with others to succeed in achieving goals.

Psychological reactance: The need to reestablish one's freedom whenever it is threatened.

Qua: A conflict not only cognitively motivating, but that the resolution of the conflict is likely to be in the direction of correct performance.

Racism: Prejudice directed at people because of their ethnic membership.

Reactance: People's need to reestablish their freedom whenever it is threatened.

Receiver: The person at whom the message is aimed.

Recurring-phase theories: These theories specify the issues that dominate group interaction and that occur over and over again.

Reference group: A group people identify with, compare their attitudes to, and use as a means to evaluate those attitudes.

Referent power: Power based on the group members' identification with, attraction to, or respect for the powerholder.

Relationship actions: Consideration of group members' ideas and feelings before implementing an action.

Relativistic thinking: A type of thinking based on the premise that authorities are sometimes right and sometimes wrong but that right and wrong depend on your perspective.

Resistance: The psychological force aroused in a person that keeps him or her from being influenced.

Resource attractor: An attribute (such as ability or training) that tends to attract other resources because it gives the possessor an advantage in a competition for these other resources.

Restorative justice: The bringing together all parties affected by harm or wrongdoing, discussing what happened and how they were affected, and agreeing on what should be done to right any wrongs suffered.

Reward power: Power based on the power holder's control over the positive and negative reinforcements desired by other group members.

Risky shift: See **Group polarization.**

Role: A set of expectations defining appropriate behaviors associated with a position within a group. The part played by a member of a group. Rules or understandings about the tasks that persons occupying certain positions within a group are expected to perform.

Role conflict: When the demands of one role are incompatible with the demands of another.

Role interdependence: Group members are assigned complementary and interconnected roles.

Role playing: A tool for bringing a specific skill and its consequences into focus, and thus vital for experiential learning; a way in which one can experience concretely the type of interaction under examination. An imaginary life situation is set up in which one acts and reacts in terms of assumptions one is being asked to adopt based on the character one is asked to play.

Role position approach to leadership: A set of expected behaviors associated with a position within a hierarchial group.

Run chart: Line graph used to monitor the behavior of a selected characteristic over time.

Scapegoat: A guiltless but defenseless group that is attacked to provide an outlet for pent-up anger and frustration caused by another group.

Scatter diagram: Displays the cause-and-effect relationship between two process variables or characteristics.

Scope of justice: The extent to which a person's concepts of justice apply to specific others.

Self-actualization: The psychological need for growth, development, and utilization of potential.

Self-efficacy: The expectation of successfully obtaining valued outcomes through personal effort; the expectation that if one exerts sufficient effort, one will be successful.

Self-fulfilling prophecy: A set of actions that provokes the other to engage in behavior that confirms one's original assumptions. An example is assuming that the other is belligerent and then proceeding to engage in hostile behavior, thereby provoking the other into belligerent actions, which confirms the original assumption.

Self-help groups: Groups that focus on overcoming or coping with life stresses, such as addiction or illness.

Self-regulation: The ability to act in socially approved ways in the absence of external monitors.

Sender: The communicator.

Sender credibility: The attitude the receiver has toward the perceived trustworthiness of the sender's statement.

Sequential-stage theories: These theories specify the typical order of the phase of group development.

Sense of injustice: The sense awakened in majority members about their treatment of minority and low power group members. It requires the majority group members to become aware of their ideologies, question the ideologies, and decide that the ideologies are no longer legitimate.

Sexism: Prejudice directed at a person because of his or her gender.

Sharing: Offering your materials and resources to others in order to help them move the group toward goal accomplishment.

Sharpening: Selective perceiving and remembering of a few high points of a message while forgetting most of the rest. The reciprocal of leveling.

Situational approach to leadership: The view that the members of a group most likely to become leaders are those who can best help it to reach its major goals.

Small group: Two or more individuals in face-to-face interaction, each aware of positive interdependence as they strive to achieve mutual goals, each aware of his or her group membership, and each aware of the others who belong to the group.

Smoothing: The process of giving up a goal in order to maintain a relationship at the highest quality possible; employed when the relationship is of much greater importance than personal goals.

Social dependence: The outcome of one person is affected by the actions of a second person, but not vice versa.

Social determinism: The view that historic events are determined by social forces, social movements, and changing social values; see **Zeitgeist.**

Social exchange: A form of social interaction in which participants exchange something of value. What they exchange can range from specific goods or services to information, love, and approval.

Social facilitation: The enhancement of well-learned responses in the presence of others. Effects on performance resulting from the presence of others.

Social independence: When individuals' outcomes are unaffected by each other's actions.

Social interaction: Patterns of mutual influence linking two or more persons.

Social interdependence: When individuals share common goals and each individual's outcomes are affected by the actions of the others.

social judgment theory: Focuses on relationship among diverse individuals.

Social loafing: A reduction of individual effort when working with others on an additive group task.

Socio-emotional activity: Behavior that focuses on interpersonal relations in the group.

Sociometry: A measurement procedure developed by Moreno that is used to summarize graphically and mathematically patterns of interpersonal attraction in groups.

Status: The degree to which an individual's contribution is crucial to the success and prestige of the group, how much power that individual has, and the extent to which the person embodies some idealized or admired characteristic.

Steps of integrative negotiating: (1) Each person explains what he or she wants in a descriptive, nonevaluative way. (2) Each person explains how he or she feels in a descriptive, nonevaluative way. (3) Each person explains his or her reasons for wanting what he or she wants and for feeling the way he or she does. (4) Each person reverses perspectives by summarizing what the other person(s) wants and feels and the reasons underlying those wants and feelings. (5) The participants invent at least three good optional agreements that would maximize joint outcomes. (6) The participants choose the agreement that seems wisest and agree to abide by its conditions.

Stereotype: Set of cognitive generalizations that summarize, organize, and guide the processing of information about members of a particular group.

Substitutability: Part of Deutsch's theory of interdependence. When the actions of one person replace the actions of another.

Superordinate goals: Goals that cannot be easily ignored by members of two antagonistic groups, but whose attainment is beyond the resources and efforts of either group alone; the two groups, therefore, must join in a cooperative effort in order to attain the goals.

Superordinate identity: Group identity that transcends the personal, gender, ethnic, and religious identities of group members.

Support: The communication to others that you recognize their strengths and believe in their ability to manage productively the situation they are in.

Survey-feedback method: An organizational development procedure that focuses on describing the current state of the organization through surveys or interviews and then sharing this descriptive information through feedback.

Synthesizing: Integrating a number of different positions containing diverse information and conclusions into a new, single, inclusive position that all group members can agree on and commit themselves to.

Task actions: The initiation of structure to achieve a goal.

Task involvement: The quality and quantity of the physical and psychological energy that individuals invest in their efforts to achieve.

Team: A set of interpersonal relationships structured to achieve established goals.

Team building: The analysis of work procedures and activities to improve productivity, relationships among members, the social competence of members, and the ability of the team to adapt to changing conditions and demands.

Team training: Teaching team members the taskwork and teamwork skills that optimize efficiency, effectiveness, and improvement.

Team-based, high-performance organizational structure: A hierarchy of work teams that are tied together by linking individuals who are leaders in one team but peer-group members at the next highest organizational level; designed to promote teams that focus on continuous improvement in quality.

Theory: A set of interrelated hypotheses or propositions concerning a phenomenon or set of phenomena.

Therapy groups: Groups that focus on increased psychological adjustment and health. *Also see* Counseling.

Threat: The statement that unless you do as I say, I will engage in an act that will harm you. One individual informing another that negative actions will follow if the recipient of the threat does (or does not) behave in some manner. A negotiator stating that unless the other agrees to the proposed settlement, the negotiator will make sure the other is harmed.

Total quality management (TQM): Use of teams to continuously improve the processes by which the product or service is produced.

Traditional work group: A group whose members agree to work together, but see little benefit from doing so.

Trait approach to leadership: The belief that inborn traits determine the leadership ability of an individual.

Trait factor view of power: The belief that influence is a function of the characteristics of the person exerting the influence, the person receiving the influence, and the influence attempt itself.

Triggering event: An event (such as two group members being in competition or the expression of criticism on a sensitive point) that triggers the occurrence of a conflict.

Trust: Perception that a choice can lead to gains or losses, that whether you will gain or lose depends on the behavior of the other person, that the loss will be greater than the gain, and that the person will likely behave so that you will gain rather than lose.

Trusting behavior: Being self-disclosing and openly accepting and supportive of others.

Trustworthy behavior: Expressing acceptance, support, and cooperative intentions.

Two-way communication: A reciprocal process in which each member starts messages and tries to understand the other members' messages.

Unitary task: One that cannot be divided into subtasks. One person has to complete the entire task.

Vigilant analysis: A decision-making procedure that ensures that each alternative solution is considered to eliminate the possibility of defensive avoidance.

Vision: An ideal and unique image of the future used to clarify the missions and goals of the group.

Want: A desire for something.

Win–lose dynamic: Seeing every action of the other as a move to dominate.

Withdrawal: The process of giving up goals and a relationship in order to avoid conflict caused by the issue and interactions with the other person.

REFERENCES

Abelson, R., Dasgupta, N., Park, J., & Banaji, M. (1998). Perceptions of the collective other. **Personality and Social Psychology Review, 2**(4), 243–250.

Abrams, D., Hopthrow, T., Hulbert, L., & Frings, D. (2006). Groupdrink? The effect of alcohol on risk attraction among groups versus individuals. **Journal of Studies on Alcohol, 67**, 628–636.

Achenback, T., & Edelbrock, C. (1981). Behavioral problems and competencies reported by parents of normal and disturbed children aged four through sixteen. **Monographs of the Society for Research in Child Development, 46**(1, Serial No. 188).

Agnew, C., Van Lange, P., Rusbult, C., & Langston, C. (1998). Cognitive interdependence: Commitment and the mental representation of close relationship. **Journal of Personality and Social Psychology, 74**, 939–954.

Alberti, R., & Emmons, M. (1978). **Your perfect right**. San Luis Obispo, CA: Impact Publishers.

Aldag, R., & Fuller, S. (1993). Beyond fiasco: A reappraisal of the groupthink phenomenon and a new model of group decision processes. **Psychological Bulletin, 113**, 533–552.

Alexopoulou, E., & Driver, R. (1996). Small-group discussion in physics: Peer interaction modes in pairs and fours. **Journal of Research in Science Teaching, 33**, 1099–1114.

Allen, R. (2001, Fall). Technology and learning. Curriculum Update, 1–3, 6–8. Association for Supervision and Curriculum Development.

Allen, V. (1965). Situational factors in conformity. In L. Berkowitz (Ed.), **Advances in experimental social psychology** (Vol. 2) (pp. 133–175). New York: Academic Press.

Allport, F. (1924). **Social psychology**. Boston: Houghton Mifflin.

Allport, G. (1954). **The nature of prejudice.** Cambridge, MA: Addison-Wesley.

Allport, G., & Kramer, B. (1946). Some roots of prejudice. **Journal of Psychology, 22**, 9–39.

Allport, G., & Postman, L. (1945). The basic psychology of rumor. **Transactions of the New York Academic Sciences**, Series II, **8**, 61–81.

Altman, L., & Churchman, A. (Eds.), (1994). **Human behavior and the environment: Advances in theory and research, place attachment** (Vol. 12). New York: Plenum.

Altman, L., & Taylor, D. (1973). **Social penetration: The development of interpersonal relationships**. New York: Holt, Rinehart, & Winston.

Amabile, T. M. (1996). Creativity in context. Boulder, CO: Westview Press.

Amason, A., & Schweiger, D. M. (1994). Resolving the paradox of conflict, strategic decision making, and organizational performance. **International Journal of Conflict Management, 5**, 239–253.

Ames, G., & Murray, F. (1982). When two wrongs make a right: Promoting cognitive change by social conflict. **Developmental Psychology, 18**, 894–897.

Amir, Y. (1969). Contact hypothesis in ethnic relations. **Psychological Bulletin, 71**, 319–352.

Amir, Y. (1976). The role of intergroup contact in change in prejudice and ethnic relations. In P. Katz (Ed.), **Towards the elimination of racism** (pp. 245–308). New York: Pergamon.

Anderson, C. A., Anderson, K. B., Dorr, N., DeNeve, K. M., & Flanagan, M. (2000). Temperature and aggression. **Advances in Experimental Social Psychology, 32**, 63–133.

Anderson, C. A., Benjamin, A. J. & Bartholow, B. D. (1998) Does the gun pull the trigger? Automatic priming effects of weapon pictures and weapon names. **Psychological Science, 9**, 308–314.

Anderson, L., & Blanchard, P. (1982). Sex differences in task and social-emotional behavior. **Basic and Applied Social Psychology, 3**, 109–139.

Anderson, N., & Graesser, C. (1976). An information integration analysis of attitude change in group discussion. **Journal of Personality and Social Psychology, 34**, 210–222.

Angell, R. B. (1964). **Reasoning and logic**. New York: Appleton-Century-Crofts. *Appodaca, Cooper, & Madder v. Oregon*, 406, U. S., 404 (1972).

Archer-Kath, J., Johnson, D. W., & Johnson, R. (1994). Individual versus group feedback in cooperative groups. **Journal of Social Psychology**, **134**(5), 681–694.

Argyris, C. (1964). **Integrating the individual and the organization**. New York: Wiley.

Aristotle (384–322 B.C./1991). **The art of rhetoric** (H. C. Lawson-Tancred, Trans.). New York: Penguin Books.

Arkes, H. R., & Blumer, C. (1985). The psychology of sunk cost. **Organizational Behavior and Human Decision Processes, 35**, 124–140.

Aronson, E. (1972). **The social animal**. San Francisco: Freeman.

Aronson, E., Blaney, N., Stephan, C., Sikes, J., & Snapp, M. (1978). **The jigsaw classroom.** Beverly Hills, CA: Sage.

Arriaga, X., & Rusbult, C. (1998). Standing in my partner's shoes: Partner perspective taking and reactions to accommodative dilemmas. **Personality and Social Psychology Bulletin, 24**(9), 927–948.

Asarnow, J. & Callan, J. (1985). Boys with peer adjustment problems: Social cognitive processes. **Journal of Consulting and Clinical Psychology**, **53**, 80–87.

Asch, S. (1951). Effects of group pressure upon the modification and distortion of judgments. In H. Guetzkow (Ed.), **Groups, leadership, and men**. Pittsburgh: Carnegie Press (pp. 177–190).

Asch, S. (1952). **Social psychology**. New York: Prentice-Hall.

Asch, S. (1956). Studies of independence and conformity: A minority of one against a unanimous majority. **Psychological Monographs**, **70**, v416.

Asch, S. (1957). An experimental investigation of group influence. In the **Symposium on preventive and social psychiatry**, Walter Reed Army Institute of Research. Washington, DC: U.S. Government Printing Office, 17–24.

Ashmore, R., & Del Boca, F. (1979). Sex stereotypes and implicit personality theory: Toward a cognitive-social psychological conceptualization. **Sex Roles, 5**, 219–248.

Asterhan, C. S. C., & Schwarz, B. (2007). The effects of monological and dislogical argumentation on concept learning in evolutionary theory. **Journal of Educational Psychology, 99**, 626–639.

Atkinson, J., & Raynor, J. (Eds.). (1974). **Motivation and achievement**. Washington, DC: Winston.

Avery, P., Freeman, C., Greenwalt, K., & Trout, M. (2006, April). The "Deliberating in a Democracy Project." **Paper presented at the annual meeting of the American Educational Research Association**, San Francisco.

Avolio, B. J. (2007). Promoting more integrative strategies for leadership theory-building. **American Psychologist, 62**(1), 25–33.

Axelrod, R. (1984). **The evolution of cooperation**. New York: Basic Books.

Babchuk, N., & Good, W. (1951). Work incentives in a self-determined group. **American Journal of Sociology, 16**, 679–687.

Bahn, C. (1964). **The interaction of creativity and social facilitation in creative problem solving.** (Doctoral dissertation, Columbia University). Dissertation Abstracts International. (University Microfilms No. 65–7499). V24, 57.

Baker, M. (2009). Argumentative interactions and the social construction of knowledge. In N. M. Mirza & A. N. Perret-Clermont (Eds.), **Argumentation and education: Theoretical foundations and practices** (pp. 127–144). New York: Springer.

Baker, S. & Petty, R. (1994). Majority and minority influence: Source-position imbalance as determinant of message scrutiny. **Journal of Personality and Social Psychology, 67**, 5–19.

Balderston, G. (1930). **Group incentives, some variations in the use of group bonus and gang piece work.** Philadelphia: University of Pennsylvania Press.

Baldwin, T., & Ford, J. (1988). Transfer of training: A review and directions for future research. **Personality Psychology, 41**, 63–105.

Bales, R. (1950). **Interaction process analysis.** Reading, MA: Addison-Wesley.

Bales, R. (1952). Some uniformities of behavior in small social systems. In G. Swanson, T. Newcomb, and E. Hartley (Eds.), **Readings in social psychology** (pp. 437–446). New York: Holt.

Bales, R. (1953). The equilibrium problem in small groups. In T. Parsons, R. Bales, & E. Shils (Eds.), **Working papers in the theory of action** (pp. 111–162). Glencoe, IL: Free Press.

Bales, R. (1955). How people interact in conferences. **Scientific American**, **192**, 31–35.

Bales, R. (1965). The equilibrium problem in small groups. In A. Hare, E. Borgatta & R. Bales (Eds.), **Small groups: Studies in social interaction** (pp. 444–476). New York: Knopf.

Bales, R., & Borgatta, E. (1955). Size of group as a factor in the interaction profile. In A. Hare, E. Borgatta, and R. Bales (Eds.), **Small groups** (pp. 396–413). New York: Knopf.

Bales, R., & Slater, P. (1955). Role differentiation in small decision-making groups. In T. Parsons & R. Bales (Eds.), **The family, socialization, and interaction process** (pp. 159–306). Glencoe, IL: Free Press.

Bales, R., & Strodtbeck, F. (1951). Phases in group problem solving. **Journal of Abnormal and Social Psychology**, **46**, 485–495.

Baltes, B., Dickson, M., Sherman, M., Bauer, C., & LaGanke, J. (2002). Computer-mediate communication and group decision making: A meta-analysis. **Organizational Behavior and Human Decision Processes**, **87**, 156–179.

Banas, P. (1988). Employee involvement: A sustained labor/management initiative at the Ford Motor Company. In J. Campbell & R. Campbell (Eds.), **Productivity in organizations: New perspectives from industrial and organizational psychology (pp. 388–416)**. San Francisco: Jossey-Bass.

Bandura, A. (1965). Vicarious processes: A case of no-trial learning. In L. Berkowitz (Ed.), **Advances in experimental social psychology** (Vol. 2, pp. 3–55). New York: Academic Press.

Bandura, A. (1969). **Principles of behavior modification.** New York: Holt, Rinehart & Winston.

Bandura, A. (1976). **Social learning theory.** Englewood Cliffs, NJ: Prentice-Hall.

Bandura, A. (2006). **Psychological modeling: Conflicting theories**. New York: Transaction Publishers.

Bantel, K., & Jackson, S. (1989). Top management and innovations in banking: Does the composition of the top team make a difference? **Strategic Management Journal**, **10**, 107–124.

Barnlund, D. (1959). A comparative study of individual, majority and group judgment. **Journal of Abnormal and Social Psychology 58**, 55–60.

Baron, R. (1986). Distraction-conflict theory: Progress and problems. In L. Berkowitz (Ed.), **Advances in experimental social psychology** (Vol. 19, pp. 1–40). New York: Academic Press.

Baron, R. S. (2005). So right it's wrong: Groupthink and the ubiquitous nature of polarized group decision making. **Advances in Experimental Social Psychology, 37**, 219–253.

Baron, R. A. (1991). Positive effects of conflict: A cognitive perspective. **Employee Responsibilities and Rights Journal, 4**, 25–36.

Baron, R., & Ball, R. (1974). The aggression-inhibiting influence of nonhostile humor. **Journal of Experimental Social Psychology, 10**(1), 23–33.

Baron, R., Baron, P., & Miller, N. (1973). The relation between distraction and persuasion. **Psychological Bulletin, 80**, 310–323.

Baron, R., Kerr, N., & Miller, N. (1992). **Group process, group decision, group action**. Pacific Grove, CA: Brooks/Cole.

Baron, R., Moore, D., & Sanders, G. (1978). Distraction as a source of drive in social facilitation research. **Journal of Personality and Social Psychology**, **36**, 816–824.

Baron, R., & Richardson, D. (1994). **Human aggression** (2nd ed.). New York: Plenum.

Baron, R., Roper, G., & Baron, P. (1974). Group discussion and the stingy shift. **Journal of Personality and Social Psychology**, **30**, 538–545.

Bartlett, F. (1932). **Remembering.** Cambridge: Cambridge University Press.

Bass, B. (1960). **Leadership, psychology, and organizational behavior.** New York: Harper & Row.

Bass, B. (1982). Individual capability, team performance, and team productivity. In E. Fleishman & M. Dunnette (Eds.), **Human performance and productivity: Human capability assessment** (pp. 179–232). Hillsdale, NJ: Erlbaum.

Batson, C., Early, S., & Salvarani, G. (1997). Perspective taking: Imagining how another feels versus imagining how you would feel. **Personality and Social Psychology Bulletin, 23**(7), 751–758.

Baum, A., Singer, J., & Baum, C. (1982). Stress and the environment. **Journal of Social Issues, 37**(1), 4–35.

Baumeister, R., Smart, L., & Boden, J. (1996). Relation of threatened egotism to violence and aggression: The dark side of high self-esteem. **Psychological Review, 103**, 5–33.

Bavelas, A. (1942). Morale and training of leaders. In G. Watson (Ed.), **Civilian morale.** (pp. 143–165). Boston: Houghton Mifflin.

Bavelas, A. (1948). A mathematical model for group structures. **Applied Anthropology, 7,** 16–30.

Bavelas, A., Hostoft A., Gross, A., & Kite, W. (1965). Experiments on the alteration of group structure. **Journal of Experimental Social Psychology, 1,** 55–70.

Beach, S., & Tesser, A. (1993). Decision making power and marital satisfaction: A self-evaluation maintenance perspective. **Journal of Social and Clinical Psychology**, 12, 471–494.

Beckhard, R. (1969). **Organizational development.** Reading, MA: Addison-Wesley.

Bednar, R., & Kaul, T. (1994). Experiential group research: Can the cannon fire? In S. Garfield & A. Bergin (Eds.), **Handbook of psychotherapy and behavior change** (4th ed., pp. 631–663). New York: Wiley.

Beer, M. (1976). The technology of organization development. In M. Dunnette (Ed.), **Handbook of industrial and organizational psychology** (pp. 937–994). Chicago: Rand McNally.

Beer, M. (1980). **Organization change and development: A systems view.** Glenview, IL: Scott, Foresman.

Beer, M. & Eisenstat, R.A. (2000). The silent killers of strategy implementation and learning. **Sloan Management Review**, Summer, 29–40.

Bekhterev, W., & DeLange, M. (1924). Die ergebnisse des experiments auf dem gebiet der kollektiven reflexologie. **Zeitschrift fur Angewandte Psychologie, 24,** 305–344.

Bem, D. (1972). Self-perception theory. In L. Berkowitz (Ed.), **Advances in experimental social psychology** (Vol. 6, pp. 2–62). New York: Academic Press.

Ben-Yoav, O., & Pruitt, D. (1984a). Resistance to yielding and the expectation of cooperative future interaction in negotiation. **Journal of Experimental Social Psychology**, 20, 323–353.

Ben-Yoav, O., & Pruitt, D. (1984b). Accountability to constituents: A two-edged sword. **Organizational Behavior and Human Performance**, 34, 282–295.

Bengston, V., & Lovejoy, M. (1973). Values, personality and social structure: An intergenerational analysis. **American Behavioral Scientist**, 16, 880–912.

Benne, K., & Sheats, P. (1948). Functional roles of group members. **Journal of Social Issues, 4**(2), 41–49.

Bennett, E. (1955). Discussion, decision, commitment and consensus in "group decision." **Human Relations, 8,** 251.

Bennis, W. (1998) **On Becoming a Leader**, London: Arrow.

Berger, J., Rosenholtz, S., & Zelditch, M. (1980). Status organizing processes. **Annual review of Sociology, 6**, 479–508.

Berkowitz, L. (1978). Whatever happened to the frustration-aggression hypothesis? **American Behavioral Scientist, 32,** 691–708.

Berkowitz, L. (1993) **Aggression: Its causes, consequences, and control**. New York: McGraw-Hill.

Berkowitz, L., & LePage, A. (1967). Weapons as aggression eliciting stimuli. **Journal of Personality and Social Psychology, 7**, 202–207.

Berkowitz, M., & Gibbs, J. (1983). Measuring the developmental features of moral discussion. **Merrill-Palmer Quarterly, 29**, 399–410.

Berkowitz, M., Gibbs, J., & Broughton, J. (1980). The relation of moral judgment stage disparity to developmental effects of peer dialogues. **Merrill-Palmer Quarterly, 26**, 341–357.

Berlyne, D. (1965). Curiosity and education. In J. Krumboltz (Ed.), **Learning and the educational process** (pp. 67–89). Chicago: Rand McNally.

Berlyne, D. (1966). Notes on intrinsic motivation and intrinsic reward in relation to instruction. In J. Bruner (Ed.), **Learning about learning** (Cooperative Research Monograph No. 15). Washington, DC: U.S. Department of Health, Education, and Welfare, Office of Education.

Berlyne, D. (1971). **Aesthetics and psychobiology**. New York: Appleton-Century-Crofts.

Bernstein, A. (1991, April). Quality is becoming job one in the office, too. **Business Week**, pp. 52–56.

Berscheid, E., & Walster, E. (1969). **Interpersonal attraction.** Reading, MA: Addison-Wesley.

Berscheid, E., & Walster, E. (1974). Physical attractiveness. In L. Berkowitz (Ed.), **Advances in experimental social psychology** (Vol. 7, pp. 158–215). New York: Academic Press.

Bettencourt, B., Brewer, M., Croak, M., & Miller, N. (1992). Cooperation and reduction of intergroup bias: The role of reward structure and social orientation. **Journal of Experimental Social Psychology, 28**, 301–319.

Bettencourt, B., Charlton, K., & Kernahan, C. (1997). Numerical representation of groups in cooperative settings: Social orientation effects on ingroup bias. **Journal of Experimental Social Psychology**, 33(6), 630–659.

Bettencourt, B., & Dorr, N. (1998). Cooperative interaction and intergroup bias: Effects of numerical representation and cross-cut role assignment. **Personality and Social Psychology Bulletin,** 24(12), 1276–1293.

Bettencourt, B., & Miller, N. (1996). Gender differences in aggression as a function of provocation: A meta-analysis. **Psychological Bulletin, 119**, 422–447.

Bezrukova, K., Jehn, K. A., Zanutto, E. L., & Thatcher, S.M.B. (2009). Do workgroup faultlines help or hurt? A moderated model of faultlines, team identification, and group performance. **Organization Science, 20**, 35–50.

Bickman, L. (1974). The social power of a uniform. **Journal of Applied Social Psychology, 4**, 47–61.

Bierman, K. (2004). **Peer rejection: Processes and intervention strategies**. New York: Guilford Press.

Bierman, R. (1962a). Comprehension of points of commonality in competing solutions. **Sociometry, 25,** 56–63.

Bierman, R. (1962b). The intergroup dynamics of win-lose conflict and problem-solving collaboration in union-management relations. In M. Sherif (Ed.), **Intergroup relations and leadership**. New York: Wiley.

Bierman, R. (1969). Dimensions for interpersonal facilitation in psychotherapy in child development. **Psychological Bulletin, 72,** 338–352.

Bion, W. (1961). **Experiences in groups.** New York: Basic Books.

Bird, C. (1940). **Social Psychology.** New York: Appleton-Century-Crofts.

Blake, R., & Mouton, J. (1962). The intergroup dynamics of win-lose conflict and problem-solving collaboration in union-management relations. In M. Sherif (Ed.), **Intergroup relations and leadership** (5, 94–140). New York: John Wiley.

Blake, R., & Mouton, J. (1964). **The managerial grid**. Houston, TX: Gulf.

Blake, R., & Mouton, J. (1983). Lateral conflict. In D. Tjosvold & D. W. Johnson (eds.), **Productive conflict management: Perspectives for organizations** (pp. 91–149). Edina, MN: Interaction Book Company.

Blanchard, F., Weigal, R., & Cook, S. (1975). The effect of relative competence of group members upon interpersonal attraction in cooperating interracial groups. **Journal of Personality and Social Psychology, 32**, 519–530.

Blanchard, F., Lilly, T., & Vaughn, L. (1991). Reducing the expression of racial prejudice. **Psychological Science, 2**, 101–105.

Blanton, H., Buunk, B. P., Gibbons, F. X., & Kuyper, H. (1999). When better-than-others compare upward: Choice of comparison and comparative evaluation as independent predictors of academic performance. **Journal of Personality and Social Psychology, 76**, 420–430.

Blascovich, J., Mendes, W., Hunter, S., & Salomon, K. (1999). Social "facilitation" as challenge and threat. **Journal of Personality and Social Psychology, 77**, 68–77.

Blau, P. (1954). Co-operation and competition in a bureaucracy. **American Journal of Sociology, 59**, 530–535.

Bloch, S., Browning, S., & McGrath, G. (1983). Humor in group psychotherapy. **British Journal of Mediation Psychology, 56**, 89–97.

Bolen, L., & Torrance, E. (1978, April). **An experimental study of the influence of locus of control, dyadic interaction, and sex on creative thinking.** Paper presented at the Annual Meeting of the American Educational Research Association, San Francisco.

Bond, C. (1982). Social facilitation: A self-presentational view. **Journal of Personality and Social Psychology**, **42**, 1042–1050.

Bond, C., Atoum, A., & Van Leeuwen, M. (1996). Social impairment of complex learning in the wake of public embarrassment. **Basic and Applied Social Psychology, 18**, 31–44.

Bond, C., & Titus, L. (1983). Social facilitation: A meta-analysis of 241 studies. **Psychological Bulletin**, **94**, 265–292.

Bond, R. & Smith, P. B. (1996). Culture and conformity: A meta-analysis of studies using Asch's (1952b, 1956) line judgment task. **Psychological Bulletin, 119**, 111–137.

Bonk, C., & King, K. (Eds.). (1998). **Electronic collaborators: Learner-centered technologies for literacy, apprenticeship, and discourse.** Hillsdale, NJ: Lawrence Erlbaum.

Bonner, H. (1959). **Group dynamics: Principles and applications.** New York: Ronald Press.

Bonoma, T., Tedeschi, J., & Helm, B. (1974). Some effects of target cooperation and reciprocated promises on conflict resolution. **Sociometry**, **37**, 251–261.

Borgatta, E., & Bales, R. (1953). Task and accumulation of experience as factors in the interacting of small groups. **Sociometry**, **26**, 239–252.

Boster, F., & Hale, J. (1989). Responsive scale ambiguity as a moderator of the choice shift. **Communication Research**, **16**(4), 532–551.

Botkin, B. (1957). **A treasury of American anecdotes**. New York: Random House.

Brauer, M., Judd, C., & Jacquein, V. (2001). The communication of social stereotypes: The effects of group discussion and information distribution on stereotype appraisals. **Journal of Personality and Social Psychology**, **81**, 463–475.

Brauner, M., Judd, C. M., & Gliner, M. D. (1995). The effects of repeated expressions on attitude polarization during group discussions. **Journal of Personality and Social Psychology, 68**, 1014–1029.

Bray, R., Kerr, N., & Atkin, S. (1978). Group size, problem difficulty, and group performance on unitary disjunctive tasks. **Journal of Personality and Social Psychology**, **36**, 1224–1240.

Brehm, J. (1966). **A theory of psychological reactance.** New York: Academic Press.

Brehm, J. (1976). Responses to loss of freedom: A theory of psychological reactance. In J. Thibaut, J. Spence, & R. Carson (Eds.), **Contemporary topics in social psychology.** Morristown, NJ: General Learning Press.

Brehm, J., & Sensenig, J. (1966). Social influence as a function of attempted and implied usurpation of choice. **Journal of Personality and Social Psychology, 4,** 703–707.

Brehm, S., & Brehm, J. (1981). **Psychological reactance: A theory of freedom and control.** New York: Academic Press.

Brett, J., & Rognes, J. (1986). Intergroup relations in organizations. In P. Goodman (Ed.), **Designing effective work groups** (pp. 202–236). San Francisco: Jossey-Bass.

Brewer, M. (1988). A dual process model of impression formation. In T. Srull & R. Wyer, Jr. (Eds.), **Advances in social cognition** (Vol. 1, pp. 1–36). Hillsdale, NJ: Erlbaum.

Brewer, M. (1991). The social self: On being the same and different at the same time. **Personality and Social Psychology Bulletin, 17**, 475–482.

Brewer, M. (1996). Managing diversity: The role of social identities. In S. Jackson & M. Ruderman (Eds.), **Diversity in work teams** (pp. 47–68). Washington, DC: American Psychological Association.

Brewer, M. (1997). The social psychology of intergroup relations: Can research inform practice? **Journal of Social Issues, 33**(1), 197–211.

Brewer, M. (2001). Ingroup identification and intergroup conflict: When does ingroup love become outgroup hate? In R. Ashmore & L. Jussim (Eds.), **Social identity, intergroup conflict, and conflict resolution** (pp. 554–594). New York: Oxford University Press.

Brewer, M., Ho, H., Lee, J., & Miller, N. (1987). Social identity and social distance among Hong Kong schoolchildren. **Personality and Social Psychology Bulletin, 13**, 156–165.

Brewer, M., & Kramer, R. (1985). The psychology of intergroup attitudes and behavior. **Annual Review of Psychology, 36,** 219–243.

Brewer, M., & Kramer, R. (1986). Choice behavior in social dilemmas: Effects of social identity, group size, and decision framing. **Journal of Personality and Social Psychology, 50,** 543–549.

Brewer, M., Manzi, K., & Shaw, J. (1993). Ingroup identification as a function of depersonalization, distinctiveness, and status. **Psychological Science, 4,** 88–92.

Brewer, M., & Miller N. (1984). Beyond the contact hypothesis: Theoretical perspectives on desegregation. In N. Miller & M. Brewer (Eds.), **Groups in contact: The psychology of desegregation** (pp. 281–302). Orlando, FL: Academic Press.

Brickner, M. (1987). **Locked into performance: Goal setting as a moderator of the social loafing effect.** Paper presented at the annual meeting of the Midwestern Psychological Assocation, Chicago.

Brickner, M., Harkins, S., & Ostrom, T. (1986). Effects of personal involvement: Thought-provoking implications for social loafing. **Journal of Personality and Social Psychology, 51,** 763–769.

Brockner, J. (1995). How to stop throwing good money after bad: Using theory to guide practice. In D. A. Schroeder (Ed.), Social dilemmas: Perspectives on individuals and groups (pp. 163–182). Westport, CT: Praeger.

Brodbeck, F. C., Kerschreiter, R., Mojzisch, A., Frey, D., & Schulz-Hardt, S. (2002). The dissemination of critical, unshared information in decision-making groups: The effects of prediscussion dissent. **European Journal of Social Psychology, 32,** 35–56.

Bronowski, J. (1973). **The ascent of man.** Boston: Little Brown.

Broome, R., & Fullbright, L. (1995). A multistage influence model of barriers to group problem solving: A participant-generated agenda for small group research. **Small Group Research, 26,** 25–55.

Brophy, J. (1945). The luxury of anti-Negro prejudice. **Public Opinion Quarterly, 9,** 456–466.

Brown, B. (1968). The effects of the need to maintain face on interpersonal bargaining. **Journal of Experimental Social Psychology, 4,** 107–122.

Brown, C., Dovidio, J., & Ellyson, S. (1990). Reducing sex differences in visual displays of dominance: Knowledge is power. **Personality and Social Psychology Bulletin, 16,** 358–368.

Brown, R. (1984). The role of similarity in intergroup relations. In H. Tajfel (Ed.), **The social dimension** (Vol2, pp. 603–623). Cambridge, England: Cambridge University Press.

Brown, V., & Paulus, P. (2002). Making group brainstorming more effective: Recommendations from an associative memory perspective. **Current Directions in Psychological Science, 11**(6), 208–212.

Brownstein, A. (2003). Biased predecisoin processing. **Psychological Bulletin, 129,** 545–568.

Bruner, J., & Minturn, A. (1955). Perceptual identification and perceptual organization. **Journal of Genetic Psychology, 53,** 21–28.

Buller, P., & Bell, C. (1986). Effects of team building and goal setting on productivity: A field experiment. **Academy of Management Journal, 29,** 305–328.

Burke, P. (1972). Leadership role differentiation. In C. McClintock (Ed.), **Experimental social psychology** (pp. 514–546). New York: Holt, Rinehart & Winston.

Burke, P. (1974). Participation and leadership in small groups. **American Sociological Review, 39,** 832–842.

Burke, R. (1969, July). Methods of resolving interpersonal conflict. **Personnel Administration,** pp. 48–55.

Burke, R. (1970). Methods of resolving superior-subordinate conflict: The constructive use of subordinate differences and disagreements. **Organizational Behavior and Human Performance, 5,** 393–411.

Burke, R., & Day R. (1986). A cumulative study of the effectiveness of managerial training. **Journal of Applied Psychology, 71,** 232–245.

Burnstein, E., & Vinokur, A. (1973). Testing two classes of theories about group-induced shifts in individual choice. **Journal of Experimental Social Psychology, 9,** 123–137.

Burnstein, E., & Vinokur, A. (1977). Persuasive arguments and social comparison as determinants of attitude polarization. **Journal of Experimental Social Psychology, 13,** 315–332.

Burnstein, E., & Vinokur, A. (1977). Persuasive argumentation and social comparison as determinants of attitude polarization. **Journal of Experimental Social Psychology, 13,** 315–332.

Bushman, B. (1984). Perceived symbols of authority and their influence on compliance. **Journal of Applied Social Psychology**, **14**, 501–508.

Bushman, B., & Anderson, C. (2001). Is it time to pull the plug on hostile versus instrumental aggression dichotomy? **Psychological Review, 108**, 273–279.

Butera, F., & Mugny, G. (2001). Conflicts and social influences in hypothesis testing. In C. K. W. De Dreu & N. K. De Vries (Eds.), **Group consensus and minority influence. Implications for innovation** (pp. 161–182). Oxford : Blackwell

Butler, T., & Fuhriman, A. (1983a). Curative factors in group therapy: A review of the recent literature. **Small Group Behavior**, **14**, 131–142.

Butler, T., & Fuhriman, A. (1983b). Level of functioning and length of time in treatment variables influencing patients' therapeutic experience in group psychotherapy. **International Journal of Group Psychotherapy**, **33**, 489–505.

Buunk, B. (1995). Comparison direction and comparison dimension among disable individuals: Toward a refined conceptualization of social comparison under stress. **Personality and Social Psychology Bulletin, 21**, 316–330.

Byrne, D. (1969). Attitudes and attraction. In L. Berkowitz (Ed.), **Advances in experimental social psychology** (Vol. 4, pp. 36–90). New York: Academic Press.

Byrne, D. (1971). **The attraction paradigm**. New York: Academic Press.

Campbell, D. (1958). Common fate, similarity, and other indices of status of aggregates of persons as social entities. **Behavioral Science, 3**, 14–25.

Campbell, D. (1965). Ethnocentric and other altruistic motives. In D. Levine (Ed.), **Nebraska symposium on motivation**. Lincoln: University Nebraska Press.

Campbell, D. (1978). On the genetics of altruism and the counterhedonic components in human culture. In L. Wispe (Ed.), **Altruism, sympathy, and helping**. New York: Academic Press.

Cantor, N., & Harlow, R. (1994). Personality, strategic behavior, and daily-life problem solving. **Curriculum Development and Psychological Science, 3**, 169–172.

Cantor, N., & Norem, J. (1989). Defensive pessimism and stress and coping. **Social Cognition, 7,** 92–112.

Cantril, H. (1940). **The invasion from Mars: A study in the psychology of panic**. Princeton, NJ: Princeton University Press.

Cantril, H. (1941). **The psychology of social movements**. New York: Wiley.

Carlopio, J. (1996). Construct validity of a physical work environment satisfaction questionnaire. **Journal of Occupational Health Psychology, 1**, 330–344.

Carlson, M., Marcus-Newhall, A., & Miller, N. (1990). Effects of situational aggression cues: A quantitative review. **Journal of Personality and Social Psychology, 58**, 622–633.

Carlyle, T. (1849). **On heroes, hero-worship, and the heroic in history**. Boston: Houghton-Mifflin.

Carnegie Foundation. (1995). **Report of the Carnegie task force on learning in the primary grades**. New York: Author.

Carnevale, P., & Keenan, P. (1990). **Frame and motive in integrative bargaining: The likelihood and the quality of agreement**. Paper presented at the Third Annual Meeting of the International Association for Conflict Management, Vancouver, British Columbia.

Carnevale, P., & Pegnetter, R. (1985). The selection of mediation tactics in public sector disputes: A contingency analysis. **Journal of Social Issues, 41**(2), 65–81.

Carnevale, P. J., & Probst, T. M. (1998). Social values and social conflict in creative problem solving and categorization. **Journal of Personality and Social Psychology, 74**, 1300–1309.

Carter, S. M., & West, M. A. (1998). Reflexivity, effectiveness and mental health in BBC production teams. **Small Group Research**, **29**, 583–601.

Cartwright, D. (1959). A field theoretical conception of power. In D. Cartwright (Ed.), **Studies in social power.** Ann Arbor: University of Michigan Press.

Cartwright, D. (1968). The nature of group cohesiveness. In D. Cartwright and A. Zander (Eds.), **Group dynamics: Research and theory** (3rd ed., pp. 91–109). New York: Harper & Row.

Cartwright, D., & Zander, A. (Eds.). (1968). **Group dynamics: Research and theory** (3rd ed.). New York: Harper & Row.

Caspi, A. (1984). Contact hypothesis and inter-age attitudes: A field study of cross-age contact. **Social Psychology Quarterly, 47**, 74–80

Cassel, R. & Shafer, A. (1961). An experiment in leadership training. **Journal of Psychology, 51**, 299–305.

Cattell, R. (1951). New concepts for measuring leadership, in terms of group syntality. **Human Relations, 4**, 161–184.

Chaiken, S. (1980). Heuristic versus systematic information processing and the use of source versus message cues in persuasion. **Journal of Personality and Social Psychology, 39**, 752–766.

Charlesworth, W. (1996). Cooperation and competition: Contributions to an evolutionary and developmental model. **International Journal of Behavioral Development**, 19, 25–39.

Chasnoff, R. (Ed.) (1979). **Structuring cooperative learning: The 1979 handbook.** New Brighton, MN: Interaction Book Company.

Chertkoff, J., & Esser, J. (1976). A review of experiments in explicit bargaining. **Journal of Experimental Social Psychology, 12**, 464–487.

Chesler, M., & Franklin, J. (1968, August). **Interracial and intergenerational conflict in secondary schools.** Paper presented at the Annual Meeting of the American Sociological Association, Boston.

Chinn, C. A. (2006). Learning to argue. In A. M. O'Donnell, C. E. Hmelo-Silver, & G. Erkens, (Eds.), **Collaborative learning, reasoning, and technology** (pp. 355–383). Mahwah, NJ: Erlbaum.

Choi, J., Johnson, D. W., & Johnson, R. (2011). Relationship among cooperative learning experiences, social interdependence, children's aggression, victimization, and prosocial behaviors. **Journal of Applied Social Psychology**. 41(4) 976–1003.

Christie, R., & Geis, F. (1970). **Studies in Machiavellianism.** New York: Academic Press.

Clark, K. (1953). Desegregation: An appraisal of the evidence. **Journal of Social Issues, 9**(4), 2–8.

Clement, D., & Schiereck, J. (1973). Sex composition and group performance in a visual signal detection task. **Memory and Cognition, 1**, 251–255.

Cline, R. (1999). Communication in social support groups. In L. Frey (Ed.), **Handbook of group communication theory and research** (pp. 516–538). Thousand Oaks, CA: Sage.

Coch, L., & French, J. (1948). Overcoming resistance to change. **Human Relations, 1,** 512–533.

Cohen, E. (1984). Talking and working together: Status, interaction and learning. In P. Peterson, L. Wilkinson, & M. Hallinan (Eds.), **The social context of instruction: Group organization and group processes** (pp. 171–187). New York: Academic Press.

Cohen, S., & Bailey, D. (1997). What makes teams work: Group effectiveness research from the shop floor to the executive suite. **Journal of Management** 23, 239–290.

Cohen, S., & Weinstein, N. (1981). Nonauditory effects of noise on behavior and health. **Journal of Social Issues, 37**(1), 36–70.

Coie, J., & Kupersmidt, J. (1983). A behavioral analysis of emerging social status in boys' groups. **Child Development, 54,** 1400–1416.

Coleman, J. (1961). **The adolescent society**. New York: Macmillan.

Coleman, P. (1997). Psychological resistance to and facilitation of power-sharing in organizations. Dissertation Abstracts.

Coleman, P. (2000). Power and conflict. In M. Deutsch & P. Coleman (Eds.), **The handbook of conflict resolution: Theory and practice** (pp. 108–130). San Francisco: Jossey-Bass.

Coleman, P., & Tjosvold, D. (2000, July). **Positive power: Mapping the dimensions of constructive power relations**. Paper presented at the Social Interdependence Theory Conference, Silver Wind Farm, Minnesota.

Collins, B. (1970). **Social psychology.** Reading, MA: Addison-Wesley.

Collins, J. C. & Porras, J. I. (1994). **Built to last: Successful habits of visionary companies**. New York: Harper Collins Publisher.

Collins, N. (1996). Working models of attachment: Implications for explanation, emotion, and behavior. **Journal of Personality and Social Psychology, 71**, 810–832.

Cook, H., & Murray, F. (1973, March). Acquisition of conservation through the observation of conserving models. Paper presented at the meetings of the American Educational Research Association, New Orleans.

Cook, S. (1957). Desegregation: A psychological analysis. **American Psychologist, 12,** 1–13.

Cook, S. (1969). Motives in a conceptual analysis of attitude-related behavior. In W. Arnold & D. Levine (Eds.), **Nebraska symposium on motivation**. Lincoln: University of Nebraska Press.

Cook, S. (1978). Interpersonal and attitudinal outcomes in cooperating interracial groups. **Journal of Research in Developmental Education, 12,** 87–113.

Cook, S., & Pelfrey, M. (1981, August). **Determinants of respect and liking in cooperative interracial groups.** Paper presented at the meeting of the American Psychological Association, Los Angeles.

Copeland, L., Lamm, L. W., & McKenna, S. J. (1999). **The world's great speeches** (4th ed.). New York: Dover Publications.

Corey, M., & Corey, G. (2005). **Groups: Process and practice** (7th ed.). Pacific Grove, CA: Brooks/Cole.

Cosier, R. (1981). Dialectical inquiry in strategic planning: A case of premature acceptance? **Academy of Management Review, 6,** 643–648.

Cosier, R., & Ruble, T. (1981). Research on conflict handling behavior: An experimental approach. **Academy of Management Journal, 24,** 816–831.

Cottrell, N. (1972). Social facilitation. In C. McClintock (Ed.), **Experimental social psychology** (pp. 185–236). New York: Holt.

Cottrell, N., Wack, D., Sekerak, G., & Rittle, R. (1968). Social facilitation of dominant responses by the presence of an audience and the mere presence of others. **Journal of Personality and Social Psychology, 9,** 245–250.

Covington, M. (1992). Making the grade: A self-worth perspective on motivation and school reform. New York: Cambridge University Press.

Cox, C. (1926). **The early mental traits of three hundred geniuses.** Stanford, CA: Stanford University Press.

Crocker, J., & Luhranen, R. (1990). Collection self-esteem and ingroup bias. **Journal of Personality and Social Psychology, 58,** 60–67.

Croizet, J. & Claire, T. (1998). Extending the concept of stereotype threat to social class: The intellectual under-performance of students from low socioeconomic backgrounds. **Personality and Social Psychology Bulletin, 24**(6), 588–594.

Crombag, H. (1966). Cooperation and competition in means-interdependent triads: A replication. **Journal of Personality and Social Psychology, 4,** 692–695.

Dahl, R. (1957). The concept of power. **Behavioral Science, 2,** 201–218.

Dalkey, N. (1969). An experimental study of group opinion: The Delphi Method. **Futures, 1**(3), 408–426.

Dalkey, N. (1975). Toward a theory of group estimation. In H. Linstone & M. Turoff (Eds.), **The Delphi method: Techniques and applications** (pp. 236–257). Reading, MA: Addison-Wesley.

Dalton, R. (2007). **The good citizen: How a younger generation is reshaping American politics.** Washington, DC: CQ Press.

Dance, F. (1970). The "concept" of communication. **Journal of Communication, 20,** 201–210.

Darley, J., & Latané, B. (1968). Bystander intervention in emergencies: Diffusion of responsibility. **Journal of Personality and Social Psychology, 8,** 377–383.

Darwin, C. (1859). **The origin of species.** London: John Murray.

David, G., & Houtman, S. (1968). **Thinking creatively: A guide to training imagination.** Madison: Wisconsin Research and Development Center for Cognitive Learning.

Davis, J. (1969). **Group performance.** Reading, MA: Addison-Wesley.

Davis, M., Conklin, L., Smith, A., & Luce, C. (1996). The effect of perspective taking on the cognitive representation of persons: A merging of self and other. **Journal of Personality and Social Psychology, 70,** 213–226.

DeCecco, J., & Richards, A. (1974). **Growing pains: Uses of school conflict.** New York: Aberdeen Press.

DeCecco, J., & Richards, S. (1975). Civil war in the high schools. **Psychology Today, 9,** 51–81.

De Cremer, D., & Van Dijk, E. (2002). Reactions to group success and failure as a function of group identification: A test of the goal-transformation hypothesis in social dilemmas. **Journal of Experimental Social Psychology, 38,** 435–442.

De Cremer, D., & Van Vugt, M. (1999). Social identification effects in social dilemmas: A transformation of motives. **European Journal of Social Psychology, 29,** 871–893.

De Dreu, C. K. W., & Nauta, A. (2009). Self-interest and other-orientation in organizational behavior: Implications for job performance, prosocial behavior, and personal initiative. **Journal of Applied Psychology, 94,** 913–926.

De Dreu, C. K. W., Weingart, L. R., & Kwon, S. (2000). Influence of social motives on integrative negotiation: A meta-analytic review and test of two theories. **Journal of Personality and Social Psychology, 76,** 889–905.

De Dreu, C. K. W. & Weingart, L. R. (2003). Task versus relationship conflict, team performance, and team member satisfaction: A meta-analysis. **Journal of Applied Psychology, 88,** 741–749.

De Dreu, C. K. W., & West, M. (2001). Minority dissent and team innovation: The importance of participation in decision making. **Journal of Applied Psychology, 86,** 1191–1201.

De Dreu, C. K. W. & West, M. A. (2001). Minority dissent and team innovation: The importance of participation in decision making. **Journal of Applied Psychology, 86,** 1191–1201.

DeFoe, D. (1908). **The life and strange surprising adventures of Robinson Crusoe.** Boston: Houghton-Mifflin.

Dehue, F., McClintock, C., & Liebrand, W. (1993). Social value related response latencies: Unobtrusive evidence for individual differences in information processes. **European Journal of Social Psychology, 23,** 273–294.

De La Paz, S. (2005). Effects of historical reasoning instruction and writing strategy mastery in culturally and academically diverse middle school classrooms. **Journal of Educational Psychology, 97,** 139–156.

Delbecq, A., Van de Ven, A., & Gustafson, D. (1975). **Group techniques for program planning.** Glenview, IL: Scott, Foresman.

Den Hartog, D. N., & Koopman, P. L. (2001). Leadership in organizations. In N. Anderson, D. S. Ones, H. K. Sinangil, & C. Visweswaran (Eds.), **Handbook of industrial, work, and organizational psychology, Vol. 2: Organizational psychology** (pp. 166–187). Thousand Oaks, CA: Sage.

Dension, D., & Sutton, R. (1990). Operating room nurses. In J. Hackman (Ed.), **Groups that work (and those that don't): Creating conditions for effective teamwork** (pp. 293–308). San Francisco: Jossey-Bass.

Deschamps, J. (1977). Effect of crossing category membership on quantitative judgment. **European Journal of Social Psychology, 22,** 189–195.

Deschamps, J., & Doise, W. (1978). Crossed category memberships in intergroup relations. In H. Tajfel (Ed.), **Differentiation between social groups: Studies in the social psychology of intergroup relations** (pp. 141–158). New York: Academic Press.

Desforges, D., Lord, C., Ramsey S., Mason, J., Van Leeuwen, M., West, S., & Lepper, M. (1991). Effects of structured cooperative contact on changing negative attitudes toward stigmatized social groups. **Journal of Personality and Social Psychology, 60,** 531–544.

Detert, J. R., & Trevino, L. K. (2010). Speaking up to higher ups: How supervisors and skip-level leaders influence employee voice. **Organization Science, 21.1,** 249–270.

Deutsch, M. (1949a). A theory of cooperation and competition. **Human Relations, 2,** 129–152.

Deutsch, M. (1949b). An experimental study of the effects of cooperation and competition upon group process. **Human Relations, 2,** 199–231.

Deutsch, M. (1958). Trust and suspicion. **Journal of Conflict Resolution, 2,** 265–279.

Deutsch, M. (1960). The effects of motivational orientation upon trust and suspicion. **Human Relations, 13,** 123–139.

Deutsch, M. (1962). Cooperation and trust: Some theoretical notes. In M. R. Jones (Ed.), **Nebraska Symposium on Motivation,** 275–320. Lincoln: University of Nebraska Press.

Deutsch, M., & Krauss, R. (1965). **Theories in social psychology,** New York: Basic Books.

Deutsch, M. (1968). Field theory in social psychology. In G. Lindzey & E. Aronson (Eds.), **Handbook of Social Psychology,** (2nd ed.), vol. 1. Reading, MA: Addison-Wesley.

Deutsch, M. (1969). Conflicts: Productive and destructive. **Journal of Social Issues, 25,** 7–43.

Deutsch, M. (1973). **The resolution of conflict.** New Haven, CT: Yale University Press.

Deutsch, M. (1975). Equity, equality, and need: What determines which value will be used as the basis of distributive justice? **Journal of Social Issues, 31,** 137–149.

Deutsch, M. (1979). Education and distributive justice: Some reflections on grading systems. **American Psychologist, 34,** 391–401.

Deutsch, M. (1985). **Distributive justice: A social psychological perspective.** New Haven, CT: Yale University Press.

Deutsch, M. (2003). Content, yes! And theory, yes! **Journal of Dispute Resolution,** 367–375.

Deutsch, M. (2006). A framework for thinking about oppression and its change. **Social Justice Research, 19**(1), 7–41.

Deutsch, M. (2006). Justice and Conflict. In M. Deutsch, Coleman, P., Marcus, E. C. (Eds.), *The Handbook of Conflict Resolution: Theory and Practice* (2nd ed.) (pp. 43–68). San Francisco: Jossey-Bass, 2000.

Deutsch, M., Canavan, D., & Rubin, J. (1971). The effects of size of conflict and sex of experimenter upon interpersonal bargaining. **Journal of Experimental Social Psychology, 7,** 258–267.

Deutsch, M. & Collins, M. (1951). **Interracial housing: A psychological evaluation of a social experiment.** Minneapolis: University of Minnesota Press.

Deutsch, M., & Krauss, R. (1960). The effect of threat upon interpersonal bargaining. **Journal of Abnormal and Social Psychology, 61,** 181–189.

Deutsch, M., & Krauss, R. (1962). Studies of interpersonal bargaining. **Journal of Conflict Resolutions, 6,** 52–76.

Deutsch, M., & Lewicki, R. (1970). "Locking in" effects during a game of chicken. **Journal of Conflict Resolution, 14,** 367–378.

Devine, P., Monteith, M., Zuwerink, J., & Elliot, A. (1991). Prejudice with and without compunction. **Journal of Personality and Social Psychology, 60,** 817–830.

DeVries, D., & Edwards, K. (1973). Learning games and student teams: Their effects on classroom process. **American Educational Research Journal, 10,** 307–318.

DeVries, D., & Edwards, K. (1974). Student teams and learning games: Their effects on cross-race and cross-sex interaction. **Journal of Educational Psychology,** 66, 741–749.

De Waal, F. B. M. (2000). The first kiss. In F. Aureli, & F. B. M. de Waal (Eds.), **Natural conflict resolution** (pp. 13–33). Berkeley, CA: University of California Press.

Diehl, M., & Stroebe, W. (1987). Productivity loss in brainstorming groups: Toward solution of a riddle. **Journal of Personality and Social Psychology,** 53, 497–509.

Diesing, P. (1962). **Reason in society.** Urbana: University of Illinois Press.

Dion, D., Baron, R., & Miller, N. (1970). Why do groups make riskier decisions than individuals? In L. Berkowitz (Ed.), **Advances in experimental social psychology** (pp. 306–378). New York: Academic Press.

Dodge, K. (1983). Behavioral antecedents of peer social status. **Child Development,** 54, 1386–1389.

Doise, W., Mugny, G., & Perret-Clermont, A.(1976). Social interaction and cognitive development: Further evidence. **European Journal of Social Psychology 6,** 245–247.

Doise, W., Mugny, G. (1979). Individual and collective conflicts of centrations in cognitive development. **European Journal of Psychology, 9,** 105–108.

Dollard, J., Doob, L., Miller, N., Mowrer, O., & Sears, R. (1939). **Frustration and aggression.** New Haven, CT: Yale University Press.

Dooley, R. S., & Fryxell, G. E. (1999). Attaining decision quality and commitment from dissent: The moderating effects of loyalty and competence in strategic decision-making teams. **Academy of Management Journal, 42,** 389–402.

Dovidio, J., & Gaertner, S. (1991). Changes in the expression and assessment of racial prejudice. In H. Knopke, R. Norrell, & R. Rogers (Eds.), **Opening doors: Perspectives on race relations in contemporary America** (pp. 119–148). Tuscaloosa: University of Alabama Press.

Driskell, J., Hogan, R., & Salas, E. (1987). Personality and group performance. In C. Hendrick (Ed.), **Group processes and intergroup relations** (pp. 91–112). Newbury Park, CA: Sage.

Drucker, P. (1974). Multinationals and developing countries: Myths and realities. **Foreign Affairs, 53**, 121–134.

Druckman, D., Rozelle, R., & Baxter, J. (1982). **Non-verbal communication: Survey, theory, and research**. Beverly Hills, CA: Sage.

Dumaine, B. (1989, February). How managers can succeed through speed. **Fortune**, pp. 54–59.

Dunnette, M., Campbell, J., & Jaastad, K. (1963). The effect of group participation on brainstorming effectiveness of two industrial samples. **Journal of Applied Psychology, 47,** 30–37.

Dunning, D., & Ross, L. (1988). Overconfidence in individual and group prediction: Is the collective any wiser? Unpublished manuscript, Cornell University.

Durkheim, E. (1897, 1966). **Suicide.** New York: Free Press.

Durkheim, E. (1898). **The rules of sociological method**. New York: Free Press.

Durkheim, E. (1953). Individual and collective representations. In D. F. Pocock (Trans.), **Sociology and philosophy**. New York: Free Press. (Reprinted from Revue de Metaphysique, 1898, 6, 274–302).

Duval, S., & Wicklund, R. (1972). **A theory of objective self-awareness**. New York: Academic Press.

Dyer, W. (1994). **Team building: Issues and alternatives** (3rd ed.). Reading, MA: Addison-Wesley.

Dyer, J., & Singh, H. (1998). The relationship view: Cooperative strategies and sources of interorganizational competitive advantage. **Academy of Management Review, 23**(4), 660–679.

Eagly, A. (1987). **Sex differences in social behavior: A social role interpretation**. Hillsdale, NJ: Erlbaum.

Ehrlich, H., & Lee, D. (1969). Dogmatism, learning, and resistance to change: A review and a new paradigm. **Psychological Bulletin, 71**(4), 249–260.

Eichler, G., & Merrill, R. (1933). Can social leadership be improved by instruction in its technique? **Journal of Educational Sociology, 7,** 233–236.

Eisbach, K. D., & Hargadon, A. B. (2006). Enhancing creativity through "mindless" work: A framework of workday design. **Organization Science, 17,** 470–483.

Eisenberg, N. & Mussen, P. (1995). **The roots of prosocial behavior in children**. Cambridge, MA: Cambridge University Press.

Elder, G. (1974). **Children of the great depression**. Chicago: University of Illinois Press.

Elder, G. (1975). Age differentiation and the life course. **Annual Review of Sociology**, **1**, 165–190.

Ellis, A. (1995). Rational emotive behavior therapy. In R. Corsini & D. Wedding (Eds.), **Current psychotherapies** (5th ed., pp. 162–196). Itasca, IL: Peacook.

Ellis, A. (1996). **Better, deeper, and more enduring belief therapy: The rational emotive behavior therapy approach**. New York: Brunner/Mazel.

Ellis, A. (1997). The evolution of Albert Ellis and rational emotive behavior therapy. In J. Zeig (Ed.), **The evolution of psychotherapy: The third conference** (pp. 69–82). New York: Runner/Mazel.

Emerson, R. (1954). Deviation and rejection: An experimental replication. **American Sociological Review, 19,** 688–693.

Enright, R. D., Gassin, E. A., & Knutson, J. A. (2003). Waging peace through forgiveness education in Belfast, Northern Ireland: A review and proposal for mental health improvement of children. **Journal of Research in Education, 13,** 1–11.

Enright, R. D., Gassin, E. A., & Knutson, J. A. (2004). Waging peace through forgiveness education in Belfast, Northern Ireland: A review and proposal for mental health improvement of children. **Journal of Research in Education, 13**(1), 51–61.

Epstein, S., & Taylor, S. (1967). Instigation to aggression as a function of degree of defeat and perceived aggressive intent of the opponent. **Journal of Personality, 35**, 265–289.

Erb, H. P., Bohner, G., Rank, S., & Einwiller, S. (2002). Processing minority and majority communications: The role of conflict with prior attitudes. **Personality and Social Psychology Bulletin, 28,** 1172–1182.

Espenshade, T., & Calhoun, C. (1993). An analysis of public opinion toward undocumented immigration. **Population Research and Policy Review, 12**, 189–224.

Falbe, C., & Yukl, G. (1992). Consequences for managers of using single influence tactics and combination of tactics. **Academy of Management Journal, 35**, 638–652.

Falk, D., & Johnson, D. W. (1977). The effects of perspective-taking and egocentrism on problem solving in heterogeneous and homogeneous groups. **Journal of Social Psychology, 102**, 63–72.

Falloon, I., Lindley, P., McDonald, R., & Marks, I. (1977). Social skills training of out-patient groups: A controlled study of rehearsal and homework. **British Journal of Psychiatry, 131**, 599–609.

Faucheux, C., & Moscovici, S. (1967). The style of behavior of a minority and its influence on majority responses. **Bulletin Du C.E.R.P, 16**, 337–361.

Fay, A. (1970). **Effects of cooperation and competion on learning and recall.** Unpublished master's thesis, George Peabody College, Nashville, TN.

Fay, B. (1929). **Benjamin Franklin: The apostle of modern times.** Boston: Little, Brown.

Fenelon, J., & Megaree, E. (1971). Influence of race on the manifestation of leadership. **Journal of Applied Psychology, 55**, 353–358.

Festinger, L. (1950). Informal social communication. **Psychological Review**, 57, 271–292.

Festinger, L. (1954). A theory of social comparison processes. **Human Relations**, 7, 117–140.

Festinger, L. (1957). **A theory of cognitive dissonance.** Evanston, IL: Row, Peterson.

Festinger, L., Pepitone, A., & Newcomb, T. (1952). Some consequences of deindividuation in a group. **Journal of Abnormal and Social Psychology, 47**, 382–389.

Festinger, L., Schachter, S., & Back. K. (1950). **Social pressures in informal groups: A study of human factors in housing.** New York: Harper-Collins.

Fiedler, F. (1964). A contingency model of leadership effectiveness. In L. Berkowitz (Ed.), **Advances in experimental social psychology** (Vol. 1, pp. 149–190). New York: Academic Press.

Fiedler, F. (1967). **A theory of leadership effectiveness.** New York: McGraw-Hill.

Fiedler, F. (1969). Style of circumstance: The leadership enigma. **Psychology Today, 2**(10), 38–46.

Fiedler, F. (1978). The contingency model and the dynamics of the leadership process. **Advances in Experimental Social Psychology, 12**, 59–112.

Fiedler, R., Meuwese, W., & Conk, S. (1961). An exploratory study of group creativity in laboratory tasks. **Acta Psychologie, 18**, 100–119.

Filley, A. (1975). **Interpersonal conflict resolution.** Glenview, IL: Scott Foresman.

Filley, A., House, R., & Kerr, S. (1976). **Managerial process and organizational behavior.** Glenview, IL: Scott Foresman.

Fine, G. (1979). The Pinkston settlement: An historical and social psychological investigation of the contact hypothesis. **Phylon, 40**, 229–242.

Fisher, R., & Ury, W. (1981). **Getting to yes: Negotiating agreement without giving in.** Boston: Houghton-Mifflin.

Fiske, S. (1993). Controlling other people: The impact of power on stereotyping. **American Psychologist, 48**, 621–628.

Fiske, S., & Morling, B. (1996). Stereotyping as a function of personal control motives and capacity constraints: The odd couple of power and anxiety. In R. Sorrentino & E. Higgins (Vol. Eds.), **Handbook of motivation and cognition: Vol. 3. The interpersonal context** (pp. 322–346). New York: Guilford.

Fiske, S., & Neuberg, S. (1990). A continuum of impression formation, from category-based to individuating processes: Influences of information and motivation on attention and interpretation. In M. Zanna (Ed.), **Advances in experimental social psychology** (Vol. 23, pp. 1–74). New York: Academic Press.

Flanders, N. (1964). Some relationships among teacher influence, pupil attitudes, and achievement. In B. Biddle & W. Ellena (Eds.), **Contemporary research on teacher effectiveness,** (pp. 196–231). New York: Holt, Rinehart & Winston.

Flowers, M. (1977). A laboratory test of some implications of Janis' groupthink hypothesis. **Journal of Personality and Social Psychology, 35**, 888–896.

Flynn, F. & Chatman, J. (2001). Strong cultures and innovation: Oxymoron or opportunity? In S. Cartwright et.al. (Eds.) **International Handbook of Organizational Culture and Climate.** Sussex, England: John Wiley & Sons.

Frese, M. & Fay, D. (2001). Personal initiative: An active performance concept for work in the 21st century. In B. M. Staw & R. I. Sutton (Eds.), **Research in organizational behavior** (Vol. 23, pp. 133–187). San Diego, CA, US: Elsevier Academic Press.

Foley, J., & MacMillan, F. (1943). Mediated generalization and the interpretation of verbal behavior: V. Free association as related to differences in professional training. **Journal of Experimental Psychology, 33,** 299–310.

Follett, M. (1973). Power. In E. Fox & L. Urwick (Eds.), **Dynamic administration: The collected papers of Mary Parker Follett** (pp. 50–75) New York: Pitman (originally published in 1924).

Follet, M. (1940). Constructive conflict. In H. Metcalf & L Urwick (Eds.), **Dynamic administration: The collected papers of Mary Parker Follet** (pp. 30–49). New York: Pitman (originally published in 1924).

Footlick, J. (1990). What happened to the family? **Newsweek**, v. 114, 21, pp.14–20.

Fox, D. (1985). Psychology, ideology, utopia, and the commons. **American Psychologist, 40,** 48–58.

Fox, D., & Lorge, I. (1962). The relative quality of decisions written by individuals and by groups as the available time for problem solving is increased. **Journal of Social Psychology, 57,** 227–242.

Frable, D., Platt, L., & Hoey, S. (1998). Concealable stigmas and positive self-perceptions: Feeling better around similar others. **Journal of Personality and Social Psychology**, 74, 909–922.

Frank, M. (1984). **A comparison between an individual and group goal structure contingency that differed in the behavioral contingency and performance-outcome components.** Unpublished doctoral thesis, University of Minnesota, Minneapolis.

Frankfort, H., Frankfort, H., Wilson, J., & Jacobson, T. (1949). **Before philosophy.** Baltimore, MD: Penguin.

Franko, D. (1987). Anorexia nervosa and bulimia: A self-help group. **Small Group Behavior**, 18, 398–407.

Fraser, C. (1971). Group risk-taking and group polarization. **European Journal of Social Psychology, 1,** 493–510.

Freeman, E. (1936). **Social psychology.** New York: Holt.

Freeberg, N., & Rock, D. (1987). **Development of a small-group team performance taxonomy based on meta-analysis**. Princeton, NJ: Educational Testing Service, Final Report to the Office of Naval Research,.

Freese, M., & Fay, D. (2001). Personal initiative (PI): An active performance concept for work in the 21st century. **Research in Organizational Behavior, 23,** 133–187.

French, J. (1941). The disruption and cohesion of groups. **Journal of Abnormal Social Psychology, 36,** 361–377.

French, J. (1951). Group productivity. In H. Guetzkow (Ed.), **Groups, leadership and men** (pp. 44–55). Pittsburgh: Carnegie Press.

French, J., & Coch, L. (1948). Overcoming resistance to change. **Human Relations, 1**, 512–532.

French, J., & Raven, B. (1959). The basis of social power. In D. Cartwright (Ed.), **Studies in social power** (pp. 150–167). Ann Arbor: University of Michigan Press.

Freud, S. (1922). **Group psychology and the analysis of the ego**. London: Hogarth.

Frey, D., & Schulz-Hardt, S. (2001). Confirmation bias in group information seeking and its implications for decision making in administration, business, and politics. In F. Butera & G. Mugny (Eds.), **Social influence in social reality: Promoting individual and social change** (pp. 53–73). Ashland, OH: Hogrefe & Huber Publishers.

Frick, F. (1973). **Study of peer training with the Lincoln Training System** (AFATC Report KE 73–116). Harrison, MS: Keesler Air Force Base.

Friedkin, N. (1999). Choice shift and group polarization. **American Sociological Review, 64**, 856–875.

Frost, D., & Stahelski, A. (1988). The systematic measurement of French and Raven's bases of social power in workgroups. **Journal of Applied Social Psychology**, 18, 375–389.

Fuhriman, A., & Burlingame, G. (1994a). Group psychotherapy: Research and practice. In A. Fuhriman & G. Burlingame (Eds.), **Handbook of group psychotherapy: An empirical and clinical synthesis** (pp. 3–40). New York: Wiley.

Fuhriman, A., & Burlingame, G. (Eds.). (1994b). **Handbook of group psychotherapy: An empirical and clinical synthesis**. New York: Wiley

Gabbert, B., Johnson, D., & Johnson, R. (1986). Co-operative learning, group-to-individual transfer, process gain, and the acquisition of cognitive reasoning strategies. **Journal of Psychology**, **120**, 265–278.

Gabrenya, W. K., Wang, Y., & Latané, B. (1983). Social loafing in cross-cultural perspective: Chinese on Taiwan. **Journal of Cross Cultural Psychology**, **14**(3), 368–384.

Gaertner, L., & Schopler, J. (1998). Perceived ingroup entitativity and intergroup bias: An interconnection of self and others. **European Journal of Social Psychology, 28,** 963–980.

Gaertner, S., & Dovidio, J., (1986). The aversive form of racism. In J. Dovidio & S. Gaertner (Eds.), **Prejudice, discrimination, and racism** (pp. 61–89). New York: Academic Press.

Gaertner, S., Dovidio, J., Anastasio, P., Bachman, B., & Rust, M. (1993). The common ingroup identity model: Recategorization and the reduction of intergroup bias. In W. Stroebe & M. Hewstone (Eds.), **European review of social psychology** (Vol. 4, pp. 1–26). Chichester, England: Wiley.

Galinsky, A. D., Maddux, W. W., Gilin, D., & White, J. B. (2008). Why it pays to get inside the head of your opponent: The differential effects of perspective taking and empathy in negotiations. *Psychological Science, 19* (1), 378–384.

Galton, F. (1869). **Hereditary genius**. New York: Appleton.

Gardin, J., Kaplan, K., Firestone, I., & Cowan, G. (1973). Proxemic effects on cooperation, attitude, and approach-avoidance in a prisoner's dilemma game. **Journal of Personality and Social Psychology, 27,** 13–18.

Gardner, J. W. (1990). **On leadership**. New York: Free Press.

Gavin, M., Green, S., & Fairhurst, G. (1995). Managerial control strategies for poor performance over time and the impact on subordinate reactions. **Organizational Behavior and Human Decision Processes**, **63**, 207–221.

Geen, R. (1976). Test anxiety, observation, and range of cue utilization. **British Journal of Social and Clinical Psychology**, **15**, 253–259.

Geen, R. (1980). The effects of being observed on performance. In P. Paulus (Ed.), **Psychology of group influence**, (pp. 61–97). Hillsdale, NJ: Erlbaum.

Georgesen, J., & Harris, M. (1998). Why's my boss always holding me down? A meta-analysis of power effects on performance evaluations. **Personality and Social Psychology Review, 2**(3), 184–195.

Gerard, H., & Hoyt, M. (1974). Distinctiveness of social categorization and attitude toward ingroup members. **Journal of Personality and Social Psychology, 27**, 836–842.

Gerard, H., Wilhelmy, R., & Conolley, E. (1968). Conformity and group size. **Journal of Personality and Social Psychology, 8**(1), 79–82.

Gersick, C. (1988). Time and transition in work teams: Toward a new model of group development. **Academy of Management Journal, 32**, 274–309.

Gersick, C. J., & Hackman, J. R. (1990). Habitual routines in task-performing groups. **Organizational Behavior and Human Decision Processing, 47**, 65–97.

Ghiselli, E., & Lodahl, T. (1958). Patterns of managerial traits and group effectiveness. **Journal of Abnormal and Social Psychology, 57**, 61–66.

Gibb, J. (1951). The effects of group size and of threat upon certainty in a problem-solving situation. **American Psychologist**, 6, 324.

Gibb, J. (1961). Defensive and supportive climates. **Journal of Communication, 11,** 141–148.

Gibbons, E., & Gerrard, M. (1989). Effects of upward and downward social comparison on mood states. **Journal of Social and Clinical Psychology, 8**, 14–31.

Giffin, K. (1967). The contribution of studies of source credibility to a theory of interpersonal trust in the communication process. **Psychological Bulletin, 68**, 104–121.

Gilbert, D., & Malone, P. (1995). The correspondence bias. **Psychological Bulletin, 117**, 21–38.

Gilbert, D., McNulty, S., Giuliano, T., & Benson, J. (1992). Blurry words and fuzzy deeds: The attribution of obscure behavior. **Journal of Personality and Social Psychology, 62**, 18–25.

Gilbert, M. (1997). Coalescent argument. Mahwah, NJ: Erlbaum.

Gilbert, P. (1992). **Depression: The evolution of powerlessness**. New York: Guilford.

Giles, M., & Buckner, M. (1993). "David Duke and Black Threat: An Old. Hypothesis Revisited." **Journal of Politics, 55,** 702–713.

Giles, M., & Hertz, K. (1994). Racial threat and partisan identification. **American Political Science Review, 88,** 317–326.

Glass, D., & Singer, J. (1973). Experimental studies of uncontrollable and unpredictable noise. **Representative Research in Social Psychology, 4**(1), 165–183.

Glass, G. (1977). Integrating findings: The meta-analysis of research. In L. Schulman (Ed.), **Review of research in education** (vol. 5, pp. 351–379). Itasca, IL: Peacock.

Glasser, W. (1984). **Control theory.** New York: Harper & Row.

Glasser, W. (1998). **Choice theory: A new psychology of personal freedom.** New York: Harper Collins.

Glidewell, J. (1953). **Group emotionality and productivity.** Unpublished doctoral dissertation, University of Chicago.

Golanics, J. D., & Nussbaum, E. M. (2008). Enhancing collaborative online argumentation through question elaboration and goal instructions. **Journal of Computer Assisted Learning, 24,** 167–180.

Goldberg, L. (1968). Ghetto riots and others: The faces of civil disorder in 1967. **Journal of Peace Research, 2,** 116–132.

Goldman, M. (1965). A comparison of individual and group performance for varying combinations of initial ability. **Journal of Personality and Social Psychology, 1,** 210–216.

Goldman, M., Dietz, D., & McGlynn, A. (1968). Comparison of individual and group performance related to heterogeneous-wrong responses, size, and patterns of interaction. **Psychological Reports, 23**(2), 459–465.

Goncalo, J. A. & Staw, B. M. (2006). Individualism-collectivism and group creativity. Organizational Behavior and Human Decision Processes, 100, 96–109.

Goodman, G., & Jacobs, M. (1994). The self-help, mutual-support group. In A. Fubriman & G. Burlingame (Eds.), **Handbook of group psychotherapy: An empirical and clinical synthesis** (pp. 489–526). New York: Wiley.

Goodman, P., & Leyden, D. (1991). Familiarity and group productivity. **Journal of Applied Psychology,** 76, 578–586.

Gordon, K. (1924). Group judgments in the field of lifted weights. **Journal of Experimental Psychology, 7,** 398–400.

Gordon, W. (1961). **Synectics.** New York: Harper & Row.

Gottman, J. (1993). The roles of conflict engagement, escalation, and avoidance in marital interaction: A longitudinal view of five types of couples. **Journal of Consulting and Clinical Psychology, 61**(1), 6–15.

Gottschalk, L. (1966). Psychoanalytic notes on T-groups at the Human Relations Laboratory, Bethel, Maine. **Comprehensive Psychiatry, 7**(6), 472–487.

Gouran, D., & Hirokawa, R. (1996). Functional theory and communication in decision-making and problem-solving groups: An expanded view. In R. Hirokawa & M. Poole (Eds.), **Communication and group decision making** (2nd ed., pp. 53–80). Thousand Oaks, CA: Sage.

Graham, S. (1991). A review of attribution theory in achievement contexts. **Educational Psychology Review, 3,** 5–39.

Grant, A. M., & Berry, J. W. (2011). The necessity of others is the mother of invention: Intrinsic and prosocial motivations, perspective-taking, and creativity. **Academy of Management Journal, 54,** 73–96.

Gray, J., & Thompson, A. (1953). The ethnic prejudices of white and Negro college students. **Journal of Abnormal and Social Psychology, 48,** 311–313.

Green, D. (1977). The immediate processing of sentences. **Quarterly Journal of Experimental Psychology, 29,** 135–146.

Greenberg, J., & Pyszczynski, T. (1985). Persistent high self-focus after failure and low self-focus after success: The depressive self-focusing style. **Journal of Personality and Social Psychology, 50,** 1039–1044.

Greer, L. L., Jehn, K. A. & Mannix, E. A. (2008). Conflict transformation: A longitudinal investigation of the relationships between different types of intragroup conflict and the moderating role of conflict resolution. **Small Group Research, 39,** 278–302.

Greitemeyer, T., & Schulz-Hardt, S. (2003). Preference-consistent evaluation of information in the hidden profile paradigm: Beyond group-level explanations for the dominance of shared information in group decision. **Journal of Personality and Social Psychology, 84,** 322–339.

Greitemeyer, T., Schulz-Hardt, S., Brodbeck, F. C., & Frey, D. (2006). Information sampling and group decision making: The effects of an advocacy decision procedure and task experience. **Journal of Experimental Psychology: Applied, 12,** 21–42.

Grint, K. (2005). **Leadership: Limits and possibilities.** Hong Kong, China: Palgrave Macmillan.

Grossack, M. (1953). Some effects of cooperation and competition upon small group behavior. **Journal of Abnormal and Social Psychology,** 49, 341–348.

Gruber, H. E. (2006). Creativity and conflict resolution: The role of point of view. In M. Deutsch & P. T. Coleman (Eds.), **The handbook of conflict resolution: Theory and practice** (pp. 391–401). San Francisco: Jossey-Bass.

Gruenfeld, D. H. (1995). Status, ideology and integrative complexity on the U.S. Supreme Court: Rethinking the politics of political decision making. **Journal of Personality and Social Psychology, 68,** 5–20.

Gruner, C. (1965). An experimental study of satire as persuasion. **Speech Monographs, 32**(2), 149–153.

Guimond, S., Dambrun, M., Michinov, N., & Duarte, S. (2003). Does social dominance generate prejudice? Integrating individual and contextual determinants of intergroup cognitions. **Journal of Personality and Social Psychology, 84,** 697–721.

Gully, S., Devine, D., & Whitney, D. (1995). A meta-analysis of cohesion and performance: Effects of level of analysis and task interdependence. **Small Groups Research, 26,** 497–520.

Gump, P. (1964). Environmental guidance of the classroom behavioral system. In B. Biddle and W. Ellena (Eds.), **Contemporary research on teacher effectiveness** (pp. 165–195). New York: Holt, Rinehart & Winston.

Gundlach, R. (1950). The effect of on-the-job experience with Negroes upon social attitudes of white workers in union shops. **American Psychologist, 5,** 300.

Gurwitch, R. H., Sitterle, K. A., Young, B. H., & Pfefferbaum, B. (2002). The aftermath of terrorism. In A. M. LaGreca, W. K. Silverman, E. M. Vernberg, &

M. C. Roberts (Eds.), **Helping children cope with disasters and terrorism** (pp. 327–358). Washington, DC: American Psychological Association.

Gurtner, A., Tschan, F., Semmer, N. K., & Nägele, C. (2007). Getting groups to develop good strategies: Effects of reflexivity interventions on team process, team performance, and mental models. **Organizational Behavior and Human Decision Processes, 102,** 127–142.

Hackman. J. (1987). The design of work teams. In J. Lorsch (Ed.), **Handbook of organizational behavior** (pp. 315–342). New York: Prentice-Hall.

Hackman, J. (1989). **Groups that work (and those that don't).** San Francisco: Jossey-Bass.

Hackman, J. R. (2002). **Leading teams: Setting the stage for great performances.** Boston: Harvard Business School Press.

Hackman, J., & Morris, C. (1975). Group tasks, group interaction process and group performance effectiveness: A review and proposed integration. In L. Berkowitz (Ed.), **Advances in Experimental Social Psychology** (Vol. 8, pp. 47–99). New York: Academic Press.

Hackman, J., & Oldham, G. (1980). **Work redesign.** Reading, MA: Addison-Wesley.

Hackman, J., & Walton, R. (1986). Leading groups in organizations. In P. Goodman (Ed.), Designing effective work groups (pp. 72–119). San Francisco: Jossey-Bass.

Hackman, J. R., & Wageman, R. (2005). When and how team leaders matter. **Research in Organizational Behavior, 26,** 37–74.

Hagman, J., & Hayes, J. (1986). **Cooperative learning: Effects of task, reward, and group size on individual achievement** (Technical Report 704). Boise, ID: Scientific Coordination Office, U.S. Army Research Institute for the Behavioral and Social Sciences (ERIC Document Reproduction Service No. ED 278 720).

Hall, J. & Veccia, E. (1990). More "touching observations: New insights on men, women, and interpersonal touch. **Journal of Personality and Social Psychology,** 59, 1155–1162.

Hall, J., & Williams, M. (1966). A comparison of decision making performance in established and ad hoc groups. **Journal of Personality and Social Psychology,** 3, 214–222.

Hall, J., & Williams, M. (1970). Group dynamics training and improved decision making. **Journal of Applied Behavioral Science, 6**, 39–68.

Halle, L. J. (1967, June). Overestimating the power of power. **The New Republic,** 15–17.

Halpern, D. (1995). **Mental health and the built environment: More than bricks and mortar?** London: Taylor & Francis.

Hamilton, D. (1979). A cognitive-attributional analysis of stereotyping. In L. Berkowitz (Ed.), **Advances in experimental social psychology** (Vol. 12) (pp. 53–84). New York: Academic Press.

Hamilton, D., & Sherman, J. (1994). Stereotypes. In R. Wyer, Jr., & T. Srull (Eds.), **Handbook of social cognition** (2nd ed., vol. 2, pp. 1–68). Hillsdale, NJ: Erlbaum.

Hamilton, D., & Sherman, J. (1996). Perceiving person and groups. **Psychological Review, 103**, 336–355.

Haney, C., Banks, C., & Zimbardo, P. (1973). Interpersonal dynamics in a simulated prison. **International Journal of Criminology and Psychology, 1**, 69–97.

Harding, J. & Hogerge, R. (1952). Attitudes of white department store employees toward Negro co-workers. **Journal of Social Issues, 8,** 18–28.

Hare, A. (1976). **Handbook of small group research** (2nd ed.). New York: Free Press.

Harkins, S. (1987). Social loafing and social facilitation. **Journal of Experimental Social Psychology, 23**, 1–18.

Harkins, S., & Jackson, J. (1985). The role of evaluation in eliminating social loafing. **Personality and Social Psychology Bulletin, 11**, 457–465.

Harkins, S., & Petty, R. (1982). The effects of task difficulty and task uniqueness on social loafing. **Journal of Personality and Social Psychology, 43**, 1214–1229.

Harkins, S. (1981, October). The role of intrinsic motivation in eliminating social loafing. **Ohio State Social Psychology Colloquium Series.**

Harkins, S., & Szymanski, K. (1987). Social loafing and self-evaluation with an objective standard. **Journal of Experimental Social Psychology, 24**, 354–365.

Harkins, S., & Szymanski, K. (1989). Social loafing and group evaluation. **Journal of Personality and Social Psychology, 56**, 934–941.

Harlan, H. (1942). Some factors affecting attitude toward Jews. **American Sociological Review, 7**, 816–827.

Harris, M., & Schaubroeck. J. (1988). A meta-analysis of self-supervisor, self-peer, and peer-supervisor ratings. **Personnel Psychology, 41**, 43–62.

Hart, W., Albarracin, D., Eagly, A., Brechan, I., Lindberg, M., and Merrill, L. (2009). Feeling validated versus being correct: A meta-analysis of selective exposure to information. **Psychological Bulletin, 135**, 555–588.

Hartig, T., Mang, M., & Evans, G. (1991). Restorative effects of natural environment experience. **Environment and Behavior, 23**, 3–26.

Harvey, J. (1999). **Civilized oppression**. Lanham, MD: Rowman and Littlefield.

Haslam, N. (2006). Dehumanization: An integrative review. **Personality and Social Psychology Review, 10**, 252–264.

Haslam, S. A. (2004). **Psychology in organizations: The social identity approach** (2nd ed.). Thousand Oaks, CA: Sage.

Haslam, S. A., Ryan, M. K., Postmes, T., Spears, R., Jetten, J., & Webley, P. (2006). Sticking to our guns: Social identity as a basis for the maintenance of commitment to faltering organizational projects. **Journal of Organizational Behavior, 27**, 607–628.

Hastorf, A., & Cantril, H. (1954). They saw a game. **Journal of Abnormal and Social Psychology, 49**, 129–134.

Hastorf, A., Northcraft, G., Picciotot, S. (1979). Helping the handicapped: How realistic is the performance feedback? **Personality and Social Psychology Bulletin, 5**, 373–376.

Haunschild, P., Moreland, R., & Murrell, A. (1994). Sources of resistance to mergers between groups. **Journal of Applied Social Psychology, 24**, 1150–1178.

Hawley, P. (1999). The ontogenesis of social dominance: A strategy-based evolutionary perspective. **Developmental Review, 19**, 97–132.

Haythorn, W. (1968). The composition of groups: A review of the literature. **Acta Psychologica, 28**, 97–128.

Hedges, L., & Olkin, I. (1985). **Statistical methods for meta-analysis**. New York: Academic Press.

Heider, F. (1958). **The psychology of interpersonal relations.** New York: Wiley.

Helson, R. (1996). In search of the creative personality. **Creativity Research Journal, 9,** 295–306.

Henningsen, D. D., & Henningsen, M. L. M. (2003). Examining social influence in information-sharing contexts. **Small Group Research, 34,** 391–412.

Henningsen, D. D., & Henningsen, M. L. M. (2007). Do groups know what they don't know? Dealing with missing information in decision-making groups. **Communication Research, 34,** 507–525.

Henningsen, D. D., Henningsen, M. L. M., Eden, J., & Cruz, M. G. (2006). Examining the symptoms of groupthink and retrospective sensemaking. **Small Group Research, 37,** 36–64.

Hepworth, J., & West, S. (1988). Lynching and the economy: A time-series reanalysis of Hovland and Sears (1940). **Journal of Personality and Social Psychology, 55,** 239–247.

Herek, G., & Capitanio, J. (1996). "Some of my best friends": Intergroup contact, concealable stigma, and heterosexuals' attitudes toward gay men and lesbians. **Personality and Social Psychology Bulletin, 22,** 412–424.

Herek, G., Janis, I., & Huth, P. (1987). Decision-making during international crises: Is quality of process related to outcome? **Journal of Conflict Resolution, 31,** 203–226.

Hertel, G., Kerr, N., & Messe, L. (2000). Motivation gains in performance groups: Paradigmatic and theoretical developments on the Kohler effect. **Journal of Personality and Social Psychology 79,** 580–601.

Herzog, T., & Bosley, P. (1992). Tranquility and preference as affective qualities of natural environment. **Journal of Environmental Psychology, 12,** 115–127.

Hewstone, M., & Brown, R. (Eds.). (1986). **Contact and conflict in intergroup relations.** Oxford, England, Basil Blackwell.

Hewstone, M., & Martin, R. (2008). Social influence. In M. Hewstone, W. Stroebe & K. Jonas (Eds.). **Introduction to social psychology** (4th ed., pp. 216–243). Malden, MA: Blackwell Publishing.

Hill, G. (1982). Group versus individual performance: Are n + 1 heads better than one? **Psychological Bulletin, 91,** 517–539.

Hill, W., & Gruner, L. (1973). A study of development in open and closed groups. **Small Group Behavior, 4,** 355–381.

Hinkin, R., & Schriesheim, C. (1989). Development and application of new scales to measure the French and Raven (1959) bases of social power. **Journal of Applied Psychology, 74,** 561–567.

Hirst, G., Mann, L., Bain, P., Pirola-Merlo, A., & Richter, A. (2004). Learning to lead: The development and testing of a model of leadership learning. **Leadership Quarterly, 15,** 311–327.

Hoerr, J. (1989, July). The payoff from teamwork. **Business Week,** pp. 56–62.

Hoffer, E. (1951). **The true believer.** New York: Harper & Row.

Hoffman, L. (1959). Group problem solving. In L. Berkowitz (Ed.), **Advances in experimental social psychology: Vol. 2** (pp. 99–132). San Diego, CA: Academic Press.

Hoffman, L. (1961). Conditions for creative problem solving. **Journal of Psychology, 52,** 429–444.

Hoffman, L. (1979). Applying experimental research on group problem solving to organizations. **Journal of Applied Behavioral Science, 15,** 375–391.

Hoffman, L., Harburg, E., & Maier, N. (1962a). Differences and disagreement as factors in creative problem solving. **Journal of Abnormal and Social Psychology, 64,** 206–214.

Hoffman, L., Harburg, E., & Maier, N. (1962b). Quality and acceptance of problem solutions by members of homogeneous and heterogeneous groups. **Journal of Abnormal and Social Psychology, 64,** 206–214.

Hoffman, L., & Maier, N. (1961). Quality and acceptance of problem solutions by members of homogeneous and heterogeneous. **Journal of Abnormal and Social Psychology, 62**(2), 401–407.

Hollander, E., & Willis, R. (1967). Some current issues in the psychology of conformity and nonconformity. **Psychological Bulletin, 68,** 62–76.

Hollingshead, A., Fulk, J., & Monge, P. (2002). Fostering intranet knowledge sharing: An integration of transactive memory and public goods approaches. In P. Hinds & S. Kiesler (Eds.), Distributed work (pp. 335–355). Cambridge, MA: MIT Press.

Homan, A. C., van Knippenberg, D., Van Kleef, G. A., & De Dreu, C. K. W. (2007a). Bridging faultlines by valuing diversity: The effects of diversity beliefs on information elaboration: The effects of diversity belies on information elaboration and performance in diverse work groups. **Journal of Applied Psychology, 92**, 1189–1199.

Homan, A. C., van Knippenberg, D., Van Kleef, G. A., & De Dreu, C. K. W. (2007b). Interacting dimensions of diversity: Cross-categorization and the functioning of diverse work groups. **Group Dynamics: Theory, Research, and Practice, 11**, 79–94.

Homans, G. (1950). **The human group.** New York: Harcourt, Brace.

Homans, G. (1961). **Social behaviors: Its elementary forms.** New York: Harcourt, Brace & World.

Homans, G. (1974). **Social behavior: Its elementary forms** (rev.ed.). New York: Harcourt Brace Jovanovich.

Hong, O., & Harrod, W. (1988). The role of reasons in the in-group bias phenomenon. **European Journal of Social Psychology, 18**, 537–545.

Hook, S. (1955). **The hero in history**. Boston: Beacon Press.

Hooper, S., Ward, T., Hannafin, M., & Clark, H. (1989). The effects of aptitude composition on achievement during small group learning. **Journal of Computer-Based Instruction, 16**, 102–109.

Hopper, R. (1950). The revolutionary process. **Social Forces, 28**, 270–279.

Hopthrow, T., Abrams, D., Fings, D., & Hulbert, L. G. (2007). Groupdrink: The effects of alcohol on intergroup competitiveness. **Psychology of Addictive Behaviors, 21**, 272–276.

Horai, J. (1977). Attributional conflict. **Journal of Social Issues, 33**(1), 88–100.

Hornstein, H., & Johnson, D. W. (1966). The effects of process analysis and ties to his group upon the negotiator's attitudes toward the outcomes of negotiations. **Journal of Applied Behavioral Science, 2**, 449–465.

Horowitz, E. (1936). The development of attitude toward the Negro. **Archives of Psychology**, (Whole No. 194).

Horwitz, M. (1954). The recall of interrupted group tasks: An experimental study of individual motivation in relation to group goals. **Human Relations, 7**, 3–38.

Hovhannisyan, A., Varrella, G., Johnson, D. W., & Johnson, R. (2005). Cooperative learning and building democracies. **The Cooperative Link, 20**(1), 1–3.

Hovland, C., Janis, I., & Kelley, H. (1953). **Communication and persuasion.** New Haven, CT: Yale University Press.

Hovland, C., Lumsdaine, A., & Sheffield, F. (1949). **Experiment on mass communication.** Princeton, NJ: Princeton University Press.

Hovland, C., & Sears, R. (1940). Minor studies in aggression: VI. Correlation of lynchings with economic indices. **Journal of Psychology, 9**, 301–310.

Hovland, C., & Weiss, W. (1952). The influence of source credibility on communication effectiveness. **Public Opinion Quarterly, 15**, 635–650.

Howell, J. M., & Shamir, B. (2005). The role of followers in the charismatic leadership process: Relationships and their consequences. **Academy of Management Review, 30**, 96–112.

Howells, L., & Becker, S. (1962). Seating arrangement and leadership emergence. **Journal of Personality and Social Psychology, 64,** 148–150.

Hulten, B., & DeVries, D. (1976). **Team competition and group practice: Effects on student achievement and attitudes.** Johns Hopkins University, Center for Social Organization of Schools, Report #212.

Hunt, P., & Hillery, J. (1973). Social facilitation in a coaction setting: An examination of the effects over learning trials. **Journal of Experimental Social Psychology, 9**, 563–571.

Hwong, N., Caswell, A., Johnson, D. W., & Johnson, R. (1993). Effects of cooperative and individualistic learning on prospective elementary teachers' music achievement and attitudes. **Journal of Social Psychology, 133**, 53–64.

Ichheiser, G. (1949). Misunderstandings in human relations: A study in false social perceptions. **American Journal of Sociology** (Supplement), **55**, 1–70.

Ilgen, D. (1986). Small groups in an individualistic world. In R. McGlynn & B. George (Eds.), **Interfaces in psychology: Organizational psychology and small**

group behavior (pp. 149–169). Lubbock: Texas Tech University Press.

Illing, H. (1957). C. Jung on the present trends in group psychotherapy. **Human Relations, 10,** 77–84.

Indik, B. (1965). Organization size and member participation: Some empirical tests of alternative explanations. **Human Relations,** 18(4), 339–350.

Ingham. A., Levinger, G., Graves, J., & Peckham, V. (1974). The Ringelmann effect: Studies of group size and group performance. **Journal of Experimental Social Psychology,** 10, 371–384.

Irish, D. (1952). Reactions of Caucasian residents to Japanese-American neighbors. **Journal of Social Issues, 8,** 10–17.

Isenberg, D. (1986). Group polarizaiton: A critical review and meta-analysis. **Journal of Personality and Social Psychology,** 50, 1141–1151.

Islam, M., & Hewstone, M. (1993). Intergroup attributions and affective consequences in majority and minority groups. **Journal of Personality and Social Psychology, 64**, 936–950.

Iverson, M., & Schwab, H. (1967). Ethnocentric dogmatism and binocular fusion of sexually and racially discrepant stimuli. **Journal of Personality and Social Psychology, 7,** 73–81.

Jackman, M., & Crane, M. (1986). "Some of my best friends are black . . ." Interracial friendship and whites' racial attitudes. **Public Opinion Quarterly, 50**, 459–486.

Jackson, S. (1992). Team composition in organizational settings: Issues in managing an increasingly diverse work force. In S. Worchel, W. Wood, & J. Simpson (Eds.), **Group process and productivity** (pp. 138–173). Newbury Park, CA: Sage.

Jackson, J., & Williams, K. (1985). Social loafing on difficult tasks: Working collectively can improve performance. **Journal of Personality and Social Psychology,** 49, 937–942.

Jackson, J., & Williams, K. (1986). **A review and theoretical analysis of social loafing**. Unpublished manuscript, Fordham University.

Jackson, S., Brett, J., Sessa, V., Cooper, D., Julin, J., & Peyronnin, K. (1991). Some differences make a difference: Interpersonal dissimilarity and group heterogeneity as correlates of recruitment, promotion, and turnover. **Journal of Applied Psychology, 76**, 675–689.

Jackson, S., May, K., & Whitney, K. (1995). Understanding the dynamics of diversity in decision-making teams. In R. Guzzo, E. Salas, and associates (Eds.), **Team effectiveness and decision making in organizations** (pp. 204–261). San Francisco: Jossey-Bass.

Jacobson, N., & Margolin, G. (1979). **Marital therapy: Strategies based on social learning and behavior exchange principles**. New York: Brunner/Mazel.

Jahoda, M., & West, P. (1951). Race relations in public housing. **Journal of Social Issues, 7,** 132–139.

James, W. (1880, October). Great men, great thoughts and their environment. **Atlantic Monthly, 46**, 441–459.

Janis, I. (1971). Groupthink. **Psychology Today, 5**(6), 43–46, 74–76.

Janis, I. L. (1972). **Victims of groupthink: A psychological study of foreign-policy decisions and fiascoes**. Oxford: Houghton Mifflin.

Janis, I. L. (1982). **Groupthink** (revised and enlarged edition of **Victims of groupthink**). Boston: Houghton-Mifflin.

Janis, I., & Mann, L. (1977). **Decision making.** New York: Free Press.

Janz, T., & Tjosvold, D. (1985). Costing effective vs. ineffective work relationships: A method and first look. **Canadian Journal of Administrative Sciences,** 2, 53–51.

Jehn, K. A. & Bezrukova, K. (2010). The faultline activation process and the effects of activated faultlines on coalition formation, conflict, and group outcomes. **Organizational Behavior and Human Decision Making Processes, 112**, 24–42.

Jehn, K. (1995). A multi-method examination of the benefits and detriments of intragroup conflict. **Administrative Science Quarterly, 40**, 256–282.

Jehn, K. (1997). A qualitative analysis of conflict types and dimensions in organizational groups. **Administrative Science Quarterly, 42**, 530–557.

Jehn, K. A., & Bendersky, C. (2003). Intragroup conflict in organizations: A contingency perspective on the conflict-outcome relationship. In R. M. Kramer &

B. M. Staw (Eds.), **Research in organizational behavior: An annual series of analytical essays and critical reviews**, Vol 25. Research in organizational behavior (pp. 187–242). Oxford, England: Elsevier Science Ltd.

Jehn, K. A. & Mannix, E. A. (2001). The dynamic nature of conflict: A longitudinal study of intra-group conflict and group performance. **Academy of Management Journal, 44** (2), 238–251.

Jehn, K., Northcraft, G., & Neale, M. (1999). Why differences make a difference: A field study of diversity, conflict, and performance in workgroups. **Administrative Science Quarterly, 44**, 741–763.

Jetten, J., Hornsey, M. J., Spears, R., Haslam, S. A., & Cowell, E. (2010). Rule transgressions in groups: The conditional nature of newcomers' willingness to confront deviance. **European Journal of Social Psychology, 40,** 338–348.

Johnson, D., & Rusbult, C. (1989). Resisting temptation: Devaluation of alternative partners as a means of maintaining commitment in close relationships. **Journal of Personality and Social Psychology, 57**, 967–980.

Johnson, D. W. (1967). The use of role reversal in intergroup competition. **Journal of Personality and Social Psychology, 7**, 135–141.

Johnson, D. W. (1970). **The social psychology of education**. New York: Holt, Rinehart & Winston.

Johnson, D. W. (1971a). Role reversal: A summary and review of the research. **International Journal of Group Tensions**, 1, 318–334.

Johnson, D. W. (1971b). The effectiveness of role reversal: The actor or the listener. **Psychological Reports**, 28, 275–282.

Johnson, D. W. (1972). **The effects of role reversal on seeing a conflict from the opponent's frame of reference.** Unpublished manuscript, University of Minnesota.

Johnson, D. W. (1973). **Contemporary social psychology**. Philadelphia: Lippincott.

Johnson, D. W. (1974). Communication and the inducement of cooperative behavior in conflicts. **Speech Monographs**, 41, 64–78.

Johnson, D. W. (1977). Distribution and exchange of information in problem solving dyads. **Communication Research, 4**, 283–298.

Johnson, D. W. (1978). **Human relations and your career** (1st ed.). Englewood Cliffs, NJ: Prentice-Hall.

Johnson, D. W. (1979). **Educational psychology**. Englewood Cliffs, NJ: Prentice-Hall.

Johnson, D. W. (1980a). Group processes: Influences on student-student interaction on school outcomes. In J. McMillan (Ed.), **Social psychology of school learning** (pp. 123–168). New York: Academic Press.

Johnson, D. W. (1980b). Attitude modification methods. In F. Kanfer and A. Goldstein (Eds.), **Helping people change** (pp. 51–88). New York: Pergamon Press.

Johnson, D. W. (1991). **Human relations and your career** (3rd ed.). Englewood Cliffs, NJ: Prentice-Hall.

Johnson, D. W. (2003). Social interdependence: The interrelationships among theory, research, and practice. **American Psychologist, 58**(11), 931–945.

Johnson, D. W. (2009). **Reaching out: Interpersonal effectiveness and self-actualization** (10th ed.). Boston: Allyn & Bacon.

Johnson, D. W., & Allen, S. (1972). Deviation from organizational norms concerning the relations between status and power. **Sociological Quarterly, 13**, 174–182.

Johnson, D. W., Johnson, F., & Johnson, R. (1976). Promoting constructive conflict in the classroom. **Notre Dame Journal of Education**, 7, 163–168.

Johnson, D. W., & Johnson, R. (1974). Instructional goal structure: Cooperative, competitive, or individualistic. **Review of Educational Research, 44**, 213–240.

Johnson, D. W., & Johnson, R. (1978). Cooperative, competitive, and individualistic learning. **Journal of Research and Development in Education, 12,** 3–15.

Johnson, D. W., & Johnson, R. (1979). Conflict in the classroom: Controversy and learning. **Review of Educational Research, 49**, 51–70.

Johnson, D. W., & Johnson, R. (1980). **Belonging** [film]. Edina, MN: Interaction Book Company.

Johnson, D. W., & Johnson, R. (1981). Effects of cooperative and individualistic learning experiences on interethnic interaction. **Journal of Educational Psychology, 73**, 454–459.

Johnson, D. W., & Johnson, R. (1983). The socialization and achievement crisis: Are cooperative learning experiences the solution? In L. Bickman (Ed.), **Applied social psychology annual 4** (pp. 119–164). Beverly Hills, CA: Sage Publications.

Johnson, D. W., & Johnson, R. (1985). Classroom conflict: Controversy versus debate in learning groups. **American Educational Research Journal, 22,** 237–256.

Johnson, D. W., & Johnson, R. (1987). **Creative conflict**. Edina, MN: Interaction Book Company.

Johnson, D. W., & Johnson, R. (1989). **Cooperation and competition: Theory and research**. Edina, MN: Interaction Book Company.

Johnson, D. W., & Johnson, R. (1990). **Cooperative learning: Warm-ups, grouping strategies and group activities** (2nd ed.). Edina, MN: Interaction Book Company.

Johnson, D. W., & Johnson, R. (1992a). **Positive interdependence: The heart of cooperative learning.** Edina, MN: Interaction Book Company.

Johnson, D. W., & Johnson, R. (1992b). **Positive interdependence: The heart of cooperative learning** (video). Edina, MN: Interaction Book Company.

Johnson, D. W., & Johnson, R. (1994). **Leading the cooperative school** (2nd ed). Edina, MN: Interaction Book Company.

Johnson, D. W., & Johnson, R. (1996). **Meaningful and manageable assessment through cooperative learning**. Edina, MN: Interaction Book Company.

Johnson, D. W., & Johnson, R. (1997). **Learning to lead teams: Developing leadership skills**. Edina, MN: Interaction Book Company.

Johnson, D. W., & Johnson, R. (1998). Cooperative learning and social interdependence theory. In R. Tindale, L. Heath, J. Edwards, E. Posavac, F. Bryant, Y. Suzrez-Balcazar, E. Henderson-King, & J. Myers (Eds.), **Theory and research on small groups** (pp. 9–36). New York: Plenum.

Johnson, D. W., & Johnson, R. (1999a). **Learning together and alone: Cooperative, competitive, and individualistic learning** (6th ed.). Boston: Allyn & Bacon.

Johnson, D. W., & Johnson, R. (1999b). **Human relations: Valuing diversity**. Edina, MN: Interaction Book Company.

Johnson, D. W., & Johnson, R. (2000). Civil political discourse in a democracy: The contribution of psychology. **Peace and Conflict: Journal of Peace Psychology, 6**(4), 291–317.

Johnson, D. W., & Johnson, R. (2002). **Meaningful And Manageable Assessment Through Cooperative Learning** (2nd ed.). Edina, MN: Interaction Book Company

Johnson, D. W., & Johnson, R. (2003a). Controversy and peace education. **Journal of Research in Education, 13**(1), 71–91.

Johnson, D. W., & Johnson, R. (2003b). Student motivation in cooperative groups: Social interdependence theory. In R. Gillies & A. Ashman (Eds.). **Cooperative learning: The social and intellectual outcomes of learning in groups** (pp. 136–176). New York: RoutledgeFalmer.

Johnson, D. W., & Johnson, R. (2003c). Training for cooperative group work. In M. West, D. Tjosvold, & K. Smith, **International handbook of organizational teamwork and cooperative working** (pp. 167–183). London: John Wiley.

Johnson, D. W., & Johnson, R. T. (2005a). New developments in social interdependence theory. **Genetic, Social, and General Psychology Monographs, 131**(4), 285–358.

Johnson, D. W., & Johnson, R. T. (2005b). **Teaching students to be peacemakers** (4th ed). Edina, MN: Interaction Book Company.

Johnson, D. W., & Johnson, R. (2006). Peace education for consensual peace: The essential role of conflict resolution. **Journal of Peace Education, 3**(2), 147–174.

Johnson, D. W., & Johnson, R. T. (2007). **Creative controversy: Intellectual challenge in the classroom** (4th ed.). Edina, MN: Interaction Book Company.

Johnson, D. W., & Johnson, R. T. (2008). Cooperation and the use of technology. In Spector, J. M., Merrill, M. D., van Merrienboer, J. J. G., Driscoll, M. P. (Eds.). **Handbook of Research on Educational Communications and Technology** (3rd ed.). (pp. 401–423). New York: Lawrence Erlbaum (Taylor & Francis).

Johnson, D. W., & Johnson, R. T. (2009a). Energizing learning: The instructional power of conflict. **Educational Researcher, 38**(1), 37–51.

Johnson, D. W., & Johnson, R. T. (2009b). An educational psychology success story: Social interdependence theory and cooperative learning. **Educational Researcher, 38**(5), 365–379.

Johnson, D. W., & Johnson, R. T. (2010). The impact of social interdependence on value education and student wellbeing. In T. Lovat, R. Toomey, & N. Clement (Eds.), **International research handbook of values education and student wellbeing** (pp. 825–848). New York: Springer Press.

Johnson, D. W., & Johnson, R. T. (2011). Restorative justice in the classroom: Necessary roles of cooperative context, constructive conflict, and civic values. **Negotiation and Conflict Management Research Journal**, in press.

Johnson, D. W., Johnson, R. T., Buckman, L., & Richards, P. (1986). The effect of prolonged implementation of cooperative learning on social support within the classroom. **Journal of Psychology, 119,** 405–411.

Johnson, D. W., Johnson, R. T., & Holubec, E. (1994). **Nuts and bolts of cooperative learning**. Edina, MN: Interaction Book Company.

Johnson, D. W., Johnson, R., & Holubec, E. (2008). **Cooperation in the classroom** (7th ed.). Edina, MN: Interaction Book Company.

Johnson, D. W., Johnson, R., & Holubec, E. (2008). **Advanced cooperative learning** (5th ed.). Edina, MN: Interaction Book Company.

Johnson, D. W., Johnson, R. T., & Holubec, E. J. (2009). **Circles of learning: Cooperation in the classroom** (9th ed.). Edina, MN: Interaction Book Company.

Johnson, D. W., Johnson, R., & Johnson, F. (1976). Promoting constructive conflict in the classroom. **Notre Dame Journal of Education, 7,** 163–168.

Johnson, D. W., Johnson, R., & Maruyama, G. (1983). Interdependence and interpersonal attraction among heterogeneous and homogeneous individuals: A theoretical formulation and a meta-analysis of the research. **Review of Educational Research, 53,** 5–54.

Johnson, D. W., Johnson, R., Ortiz, A., & Stanne, M. (1991). Impact of positive goal and resource interdependence on achievement, interaction, and attitudes. **Journal of General Psychology, 118**(4), 341–347.

Johnson, D. W., Johnson, R., & Skon, L. (1979). Student achievement on different types of tasks under cooperative, competitive, and individualistic conditions. **Contemporary Educational Psychology, 4,** 99–106.

Johnson, D. W., Johnson, R., & Smith, K. (1987). Academic conflict among students: Controversy and learning. In R. Feldman (Ed.), **Social psychological applications to education** (pp. 199–231). Cambridge: Cambridge University Press.

Johnson, D. W., Johnson, R., & Smith, K. (1998). **Active learning: Cooperation in the college classroom** (2nd ed.). Edina, MN: Interaction Book Company.

Johnson, D. W., Johnson, R., & Smith, K. (2000). Constructive controversy: The educative power of intellectual conflict. **Change, 32**(1), 28–37.

Johnson, D. W., Johnson, R., & Smith, K. (2006). **Active learning: Cooperative learning in the college classroom** (3rd edition). Edina, MN: Interaction Book Company.

Johnson, D. W., Johnson, R., Stanne, M., & Garibaldi, A. (1990). Impact of group processing on achievement in cooperative groups. **Journal of Social Psychology, 130,** 507–516.

Johnson, D. W., Johnson, R., & Tjosvold, D. (2000). Constructive controversy: The value of intellectual opposition. In M. Deutsch, & P. Coleman (Eds.), **Handbook of constructive conflict resolution: Theory and practice** (pp. 65–85). San Francisco: Jossey-Bass.

Johnson, D. W., Kavanagh, J., & Lubin, B. (1973). Tests, t-groups, and tension. **Comparative Group Studies, 4,** 81–88.

Johnson, D. W., & Lewicki, R. (1969). The initiation of superordinate goals. **Journal of Applied Behavioral Science, 5,** 9–24.

Johnson, D. W., Maruyama, G., Johnson, R., Nelson, D., & Skon, L. (1981). Effects of cooperative, competitive, and individualistic goal structures on achievement: A meta-analysis. **Psychological Bulletin, 89,** 47–62.

Johnson, D. W., & Matross, R. (1977). The interpersonal influence of the psychotherapist. In A. Gurman and A. Razin (Eds.), **Effective psychotherapy: A handbook of research** (pp. 395–432). Elmsford, NY: Pergamon Press.

Johnson, D. W., McCarty, K., & Allen, T. (1976). Congruent and contradictory verbal and nonverbal communications of cooperativeness and competitiveness in negotiations. **Communication Research**, **3**, 275–292.

Johnson, D. W., & Noonan, P. (1972). Effects of acceptance and reciprocation of self-disclosures on the development of trust. **Journal of Counseling Psychology**, **19**, 411–416.

Johnson, D. W., & Norem-Hebeisen, A. (1981). The relationship between cooperative, competitive, and individualistic attitudes and differentiated aspects of self-esteem. **Journal of Personality**, **49**, 415–426.

Johnson, D. W., Skon, L., & Johnson, R. (1980). The effects of cooperative, competitive and individualistic goal structures on student achievement on different types of tasks. **American Educational Research Journal, 17,** 83–93.

Johnson, R., Johnson, D. W., Scott, L., & Ramolae, B. (1985). Effects of single-sex and mixed-sex cooperative interaction on science achievement and attitudes and cross-handicap and cross-sex relationship. **Journal of Research in Science Teaching**, **22**, 207–220.

Johnson, S., & Johnson, D. W. (1972). The effects of other's actions, attitude similarity, and race on attraction towards the other. **Human Relations, 25,** 121–130.

Jones, E., & Gerard, H. (1967). **Foundations of social psychology.** New York: John Wiley.

Jones, E., & Nesbett, R. (1972). The actor and the observer: Divergent perceptions of the causes of behavior. In E. Jones, D. Kanouse, H. Kelley, R. Nisbett, S. Valins, & B. Weiner (Eds.), **Attribution: Perceiving the causes of behavior** (pp. 79–94). Morristown, NJ: General Learning Press.

Jones, M. (1974). Regressing group on individual effectiveness. **Organizational Behavior and Human Performance**, **11**, 426–451.

Kahpor-Klein, F. & Kahlon, M. (2004). **Discrimination and Americans' dreams. HOW FAIR.** Level Playing Field Institute and the University of Connecticut.

Kameda, T., & Tamura, R. (2007). "To eat or not to be eaten?" Collective risk-monitoring in groups. **Journal of Experimental Social Psychology 43**, 168–179.

Kantor, R.M. (1988). When a thousand flowers bloom: Structural, collective and social conditions for innovation in organizations. In B. Staw & L. L. Cummings (Eds.), Research in Organizational Behavior, 10, 169–211. Greenwich, CT: JAI Press.

Kantor, R. (1977). **Men and women of the corporation.** New York: Basic Books.

Kaplan, M. (1977). Discussion polarization effects in a modern jury decision paradigm: Informational influences. **Sociometry, 40**, 262–271.

Kaplan, M., & Miller, C. (1977). Group decision making and normative versus information influence: Effects of type of issue and assigned decision rule. **Journal of Personality and Social Psychology**, **53**, 306–313.

Kaplan, M., & Miller, C. (1977). Judgments and group discussion: Effect of presentation and memory factors on polarization. **Sociometry, 40,** 337–343

Karau, S., & Williams, K. (1993). Social loading: A meta-analytic review and theoretical integration. **Journal of Personality and Social Psychology, 65**, 681–706.

Karau, S., & Williams, K. (2001). Understanding individual motivation in groups: The collective effort model. In M. Turner (Ed.), **Groups at work: Theory and research** (pp. 113–141). Mahwah, NJ: Erlbaum.

Katz, D., & Braly, K. (1933). Racial stereotypes of 100 college students. **Journal of Abnormal and Social Psychology, 28**, 280–290.

Katz, I., & Hass, R. (1988). Racial ambivalence and American value conflict: Correlational and priming studies of dual cognitive structures. **Journal of Personality and Social Psychology, 55**, 893–905.

Katz, I., Wachenhut, J., & Hass, R. (1986). Racial ambivalence, value duality, and behavior. In J. Dovidio & S. Gaertner (Eds.), **Prejudice, discrimination, and racism** (pp. 35–60). New York: Academic Press.

Katzenbach, J., & Smith, D. (2003). **The wisdom of teams.** Cambridge, MA: Harvard Business School Press.

Kaul, T., & Bednar, R. (2003). Experiential group research: Results, questions, and suggestions. In S. Garfield & A Bergin (Eds.), **Handbook of psychotherapy and behavior change** (5th ed., pp. 671–714). New York: Wiley.

Kellerman, B. (2004). **Bad leadership: What it is, how it happens, why it matters**. Boston: Harvard Business School Press.

Kelley, H. (1968). Interpersonal accommodation. **American Psychologist, 23**, 399–410.

Kelley, H. (1979). **Personal relationships**. Hillsdale, NJ: Erlbaum.

Kelley, H., & Stahelski, A. (1970). Social interaction basis of cooperators' and competitors' beliefs about others. **Journal of Personality and Social Psychology, 16**, 66–91.

Kelley, H., & Thibaut, J. (1978). **Interpersonal relations: A theory of interdependence**. New York: Wiley.

Kelly, J., & Karau, S. (1999). Group decision making: The effects of initial preferences and time pressure. **Personality and Social Psychology Bulletin, 25**, 1342–1354.

Kerr, N. (1983). The dispensability of member effort and group motivation losses: Free-rider effects. **Journal of Personality and Social Psychology, 44**, 78–94.

Kerr, N. (1989). Illusions of efficacy: The effects of group size on perceived efficacy in social dilemmas. **Journal of Experimental Social Psychology, 35**, 287–313.

Kerr, N. (2001). Social loafing and social striving: Motivational processes in task performing groups. In J. Forgas, K. Williams, & L. Wheeler (Eds.), **The social mind: Cognitive and motivational aspects of interpersonal behavior.** New York: Cambridge University Press.

Kerr, N., Atkin, R., Stasser, G., Meek, D., Holt, R., & Davis, J. (1976). Guilt beyond a reasonable doubt: Effects of concept definition and assigned decision rule on the judgments of mock jurors. **Journal of Personality and Social Psychology, 34**, 282–294.

Kerr, N., & Bruun, S. (1981). Ringelmann revisited: Alternative explanations for the social loafing effect. **Personality and Social Psychology Bulletin, 7**, 224–231.

Kerr, N., & Bruun, S. (1983). The dispensability of member effort and group motivation losses: Free-rider effects. **Journal of Personality and Social Psychology, 44,** 78–94.

Kerr, N., Davis, J., Meek, D., & Rissman, A. (1975). Group position as a function of member attitudes: Choice shift effects from the perspective of social decision scheme theory. **Journal of Personality and Social Psychology, 31**, 574–593.

Key, V. (1949). **Southern politics in state and nation**. New York: Knopf.

Keyton, J. (1999). Relational communication in groups. In L. Frey, D. Gouran, & M. Poole, (Eds.), **The handbook of group communication theory and research** (pp. 192–222). Thousand Oaks, CA: Sage.

Kiesler, S., Siegel, J., & McGuire, T. (1984, October). Social psychological aspects of computer-mediated communication. **American Psychologist, 39**(10), 1123–1134.

Kim, S., Smith, R., & Brigham, N. (1998). Effects of power imbalance and the presence of third parties on reactions to harm: Upward and downward revenge. **Personality and Social Psychology Bulletin, 24**(4), 353–361.

Kimberly, J., & Evanisko, M. (1981). Organizational innovation: The influence of individual, organizational, and contextual factors on hospital adoption of technological and administrative innovations. **Academy of Management Journal, 24**, 689–713.

Kinlaw, D.C. (1991). **Developing superior work teams: Building quality and the competitive edge**. Lexington, MA: Lexington Books.

Kipnis, D. (1972). Does power corrupt? **Journal of Personality and Social Psychology, 24**, 33–41.

Kipnis, D. (1984). The use of power in organizations and in interpersonal settings. **Applied Social Psychology Annual, 5**, 179–210.

Kipnis, D. (1987). Psychology and behavioral technology. **American Psychologist, 42**, 30–36.

Kipnis, D., Castell, J., Gergen, M., & Mauch, D. (1976). Metamorphic effects of power. **Journal of Applied Psychology, 61**, 127–135.

Kipnis, D., Schmidt, S., Prince K., & Stitt, C. (1981). Why do I like thee: Is it your performance or my orders? **Journal of Applied Psychology, 66**, 324–328.

Kirkpatrick, S. A., & Locke, E. A. (1991). Leadership: Do traits matter? **Academy of Management Executive, 5**, 48–60.

Kivlighan, D., & Mullison, D. (1988). Participants' perception of therapeutic factors in group counseling: The role of interpersonal style and stage of group development. **Small Group Behavior**, **19**, 452–468.

Kivlighan, D., Multon, K., & Brossart, D. (1996). Helpful impacts in group counseling: Development of a multidimensional rating system. **Journal of Counseling Psychology**, **43**, 347–355.

Kloche, U. (2007). How to improve decision making in small groups: Effects of dissent and training interventions. **Small Group Research, 38**, 437–468.

Kohn, A. (1992). **No contest: The case against competition** (2nd ed.). Boston: Houghton Mifflin.

Kohn, A. (1993). **Punished by rewards**. Boston: Houghton Mifflin.

Kolb, D. (1985). To be a mediator: Expressive tactics in mediation. **Journal of Social Issues, 41**(2), 11–26.

Kostick, M. (1957). An experiment in group decision. **Journal of Teacher Education, 8**, 67–72.

Kouzes, J., & Posner, B. (1987). **The leadership challenge**. San Francisco: Jossey-Bass.

Kramer, G. (1951). **Residential contact as a determinant of attitudes toward Negroes.** Unpublished doctoral dissertation, Harvard University.

Kramer, R. (1996). Divergent realities and convergent disappointments in the hierarchic relation: Trust and the intuitive auditor at work. In R. Kramer & T. Tyler (Eds.), **Trust in organizations: Frontiers of theory and research** (pp. 216–245). Thousand Oaks, CA: Sage.

Kramer, R., & Brewer, M. (1984). Effects of group identity on resource use in a simulated commons dilemma. **Journal of Personality and Social Psychology, 46**, 1044–1057.

Kramer, R., & Brewer, M. (1986). Social group identity and the emergence of cooperation in resource conservation dilemmas. In H. Wilke, D. Messick, & C. Rutte (Eds.), **Experimental social dilemmas** (pp. 205–234). Frankfurt am Main: Verlag Peter Lang.

Krause, C. (1978). **Guyana massacre: The eyewitness account.** Washington, DC: The Washington Post.

Krauss, R., & Deutsch, M. (1966). Communication in interpersonal bargaining. **Journal of Personality and Social Psychology, 4**, 572–577.

Kray, L., & Gallinsky, A. (2003). The debiasing effect of counterfactual mind-sets: Increasing the search for disconfirmatory information in group decisions. **Organizational Behavior and Human Decision Processes, 91**, 69–81.

Kressel, K., & Pruitt, D. (1985). Themes in the mediation of social conflict. **Journal of Social Issues, 41**(2), 179–198.

Kropotkin, P. (1902). **Mutual aid: A factor of evolution**. London: Doubleday.

Kruglanski, A. W., Pierro, A., Mannetti, L., & DeGrada, E. (2006). Groups as epistemic providers: Need for closure and the unfolding of group-centrism. **Psychological Review, 113**, 84–100.

Labarre, W. (1972). **The ghost dance**. New York: Delta.

Lakin, M. (1972). **Interpersonal encounter: Theory and practice in sensitivity training.** New York: McGraw-Hill.

Lamm, H., & Trommsdorff, G. (1973). Group versus individual performance on tasks requiring ideational proficiency (brainstorming): A review. **European Journal of Social Psychology, 3**, 361–388.

Lampert, M. L., Rittenhouse, P., & Crumbaugh, C. (1996). Agreeing to disagree: Developing sociable mathematical discourse. In D. R. Olson & N. Torrance (Eds.), **Handbook of human development in education** (pp. 731–764). Cambridge, MA: Blackwell.

Langer, E., & Benevento, A. (1978). Self-induced dependence. **Journal of Personality and Social Psychology, 36**, 886–893.

Langer, E., Blank, A., & Chanowitz, B. (1978). The mindlessness of ostensibly thoughtful action: The role of "placebic" information in interpersonal interaction. **Journal of Personality and Social Psychology, 36**, 635–642.

Langer, E., & Rodin, J. (1976). The effects of choice and enhanced personal responsibility for the aged: A field experiment in an institutional setting. **Journal of Personality and Social Psychology, 34**(2), 191–198.

Langewiesche, W. (2003). Columbia's last flight. **The Atlantic Monthly, 292**, 58–87.

Larson, J. R., Christensen, C., Franz, T., & Abbott, A. (1998). Diagnosing groups: The pooling, management, and impact of shared and unshared case information in team-based medical decision making. **Journal of Personality and Social Psychology, 75**, 93–108.

Larson, J. R., Foster-Fishman, P. G., & Franz, T. (1998). Leadership style and the discussion of shared and unshared information in decision-making groups. **Personality and Social Psychology Bulletin, 24**, 482–495.

Larson, J. R., Foster-Fishman, P. G., & Keys, C. B. (1994). The discussion of shared and unshared information in decision-making groups. **Journal of Personality and Social Psychology, 67**, 446–461.

Lasswell, H. D., & Kaplan A. (1950). **Power and society: A framework for political inquiry**. New Haven, CT: Yale University Press.

Latané, B. (1981). The psychology of social impact. **American Psychologist, 36**, 343–356.

Latané, B., & Nida, S. (1981). Ten years of research on group size and helping. **Psychological Bulletin, 89**, 308–324.

Latané, B., Williams, K., & Harkins, S. (1979). Many hands make light the work: The causes and consequences of social loafing. **Journal of Personality and Social Psychology, 37**, 822–832.

Latham, G., & Baldes, J. (1975). The "practical significance" of Locke's theory of goal setting. **Journal of Applied Psychology, 60**, 122–124.

Laughlin, P. (1980). Social combination processes of cooperative problem-solving groups on verbal intellective tasks. In M. Fishbein (Ed.), **Progress in social psychology** (Vol. 1, pp. 127–155). Hillsdale, NJ: Erlbaum.

Laughlin, P., & Adamopoulos, J. (1980). Social combination processes and individual learning for six-person cooperative groups on an intellective task. **Journal of Personality and Social Psychology, 38**, 941–947.

Laughlin, P., & Bitz, D. (1975). Individual versus dyadic performance on a disjunctive task as a function of initial ability level. **Journal of Personality and Social Psychology, 31**, 487–496.

Laughlin, P., Branch, L., & Johnson, H. (1969). Individual versus triadic performance on a unidimensional complementary task as a function of initial ability level. **Journal of Personality and Social Psychology, 12**, 144–150.

Laughlin, P., & Early, P. (1982). Social combination models, persuasive arguments theory, social comparison theory and choice shift. **Journal of Personality and Social Psychology, 42**, 273–280.

Lawler, E., & Yoon, J. (1993). Power and the emergence of commitment behavior in negotiated exchange. **American Sociological Review, 58**, 465–481.

Lawrence, P., & Lorsch, J. (1967). **Organization and environment: Managing differentiation and integration.** Cambridge: Harvard University, Division of Research, Graduate School of Business Administration.

Leana, C. (1985). A partial test of Janis' groupthink model: Effects of group cohesiveness and leader behavior on defective decision making. **Journal of Management, 11**, 5–17.

Leavitt, H. (1951). Some effects of certain communication patterns on group performance. **Journal of Abnormal and Social Psychology, 46,** 38–50.

Le Bon, G. (1895). **The crowd: A study of the popular mind**. London: T. Fisher Unwin.

Le Bon, G. (1960). **The crowd**. New York: The Viking Press. (Original work published in 1895)

Lee, C. (1989). The relationship between goal setting, self-efficacy, and female field-hockey team performance. **International Journal of Sport Psychology, 20**(2), 147–161.

Leichtentritt, J., & Shechtman, Z. (1998). Therapist, trainee, and child very response modes in child group therapy. **Group Dynamics: Theory, Research, and Practice, 2**, 36–47.

LePine, J. A. & Van Dyne, L. (2001). Voice and cooperative behavior as contrasting forms of contextual performance: Evidence of differential relationships with Big 5 personality characteristics and cognitive ability. **Journal of Applied Psychology, 86**, 326–336. *Johnson v. Louisiana*, 406, U.S., 356 (1972).

Levine, J., & Butler, J. (1952). Lecture vs. group decision in changing behavior. **Journal of Applied Psychology, 36**, 29–33.

Levine, J., & Moreland, R. (1998). Small groups. In D. Gilbert, S. Fiske, & G. Lindzey (Eds.), **The handbook of social psychology** (4th ed., Vol. 2, pp. 415–469). New York: McGraw-Hill.

Levine, R., Chein, I., & Murphy, G. (1942). The relation of the intensity of a need to the amount of perceptual distortion: A preliminary report. **Journal of Psychology, 13,** 283–293.

Levinger, G. (1980). Toward the analysis of close relationships. **Journal of Experimental Social Psychology, 16,** 510–544.

Lew, M., Mesch, D., Johnson, D. W., & Johnson, R. (1986a). Postive interdependence, academic and collaborative-skills group contingencies and isolated students. **American Educational Research Journal, 23,** 476–488.

Lew, M., Mesch, D., Johnson, D. W., & Johnson, R. (1986b). Components of cooperative learning: Effects of collaborative skills and academic group contingencies on achievement and mainstreaming. **Contemporary Educational Psychology, 11,** 229–239.

Lewin, K. (1935). **A dynamic theory of personality.** New York: McGraw-Hill.

Lewin, K. (1943). Forces behind food habits and methods of change. **Bulletin of the National Research Council, 108,** 35–65. (Washington, DC: National Research Council: Committee on Food Habits)

Lewin, K. (1944). Dynamics of group action. **Educational Leadership, 1,** 195–200.

Lewin, K. (1948). **Resolving social conflicts.** New York: Harper.

Lewin, K. (1951). **Field theory in social science.** New York: Harper.

Lewin, K., Dembo, T., Festinger, L., & Sears, P. (1944). Level of aspiration. In J. Hunt (Ed.), **Personality and the behavior disorders** (pp. 333–378). New York: Ronald Press.

Lewin, K., & Grabbe, P. (1945). Conduct, knowledge, and acceptance of new values. **Journal of Social Issues, 1,** 56–64.

Lewin, K., Lippitt, R., & White, R. (1939). Patterns of aggressive behavior in experimentally created "social climates." **Journal of Social Psychology, 10,** 271–299.

Lewis, H. (1944). An experimental study of the role of the ego in work. I. The role of the ego in cooperative work. **Journal of Experimental Psychology, 34,** 113–126.

Lewis, H., & Franklin, M. (1944). An experimental study of the role of the ego in work. II. The significance of task-orientation in work. **Journal of Experimental Psychology, 34,** 195–215.

Lewis, S., & Pruitt, D. (1971). Organization, aspiration level, and communication freedom in integrative bargaining. **Proceedings of the 79th Annual Convention of the American Psychological Association, 6,** 221–222.

Lickel, B., Hamilton, D., Wieczorkowska, G., Lewis, A., Sherman, S., & Uhles, A. (2000). Varieties of groups and the perception of group entitativity. **Journal of Personality and Social Psychology, 78,** 223–246.

Lickel, B., Schmader, T., & Miller, N. (2003). **Vicarious retribution: The role of collective blame in intergroup aggression.** Research report, University of Southern California.

Lieberman, M. (1993). Self-help groups. In H. Kaplan & MN. Sadock (Eds.), **Comprehensive group psychotherapy** (3rd ed., pp. 292–304). Baltimore: Williams & Wilkins.

Lieberman, M., Lakin, M., & Whitaker, D. (1968). The group as a unique context for therapy. **Psychotherapy: Theory, Research and Practice, 5**(1), 29–36.

Lieberman, M., Yalom, I., & Miles, M. (1973). **Encounter groups: First facts.** New York: Basic Books.

Lieberman, M., Yalom, I., & Miles, M. (1980). Group methods. In F. Kanfer & A. Goldstein (Eds.), **Helping people change** (pp. 433–485). New York: Pergamon Press.

Likert, R. (1961). **New patterns of management.** New York: McGraw-Hill.

Lindbloom, D. (1959). The science of muddling through. **Public Administrative Review, 15,** 79–88.

Lindeman, A. (1997). Ingroup bias, self-enhancement, and group identification. **European Journal of Social Psychology, 27,** 337–355.

Lindskold, S., & Aronoff, J. (1980). Conciliatory strategies and relative power. **Journal of Experimental Social Psychology, 16,** 187–198.

Linville, P. (1982). The complexity-extremity effect and age-based stereotyping. **Journal of Personality and Social Psychology, 42,** 193–211.

Linville, P., & Jones, E. (1980). Polarized appraisals of out-group members. **Journal of Personality and Social Psychology, 38,** 689–703.

Linville, P., Fisher, G., & Salovey, P. (1989). Perceived distribution of the characteristics of in-group and out-group members: Empirical evidence and a computer simulation. **Journal of Personality and Social Psychology, 57,** 165–188.

Lippmann, W. (1922). **Public opinion.** New York: Harcourt, Brace, Javanovich.

Lissner, K. (1933). The resolution of needs by substitutive acts: Studies of action and affect psychology, edited by K. Lewin. **Psychologische Fortung, 18,** 27–87.

Littlepage, G., & Mueller, A. (1997). Recognition and utilization of expertise in problem-solving groups: Expert characteristics and behavior. **Group Dynamics: Theory, Research, and Practice,** 1, 324–328.

Littlepage, G., Robison, W., & Reddington, KI. (1997). Effects of task experience and group experience on group performance, member ability, and recognition of expertise. **Organizational Behavior and Human Decision Processes, 69,** 133–147.

Littlepage, G., & Silbiger, H. (1992). Recognition of expertise in decision-making groups: Effects of group size and participation patterns. **Small Group Research, 23,** 344–355.

Locke, E., & Latham, G. (1985). The application of goal setting to sports. **Journal of Sport Psychology,** 7(3), 205–222.

Lockhead, J. (1983). **Beyond Emile: Misconceptions of education in the 21st century.** Paper presented at the annual meeting of the American Education Research Association, Montreal, Quebec.

London, P. (1969). **Behavior control.** New York: Harper & Row.

Longley, J., & Pruitt, D. (1980). Groupthink: A critique of Janis's theory. In L. Wheeler (Ed.), **Review of Personality and Social Psychology,** 1. Beverly Hills, CA: Sage.

Lord, C., Ross, L., & Lepper, M. (1979). Biased assimilation and attitude polarization: The effects of prior theories on subsequently considered evidence. **Journal of Personality and Social Psychology, 37**(11), 2098–2109.

Lorge, I., Fox, D., Davitz, J., & Brenner, M. (1958). A survey of studies contrasting the quality of group performance and individual performance, 1920–1957. **Psychological Bulletin,** 55, 337–372.

Lott, A., & Lott, B. (1965). Group cohesiveness and interpersonal attraction: A review of relationships with antecedent and consequent variables. **Psychological Bulletin, 64,** 259–302.

Lovelace, K., Shapiro, D., & Weingart, L. R. 2001. Maximizing cross-functional new product teams innovativeness and constraint adherence: A conflict communications perspective. **Academy of Management Journal, 44**(4): 779–783.

Lowry, N., & Johnson, D. W. (1981). Effects of controversy on epistemic curiosity, achievement, and attitudes. **Journal of Social Psychology, 115,** 31–43.

Luce, R. & Raiffa, H. (1957). **Games and decisions.** New York: Wiley.

Luchins, A. (1942). Mechanization in problem solving: The effect of Einstellung. **Psychological Monographs, 54** (Whole No. 248).

Lull, P. E. (1940). The effectiveness of humor in persuasive speech. **Speech Monographs, 7,** 20–40.

Lyons, V. (1980). **Structuring cooperative learning: The 1980 handbook.** New Brighton, MN: Interaction Book Company.

MacKenzie, B. (1948). The importance of contact in determining attitudes toward Negroes. **Journal of Abnormal and Social Psychology, 43,** 417–441.

Mackie, D. M. (1987). Systematic and nonsystematic processing of majority and minority persuasive communications. **Journal of Personality and Social Psychology, 53,** 41–52.

Maehr, M., & Midgley, C. (1991). Enhancing student motivation: A school-work approach. **Educational Psychologist, 26,** 399–427.

Magnuson, E. (1986) "Fixing NASA." **Time, 9** June: 14ff.

Mahler, W. (1933). Substitution acts of a different degree of reality. Students of action and affect psychology, edited by K. Lewin. **Psychologishe Fortschung, 18,** 27–89.

Maier, N. (1930). Reasoning in humans. **Journal of Comparative Psychology, 10,** 115–143.

Maier, N. (1950). The quality of group decisions as influenced by the discussion leader. **Human Relations, 3**, 155–174.

Maier, N. (1970). **Problem solving and creativity in individuals and group.** Belmont, CA: Brooks/Cole.

Maier, N., & Hoffman, L. (1964). Financial incentives and group decision in motivating change. **Journal of Social Psychology, 64,** 369–378.

Maier, N., & Solem, A. (1952). The contribution of a discussion leader to the quality of group thinking: The effective use of minority opinions. **Human Relations, 5,** 277–288.

Maier, N., & Thurber, J. (1969). Innovative problemsolving by outsiders: A study of individuals and groups. **Personal Psychology, 22**(3), 237–249.

Major, B., Schmidlin, A., & Williams, L. (1990). Gender patterns in social touch: The impact of setting and age. **Journal of Personality and Social Psychology**, 58, 634–643.

Mann, L., & Janis, I. (1983). Decisional conflict in organizations. In D. Tjosvold and D. Johnson (Eds.), **Productive conflict management** (pp. 16–45). New York: Irvington.

Mann, R. (1959). A review of the relationship between personality and performance in small groups. **Psychological Bulletin, 56,** 241–270.

Mannheimer, D., & Williams, R. (1949). A note on Negro troops in combat. In S. Stouffer, E. Suchman, L. DeVinney, S. Star, & R. Williams (Eds.), **The American Soldier,** Vol. 1. Princeton, N.J.: Princeton University Press.

Maoz, I. (2009). Does contact work in protracted asymmetrical conflict? Appraising 20 years and four major models of reconciliation aimed planned encounters between Israeli Jews and Palestinians. Unpublished manuscript. Department of Communication and Journalism Hebrew University of Jerusalem, Israel.

Marcus-Newhall, A., Miller, N., Holtz, R., & Brewer, M. (1993). Cross-cutting category membership with role assignment: A means of reducing intergroup bias. **British Journal of Social Psychology, 32**, 124–146.

Marcus-Newhall, A., Pedersen, W., Carlson, M., & Miller, N. (2000). Displaced aggression is alive and well: A meta-analytic review. **Journal of Personality and Social Psychology,** 78, 670–689.

Markman, H. (1981). Prediction of marital distress: A 5-year follow-up. **Journal of Consulting and Clinical Psychology, 49,** 760–762.

Markus, H. (1978). The effect of mere presence on social facilitation: An unobtrusive test. **Journal of Experimental Social Psychology, 14,** 389–397.

Marrow, A. (1957). **Making management human**. New York: McGraw-Hill.

Marrow, A. (1969). **The practical theorist: The life and work of Kurt Lewin**. New York: Basic Books.

Martin, R., Gardikiotis, A., & Hewstone, M. (2002). Levels of consensus and majority and minority influence. **European Journal of Social Psychology, 32**, 645–665.

Magnuson, Ed., (1986). Fixing NASA. **Time, 9** June: 14ff.

Maslach, C., Stapp, J., & Santee, R. (1985). Individuation: Conceptual analysis and assessment. **Journal of Personality and Social Psychology, 49,** 729–738.

Maslow, A. (1954). **Motivation and personality**. New York: Harper & Row.

Maslow, A. (1962). **Toward a psychology of being.** Princeton, NJ: Van Nostrand.

Matsui, N., Kakuyama, T., & Onglateo, M. (1987). Effects of goals and feedback on performance in groups. **Journal of Applied Psychology, 72**(3), 416–425.

Mayerson, N., & Rhodewalt, F. (1988). The role of self-protective attributions in the experience of pain. **Journal of Social Clinical Psychology, 6**, 203–218.

McCain, B., O'Reilly, C., & Pfeffer, J. (1983). The effects of departmental demography on turnover. **Academy of Management Journal,** 26, 626–641.

McCauley, C. (1989). The nature of social influence in groupthink: Compliance and internalization. **Journal of Personality and Social Psychology, 57,** 250–260.

McClelland, D. (1975). **Power: The inner experience**. New York: Irvington.

McClelland, D. (1985). How motives, skills, and values determine what people do. **American Psychologist, 40,** 812–825.

McClelland, D., & Atkinson, J. (1948). The projective expression of needs: I. The effect of different intensities of the hunger drive on perception. **Journal of Psychology**, **25**, 205–222.

McConahay, J. (1986). Modern racism, ambivalence, and the modern racism scale. In J. Dovidio & S. Gaertner (Eds.), **Prejudice, discrimination, and racism** (pp. 91–125). New York: Academic Press.

McCown, W., & Johnson, J. (1991). Personality and chronic procrastination by university students during an academic examination period. **Personality and Individual Differences, 12**, 413–415.

McDavid, J., & Harari, H. (1968). **Social psychology: Individuals, groups, societies.** New York: Harper & Row.

McGrath, J. E. (1962). **Leadership behavior: Some requirements for leadership training.** Washington, DC: U.S. Civil Service Commission.

McGrath, J. E. (1984). **Groups: Interaction and performance.** Englewood Cliffs, NJ: Prentice-Hall.

McGregor, D. (1967). **The human side of enterprise.** New York: McGraw-Hill.

McGuire, W. (1964). Inducing resistance to persuasion. In L. Berkowitz (Ed.), **Advances in experimental social psychology** (Vol. 1, pp. 192–232). New York: Academic Press.

McGuire, W. (1969). The nature of attitudes and attitude change. In B. Lindsey and E. Aronson (Eds.), **Handbook of social psychology** (Vol. 3, pp. 136–314). Reading, MA: Addison-Wesley.

McGuire, W. (1985). Attitudes and attitude change. In G. Lindzey & E. Aronson (Eds.), **The handbook of social psychology** (3rd ed., Vol. 2, pp. 233–346). New York: Random House.

McGuire, T., Kiesler, S., & Siegel, J. (1987). Group and computer-mediated discussion effects in risk decision making. **Journal of Personality and Social Psychology, 52**, 917–930.

McGuire, W., McGuire, C., Child, P., & Fujioka, P. (1978). Salience of ethnicity in he spontaneous self-concept as a function of one's ethnic distinctiveness in the social environment. **Journal of Personality and Social Psychology, 36**, 511–520.

McGuire, W., McGuire, C., & Winton, W. (1979). Effects of household sex composition on the salience of one's gender in the spontaneous self-concept. **Journal of Experimental Social Psychology, 15**, 77–90.

McRoberts, C., Burlingame, G., & Hoag, M. (1998). Comparative efficacy of individual and group psychotherapy: A meta-analysis. **Group Dynamics: Theory, Research, and Practice, 2**, 101–117.

Meer, B., & Freedman, E. (1966). The impact of Negro neighbors on White house owners. **Social Forces, 45**, 11–19.

Medalia, N., & Larson, O. (1958). Diffusion and belief in a collective delusion: The Seattle windshield pitting epidemic. **American Sociological Review, 23**, 180–186.

Medin, D. (1988). Social categorization: Structures, processes, and purposes. In R. Wyer, Jr., & T. Srull (Eds.), **Handbook of social cognition** (2nd ed., Vol. 2, pp. 1–68). Hillsdale, NJ: Erlbaum.

Mehrabian, A. (1971). **Silent messages**. Belmont, CA: Wadsworth.

Mesch, D., Johnson, D. W., & Johnson, R. (1988). Impact of positive interdependence and academic group contingencies on achievement. **Journal of Social Psychology, 128**, 345–352.

Mesch, D., Lew, M., Johnson, D. W., & Johnson, R. (1986). Isolated teenagers, cooperative learning and the training of social skills. **Journal of Psychology, 120**, 323–334.

Mesch, D., Lew, M., Johnson, D. W., & Johnson, R. (1993). Effects of cooperative learning on isolated teens. In J. Cohen & M. Fish (Eds.), **Handbook of school-based interventions**. San Francisco, CA: Jossey-Bass (pp. 404–405).

Messe, L., Hertel, G., Kerr, N., Lount R., & Park, E. (2002). Knowledge of partner's ability as a moderator of group motivation gains: An exploration of the Koehler discrepancy effect. **Journal of Personality and Social Psychology, 82**, 935–946.

Messe, L., Kerr, N., & Sattler, D. (1992). "But some animals are more equal than others": The supervisor as a privileged status in group contexts. In S. Worchel, W. Wood, & J. Simpson (Eds.), **Group process and productivity** (pp. 203–223). Newbury Park, CA: Sage.

Messe, L., Stollak, G., Larson, R., & Michaels, G. (1979). Interpersonal consequences of person perception in two social contexts. **Journal of Personality and Social Psychology, 37**, 369–379.

Messick, D., & Brewer, M. (1983). Solving social dilemmas: A review. In L. Wheeler & P. Shaver (Eds.),

Review of Personality and Social Psychology (Vol. 4, pp. 11–44). Newbury Park, CA: Sage.

Michels, R. (1915/1959). **Political parties: A sociological study of the oligarchical tendencies of modern democracy**. New York: Dover.

Michener, H., & Burt, M. (1975). Components of "authority" as determinants of compliance. **Journal of Personality Psychology, 31**, 606–614.

Milgram, S. (1974). **Obedience to authority**. New York: Harper & Row.

Mill, J.S. (1979). **On liberty**. New York: Penguin Press (originally published 1859).

Miller, N. (2002). Personalization and the promise of contact theory. **Journal of Social Issues, 58**(2), 387–410.

Miller, N., & Brewer, M. (Ed.). (1984). **Groups in contact: The psychology of desegregation**. New York: Academic Press.

Miller, N., Brewer, M., & Edwards, K. (1985). Cooperative interaction in desegregated settings: A laboratory analogue. **Journal of Social Issues, 41**(3), 63–79.

Miller, N., & Davidson-Podgorny, G. (1987). Theoretical models of intergroup relations and the use of cooperative teams as an intervention for desegregated settings. In C. Hendrick (Ed.), **Annual review of personality and social psychology: Group processes and intergroup relations** (Vol. 9, pp. 23–39). Newbury Park, CA: Sage.

Mills, T. (1967). **The sociology of small groups**. Englewood Cliffs, NJ: Prentice-Hall.

Minard, R. (1952). Race relationships in the Pocahontas coal field. **Journal of Social Issues, 8**, 29–44.

Mitchell, T., & Silver, W. (1990). Individual and group goals when workers are interdependent: Effects on task strategies and performance. **Journal of Applied Psychology, 75**(2), 185–193.

Mobley, W., Griffith, R., Hand, H., & Miglino, B. (1979). Review and conceptual analysis of the employee turnover process. **Psychological Bulletin, 86**, 493–522.

Moede, W. (1920). **Experimentelle massenpsychologie.** Leipzig: S. Hirzel.

Moede, W. (1927). Die richtlinien der leistungspsycholgie. **Industrielle Psychotechnik, 4**, 193–207.

Monteith, M. (1996a). Affective reactions to prejudice-related discrepant resonses: The impact of standard salience. **Personality and Social Psychology Bulletin, 22**, 48–59.

Monteith, M. (1996b). Contemporary forms of prejudice-related conflict: In search of a nutshell. **Personality and Social Psychology Bulletin, 22**, 416–473.

Monteith, M., Devine, P., & Zuwerink, J. (1993). Self-directed versus other-directed affect as a consequence of prejudice-related discrepancies. **Journal of Personality and Social Psychology, 64**, 198–210.

Monteith, M., & Walters, G. (1998). Egalitarianism, moral obligation, and prejudice-related personal standards. **Personality and Social Psychology Bulletin, 24**(2), 186–199.

Moreland, R., & Levine, J. (1982). Socialization in small groups: Temporal changes in individual-group relations. In L. Berkowitz (Ed.), **Advances in experimental social pscyhology** (Vol. 15, pp. 137–192). New York: Academic Press.

Moreland, R., & Levine, J. (1988). Group dynamics over time: Development and socialization in small groups. In J. McGrath (Ed.), **The social psychology of time** (pp. 151–181). Newbury Park, CA: Sage.

Moreland, R., & Levine, J. (1989). Newcomers and oldtimers in small groups. In P. Paulus (Ed.), **Psychology of group influence** (2nd ed., pp. 143–185). Hillsdale, NJ: Erlbaum.

Moreno, J. (1932/1953). **Who shall survive? Foundations of sociometry, group psychotherapy, and sociodrama** (2nd ed.). Beacon, NY: Beacon House.

Morgan, B., Coates, G., & Rebbin, T. (1970). **The effects of Phlebotomus fever on sustained performance and muscular output** (Tech. Rep. No. ITR-70–14). Louisville, KY: University of Louisville, Performance Research Laboratory.

Morrison, J. (1993). **Group composition and creative performance**. Unpublished doctoral dissertation, University of Tulsa, Tulsa, OK.

Morrison, B., & Ahmed, E. (2006). Restorative justice and civil society: Emerging practice, theory, and evidence. **Journal of Social Issues, 62**(2), 209–215.

Morrison, E. W., & Milliken, F. J. (2000). Organizational silence: A barrier to change and development in a pluralistic world. **Academy of Management Review, 25** (4), 706–725.

Moscovici, S. (1980). Toward a theory of conversion behavior. In L. Berkowitz (Ed.), **Advances in Experimental Social Psychology, 13**, New York: Academic Press.

Moscovici, S. (1985a). Innovation and minority influence. In S. Moscovici, G. Mugny, & E. Van Avermaet (Eds.), **Perspectives on minority influence** (pp. 9–51). Cambridge: Cambridge University Press.

Moscovici, S. (1985b). Social influence and conformity. In G. Lindzey & E. Aronson, (Eds.), **The Handbook of Social Psychology** (3rd ed., Vol. 2, pp. 347–412). New York: Random House.

Moscovici, S., & Faucheux, C. (1972). Social Influence, conforming bias, and the study of active minorities. In L. Berkowitz (Ed.), **Advances in Experimental Social Psychology** (Vol. 13), New York: Academic Press.

Moscovici, S., Lage, E., & Naffrechoux, M. (1969). Influence of a consistent minority on the responses of a majority in a color perception task. **Sociometry, 32**, 365–380.

Moscovici, S., Mucchi-Faina, A., & Maass, A. (Eds.). (1994). **Minority influence**. Chicago: Nelson-Hall.

Moscovici, S., & Nemeth, C. (1974). **Social influence: II. Minority influence**. Oxford, England: Rand McNally.

Moscovici, S., & Zavalloni, M. (1969). The group as a polarizer of attitudes. **Journal of Personality and Social Psychology, 12**, 125–135.

Mugny, G. (1982). **The power of minorities**. London: Academic Press.

Mugny, G., Doise, W., & Perret-Clermont, A. N. (1975–1976). Conflit de centrations et progrès congnitif [Conflict of centrations and cognitive progress]. **Bulletin de Psychologie, 29**, 199–204.

Mugny, G., Levy, M., & Doise, W. (1978). Conflit socio-cognitif et developpement cognitif [Socio-cognitive conflict and cognitive development]. **Swiss Journal of Psychology, 37**, 22–43.

Mugny, G., & Papastamou, S. (1980). When rigidity does not fail: Individualization and psychologization as resistances to the diffusion of minority innovations. **European Journal of Social Psychology, 10**, 43–61.

Mugny, G., & Perez, J.A. (1991). **The social psychology of minority influence**. New York: Cambridge University Press.

Mullan, F. (1992). Rewriting the social contract in health. In A. Katz, H. Hedrick, D. Isenberg, L. Thompson, T. Goodrich, & A. Kutscher (Eds.), **Self-help: Concepts and applications** (pp. 61–67). Philadelphia: Charles Press.

Mullen, B. (1983). Operationalizing the effect of the group on the individual: A self-attention perspective. **Journal of Experimental Social Psychology, 19**, 295–322.

Mullen, B., Brown, R., & Smith, C. (1992). Ingroup bias as a function of salience, relevance, and status: An integration. **European Journal of Social Psychology, 22**, 103–122.

Mullen, B., & Cooper, C. (1994). The relation between group cohesiveness and performance: An integration. **Psychological Bulletin, 115**(2), 210–227.

Mullen, B., Johnson, C., & Salas, E. (1991). Productivity loss in brainstorming groups: A meta-analytic integration. **Basic and Applied Social Psychology, 12**, 3–25.

Murnighan, J., & Pillutla, M. (1995). Fairness versus self-interest: Asymmetric moral imperatives in ultimatum bargaining. In R. Kramer & D. Messick (Eds.), **Negotiation as a social process** (pp. 240–267). Thousand Oaks, CA: Sage.

Murray, F. (1972). The acquisition of conservation through social interaction. Developmental Psychology, 6, 1–6.

Murray, F. (1983). **Cognitive benefits of teaching on the teacher**. Paper presented at American Educational Research Association Annual Meeting, Montreal, Quebec.

Murray, F., Ames, G., & Botvin, G. (1977). Acquisition of conservation through cognitive dissonance. **Journal of Educational Psychology, 69**, 519–527.

Myers, D. (1978). The polarizing effects of social comparison. **Journal of Experimental Social Psychology**, 14, 554–563.

Myers, D. (1987). **Social psychology** (2nd ed). New York: McGraw-Hill.

Myers, D., & Bishop, G. (1970). Discussion effects on racial attitudes. **Science, 169,** 778–789.

Myers, D. G. (1982). Polarizing effects of social interaction. In H. Brandstatter, J. H. Davis, & G. Stocker-Kreichgauer (Eds.), **Group decision making** (pp. 125–161). New York: Academic Press.

Myers, D. G., & Lamm, H. (1976). The group polarization phenomenon. **Psychological Bulletin, 83**, 602–627.

Myers, R. (1969). **Some effects of seating arrangements in counseling.** Unpublished doctoral dissertation, University of Florida, Gainesville.

Myrdal, G. (1944). **An American dilemma: The Negro problem and modern democracy.** New York: Harper.

Nadler, D., Hackman, J., & Lawler, E. (1979). **Managing organizational behavior. Boston:** Little, Brown.

National Center for Manufacturing Sciences. (1989). **Making the Grade: Student perspectives on the state of manufacturing engineering education in America.** Ann Arbor, MI.

Nauta, A, De Dreu, C. K. W., & Van der Vaart, T. (2002). Social value orientation, organizational goal concerns, and interdepartmental problem-solving behavior. **Journal of Organizational Behavior, 23**, 199–213.

Neisser, U. (1954). On experimental distinction between perceptual process and verbal response. **Journal of Experimental Psychology, 47**, 399–402.

Nemeth, C. (1976). **A comparison between conformity and minority influence**. Paper presented to the International Congress of psychology, Paris, France.

Nemeth, C. (1977). Interactions between jurors as a function of majority vs. unanimity decision rules. **Journal of Applied Social Psychology, 7,** 38–56.

Nemeth, C. (1995). Dissent as driving cognition, attitudes and judgments. Social Cognition, 13, 273–291.

Nemeth, C. J. (1977). Interaction between jurors as a function of majority vs. unanimity decision rules. **Journal of Applied Social Psychology, 7,** 38–56.

Nemeth, C. J. (1986). Differential contributions of majority and minority influence. **Psychological Review, 93**, 23–32.

Nemeth, C. J. (1992). Minority dissent as a stimulant to group performance. In S. Worchel, W. Wood, & J. Simpson (Eds.), **Group process and productivity** (pp. 95–111). Newbury Park, CA: Sage.

Nemeth, C. J. (1997). **Managing innovation: When less is more**. California Management Review, 40.

Nemeth, C. J. (2003). "The Requirement of Unanimity, Protection of Minority Views and the Quality of the Decision Making." Invited address, Jury Research Conference, University of Sydney Law School, Australia, October 2003.

Nemeth, C., Brown, K., & Rogers, J. (2001). Devil's advocate versus authentic dissent: Stimulating quantity and quality. **European Journal of Social Psychology, 31**, 707–720.

Nemeth, C., & Chiles, C. (1988). Modeling courage: The role of dissent in fostering independence. **European Journal of Social Psychology, 18**, 275–280.

Nemeth, C. J., & Goncalo, J. A. (2004). Influence and persuasion in small groups. In S. Shavitt & T. C. Brock (Eds.), **Persuasion: Psychological Insights and Perspectives**. Boston: Allyn & Bacon.

Nemeth, C. J., & Goncalo, J. A. (2005). Influence and persuasion in small groups. In T. C. Brock and M .C. Green (Eds.), **Persuasion: Psychological insights and perspectives** (pp. 171–194). London: Sage Publications.

Nemeth, C. J., & Goncalo, J. A. (2011). Rogues and heroes: Finding value in dissent. In J. Jetten & M. Hornsey (Eds.), **Rebels in groups: Dissent, deviance, difference, and defiance** (pp. 17–36). London: Blackwell.

Nemeth, C. J., & Kwan, J. L. (1985). Originality of word associations as a function of majority vs minority influence. **Social Psychology Quarterly, 48**, 277–282.

Nemeth, C. J., & Kwan, J. L. (1987). Minority influence, divergent thinking and detection of correct solutions. **Journal of Applied Social Psychology, 17**, 788–799.

Nemeth, C., & Owens, P. (1996). Making work groups more effective: The value of minority dissent. In M. West (Ed.), *Handbook of work group psychology* (pp. 125–142). Chichester, UK: John Wiley.

Nemeth, C. J., Personnaz, M., Personnaz, B. & Goncalo, J. A. (2004). The liberating role of conflict in group creativity: A study in two countries. **European Journal of Social Psychology, 34**, 365–374.

Nemeth, C., & Rogers, J. (1996). Dissent and the search for information. **British Journal of Social Psychology. Special Issue: Minority Influences, 35**, 67–76.

Nemeth, C.J. & Staw, B.M. (1989). The tradeoffs of social control and innovation in small groups and organizations. In L. Berkowitz (Ed.), **Advances in experimental social psychology,** vol. 22, (pp. 175–210). New York: Academic Press.

Nemeth, C., Swedlund, M., & Kanki, B. (1974). Patterning of a minority's responses and their influence on the majority. **European Journal of Social Psychology, 4,** 53–64.

Nemeth, C., & Wachtler, J. (1974). Creating the perceptions of consistency and confidence: A necessary condition for minority influence. **Sociometry, 37,** 529–540.

Nemeth, C. J., & Wachtler, J. (1983). Creative problem solving as a result of majority vs. minority influence. **European Journal of Social Psychology, 13,** 45–55.

Nesbitt, P., Pond, A., & Allen, W. (1959). **The survival book.** New York: Funk & Wagnalls.

Newcomb, T. (1943). **Personality and social change.** New York: Dryden.

Newcomb, T. (1956). The prediction of interpersonal attraction. **American Psychologist, 11,** 575–586.

Newcomb, T. (1961). **The acquaintance process.** New York: Holt, Rinehart, & Winston.

Nijhof, W., & Kommers, P. (1982, July). **Analysis of cooperation in relation to cognitive controversy**. Paper presented at International Conference on Cooperation in Education, Provo, UT.

Norem, J., & Illingworth, K. (1993). Strategy-dependent effects of reflecting on self and tasks: Some implications of optimism and defensive pessimism. **Journal of Personality and Social Psychology, 65,** 822–835.

Nussbaum, E. M. (2011). Argumentation, dialogue theory, and probability modeling: Alternative frameworks for argumentation research in education. **Educational Psychologist 46**(2), 84–106.

Oakes, P. (1987). The salience of social categories. In J. Turner, M. Hogg, P. Oakes, S. Reicher, & M. Wetherell (Eds.), **Rediscovering the social group: A self-categorization theory** (pp. 117–141). Oxford, UK: Basil Blackwell.

Oakes, P., & Turner, J. (1986). Distinctiveness and the salience of social category memberships: Is there an automatic perceptual bias toward novelty? **European Journal of Social Psychology, 16,** 325–344.

Oakes, P., Turner, J., & Haslam, S. (1991). Perceiving people as group members: The role of fit in the salience of social categorizations. **British Journal of Social Psychology, 30,** 125–144.

Ohbuchi, K., & Saito, M. (1986). Power imbalance, its legitimacy, and aggression. **Aggressive Behavior, 12,** 33–40.

O'Keefe, D. J. (1982). The concept of argument and arguing. In J. R. Cox & C. A. Willard (Eds.), **Advances in argumentation theory and research** (pp. 3–23). Carbondale, IL: Southern Illinois University Press.

Olson, M. (1965). **The logic of collective action: Public goods and the theory of groups**. Cambridge, MA: Harvard University Press.

Olzak, S. (1992). **The dynamics of ethic competition and conflict**. Stanford, CA: Stanford University Press.

Opotow, S. (1990). Moral exclusion and injustice: An introduction. **Journal of Social Issues, 46,** 1–20.

Opotow, S. (1993). Animals and the scope of justice. **Journal of Social Issues, 49,** 71–85.

Opotow, S., & Weiss, L. (2000). Denial and exclusion in environmental conflict. **Journal of Social Issues, 56,** 475–490.

O'Quin, K., & Aronoff, J. (1981). Humor as a technique of social influence. **Social Psychology Quarterly, 44**(4), 349–357.

O'Reilly, C., Caldwell, D., & Barnett, W. (1989). Work group demography, social integration, and turnover. **Administrative Science Quarterly, 34,** 21–37.

Ortiz, A., Johnson, D. W., & Johnson, R. (1996). Effects of positive goal and resource interdependence on individual performance. **Journal of Social Psychology, 136**(2), 243–249.

Orvis, B., Kelley, H., & Butler, D. (1976). Attributional conflict in young couples. In J. Harvey, W. Ickles, & R. Kidd (Eds.), **New directions in attribution research** (Vol. 1). Hillsdale, NJ: Erlbaum.

Packer, D.J. (2008) On being both with us and against us: A normative conflict model of dissent in social groups. **Personality and Social Psychology Review, 12,** 50.

Parker, W. C. (2006). Public discourses in schools: Purposes, problems, possibilities. **Educational Researcher, 35**(8), 11–18.

Paulson, P.B., & Nigstad, B.A. (2003). Group Creativity: Innovation through Collaboration. New York: Oxford University Press.

Pearsall, M. J., Ellis, A. P. J., & Evans, J. M. (2008). Unlocking the effects of gender faultlines on team creativity: Is activation the key? **Journal of Applied Psychology, 93**, 225–234.

Pelz, D. (1956). Some social factors related to performance in a research organization. **Administrative Science Quarterly**, **1**, 310–325.

Pelz, E. (1958). Some factors in "group decision." In E. Maccoby, T. Newcomb, and E. Hartley (Eds.), **Readings in social psychology** (pp. 212–218). New York: Holt.

Pelz, E., & Andrews, F. (1966). **Scientists in organizations.** New York: John Wiley.

Pennebaker, J. W. (1982) Social and perceptual factors affecting symptom reporting and mass psychogenic illness. In M. J. Colligan, J. W. Pennebaker, & L. R. Murphy (Eds.), **Mass psychogenic illness: A social psychological analysis** (pp. 139–153). Hillsdale, NJ: Erlbaum.

Pennington, D., Haravey, F., & Bass, B. (1958). Some effects of decision and discussion on coalescence, change, and effectiveness. **Journal of Applied Psychology, 42**, 404–408.

Pepinski, P., Hemphill, J., & Shevitz, R. (1958). Attempts to lead, group productivity, and morale under conditions of acceptance and rejection. **Journal of Abnormal and Social Psychology, 57, 47**–54.

Pepitone, A. (1952). **Responsibility to the group and its effects on the performance of members.** Unpublished doctoral dissertation, University of Michigan, Ann Arbor.

Pepitone, E. (Ed.) (1980). **Children in cooperation and competition.** Lexington, MA: Lexington Books.

Pepitone, A. & Reichling, G. (1955). Group cohesiveness and the expression of hostility. **Human Relations, 8**, 327–337.

Perdue, C., Dovidio. J., Gutman, M., & Tyler, R. (1990). Us and them: Social categorization and the process of intergroup bias. **Journal of Personality and Social Psychology**, 59, 475–486.

Perls, F. (1969). **Gestalt therapy verbatim**. Lafayette, CA: Real People Press.

Perry-Smith, J.E. (2006). Social yet creative: The role of social relationships in facilitating individual creativity. **Academy of Management Journal, 49**: 85–101.

Peters, D. (1966). **Identification and personal change in laboratory training.** Unpublished doctoral dissertation, Massachusetts Institute of Technology, Boston.

Peters, R., & Torrance, E. (1972). Dyadic interaction of preschool children and performance on a construction task. **Psychological Reports, 30**, 747–750.

Peters, T. (1987). **Thriving on chaos**. New York: Knopf.

Peterson, R., Johnson, D. W., & Johnson, R. (1991). Effects of cooperative learning on perceived status of male and female pupils. **Journal of Social Psychology**, **13**, 717–735.

Peterson, R. S., & Nemeth, C. J. (1996). Focus versus flexibility: Majority and minority influence can both improve performance. **Personality and Social Psychology Bulletin, 22,** 14–23.

Peterson, R. S., Owens, P. D., Tetlock, P. E., Fan, E. T., & Martorana, P.V. (1998). Group dynamics in top management teams: Groupthink, vigilance and alternative models of organizational failure and success. **Organizational Behavior and Human Decision Processes, 73**, 272–305.

Pettigrew, T. (1969). Racially separate or together? **Journal of Social Issues, 25**, 43–69.

Pettigrew, T. (1997). Generalized intergroup contact effects on prejudice. **Personality and Social Psychology Bulletin, 23**(2), 173–185.

Pettigrew, T. (1998). Intergroup contact theory. **Annual Review of Psychology, 49**, 65–85.

Pettigrew, T., & Meertens, R. (1995). Subtle and blatant prejudice in Western Europe. **European Journal of Social Psychology, 25**, 57–75.

Petty, M., Harkins, S., Williams, K., & Latané, B. (1977). Effects of group size on cognitive effort and evaluation. **Journal of Personality and Social Psychology, 3**(4), 579–582.

Petty, R., Cacioppo, J., & Krasmer, J. (1985). **Individual differences in social loafing on cognitive tasks**. Paper presented at the annual meeting of the Midwestern Psychological Association, Chicago.

Petty, R. E., & Cacioppo, J. T. (1981). **Attitudes and persuasion - classic and contemporary approaches**. Dubuque, IA: William C. Brown.

Phoon, W. H. (1982) Outbreaks of mass hysteria at workplaces in Singapore: Some patterns & modes of presentation. In M. J. Colligan, J. W. Pennebaker, & L. R. Murphy (Eds.), **Mass psychogenic illness: A social psychological analysis** (pp. 21–31). Hillsdale, NJ: Erlbaum.

Piore, M., & Sabel, C. (1984). **The second industrial divide: Possibilities for prosperity**. New York: Basic Books.

Poole, M. (1998). The small group should be the fundamental unit of communication research. In J. Trent (Ed.), **Communication: Views from the helm in the 21st century** (pp. 94–97). Boston: Allyn & Bacon.

Poole, M. (1999). Group communication theory. In L. Frey, D. Gouran, & M. Poole (Eds.), **The handbook of group communication theory and research** (pp. 37–70). Thousand Oaks, CA: Sage.

Postmes, T., Spears, R., & Cihangir, S. (2001). Quality of group decision making and group norms. **Journal of Personality and Social Psychology, 80**(6), 918–930.

Pratto, F., Lio, J., Levin, S., Sidanius, J., Shih, M., & Bachrach, H. (1998). **Social dominance orientation and legitimization of inequality across cultures**. Unpublished manuscript, Stanford University.

Pratto, F., Sidanius, J., Stallworth, L., & Malle, B. (1994). Social dominance orientation: A personality variable predicting social dn political attitudes. **Journal of Personality and Social Psychology, 67,** 741–763.

Preston, M., & Heintz, R. (1949). Effects of participatory vs. supervisory leadership on group judgment. **Journal of Abnormal and Social Psychology, 44,** 345–355.

Pruitt, D. (1981). **Negotiation behavior**. New York: Academic Press.

Pruitt, D., & Johnson, D. (1970). Mediation as an aid to face saving in negotiation. **Journal of Personality and Social Psychology, 14,** 239–246.

Pruitt, D., & Rubin, J. (1986). **Social conflict**. New York: Random House.

Pruitt, D., & Syna, H. (1983). Successful problem solving. In D. Tjosvold & D. W. Johnson (Eds.), **Conflict in Organizations** (pp. 62–81). New York: Irvington.

Pruitt, D. G., Rubin, J., & Kim, S. H. (2004). **Social conflict: Escalation, stalemate, and settlement** (3rd ed.). New York: McGraw-Hill.

Prusak, L., & Cohen, D. (2001). **In good company: How social capital makes organizations work**. Cambridge, MA: Harvard Business School Press.

Putnam, J., Rynders, J., Johnson, D. W., & Johnson, R. (1989). Collaborative skills instruction for promoting positive interactions between mentally handicapped and nonhandicapped children. **Exceptional Children, 55,** 550–557.

Qin, A., Johnson, D. W., & Johnson, R. (1995). Cooperative versus competitive efforts and problem solving. **Review of Educational Research, 65**(2), 129–143.

Quattrone, G. & Jones, E. (1980). The perception of variability within in-groups and out-groups: Implications for the law of small numbers. **Journal of Personality and Social Psychology, 38,** 141–152.

Quinn, A., & Schlenker, B. (2002). Can accountability produce independence? Goals as determinants of the impact of accountability on conformity. **Personality and Social Psychology Bulletin, 28,** 472–483.

Radke, M., & Klisurich, D. (1947). Experiments in changing food habits. **Journal of the American Dietetics Association, 23,** 403–409.

Rafalides, M., & Hoy, W. (1971). Student sense of alienation and pupil control orientation of high schools. **The High School Journal, 55**(3), 101–111.

Rahim, M. (1983). A measure of styles of handling interpersonal conflict. **Academy of Management Journal, 26,** 368–376.

Rahim, M. (1989). Relationships of leader power to compliance and satisfaction with supervision: Evidence from a national sample of managers. **Journal of Management, 15,** 545–556.

Rapoport, A., & Bornstein, B. (1987). Intergroup competition for the provision of binary public goods. **Psychological Review, 94,** 291–299.

Raven, B. (1992). A power/interaction model of interpersonal influence: French and Raven thirty years later. **Journal of Social Behavior and Personality, 7,** 217–244.

Raven, B. (1993). The origins of power: Origins and recent developments. **Journal of Social Issues, 49,** 227–251.

Raven, B., & Kruglanksi, A. (1970). Conflict and power. In P. Swingle (Ed.), **The structure of conflict** (pp. 69–110). New York: Academic Press.

Raven, B., & Rietsema, J. (1957). The effects of varied clarity of group goal and group path upon the individual and his relation to his group. **Human Relations, 10,** 29–44.

Raven, B., & Rubin, J. (1976). **Social psychology: People in groups**. New York: Wiley.

Rawls, J. (1971). **A theory of justice.** Cambridge: Harvard University Press.

Read, P. (1974). **Alive.** New York: Avon.

Reed, B. (1947). Accommodation between Negro and white employees in a west coast aircraft industry, 1942–1944. **Social Forces, 26,** 76–84.

Reeder, G. (1993). Trait-behavior relations and dispositional inference. **Personality and Social Psychology Bulletin, 19,** 586–593.

Regan, D., & Totten, J. (1975). Empathy and attribution: Turning observers into actors. **Journal of Personality and Social Psychology, 32,** 850–856.

Reimer, T., Reimer, A., & Hinsz, V. B. (2008). Presenting decision tasks in meetings as old versus new business instigates different group processes in the hidden-profile paradigm. Unpublished manuscript. Berlin, Germany: Max Planck Institute for Human Development.

Reisman, D. (1950). **The lonely crowd**. New Haven, CT: Yale University Press.

Rest, J. R., Narvaez, D., Bebeau, M. J., & Thoma, S. J. (1999). **Postconventional moral thinking: Neo-Kohlbergian approach.** Hillsdale, NJ: Lawrence Erlbaum.

Rhodewalt, F., Morf, C., Hazlett, S., Fairfield, M. (1991). Self-handicapping: The role of discounting and augmentation in the preservation of self-esteem. **Journal of Personality and Social Psychology, 61,** 122–131.

Rice, O. (1978). **The Hatfields and the McCoys.** Lexington: University Press of Kentucky.

Richardson, F., & Manaster, G. (1997). Back to the future: Alfred Adler on freedom and commitment. **Individual Psychology: The Journal of Adlerian Theory, Research, & Practice, 53**(3), 286–309.

Richter, F., & Tjosvold, D. (1981). Effects of student participation in classroom decision-making on attitudes, peer interaction, motivation, and learning. **Journal of Applied Psychology, 65,** 74–80.

Riess, M. (1982). Seating preferences as impression management: A literature review and theoretical integration. **Communication, 11,** 85–113.

Riess, M., & Rosenfeld, P. (1980). Seating preferences as nonverbal communication: A self-presentational analysis. **Journal of Applied Communications Research, 8,** 22–30.

Ringelmann, M. (1913). Research on animate sources of power: The work of man. **Annales de L'Instise National Agronomique, 2e, serietome** XII, 1–40.

Roark, A., & Sharah, H. (1989). Factors related to group cohesiveness. **Small Group Behavior, 20,** 62–69.

Robins, J., et al. (1984). Lifetime prevalence of specific psychiatric disorders in three sites. **Archives of General Psychiatry, 41,** 949–958.

Rodin, J., & Langer, E. (1977). Long-term effects of a control-relevant intervention with the institutionalized aged. **Journal of Personality and Social Psychology, 35,** 897–902.

Rodin, J., Solomon, J., & Metcalf, J. (1978). Role of control in mediating perceptions of density. **Journal of Personality and Social Psychology, 36**(9), 988–999.

Roethlisberger, F., & Dickson, W. (1939). **Management and the worker.** Cambridge, MA: Harvard University Press.

Roff, J., & Wirt, R. (1984). Childhood aggression and social adjustment antecedents of delinquency. **Journal of Abnormal Child Psychology, 12**(1), 111–126.

Rogers, C. (1961). **On becoming a person: A therapist's view of psychotherapy.** Boston: Houghton Mifflin.

Rogers, C. (1970a). Towards a theory of creativity. In P. Vernon (Ed.), **Creativity: Selected readings** (pp. 137–151). London: Penguin.

Rogers, C. (1970b). **Encounter groups.** New York: Harper & Row.

Rogers, E., & Shoemaker, F. (1971). **Communications and innovations.** New York: Free Press.

Rogers, M., Hennigan, K., Bosman, C., & Miller, N. (1984). Intergroup acceptance in classroom and playground settings. In N. Miller & M. Brewer (Eds.), **Groups in contact: The psychology of desegregation** (pp. 187–212). Orlando, FL: Academic Press.

Rokeach, M. (1954). The nature and meaning of dogmatism. **Psychological Review, 61,** 194–204.

Rokeach, M. (1960). **The open and closed mind.** New York: Basic Books.

Rokeach, M. (1968). **Beliefs, attitudes, and values.** San Francisco: Jossey-Bass.

Rose, A. (1948). Race relations in a Chicago industry. In M. Rose (Ed.), **Studies in the reduction of prejudice.** Chicago: American Council on Race Relations.

Rosenberg, L. (1961). Group size, prior experience, and conformity. **Journal of Abnormal and Social Psychology, 63**(2), 436–447.

Rosenblith, J. (1949). A replication of "some roots of prejudice." **Journal of Abnormal and Social Psychology, 44,** 470–489.

Roseth, C. J., Johnson, D. W., & Johnson, R. T. (2008). The relationship between interpersonal relationships and achievement within cooperative, competitive, and individualistic conditions: A meta-analysis. **Psychological Bulletin, 134**(2), 223–246.

Roseth, C. J., Pellegrini, A. D., Dupusi, D. N., Boh, C. M., Hickey, M. C., Hilk, C. L., & Peshkam, A. (2010). Preschoolers' bistrategic resource control, reconciliation, and peer regard. **Social Development, 19,** 1–27.

Roskow-Ewoldsen, D., & Fazio, R. (1992). The accessibility of source likeability as a determinant of persuasion. **Personality and Social Psychology Bulletin, 18,** 19–25.

Ross, L. (1977). The intuitive psychologist and his shortcomings: Distortions in the attributional process. In L. Berkowitz (Ed.), **Advances in experimental social psychology** (Vol. 10, pp. 174–220). New York: Academic Press.

Ross, L., & Nisbett, R. (1991). **The person and the situation.** New York: McGraw-Hill.

Rothbart, M., Evans, M., & Fulero, S. (1979). Recall for confirming events: Memory processes and the maintenance of social stereotypes. **Journal of Experimental Social Psychology, 15,** 343–355.

Rothbart, M., Fulero, S., Jensen, C., Howard, J., & Birrell, P. (1978). From individual to group impressions: Availability heuristics in stereotype formation. **Journal of Experimental Social Psychology, 14,** 237–255.

Rothgerber, H., & Worchel, S. (1997). The view from below: Intergroup relations from the perspective of the disadvantaged group. **Journal of Personality and Social Psychology, 73,** 1191–1205.

Rotter, J. (1971). Generalized expectancies for interpersonal trust. **American Psychologist, 26,** 443–452.

Rubin, J., & Brown, B. (1975). **The social psychology of bargaining and negotiation.** New York: Academic Press.

Rubin, J., Pruitt, D., & Kim, S. (1994). **Social conflict.** New York: McGraw-Hill.

Rusbult, C., Johnson, D., & Morrow, G. (1986). Predicting satisfaction and commitment in adult romantic involvements: An assessment of the generalizability of the investment model. **Social Psychology Quarterly, 49,** 81–89.

Rusbult, C., & Van Lange, P. (1996). Interdependent processes. In E. Higgins & A. Kruglanski (Eds.), **Social psychology: Handbook of basic principles** (pp. 564–596). New York: Guilford.

Rusbult, C., Yovetich, N., & Verette, J. (1996). An interdependence analysis of accommodation processes. In G. Fletcher & J. Fitness (Eds.), **Knowledge structures in close relationships: A social psychological approach** (pp. 63–90). Mahwah, NJ: Lawrence Erlbaum.

Russell, B. (1938). **Power: A new social analysis.** New York: Norton.

Rutstrum, C. (1973). **The new ways of the wilderness.** New York: Collier.

Sachdev, I., & Bourhis, R. (1984). Minimal majorities and minorities. **European Journal of Social Psychology, 14,** 35–52.

Sachdev, I., & Bourhis, R. (1991). Power and status differentials in minority and majority group relations. **European Journal of Social Psychology, 21,** 1–24.

Salomon, G. (1981). **Communication and education: Social and psychological interactions.** Beverly Hills, CA: Sage.

Sanders, G. (1981). Driven by distraction: An integrative review of social facilitation theory and research. **Journal of Experimental Social Psychology, 17,** 227–251.

Sanders, G. S., & Baron, R. S. (1975). The motivating effects of distraction on task performance. **Journal of Personality and Social Psychology, 32,** 956–963.

Sanders, G. S., & Baron, R. S. (1977). Is social comparison irrelevant for producing choice shifts? **Journal of Experimental Social Psychology, 13,** 303–314.

Sarachek, G. (1968). Greek concepts of leadership. **Academy of Management Journal, 11,** 39–48.

Sarason, I., & Potter, E. (1983). **Self-monitoring: Cognitive processes and performance.** Seattle: University of Washington Press.

Sargis, E., & Larson, J. (2002). Informational centrality and member participation during group dicision making. **Group Processes and Intergroup Relations, 5,** 333–347.

Sashkin, M. (1984). Participative management in an ethical imperative. **Organizational Dynamics, 12**(4), 4–22.

Sayette, M. A., Kirchner, T. R., Moreland, R. L., Levine, J. M., & Travis, T. (2004). Effects of alcohol on risk-seeking behavior: A group-level analysis. **Psychology of Addictive Behaviors, 18,** 190–193.

Schachter, S. (1951). Deviation, rejection, and communication. **Journal of Abnormal and Social Psychology, 46,** 190–207.

Schachter, S. (1959). **The Psychology of Affiliation: Experimental Studies of the Sources of Gregariousness.** Stanford: Stanford University Press.

Schachter, S., Ellertson, N., McBride, D., & Gregory, D. (1951). An experimental study of cohesiveness and productivity. **Human Relations, 4,** 229–238.

Schachter, S., Nuttin, J., de Monchaux, C., Maucorps, P., Osmer, D., Duijker, H., Rommetveit, R., & Israel, J. (1954). Cross-cultural experiments on threat and rejection. **Human Relations, 7,** 403–439.

Schein E. (1969). **Process consultation.** Reading, MA: Addison-Wesley.

Schippers, M. C. (2003). **Reflexivity in teams.** Dissertation, Vrije Universiteit, Amsterdam.

Schippers, M. Hartog, D. N., Koopman, P. L. (2007). Reflexivity in teams: A measure and correlates. **Applied Psychology: An International Review, 56**(2), 189–211.

Schippers, M. C., Hartog, D. N., Koopman, P. L., & Wienk, J. A. (2003). Diversity and team outcomes: The moderating effects of outcome interdependence and group longevity and the mediating effect of reflexivity. **Journal of Organizational Behavior, 24,** 779–802.

Schippers, M. C., Edmondson, A. C., & West, M. A. (2006). **The role of reflexivity in team information processing.** Paper presented at the Academy of Management Meeting. Atlanta.

Schmidt, W. (1974). Conflict: A powerful process for (good and bad) change. **Management Review, 63,** 4–10.

Schneider, J. (1937). The cultural situation as a condition for the achievement of fame. **American Sociological Review, 2,** 480–491.

Scholten, L., van Knippenberg, D., Nijstad, B. A., & De Dreu, C.K.W. (2007). Motivated information processing and group decision-making: Effects of process accountability on information processing and decision quality. **Journal of Experimental Social Psychology, 43,** 539–552.

Schopler, J., Insko, C. A., Wieselquist, J., Pemberton, M. B., Witcher, B., Lozar, R., et al. (2001). When groups are more competitive than individuals: The domain of the discontinuity effect. **Journal of Personality and Social Psychology, 80,** 632–644.

Schroeder, J., Insko, C. A., Wieselquist, J., Pemberton, M., Witcher, B., Kozar, R., Roddenberry, C., & Wildschut, T. (2001). When groups are more competitive than individuals: The domain of the discontinuity effect. **Journal of Personality and Social Psychology, 80,** 632–644.

Schultz, W. (1958). **FIRO: A three dimensional theory of interpersonal behavior.** New York: Rinehart.

Schultz, W. (1966). **The interpersonal underworld.** Palo Alto, CA: Science and Behavior Books.

Schulz-Hardt, S., Frey D., Luethgens, C., & Moscovici, S. (2000). Biased information search in group decision making. **Journal of Personality and Social Psychology, 78,** 655–669.

Schulz-Hardt, S., Jochims, M., & Frey, D. (2002). Productive conflict in group decision making: Genuine and contrived dissent as strategies to counteract biased information seeking. **Organizational Behavior and Human Decision Processes, 88**, 563–586.

Schwarz, B. B., Neuman, Y., & Biezuner, A. (2000). Two wrongs may make a right. If they argue together! **Cognition and Instruction, 18**, 461–494.

Schweitzer, M. E., & Kerr, J. L. (2000). Bargaining under the influence: The role of alcohol in negotiations. **The Academy of Management Executive, 14**, 47–57.

Schweiger, D., Sandberg, W., & Rechner, P. (1989). Experiential effects of dialectical inquiry, devil's advocacy, and consensus approaches to strategic decision making. **Academy of Management Journal, 32**, 722–745.

Schwenk, C. (1983). Laboratory research on ill-structured decision aids: The case of dialectical inquiry. **Decision Sciences, 14**, 140–144.

Seashore, S. (1954). **Group cohesiveness in the industrial work group.** Ann Arbor, MI: Institute for Social Research.

Seligman, M. (1975). **On depression, development, and death.** San Francisco: Freeman.

Seligman, M. (1988). Boomer blues. **Psychology Today, 22**, 50–55.

Seligman, M. (1995). **The optimistic child.** New York: Houghton Mifflin.

Selman, R. (1981). The development of interpersonal competence: The role of understanding in conduct. **Departmental Review, 1**, 401–422.

Seta, J., Paulus, P., & Schkade, J. (1976). Effects of group size and proximity under cooperative and competitive conditions. **Journal of Personality and Social Psychology, 34,** 47–53.

Shaffer, J., & Galinsky, M. (1989). **Models of group therapy** (2nd ed.). Englewood Cliffs, NJ: Prentice-Hall.

Shambaugh, P. (1978). The development of the small group. **Human Relations, 31,** 283–295.

Shaw, M. (1932). A comparison of individuals and small groups in the rational solution of complex problems. **American Journal of Psychology, 44,** 491–504.

Shaw, M. (1964). Communication networks. In L. Berkowitz (Ed.), **Advances in experimental social psychology** (Vol. 1, pp. 111–147). New York: Academic Press.

Shaw, M. (1976, 1981). **Group dynamics: The psychology of small group behavior.** New York: McGraw-Hill.

Sheingold, K., Hawkins, J., & Char, C. (1984). "I'm the thinkist, you're the typist": The interaction of technology and the social life of classrooms. **Journal of Social Issues, 40**(3), 49–61.

Shepperd, J. (1993). Productivity loss in performance groups: A motivation analysis. **Psychological Bulletin, 113**(1), 67–81.

Sherif, C. (1978). The social context of competition. In R. Martens (Ed.), **Joy and sadness in children's sports** (pp. 81–97). Champaign, IL: Human Kinetics.

Sherif, M. (1936). **The psychology of group norms.** New York: Harper.

Sherif, M. (1966). **In common predicament.** Boston: Houghton Mifflin.

Sherif, M., Harvey, O., White, B., Hood W., & Sherif, C. (1961/1988). **The robber's cave experiment: Intergroup conflict and cooperation.** CT: Wesleyan University Press.

Sherif, M., & Sherif, C. (1956). **An outline of social psychology.** New York: Harper & Row.

Sherif, M., & Sherif, C. (1969). **Social psychology.** New York: Harper & Row.

Sherman, J. (1996). Development and mental representation of stereotypes. **Journal of Personality and Social Psychology, 70**, 1126–1141.

Sherman, J., Lee, A., Bessenoff, G., & Frost, L. (1998). Stereotype efficiency reconsidered: Encoding flexibility under cognitive load. **Journal of Personality and Social Psychology, 75**(3), 589–606.

Shinagawa, L. (1997). **Atlas of American diversity.** Thousand Oaks, CA: Sage.

Short, J., Williams, E., & Christie, B. (1976). **The social psychology of telecommunications.** London: Wiley.

Sidanius, J., & Pratto, F. (1999). **Social dominance: An intergroup theory of social hierarchy and oppression.** New York: Cambridge University Press.

Siegel, J., Dubrovsky, V., Kiesler, S., & McGuire, T. (1986). Group processes in computer-mediated communication. **Organizational Behavior and Human Decision Processes**, *37*, 157–187.

Sigelman, L., & Welch, S. (1993). The contact hypothesis revisited: Black-White interaction and positive racial attitudes. **Social Forces, 71**, 781–795.

Simon, H. (1976). **Administrative behavior: A study of decision-making processes in administrative organization** (3rd ed.). New York: Free Press.

Simon, H. (1979). **The science of the artificial** (2nd ed.). Cambridge, MA: Massachusetts Institute of Technology Press.

Simons, T., & Peterson, R. (2000). Task conflict and relationship conflict in top management teams: The pivotal role of intragroup trust. **Journal of Applied Psychology, 83**, 102–111.

Simonton, D. (1979). Multiple discovery and invention: Zeitgeist, genius or chance? **Journal of Personality and Social Psychology, 37**, 1603–1616.

Singh, R., Choo, W., & Poh, L. (1998). In-group bias and fair-mindedness as strategies of self-presentation in intergroup perception. **Personality and Social Psychology Bulletin, 24**(2), 147–162.

Sirota, Alper, & Pfau, Inc. (1989). **Report to respondents: Survey of views towards human resources policies and practices**. New York: Author.

Skinner, B. (1953). **Science and human behavior**. New York: Macmillan.

Skinner, B. (1968). **The technology of teaching**. New York: Appleton-Century-Crofts.

Skinner, B. (1971). **Beyond freedom and dignity**. New York: Knopf.

Skon, L., Johnson, D.W., & Johnson, R. (1981). Cooperative peer interaction versus individual competition and individualistic efforts: Effects of the acquisition of cognitive reasoning strategies. **Journal of Educational Psychology, 73**, 83–92.

Slavin, R. (1986). **Using student team learning**. Baltimore, MD: Center for Research on Elementary & Middle Schools, Johns Hopkins University.

Smiles, S. (1866). Self-help: With illustrations of character, conduct, and perseverance (2nd ed.). London: Murray.

Smith, C. M. (2008). Adding minority status to a source of conflict: An examination of influence processes and product quality in dyads. **European Journal of Social Psychology, 38**, 75–83.

Smith, C. M., & Powell, L. (1988). The use of disparaging humor by group leaders. **Southern Speech Communication Journal, 53**, 279–292.

Smith, F. (1943). **An experiment in modifying attitudes toward the Negro** (Teachers College Contributions to Education, 887). New York: Columbia University.

Smith, K., Johnson, D. W., & Johnson, R. (1981). Can conflict be constructive? Controversy versus concurrence seeking in learning groups. **Journal of Educational Psychology, 73,** 651–663.

Smith, K., Johnson, D. W., & Johnson, R. (1984). Effects of controversy on learning in cooperative groups. **Journal of Social Psychology, 122,** 199–209.

Smith, M. (1945). Social situation, social behavior, and social group. **Psychological Review, 52**, 224–229.

Sniezek, J. A. (1992). Groups under uncertainty: An examination of confidence in group decision making. **Organizational Behavior and Human Decision Processes, 52**, 124–155.

Snyder, C., Cheavens, J., & Sympson, S. (1997). Hope: An individual motive for social commerce. **Group Dynamics: Theory, Research, and Practice, 1**, 107–118.

Somech, A. (2006). The effects of leadership style and team process on performance and innovation in functionally heterogeneous teams. **Journal of Management, 32,** 132–157.

Sommer, R. (1967). Small group ecology. **Psychological Bulletin, 67**, 145–152.

Sonstegard, M., & Bitter, J. (1998). Counseling children in groups. **Journal of Individual Psychology, 54**(2), 251–267.

Sonstegard, M., Dreikurs, R., & Bitter, J. (1982). The teleanalytic group counseling approach. In G. Gazda (Ed.), **Basic approaches to group psychotherapy and counseling** (3rd ed., pp. 507–551). Springfield, IL: Charles C. Thomas.

Sorrentino, R., & Boutillier, R. (1975). The effect of quantity and quality of verbal interaction on ratings of leadership ability. **Journal of Experimental Social Psychology, 11,** 403–411.

South, E. (1972). Some psychological aspects of committee work. **Journal of Applied Psychology, 11,** 348–368, 437–464.

Spencer, S., Fein, S., Wolfe, C., Fong, C., & Dunn, M. (1998). Automatic activation of stereotypes: The role of self-image threat. **Personality and Social Psychology Bulletin, 24**(11), 1139–1152.

Sprink, K., & Carron, A. (1994). Group cohesion effects in exercise classes. **Small Group Research, 25,** 26–42.

Spurlin, J., Dansereau, D., Larson, C., & Brooks, L. (1984). Cooperative learning strategies in processing descriptive text: Effects of role and activity level of the learner. **Cognition and Instruction,** 1, 451–463.

Stanne, M., Johnson, D. W., & Johnson, R. (1999). Does competition enhance or inhibit motor performance: A meta-analysis. **Psychological Bulletin, 125**(1), 1–22.

Star, S., Williams, R., & Stouffer, S. (1965). Negro infantry platoons in white companies. In H. Proshansky & B. Seidenberg (Eds.), **Basic studies in social psychology** (pp. 680–684). New York: Holt, Rinehart & Winston.

Stasser, G. (2000). Information distribution, participation, and group decision: Explorations with the DISCUSS and SPEAK models. In D. Ilgen & C. Hulin (Eds.), **Computational modeling of behavior in organizations: The third scientific discipline** (pp. 135–161). Washington, D. C.: American Psychological Association.

Stasser, G., & Titus, W. (1987). Effects of information load and percentage shared information on the dissemination of unshared information during discussion. **Journal of Personality and Social Psychology,** 53, 81–93.

Staw, B. M. (1995). Why no one really wants creativity. In C. M. Ford & D. A. Gioia (Eds.), **Creative Action in Organizations: Ivory Tower Visions & Real World Voices** (pp.161–172). Thousand Oaks, CA: Sage.

Steele, C., & Aronson, J. (1995). Stereotype threat and the intellectual test performance of African Americans. **Journal of Personality and Social Psychology,** 69, 797–811.

Stein, M. (1968). **The creative individual.** New York: Harper & Row.

Stein, R., & Heller, T. (1979). An empirical analysis of the correlations between leadership status and participation rates reported in the literature. **Journal of Personality and Social Psychology,** 37, 1993–2002.

Steiner, I. (1959). Human interaction and interpersonal perception. **Sociometry, 22,** 230–235.

Steiner, I. (1966). Models for inferring relationships between group size and potential group productivity. **Behavioral Science,** 11, 273–283.

Steiner, I. (1972). **Group process and productivity.** New York: Academic Press.

Steiner, I. (1974). Whatever happened to the group in social psychology? **Journal of Experimental Social Psychology, 10,** 94–108.

Steiner, I. (1976). Task-performing groups. In J. Thibaut, J. Spence, & R. Carson (Eds.), **Contemporary topics in social psychology.** Morristown, NJ: General Learning Press.

Steinzor, B. (1950). The spatial factor in face-to-face discussion groups. **Journal of Abnormal and Social Psychology, 45,** 552–555.

Stephan, F., & Mishler, E. (1952). The distribution of participation in small groups: An exponential approximation. **American Sociological Review,** 17, 598–608.

Stephan, W. (1978). School desegregation: An evaluation of predictions made in Brown vs. Board of Education. **Psychological Bulletin, 85,** 217–238.

Sternberg, R. J. (2007). A systems model of leadership. **American Psychologist, 62**(1), 34–42.

Stevens, C. (1963). **Strategy and collective bargaining negotiation.** New York: McGraw-Hill.

Stogdill, R. (1948). Persoanl factors associated with leadership: A survey of the literature. **Journal of Psychology, 25,** 35–71.

Stogdill, R. (1959). **Individual behavior and group achievement.** New York: Oxford University Press.

Stogdill, R. (1974). **Handbook of leadership.** New York: Free Press.

Storm, H. (1972). **Steven arrows**. New York: Ballantine Books.

Storms, M. (1973). Videotape and the attribution process: Reversing actors' and observers' points of view. **Journal of Personality and Social Psychology, 27**, 165–175.

Stoner, J. (1961). **A comparison of individual and group decisions involving risk.** Unpublished master's thesis, Massachusetts Institute of Technology, Boston.

Stotle, J. (1978). Power structure and personal competence. **Journal of Social Psychology, 38,** 72–83.

Strodtbeck, F., & Hook, L. (1961). The social dimensions of a twelve man jury table. **Sociometry, 24,** 397–415.

Stroebe, W., Diehl, M., & Abukoumkin, G. (1992). The illusion of group effectivity. **Personality and Social Psychology Bulletin, 18**, 643–650.

Sundstrom, E., Perkins, M., George, J., Futrell, D., & Hoffman, D. (1990, April). **Work-team context, development, and effectiveness in a manufacturing organization**. Paper presented at the Fifth Annual Conference of the Society for Industrial and Organizational Psychology, Miami.

Sunstein, C. R. (2002). The Law of Group Polarization. **Journal of Political Philosophy, 10:** 175–195.

Swann, W. (1984). Quest for accuracy in person perception: A matter of pragmatics. **Psychological Review, 91**, 457–477.

Sweeney, J. (1973). An experimental investigation of the free-rider problem. **Social Science Research, 2**, 277–292.

Swim, K., Aikin, K., Hall, W., & Hunter, B. (1995). Sexism and racism: Old fashioned and modern prejudices. **Journal of Personality and Social Psychology, 68**, 199–214.

Szymanski, K., & Harkins, S. (1987). Social loafing and self-evaluation with a social standard. **Journal of Personality and Social Psychology, 53**, 891–897.

Tajfel, H. (1969). Cognitive aspects of prejudice. **Journal of Social Issues, 25**, 79–87.

Tajfel, H. (1970). Experiments in intergroup discrimination. **Scientific American, 223**, 96–102.

Tajfel, H. (1974). Social identity and intergroup behavior. **Social Science Information, 13**, 65–93.

Tajfel, H. (1978). Social categorization, social identity, and social comparison. In H. Tajfel (Ed.), **Differentiation between social groups** (pp. 61–76). London: Academic Press.

Tajfel, H. (1981). **Human groups and social categories**. Cambridge, UK: Cambridge University Press.

Tajfel, H. (1982a). Social psychology of intergroup relations. **Annual Review of Psychology, 33**, 1–39.

Tajfel, H. (Ed.). (1982b). **Social identity and intergroup relations**. Cambridge, England: Cambridge University Press.

Tajfel, H., Billig, M., Bundy, R., & Flament, C. (1971). Social categorization and intergroup behavior. **European Journal of Social Psychology, 1**, 149–178.

Tajfel, H., & Turner, J. (1979). An integrative theory of intergroup conflict. In W. Austin & S. Worchel (Eds.), **Psychology of intergroup relations** (pp. 33–47). Monterey, CA: Brooks/Cole.

Tajfel, H., & Turner, J. (1986). The social identity theory of intergroup relation. In S. Worchel & W. Austin (Eds.), **Psychology of intergroup relations** (pp. 7–24). Chicago: Nelson-Hall.

Taylor, D., & Faust, W. (1952). Twenty questions: Efficiency in problem solving as a function of size of group. **Journal of Experimental Psychology, 44**, 360–368.

Taylor, S. (1980). The interface of cognitive and social psychology. In J. H Harvey (Ed.), **Cognition, social behavior, and the environment** (pp. 189–211). Hillsdale, NJ: Erlbaum.

Taylor, S., & Lobel, M. (1989). Social comparison activity under threat: Downward evaluation and upward contacts. **Psychological Review, 96**, 569–575.

Teger, A. (1980). **Too much invested to quit.** New York: Pergamon.

Terborg, J., Castore, C., & DeNinno, J. (1976). A longitudinal field investigation of the impact of group composition on group performance and cohesion. **Journal of Personality and Social Psychology, 34**, 782–790.

Terman, L., & Odor, M. (1947). **The gifted child grows up.** Stanford, CA: Stanford University Press.

Tetlock P. (1979). Identifying victims of group-think from public statements of decision makers. **Journal of Personality and Social Psychology, 37,** 1314–1324.

Thernstrom, S. (1973). **The other Bostonians: Poverty and progress in the American metropolis, 1880–1970.** Cambridge, MA: Harvard University Press.

Thibaut, J., & Kelly, H. (1959). **The social psychology of groups.** New York: John Wiley.

Thomas, E., & Fink, C. (1961). Models of group problem solving. **Journal of Abnormal and Social Psychology, 63,** 53–63.

Thomas, K. (1976). Conflict and conflict management. In M. Dunnette (ed.), **Handbook of industrial and organizational psychology** (pp. 889–935). Chicago: Rand McNally.

Thompson, T., Davidson, J., & Barber, J. (1995). Self-worth protection in achievement motivation: Performance effects and attitudinal behavior. **Journal of Educational Psychology, 87,** 598–610.

Thompson, L., Levine, J., & Messick, D. (1999). **Shared cognition in organizations: The management of knowledge.** Mahwah, NJ: Erlbaum.

Thorndike, R. (1938). On what type of task will a group do well? **Journal of Abnormal Social Psychology, 30,** 409–413.

Tichy, M., Johnson, D. W., Johnson, R. T., & Roseth, C. (in press). The impact of constructive controversy on moral development. **Journal of Applied Social Psychology.**

Tjosvold, D. (1974). Threat as a low-power person's strategy in bargaining: Social face and tangible outcomes. **International Journal of Group Tensions, 4,** 494–510.

Tjosvold, D. (1977). Low-power person's strategies in bargaining: Negotiability of demand, maintaining face, and race. **International Journal of Group Tensions, 7,** 29–42.

Tjosvold, D. (1978). Alternative organizations for schools and classrooms. In D. Bar-Tal & L. Saxe (Eds.), **Social psychology of education: theory & research** (pp. 275–298). Washington, DC: Hemisphere.

Tjosvold, D. (1981). Unequal power relationships within a cooperative or competitive context. **Journal of Applied Social Psychology, 11,** 137–150.

Tjosvold, D. (1982). Effects of approach to controversy on superiors' incorporation of subordinates' information in decision making. **Journal of Applied Psychology, 67,** 189–193.

Tjosvold, D. (1985a). The effects of attribution and social context on superiors' influence and interaction with low performing subordinates. **Personnel Psychology, 38,** 361–376.

Tjosvold, D. (1985b). Power and social context in superior-subordinate interaction. **Organizational Behavior and Human Decision Processes, 35,** 281–293.

Tjosvold, D. (1986). **Working together to get things done.** Lexington, MA: Lexington.

Tjosvold, D. (1989). Interdependence and power between managers and employees: A study of the leader relationship. **Journal of Management, 15,** 49–62.

Tjosvold, D. (1990a). Power in cooperative and competitive organizational contexts. **Journal of Social Psychology, 130,** 249–258.

Tjosvold, D. (1990b). **The team organization: Applying group research to the workplace.** New York: Wiley.

Tjosvold, D. (1991a). **Team organization.** New York: Wiley.

Tjosvold, D. (1991b). **The conflict-positive organization.** Reading, MA: Addison-Wesley.

Tjosvold, D. (1993). Experiencing a given base of power as a reward or punishment. **Psychological Reports, 73,** 178.

Tjosvold, D. (1995a). Cooperation theory, constructive controversy, and effectiveness: Learning from crisis. In R. Guzzo & E. Salas (Eds.), **Team effectiveness and decision making in organizations** (pp. 79–112). San Francisco: Jossey-Bass.

Tjosvold, D. (1995b). Effects of power to reward and punish in cooperative and competitive contexts. **Journal of Social Psychology, 135**(6), 723–736.

Tjosvold, D. (1996). **Managing anger for teamwork in Hong Kong: Provocations, intensity, aggression and open-mindedness.** Research Report, Lingnam University, Hong Kong.

Tjosvold, D., Coleman, P., & Sun, H. (2003). Effects of organizational values on leader's use of information power to affect performance in China. **Group Dynamics: Theory, Research, and Practice, 7**, 152–167.

Tjosvold, D., & Johnson, D. W. (1978). Controversy within a cooperative or competitive context and cognitive perspective-taking. **Contemporary Educational Psychology, 3**, 376–386.

Tjosvold, D., & Johnson, D. W.(1982). **Productive conflict**. New York: Irvin.

Tjosvold, D., Johnson, D. W., & Johnson, R. (1981). Effect of partner's effort and ability on liking for partner after failure on a cooperative task. **Journal of Psychology, 109**, 147–152.

Tjosvold, D., Johnson, D. W., & Johnson, R. (1984). Influence strategy, perspective-taking, and relationships between high and low power individuals in cooperative and competitive contexts. **Journal of Psychology, 116**, 187–202.

Tjosvold, D., Johnson, D. W., Johnson, R., & Sun, H. (2003). Can interpersonal competition be constructive within organizations? **Journal of Psychology, 137**(1), 63–84.

Tjosvold, D., Johnson, D. W., Johnson, R., & Sun, H. (2006). Competitive motives and strategies in organizations: Understanding constructive interpersonal competition. **Group Dynamics: Theory, Research, & Practice**, 10(2), 87–99.

Tjosvold, D., & Sagaria, D. (1978). Effects of relative power of cognitive perspective-taking. **Personality and Social Psychology Bulletin, 4**, 256–259.

Tjosvold, D., Tang, M.M.L., & West, M. A. (2004). Reflexivity for team innovation in China: The contribution of goal interdependence. **Group and Organization Management, 29**(5), 540–559.

Tjosvold, D., XueHuang, Y., Johnson, D. W., & Johnson, R. T. (2008). Social interdependence and orientation toward life and work. **Journal of Applied Social Psychology**, 32(2), 409–435.

Torrance, E. (1954). Some consequences of power differences in decision making in permanent and temporary three-man groups. **Research Studies, State College of Washington, 22**, 130–140.

Torrance, E. (1957). Group decision-making and disagreement. **Social Forces, 35**, 314–318.

Torrance, E. (1961). Can grouping control social stress in creative activity? **Elementary School Journal, 62**, 391–394.

Torrance, E. P. (1970). Influence of dyadic interaction on creative functioning. **Psychological Reports, 26**, 391–394.

Torrance, E. P. (1971). Stimulation, enjoyment, and originality in dyadic creativity. **Journal of Educational Psychology, 62**, 45–48.

Torrance, E. P. (1973, February). **Dyadic interaction in creative thinking and problem solving.** Paper presented at the annual meeting of the American Educational Research Association, New Orleans, LA.

Toulmin, S. (1958). **The uses of argument**. New York: Cambridge University Press.

Treffinger, D., Speedie, S., & Brunner, W. (1974). Improving children's creative problem solving ability: The Purdue creativity project. **The Journal of Creative Behavior, 8**, 20–29.

Trevino, L., Lengel, R., & Draft, R. (1987). Media symbolism, media richness, and media choice in organizations: A symbolic interactionist perspective. **Communication Research**, 14, 553–574.

Triandis, H., Bass, A., Ewen, R., & Mieksele, E. (1963). Teaching creativity as a function of the members. **Journal of Applied Psychology, 47**, 104–110.

Triandis, H., Hall, D. & Ewen, R. (1965). Member heterogeneity and dyadic creativity. **Human Relations, 18**, 33–55.

Triplett, N. (1898). The dynamogenic factors in peacemaking and competition. **American Journal of Psychology, 9**, 507–533.

Tschuschke, V., & Dies, R. (1994). Intensive analysis of therapeutic factors and outcome in long-term inpatient groups. **International Journal of Group Psychotherapy, 44**, 185–208.

Tsekeris, C. (2010). Reflections on reflexivity. **Sociological Issues and Perspectives, Contemporary Issues, 3**(1), 28–37.

Tuckman, B. (1965). Developmental sequence in small groups. **Psychological Bulletin, 63**, 384–399.

Tuckman, B. & Jensen, M. (1977). Stages of small group development revisited. **Group and Organizational Studies, 2**, 419–427.

Turk, S., & Sarason, I. (1983). **Test anxiety and causal attributions**. Unpublished manuscripts, University of Washington, Department of Psychology, Seattle, WA.

Turner, J. (1978). Social comparison, similarity and ingroup favoritism. In H. Tajfel (Ed.), **Differentiation between social groups** (pp. 235–250). London: Academic Press.

Turner, J. (1985). Social categorization and the self-concept: A social cognitive theory of group behavior. In E. Lawler (Ed.), **Advances in group processes** (Vol. 2, pp. 77–122). Greenwich, CT: JAI Press.

Turner, J. (1987). **Rediscovering the social group: A self-categorization theory**. New York: Basil Blackwell.

Turner, J., Brown, R., & Tajfel, H. (1979). Social comparison and group interest in ingroup favouritism. **European Journal of Social Psychology, 9**, 187–204.

Turner, J., & Oakes, P. (1989). Self-categorization theory and social influence. In P. Paulus (Ed.), **Psychology of group influence** (2nd ed., pp. 233–275). Hillsdale, NJ: Erlbaum.

Turner, M. E., & Pratkanis, A. R. (1998). A social identity maintenance model of groupthink. **Organizational Behavior and Human Decision Processes, 73**(2–3), 210–235.

Turner, M. E., Pratkanis, A. R., Probasco, P., & Leve, C. (1992). Threat, cohesion, and group effectiveness: Testing a social identity maintenance perspective on groupthink. **Journal of Personality and Social Psychology, 63**, 781–796.

Turner, R., & Killian, L. (1972/1987). **Collective behavior** (3rd ed.). Englewood Cliffs, NJ: Prentice-Hall.

Tversky, A., & Kahneman, D. (1981). The framing of decisions and the psychology of choice. **Science, 211**, 453–458.

Tyler, T. (1997). The psychology of legitimacy: A relational perspective on voluntary deference to authorities. **Personality and Social Psychology Review, 1**, 323–345.

Tyler, T., & Degoey, P. (1996). Trust in organizational authorities: The influence of motive attributions on willingness to accept decisions. In R. Kramer & T. Tyler (Eds.), **Trust in organizational authorities** (pp. 331–356). Thousand Oaks, CA: Sage.

Tyler, T., Lind, E., Ohbuchi, K., Sugawara, I., & Huo, Y. (1998). Conflict with outsiders: Disputing within and across cultural boundaries. **Personality and Social Psychology Bulletin, 24**(2), 137–146.

Umbright M.S. (1995). **Mediating interpersonal conflicts: A pathway to peace**. West Concord, MN: CPI Publishing.

Urban, L., & Miller, N. (1998). A theoretical analysis of crossed categorization effects: A meta-analysis. **Journal of Personality and Social Psychology, 74**, 894–908.

Vacchiano, R.B., Strauss, P.S., & Hochman, L. (1968). The open and closed mind: A review of dogmatism. **Psychological Bulletin, 71**(4), 261–273.

Vanbeselaere, N. (1987). The effects of dichotomous and crossed social categorizations upon intergroup discrimination. **European Journal of Social Psychology, 17**, 143–156.

Vanbeselaere, N. (1991). The different effects of simple and crossed categorization: A result of the category differentiation process or of differential category salience? In W. Stroebe & M. Hewstone (Eds.), **European review of social psychology** (Vol. 2, pp. 143–156). Chichester, UK: Wiley.

Van Blerkom, M., & Tjosvold, D. (1981). The effects of social context on engaging in controversy. **Journal of Psychology, 107,** 141–145.

Van Dyne, L., Ang, S. & Botero, I.C. (2003). Conceptualizing employee silence and employee voice as multi-dimensional constructs. **Journal of Management Studies, 40**, 1360–1392.

Van Dyne, L. & LePine, J.A. (1998). Helping and voice extra-role behavior: Evidence of a construct and predictive validity. **Academy of Management Journal, 41**, 108–119.

Van Dyne, L. & Saavedra, R. (1996). A naturalistic minority influence experiment: Effects of divergent thinking, conflict and originality in work groups. **British Journal of Social Psychology, 35**, 151–168.

Villasenor, V. (1977). **Jury: The people vs. Juan Corona**. New York: Bantam.

Vinokur, A., & Burnstein, E. (1974). The effects of partially shared persuasive arguments on group-induced shifts: A group-problem-solving approach. **Journal of Personality and Social Psychology, 29**, 305–315.

Vinokur, A., & Burnstein, E. (1978). Depolarization of attitudes in groups. **Journal of Personality and Social Psychology, 36,** 872–885.

Vinton, K. (1989). Humor in the workplace: It is more than telling jokes. **Small Group Research**, 20, 151–166.

Voiers, W. (1956). **Bombing accuracy as a function of the group-school proficiency structure of the B-29 bomb team.** (Research Report AFDTRC-TN-56-4.) Lackland Air Force Base, TX: Air Force Personnel and Training Research Center.

Von Hippel, E., Thomke, S. & Sonnack, M. (1999). Creating Breakthroughs at 3M. **Harvard Business Review, 77**(5), September-October, 47–57.

Von Mises, L. (1949). **Human action: A treatise on economics.** New Haven, CT: Yale University Press.

Vroom, V., & Pahl, B. (1971). Relationship between age and risk-taking among managers. **Journal of Applied Psychology, 55,** 399–405.

Vroom, V., & Yetton, P. (1973). **Leadership and decision making.** Pittsburgh, PA: University of Pittsburgh Press.

Vrugt, A., & Koenis, S. (2002). Perceived self-efficacy, personal goals, social comparison, and scientific productivity. **Applied Psychology: An International Review,** 51, 593–607.

Vye, N. J., Goldman, S. R., Voss, J. F., Hmelo, C., Wiolliams, S., & the Cognition and Technology Group at Vanderbilt. (1997). Complex mathematical problem solving by individuals and dyads. **Cognition and Instruction, 15,** 485–484.

Vygotsky, L. (1962). **Thought and language**. Cambridge, MA: MIT Press.

Wagner, U., Hewstone, M., & Machleit, U. (1989). Contact and prejudice between Germans and Turks. **Human Relations, 42,** 561–574.

Wagner, W. G., Pfeffer, J., and O'Reilly, C. A. (1984). Organizational demography and turnover in top-management groups. **Administrative Science Ouarterly 29,** 74–92.

Walker, L. (1983). Sources of cognitive conflict for stage transition in moral development. **Developmental Psychology, 19,** 103–110.

Wallach, M., Kogan, N., & Bem, D. (1962). Group influence on individual risk taking. **Journal of Abnormal and Social Psychology, 65**, 75–86.

Walton, D. (2007). **Dialogue theory for critical argumentation**. Philadelphia, PA: John Benjamins.

Walton, D. (2010). A dialogue model of belief. **Argument and Computation, 1**, 23–46.

Walton, R. (1969). **Interpersonal peacemaking.** Reading, MA: Addison-Wesley.

Walton, R. (1985). From control to commitment in the workplace. **Harvard Business Review**, 63, 76–84.

Walton, R. (1987). **Managing conflict**. Reading, MA: Addison-Wesley.

Walton, R., & McKersie, R. (1965). **A behavioral theory of labor negotiations.** New York: McGraw-Hill.

Walzer, M. (2004). *Politics and passion: Toward a more egalitarian liberalism.* New Haven, CT: Yale University Press.

Warriner, C. (1956). Groups are real: A reaffirmation. **American Sociological Review**, 21, 349–354.

Watson, D., & Tharp, R. (1997). **Self-directed behavior: Self-modification for personal adjustment** (7th ed.). Pacific Grove, CA: Brooks/Cole.

Watson, D. & Tharp, R. (1997). **Self-directed behavior: Self-modification for personal adjustment** (7th ed.). Pacific Grove, CA: Brooks/Cole.

Watson, G. (1928). Do groups think more effectively than individuals? **Journal of Abnormal and Social Psychology, 23,** 328–336.

Watson, G. (1931). Do groups think more effectively than individuals? In G. Murphy & L. Murphy (Eds.), **Experimental social psychology**. New York: Harper.

Watson, G. (1947). **Action for unity.** New York: Harper.

Watson, G., & Johnson, D.W. (1972). **Social psychology: Issues and insights** (2nd ed.). Philadelphia: Lippincott.

Watson, W., Kumar, K., & Michaelsen, L. (1993). Cultural diversity's impact on interaction process and performance: Comparing homogeneous and diverse task groups. **Academy of Management Journal, 36**, 590–602.

Watson, W., Michaelsen, L., & Sharp, W. (1991). Member competence, group interaction, and group decision making: A longitudinal study. **Journal of Applied Psychology, 76**, 803–809.

Webb, N. (1977). **Learning in individual and small group setting** (Tech. Report No. 7). Stanford, CA: Stanford University, School of Education, Aptitude Research Project.

Webb, N., Ender, P., & Lewis, S. (1986). Problem-solving strategies and group processes in small group learning computer programming. **American Educational Research Journal, 23**(2), 243–261.

Weber, M. (1946). The sociology of charismatic authority. In H. Gert & C. Mills (Trans. & Eds.), **From Max Weber: Essay in sociology** (pp. 245–252). New York: Oxford University Press (original work published 1921).

Weber, M. (1947). **The theory of social and economic organization** (A. M. Henderson & T. Parsons, Trans.). New York: Oxford University Press (original work published 1924).

Wegner, D. (1995). A computer network model of human transactive memory. **Social Cognition, 13**, 319–339.

Weick, K. (1990). The vulnerable system: An analysis of the Tenerife air disaster. **Journal of Management, 16**, 571–593.

Weigel, R., & Howes, P. (1985). Conceptions of racial prejudice. **Journal of Social Issues, 41**(3), 117–138.

Weigold, M. F., & Schlenker, B. R. (1991). Accountability and risk taking. **Personality and Social Psychology Bulletin, 17**, 25–29.

Weiner, N., Pandy, J., & Lantané, B. (1981). **Individual and group productivity in the United States and India**. Paper presented at the annual meeting of the American Psychological Association, Los Angeles.

Welbourne, J. (1999). The impact of perceived entitativity on inconsistency resolution for groups and individuals. **Journal of Experimental Social Psychology, 35**, 481–508.

Wentzel, K. (1994). Relations of social goal pursuit to social acceptance, classroom behavior, and perceived social support. **Journal of Educational Psychology, 86**, 173–182.

Wessells, M. (2002). Recruitment of children as soldiers in sub-Saharan Africa: An ecological analysis. In L. Mjoset & S. Van Holde (Eds.), **The comparative study of conscription in the armed forces (Comparative Social Research,** Vol. 20) (pp. 237–254). Amsterdam: Elsevier.

West, C., & Zimmerman, D. (1983). Small insults: A study of interruptions in cross-sex conversations between unacquainted persons. In B. Thorne, C. Dramarge, & N. Henley (Eds.), **Language, gender, and society** (pp. 102–117). Rowley, MA: Newbury House.

Wheeler, D. D., & Janis, I. L. (1980). A practical guide for making decisions. New York: Free Press.

Wheeler, R., & Ryan, F. (1973). Effects of cooperative and competitive classroom environments on the attitudes and achievement of elementary school students engaged in social studies inquiry activities. **Journal of Educational Psychology, 65,** 402–407.

Whitman, W. (1860) Leaves of grass. Whitman, Walt. **Leaves of Grass: Facsimile Edition of the 1860 Text**. Ed. Roy Harvey Pearce. Ithaca, N.Y.: Cornell UP, 1961.

Whyte, W.F. (1943). **Street corner society.** Chicago: University of Chicago Press.

Wiersema, M., & Bantel, K. (1992). Top management team demography and corporate strategic change. **Academy of Management Journal, 35**, 91–121.

Wiggam, A. (1931). The biology of leadership. In H. Metcalf (Ed.), **Business leadership**. New York: Pitman.

Wilder, D. (1977). Perception of group, size of opposition, and social influence. **Journal of Experimental Social Psychology, 13**, 253–268.

Wilder, D. (1978a). Perceiving persons as a group: Effects on attributions of causality and beliefs. **Social Psychology, 41**, 13–33.

Wilder, D. (1978b). Reduction of intergroup discrimination through individuation of the out-group.

Journal of Personality and Social Psychology, 36, 1361–1374.

Wilder, D. (1986). Social categorization: Implications for creation and reduction of intergroup bias. **Advances in Experimental Social Psychology, 19,** 291–355.

Wilder, D. (1990). Some determinants of the persuasive power of in-groups and the out-groups: Organization of information and attribution of independence. **Journal of Personality and Social Psychology, 59,** 1202–1213.

Wilder, D. (1993). Freezing intergroup evaluations: Anxiety and resistance to counterstereotypic information. In M. Hogg & D. Abrams (Eds.), **Group motivation: Social psychological perspectives** (pp. 68–86). London: Harvester Wheatsheaf.

Wilder, D., & Shapiro, P. (1989a). Effects of anxiety on impression formation in a group context: An anxiety-assimilation hypothesis. **Journal of Experimental Social Psychology, 25,** 481–499.

Wilder, D., & Shapiro, P. (1989b). Role of competition-induced anxiety in limiting the beneficial impact of positive behavior by an out-group member. **Journal of Personality and Social Psychology, 56,** 60–69.

Wilder, D., & Shapiro, P. (1991). Facilitation of out-group stereotypes by enhanced ingroup identity. **Journal of Experimental Social Psychology, 27,** 431–452.

Wiley, J., & Voss, J. F. (1999). Constructing arguments from multiple sources: Tasks that promote understanding and not just memory for text. **Journal of Educational Psychology, 91,** 301–311.

Wilkinson, I., & Kipnis, D. (1978). Interfirm use of power. **Journal of Applied Psychology, 63,** 315–320.

Willems, E., & Clark, R. (1971). Shift toward risk and heterogeneity of groups. **Journal of Experimental and Social Psychology, 7,** 304–312.

Williams, D. (1948). The effect of an interracial project upon the attitudes of Negro and white girls within the YWCA. In A. Rose (Ed.), **Studies in the reduction of prejudice**. Chicago: American Council of Race Relations.

Williams, K. (1981). Developmental characteristics of a forward roll. **Research Quarterly for Exercise and Sport, 51**(4), 703–713.

Williams, K., Harkins, S., & Latané, B. (1981). Identifiability as a deterrent to social loafing: Two cheering experiments. **Journal of Personality and Social Psychology, 40,** 303–311.

Williams, K., & Williams, K. (1984). **Social loafing in Japan: A cross-cultural development study**. Paper presented at the Midwestern Psychological Association, Chicago.

Williams, K. D., Forgas, J. P., & von Hippel, W. (2005). **The social outcast: Ostracism, social exclusion, rejection, and bullying.** New York: Psychology Press.

Williams, R. (1947). **Reduction of intergroup tension: A survey of research on problems of ethnic, racial, and religious group relations**, Bulletin 57. New York: Social Science Research Council.

Williams, R. (1964) **Strangers next door.** Englewood Cliffs, NJ: Prentice-Hall.

Williams, R., & Ryan, M. (Eds.) (1954). **Schools of transition: Community experiences in desegregation.** Chapel Hill: University of North Carolina Press.

Wilner, D., Walkley, R., & Cook, S. (1952). Residential proximity and intergroup relations in public housing projects. **Journal of Social Issues, 8,** 45–69.

Wilson, S. (1955, 1991). **The man in the grey flannel suit**. Mattituck, NY: Amereon.

Winder, A. (1952). White attitudes toward Negro-white interaction in an area of changing racial composition. **American Psychologist, 7,** 330–331.

Winquist, J. R., & Larson, J. R., Jr. (1998). Information pooling: When it impacts group decision making. **Journal of Personality and Social Psychology, 74,** 371–377.

Wittenbaum, G. M., Hollingshead, A. B., & Botero, I. C. (2004). From cooperative to motivated information sharing in groups: Moving beyond the hidden profile paradigm. **Communication Monographs, 71,** 286–310.

Wolfe, J., & Box, T. (1988). Team cohesion effects on business game performance. **Simulation and Games, 19**(1), 82–98.

Wolman, B., & Stricker, G. (Eds.), (1983). **Handbook of family and marital therapy**. New York: Plenum.

Wood, J., Taylor, S., & Lichtman, R. (1985). Social comparison in adjustment to breast cancer. **Journal of Personality and Social Psychology, 49,** 1169–1183.

Wood, R., Mento, A., & Locke, E. (1987). Task complexity as a moderator of goal effects: A meta-analysis. **Journal of Applied Psychology, 72**(3), 416–425.

Wood, W. (1987). Meta-analytic review of sex differences in group performance. **Psychological Bulletin, 102**, 53–71.

Wood, W., Lundgren, S., Ouelletter, J., Busceme, S., & Blackstone, T. (1994). Minority influence: A meta-analytic review of social influence processes. **Psychological Bulletin, 115**(3), 323–345.

Woods, F. (1913). **The influence of monarchs.** New York: Macmillan.

Worchel, S., Andreoli, V., & Folger, R. (1977). Intergroup cooperation and intergroup attraction: The effect of previous interaction and outcome on combined effort. **Journal of Experimental Social Psychology, 13**, 131–140.

Worchel, S., & Brehm, J. (1971). Direct and implied social restoration of freedom. **Journal of Personality and Social Psychology, 18**, 294–304.

Worchel, S., Coutant-Sassic, D., & Grossman, M. (1992). A developmental approach to group dynamics: A model and illustrative research. In S. Worchel, W. Wood, & J. Simpson (Eds.), **Group process and productivity** (pp. 181–202). Newbury Park, CA: Sage.

Wright, J. (1979). **On a clear day you can see General Motors.** New York: Avon.

Wright, S., Aron, A., McLaughlin-Volpe, T., & Ropp, S. (1997). The extended contact effect: Knowledge of cross-group friendships and prejudice. **Journal of Personality and Social Psychology, 73**(1), 73–90.

Yager, S., Johnson, D. W., & Johnson, R. (1985). Oral discussion, group-to-individual transfer, and achievement in cooperative learning groups. **Journal of Educational Psychology, 77**, 60–66.

Yager, S., Johnson, D. W., Johnson, R., & B. Snider. (1986). The impact of group processing on achievement in cooperative learning groups. **Journal of Social Psychology, 126**(3), 389–398.

Yalom, I., & Leszoz, M. (2005). **The theory and practice of group psychotherapy** (5th ed.). New York: Basic Books.

Yalom, I. D., Miles, M., B., & Licherman, M. A. (1973). **Encounter groups: First facts.** New York: Basic Books.

Yarrow, M., Campbell, J., & Yarrow, L. (1958). Interpersonal dynamics in racial integration. In |E. Maccoby, T. Newcomb, & E. Hartley (Eds.), **Readings in social psychology** (pp. 623–635). New York: Holt, Rinehart, & Winston.

Young, D. (1932). **American minority people: A study in racial and cultural conflicts in the United States.** New York: Harper.

Yovetich, N., & Rusbult, C. (1994). Accommodative behavior in close relationships: Exploring transformation of motivation. **Journal of Experimental Social Psychology, 30**, 138–164.

Yukl, G. (2005). **Leadership in organizations** (6th ed.). Englewood Cliffs, NJ: Prentice-Hall.

Yukl, G., & Falbe, C. (1990). Influence tactics and objectives in upward, downward, and lateral influence attempts. **Journal of Applied Psychology, 75**, 132–140.

Yukl, G., & Falbe, C. (1991). Importance of different power sources in downward and lateral relations. **Journal of Applied Psychology, 76**, 416–423.

Yukl, G., & Tracey, J. (1992). Consequences of influence attempts used with subordinates, peers, and the boss. **Journal of Applied Psychology, 77**, 525–535.

Zaccaro, S. J. (1984). Social loafing: The role of task attractiveness. **Personality and Social Psychology Bulletin, 10**, 99–106.

Zaccaro, S. J. (2007). Trait-based perspectives of leadership. **American Psychologist, 62**(1), 6–16.

Zaccaro, S. J., Kemp, C., & Bader, P. (2004). Leader traits and attributes. In J. Antonakis, A. T. Cianciolo, & R. J. Sternberg (Eds.), **The nature of organizational leadership: Understanding the performance imperatives confronting today's leaders** (pp. 3–41). Thousand Oaks, CA: Sage.

Zajonc, R. (1960). The process or cognitive tuning in communication. **Journal of Abnormal and Social Psychology, 61**, 159–167.

Zajonc, R. (1965). Social facilitation. **Science, 149**, 269–272.

Zander, A. (1971). **Motives and goals in groups.** New York: Academic Press.

Zander, A. (1974). Team spirit vs. the individual achiever. **Psychology Today, 8**(6), 64–68.

Zander, A. (1977). **Groups at work**. San Francisco: Jossey-Bass.

Zander, A. (1979). The psychology of group process. In A. Inkeles, J. Coleman, & R. Turner (Eds.), **Annual review of sociology** (Vol. 5, pp. 417–451). Palo Alto, CA: Annual Review Inc.

Zander, A., & Armstrong, W. (1972). Working for group pride in a slipper factory. **Journal of Applied Social Psychology**, 2, 293–307.

Zander, A., & Medow, H. (1963). Individual and group levels of aspiration. **Human Relations**, **16**, 89–105.

Zdep, S., & Oakes, W. (1967). Reinforcement of leadership behavior in group discussion. **Journal of Experimental Social Psychology, 3,** 310–320.

Zeleny, L. (1940). Experimental appraisal of a group learning plan. **Journal of Educational Research**, **34**, 37–42.

Zenger, T., & Lawrence, B. (1989). Organizational demography: The differential effects of age and tenure distribution on technical communication. **Academy of Management Journal, 32**, 353–376.

Ziller, R. (1957). Group size: A determinant of the quality and stability of group decision. **Sociometry**, **20,** 165–173.

Ziller, R., Behringer, R., & Goodchilds, J. (1962). Group creativity under conditions of success or failure and variations in group stability. **Journal of Applied Psychology**, **46**, 43–49.

Zimbardo, P. (1970). The human choice: Individuation, reason, and order versus deindividuation, impulse, and chaos. In W. Arnold & D. Levine (Eds.), **Nebraska symposium on motivation** (pp. 237–307). Lincoln: University of Nebraska Press.

Zimbardo, P. (1975). Transforming experimental research into advocacy for social change. In M. Deutsch & H. Hornstein (Eds.), **Applying social psychology** (pp. 33–66). Hillsdale, N.J.: Erlbaum.

Zuwerink, J., Monteith, M., Devine, P., & Cook, D. (1996). Prejudice towards Blacks: With and without compunction? **Basic and Applied Social Psychology**, **18**, 131–150.

NAME INDEX